Aztec Philosophy

Aztec Philosophy

UNDERSTANDING A WORLD IN MOTION

James Maffie

UNIVERSITY PRESS OF COLORADO
Boulder

© 2014 by University Press of Colorado

Published by University Press of Colorado
5589 Arapahoe Avenue, Suite 206C
Boulder, Colorado 80303

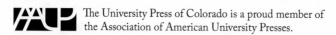 The University Press of Colorado is a proud member of
the Association of American University Presses.

The University Press of Colorado is a cooperative publishing enterprise supported, in part, by
Adams State University, Colorado State University, Fort Lewis College, Metropolitan State
University of Denver, Regis University, University of Colorado, University of Northern Colorado,
Utah State University, and Western State Colorado University.

∞ The paper used in this publication meets the minimum requirements of the American
National Standard for Information Sciences – Permanence of Paper for Printed Library
Materials. ANSI Z39.48-1992

Library of Congress Cataloging-in-Publication Data

Maffie, James.
  Aztec philosophy: understanding a world in motion / James Maffie.
    pages cm
  Includes bibliographical references and index.
  ISBN 978-1-60732-222-1 (cloth: alk. paper) — ISBN 978-1-60732-461-4 (pbk) —
ISBN 978-1-60732-223-8 (ebook)
  1. Aztec philosophy. 2. Aztecs—Folklore. I. Title.
  F1219.76.P55M35 2013
  199'.7208997452—dc23
                          2013018407

24   23   22   21   20   19   18   17   16   15   10   9   8   7   6   5   4   3   2   1

Cover photo credit: *Almena en forma de caracol cortado*, El Museo del Templo Mayor, Mexico City,
Mexico. Photograph by Jorge Pérez de Lara Elías.

To my mother, Elaine Wack Maffie,
and the memory of my father, Cornelius Michael Maffie.

Contents

This work would not have been possible without the monumental achievements of Miguel León-Portilla and Alfredo López Austin. They are the giants upon whose shoulders Aztec scholarship rests. Although I know neither personally, I found myself in constant dialogue with them while writing this book. I also owe intellectual debts to the work of Cecelia Klein, Willard Gingerich, David Hall, Roger Ames, Thelma Sullivan, Eva Hunt, Alan Sandstrom, Pamela Effrein Sandstrom, Barbara Tedlock, Dennis Tedlock, Timothy Knab, Louise Burkhart, Davíd Carrasco, H. B. Nicholson, Jill McKeever Furst, Kay Read, Doris Heyden, Vine Deloria Jr., and Peter Furst.

Although trained in Western epistemology, metaphysics, and philosophy of science, I have always harbored a deep interest in non-Western philosophies. It was my chancing upon León-Portilla's *Aztec Thought and Culture* that led me to decide to pursue Aztec (Nahua) philosophy. Such a pursuit is tantamount to philosophical heresy and career suicide from the perspective of academic philosophy in the USA. My previous colleagues at Colorado State University – Grant Lee, Pat McKee, Ron Williams, James Boyd, Richard Kitchener, Jane Kneller, Michael Losonsky, and Bernie Rollins – wholeheartedly supported my retraining myself as a Nahuatlist.

My thinking over the years has benefited from discussions with Sandra Harding, David Hall, Barry Hallen, Ben-Ami Scharfstein, Helen Verran, David Turnbull, Alberto Hernández-Lemus, Henry Odera Oruka, Shari Stone-Mediatore, Norman Swazo, Helmut Wautischer, Zeno Vendler, Oscar Martí, Alicia Matsunaga, Susana Nuccetelli, Ofelia Schutte, Elizabeth Milan-Zaibert,

Larry Laudan, Vinay Lal, Susantha Goonatilake, Meera Nanda, Bryce Hubner, Robert Batterman, Lawrence Sklar, William R. Carter, Xuan Wang, Deepak Mirchandani, Sara Castro-Klaren, and Alejandro Cañeque. For as long as I can remember, Julie Greene, Howard Brick, Paul Roth, William E. Morris, and Alex Greene have challenged me to rethink my ideas with greater rigor.

For stimulating discussions I'd like to thank audience members at the Pratt Institute; the 2013 Northeastern Group of Nahuatl Studies Conference, Yale University; the Johns Hopkins University; American University; University of Colorado, College Springs; University of San Diego; University of Alaska, Fairbanks; Colorado College; Texas State University, San Marcos; Ohio Wesleyan University; Colorado State University; the Precolumbian Society of Washington, DC; University of Maryland; Caribbean Philosophy Association Meetings, Rutgers University; New Directions in Critical Theory Conference, University of Arizona; American Philosophical Association, Eastern Division Meetings; Nahuatl Workshop 1, University of Maryland; Latin American Studies Association Meetings, Montreal; Society for Iberian and Latin American Thought, American Philosophical Association, Pacific Division Meetings; Rocky Mountain Council for Latin American Studies, Santa Fe; and Third Annual St. Louis Philosophy of Social Science Roundtable.

I am deeply grateful for the support given to me by the University of Maryland, College Park. Dean James Harris and Richard Price, Chair of the Department of History, arranged a two-year research fellowship that enabled me to devote myself to researching and writing this book. Mary Kay Vaughn, Karin Rosemblatt, Daryl Williams, and Sandra Cypess welcomed me to my new home in the Latin American Studies Center. As successive directors of the Latin American Studies Center, Mary Kay and Karin have sponsored two Nahua Workshops. The Department of Philosophy offered me a place to teach world philosophies. Christopher Morris and Allen Stairs have been especially welcoming. Students in my World Philosophies, Aztec Thought, Indigenous Thought of the Americas, and Contemporary Latin and Caribbean Philosophy courses have helped me sharpen and clarify my ideas. Nancy Struna, Chair of the Department of American Studies, and Maxine Grossman, Director of the Religious Studies Program, have also extended welcome mats to me. Finally, the members of the Precolumbian Society of Washington, DC, provided me with an instant community here in the greater Washington, DC, area.

I'd like to thank Darrin Pratt, Jessica d'Arbonne, Laura Furney, Daniel Pratt, and Karl Yambert at the University Press of Colorado for patiently guiding the manuscript through publication and the two anonymous referees who read an early draft and made insightful suggestions regarding its improvement.

Special thanks go to my teachers of Nahuatl at IDIEZ: John Sullivan, Urbano Francisco Martínez, Delfina de la Cruz de la Cruz, Andrés Francisco Martínez, and the extended Francisco Martínez family of San Luis Potosí. I have many Mesoamericanists to thank. At one time or another Alfredo López Austin, Richard Townsend, John F. Schwaller, Jonathan Amith, Frances Berdan, Frances Karttunen, Jane Hill, Alejandro Santana, Kim Goldsmith, Davíd Carrasco, Leisa Kauffmann, Gordon Brotherston, Richard Haly, Patricia Anawalt, Viviana Díaz-Balsera, Alejandro Santana, Michael Smith, Jacqueline Messing, Catherine DiCesare, and John Millhauser have improved my understanding of Aztec philosophy. Joe Campbell generously shared many of his concordances of Nahuatl words. These – along with his amazing *A Morphological Dictionary of Classical Nahuatl* – were absolutely indispensable to formulating and testing my ideas.

Academics are commonly concerned with guarding their boundaries and wary of outsiders. I have been extremely fortunate to find a group of Nahuatlists who exemplify quite the opposite. I owe very special thanks to James Taggart, Cecelia Klein, the late Elizabeth Brumfiel, Jerome Offner, Joanna Sánchez, and Camilla Townsend for warmly welcoming me and generously sharing with me their understanding of all matters Aztec. I spent several wonderful days at the Pratt Institute exchanging ideas with Janice Robertson. I have benefited immensely from Pamela Sandstrom's first-hand knowledge of contemporary Nahua culture, and my manuscript has benefited equally from her expert indexing. John Sullivan repeatedly rescued me from Nahuatl words I found hopelessly impenetrable and along the way helped me appreciate the marvelous nuances of Nahuatl. Among this group, however, two individuals particularly stand out. Willard Gingerich enthusiastically welcomed me to the community of Nahua scholars and legitimized my desire to approach Aztec thought from a philosopher's perspective. Willard has always been generously forthcoming with his highly original and subtle understanding of Aztec literature, poetry, and philosophy. Alan Sandstrom introduced me to the community of Nahua scholars by publishing two of my articles in *The Nahua Newsletter*. Alan repeatedly assured me that the conversation among contemporary Nahuatlists needed a philosopher's voice, and he selflessly supported my developing this voice. His vast, insightful, and detailed understanding of both historical and contemporary Nahua matters helped me overcome more than one intellectual impasse. Along the way both Alan and Pamela have become cherished friends.

I owe my greatest debt of gratitude to my mother, Elaine Maffie, and my late father, Cornelius Maffie. This book is lovingly dedicated to them. Julie Greene and I have shared our lives and work for so long that they have become nearly indistinguishable. Julie's scholarly acumen, practical wisdom, and personal support appear on every page of this book. Sophie Florence Meinsen Maffie, our daughter, enriches our lives beyond measure.

Aztec Philosophy

0.1 AZTEC METAPHYSICS

The indigenous peoples of what is now Mexico enjoy long and rich traditions of philosophical reflection dating back centuries before being characterized by their European "discoverers" as "barbarians" or "primitives" incapable of or unmotivated to think rationally, abstractly, or philosophically.[1] Pre-Columbian societies contained individuals who reflected systematically upon the nature of reality, human existence, knowledge, right conduct, and goodness. The Nahuatl-speaking peoples of Central Mexico – including those residing in Mexico-Tenochtitlan known today as the "Aztecs" – were no exception. Nahua societies included individuals called *tlamatinime* ("knowers of things," "sages," or "philosophers"; sing. *tlamatini*) given to puzzling over such questions as, what is the nature of things? where did we come from? what is the proper path for us to follow? and what are we able to know?

Nahua metaphysics served as the backdrop of Nahua religious, theological, and philosophical thought (including moral, political, epistemological, and aesthetic thought) as well as Nahua ritual praxis.[2] Indeed, I argue one cannot adequately understand the latter without first understanding the former. More prosaic, everyday practices such as weaving, farming, hunting, and childrearing likewise presupposed (albeit perhaps only tacitly) metaphysical views. What is metaphysics? Metaphysics investigates the nature, structure, and constitution of reality at the broadest, most comprehensive, and most synoptic level.[3] It aims to advance our understanding of the nature of things broadly construed. Questions concerning the nature of reality, existence, being qua being, causality, time, space, personal

DOI: 10.5876_9781607322238.c000

1

identity, the self, God, free will, mind, and body are among the questions traditionally assigned to metaphysics by Western philosophers. Nahua metaphysics
thus consists of the Nahuas' understanding of the nature, structure, and consti
tution of reality.[4]

Because one cannot adequately understand Nahua theology, religion, and
ritual as well as ethical, political, epistemological, and aesthetic thinking and
activity without first understanding Nahua metaphysics, I devote this work to
Nahua metaphysics. Nahua ethics, epistemology, political philosophy, and aes
thetics will be the focus of a later work. This work's conclusion sketches in broad
outlines how Nahua metaphysics shapes these latter areas of inquiry.

I aim to approximate Nahua views about the nature, structure, and ultimate
constituents of reality at the time of the Conquest. Given its greater name
recognition, I adopt the term *Aztec* in place of *Nahua* with the caution that
it is both clumsy and inaccurate. *Aztec* refers specifically to the Nahuatl
speaking residents of Mexico-Tenochtitlan, the Mexica-Tenocha, but not to
the Nahuatl-speaking residents of Chalco, Cholula, or Tlaxcala, for example
The term's use also imposes an artificial unity upon Mexica-Tenocha thinking
Views about the nature of things were fragmented since they obviously dif
fered between nobility and commoners; priests, warriors, merchants, artisans
and farmers; men and women; dominant and subordinate city-states; regional
and ethnic subgroups; and finally, even between individuals themselves.[5] They
were contested and resisted by various groups in various ways and in varying
degrees. What's more, metaphysical views are living works in progress and thus
are continually changing over time. Some scholars contend, for example, that
at the time of the Conquest Aztec philosophy was becoming more hierarchi
cal, militaristic, and masculinist – as evidenced by the increasing prominence
of Huitzilopochtli (the Sun-War God) in Aztec religious affairs – due to the
increasingly hierarchical social and political stratification of Aztec society, the
emergence of a hereditary ruling elite, and the ruling elite's greater emphasis
upon war and military conquest.[6] This contention notwithstanding, I submit
that the central concepts and organizing metaphors employed by Aztec philos
ophers in thinking about the nature of things were rooted squarely in ordinary
ways of thinking and speaking about everyday activities such as living, dying
eating, weaving, farming, hunting, sexual reproduction, and warfare. Therefore
while I consider the metaphysical views presented here as an approximation
of the more or less shared understanding of the upper elite of Aztec priests
scholars, and educated nobility, I nevertheless maintain that these views were
firmly anchored in non-elite views about the nature and way of things. The
former group simply had more opportunity to refine and articulate their views

than did the latter. Their views accordingly differed in degree of refinement, not in substance.

Our current scholarly understanding of Aztec thought and culture is the product of a rich and sophisticated interdisciplinary conversation between anthropologists, archaeologists, archaeoastronomers, art historians, historians, linguists, literary theorists, and religionists. This book draws deeply and openly from this ongoing conversation. Noticeably absent from this conversation, however, is the voice of academic philosophy. This study seeks to fill this absence. How then does it differ from existing scholarship?

I come to Aztec metaphysics as someone trained in contemporary academic Anglo-American analytic philosophy, history of Western philosophy, and comparative world philosophy. What makes mine a *philosophical* rather than a historical, religionist, or anthropological examination and interpretation is the fact that I bring to bear upon our understanding of Aztec metaphysics the analytical tools, concepts, hermeneutical strategies, lessons, and insights of these areas of academic philosophy. Doing so, I hope, enables me to shed new light upon the Aztecs' views about the nature, constitution, and structure of reality. This project *reconstructs* Aztec metaphysics in the sense of presenting and explicating the concepts and claims of Aztec metaphysics in a manner not necessarily identical with the Aztecs' manner of presentation. Doing so inevitably involves highlighting and making explicit certain aspects of Aztec metaphysics at the expense of others. What's more, many of the terms and concepts I employ – beginning with the concept of metaphysics itself – are alien to Aztec thought. This is unavoidable in any explication that involves interpreting and translating one way of thinking about things into an alien system of thinking about things. Although alien, my hope is that the terms and concepts I employ are not hostile to and do minimal violence to Aztec metaphysics. I will let my critics determine the degree of violence my interpretative translation of Aztec metaphysics into non-Aztec metaphysics wreaks upon Aztec metaphysics.

I approach Aztec metaphysics as a systematic, unified, and coherent corpus of thought, worthy of consideration in its own terms and for its own sake (quite apart from what contemporary Western readers may find instructive or valuable in it). I accordingly aim to understand the internal logic and structure of Aztec metaphysics – that is, how its claims, concepts, metaphors, and arguments fit together – rather than *causally explain* Aztec metaphysics in terms such as genes, memes, collective unconsciousness, dietary needs, social-political function, mode of production, or physical environment. Before explaining causally *why* the Aztecs believed as they did, one must *first* correctly apprehend *what* they believed. I examine the internal logic of Aztec metaphysics in the same manner that Euro-American academic philosophers engaged in "normal" (in the Kuhnian sense[7]) history of philosophy routinely examine the internal logic of the metaphysics of Plato, Spinoza, Hegel, or Russell. The project is cut from the same cloth as these projects; it is no more and no less a history of philosophy – or anthropology or intellectual history, for that matter – than are they.

Approaching Aztec metaphysics in this manner does not commit one to an idealist view of philosophy that sees philosophers and their views as operating autonomously from the exigencies of history, politics, economics, culture, and natural environment. Aztec philosophy, like all philosophies, emerges in response to everyday life problems and challenges and admits of naturalistic explanation in terms of these. However, naturalistic explanations of philosophies advanced by anthropologists and sociologists of knowledge, neuroscientists, intellectual historians, and evolutionary psychologists remain a thoroughly Western scientific project. And by forcing Aztec and other non-Western philosophies upon the Procrustean bed of Western metaphysical and epistemological assumptions in this manner, such naturalistic explanations inevitably privilege Western metaphysical and epistemological assumptions to the detriment of non-Western philosophies. Yet such privileging of the Western is a priori unwarranted and question-begging. By parity of reasoning we must be willing to give equal consideration to non-Western (e.g., Aztec or Daoist) explanations of Western philosophies.[8]

Finally, this study focuses upon what I consider to be the central tenets and concepts of Aztec metaphysics. It does not purport to be exhaustive. I see it as complementing the closely related and often times overlapping work of other scholars in the field.

0.2 AZTEC THOUGHT AS PHILOSOPHY

Contemporary Anglo-American and European academic philosophers routinely distinguish *having* a philosophy, in the sense of holding an implicit worldview, ideology, or "*cosmovisión*," from *doing* philosophy, in the sense of self-consciously and critically reflecting upon and speculating about the nature, structure, and constitution of reality, the nature of truth, the nature of right and wrong, the possibility of human knowledge, the meaning of life, and so on. They contend that while all cultures *have* a philosophy, not all cultures contain individuals who think philosophically and thus *do* philosophy. The former emerges haphazardly and un-self-consciously without systematic or sustained critical reflection. In contrast, doing philosophy – that is, philosophy *properly speaking* – is the sole invention and possession of Western culture beginning with

Socratics and the Sophists. As though channeling sixteenth-century European "discoverers," these modern-day schoolmen argue that non-Western peoples are in effect unreasoning, philosophical sleepwalkers. This view is crisply articulated by prominent Western philosophers such as Edmund Husserl, who claimed that the expression *Western philosophy* is tautologous while the expression *non-Western philosophy* is oxymoronic;[9] Emmanuel Levinas, who once remarked, "I always say – but in private – that the Greeks and the Bible are all that is serious in humanity. Everything else is dancing";[10] and Richard Rorty who claimed that looking for philosophy outside of the West is "pointless" since philosophy is unique to Western culture.[11] According to Robert Bernasconi, "Western philosophy traps [non-Western philosophy] in a double bind: either [non-Western philosophy] is so similar to Western philosophy that it makes no distinctive contribution and effectively disappears; or it is so different that its credentials to be genuine philosophy will always be in doubt."[12] Either way, Western philosophers think and speak for all humanity. This view is not confined to academic philosophers, of course. Western anthropologists, religionists, and historians of ideas also commonly contend that while non-Western peoples are capable of religious and mythopoeic thought, they are clearly incapable of philosophical thought.[13]

In his groundbreaking 1956 book, *La filosofía náhuatl*, Miguel León-Portilla argued that Nahua culture included individuals who were every bit as philosophical as Socrates and the Sophists.[14] Nezahualcoyotl, Tochihuitzin Coyolchiuhqui, Ayocuan Cuetzpaltzin, and other Nahuas reflected self-consciously, critically, and generally upon the nature of existence, truth, knowledge, and the reigning mythical-religious views of their day. By attacking the dominant orthodoxy among Western academic philosophers and their epigones regarding the West's monopoly on philosophical activity, León-Portilla brought upon himself a firestorm of calumny and condemnation. In *The Aztec Image in Western Thought* Benjamin Keen, for example, scathingly upbraids León-Portilla for comparing "the highest thought achieved by an Upper Stone Age people" with the "climactic intellectual achievements" of the ancient Greeks.[15] Presumably under pressure from its North American publisher, the book's 1963 English title, *Aztec Thought and Culture: A Study of the Ancient Nahuatl Mind*, backed away from this controversy and steered the book toward university courses in anthropology and history. Judging from the English title, León-Portilla's book was no longer a study of Aztec philosophy. It was now conceived more appropriately as a study of Aztec "thought." Fortunately, however, the text itself remained steadfast in its commitment to the heterodoxy that the Aztecs *did* philosophy.

Why does this issue generate so much heat? Why does it matter who is, and who is not, deemed a philosopher? As countless scholars have argued, philosophy plays a vital role in the modern West's conception of itself and of the non-Western *Other*.[16] What is at stake here is nothing less than the modern West's self-image as rational, self-conscious, civilized, cultured, human disciplined, modern, and masculine in contrast with the non-West as irrational, appetitive, emotional, instinctive, uncivilized, savage, primitive, nonhuman, undisciplined, backward, feminine, and closer to nature. Philosophy, "the queen of the sciences," as Aristotle so marvelously characterized it, represents the pinnacle of humanity's intellectual and rational achievement. For the European Enlightenment, philosophy represents the intellect's emancipation from the fantasies of myth and shackles of religious dogma. Western culture's philosophy versus nonphilosophy binary is thus a social-historical tool constructed to celebrate and legitimize the West and its imperial hegemony while at the same time denigrating "the Rest" and legitimizing its heteronomy.

The reaction to León-Portilla together with the West's attitude toward the philosophical capabilities of non-Western peoples is all the more puzzling in light of the fact that Western academic philosophers are unable to agree among themselves upon a suitable definition of philosophy. All they seem to be able to agree upon is that non-Western thinkers do not (cannot) do it! Even self-styled, antiphilosophical establishment rebels such a Richard Rorty who maintain that philosophy has no essence nevertheless join the chauvinistic chorus denying membership in Club Philosophy to non-Western thinkers.[17] Upon inspection, however, philosophy turns out to be infuriatingly difficult, if not impossible, to define. Indeed, defining philosophy is itself a *philosophical* issue: the sort Western philosophers call a "metaphilosophical problem." Is philosophy to be defined in terms of its aims, subject matter, origin, or method? Is philosophy even the sort of thing that even admits of definition? How do we decide? And more to the point, who gets to decide? Whose definitions and answers count, and why? Whose standards govern the discussion? Who is included and who is excluded from the discussion, and on what grounds? Equally crucially, who poses and entertains as worthwhile questions such as, Are non-Western people philosophical? And why do they pose them? In short, it is far from clear that this issue can be resolved in a non-ethnocentric and noncircular way.

This is obviously not the place to resolve this issue. However, it would seem that those traditionally excluded from Club Philosophy may pursue either of two strategies. They may seek admission into the club by arguing that what they do sufficiently resembles what bona fide club members do. León-Portilla pursues this strategy on behalf of the Aztecs. Or they may reject the philosophy versus nonphilosophy binary – along with the entire debate – as a now discredited, self-serving relic of Western colonialism (racism, modernism, paternalism, etc.), not worry about whether or not what they do qualifies as "real" philosophy, and continue doing what they have always been doing.

I reject the rational-civilized-masculine versus irrational-savage-feminine binary yet also refuse to cede philosophical inquiry to the West. Like León-Portilla, I maintain the Aztecs not only had a philosophy but also *did* philosophy. They engaged in self-consciously reflective and critical endeavors that satisfy the definition of philosophy advanced by North American philosopher Wilfred Sellars: "The aim of philosophy, abstractly formulated, is to understand how things in the broadest possible sense of the term hang together in the broadest possible sense of the term."[18] Their endeavors likewise satisfy William James' definition of philosophy as "the unusually stubborn attempt to think clearly."[19] Indigenous North American philosophers Thurman Lee Hester Jr. and Dennis McPherson claim the thought systems of indigenous North American peoples satisfy the basic definition of philosophy lying at the roots of the Euro-American tradition: "a thoughtful interaction with the world." Every culture has people who give themselves to reflecting upon the world in this manner. "These are their philosophers."[20] Granted, the Aztecs' philosophical journey took a different form and took them to a different set of answers.[21] Yet this is irrelevant. As John Dewey once noted, "I think it shows a remarkable deadness of imagination to suppose that philosophy [must] revolve within the scope of the problems and systems that two thousand years of European history have bequeathed to us."[22] Aztec and European philosophies represent two alternative philosophical orientations and trajectories rooted in two alternative forms of life or ways of being human in the world. Aztec philosophy need not ape European philosophy in order to count as "real" philosophy. There is no law of reason, thought, or culture requiring that all peoples think alike or follow the same path of philosophical development.

It is also sometimes argued that the Aztecs' religiosity precluded their thinking philosophically. Philosophy, as the West's self-narrative often goes, begins where religion ends. This view assumes, however, that religion and philosophy are mutually exclusive. The Aztecs' religiosity no more precluded their doing philosophy than did the religiosity of St. Augustine, Maimonides, St. Aquinas, Ockham, Descartes, Spinoza, Kant, or Whitehead (to name only a few bona fide philosophers by Western lights). What's more, the possibility that Aztec metaphysical speculation operated within the bounds of Aztec religion and served as its "handmaiden" (to borrow Locke's telling phrase) no more disqualifies it as "real" philosophy than does the fact that the lion's share of contemporary Anglo-American philosophy operates within the bounds of science and serves as *its* "handmaiden" disqualifies it as "real" philosophy.

Finally, the cogency of the interpretation of Aztec metaphysics advanced here does not hinge upon one's accepting the thesis that the Aztecs *did* philoso phy. Regardless of one's view on this matter, it is undeniable that the Aztecs *had* a metaphysics, that is, a systematic and coherent understanding of how things in the broadest possible sense hang together.

0.3 METHODOLOGICAL CONSIDERATIONS IN INTERPRETING AZTEC METAPHYSICS

Metaphysical views about the nature, constitution, and structure of reality are by their very nature highly general, abstract, and theoretical. They seem far removed from what we like to think of as the pushes and pulls of everyday immediate experience and people's practical beliefs concerning farming, house building, weaving, and cooking. And this distance, it seems, makes them all the more difficult to access.[23] How then does one access the Aztecs' metaphysical views, and how does one justify one's interpretation of them? Let's begin by tak ing a short stroll through recent Anglo-American philosophy of science.

The late North American philosopher of science, language, and logic, W.V.O Quine, proposed that we think of the structure of what he called "total sci ence" (including logic, mathematics, and the natural and human sciences) as a "man-made fabric" or "field of force."[24] Sense experience impinges upon this grand *web of belief* only along the edges. Our beliefs about the contents of our sense experiences also occur along the web's edge. More-general theoretical speculation and belief occur further within the interior of the web. The prin ciples of logic (such as the law of excluded middle) and theoretical-speculative metaphysical beliefs about the world (such as those concerning quarks and dark matter, gravitational fields, and the relativistic nature of space-time) occur in the interior-most portion of the web, far removed from the concrete sense experiences we customarily associate with scientific testing and experimenta tion. What's more, no particular sense experiences are directly linked with any particular beliefs in the web's interior. They are linked only indirectly by means of considerations of "equilibrium" affecting the web as a whole. Conflicts with experience "occasion," as Quine puts it, readjustments within the interior of the web. Beliefs about sensory experiences, beliefs about physical objects, and beliefs about quarks, quantum phenomena, and the nature of causality all con tribute to the makeup of the total web. As such they occur along an epistemo logical continuum. No in-principle epistemological distinction divides them

Theory and data are united epistemologically within one and the same overall web of belief.

Quine's conception of total science as a web of belief has, to one degree or another, become widely accepted by contemporary Anglo-American philosophers of science.[25] Also universally accepted by philosophers of science is another key tenet of Quine's philosophy of science: the underdetermination of theory by sense experience. Following the late nineteenth-century French philosopher of science Pierre Duhem, Quine argues that empirical evidence does not uniquely determine theory. Faced with unacceptable empirical consequences, scientists have a choice regarding how to respond. "The total field is so underdetermined by its boundary conditions, experience, that there is much latitude of choice as to what statements to reëvaluate in the light of a single contrary experience."[26] Empirical adequacy alone does not therefore suffice as an epistemological criterion in scientific decision-making. "The edge of the system must be squared with experience," writes Quine, "the rest, with all its elaborate myths or fictions, has as it objective the simplicity of laws."[27] Scientists accordingly appeal to nonempirical criteria when choosing between rival theories.

On what additional grounds do scientists choose between alternative scientific theories and webs of belief? On what additional grounds do they choose, for example, between alternative logics (e.g., two-valued as opposed to three-valued), alternative theories of space-time (e.g., relational as opposed to substantive), alternative conceptions of natural laws (e.g., deterministic as opposed to irreducibly probabilistic), or alternative theories of causality (e.g., allowing as opposed to not allowing causation backward in time)? The current consensus among philosophers of science maintains that scientists appeal to a variety of competing, non-algorithmically ordered values when making such decisions: empirical adequacy (how well does the theory capture the sense experience?); logical consistency; simplicity (Occam's razor, or to what extent does the theory provide a unified and common treatment of diverse phenomena as opposed to treating each phenomena separately and independently?); conservatism (how well does the theory preserve existing views?); unification (how well does it unify our beliefs into a coherent whole by bringing together apparently diverse phenomena under a single account?); generality; fecundity (how productive of new areas of inquiry is it? What new problems does it enable us to solve?); and explanatory power (how well does it explain why things happen as they do?).[28]

Let's focus on the explanatory role of theory. Theory explains and makes intelligible empirical data. Theory without empirical data is, of course, empty, but empirical data without theory are blind. Whether a given sensory experience counts as information (data) and hence is evidentially significant, as opposed to

mere noise, depends upon whether or not the sense experience may be incorpo
rated within a theory. All information is thus theory laden since theory cuts all
the way down. Empirical input is not epistemologically self-standing.

As we saw, one criterion for selecting theories is explanatory power. Philos
ophers of science such as Richard Boyd defend what they call the principle
of inference to the best explanation.[29] Given a choice between two competing
theories, one is justified in adopting the theory that offers us the best explana
tion of the empirical data. For example, we are justified in adopting theories
that posit the existence of unobservable (so-called theoretical) entities or forces
such as quarks, antimatter, gravity, or even more humble middle-sized physical
objects (such as rocks, skyscrapers, and trees) and hence justified in believing
that these unobservables exist to the degree that the relevant theories offer us
a better explanation of the relevant sense experiences than do those compet
ing theories that do not posit their existence. Consider the prosaic example
of middle-sized physical objects. We are justified in positing the existence of
middle-sized physical objects (such as mountains, insects, and houses) and thus
believing that middle-sized physical objects exist if doing so better explains the
relevant phenomena (our sense experiences) than do rival theories such as that
which posits the existence of a Cartesian-style, omnipotent, and malevolent
devil who causes these experiences, or that which claims all our sense experi
ences are the products of dreams or hallucinations. Such an explanation, argue
Boyd and others, increases the coherence and unification of our entire system of
belief and thus increases our understanding of the phenomena.

How does this detour through contemporary philosophy of science bear
upon justifying an interpretation of Aztec metaphysics? Given the general,
abstract, and theoretical speculative nature of metaphysical views, we should
expect Aztec views about the nature, structure, and ultimate constituents of
reality to be abstract, general, and theoretical-speculative. Consequently, we
should not expect them to be immediately apparent from the empirical evi
dence available to contemporary researchers.[30] We should not expect them to
appear on the surface of what is immediately observable. As students of Aztec
metaphysics we must therefore recognize the necessity of having to theorize
about the Aztecs' theorizing on the basis of the available evidence. And what is
our available evidence?

Generally speaking, our understanding of Aztec philosophy, religion, and cul
ture is constrained by the fact that we lack pre-Contact Aztec primary sources
written in Nahuatl. Reconstructing Aztec metaphysics therefore requires tri
angulating from a host of alternative sources. First, we have the ethnohistories
and dictionaries of early Spanish and mestizo chroniclers such as Bernardino

de Sahagún, Diego Durán, Toribio de Benavente (Motolinía), Alonso de Molina, Fernando de Alva Ixtlilxochitl, Gerónimo Mendieta, Hernando Alvarado Tezozomoc, and Juan de Torquemada. Second, we have Aztec and other Conquest-era indigenous pictorial histories, ritual calendars, maps, and tribute records. Third, we have archaeological evidence such as architecture, statues, pottery, weaving tools, jewelry, tools, and human remains. Fourth, we have the correlations between ancient and modern astronomies culled by contemporary ethnoastronomers. And finally, we have ethnographies of contemporary Nahuatl-speaking and other non-Nahuatl-speaking indigenous peoples of Mesoamerica.[31] I avail myself of all these in constructing my interpretation of Aztec metaphysics.

How do we assess the evidential credentials of alternative interpretations of Aztec metaphysics? Our detour through contemporary philosophy of science suggests that we assess theoretical interpretations of Aztec metaphysics in such terms as empirical adequacy, conservatism, simplicity, internal coherence, unification, fecundity, and explanatory power.[32] We should expect a scholarly interpretation of Aztec metaphysics to capture as much of the empirical data as possible; to preserve as much previously established scholarship as possible; to suggest new questions and avenues of research; to be consistent in the sense of maximizing the internal, logical consistency of Aztec metaphysical beliefs; to be simple in the sense of providing a unified, common treatment of different phenomena; and to be coherent in the sense of attributing to the Aztecs an intelligible metaphysics, that is, one that makes sense of itself in its own terms. Finally, we should expect an interpretation of Aztec metaphysics to offer us an explanation of Aztec behavior broadly construed, that is, their ritual, religious, cultural, social, and, yes, even their agricultural, military, and craft practices.

Consequently, although there is admittedly no direct empirical evidence for our interpretive claims about Aztec metaphysics (just as there is no direct empirical evidence for our theoretical claims concerning, quarks, black holes, or curved space-time), there is nevertheless (as contemporary philosophers of science argue) indirect evidence for deciding between better and worse interpretations relative to the foregoing criteria of theory choice. The absence of direct empirical evidence should no more deter us from theorizing about the contents of Aztec metaphysics than it should deter physicists from theorizing about the nature of elementary forces, the Big Bang, and the deep structure of the universe.

It is therefore in the light of the aforementioned evidential criteria that we need to ask, to which did Aztec metaphysics subscribe: polytheism or pantheism? Ontological monism or pluralism? Constitutional monism or dualism?

Substantival or relational conception of time and space? Which of these offers us a better theoretical account of Aztec metaphysics? Which offers us a better explanation and understanding of Aztec practices broadly construed? Which provides a unified, common treatment of different phenomena? Which attributes to the Aztecs a metaphysics that makes sense of itself in its own terms? I contend the interpretation of Aztec metaphysics advanced here is justified by the foregoing evidential criteria.

0.4 CHAPTER OUTLINE

The Aztecs advanced a systematic, coherent, and sophisticated metaphysics. Chapter 1 argues that at the heart of Aztec metaphysics stands the ontological thesis that there exists at bottom just one thing: dynamic, vivifying, eternally self-generating and self-regenerating sacred power, force, or energy. The Aztecs referred to this power as *teotl*. Reality and thus the cosmos and all its inhabitants are identical with and consist of teotl. Since teotl is constitutionally uniform, reality consists ultimately of just one kind of stuff: energy. Aztec metaphysics thus embraces an ontological and constitutional monism. Since only teotl exists and teotl is constitutionally uniform, it follows that Aztec philosophy also embraces a nonhierarchical metaphysics, that is, one that denies any principled metaphysical distinction between transcendent and immanent, higher and lower, or supernatural and natural realities, degrees of being, or kinds of stuff.

Process, movement, change, and transformation define teotl. That which is real is that which becomes, changes, and moves. Reality is characterized by *becoming* – not by *being* or "is-ness." To exist – to be real – is to become, to move, to change. Teotl and hence reality, cosmos, and all existing things are defined in terms of becoming. They are essentially dynamic: always moving, always changing. Aztec philosophy thus embraces what Western philosophers call a *process metaphysics*. Process metaphysics holds that processes rather than perduring objects, entities, or substances are ontologically fundamental. Lastly, chapter 1 anticipates and responds to several possible objections to this interpretation.

Chapter 2 contends Aztec metaphysics is better understood as pantheistic rather than polytheistic. Everything that exists constitutes a single, all-inclusive and interrelated unity. This single all-encompassing unity is substantively constituted by teotl and is ontologically identical with teotl. It is genealogically unified by teotl since it emerges from teotl. Teotl is not the "creator" ex nihilo of the cosmos in a theistic sense but rather the immanent engenderer of the cosmos. Teotl is not a minded or intentional agent, being, or deity. The history of the cosmos is nothing more than the self-unfolding and self-presenting of teotl. This single, all-inclusive unity is sacred because teotl is sacred. Chapter 2 also anticipates and responds to several possible objections to this view.

Teotl's ceaseless becoming and self-transforming are characterized by what I call *agonistic inamic unity*. Chapter 3 explores this notion. An *inamic* is a power, force, or influence that is by definition matched or paired with a second power, force, or influence. Each is conceived as the complementary polar opposite of the other. Each is the inamic of the other. Together, the two constitute an inamic pair, or set of paired inamic partners. Male and female, for example, are each other's inamic. Male is the inamic of female; female the inamic of male. Each is the inamic partner of the other. Since the concept of inamic is relational (e.g., like sisterhood), nothing can be an inamic by itself. Inamic partners by definition come in pairs. Other inamic pairs include life/death, dry/wet, hot/cold, being/nonbeing, and order/disorder. Each inamic is mutually arising, interdependent, and complementary as well as mutually competitive (antagonistic) with its partner inamic. What's more, each pair of inamic partners forms a unity, albeit an unstable one. Paired inamic forces perpetually struggle against one another. Because inamic partners coexist alongside one another, they are properly understood neither as contraries nor as contradictories as these relationships are standardly defined by Western philosophy. The transformation and becoming of reality and cosmos consist of the nonteleological struggle (agon) between inamic partners as well as the alternating dominance of each inamic over its partner. All existing things (e.g., suns, humans, trees, and corn) are constituted by the agonistic unity of inamic partners and consequently constitutionally unstable and ambiguous. Indeed, reality itself is irreducibly ambiguous. In keeping with Aztec philosophy's ontological and constitutional monism, inamic partners represent *dual aspects of teotl* – not two metaphysically distinct substances.

Inamic partners struggle against one another and unite with one another in three principal ways: *olin*, *malinalli*, and *nepantla*. These represent three different patterns of motion and change or what I call *motion-change* (seeing as how Aztec metaphysics regards qualitative change as a species of motion broadly construed). They define the dynamics of reality and cosmos. Teotl's sacred energy and agonistic inamic forces circulate throughout the cosmos in these three ways. I devote chapters 4, 5, and 6 to each (respectively). Olin is curving, swaying, oscillating, pulsating, and centering motion-change. It is exemplified by bouncing balls, pulsating hearts, respiring chests, earthquakes, labor contractions, and the daily movement of the Fifth Sun. Olin is also the motion-change of fourfold cyclical completion and transformation *within* and *across* olin-defined life-death cycles. Since all things in the Fifth Age are alive, all things are defined by a four-phased olin-defined life-death cycle. As the defining pattern of motion-change in the Fifth Age, olin constitutes the biorhythm of the Fifth Sun, the Fifth Age, and all inhabitants of the Fifth Age. Malinalli is twisting, spinning, gyrating, coiling, whirling, and spiraling motion-change. It is exemplified by spinning fiber into thread, cooking and digesting food, blowing life into things, drilling fire, burning incense, and ritual music, speech, and song (*in xochitl in cuicatl*). Malinalli is the motion-change involved in energy transmission between olin-defined life-death cycles of different things (e.g., from sun to grass to rabbit to human to sun, and so on), between vertical layers of the cosmos, and between different conditions of the same thing (e.g., raw cotton into spun thread). Malinalli motion-change initiates, nourishes, and feeds olin-defined life-death cycles. It is also the energy-conveying, life-sustaining bloodstream and foodstream of the Fifth Age. Nepantla is middling, intermixing, and mutually reciprocating motion-change. It binds together inamic pairs in the simultaneously creative-and-destructive agonistic tension of transformation. Nepantla motion-change is exemplified by mixing and shaking things together, weaving (interlacing), and sexual commingling. Nepantla is metaphysically speaking the most fundamental of the three. It cosmogonically precedes and incorporates olin and malinalli. Nepantla motion-change defines and explains teotl's – and hence reality's – continual self-generation, self-regeneration, and self-transformation. Nepantla holds the key to understanding Aztec metaphysics.

Chapter 7 argues that Aztec metaphysics conceives time and space as a single, seamless unity: what I call *time-place*. Time-place is a pattern in the modus operandi of teotl's continual becoming, processing, and moving-changing. Time-place is a matter of *how* teotl moves and is therefore relational, not substantive. The *tonalpohualli* (or 260-day calendar count), *xiuhpohualli* (or 360+5-day calendar count), and *xiuhmolpilli* (52-year calendar count) represent patterns in the unfolding of teotl.

Finally, chapter 8 argues that Aztec metaphysics conceives teotl as a grand cosmic weaver who by means of nepantla motion-change generates and regenerates reality, the cosmos, the Five Ages of the cosmos, and all existing things. *Teotl is the weaver, the weaving, and the woven.* The cosmos per se is a grand weaving in progress. Weaving serves as one of the principal organizing metaphors of Aztec metaphysics. Aztec metaphysics conceives the Fifth Age in particular as a grand weaving in progress and conceives teotl as its grand cosmic weaver. Aztec metaphysics models the continuing generation and regeneration of the Fifth Age upon backstrap weaving. Because weaving is an instance of nepantla motion-change, it follows that Aztec metaphysics conceives the Fifth Age as a grand nepantla-defined weaving in progress and conceives teotl as a grand cosmic weaver who, by means of nepantla motion-change, generates and regenerates the Fifth Age and all its inhabitants. Nepantla motion-change constitutes the creative interlacing of warp and weft into the agonistic inamic unity that is reality. Nepantla motion-change generates as well as defines the fabric of the cosmos. As such, weaving (nepantla motion-change) is the fundamental and all-encompassing, creative, and transformative motion-change of the Fifth Age. How do olin and malinalli figure into the weaving of the Fifth Age? Weaving fabric involves interlacing weft (horizontal) and warp (vertical) fibers. Olin motion-change constitutes the horizontal weft-related activities that contribute to the weaving the Fifth Age. It functions as the Fifth Age's weft. The wefting of the Fifth Age is carried out by the Fifth Sun's olin-defined oscillating path about the earth. Malinalli motion-change, in turn, constitutes the vertical warp-related activities that contribute to the weaving of the Fifth Age. Malinalli motion-change thus functions as the Fifth Age's warp. The tonalpohualli, xiuhpohualli, and xiuhmolpilli represent warp patterns in teotl's weaving of the Fifth Age.

I conclude by suggesting that nepantla holds the key not only to understanding Aztec metaphysics but also to Aztec philosophy generally. Aztec tlamatinime defined the human existential condition in terms of nepantla, and accordingly fleshed out what Western philosophers call wisdom, moral philosophy, social and political philosophy, epistemology, and aesthetics in terms of nepantla.

NOTES

1. See Anthony Pagden (*The Fall of Natural Man* [Cambridge: University of Cambridge Press, 1982]) and Benjamin Keen (*The Aztec Image in Western Thought* [New Brunswick, NJ: Rutgers University Press, 1971]) for discussion of European attitudes toward the indigenous peoples of Europe's "New World."

2. It is not obvious that these categories apply to Aztec thought. They reflect, after all, our way of thinking about things, not necessarily the Aztecs'.

3. As with all matters philosophical, the definition of metaphysics is itself controversial. For discussion, see Jaegwon Kim and Ernest Sosa, eds., *A Companion to Metaphysics* (Oxford: Blackwell, 1995); Robert Audi, ed., *The Cambridge Dictionary of Philosophy* (Cambridge: Cambridge University Press, 1995); and Nicholas Rescher, *Process Metaphysics: An Introduction to Process Philosophy* (Albany: State University of New York Press, 1996), 8.

4. Metaphysics is more abstract than the notion of *cosmovisión* employed by scholars such as Johanna Broda, "Astronomy, *Cosmovisión*, and Ideology in Pre-Hispanic Mesoamerica," in *Ethnoastronomy and Archaeoastronomy in the American Tropics*, ed. Anthony

Aveni and Gary Urton, Annals of the New York Academy of Sciences, No. 38 (New York: New York Academy of Sciences, 1982), 81–110; Broda, "Astronomical Knowledge, Calendrics, and Sacred Geography in Ancient Mesoamerica," in *Astronomies and Cultures*, ed. Clive N. Ruggles and Nicholas J. Saunders (Niwot: University Press of Colorado 1993), 253–95; Alfredo López Austin, *The Human Body and Ideology: Concepts of the Ancient Nahuas*, 2 vols., trans. Thelma Ortiz de Montellano and Bernard R. Ortiz de Montellano (Salt Lake City: University of Utah Press, 1988); López Austin, *Tamoanchan, Tlalocan: Places of Mist*, trans. Bernard R. Ortiz de Montellano and Thelma Ortiz de Montellano (Niwot: University Press of Colorado, 1997); López Austin, "Cosmovision," trans. Scott Sessions, in *The Oxford Encyclopedia of Mesoamerican Cultures: The Civilizations of Mexico and Central America*, ed. Davíd Carrasco (Oxford: Oxford University Press, 2001), 1: 268–74; Davíd Carrasco, *Religions of Mesoamerica: Cosmovision and Ceremonial Centers* (San Francisco: Harper and Row, 1990); and Carrasco, *City of Sacrifice: The Aztec Empire and the Role of Violence in Civilization* (Boston: Beacon Press, 1999).

5. See Elizabeth M. Brumfiel, "Huitzilopochtli's Conquest: Aztec Ideology in the Archaeological Record," *Cambridge Archaeological Journal* 8, no. 1 (1998): 3–13; Inga Clendinnen, *Aztecs: An Interpretation* (Cambridge: Cambridge University Press, 1991); Nancy Gonlin and Jon C. Lohse, eds., *Commoner Ritual and Ideology in Ancient Mesoamerica* (Boulder: University Press of Colorado, 2007); López Austin, *Human Body and Ideology*; López Austin, *The Rabbit on the Face of the Moon: Mythology in the Mesoamerican Tradition*, trans. Bernard R. Ortiz de Montellano and Thelma Ortiz de Montellano (Salt Lake City: University of Utah Press, 1996), 112–13; Kay A. Read, *Time and Sacrifice in the Aztec Cosmos* (Bloomington: Indiana University Press, 1998); and more generally James C. Scott, *Domination and the Arts of Resistance: Hidden Transcripts* (New Haven, CT: Yale University Press, 1990), for discussion of demographic differences in beliefs. Miguel León-Portilla (*Aztec Thought and Culture: A Study of the Ancient Nahuatl Mind* [Norman: University of Oklahoma Press, 1963]) argues official Aztec philosophy changed over time under the influence of different *tlatoani* or speaker-ruler-kings. Alfonso Caso (*The Aztecs: People of the Sun*, trans. Lowell Dunham [Norman: University of Oklahoma Press, 1958], 7), León-Portilla (*Aztec Thought and Culture*), and J. Jorge Klor de Alva ("Christianity and the Aztecs," *San Jose Studies* 5 [1979]: 7–21) argue polytheism was embraced by the masses but not by the elite. Their argument rests upon the assumption that common folk are insufficiently intelligent and abstract-minded to grasp pantheism and are consequently capable of holding only a more simple-minded polytheism. This assumption is challenged by Alan Sandstrom (*Corn Is Our Blood: Culture and Ethnic Identity in a Contemporary Aztec Indian Village* [Norman: University of Oklahoma Press, 1991]), Viola Cordova ("The European Concept of *Usen*: An American Aboriginal Text," in *Native American Religious Identity: Unforgotten Gods*, ed. Jace Weaver [Maryknoll, NY: Orbis, 1998], 26–32), and Brian Yazzie Burkhart ("The Physics of the Spirit: The

Indigenous Continuity of Science and Religion," in *The Routledge Companion to Religion and Science*, ed. James W. Hagg, Gregory R. Peterson, and Michael L. Spezio [New York: Routledge, 2011], 34–42). I believe both commoners and elite embraced pantheism to the same extent.

6. For example: León-Portilla (*Aztec Thought and Culture*); Brenda Rosenbaum ("Women and Gender in Mesoamerica," in *The Legacy of Mesoamerica: History and Culture of a Native American Civilization*, ed. Robert Carmack, Janine Gasco, and Gary H. Gossen [Upper Saddle River, NJ: Prentice Hall, 1996], 325–26); and Alan Sandstrom (personal correspondence).

7. Thomas S. Kuhn, *The Structure of Scientific Revolutions*, 2nd enlarged ed. (Chicago: University of Chicago Press, 1970).

8. For further discussion, see James Maffie, "'Whatever Happens, We Have the Gatlin Gun, and They Have Not': Future Prospects for Indigenous Knowledges," special issue, *Futures: The Journal of Policy and Planning, and Future Studies* 41 (2009): 53–65; Vine Deloria Jr., *God Is Red: A Native View of Religion* (Golden, CO: Fulcrum Publishing, 1994); and Laurie Ann Whitt, "Indigenous Peoples and the Cultural Politics of Knowledge," in *Issues in Native American Cultural Identity*, ed. Michael K. Green (New York: Peter Lang, 1995), 223–71. Many indigenous thinkers claim scientific-style explanations of indigenous philosophies perpetuate the West's colonization of indigenous philosophies. See Cecil King, "Here Come the Anthros," in *Indians and Anthropologists: Vine Deloria, Jr., and the Critique of Anthropology*, ed. Thomas Biolsi and Larry J. Zimmerman (Tucson: University of Arizona, 1997), 115–19; and Huanani-Kay Trask, *From a Native Daughter: Colonialism and Sovereignty in Hawai'i* (Honolulu: University of Hawai'i Press, 1999).

9. Quoted in Bina Gupta and J. N. Mohanty, eds., *Philosophical Questions East and West* (Lanham, MD: Rowman and Littlefield, 2000), xi.

10. Quoted in Robert Bernasconi, "African Philosophy's Challenge to Continental Philosophy," in *Postcolonial African Philosophy: A Critical Reader*, ed. Emmanuel Chukwadi Eze (Oxford: Blackwell, 1997), 185.

11. Quoted in Barry Hallen, "'Philosophy Doesn't Translate': Richard Rorty and Multiculturalism," *SAPINA* 8, no. 3 (1995): 17.

12. Bernasconi, "African Philosophy's Challenge," 188, brackets mine. For their part, Western social scientists and philosophers construct various conceptual dichotomies such as rational versus irrational, intellectualist versus symbolist, logical versus mythopoeic, linear versus non-linear, traditional versus modern, and open versus closed – into which they try to force non-Western thinking. For discussion, see David L. Hall and Roger T. Ames, *Thinking through Confucius* (Albany: State University of New York Press, 1987); Hall and Ames, *Thinking from the Han: Self, Truth and Transcendence in Chinese and Western Culture* (Albany: SUNY Press, 1998); Brian Morris, *Anthropological Studies*

of Religion: An Introductory Text (Cambridge: Cambridge University Press, 1987); Hallen, "'Philosophy Doesn't Translate'"; Donald Fixico, *The American Indian Mind in a Linear World* (New York: Routledge, 2003); Thomas Norton-Smith, *The Dance of Person and Place: One Interpretation of American Indian Philosophy* (Buffalo: SUNY Press, 2010); Burkhart, "The Physics of the Spirit"; Cordova, "The European Concept of *Usen*"; and Deloria, *God Is Red*.

13. Lucien Lévy-Bruhl (*How Natives Think*, trans. Lilian A. Clare with an introduction by Ruth L. Bunzel [New York: Washington Square Press, 1966]), Henri Frankfort and H. A. Frankfort ("Myth and Reality" and "The Emancipation of Thought from Myth," in *The Intellectual Adventure of Ancient Man*, ed. Henri Frankfort, H.A. Frankfort, John A. Wilson, Thorkild Jacobsen, and William A. Irwin [Chicago: University of Chicago, 1977], 3–30, 363–88), and Keen (*Aztec Image in Western Thought*) advance such a view.

14. Miguel León-Portilla, *La filosofía náhuatl: Estudiada en sus fuentes con nuevo apéndice*, new ed., prologue by Angel María Garibay K. (México, DF: Universidad Nacional Autónoma de México, 2001 [1956]); León-Portilla, *Aztec Thought and Culture*; León-Portilla, *Fifteen Poets of the Aztec World* (Norman: University of Oklahoma Press, 1992).

15. Keen, *Aztec Image in Western Thought*, 40. Keen does not hazard an explanation of the putative connection between technological and philosophical sophistication.

16. As the late Standing Rock Sioux scholar Vine Deloria Jr. writes, "Tribal peoples have traditionally been understood by Westerners as the last remnants of a . . . 'primitive stage' of human development . . . [T]he stereotype of primitive peoples anchors the whole edifice of Western social thought" (Vine Deloria Jr., "Philosophy and the Tribal Peoples," in *American Indian Thought*, ed. Anne Waters [Oxford: Blackwell, 2004], 3). See also Edward Said, *Orientalism* (New York: Vintage, 1978); Sandra Harding, *Is Science Multicultural? Postcolonialisms, Feminisms, and Epistemologies* (Bloomington: Indiana University Press, 1988); Charles W. Mills, *The Racial Contract* (Ithaca, NY: Cornell University Press, 1997); Bernasconi, "African Philosophy's Challenge"; Walter D. Mignolo, "Philosophy and the Colonial Difference," in *Latin American Philosophy*, ed. Eduardo Mendieta (Bloomington: Indiana University Press, 2003); Paget Henry, *Caliban's Reason: Introducing Afro-Caribbean Philosophy* (London: Routledge, 2000); Hallen, "'Philosophy Doesn't Translate'"; James Maffie, "Ethnoepistemology," *The Internet Encyclopedia of Philosophy* (2005, http://www.iep.utm.edu/ethno-ep); Maffie, "'Whatever Happens'"; and Maffie, "In *Huehue Tlamanitiliztli* and *la Verdad*: Nahua and European Philosophies in Fray Bernardino de Sahagún's *Colloquios y doctrina cristiana*," *Inter-America Journal of Philosophy* 3 (June 2012): 1–33.

17. Richard Rorty, *Objectivity, Relativism, and Truth* (Cambridge: Cambridge University Press, 1991); Rorty, "A Pragmatist View of Rationality and Cultural Difference," *Philosophy East and West* 42 (1992): 581–89; Rorty, "Stories of Difference: A Conversation

with Richard Rorty," ed. Gaurav Desai, *SAPINA Bulletin* 2–3 (1993): 23–45. For critical discussion, see Hallen, "'Philosophy Doesn't Translate.'"

18. Wilfrid Sellars, *Science, Perception and Reality* (London: Routledge and Kegan Paul, 1963), 1.

19. Quoted in Hall and Ames, *Thinking through Confucius*, 68.

20. Thurman Lee Hester Jr. and Dennis McPherson, "Editorial: The Euro-American Philosophical Tradition and Its Ability to Examine Indigenous Philosophy," *Ayaangwaamizin: The International Journal of Indigenous Philosophy* 1 (1997): 9. See also Norton-Smith, *The Dance of Person and Place*; Burkhart, "The Physics of the Spirit"; Henry, *Caliban's Reason*; Viola Cordova, "Approaches to Native American Philosophy," in *American Indian Thought*, ed. Anne Waters (Oxford: Blackwell, 2004), 27–33; Paul Radin, *Primitive Man as Philosopher* (New York: Dover Publications, 1957); Barbara Deloria, Kristen Foehner, and Sam Scinta, eds., *Spirit and Reason: A Vine Deloria Jr. Reader* (Golden, CO: Fulcrum Publishers, 1999); and Hallen, "'Philosophy Doesn't Translate.'" Alejandro Santana (in "Did the Aztecs Do Philosophy?," *American Philosophical Association Newsletter on Hispanic/Latino Issues in Philosophy* 8, no. 1 [2008]: 2–9), presents a marvelous review of definitions of philosophy culled from recent introductory philosophy college textbooks. He argues Aztec theorizing satisfies all these criteria and so handily qualifies as "real" philosophy by these standards.

21. I argue (in Maffie, "Ethnoepistemology"; Maffie, "'Whatever Happens'"; and Maffie, "In *Huehue Tlamanitiliztli* and *la Verdad*") that the Aztecs conceived philosophy as a way-seeking enterprise while Euro-American philosophers overwhelmingly conceive philosophy as a truth-seeking enterprise.

22. L. A. Hickman and T. A. Alexander, eds., *The Essential Dewey*, vol. 1 (Bloomington: Indiana University Press, 1998), 21.

23. In this respect metaphysics resembles religion and theology.

24. See W.V.O. Quine, *From a Logical Point of View*, 2nd ed., rev. (Cambridge, MA: Harvard University Press, 1961), 42–46; see also W.V.O. Quine, *Word and Object* (Cambridge, MA: MIT Press, 1960). See W. H. Newton-Smith, ed., *A Companion to the Philosophy of Science* (Oxford: Blackwell, 2000), for discussion.

25. For discussion of these issues see Quine, *From a Logical Point of View*; Philip Kitcher, *Abusing Science: The Case against Scientific Creationism* (Cambridge, MA: MIT Press, 1982); and Newton-Smith, *A Companion to the Philosophy of Science*.

26. Quine, *From a Logical Point of View*, 42–43.

27. Ibid., 45.

28. See Quine, *Word and Object*; Quine, *From a Logical Point of View*; Kitcher, *Abusing Science*; Alison Wylie, *Thinking from Things: Essays in the Philosophy of Archaeology* (Berkeley: University of California Press, 2002); and Newton-Smith, *Companion to the Philosophy of Science*, for further discussion.

29. Richard Boyd, "The Current Status of Scientific Realism," in *Scientific Realism*, ed. Jarrett Leplin (Berkeley: University of California Press, 1984). See Newton-Smith, *Companion to the Philosophy of Science*, for discussion.

30. See Quine, *Word and Object*.

31. For further discussion of available sources, see Davíd Carrasco, ed., *The Oxford Encyclopedia of Mesoamerican Cultures: The Civilizations of Mexico and Central America* (Oxford: Oxford University Press, 2001); López Austin, *Human Body and Ideology*; López Austin, *Tamoanchan, Tlalocan*; and Michael E. Smith, *The Aztecs* (Oxford: Blackwell, 1996).

32. I see no in-principle epistemological distinction between the natural and social sciences. For further discussion of the epistemology of the social sciences, see Brian Fay, *Contemporary Philosophy of Social Science* (Oxford: Blackwell, 1996); Quine, *From a Logical Point of View*; Quine, *Word and Object*; and Newton-Smith, *Companion to the Philosophy of Science*. Alison Wylie (*Thinking from Things*) applies these lessons from contemporary epistemology of science to archaeology.

Let's begin our examination of Aztec metaphysics. Western philosophy standardly defines *metaphysics* as the study of the nature, structure, and constitution of reality at the most comprehensive and synoptic level. Metaphysics aims to advance our understanding of the nature of things broadly construed. Metaphysicians seek answers to puzzles concerning the nature of existence, causality, consciousness, space, time, God, personal identity, and the relationship between human beings and the world. *Ontology* is a branch of metaphysics that focuses more narrowly on the nature of being per se and on what things exist and the kind of existence they enjoy.[1] Aztec metaphysics accordingly consists of the Aztecs' view of the nature, structure, and constitution of reality. Aztec ontology consists of the Aztecs' view concerning what exists and the kind of existence that existing things enjoy.

Section 1.1 sketches in broad strokes the general contours and fundamental features of my interpretation of Aztec metaphysics. My defense of this interpretation begins in section 1.2 and continues throughout the remainder of the book. Section 1.2 situates my understanding within existing scholarship on Aztec metaphysics. Section 1.3 discusses the artistic and shamanic elements of Aztec metaphysics, while section 1.4 explores several salient implications of along with several objections against my interpretation. Section 1.5 briefly summarizes the chapter's findings.

1.1. TEOTL

At the heart of Aztec metaphysics stands the ontological thesis that there exists just one thing: continually

DOI: 10.5876_9781607322238.c001

dynamic, vivifying, self-generating and self-regenerating sacred power, force, or energy. The Aztecs referred to this energy as *teotl*. Teotl is identical with real ity per se and hence identical with everything that exists. What's more, teotl is the basic stuff of reality. That which is real, in other words, is both identi cal with teotl and consists of teotl. Aztec metaphysics thus holds that there exists *numerically* only one thing – energy – as well as only one *kind* of thing - energy. Reality consists of just one thing, teotl, and this one thing is metaphysi cally homogeneous. Reality consists of just one kind of stuff: power or force Taking a page from the metaphysical views of contemporary Mixtec-speaking Nuyootecos of the Mixteca Alta, we might think of teotl as something akin to electricity. Nuyootecos speak of a single, all-encompassing energy, *yɨɨ*, which they liken to electricity.[2] What's more, the Aztecs regarded teotl as sacred Although everywhere and in everything, teotl presents itself most dramatically – and is accordingly sensed most vibrantly by humans – in the vivifying potency of water, sexual activity, blood, heat, sunlight, jade, the singing of birds, and the iridescent blue-green plumage of the quetzal bird. As the single, all-encom passing life force of the cosmos, teotl vivifies the cosmos and all its contents Everything that happens does so through teotl's perpetual energy-in-motion Teotl is the continuing "life-flow of creation":[3] "a vast ocean of impersonal cre ative energy."[4]

Aztec metaphysics is therefore monistic in two distinct senses. First, it claims that there exists only one *numerically countable* thing: teotl. I call this claim *ontological monism*. Aztec metaphysics thus rejects *ontological pluralism* or the view that there exists more than one numerically countable thing. Second, it claims that this single existing thing – teotl – consists of just one *kind of stuff*, to wit, force, energy or power. Teotl is metaphysically uniform and homogenous I call this view *constitutional monism*. Since the cosmos and all its contents are identical with teotl as well as constituted by teotl, it follows that the cosmos and all its contents consist uniformly of energy, power, or force. Everything consists of electricity-like energy-in-motion. Aztec metaphysics thus denies *constitutional pluralism* or the thesis that reality consists of more than one kind of stuff (e.g., spiritual stuff and physical stuff). Together, ontological and constitutional monism entail that the apparent plurality of existing things (e.g., sun, moun tains, trees, stones, and humans) as well as plurality of different kinds of stuff (e.g., spiritual vs. material) are both derivable from and hence explainable in terms of one existent and one kind of stuff: teotl. In the final analysis, the nature of things is to be understood in terms of teotl.

Teotl is nonpersonal, nonminded, nonagentive, and nonintentional. It is not a deity, person, or subject possessing emotions, cognitions, grand intentions, or goals. It is not an all-powerful benevolent or malevolent god.[5] It is neither a legislative agent characterized by free will nor an omniscient intellect. Teotl is thoroughly amoral, that is, it is wholly lacking in moral qualities such as good and evil. Like the changing of the seasons, teotl's constant changing lacks moral properties.[6]

Teotl is essentially power: continually active, actualized, and actualizing energy-in-motion. It is essentially dynamic: ever-moving, ever-circulating, and ever-becoming. As ever-actualizing power, teotl consists of creating, doing, making, changing, effecting, and destroying. Generating, degenerating, and regenerating are what teotl does and therefore what teotl *is*. Yet teotl no more chooses to do this than electricity chooses to flow or the seasons choose to change. This is simply teotl's nature. The power by which teotl generates and regenerates itself and the cosmos is teotl's essence. Similarly, the power by which teotl and all things exist is also its essence.[7] In the final analysis, then, the existence and nature of all things are functions of and ultimately explainable in terms of the generative and regenerative power of teotl.

Teotl is a *process* like a thunderstorm or flowing river rather a static, perduring *substantive entity* like a table or pebble. Moreover, it is continuous and ever-continuing process. Since there exists only one thing – namely, teotl – it follows that teotl is self-generating. After all, there is nothing outside of teotl that could act upon teotl. Teotl's tireless process of flowing, changing, and becoming is ultimately a process of self-unfolding and self-transforming. This self-becoming does not move toward a predetermined goal or ineluctable end (*telos*) at which point teotl realizes itself (like Hegel's absolute spirit) or at which point history or time comes to an end. Teotl's tireless becoming is not linear in this sense. Like the changing of the seasons, teotl's becoming is neither teleological nor eschatological. Teotl simply becomes, just as the seasons simply change. Teotl's becoming has both positive and negative consequences for human beings and is therefore ambiguous in this sense. Creative energy and destructive energy are not two different kinds of energy but two aspects of one and the same teotlizing energy.

Teotl continually and continuously generates and regenerates as well as permeates, encompasses, and shapes reality as part of its endless process of self-generation-and-regeneration. It creates the cosmos and all its contents *from within* itself as well as *out of* itself. It engenders the cosmos without being a "creator" or "maker" in the sense of an intentional agent with a plan. Teotl does not stand apart from or exist outside of its creation in the manner of the Judeo-Christian god. It is completely coextensive with created reality and cosmos. Teotl is wholly concrete, omnipresent, and immediate. Everything that humans touch, taste, smell, hear, and see consists of and is identical with teotl's electricity-like energy. Indeed, even humans are composed of and ultimately one with teotl and, as such, exist as aspects or facets of teotl. Teotl's cease less changing and becoming, its ceaseless generating and regenerating of the cosmos, is a process of ceaseless self-metamorphosis or self-transformation and-retransformation. In short, teotl's becoming consists of a particular kind of becoming, namely transformative becoming; its power, a particular kind of power, namely transformative power.

Since teotl generates and regenerates the cosmos out of itself, it would be incorrect to think that it creates the cosmos ex nihilo. Contrasting the Quiché Maya concept of creation in the *Popol Vuh* with the Judeo-Christian concept creation in the Bible, Dennis Tedlock notes that for the Maya the cosmos does not begin with a "maelstrom" of "confusion and chaos."[8] The same holds for Aztec metaphysics. The cosmos does not begin from chaos or nothingness; it burgeons forth from an *always already existing* teotl. Consequently Aztec meta physics may aptly be described as lacking a cosmogony, if by *cosmogony* one means the creation of an ordered cosmos from nothingness or primordial chaos There are no absolute beginnings – or absolute endings, for that matter – in Aztec metaphysics. There are only continuings. Death, for example, is not an ending but a change of status, as that which dies flows into and feeds that which lives. All things are involved in a single, never-ending process of recycling and transformation. There is furthermore no time prior to or after teotl since time is defined wholly in terms of teotl's becoming. Nor is there space outside of teotl since space, too, is defined wholly in terms of teotl's becoming.

Teotl continually generates and regenerates as well as permeates, encom passes, and shapes the cosmos as part of its endless process of self-generation and-regeneration. It penetrates deeply into every detail of the cosmos and exists within the myriad of existing things. All existing things are merely momentary arrangements of this sacred energy. Reality and hence the cosmos and all its inhabitants are not only wholly exhausted by teotl, they are at bottom *identical with* teotl. That which we customarily think of as the cosmos – sun, earth, rain humans, trees, sand, and so on – is generated *by* teotl, *from* teotl as one aspect facet, or moment of teotl's endless process of self-generation-and-regeneration The power of teotl is thus multifaceted, seeing as it presents itself in a multi tude of different ways: for example, as heat, water, wind, fecundity, nourishment humans, and tortillas. Yet teotl is more than the unified, kaleidoscopic totality of these aspects. It is identical with everything and everything is identical with it.

Process and transformation thus define the essence of teotl. Teotl is becom ing, and as becoming it is *neither* being *nor* nonbeing yet at the same time *both* being *and* nonbeing. As becoming, teotl neither *is* nor *is not*, and yet at the same time it both *is* and *is not*. Aztec metaphysics, in other words, embraces a *metaphysics of becoming* instead of a *metaphysics of being*. Teotl *processes*, where *to process* is understood as an intransitive verb such as "to become," "to proceed," or "to walk in a procession." Teotl's processing does not represent the activity or doing of an agent. Nor does it have a direct object. Teotl's processing is a *nonagentive* process such as the changing of the seasons, the coming and going of the tides, and fluctuations in a magnetic field. Because identical with teotl, reality is essentially process, movement, becoming, change, and transformation. Because identical with teotl, the cosmos is processive and as a consequence lacks entities, structures, and states of affairs that are static, immutable, and permanent. Everything that teotl creates out of itself – from cosmos and sun to all earth's inhabitants – is processive, unstable, evanescent, and doomed to degeneration and destruction.

David Cooper proposes that we understand the term, *God*, in the mystical teachings of the Jewish Kabbalah as a verb rather than as a noun. He suggests *God* be understood along the lines of "raining" and "digesting" rather than "table" or "planet." Doing so better captures the dynamic, processive nature of the deity discussed in these teachings.[9] Similarly, David Hall argues in his study of classical Daoism that we better understand the term *dao* as "primarily gerundive and processive" rather than as nominative and substantive. *Dao* signifies a "moving ahead in the world, forging a way forward, road building."[10] Since doing so better reflects the dynamic nature of teotl, I propose we think of the word *teotl* as primarily gerundive, processive, and denoting a process (rather than as nominative and denoting a static substantive entity). *Teotl* refers to the eternal, all-encompassing process of teotlizing. Since the cosmos and all its contents are merely moments in teotl's teotlizing, they, too, are properly understood as processes.[11]

Aztec metaphysics' understanding of teotl is shaped by several further fundamental guiding intuitions. First, it subscribes to the notion that that which is real is that which becomes, changes, and moves. Reality is defined by *becoming* – not by *being* or "is-ness." To be real is to become, to move, and to change. In short, Aztec metaphysics embraces a metaphysics of Becoming. It embraces flux, evanescence, and change by making them *defining* characteristics of existence and reality – rather than marginalizing them by denying them existence and reality. It maintains the ontological priority of process and change over rest and permanence. It squarely identifies the real with the constant flux of things.[12] Since teotl is sacred, it follows that the sacred is defined by becoming, change, and motion as well.

The Aztecs' metaphysics of Becoming stands in dramatic contrast with the metaphysics of Being that characterizes the lion's share of Western metaphysics since Plato and Aristotle. The latter defines reality in terms of being or is-ness. On this view to be real is to be permanent, immutable, static, eternal, and at rest (E.g., real love, as popular sentiment would have it, is eternal, immutable, and undying love.) That which becomes, changes, perishes, or moves is *not* real – or at least not wholly or fully so. Mutability, evanescence, and expiry are criteria of non- or partial reality, whereas immutability, permanence, and eternality are criteria of reality. Plato's metaphysics serves as a paradigmatic expression of this intuition. It denies complete reality, is-ness, and being to all things that change and assigns them to an ontologically inferior realm of semireality. Perishable and mutable things occupy his famous Cave where they suffer from semireality and semiexistence. This is the realm of Appearances. Eternally unchanging things occupy his famous the realm of the Forms, where they enjoy complete reality and is-ness. This is the realm of the Real.[13]

One's view on this issue has important implications for one's understanding of the sacred. For example, if one upholds a metaphysics of Being and if one also defends the reality of the sacred (e.g., the gods), then one must a fortiori see the sacred as eternal, immutable, and defined by pure Being. The sacred can not therefore be identified with that which becomes, changes, and perishes. The latter must be characterized as nonsacred or profane. Furthermore, if the world about us changes then the sacred must be metaphysically divorced from the world and instead identified with a transcendent, metaphysically distinct realm of Being. On the other hand, if one upholds a metaphysics of Becoming, then one may identify the sacred with the mutable, evanescent, and perishable, and hence with the changing world about us.

Second, Aztec metaphysics equates reality with the exercise of power, that is being real with making things happen, influencing things, acting upon things and effecting change in things. As always active, actualized, and actualizing power, teotl is continually doing, effecting, and making happen. Carl Jung articulates the intuition nicely: "Everything that exists acts, otherwise it would not *be*. It can *be only* by virtue of its inherent energy."[14]

A third intuition claims essence follows from function. That is, what something *is* follows from *what* it does as well as *how* it does it. This intuition replaces the traditional Western metaphysical principle *operari sequitar esse* ("function ing follows being") with its own principle *esse sequitar operari* ("being follows from operation").[15] Teotl therefore *is* what teotl *does*. And what does teotl do? Teotl makes everything happen as well as happen the way it does. Teotl is the happening of all things, the patterns in the happening of all things, and the co-relatedness between the happenings of all things. It vivifies all things and is essentially vivifying energy. It energizes the life cycles of plants, animals, and humans; the cycles of the seasons and time; and the creation and destruction of the five Suns and their respective Ages or what I call (for reasons that will become clear in chapter 4) "Sun-Earth Orderings." Teotl is the power behind and the power of the becoming, changing, and transforming of all things above the earth, on the surface of the earth, and below the earth.[16]

The foregoing suggests Aztec philosophy embraces what Western philosophers call a *process metaphysics*.[17] Process metaphysics views processes rather than perduring objects, things, or substances as ontologically basic. What seem to be perduring things are really nothing more than stability patterns in processes. As the products of processes, entities are derivative. Process metaphysics treats *dynamic* notions such as becoming, power, activity, change, flux, fluidity, unfolding, creation, destruction, transformation, novelty, interactive interrelatedness, evanescence, and emergence as central to understanding reality and how everything hangs together. What's more, processes *are* what processes *do*. Essence follows function. This intuition, like others we've seen, contradicts the dominant view in the history of Western philosophy since Plato and Aristotle, namely, *substance metaphysics*. Substance metaphysics views perduring things or substances as ontologically basic and processes as ontologically derivative.

Teotl, and hence reality, cosmos, and all existing things are processes. Teotl is not a perduring entity that underlies the various changes in the cosmos the way that say a table, according to Aristotelian metaphysics, underlies changes in its attributes (e.g., color). Nor is it a perduring substance that undergoes the various changes in the cosmos the way that say wood, according to Aristotelian metaphysics, undergoes changes from tree to lumber to table. We therefore need to resist the temptation to reify teotl. Sun, earth, humans, maize, insects, tortillas and stones are processes. What's more, teotl is a *transformational* process that changes the form, shape or "face" (*ixtli*) of things.[18] As such, it is simultaneously creative and destructive. Transformational processes involve the destruction of something prior in the course of creating something posterior.

Fourth, Aztec metaphysics sees reality as ex hypothesi ineliminably and irreducibly *ambiguous*. The ambiguity of things cannot be explained away as a product of human misunderstanding, ignorance, or illusion. Teotl, reality, cosmos, and all existing things are characterized simultaneously by inamic pairs such as being *and* nonbeing, life *and* death, male *and* female, and wet *and* dry. This contradicts the reigning intuition in Western metaphysics since Plato that holds that that which is real is ex hypothesi unambiguous, pure, and unmixed. It is only appearances and illusions that are contradictory, ambiguous, impure, and mixed.

Fifth, Aztec metaphysics views reality in *holistic* terms. Holism claims reality consists of a special kind of unity or whole: namely, one in which all individual components are *essentially* interrelated, interdependent, correlational, interactive, and thus defined in terms of one another.[19] Holists commonly cite biological organisms and ecological systems as examples of the kind of unity they have in mind, and accordingly liken reality to a grand biological organism or ecosystem. They claim wholes are ontologically primary and individuals are ontologically secondary, and that individuals are defined in terms of the wholes in which they participate. Houses, trees, and humans, for example, do not enjoy independent existence apart from the wholes of which they are *essentially* parts and in which they *essentially* participate. By contrast, atomism views reality as the summative product of its individual parts. Individuals, not wholes, are basic. Atomists commonly cite sets or collections of things such as the coins in one's pocket as paradigmatic examples of atomistic unities.

For holists, individuals cannot be properly understood apart from how they function in the constellation of interrelated and intercorrelated processes that define the whole and in which they essentially participate. Individuals' relationships with one another are *intrinsic* to them and exhaustively *define* them. What's more, an individual's relations extend throughout the entire cosmos. In the preceding I claimed the fundamental concepts for understanding reality are *dynamic* ones such as becoming, power, transformation, and emergence. I want now to add to this list *holistic* concepts such as interdependence, mutual arising, covariance, interconnectedness, interdependence, complementarity, and correlationalism.

How does this bear upon Aztec metaphysics? For starters, since reality is processive, it follows that Aztec metaphysics' holism is a processive holism. And since teotl is nonteleological and identical with reality per se, it follows that reality is a nonteleological processive whole: a "unified macroprocess consisting of a myriad of duly coordinated subordinate microprocesses."[20] The same also holds for the cosmos. These microprocesses are mutually arising, interconnected, interdependent, interpenetrating, and mutually correlated. They are interwoven one with one another like threads in a total fabric, where teotl is not only the total woven fabric but also the *weaver* of the fabric and the *weaving* of the fabric. Weaving is especially apropos since (as I argue in chapters 3 and 8) weaving functions as a root organizing metaphor of Aztec metaphysics. Alternatively seeing as biological organisms function as another organizing metaphor in Aztec metaphysics, we may view these processes as mutually interdependent and interpenetrating like the processes composing an individual biological organism. It is in this vein that Kay Read claims Aztec metaphysics conceives the cosmos as a "biologically historical" process.[21] In sum, Aztec metaphysics advances a nonteleological *ecological holism*.

If the foregoing is correct, it follows that teotl is metaphysically *immanent* in several significant senses.[22] First, teotl does not exist apart from or independently of the cosmos. Teotl is fully *copresent* and *coextensional* with the cosmos. Second, teotl is *not* correctly understood as *supernatural* or otherworldly. Teotl is identical with and hence fully coextensional with creation: hence no part of teotl exists apart from creation. Teotl does not exist outside of space and time. It is as concrete and immediate as the water we drink, air we breathe, and food we eat. Teotl is neither abstract nor transcendent.

Third, teotl is metaphysically homogeneous, consisting of just one kind of stuff: always actual, actualized, and actualizing energy-in-motion. The fact that teotl has various aspects does not gainsay its homogeneity. Teotl does not bifurcate into two essentially different kinds of stuff – "natural" and "supernatural" – and thus neither do reality and cosmos. Indeed, the very nature of teotl precludes the drawing of any qualitative metaphysical distinction between "natural" and "supernatural."[23] The natural versus supernatural dichotomy, so cherished by Western metaphysics and theology, simply does not apply. While Aztec tlamatinime did claim that certain aspects of teotl are *imperceptible to* and so *hidden from* humans under ordinary perceptual conditions, and accordingly made an *epistemological* distinction between different aspects of teotl, this does not mean that Aztec tlamatinime drew a principled metaphysical distinction between perceptible and imperceptible aspects of teotl or that they believed that the imperceptible aspects were "supernatural" because they consisted of a different kind of stuff.

Fourth, teotl is immanent in the sense that it generates and regenerates the cosmos out of itself. The history of the cosmos consists of the self-unfolding and self-becoming of teotl; of the continual unfolding and burgeoning of teotl *out of* teotl. Teotl is identical with creation since teotl is identical with itself. There do not therefore exist two metaphysically distinct things: teotl and its creation. There is only one thing: teotl.

Fifth, although teotl is sacred, it is not transcendent in the sense of being metaphysically divorced from a profane, immanent world. Aztec metaphysics does not embrace a dichotomy of sacred versus profane. Given that teotl is sacred, that everything is identical with teotl, and that teotl is homogeneous, it follows that *everything* is sacred. The Aztecs saw sacredness everywhere and in everything. Whereas Christianity's dualistic (and as we will see hierarchical) metaphysics effectively removes the sacred from the earthly and characterizes the earthly in terms of the absence of the sacred, the Aztecs' monistic (and as we will see nonhierarchical) metaphysics makes the sacred present everywhere.[24] Aztec metaphysics lacks the conceptual resources for constructing a grand metaphysical distinction between two essentially different kinds of stuff: sacred and profane. The sacred versus profane dichotomy, venerated by the metaphysical systems underlying many religions, simply does not obtain. This dichotomy is commonly underwritten by a Platonic-style, metaphysical dualism between two ontologically different kinds of stuff, one sacred, the other profane. But Aztec metaphysics rejects all manner of ontological dualisms. There is, however, one quite limited and insignificant sense in which teotl may be said to be transcendent. Teotl is neither exhausted by nor limited to any one existing thing at any given time or place: for example, any one given tree, human, or even cosmic era.

Consonant with the foregoing, Aztec philosophy embraces a *nonhierarchical* metaphysics.[25] That is, it denies the existence of a principled, ontological distinction between "higher" and "lower" realms, realities, degrees of being, or kinds of stuff. A hierarchical metaphysics, by contrast, upholds the existence of a principled hierarchy of "higher" and "lower" realities, degrees of being, and so on. Plato's Middle Period metaphysics serves as a paradigmatic instance of a hierarchical metaphysics, one that has exerted tremendous influence upon the metaphysics of Christianity and Western philosophy.[26] Hierarchical metaphysics are characterized by what Arthur Lovejoy calls a "great chain of being" and "great scale of being."[27] They standardly defend metaphysical dualism and the transcendence of the real and the sacred. Teotl's ontological monism and homogeneity, as well as its radical immanence preclude any such hierarchicalness. This helps us understand why, for example, "Christian transcendentalism was meaningless to the Nahuas," as Louise Burkhart claims.[28]

The assertion that Aztec metaphysics is nonhierarchical appears inconsistent with sources such as the *Historia de los mexicanos por sus pinturas* and *Histoyre du Mechique* that speak of the cosmos as being divided vertically into distinct layers: thirteen above and nine below the earthly layer (*tlalticpac*).[29] These layers are alternatively characterized as nine upper skies, four lower skies and the surface of the earth, and nine lower layers of the underworld. Claims regarding the hierarchical layering of the Aztec cosmos are also routinely based upon the depiction of cosmos with vertical layers (and accompanying commentary) on pages 1 and 2 of the *Codex Vaticanus 3738 A*.[30]

How do I respond to this? Chapter 8 argues the vertical layers of the cosmos are merely *folds* in the single, metaphysically homogeneous energy of teotl. This folding is analogous to the folding of a blanket or skirt that consists of one and the same kind of material (e.g., cotton). The fact that the Aztecs cosmologists assigned different names to the folds does not mean they defended the meta-physical heterogeneity of the folds.

I.2. SUPPORTING SCHOLARSHIP

Supporting Scholarship on the Aztecs

My understanding of teotl builds upon the foundational work of many scholars. First and foremost, Arild Hvidtfeldt observes that *teotl* is standardly translated as "god" (*dios*) and occurs commonly in compounds such as *teocalli*, "god's house, temple." Although "god's" is commonly used in translating such compounds, Hvidtfeldt argues that "sacred, sacral, or ritual" would be better: for example, *teopan* as "sacred place" rather than as "god's place"; "*teoquemitl*" as "ritual garment" rather than as "god's garment"; and *teocalli* as "sacred house" rather than as "god's house."[31] Less commonly, teotl can also mean "sun" and occurs in such compounds as *teotlac*, "at sunset." In other compounds *teo-* entails "high potency, intensification, excellence."[32] In this respect, according to Hvidtfeldt, the notion resembles the Polynesian notion of *mana*. He concludes by suggesting that teotl be understood as a manalike power and that *teotl* be translated as "mana" (rather than as "god").[33]

Richard Townsend argues *teotl* signifies "a numinous, impersonal force diffused throughout the cosmos" and "expresses the notion of sacred quality."[34] Conceiving the cosmos in terms of teotl is an "essentially non-theistic manner of perceiving the universe as hallowed."[35] Like Hvidtfeldt, Townsend likens teotl to mana:

> This force was preeminently manifested in the natural forces – earth, air, fire, and water – but was also found in persons of great distinction, or things, and places of unusual or mysterious configuration. *Teotl* expresses the notion of sacred quality, but with the idea that it could be physically manifested in some specific presence – a rainstorm, a mirage, a lake, or a majestic mountain. It was if the world was perceived as being magically charged, inherently alive in greater or lesser degrees with this vital force.[36]

Indeed, everything in the cosmos – from stars, lakes, humans, plants, and insects to song-poems, works of art, and effigies made of amaranth dough – manifests some "aspect of the sacred." The early Spaniards' translations of *teotl* as "god," "deity," "saint," or "demon" are therefore misconceived.

In a later work, Townsend maintains teotl plays a central role in Aztec religious thought. Teotl was designated by the word-root *teo* and commonly written with the -*tl* suffix as *teotl*.[37] Teotl is standardly associated with nature deities, sacred masks, and ritual objects (such as effigies of stone, wood, and amaranth dough). In this work Townsend denies *teotl* is adequately translated as "mana."[38] Mana – along with such notions as the numinous and the sacred – are far too narrow. He writes, "*teo* may be used to qualify almost anything mysterious, powerful, or beyond ordinary experience, such as animals of prey, a remote and awe-inspiring snowcapped mountain, a phenomenon of terrible power such as the sun or bolt of lightning."[39] What's more, *teo* was applied without equivocation to both benign *and* malign forces and objects. He concludes, "The diverse contexts of the word *teo* suggest that the Aztecs regarded the things of their world . . . as inherently charged to a greater or lesser degree with vital force or power."[40]

Since it serves as a reference point for many scholars' understanding of teotl let's briefly examine the notion of mana. In his 1891 study, *The Melanesians*, R. H Codrington writes, "*Mana* is power, *par excellence*, the genuine effectiveness of things which corroborates their practical actions without annihilating them This is what causes a net to bring in a good catch, makes the house solid and keeps the canoe sailing smoothly: in the farms it is fertility, in medicine it is either health or death."[41] Mana is an inherent and pervasive "power or influence" diffused throughout the cosmos, "present in the atmosphere of life."[42]

However, we must resist thinking of teotl wholly in terms of mana as conceived by Codrington since the two concepts differ in several important respects. Most critically, Codrington characterizes mana as "a supernatural power or influence" that "works to effect everything which is . . . outside the common processes of nature."[43] However, teotl is neither supernatural nor operates "outside the common processes of nature." Teotl does not exist apart from the natural or the commonplace. It is one with both. The concept of teotl is also incompatible with a natural versus supernatural dualism. There exists just one thing, teotl, and it is identical with and exhaustive of everything – including what Western theology, metaphysics, and anthropology standardly call the "supernatural" and the "natural." The ordinary processes of everyday nature are simply the processing of teotl. In short, Codrington's conception of mana presupposes several dualisms which, although deeply entrenched in Western theologies and metaphysics, are not shared by Aztec metaphysics.

Jorge Klor de Alva, like Townsend and Hvidtfeldt, places teotl at the heart of Aztec religiosity and a fortiori Aztec metaphysics. He writes, "*Teotl* . . . implies something more than the idea of the divine manifested in the form of a god or gods; instead it signifies the sacred in more general terms." Klor de Alva proposes the term, *teoyoism*, as a generic name "for the complex theological belief systems, the ritual practices, and mystical responses that constituted Nahua religiosity before and after the conquest." He derives the neologism *teoyoism* from *teoyotl*, the abstract form of *teotl*.[44]

Elizabeth Boone interprets teotl as "a concentration of power as a sacred and impersonal force" that charged the entire Aztec cosmos.[45] She writes, "Individual [Aztec] gods do not exist ontologically, endowed with visual appearances and physical attributes that they may or may not assume at any given time. Rather, sacred power, mana, or *teotl* (divinity)" exists.[46] The names of Aztec gods do not therefore function as proper names denoting supernatural beings but rather as "cultic terms denoting the persons and objects central to the ritual activities."[47] The various so-called deities are mere momentary ritual constructions. Louise Burkhart argues Aztec metaphysics is monistic. She writes, "A single divine principle – *teotl* – was responsible for the nature of the cosmos . . . It was a polytheistic monism: that is, the divine principle manifested itself in multiple forms, some ambivalent, some expressing opposite principles in their different manifestations. More accurate would be Klor de Alva's teoyism."[48] She proposes we translate *teotl* as "deity" or "sacred thing."[49]

Kay Read contends that although *teotl* translates literally as "powerful thing," we better understand its meaning if we add a sense of "animistic force or vitality."[50] Teotl is potent, vital, awesome, honored, and commonly beyond human ken. She writes, "The Nahua did not discuss teotl by itself, as we are doing. This was natural seeing as these powers could not be separated from physical objects. Nahuatl always includes powers in something else by using a prefix form that cannot stand alone (*teo-*). We are the ones focusing on these powers as a [metaphysical] category that can be [analytically] distinguished from the physical world."[51] Teotl permeates and vitalizes the entire cosmos including those things modern Westerners regard as inanimate such as sun, lakes, cities, and tortillas.[52] As Davíd Carrasco remarks, "divine energy and force inhabit buildings as well as people, hills as well as temples, granaries as well as pyramids, costumes as well as animal skins and feathers, stones as well as bones."[53]

In sum, at the center of Aztec metaphysics stands the ontological thesis that there exists a single, dynamic, vivifying, eternally self-generating and self-regenerating sacred power: teotl. Thunderstorms, houses, grass, and centipedes are simply momentary orderings of this sacred power.

SUPPORTING SCHOLARSHIP ON OTHER MESOAMERICAN PEOPLES

The foregoing interpretation receives additional albeit indirect support from other indigenous Mesoamerican metaphysics. That other philosophies in the Mesoamerican cultural unit embrace similar views makes my interpretation less novel and thus more plausible. If true, my interpretation attributes to the Aztecs a metaphysics not wholly unlike other indigenous Mesoamerican philosophies.

According to Alan Sandstrom, contemporary Nahuatl-speakers in the Huastecan region of Eastern Mexico view the sacred as "a single, all-pervasive principle." They call this sacred unity *totiotsij* ("our honored deity").[54] Despite its singularity, unity, and indivisibility, they nevertheless regard the sacred as multifaceted. The Nahuas' Otomí, Tepehua, Huastec, and Totonac neighbors likewise subscribe to such a notion.[55]

In his ethnography of contemporary Mixtec-speakers of the Mixteca Alta of Mexico, John Monaghan writes, "If the division between spirit and matter is axiomatic in Judeo-Christian thought, Nuyootecos begin in a different place, assuming that everything in existence is endowed with a life principle."[56] Nuyootecos call this single life principle *yïi*, which Monaghan glosses as "potency, vitality, fecundity."[57] They liken *yïi* to electricity.[58] *Yïi* possesses the properties of generative fecundity, transformative power, self-preservation, and vital heat.[59] Everything is vivified by this single, general, circulating, transforming, sacred force: wind, rain, earth, and sun as well as humans, communities, houses, birds, corn, and food. Nuyootecos also regard *yïi* as *ii* ("sacred"), suggesting something "dangerous, fragile, and easily disturbed."[60] In sum, at the core of Mixtec religious thought are notions of power, potency, vitality, force; transformative vitality and fertility; the animation of all things by a single sacred energy; and the circulation of this energy between things.

In his review of recent work on Mesoamerican religions, Monaghan claims Klor de Alva's concept of "teoyosim" more or less captures the beliefs, practices, and teachings of Mesoamerican religions.[61] The term *teotl* expresses "the proposition that reality is a unified whole, with a single divine principle responsible for the nature of the cosmos."[62] The divine is indistinct from the cosmos as well as immanent within the cosmos. What's more, this sacred principle appears to be indivisible, unitary, and fundamentally undifferentiated. Summarizing recent work on Mixtec, Zapotec, and Chatino religions at the time of the conquest, Arthur A. Joyce claims the three shared in common a fundamental belief in the existence of a vital force that animated time, the calendar, divine beings, people, plants, and animals as well as rivers, rain, light, mountains, wind, earthquakes, and clouds. The Mixtecs called this force *ini* or *yïi*; the Zapotecs, *pèe*; and the Chatinos, *cryasa*. All three terms may be glossed as "wind," "heat," and "heart."[63] Belief in this single animating energy remains a vital component of the religious views of contemporary indigenous people throughout Oaxaca. According to Joyce Marcus, the Zapotec word *pèe* refers to a single animating power found in humans, plants, hills, earthquakes, and the calendar.[64]

After observing that teotl is better understood as mana or sacred power than as a god, David Stuart asserts that "a very similar, if not identical, concept" is conveyed in Mayan languages by the word *k'uh* or *ch'uh*.[65] K'uh or ch'uh refers to holy things generally – items that are charged, sometimes even fleetingly, with a sacred essence." He adds, "This overarching concept of a divine essence and its multifaceted expression through material objects appears to be a major foundation of Mesoamerican religious thought."[66] Stephen Houston and David Stuart analyze the Maya religious notion of *ku'* or *chu'* as follows: "*Ch'u* is the foundation of the word *ch'ulel* which appears in Chol Mayan and Greater Tzeltalan languages with the meaning like 'vitality', but perhaps more literally 'holiness' .. Widely translated as 'soul' or 'spirit' it more correctly refers to the vital force or power that inhabits the blood and energizes people and a variety of objects of ritual and everyday life."[67] This concept, they add, is "essentially identical" to other concepts of divinity found across Mesoamerica, including the central Mexican notion of teotl and the contemporary Mixtec notion of *yii*.[68]

In a similar vein, Linda Schele and Ellen Miller write, "For the Maya, the world was a complex and awesome place, alive with sacred power. This power was part of the landscape, of the fabric of space and time, of things both living and inanimate, and of the forces of nature – storms, wind, mist, smoke, rain, earth, sky, and water."[69]

In sum, Mesoamerican metaphysical systems view the nature of reality in terms closely similar to those of Aztec metaphysics. My thesis that the Aztecs embraced the notion of teotl is well within the realm of Mesoamerican metaphysical thinking regarding the sacred.

Scholarship on Indigenous North American and East Asian Metaphysics

Native North American scholars attribute similar views regarding the singularity, uniformity, immanence, and vivifying potency of reality to indigenous North American philosophies. The late Standing Rock Sioux philosopher, Vine Deloria Jr., for example, argues that for indigenous peoples "the presence of energy and power is the starting point [and cornerstone] of their analyses and understanding of the world."[70] The "feeling or belief that the universe is energized by a pervading power" is basic and pervasive. It is not the abstract, theoretical conclusion of a process of scientific reasoning. Awareness of power is immediate and concrete.[71] The indigenous peoples of North America called this power *wakan orenda* or *manitou*. Deloria likens this power to "a force field" that permeates as well as constitutes everything (without distinction between so-called matter and spirit). The cosmos is the operating of this vital power and all existing things are products of its operating. Since this power is sacred so is the entire cosmos. This power is neither "spiritual" nor "material" as these terms are customarily understood by Western secular and religious metaphysical thought. Indeed, indigenous metaphysics considers this a false distinction. Nature, too, then, is neither "material" nor "spiritual." Keith Basso writes, "The distinction made by Westerners between things 'natural' and 'supernatural' has no exact equivalent in the culture of the Western Apache." Powers, mythological figures, and ghosts exist on a par metaphysically with rain, sun, and wind. "The former are not conceptualized as belonging to an order of phenomena radically opposed to that which makes up the natural world."[72] In short, Western style distinctions of sacred versus profane, spiritual versus material, and natural versus supernatural simply do not apply to indigenous North American metaphysics.[73] They are false distinctions.

Jicarilla Apache philosopher Viola Cordova argues indigenous North American metaphysics conceives the cosmos as a seamless dynamic field of energy or power that is called *usen* in Jicarilla Apache. Although standardly glossed as "great spirit" by anthropologists, she contends *usen* refers to something nonanthropomorphic and nonpersonal.[74] Usen has a tendency to "pool" and concentrate in varying degrees, creating "things" such as rocks and trees.[75] Cordova, Jace Weaver, Gregory Cajete, George Tinker, Willie Ermine, Deloria, and other Native scholars liken usen to other indigenous North American conceptions of a single, primordial, processive all-encompassing and ever-flowing creative life force including *natoji* (Blackfoot), *wakan tanka* (Sioux), *yowa* (Cherokee) *orenda* (Iroquois), and *nil'ch'i* (Navajo).[76] According to Leroy Meyer and Tony Ramírez, Sioux metaphysics conceives all objects as "distinct manifestations" of wakan tanka.[77] Once again, we see that native North American philosophies reject as false the distinctions between sacred and profane, spirit and matter, mind and body, and natural and supernatural.

My purpose in introducing these views is to suggest that the Aztec notion of teotl is well within the realm of indigenous North American metaphysical thinking about the ultimate nature of reality. I do *not* claim exact correspondence, cross-cultural influence, or the existence of a shared pan-Indian way of thinking. I am *not* arguing that my interpretation of Aztec metaphysics is correct on the grounds that North American philosophies believed something similar. Rather, showing resonance between indigenous Mesoamerican (Aztec and others) and indigenous North American metaphysics enables us to see that this kind of metaphysical picture is *not* inconceivable or even uncommon, and that it is *not* a priori out of the question to attribute such a view to the Aztecs.

My purpose is also negative in the sense of clearing the ground. I believe such comparisons help gainsay scholars such as Lucien Lévy-Bruhl, Henri and H. A. Frankfort, and Benjamin Keen, who would argue that such a view exceeds the undeveloped cognitive abilities of "prephilosophical" and "mythopoeic" peoples who are too emotionally, practically, simple-, or concrete-minded to devise a metaphysical theory about something as "abstract" as teotl.[78] The Aztecs did not regarded teotl as a bloodless, theoretical abstraction intellectually removed from the concrete, perceptible, and immediate. Rather, following Deloria Jr., I believe they sensed the immediate and concrete presence of power and life force both within and without. The idea of teotl as an "abstraction" is *ours*.

Before continuing, let's briefly examine several similar notions in classical East Asian metaphysics. First, consider classical Chinese metaphysics' notion of *qi*, traditionally translated as "breath-energy." Chad Hansen character-izes the concept of qi as the "*basic-stuff* concept" of Chinese metaphysics.[79] David Hall defines qi as a "vital, energizing field."[80] According to Ben-Ami Scharfstein, qi is the vivifying energy or life-force stuff constitutive of reality. Everything that exists – both animate and inanimate – is a "permutation" of qi. All things are momentary condensations or coagulations of qi. Qi possesses the power to assume different shapes or forms, two of which are mind and body. Qi also manifests itself in the generation, vigor, and decay of all things.[81] David Hall and Roger Ames characterize qi as the hylozoic, "continuous psy-chophysical sea of stuff that constitutes the ceaseless flow of existence."[82] Qi cuts across traditional Western dichotomies such as mind versus matter, mind versus body, spirit versus matter, and animate versus inanimate. Qi is conse-quently metaphysically ambiguous vis-à-vis these dichotomies. According to François Jullien, qi is "breath-energy," a primal, invisible, and generally diffuse flow of energy that tirelessly courses its way throughout the cosmos. Humans, rocks, and rain, for example, are nothing more than temporary concentrations or coagulations of qi. Their destruction, degeneration, and death represent the dissolving of these temporary concentrates.[83] Lastly, East Asian metaphysics commonly characterizes qi in terms of the active and passive dynamics of *yin* and *yang*.[84]

Second, Daoism speaks of *dao*, which Alan Watts characterizes as "an uncon-scious though nonetheless formative energy, like a magnetic field. Individual things are not so much entities as differentiations or forms in the unified field of the [d]ao."[85] Third, Japanese Shinto speaks of *musubi*, a creative and generative force that not only vivifies but also connects all of "Great Nature (*dasihizen*)." Humans, rivers, mountains, trees, and so forth are but aspects or manifestations of musubi.[86]

What's the point of discussing such East Asian concepts in the context of Aztec metaphysics? After all, they are obviously not equivalent to teotl, and I make no claims that they are. Nor for that matter do I defend cross-cultural influence or the existence of a cross-culturally shared, non-Western mode of thinking. There are, nevertheless, striking resemblances between these notions. All are central components of monistic metaphysical theories claiming that a single, vital, energy-like stuff comprises reality. Qi, dao, and teotl (as I argue in chapter 3) are also characterized in terms of dynamic dual polarities. In the case of dao and qi, these are yin and yang; in the case of teotl, they are inamic partners such as being and nonbeing, male and female, death and life, and so on. But what's the point of observing these similarities?

Such comparisons are useful heuristically. Listening to how Chinese philosophers characterized qi or dao offers us with new ways of thinking about teotl. I find it fruitful to think of teotl as a continuous "psychophysical sea" of vitalizing stuff that constitutes all things, or to think of the arrangement of the cosmos at any given time and place as well as the particular inhabitants of the cosmos at any given time and place (e.g., wind, earth, humans, butterflies, and corn) as nothing more than temporarily pooled, concentrated, or coagulated teotl energy-stuff. Furthermore, such comparisons offer us ways of thinking beyond such dichotomies as mind versus matter, spiritual versus physical, natural versus supernatural, and animate versus inanimate that are habitually entrenched in Western ways of thinking. Finally, such comparisons show that the idea that the cosmos is constituted and vivified by a single indivisible energy is neither unknown nor uncommon across world philosophies (and religions) – including those developed by cultures deemed "unsophisticated," "emotional," "irrational," "primitive," and "High Stone Age" by Western-trained scholars – and therefore show that it is not a priori implausible to ascribe such a view to Aztec tlamatinime.

1.3. THE COSMOS AS TEOTL'S ARTISTIC-SHAMANIC SELF-TRANSFORMATION

Teotl's continual generating and regenerating of the cosmos is also a process of tireless self-transformation and retransformation. Aztec metaphysics commonly characterizes this transformation in two closely related, if not ultimately equivalent, ways: as a process of artistic creation and as a process of shamanic form-changing or shape-shifting. Teotl is the consummate cosmic artist-shaman. Let's examine each.

The Aztecs saw teotl as a creative and artistic process since teotl endlessly fashions and refashions itself *into* and *as* the cosmos. Artistic creation is fundamentally transformative. The artist transforms disordered raw materials into well-ordered finished products: for example, raw cotton into woven fabric, words into song-poems, and mineral ore into jewelry. The artist also takes old objects and refashions them into new ones: for example, melting down old broken jewelry and refashioning it anew. Aztec metaphysics accordingly views the cosmos as teotl's *in xochitl in cuicatl* ("flower and song"). *In xochitl in cuicatl* refers broadly to creative activity such as composing-singing poetry, weaving, goldsmithing, and painting-writing. Conquest-era Nahua philosopher-poets commonly characterized the cosmos as an *amoxtli*, or sacred book of paintings, and earthly existents as figures painted-written therein. Nezahualcoyotl declares:

> You paint with flowers, with songs, Life Giver. You color the ones who'll live on
> earth, you recite them in colors, and so you're hatching eagles, jaguars, in your
> painting place [*motlacuilolpani*] . . .
> Though we vassals are alive, we are mortal. All of us are to pass away, all of us are
> to die on earth . . .
> Like paintings we're destroyed, like flowers we wither on earth.[87]

A song-poem León-Portilla attributes to Aquiauhtzin characterizes the cosmos as a *tlacuilocalitec* ("house of paintings").[88] A song-poem attributed to Xayacamach declares, "your home is here, in the midst of the paintings."[89] The contemporary Nahua poet, Natalio Hernández Hernández, expresses this idea as follows:

> I sing to life, to man
> and to nature, the mother earth;
> because life is flower and it is song,
> it is in the end: flower and song.[90]

Aztec metaphysics also understands teotl's continuing generation and regeneration of the cosmos in terms of shamanic transformation or form-changing. The cosmos is teotl's *nahual* (*nahualli* or *nagual*) – that is, teotl's "guise," "transfiguration," "double," or "mask." The word *nahual* derives from *nahualli* meaning both a form-changing shaman and the being into which a shaman transforms.[91] The concept of a nahual has its roots in indigenous Mesoamerican notions of shamanic power and transformation. As a shaman possesses the power to transform him/herself into his nahual (say, a jaguar), so teotl possesses the power to transform itself into its nahual: the cosmos. The continual becoming of the cosmos along with its myriad characteristics and inhabitants are products of teotl's continuing shamanic self-shape-shifting and self-transforming. Teotl is essentially transformative power and hence the quintessential transformer. As the ultimate shape shifter, Tezcatlipoca, "Lord of the Smoking Mirror," exemplified this shamanic power.[92]

Are teotl's transformations therefore deceptive? J. Richard Andrews and Ross Hassig reject Angel María Garibay K.'s proposal that *nahual* is rooted in an archaic verb meaning "to dissemble, to deceive" along with the idea that a nahual is by definition deceptive. *Nahualli* is a patientive noun that derives from *tla-nāhua*, meaning "to interpose something between self and public, skin and outer clothing, man and gods, the natural and supernatural, and so forth." A nahualli is simply "an entity that can be interposed."[93]

Andrews and Hassig's discussion suggests the need to be careful when thinking about masks and disguises. Raymond Fogelson writes about the traditions of Cherokee Booger masks and Iroquois (Seneca) False Faces as follows: "We do *not* understand the meaning of masks in these cultures if we treat their usage as analogous to our sense of masks as disguises, as distortions or caricatures that cover up a true reality hidden behind the mask." In these traditions masks represent "temporary incarnation[s] of cosmic reality."[94] The Seneca, argues Sam Gill, refer to their masks as *gagosa* which simply means "face."[95] "False Faces," the common name given to Seneca masks by outsiders, is therefore inaccurate and misleading. Seneca masks are living objects that "present and animate the real presence of the spirit."[96] They disclose and present a spirit, and are better thought of as *guises* than as *disguises*. The Seneca do not regard masks as coverings that are worn in order to hide, conceal, or deceive. The concept of being false or untrue plays no role. Similarly, in Hopi masking tradition the person who dons a mask is not regarded as someone impersonating a deity but as someone who loses his own personal identity in the process of becoming that deity.[97] In sum, we cannot simply assume that Aztec philosophy understands masks as necessarily deceptive or as ontologically distinct from the person donning the mask.

We customarily think about masks as by definition deceptive and as ontologically distinct from the person donning the mask. We customarily think of masks as deceptive because we see masks as concealing the identity of their wearers. One hides behind a mask; one covers one's face with a mask. Others are unable to recognize one's identity because one *interposes* the mask between one's face and them. This way of thinking about masks and masking presupposes a specific metaphysics, namely, one according to which mask and mask wearer are two ontologically distinct things. It presupposes, in other words, an ontological dualism. The *epistemological* phenomenon of deception is grounded in this *dualistic ontology*. One is able to cover and hide one's face with a mask because mask and face are two distinct things.

This way of thinking about masks and masking, however, is not Aztec philosophy's way. In brief, since Aztec philosophy is ontologically monistic and it is a fortiori precluded from thinking about masks as something ontologically distinct from teotl, teotl cannot be said to mask itself in a way that presupposes that teotl and mask are two distinct things. Teotl and mask must in the final analysis be identical with one another. Consequently, the epistemological phenomenon of deception cannot be explained metaphysically by appealing to a dualistic ontology consisting of "false" mask versus "true" wearer.

Since Aztec philosophy sees teotl's generation and regeneration of the cosmos as a process of shamanic transformation, let's turn to shamanism for further insight. When transforming himself into, say, a jaguar, a shaman does not simply assume the guise or external form of a jaguar. The shaman literally *becomes* a jaguar. Shaman and jaguar are one. And although the shaman's human identity is obscure and difficult to recognize while a jaguar, this is not the result of his concealing his identity within or behind the mask of the jaguar.

Teotl's relationship to the cosmos is analogous to the shaman's relationship to the jaguar. From this interpretation several important consequences follow for our thinking about teotl's relationship to the cosmos and its inhabitants. First, since a nahual is better understood as a guise that presents rather than as a disguise that misrepresents, to say that the cosmos and all its inhabitants are teotl's nahual is *not* to say that they are nothing but illusion (or illusory). Similarly, to say this is *not* to say that teotl *misrepresents* itself to human beings *in the guise of* the cosmos. Teotl does not hide behind the mask of the cosmos as a Halloween trick-or-treater hides behind her witch mask. Teotl is one and the same with the cosmos.

Second, it is a mistake to think of a nahual as something ontologically distinct from the shaman who assumes it. Nahual and shaman are one. The shaman literally becomes a jaguar (his nahual). Teotl literally *becomes* the cosmos. To think otherwise is to commit Aztec metaphysics to an intolerable ontological dualism. Teotl and nahual (the cosmos) are numerically one and the same thing.

Third, just as it is a mistake to think the jaguar does not really exist because it is merely illusion (or illusory), so likewise it is a mistake to think that the cosmos does not really exist because it is merely illusion (or illusory). Both jaguar and cosmos are real; both exist.

Fourth, to claim that teotl is identical with its nahual (the cosmos) and to claim that nahuals are not deceptive is *not* to claim that humans recognize this identity, recognize the cosmos as teotl's nahual, or recognize teotl in the cosmos by means of ordinary sense perception. We may express this point more sharply using the Western philosophical distinction between perception *de re* (i.e., perception of the thing) and perception *de dicto* (i.e., perception under a description; perception that the thing is such-and-such; perception of what is said or of the proposition).[98] Successful de re perception does not entail successful de dicto perception. For example, I may have seen de re President Obama entering a black limousine earlier today without having seen at the time *that* it was Obama, that is, without having seen Obama de dicto. What I saw de dicto was simply a tall, thin man entering a black limousine.

Applying this distinction to the present case, humans perceive teotl de re via ordinary sense perception. Why? Because according to ontological monism there exists only one thing to perceive de re: teotl. When humans look about themselves, there is only one thing: teotl. However, from this it does *not* follow that humans perceive teotl de dicto, that is, that they *recognize* what they see around themselves *as* teotl, as *fitting the description of* teotl, or that it *is* teotl. What they see de dicto are sun, birds, flowers, and flint knives. What they ordinarily see de dicto is teotl's nahual. But since they do not know that the cosmos and teotl are one and the same (just as I did not know that the man entering the limousine and Obama were one and the same), they do not see de dicto teotl. Deception is thus understood *epistemologically* in terms of what a perceiver is able to recognize or discern when she perceives. Deception is *not* understood *metaphysically* in terms of the existence of two distinct things: mask and person behind the mask.

That Aztec metaphysics understands teotl in terms of shaman transformation and artistic creativity is not accidental, for shamanism and artistic creation commonly go hand-in-hand in Mesoamerica thought. Shamans commonly double as artists whose creations reflect their out-of-body visions. In their study of papermaking and cut-paper figures among contemporary Nahua, Otomí, and Tepehua peoples, Alan Sandstrom and Pamela Effrein Sandstrom discuss "shaman-artists" who create the various paper figures used in religious rituals.[99] Regarded as a "person of knowledge" (*tlamátiquetl* in modern Nahuatl), the shaman cuts paper figures that reflect his out-of-body visions of the life-and-death forces operating in the cosmos.[100] The ritual efficacy of a shaman's paper-cut figures depends largely upon the accuracy of his or her visions. Sandstrom and Sandstrom write, "No shaman can establish a positive reputation without first becoming a master paper cutter."[101] Stacy Schaefer explains how Wixárika women weavers conceive weaving as a shamanic-like creative process that relies upon the weaver's out-of-body visions and apprehensions of sacred forces operating in the cosmos. Schaefer writes, "Weaving and shamanism share a basic element in common: transformation."[102]

1.4. SOME IMPLICATIONS OF AND OBJECTIONS AGAINST SEVERAL ASPECTS OF THIS INTERPRETATION OF AZTEC METAPHYSICS

METAPHYSICS OF BECOMING: AN IMPLICATION

I consider now some implications of and objections against the preceding interpretation of Aztec metaphysics. First, Aztec philosophy's metaphysics of Becoming maintains that that which is real is that which becomes, changes, transmutes, and moves. Reality is characterized essentially by becoming – not by being or is-ness. Aztec metaphysics embraces flux, evanescence, expiry, and change by making them defining characteristics of reality – rather than marginalizing them as mere illusion and unreality. This implies that Aztec metaphysics does not condemn something as unreal, semi-real, or illusory solely on the grounds that it is impermanent, evanescent, and changeable.

To think that Aztec metaphysics *does* condemn something as unreal or illusory solely on the grounds that it is impermanent is to attribute a Platonic-style metaphysics of Being to Aztec philosophy. Unfortunately, this is precisely what Miguel León-Portilla does when interpreting several song-poems collected in the *Cantares mexicanos* and *Romances de los señores de la Nueva España*.[103] Consider the following two song-poems commonly attributed to Nezahualcoyotl:

I, Nezahualcoyotl, ask this:
Is it true one really lives on the earth?
Not forever on earth,
only a little while here.
Though it be of jade it falls apart,
though it be gold it wears away,
though it be quetzal plumage it is torn asunder.
Not forever on earth,
Only a little while here.[104]

And;

I comprehend the secret, the hidden:
O my lords!
Thus we are,
we are mortal,
humans through and through
we all will have to go away,
we all will have to die on earth . . .
Like a painting
we will be erased.

Like a flower,
we will dry up
here on earth.
Like the plumed vestment of the precious bird,
that precious bird with the agile neck,
we will all come to an end . . .
Think on this, o lords,
eagles and tigers,
though you be of jade,
though you be of gold,
you will also go there,
to the place of the fleshless.
We will have to disappear,
no one can remain.[105]

León-Portilla interprets these and other song-poems attributed to Nezahual-coyotl as expressing Nezahualcoyotl's doubt about the reality of earthly exis-tence; doubts based on the widespread observation that everything earthly is evanescent, perishable, and impermanent. Quetzal plumes are torn asunder. Jade is broken. Gold is crushed. All earthly things appear and then quickly disappear like a delicate flower in the hot summer sun. Nezahualcoyotl's "keen awareness of time and change" and of the ephemerality of everything earthly, writes León-Portilla, not only causes him profound sorrow and anguish, but, more significantly, causes him to doubt the very reality of everything earthly.[106] Because earthly existence is evanescent, León-Portilla's Nezahualcoyotl reasons, it is *not* real. Nezahualcoyotl yearns for something enduring and stable – that is, something genuinely real.[107]

León-Portilla thus attributes the following syllogism to Nezahualcoyotl:

1. PREMISE: Earthly existence is evanescent, impermanent, perishable.
2. PREMISE: If something is evanescent, etc., then it is not real.
3. CONCLUSION: Hence earthly existence is not real.

Note that in order to make this song-poem express any syllogism at all, León-Portilla must supply a conclusion indicator such as "hence." In order to make it express the specific syllogism he wants, he must supply a suppressed premise: premise 2. And in order to make this song-poem express a syllogism with the conclusion he wants, León-Portilla must supply a quite specific premise drawn from the metaphysics of Being: "If something is evanescent, etc., then it is not real." None of these, however, is present in the original text.

I do not dispute León-Portilla's claim that Nezahualcoyotl expresses sorrow and anguish over the facts that human life is fleeting and that human beings ineluctably perish. Nor do I dispute León-Portilla's claim that Nezahualcoyotl yearns for a way to escape this destiny; that he yearns for something ever-lasting. What I do dispute however is the legitimacy of León-Portilla's interpretation of these song-poems in terms of a metaphysics of Being, that is, that in these song-poems Nezahualcoyotl advances a syllogism with a premise that equates reality per se with being, immutability, imperishability, and permanence. These song-poems state nothing that logically implies a metaphysics of Being. After all, Nezahualcoyotl can wish things were otherwise while woefully acknowledging that they are not. He can wish that reality were not defined by change while painfully acknowledging that it is. He can wish to avoid death while bitterly acknowledging its inevitability. Indeed, doing so is an even greater source of sorrow and anguish than finding an escape.

León-Portilla and John Bierhorst attribute the selfsame metaphysics of Being and syllogistic reasoning to a song-poem attributed to Tochihuitzin Coyolchiuhqui.[108] It reads:

We only rise from sleep,
we come only to dream,
it is not true, it is not true,
that we come on earth to live.
As an herb in springtime,
so is our nature.
Our hearts give birth, make sprout,
the flowers of our flesh.
Some open their corollas,
then they become dry.[109]

They interpret the song-poem as advancing the metaphysical argument that human life on earth is a dream (or dreamlike) and therefore not fully real: life is not real, for life is but a dream. León-Portilla reconstructs Tochihuitzin Coyolchiuhqui's reasoning as follows: "We have come to earth only to dream, and our dream vanishes quickly."[110] That which is transitory is illusion.[111] And "[s]ince what one finds on earth (in tlaltipac) is transitory," it follows that what one finds on earth is "a world of illusion."[112] That is:

1. PREMISE: Life (human existence on earth) is a dream.
2. PREMISE: Dreams are transitory.
3. PREMISE: If something is transitory, then it is illusion (illusory).

4. CONCLUSION/PREMISE: Therefore dreams are illusions (illusory).
5. PREMISE: If something is an illusion, then it is transitory.
6. PREMISE: If something is transitory, then it is not real.
7. CONCLUSION/PREMISE: Therefore illusions and dreams are not real.
8. CONCLUSION: Therefore life (human existence) on earth is not real.

In order to make this song-poem express any kind of syllogism whatsoever, León-Portilla and Bierhorst must supply conclusion indicators such as "there fore." And in order to make it express the specific syllogism they desire, they must supply several suppressed premises: premises 2, 3, 5, and 6. In order to make the song-poem express a syllogism with the precise conclusion they seek Bierhorst and León-Portilla must supply a premise drawn specifically from the metaphysics of Being, namely premise 6: "If something is transitory, then it is not real." Yet none of this is present in the original text.

Interpreting the song-poems collected in the *Cantares mexicanos* and *Romances de los señores de Nueva España* is a dicey business into which I prefer not to enter at this time. As Bierhorst observes, in their present form the song-poems gathered in the *Cantares* appear to derive mostly from the generation begin ning around 1550.[113] Before being gathered and written down, the song-poems were orally transmitted. Many clearly refer to post-Conquest events and per sons, treat Christian themes, and so appear to be colonial compositions. Others clearly appear rooted in the precolonial past. As scholars recognize, teasing out the pre-Conquest from the post-Conquest is a daunting task. I suggest that drawing conclusions about the metaphysical views espoused by their composers is equally if not more daunting.

Defending a new interpretation of these song-poems is not my aim. Rather my aim is simply to cast sufficient doubt upon León-Portilla's and Bierhorst's interpretation so as to defuse the song-poems as a potential objections against my reconstruction of Aztec metaphysics as one of Becoming rather than Being It is still possible, of course, that León-Portilla is correct when asserting that Nezahualcoyotl and Tochihuitzin Coyolchiuhqui are Socrates-like skeptics questioning the reigning ideas of their age (which if I am correct, would be a metaphysics of Becoming). And it is possible, too, that in so doing they presup poses a metaphysics of Being.[114] However, León-Portilla gives us no reasons for thinking that Tochihuitzin Coyolchiuhqui and Nezahualcoyotl were such skeptics. Furthermore, nothing stated explicitly in the song-poems entails a metaphysics of Being. I thus suggest León-Portilla and Bierhorst are guilty of unwittingly importing their own metaphysics of Being into their interpreta tion of these poems. Rather than doubting the reigning metaphysics of their day, Nezahualcoyotl and Tochihuitzin Coyolchiuhqui might have been doing nothing more (or less) philosophically profound than agonizing over the consequences for human existence implied by that metaphysics. With no afterlife obvious, yet also caught in a world beset by famine, disease, and war, they wished to live as long as possible. And so they bemoaned the fragility, evanescence, and brevity of life.

Before moving on, let's revisit Natalio Hernández Hernández's song-poem. It continues:

> We are all transient,
> all of us will go;
> for this reason we must respect,
> for this reason we must work;
> for this reasons we must gather,
> respect and conserve
> the things of life:
> the flower and the song.[115]

Here is a response to the observation that earthly existence is transient that differs significantly from the response attributed to Nezahualcoyotl and others by León-Portilla and Bierhorst. Life is transient: therefore we must work, gather, respect, and conserve "the things of life: the flower and the song." Hernández Hernández suggests an alternative way of interpreting the song-poems of the *Romances* and *Cantares*.

In conclusion, if Aztec philosophy embraces a metaphysics of Becoming as I maintain, then it appears we may well have to revisit existing interpretations and translations of Aztec song-poems as well as many of the assumptions underlying contemporary scholarship regarding Aztec thought.

Constitutional Monism: Implication 1

Aztec constitutional monism claims reality and hence the cosmos and all its contents consist of *essentially one kind of stuff*: always active, actualized, and actualizing energy. Aztec metaphysics thus rejects constitutional dualism, that is, the thesis that reality consists of *two essentially distinct and mutually exclusive kinds of stuff*: for example, mind versus matter, soul versus body, or spiritual versus physical. Unlike most versions of constitutional monism in world philosophy, Aztec constitutional monism does not maintain that reality consists of one *or* the other of the foregoing dualities. Unlike materialism, it does not claim reality consists exclusively of matter and does not aim to reduce mind to matter. Unlike idealism, it does not claim reality consists exclusively of mind and does not aim to reduce matter to mind. Aztec constitutional monism affirms that reality consists of a tertium quid, a *third kind* of stuff that is *neither* mind *nor* matter (as customarily conceived by dualists). This third kind of stuff is electricity-like energy or power. Aztec metaphysics intentionally confounds or cuts across the above dualisms since it regards them as false dualisms. As a consequence reality appears ineliminably and irreducibly ambiguous from the perspective of these nonautochthonous dualisms.

So, what about that which we customarily think of as mind and body, soul and matter, and spiritual and physical? Briefly put, they are simply two different facets or aspects of teotl. As Serge Gruzinski puts it, the Christian dualism of mind and body is replaced by an indigenous notion of a pluralism of vital forces.[116] The physical (material, corporeal) and the spiritual (mental, conscious) are simply two of the many different ways in which teotl presents itself. The Nahuatl concept of *ixtli* nicely captures this idea. The concept of ixtli is polysemous and terribly complex, and I cannot fully explore it here. For our purposes however, what is relevant is that among its meanings are "face," "countenance," "visage," "surface," "identity," "character," "eye," and "nature."[117] According to Alfredo López Austin, *ix* refers generally to the surface of things.[118] I submit mind is one ixtli of teotl, body, another. I call this view *dual aspect monism* for short.

Something like the Aztec conceptual complex of face-surface-visage-identity-character appears in other Mesoamerican conceptual systems. According to Barbara Tedlock, contemporary Quiché Maya believe each of the twenty Day Lords of the 260-day calendar has its own *uwäch uk'ij*, which she translates as "face of his day" or "his character."[119] Each day imparts its own face or character to children born on that day. The word *k'ij* in the languages of the Quiché and almost all Highland Maya, like the word *kin* in the language of the Maya of Yucatán, means not only "day" but also "sun," "time," and "aeon."[120] Each Day Lord presents one of twenty "faces" or "characters" of sun-day-time.

According to León-Portilla the Postclassic Maya notion of *kinh* (from which the contemporary Yucatec word *kin* derives) has the meaning of sun-day-time.[121] In the Postclassic period, *kinh* is associated closely with various "advocations of one and the same deity," sometimes called *Kinnich Ahua* ("Lord of the solar eye or countenance"), other times, *Kinnich Kak Moo* ("Lord of the solar countenance, fire macaw").[122] In the course of his tireless travels through the cosmos, kinh presents many faces, that is, personalities, attributes, and influences Significant divisions of time – days, months, and years – are presentations of kinh. Throughout all these changes, however, kinh himself remains unchanged León-Portilla writes, "The divine nature of kinh . . . can be distinguished in

numerable moments, each with its own face [and] attributes. Among the faces
.. are those of the solar deity in all its forms and those of the gods and goddesses
of rain, earth, corn, death, sacrifice, the great star, the moon, and hunting."[123]

Mixtec-speaking Nuyootecos embrace a like-minded view. Nuyooteco
thought starts from the assumption that everything is vivified by a single, generalized life force called *yii*,[124] which Monaghan translates as "potency, vitality,
fecundity."[125] Nuyootecos liken *yii* to electricity. *Yii* is characterized by generative fecundity, transformative power, self-preservation, and vital heat – properties represented by the Sun, Rain, Wind, and Earth. These, in turn, have a
variety of specific manifestations or "faces" (as Monaghan puts it) that are distinguished by the places where they are manifest and their associated properties.[126] Nuyootecos thus appear to embrace both constitutional and ontological monism. Reality consists of just one kind of stuff: *yii*. *Yii*'s singularity and
uniformity is compatible with the fact that *yii* manifests itself in a variety of
different faces.

Farther from home, Deloria, Weaver, Cordova, Burkhart, and other native
North American thinkers interpret many indigenous North American philosophies as upholding a like-minded constitutional monism according to which
reality consists of a single, uniform, homogenous energy or power – usen, natoji,
wakan tanka, yowa, orenda, or nil'ch'i – that is neutral between spirit and matter,
mind and body, and so on. Even farther from home, Benedict de Spinoza's ontological and constitutional monism and in particular what scholars call his "two-
aspect theory" resonate with Aztec metaphysics. Spinoza asserts that mind and
matter are not two different kinds of substance but merely two aspects, facets,
modes of a single substance, namely, God, who is neither. For Spinoza, writes
Genevieve Lloyd, mind and matter "are the same reality, though expressed in
different ways."[127] As Jaegwon Kim understands the view, mind and matter are
simply two . . . aspects of a single underlying substance that is neither mental
nor material."[128] The Chinese theory of qi likewise holds that both body (matter)
and spirit (mind, psyche) emerge from qi, the single energy-stuff of reality. They
are merely two different concentrations of qi – just as steam, liquid, and ice are
merely different condensations of water.[129] Lastly, Aztec monism resonates with
what Anglo-American metaphysicians call *neutral monism*. Neutral monism
claims reality consists of just one kind of stuff that is neutral between mind and
matter. Mind and matter are different combinations of this neutral stuff – not
essentially different kinds of stuff. David Hume, for example, maintained that
"perceptions" constituted this neutral stuff, and that minds and bodies are nothing more than "bundles" of sense perceptions.[130] William James saw the neutral
stuff as "pure experience," while Bertrand Russell saw it as "sensibilia."[131]

An Objection

My interpretation of Aztec metaphysics flies in the face of the well-respected and longstanding interpretation of López Austin. López Austin argues Meso-american thinkers generally and Aztec thinkers specifically embraced what I call constitutional dualism. He writes, "Mesoamerican thought was profoundly binary . . . Everything – including the gods – consisted of two types of sub stance . . . matter [or] essence."[132] One of these two substances is light, the other is heavy. Light substance is "divine," "subtle," and "imperceptible to humans under normal conditions." Heavy substance is "hard" and "perceptible to humans" under normal conditions. Heavy and light substances are essentially different. Uncreated things such as the gods are composed entirely of light sub-stance. Created things – humans, trees, and insects along with rocks, copal, and musical instruments, for example – are composed of a mixture of heavy and light substances. The light substance making up created things gives them their "spirit," while the heavy component gives them their "covering" (apparently as a corn husk covers the life-sustaining corn inside). This heavy covering links created things to decay, destruction, and death.[133] Although essentially different light and heavy substances are complementary. Indeed, the substantive dualism of light and heavy matter overlaps with the complementary dualisms of mascu-line/feminine, hot/cold, vital/mortal, dry/wet, and so on.[134]

Reply

I do not dispute López Austin's assertion concerning the centrality of binary complementary categories such as heavy/light and male/female in Aztec meta-physics. What I do dispute is López Austin's interpretation of these binary cat-egories as designating two essentially different kinds of metaphysical substance López Austin offers us no compelling reasons for thinking these differences must be *essential* differences and therefore no compelling reasons for thinking the Aztecs embraced constitutional dualism.

For starters, the mere existence of binary complementary properties does not entail the existence of essentially different binary substances. Why not? Because not every difference – not even every significant difference – is neces-sarily an essential difference. Not every difference need be rooted in a meta-physical difference between essentially different kinds of stuff. More argument is thus required. This is a simple point of formal logic. Yet this criticism is not fatal to López Austin seeing as no empirical theory – and I see all interpreta-tions of Aztec metaphysics as empirical theories – is ever logically entailed by its data. Rival empirical theories are adjudicated in terms of a number of criteria including empirical adequacy, simplicity, internal coherence, predictive accuracy, and what I consider most pertinent here, explanatory power – that is, which theory enables us to make more sense of the phenomena in question.[135]

I believe constitutional monism offers us a better understanding of complementary binary properties than does constitutional dualism. My constitutional monism treats López Austin's heavy and light "substances" as ultimately derivable from and understandable in terms of the single stuff of teotl. Heavy and light are simply two different intensities, coagulations, or condensations of teotl's energy-in-motion. They are no more substantively different from one another than are blue and red. Colors, after all, are nothing more than different intensities of a single stuff: electromagnetic radiation. Alternatively, heavy and light are no more substantively different from one another than are vaporous, liquid, and frozen water. Heavy and light simply refer to two different aspects, facets, or faces of teotl: hence the title *dual aspect monism*.

According to the *Historia de los mexicanos por sus pinturas*, argues López Austin, light and heavy "substances" originated in Tezcatlipoca's and Quetzalcoatl's splitting of Cipactli (the primordial caiman; in the *Histoyre du Mechique*, they split Tlaltecuhtli [Earth Lord-Lady, the great earth monster]), creating the heavens and surface of the earth. The gods that emerged from Cipactli's upper half were light, luminous, hot, and dry; those emerging from Cipactli's lower half were heavy, dark, cold, and wet.[136] López Austin alternatively tells us that heavy and light substances have a common origin in the single, primordial divine Father-Mother unity, Ometecuhtli-Omecihuatl ("Two-Lord-Two-Lady"), who is also called Ometeotl ("Two-Teotl"). Ometecuhtli-Omecihuatl dwells in Omeyocan ("two-place or place of unified twoness").[137]

Yet as I see it, the fact that heavy and light substances derive from a common, single source, Ometecuhtli-Omecihuatl or Ometeotl, suggests instead that they consist ultimately of the same stuff and that they are therefore ultimately reducible to and explainable in terms of this single stuff. Their common origin and constitution also help explain why they are inextricably bound together as well as why they are mutually arising and mutually interdependent. Constitutional dualism appears to fall short on this score, since we customarily understand essentially distinct substances as able to exist independently of and apart from one another and therefore *not* as mutually arising and interdependent. Aztec binaries appear instead to be two aspects of a single thing. Moreover, if Ometecuhtli-Omecihuatl and Ometeotl are (as I argue in chapter 2) monikers for teotl, then heavy and light are clearly derivable from the single stuff of teotl. They are nothing more than two facets or presentations of teotl. The relationship between teotl, on the one hand, and heavy and light, on the other, is analogous to the relationship (according to Spinoza) between God, on the one hand, and thought and extension, on the other; the relationship (according to Hume's neutral monism) between perceptions, on the one hand, and mind and body as bundles of perceptions, on the other; and lastly, the relationship between qi, on the one hand, and blood and breath as different concentrations of qi, on the other.

The heavy component of created things, according to López Austin, serves as a "covering" around their light component. He apparently believes this fact also suggests, if not also entails, constitutional dualism. Yet this fact alone is no more decisive than is the fact that the liquid interior of a partially frozen ice cube has a frozen covering, or the soft interior of baked bread is covered with a hard crust. Both covering and interior may consist of one and the same kind of stuff.

In *Tamoanchan, Tlalocan* López Austin relates another myth according to which a single, great, swollen, hollow tree exists in *Tamoanchan*, the "primogenital" place of origins and creation. (According to another variant, Tamoanchan is the tree itself.)[138] The tree contains two streams, one consisting of light, hot, dry substance, the other, heavy, cold, wet substance. The two streams twist around one another in helicoidal fashion. In other accounts, the single tree consists of two trunks similarly constituted and similarly intertwisting. The gods residing in Tamoanchan eventually violate this divine order, causing the tree to rupture into two halves, causing the two substances to flow like blood from the tree. This event created human time and the current cosmos.

Yet this myth does not unequivocally support constitutional dualism, either. It appears instead far more consonant with and intelligible in terms of constitutional monism. I take it as profoundly significant that both light and heavy streams are components of and hence derive from one and the same tree, that is, from singularity. They do not derive from two essentially distinct trees. What's more, if the two streams were essentially different, then they should be capable of existing without each other. Yet they are not. Indeed, the unity and inseparability of the two streams appears to be a fundamental and essential feature of the myth. They emerge from and remain tied to a single source.

López Austin appears to rest his case for the essential distinction between light and heavy substances upon the further fact that heavy matter is perceptible by humans "in their normal state of awareness" but light matter is not. How metaphysically probative is this? Not very. This distinction is *epistemological*, not metaphysical. That is, it concerns what human beings are or are not able to perceive "in their normal state of awareness" – not the way the nonhuman world is actually put together. It concerns the nature of human sense perception – not the nature of reality. And at least by the norms of Western logic, one cannot validly deduce metaphysical conclusions about the way the world is from epistemological premises about human perceptual abilities. Therefore without additional premises López Austin is not logically entitled to infer that this epistemological distinction entails – much less presupposes – a metaphysical distinction between two essentially different kinds of substance. For example, both tables and microbes consist of matter yet the former are perceptible by humans "in their normal state of awareness" yet the latter are not. In short, that which is imperceptible is not necessarily metaphysically different from that which is perceptible.

The distinction between what is and is not perceptible by humans "in their normal state of awareness" is wholly compatible with constitutional monism's claim that heavy and light are two aspects of teotl. There is perceptible energy and there is imperceptible energy. And this assertion no more entails constitutional dualism than the assertion by contemporary physics that electromagnetic radiation of certain wavelengths is visible to the naked eye (e.g., as colors) while electromagnetic radiation of other wavelengths (e.g., infrared and ultraviolet) is not. Both are constituted by one and the same stuff: electromagnetic radiation. Like the Aztecs, we are awash in a single energy, some intensities of which we are able to perceive, others of which we are not.

I see the foregoing as one of the lessons of the Quiché Maya myth of human creation: we live amidst a single stuff some of aspects of which we are ordinarily able to perceive, other aspects of which we are not. According to the *Popol Vuh*, the gods gave the first four human beings the ability to see and thereby know everything. Yet the gods later realized this enabled humans to become gods, so they decided to weaken the visual and epistemological powers of humans.

Perfectly [the first humans] saw, perfectly they knew everything under the sky, whenever they looked. The moment they turned around and looked around in the sky, on the earth, everything was seen without any obstruction. . . .

As they looked, their knowledge became intense. Their sight passed through trees, through rocks, through lakes, through seas, through mountains, through plains. [They] were truly gifted people. . . .

They understood everything perfectly, they sighted the four sides, the four corners in the sky, on the earth, and this didn't sound good to the [gods]:

"What our works and designs have said is no good:
'We have understood everything, great and small,' [the humans] say." And so the [gods] took back their knowledge. . . .

[The first humans] were [consequently] *blinded as the face of a mirror is breathed upon*. Their eyes were weakened. Now it was only when they looked nearby that things were clear.

And such was the loss of the means of understanding, along with the means of knowing everything, by the four humans.[139]

I interpret this passage as saying that humans are unable to perceive what López Austin calls "light matter" not because it consists of a substantially different kind of stuff from "heavy matter" but because humans are simply blind to certain aspects of the single stuff constituting reality. That which distinguishes light and heavy matter is not a metaphysical difference but an epistemological difference. What explains this discrepancy is something about the makeup of humans as perceivers – not something about the make-up of reality.[140]

In conclusion, López Austin offers us insufficient reasons for thinking the centrality of binary categories in Aztec thought entails or is even better explained by constitutional dualism. Constitutional monism maintains all binaries are derivable from teotl. This interpretation obviously requires further argument. The remainder of this book endeavors to do this.

Ontological Monism, the Multiplicity of Things, and the Distinction between Appearance (Illusion) and Reality: Implication 2

Aztec ontological monism maintains that there exists just one thing: teotl. From this it follows that there cannot also exist a multiplicity of discrete, independently existing things such as houses, censers, and tortillas. Simply put, if there exists only one thing, then there cannot also exist many things. However, this implication appears to contradict both ordinary sense experience and common sense, for when we look around ourselves, there certainly appears to be a multiplicity of independently existing individual things. How does Aztec metaphysics reconcile these two? How does ontological monism account for the apparent plurality of things?[141] What's more, the foregoing seems to entail that reality (teotl) is *not* as it appears to be. But if so, then it would seem that appearance and reality are not identical, that is, that they are two distinct kinds of things. But then what kind of thing are appearances? And similarly with illusion: if reality is single, then multiplicity must be an illusion. But if illusion differs from reality, then it would seem illusion and reality must be two distinct things. But then what kind of a thing is illusion? In short, what is the ontological status of appearance and illusion, and how do we account for them? (For present purposes I equate illusion and appearance and use the term *appearance* for both.)

Generally speaking, Western and non-Western philosophers commonly pursue one of two strategies for making sense of the distinction between reality and appearance: metaphysical and epistemological. The metaphysical strategy introduces an ontological distinction between appearance and reality and defends an *ontological dualism* of appearance and reality. Reality and appearance are *two* different *kinds of things*. There are two general categories or kinds of existents: the real and the apparent. The metaphysical strategy takes its clue from the statement, "Reality is not *what* it appears to be," as this suggests that appearance is a "what," that is, an existing thing of some sort. But what kind of thing is an appearance or illusion?

Plato in Book VI of *The Republic* advances what is perhaps the most famous and influential metaphysical answer to this question in Western philosophy and theology. Plato argues appearance and reality are two different kinds of existents or things. Appearances exist but do so in a less robust manner than does reality (or real things), which exists in the most robust manner possible. Appearances are only partially real or semireal, whereas reality (real things) is fully and completely real. Appearances enjoy a lower amount of being or is-ness than does reality, which possesses the highest possible amount of being or is-ness. Plato proposes a graded ontological hierarchy that he illustrates using a divided vertical line. At the top of the line sits reality (the real). Reality enjoys complete being and is-ness. It is completely, fully, or wholly real. Since Plato also adopts a metaphysics of Being, he concludes that that which is real is perfect, timeless, immutable, and permanent. In the middle of the line sit appearances (the merely apparent). Appearances enjoy only incomplete being or is-ness. They are only partially real or semireal. Plato's metaphysics of Being claims appearances are therefore imperfect, timed, mutable, and impermanent. Finally, at the bottom of the divided line sits nothingness. Nothingness represents the total absence and negation of being. It is literally no thing. Nothingness is wholly unreal since it partakes of no amount of being or is-ness whatsoever. It simply is not.[142]

In sum, Plato explains the difference between how things appear and how things really are by positing the existence of an ontological distinction between appearance and reality. In so doing, he introduces an *ontological dualism* into his metaphysics. Plato uses the notion of appearance (illusion) to characterize an inferior or lower grade of reality and existence – the semi- or partially real – and to distinguish this inferior grade of reality from a superior, higher one – the fully real. The realm of appearances is not only distinct from but also ontologically inferior to the realm of the real. His metaphysical strategy *reifies* appearances (and illusions). Appearances are a kind of thing albeit an inferior one.

As intuitive as it may be, the metaphysical strategy is not an option for ontological monists since they cannot on pain of logical inconsistency admit the existence of a plurality of things, even if those things enjoy only partial reality.

Ontological monists must therefore look elsewhere for a solution to this puzzle. They commonly pursue what I call the epistemological strategy.

The epistemological strategy takes it cue from the statement, "Reality is not *how* it appears to be," as this suggests that appearance is a "how" rather than a "what." But what, exactly, does it mean to say that appearance is a "how"? It means that appearances and illusions are a function of *how* humans perceive the single reality around them. They are a function of our *misperception* of reality. Appearance and illusion are not distinct existents or things of any kind, semireal or otherwise. They are shortcomings in *how* humans perceive – not ontologically substandard objects *that* we perceive. As such they are to be understood in *adverbial* rather than *substantive* terms. The fact that teotl is not how it appears thus says something about how we perceive teotl, not something about the existence of some discrete, independently existing things called appearances or illusions.

South Asian Advaita Vedānta likewise espouses an ontological monism (or nondualism) and so faces the same challenge of explaining the compatibility of ontological monism with the apparent multiplicity of things. Śamkara (Shankara), the eight-century South Asian philosopher and exponent of Advaita Vedānta, pursued an epistemological strategy for dissolving this apparent contradiction. He advanced the following analogy for understanding the relationship between appearance and reality, and a fortiori the relationship between the apparent multiplicity of things and the singularity (or nonduality) of Brahman.[143] Walking down a path a man approaches a rope slung upon the ground. At first he perceives the rope as a serpent. Since there is no serpent present to his consciousness, this is obviously a case of *mis*perception. The man mistakenly perceives the rope *as* a snake. Yet the man's (mis)perception is not entirely illusory, since there is, after all, a rope on the ground before him. He does perceive *something*. Upon closer examination, the man realizes his mistake. The appearance of a serpent ceases.[144]

Śamkara's point may be expressed using the distinction between perception de re (perception of the thing) and perception de dicto (perception of what is said or of the proposition; or perception under a description) introduced earlier. The man in Śamkara's example perceives de re the rope during the episode. The rope is physically present before him, his eyes are directed toward it, and electromagnetic waves reflected by the rope causally impinge upon his retinas and affect his nervous system. De re speaking, there is no illusion. In fact, there can be no illusion since illusions do not exist. This notwithstanding, the man initially perceives de dicto a snake. He perceives the rope *as* a snake; perceives that it *is* a snake; or perceives the rope *under a description* (which in this case is false). We might say that he *imposes* or *projects* a subjective description or set of categories. The snake, after all, does not exist; it is not real. Perceiving "snakely" however does.

Analogously, Śamkara reasoned that since there exists only one thing – Brahman – it follows that humans cannot perceive de re anything but Brahman. There simply is nothing else to perceive de re. This notwithstanding, humans impose various descriptions upon their de re perceptions of Brahman, and as a consequence perceive Brahman de dicto *as* a multiplicity of discrete physical objects and personal selves. Illusion and appearance are therefore functions of *how* humans perceive – *not things* that humans perceive. Appearance and illusion do exist in their own right.

Dōgen, the famous thirteenth-century Japanese Zen Master, pursued a similar epistemological strategy. He maintained there are no illusions: "there are only the *de*lusions we inflict upon ourselves."[145] Illusion resides in our interpretation and judgment, not in the things themselves. What's more, an illusion is "true" or real in the sense of being an actually occurring *mental* phenomena. What is "false" is our misinterpretation of the content of the mental phenomenon. This is how illusion arises. It arises in the cognitive activity of perceiving and judging. In short, there are not two things in the world: illusion and reality. Illusion does not refer to a separate kind of entity or level of existence. Dōgen explains illusion in terms of *how* we perceive, not *what* we perceive.

Śamkara's and Dōgen's treatments of misperception, appearance, and illusion anticipate in significant respects the treatment of illusions proffered by contemporary Gestalt psychology. Consider the stock duck/rabbit image discussed by contemporary Gestalt psychology (see Figure 1.1).[146] Strictly speaking, the figure is neither the figure of a duck nor the figure of a rabbit. And since the figure itself is objectively neither duck nor rabbit, what we perceive de re is neither duck nor rabbit. This notwithstanding, we perceive the figure *as* a duck or *as* a rabbit. That is, we perceive the figure de dicto *as* a duck or de dicto *as* a rabbit. However, since the figure itself is neither duck nor rabbit, it follows that our de dicto perceptions of a rabbit and of a duck are both illusions. We are guilty of imposing (albeit unconsciously) our own de dicto interpretations upon the figure. Perceiving the figure as a duck or as a rabbit is matter of *how* we perceive, not *what* we perceive. The illusion, in other words, is explained epistemologically, not metaphysically. We see "duckly" or "rabbitly."

The metaphysical strategy is incompatible with ontological monism. Like Śamkara, Dōgen, and Gestalt psychology, Aztec metaphysics refuses to reify appearances and illusions. Like them, it interprets illusion and appearance adverbially. Aztec metaphysics employs an epistemological strategy, the details

FIGURE 1.1. *Duck/Rabbit (Author's drawing)*

of which are dictated by conceiving teotl as shaman and cosmos as teotl's nahual. I call it a shamanic-epistemological strategy.

The shamanic-epistemological strategy consists of the following seven claims. First, the multiplicity of things is real. Individual humans, reed mats fishing nets, birds, temples, and lakes are fully real. They are not illusions; they are not mere appearances.

Second, the multiplicity of things is real because individual things are identical with teotl, and teotl is real. They are teotl's shamanic self-transformations. As we've seen, teotl is identical with its shamanic self-transformation just as a shaman is identical with his self-transformation (e.g., a jaguar). Teotl literally becomes the myriad of individual things just as the shaman literally becomes the jaguar. Individual things exist and have reality as aspects of teotl.

Third, Aztec ontological monism entails the metaphysical impossibility of humans perceiving de re anything but teotl. Teotl is the only thing that exists and hence the only thing that exists to be perceived de re. Therefore, when humans look around themselves, they perceive de re teotl and only teotl. However, since the multiplicity of things is identical with teotl, it follows that humans also perceive de re the multiplicity of things.

Fourth, the foregoing notwithstanding, humans ordinarily neglect both to perceive the identity of individual things with teotl and fail to perceive teotl itself. That is, although they perceive teotl de re, they do not perceive teotl de dicto. They do not perceive the myriad things *as aspects of teotl*. They do not perceive *that* the myriad of things and teotl are one and the same.

Fifth, what is illusory or merely appearance is the discrete, independent existence of individual things – not their existence per se. Their existence per se is not illusory since they are fully real, and they are fully real because they are self-transformative aspects of teotl and hence identical with teotl. What is illusory is their discreteness and independent existence from teotl (and one another). Although humans, dogs, and clay pots do certainly exist, they do *not* exist *as* discrete, independent things.

Sixth, Aztec philosophy employs an epistemological strategy for understanding this illusion and appearance. Illusion and appearance are functions of *how* humans perceive, not *what* they perceive.

Seventh, as functions of how humans perceive, illusion and appearance are fully real since they are actually occurring *mental* events in human perceivers. Human perceivers are fully real since identical with teotl. Here we arrive at another significant yet counterintuitive consequence of ontological monism. Given the identity of humans and the one – in our case, teotl – it follows that all human perception, both veridical and nonveridical, ultimately consists of teotl perceiving itself!

The epistemological approach is elegantly expressed in the passage quoted above from the *Popol Vuh*. The *Popol Vuh* tells us that the gods gave the first four human beings the ability to see and so know everything. Yet upon realizing that doing so enabled humans to become gods, the gods decided to weaken humans' visual and epistemological powers. And so humans were *"blinded as the face of a mirror is breathed upon."*[147] I suggest that the first four humans continued perceiving reality de re but no longer had the ability to recognize what they perceived de re since they were blinded by a mist of de dicto misperception. I suggest this analogy applies mutatis mutandis to Aztec metaphysics. For the latter, the breath on the mirror consists of the illusion that individual things exist independently of and discretely from teotl. Under normal circumstances humans are unable to see de dicto that which right in front of them, namely, teotl. Their perceptual powers have become befogged by "a cloud of unknowing" (as the anonymous fourteenth century English mystical text by the same title puts it).[148]

The *Popol Vuh* analogy neatly demonstrates how the epistemological approach is compatible with ontological monism. Imagine looking at yourself in a clean bathroom mirror. You see your face and its features clearly. Upon turning on the hot water, the bathroom fills with steam and the mirror gradually becomes more and more befogged. You continue looking at yourself while this is occurring, and as you do so you become increasingly less able to see your face clearly. Although you are still looking at yourself, you become less able to recognize yourself. How shall we understand this? Ontological monists contend you do not perceive two different faces, one clear and one obscure; rather you see the same face, first clearly and then obscurely. The difference consists of *how* you perceive *one and the same face*. Blurry face and clear face are ontologically identical and equally real.

Ontological Monism and the Nature of Dreams: Implication 3

But what about dreams? Surely dreams are not real, and so surely dreams demand a metaphysical explanation incompatible with ontological monism. How does Aztec metaphysics handle dreams? First, when one declares dreams not to be real, one does not mean that dreams do not occur, or that dreams are not actually occurring events or processes in the world. What one means is something like this: the experiences that occur while dreaming or within dreams are not real; what happens in dreams does not really happen; things are not really as they seem in dreams; or the contents of dreams are not true. Now reconsider the song-poem of Tochihuitzin Coyolchiuhqui:

> We merely come to stand sleeping, we merely come to dream. It is not true, not true that we come to live on earth.[149]

A second, anonymous song-poem collected in the *Cantares Mexicanos* expresses the same theme:

> But can what I say be real, O Life Giver? We must sleep, we were merely born to dream, and though I say it here on earth it falls on no one's ears.[150]

Earlier I discussed León-Portilla's and Bierhorst's argument that dreams are not real because dreams are ephemeral. Let's set aside that argument and focus now on the claim that life is a dream and its consequences. León-Portilla finds the following syllogism implicit in the preceding two song-poems:

1. Premise: Dreams are not real.
2. Premise: Human existence on earth is a dream.
3. Conclusion: Therefore human existence on earth is not real.[151]

I do not believe Aztec metaphysics subscribes to premise 1 and do not believe this syllogism is consistent with Aztec metaphysics.[152] Aztec metaphysics considers dreams (i.e., dream experiences or contents of dreams) to be real, and indeed every bit as real as waking experiences. Although it may seem patently true to those of us raised on Western science that the contents of dreams do not really occur, we are not entitled to assume the Aztecs shared our view. Therefore we are not entitled to assume the Aztecs regarded dreams as ontologically unreal or inferior to waking experiences, or that the Aztecs regarded dreams as epistemologically nonprobative.

In fact, quite the opposite seems true. According to López Austin, the Aztecs believed three animistic forces or energies occupy the living human body: *tonalli*, *teyolia*, and *ihiyotl*.[153] These reside in the head, heart, and liver (respectively). Tonalli is capable of temporarily leaving the body. This happens most frequently and normally during sleep. Dreaming consists of one's tonalli leaving one's body during sleep. According to López Austin, the Aztecs considered dreams "to be a perception of reality at places far removed from the one occupied by the sleeping body."[154] Dream experiences are real, and indeed just as real as waking experiences – notwithstanding the fact that the import of dreaming experiences is harder to discern than that of waking experiences. Furthermore, during dreams one's tonalli is able to communicate with the sacred as well as acquire certain kinds of knowledge. The reality of out-of-body experiences and travels during dreams is further demonstrated by the fact that they are dangerous and potentially fatal. One's tonalli might become trapped and unable to return to one's body. Finally, López Austin maintains the literal meaning of the Nahuatl verb meaning "to awaken" (*za* or *hualiza*) is "to be here" or "to come to be here."[155] He argues this supports the notion that one's tonalli undertakes bona fide out-of-body experiences and adventures during sleep.

The first line of Tochihuitzin Coyolchiuhqui's song-poem reads "*za tocochitle-huaco za tontemiquico*," which Bierhorst translates as "We merely come to stand sleeping, we merely come to dream." Bierhorst translates the Nahuatl word *toco-chitlehuaco* as "we come to stand sleeping." López Austin notes that although Siméon translates *cochitlehualiztli* as "dream," the word means etymologically "arising when one is asleep."[156] Dibble and Anderson translate *cochitlehua* as "to start up in one's sleep" but more often translate it as "to see in dreams."[157] The other word in the song-poem, *tontemiquico* ("we come to dream"), derives from *temiqui* ("to dream something").[158]

The verbs *temiqui* and *cochitlehua* (and their derivations) occur together throughout the speeches recorded in Sahagún's *Florentine Codex*, apparently functioning as a couplet.[159] Dibble and Anderson consistently translate the two as "to dream, to see in dreams" (e.g., *titemiqui ticochitlehua* as "we dream, we see in dreams").[160] The Nahuatl word *ontemictlamati*, which Dibble and Anderson translate as "they know in dreams,"[161] is also telling. For it strongly suggests the Aztecs regarded dreams as a potential source of knowledge, and in addition (assuming knowledge concerns that which is true) suggests they regarded dream experiences as at least sometimes truthful. Consistent with this, Molina contains multiple entries that distinguish between truthful dreams and false dreams: *iztlaca temictli* ("vain and nontruthful dream")[162] and *melahuacatemictli* ("truthful dream").[163] Pace León-Portilla, the fact that some kind of knowledge is attainable in dreams strongly implies that the Aztecs did *not* regard dreams as by definition unreal, illusory, false, or untrustworthy.

The Aztecs apparently regarded the ability to dream, to see in one's dreams, and to acquire knowledge through dreams as a sacred gift. A prayer addressed to Tezcatlipoca states, "And now, O master, O our lord, O lord of the near, of the nigh, may thou incline thy heart, that by thy grace for yet a while they see in dreams (*oncochitleoa*), know in dreams (*ontemictlamati*)."[164] The Aztecs devoted great energy to *temic iximati* and *temicnamictia*, that is, to interpreting and understanding the significance of the contents of dreams.[165] As Timothy Knab writes in his ethnography of contemporary Nahuatl-speakers in Sierra Norte de Puebla, "In a world where dreams are real, they are potent tools for interpretation. They are also potent explanations of the events of everyday life."[166] The fact that the significance of dreams is obscure and difficult to discern does not gainsay their veracity or their reality. The Aztecs standardized and recorded their understandings of dreams in their *temicamatl* ("book of dreams"). In Book X of the *Florentine Codex*, Sahagún's informants speak of the wise Toltecs having recorded their knowledge of dreams in their temicamatl.[167] Sahagún's informants also speak of the four wise men, Oxomoco, Cipactonal, Tlaltetecui, and Xochicahuaca, drafting a new *temicamatl* during the Mexica (Aztec) migration from the land of the Chichimeca. The book of dreams ranked in importance with the book of days (*tonalpohualli*), the book of years (*xioamatl*), and the count of the years (*xippoalli*).[168] Sahagún's *Primeros memoriales* includes a standardized list of dream interpretation.[169]

In sum, if the Aztecs considered dreams to be unreal, illusory, and false as León-Portilla and Bierhorst maintain, why then would the Aztecs devote so much effort to composing books aimed at interpreting dreams? Why would they revere these books? These practices clearly support the idea that the Aztecs regarded dreams as epistemologically probative because ontologically real.[170]

What then does Tochihuitzin Coyolchiuhqui mean when he says, "*za tocochitlehuaco za tontemiquico ahnelli ahnelli tinemico in tlalticpac*" ("We merely come to stand sleeping, we merely come to dream; it is not true, not true that we come to live on earth"?) It's difficult to say. If indeed he is likening earthly existence to dreaming, the foregoing discussion suggests that he is not attributing unreality or illusoriness to earthly existence but perhaps simply stating that life is as ephemeral as dreams. We come and go in the blink of an eye. Alternatively, he might be stating that the meaning of life on earth is as elusive as the meaning of dreams. Dreams function in these song-poems as a trope for that which is obscure and mysterious – not for that which is unreal.

1.5. CONCLUSION

Aztec metaphysics maintains there exists just one thing: the sacred energy-in-motion that is teotl. The cosmos and its inhabitants are not only constituted by but also ultimately identical with the sacred electricity-like force of teotl. Reality is defined by process, becoming, change, impermanence, and transformation. As teotl's ongoing "flower and song," the cosmos and all its inhabitants are teotl's grand, artistic-shamanic, kaleidoscopic self-presentation; teotl's ongoing work of performance art.

NOTES

1. See Alasdair MacIntyre, "Ontology," in Paul Edwards, ed.-in-chief, *Encyclopedia of Philosophy*, 8 vols. (New York: Macmillan Publishing, 1967), 5:542–43; Robert Audi, ed., *The Cambridge Dictionary of Philosophy* (Cambridge: Cambridge University Press, 1995); and Jaegwon Kim and Ernest Sosa, eds., *A Companion to Metaphysics* (Oxford: Blackwell, 1995).

2. John D. Monaghan, *The Covenants with Earth and Rain: Exchange, Sacrifice and Revelation in Mixtec Sociality* (Norman: University of Oklahoma Press, 1995), 198.

3. I borrow this phrase from Vine Deloria Jr., *God Is Red: A Native View of Religion* (Golden, CO: Fulcrum Publishing, 1994), 88.

4. I borrow this from Henry's characterization of traditional African metaphysics (Paget Henry, *Caliban's Reason: Introducing Afro-Caribbean Philosophy* [London, UK: Routledge, 2000]), 26.

5. In this respect, teotl resembles Spinoza's understanding of God. See Gilles Deleuze, *Spinoza: Practical Philosophy* (San Francisco, CA: City Lights Books, 1988), 97; Stuart Hampshire, *Spinoza* (Harmondsworth, UK: Penguin Books, 1951); Genevieve Lloyd, *Spinoza and the Ethics* (London, UK: Routledge, 1996); and Michael Levine, *Pantheism: A Non-Theistic Concept of Deity* (London, UK: Routledge, 1994).

6. I refer to teotl as *teotl* rather than *Teotl* in order to help remind us that teotl is more akin to electricity than to a deity.

7. Spinoza writes, "The power of God is . . . His essence," and God's power is to create (Benedict de Spinoza, *Ethics*, ed. James Gutman [New York: Hafner Publishing, 1949], Part I, Proposition XXXIV). For discussion, see Deleuze, *Spinoza: Practical Philosophy*; Hampshire, *Spinoza*.

8. Dennis Tedlock, "Creation in the Popol Vuh: A Hermeneutical Approach," in *Symbol and Meaning beyond the Closed Community: Essays in Mesoamerican Ideas*, ed. Gary H. Gossen (Albany, NY: Institute for Mesoamerican Studies, SUNY Press, 1986), 79. For further discussion, see Alfredo López Austin, *Tamoanchan, Tlalocan: Places of Mist*, trans. Bernard R. Ortiz de Montellano and Thelma Ortiz de Montellano (Niwot: University Press of Colorado, 1997); and Kay A. Read, *Time and Sacrifice in the Aztec Cosmos* (Bloomington, IN: Indiana University Press, 1998). Carlsen and Prechtel as well as Monaghan offer useful discussions of the role of transformation and renewal in Highland Maya religion and Nuyooteco thought (respectively). (Robert S. Carlsen and Martin Prechtel, "The Flowering of the Dead: An Interpretation of Highland Maya Culture," *Man* 26, no. 1 [1991]: 23–42; Monaghan, *Covenants with Earth and Rain*). Furst suggests this idea is rooted in Mesoamerican shamanism with its emphasis upon transformation as shamans are consummate form-changers; see Peter T. Furst, "Shamanistic Survivals in Mesoamerican Religion," *Actas del XLI Congreso Internacional de Americanistas* (Mexico: Instituto Nacional de Antropología e Historia, 1976), 3:149–57; and Furst,

"Introduction: An Overview of Shamanism," in *Ancient Traditions: Shamanism in Central Asia and the Americas*, ed. Gary Seaman and Jane S. Day (Niwot: Denver Museum of Natural History and University Press of Colorado, 1994), 1–28.

9. David A. Cooper, *God Is a Verb: Kabbalah and the Practice of Mystical Judaism* (New York: Riverhead Books, 1997), 69–73.

10. David L. Hall, "Just How Provincial *Is* Western Philosophy? 'Truth' in Comparative Context," *Social Epistemology* 15, no. 4 (2001): 293. Ames and Rosemont argue the verb-noun distinction thus gives way to a "gerundial" language: for example, *living properly* replaces *to live properly* and *proper life* (Roger T. Ames and Henry Rosemont Jr. *The Analects of Confucius: A Philosophical Translation* [New York, NY: Ballantine Books, 1998]).

11. Borrowing Rescher's terminology, I suggest we see teotl as a "verb-entity" (like "tornado" or "heat wave") rather an as a "noun-entity" (like "camel" or "bottle") (Nicholas Rescher, *Process Metaphysics: An Introduction to Process Philosophy* [Albany: State University of New York Press, 1966], 29).

12. In this respect Aztec metaphysics resembles Confucianism, Shinto, and Taoism. For discussion see Roger T. Ames, "Putting the *Te* Back into Taoism," in *Nature in Asian Traditions of Thought: Essays in Environmental Philosophy*, ed. J. Baird Callicott and Roger T. Ames (Albany: State University of New York, 1989), 113–43; James W. Boyd and Ron G. Williams, "Japanese Shinto: An Interpretation of a Priestly Perspective," *Philosophy East and West* 55, no. 1 (2005): 33–63; David L. Hall and Roger T. Ames, "Understanding Order: The Chinese Perspective," in *From Africa to Zen*, ed. Robert Solomon and Kathleen Higgins (Lanham, MD: Rowman and Littlefield, 1993), 1–23; David L. Hall and Roger T. Ames, *Anticipating China: Thinking through the Narratives of Chinese and Western Culture* (Albany: SUNY Press, 1995); and David L. Hall and Roger T. Ames, *Thinking from the Han: Self, Truth and Transcendence in Chinese and Western Culture* (Albany: SUNY Press, 1998).

13. For discussion see Richard Lewis Nettleship, *Lectures on the Republic of Plato*, 2nd ed. (London, UK: Macmillan and Co., 1963). Plato's Being-oriented metaphysics is clearly illustrated by his "divided line" and allegory of the cave in Books VI and VII of *The Republic*; (Plato, *Plato: The Collected Dialogues including the Letters*, ed. Edith Hamilton and Huntington Cairns [Princeton, NJ: Princeton University Press, 1961]).

14. Quoted in Barbara Deloria, Kristen Foehner, and Sam Scinta, eds., *Spirit and Reason: The Vine Deloria Jr., Reader* (Golden, CO: Fulcrum Publishers, 1999), 356, emphasis in original. Spores argues Mixtec religion conceives the universe as "a force field" (Ronald L. Spores, "Mixtec Religion," in *The Cloud People: Divergent Evolution of the Zapotec and Mixtec Civilizations*, ed. Kent Flannery and Joyce Marcus [New York: Academic Press, 1983], 345). According to Deloria Jr., the "tribal peoples" of North America equate power and existence (Deloria et al., *Spirit and Reason*, 356; see also

Deloria, *God Is Red*, 88). Hallowell argues the Ojibway regarded metamorphosis as an "earmark" of power (A. Irving Hallowell, *Contributions to Anthropology, Selected Papers of A. Irving Hallowell* [Chicago: University of Chicago Press, 1976], 377). Describing the Chinese notions of *qi* and *yun*, Stanley Murashige ("Philosophy of Art," in *Encyclopedia of Chinese Philosophy*, ed. Antonio S. Cua [New York: Routledge, 2003], 513) writes, "Power lives in motion." According to Placide Temples, the Bantu-speaking Baluba of the former Belgian Congo define existence in terms of force (Henry, *Caliban's Reason*, 26). Lastly, Henri Frankfort and H. A. Frankfort ("Myth and Reality," in *The Intellectual Adventure of Ancient Man*, Henri Frankfort, H. A. Frankfort, John A. Wilson, Thorkild Jacobsen, and William A. Irwin [Chicago: University of Chicago, 1977], 12) write "to be effective" is equivalent to "to be."

15. Nicholas Rescher, "Process Philosophy," in *A Companion to Metaphysics*, ed. Jaegwon Kim and Ernest Sosa (Oxford: Blackwell, 1995), 417.

16. Chapter 4 distinguishes between the cosmos per se, the Fifth Era, and the cosmos *of* the Fifth Era (i.e. the combination of middle region unique to the Fifth Era plus the upper and lower realms of the cosmos). Alan Sandstrom (personal correspondence, 8/20/11) cautions against equating teotl with (what Westerners think of as) nature since contemporary Nahuatl-speakers in eastern Mexico translate "nature" as *tlalticpac*, that is, as the earth's surface and all things on the earth's surface. I see *teotl* as far broader than this since *teotl* is identical with not only *tlalticpac* but also the realms above (*ilhuicatl*) and below (*mictlan*) tlalticpac as well as the cosmos before the creation of the Fifth Age.

17. I owe my understanding of process philosophy to Rescher, "Process Philosophy"; Rescher, *Process Metaphysics*; and Dorothy Emmet, *The Passage of Nature* (Philadelphia: Temple University Press, 1992).

18. See Read, *Time and Sacrifice*.

19. For supporting discussion of Aztec metaphysics, see Read, *Time and Sacrifice*; Bernard R. Ortiz de Montellano, *Aztec Medicine, Health, and Nutrition* (New Brunswick, NJ: Rutgers University Press, 1990); and López Austin, *Tamoanchan, Tlalocan*. For discussion of Nuyooteco metaphysics, see Monaghan, *Covenants with Earth and Rain*. Deloria (Deloria et al., *Spirit and Reason*) and Brian Yazzie Burkhart ("The Physics of the Spirit: The Indigenous Continuity of Science and Religion," in *The Routledge Companion to Religion and Science*, ed. James W. Hagg, Gregory R. Peterson, and Michael L. Spezio [New York: Routledge, 2011], 34–42) contend that indigenous North American philosophies likewise embrace holistic metaphysics. Lloyd characterizes Spinoza's closely similar metaphysics as an "ecosystem – an interconnected totality of organisms and their environment" (Genevieve Lloyd, *Part of Nature: Self-Knowledge in Spinoza's Ethics* [Ithaca, NY: Cornell University Press, 1994], 13). Hindu metaphysics defends a similar holism called "Indra's net" that Loy characterizes as a seamless, "all-

encompassing web of causal conditions" (David Loy, *Nondualism: A Study in Comparative Philosophy* [Amherst, NY: Humanities Books, 1988], 235). I borrow the notion of correlationality from Ames, "Putting the *Te* Back into Taoism"; Ames and Rosemont, *The Analects of Confucius*; Hall and Ames, *Anticipating China*; and Hall and Ames, *Thinking from the Han*.

20. I borrow this from Rescher, *Process Metaphysics*, 83.

21. Read, *Time and Sacrifice*, viii.

22. I use the definitions of immanence and transcendence in Audi, ed., *Cambridge Dictionary of Philosophy*, 361, 807.

23. For supporting ethnographic work, see John D. Monaghan, "Theology and History in the Study of Mesoamerican Religions," in *Supplement to the Handbook of Middle American Indians*, ed. John D. Monaghan (Austin: University of Texas Press, 2000), 6:27. See also Burkhart, "The Physics of the Spirit"; Deloria, *God Is Red*; and Deloria et al., *Spirit and Reason*.

24. Contrasting Christian and native Mesoamerican views of the supernatural, Andrews and Hassig write, "the native view saw supernatural power everywhere"; J. Richard Andrews and Ross Hassig, "Editor's Introduction," in *Treatise on the Heathen Superstitions that Today Live among the Indians Native to This New Spain*, Hernando Ruiz de Alarcón (Norman: University of Oklahoma Press, 1984), 24.

25. For related discussion, see Hall and Ames, *Anticipating China*, 124; James W. Boyd and Ron G. Williams, "The Art of Ritual in Comparative Context," in *Zoroastrian Rituals in Context: Proceedings of the Conference at the Internationales Wissenschaftsforum*, University of Heidelberg, April 2002, ed. Michael Stausberg (Leiden: Brill, 2004); and Boyd and Williams, "Japanese Shinto."

26. See Nettleship, *Lectures*. Plato's vertical metaphysics is dramatically illustrated by his divided line and allegory of the cave in Books VI and VII of *The Republic*; Plato, *Plato: The Collected Dialogues*. Gossen briefly contrasts Platonic metaphysics with Quiché Maya metaphysics of the *Popol Vuh*. His contrast applies *mutatis mutandis* to Aztec metaphysics. See Gary H. Gossen, "The Religious Traditions of Mesoamerica," in *The Legacy of Mesoamerica: History and Culture of a Native American Civilization*, ed. Robert Carmack, Janine Gasco, and Gary H. Gossen (Upper Saddle River, NJ: Prentice Hall, 1996), 532.

27. Arthur O. Lovejoy, *The Great Chain of Being: A Study of the History of an Idea* (New York: Harper and Row, Publishers, 1960).

28. Louise M. Burkhart, "The Amanuenses Have Appropriated the Text: Interpreting a Nahuatl Song of Santiago," in *On the Translation of Native American Literatures*, ed. Brian Swann (Washington, DC: Smithsonian Institute Press, 1992), 345.

29. *Historia de los mexicanos por sus pinturas*, in *Teogonía e historia de los mexicanos: Tres opúsculos del siglo XVI*, 1st ed., ed. Angel María Garibay K. (México: Editorial Por-

rúa, 1965), 23; *Histoyre du Mechique*, in *Teogonía e historia de los mexicanos: Tres opúsculos del siglo XVI*, 1st ed., ed. Angel María Garibay K. (México, DF: Editorial Porrúa, 1965), 102–3. For discussion, see Henry B. Nicholson, "Religion in Pre-Hispanic Central Mexico," in *Handbook of Middle American Indians*, vol. 10, ed. Robert Wauchope, Gordon F. Elkholm, and Ignacio Bernal (Austin: University of Texas Press, 1971), 407; Miguel León-Portilla, *Aztec Thought and Culture: A Study of the Ancient Nahuatl Mind*, trans. Jack Emory Davis (Norman: University of Oklahoma Press, 1963), 59; and López Austin, *Tamoanchan, Tlalocan*, 17.

30. See, for example, León-Portilla, *Aztec Thought and Culture*, 59; Davíd Carrasco with Scott Sessions, *Daily Life of the Aztecs: People of the Sun and Earth* (Westport, CT: Greenwood Press, 1998); and Eduardo Matos Moctezuma, *Life and Death in the Templo Mayor*, trans. Bernard R. Ortiz de Montellano and Thelma Ortiz de Montellano (Niwot: University Press of Colorado, 1995). To my knowledge, Read alone questions this interpretation; Read, *Time and Sacrifice*, 137–44, 269n26.

31. Arild Hvidtfeldt, *Teotl and *Ixiptlatli: Some Central Conceptions in Ancient Mexican Religion* (Copenhagen: Munksgaard, 1958), 77–78.

32. Ibid., 78n1.

33. Ibid., 100, 140; see also 25–35.

34. Richard F. Townsend, *State and Cosmos in the Art of Tenochtitlan* (Washington, DC: Dumbarton Oaks, 1979), 28. See also Burr Cartwright Brundage, *The Fifth Sun: Aztec Gods, Aztec World* (Austin: University of Texas Press, 1979), 137–144, 269n26.

35. Townsend, *State and Cosmos*, 30–31.

36. Ibid., 28.

37. Richard F. Townsend, *The Aztecs* (London: Thames and Hudson, 1992), 115.

38. Ibid., 115–16.

39. Ibid., 116.

40. Ibid.

41. Quoted in John Bowker, ed., *The Oxford Dictionary of World Religions* (Oxford: Oxford University Press, 1997), 598; see also 699.

42. Quoted in Hvidtfeldt, *Teotl and *Ixiptlatli*, 20.

43. Quoted in Ibid.

44. J. Jorge Klor de Alva, "Christianity and the Aztecs," *San Jose Studies* 5 (1979): 7.

45. Elizabeth Hill Boone, *The Aztec World* (Washington, DC: Smithsonian Books, 1994), 105.

46. Elizabeth Hill Boone, *Incarnations of the Aztec Supernatural: The Image of Huitzilopochtli in Mexico and Europe* (Philadelphia: American Philosophical Society, 1989), 4.

47. Ibid.

48. Louise M. Burkhart, *The Slippery Earth: Nahua-Christian Dialogue in Sixteenth-Century Mexico* (Tucson: University of Arizona Press, 1989), 37.

49. Ibid., 102. See also Thelma D. Sullivan, "Tlazolteotl-Ixcuina: The Great Spinner and Weaver," in *The Art and Iconography of Late Post-Classic Central Mexico*, ed. Elizabeth Hill Boone (Washington, DC: Dumbarton Oaks, 1982), 7.

50. Read, *Time and Sacrifice*, 206 and 145, respectively. Read notes that Walter Krickenberg glossed *teotl* as "kraft."

51. Read, *Time and Sacrifice*, 271n41; brackets mine.

52. Ibid., 146, 206.

53. Davíd Carrasco, "The Sacrifice of Women in the Florentine Codex: The Hearts of Plants and Players in War Games," in *Representing Aztec Ritual: Performance, Text, and Image in the Work of Sahagún*, ed. Eloise Quiñones Keber (Boulder: University Press of Colorado, 2002), 200.

54. Alan R. Sandstrom, "Sacred Mountains and Miniature Worlds: Altar Design among the Nahua of Northern Veracruz, Mexico," in *Mesas and Cosmologies in Mesoamerica*, ed. Douglas Sharon, San Diego Museum of Man Papers 42 (San Diego: San Diego Museum of Man, 2003), 56. See also Alan Sandstrom and Pamela Effrein Sandstrom, *Traditional Papermaking and Paper Cult Figures of Mexico* (Norman: University of Oklahoma Press, 1986), 276; and Alan R. Sandstrom, *Corn Is Our Blood: Culture and Ethnic Identity in a Contemporary Aztec Indian Village* (Norman: University of Oklahoma Press, 1991), 238–39.

55. Ibid. See also Sandstrom and Sandstrom, *Traditional Papermaking*.

56. Monaghan, *Covenants with Earth and Rain*, 98–99.

57. Ibid., 127.

58. Ibid., 198.

59. Ibid., 97.

60. Ibid., 104.

61. Monaghan, "Theology and History," 25.

62. Ibid., 26.

63. Arthur A. Joyce, *Mixtecs, Zapotecs, and Chatinos: Ancient Peoples of Southern Mexico* (Oxford: Wiley-Blackwell, 2010), 56.

64. Joyce Marcus, "Zapotec Religion," in *The Cloud People: Divergent Evolution of the Zapotec and Mixtec Civilizations*, ed. Kent Flannery and Joyce Marcus (New York: Academic Press, 1983). See also Monaghan, "Theology and History," 27–28. Hunt claims Zinacantecos view this sacred principle as transcending gendered divisions (Eva Hunt, *The Transformation of the Hummingbird: Cultural Roots of a Zinacatecan Mythical Poem* [Ithaca, NY: Cornell University Press, 1977], 234). See also Dennis Tedlock, *The Spoken Word and the Work of Interpretation* (Philadelphia: University of Pennsylvania Press, 1983), 268. Munro Edmonson characterizes Mixe metaphysics as a "pluralistic monism" (Munro S. Edmonson, "Foreword," in Frank J. Lipp, *The Mixe of Oaxaca: Religion, Ritual and Healing* [Austin: University of Texas Press, 1991], vii).

65. David Stuart, "Kings of Stone: A Consideration of Stelae in Ancient Maya Ritual and Representation," *RES* 29/30 Spring/Autumn (1996): 162–64.

66. Stuart, "Kings of Stone," 164.

67. Stephen Houston and David Stuart, "Of Gods, Glyphs, and Kings: Divinity and Rulership among the Classic Maya," *Antiquity* 70 (1996): 292; see also Stephen Houston and David Stuart, "The Ancient Maya Self: Personhood and Portraiture in the Classic Period," *RES* 33 (1998): 92.

68. Ibid. See also Munro S. Edmundson, "The Mayan Faith," in *South and Mesoamerican Spirituality: From the Cult of the Feathered Serpent to the Theology of Liberation*, ed. Gary H. Gossen in collaboration with Miguel León-Portilla (New York: Crossroads, 1993), 65–85.

69. Linda Schele and Ellen Miller, *The Blood of Kings: Dynasty and Ritual in Maya Art* (Fort Worth: Kimbell Art Museum, 1986), 301. See also Nancy M. Farriss, *Maya Society under Colonial Rule: The Collective Enterprise of Survival* (Princeton, NJ: Princeton University Press, 1984), 301ff.

70. Quoted in Deloria et al., *Spirit and Reason*, 356; see also 40–60 and Deloria, *God Is Red*.

71. Ibid. See also Vine Deloria Jr. and Daniel R. Wildcat, *Power and Place* (Golden, CO: American Indian Graduate Center and Fulcrum Resources, 2001); George Tinker, "Jesus, Corn Mother, and Conquest: Christology and Colonialism," in *Native American Religious Identity: Unforgotten Gods*, ed. Jace Weaver (Maryknoll, NY: Orbis, 1998), 134–54; Clara Sue Kidwell, Homer Noley, and George E. "Tink" Tinker, *A Native American Theology* (Maryknoll, NY: Orbis, 2002), 14, 89–93; and Burkhart, "The Physics of the Spirit."

72. Keith H. Basso, *The Cibecue Apache* (New York: Holt, Rinehart, and Winston, 1970), 36.

73. Deloria et al., *Spirit and Reason*, 357. Spores claims Mixtec religion sees the universe as "a force field to be revered, honored, and influenced for the benefit of humankind" (Spores, "Mixtec Religion," 345).

74. Viola Cordova, "The European Concept of *Usen*: An American Aboriginal Text," in *Native American Religious Identity: Unforgotten Gods*, ed. Jace Weaver (Maryknoll, NY: Orbis Books, 1998), 26–28.

75. Quoted in Kathleen Dean Moore, Kurt Peters, Ted Jojola, and Amber Lacy, eds. *How It Is: The Native American Philosophy of V. F. Cordova* (Tucson: University of Arizona Press, 2007), 117.

76. See Cordova, "The European Concept of *Usen*," 27; Willie Ermine, "Aboriginal Epistemology," in *First Nations Education in Canada: The Circle Unfolds*, ed. Marie Battiste and Jean Barman (Vancouver: University of British Columbia Press, 1995), 101–112; Jace Weaver, "Introduction: Notes from a Miner's Canary," in *Defending Mother Earth: Native American Perspectives on Environmental Justice*, ed. Jace Weaver (Maryknoll, NY:

Orbis Books, 1996), 10–12; Viola Cordova, "Ethics: The We and the I," in *American Indian Thought*, ed. Anne Waters (Oxford: Blackwell, 2004), 173–81; Gregory Cajete, *Native Science: Natural Laws of Interdependence* (Sana Fe, NM: Clear Light Publishers); Tinker, "Jesus, Corn Mother, and Conquest"; and Kidwell, Noley, and Tinker, *A Native American Theology*, 57.

77. Leroy N. Meyer and Tony Ramirez, "'*Wakinyan Hotan*' ('The Thunder Beings Call Out'): The Inscrutability of Lakota/Dakota Metaphysics," in *From Our Eyes: Learning from Indigenous Peoples*, ed. Sylvia O'Meara and Douglas A. West (Toronto: Garamond Press, 1996), 96.

78. See Lucien Lévy-Bruhl, *How Natives Think*, trans. Lilian A. Clare (New York: Washington Square Press, 1966); Henri Frankfort and H. A. Frankfort, "The Emancipation of Thought from Myth," in *The Intellectual Adventure of Ancient Man*, ed. Henri Frankfort et al. (Chicago: University of Chicago Press, 1977; published 1960 by Penguin Press as *Before Philosophy*), 363–88; Henri Frankfort and H. A. Frankfort, "Myth and Reality," in *Intellectual Adventure of Ancient Man*, ed. Henri Frankfort et al., 3–30; and Benjamin Keen, *The Aztec Image in Western Thought* (New Brunswick, NJ: Rutgers University Press, 1971).

79. Chad Hansen, *A Daoist Theory of Chinese Thought: A Philosophical Interpretation* (Oxford: Oxford University Press, 1992), 156.

80. Hall, "Just How Provincial *Is* Western Philosophy?," 290.

81. Ben-Ami Scharfstein, *A Comparative History of World Philosophy: From the Upanishads to Kant* (Albany: SUNY Press, 1998), 150, 290.

82. Hall and Ames, *Anticipating China*, 188. See also Roger T. Ames, "*Yin* and *Yang*," in *Encyclopedia of Chinese Philosophy*, ed. Antonio S. Cua (New York: Routledge, 2003), 846–47.

83. François Jullien, *Vital Nourishment: Departing from Happiness*, trans. Arthur Goldhammer (Cambridge: Zone Books, 2007), 76.

84. Hall, "Just How Provincial *Is* Western Philosophy?," 290.

85. Alan Watts, *Tao: The Watercourse Way* (New York: Pantheon Books, 1975), 54. See also Ku-ying Ch'en, *Lao Tzu: Text, Notes, and Comments*, intro, adapt., and transl. Rhett Y.W. Young and Roger T. Ames (San Francisco: Chinese Materials Center, 1977); David L. Hall, "Process and Anarchy: A Taoist View of Creativity," *Philosophy East and West* 28 (1978): 271–86; Roger T. Ames, "Putting the *Te* Back into Taoism," in *Nature in Asian Traditions of Thought: Essays in Environmental Philosophy*, ed. J. Baird Callicott and Roger T. Ames (Albany: State University Press of New York, 1989), 113–43; and Ames, "*Yin* and *Yang*."

86. Boyd and Williams, "Japanese Shinto," 34. See also James W. Boyd and Ron G. Williams, "Artful Means: An Aesthetic View of Shinto Purification Rituals," *Journal of Religious Studies* 13, no. 1 (1999): 37–52.

87. *Romances de los señores de la Nueva España*, fol. 35r–v, quoted in and trans. John Bierhorst, *Ballads of the Lords of New Spain: The codex romances de los señores de la Nueva España* (Austin: University of Texas Press, 2009), 149. León-Portilla attributes this song-poem to Nezahualcoyotl (Miguel León-Portilla, *Fifteen Poets of the Aztec World* [Norman: University of Oklahoma Press, 1992], 83).

88. *Cantares mexicanos*, fol. 10v, quoted in and trans. León-Portilla, *Fifteen Poets*, 282.

89. *Cantares mexicanos*, fol. 11v, quoted in and trans. León-Portilla, *Fifteen Poets*, 228.

90. Quoted in and trans. Sandstrom, *Corn Is Our Blood*, 229.

91. See Alfonso Caso, *The Aztecs: People of the Sun*, trans. Lowell Dunham (Norman: University of Oklahoma Press, 1985), 14, 39, 51; Mary Miller and Karl Taube, *An Illustrated Dictionary of the Gods and Symbols of Ancient Mexico and the Maya* (London: Thames and Hudson, 1993), 122, 172; Nicholson, "Religion," 439; Alfredo López Austin, *The Human Body and Ideology: Concepts of the Ancient Nahuas*, 2 vols., trans. Thelma Ortiz de Montellano and Bernard R. Ortiz de Montellano (Salt Lake City: University of Utah Press, 1988), I:362–75, II:292; Furst, "Shamanistic Survivals in Mesoamerican Religion"; Read, *Time and Sacrifice*; and Willard Gingerich, "*Chipahuacanemiliztli*, 'the Purified Life,' in the Discourses of Book VI, Florentine Codex," in *Smoke and Mist: Mesoamerican Studies in Memory of Thelma D. Sullivan*, Part 2, ed. J. Kathryn Josserand and Karen Dakin (Oxford: British Archaeological Reports, 1988), 517–43. Eliade writes, "Embodying an animal during seance is less a possession than a magical transformation of the shaman into that animal" (Mircea Eliade, *Shamanism: Archaic Techniques of Ecstasy* [Princeton, NJ: Princeton University Press, 1964], 99).

92. See Guilhem Olivier, *Mockeries and Metamorphoses of an Aztec God: Tezcatlipoca, "Lord of the Smoking Mirror,"* trans. Michel Besson (Niwot: University Press of Colorado, 2003).

93. Andrews and Hassig, in *Treatise, Appendix C*, 246.

94. Raymond D. Fogelson, "Person, Self, and Identity: Some Anthropological Retrospects, Circumspects, and Prospects," in *Psychosocial Theories of the Self*, ed. Benjamin Lee (New York: Plenum Press, 1982), 76, emphasis mine. See also Raymond D. Fogelson and Amelia B. Walker, "Self and Other in Cherokee Booger Masks," *Journal of Cherokee Studies* 5 (1980): 88–102.

95. Sam D. Gill, *Native American Religions: An Introduction* (Belmont, CA: Wadsworth Publishing, 1982), 69.

96. Ibid., 70–71.

97. Ibid., 71–72; see also Sam D. Gill, *Native American Religious Action: A Performance Approach to Religion* (Columbia: University South Carolina Press, 1987), 42–44.

98. See Audi, *Cambridge Dictionary of Philosophy*, 183.

99. Sandstrom and Sandstrom, *Traditional Papermaking*, 260; see also Sandstrom, *Corn Is Our Blood*; and Peter T. Furst, "The Roots and Continuities of Shamanism," in

Stones, Bones, and Skin: Ritual and Shamanic Art, ed. Anne T. Bodsky, Rose Danesewich, and Nick Johnson (Toronto: Society for Art Publications, 1977), 1–28.

100. Sandstrom, *Corn Is Our Blood*, 233–35; see also Sandstrom and Sandstrom, *Traditional Papermaking*.

101. Sandstrom and Sandstrom, *Traditional Papermaking*, 259.

102. Stacy B. Schaefer, *To Think with a Good Heart: Wixárika Women, Weavers, and Shamans* (Salt Lake City: University of Utah Press, 2002), 242. See also Gingerich, "*Chipahuacanemiliztli*"; Barbara G. Myerhoff, *Peyote Hunt: The Sacred Journey of the Huichol Indians* (Ithaca: Cornell University Press, 1974); Barbara G. Myerhoff, "The Huichol and the Quest for Paradise," *Parabola* 1, no. 1 (1976): 22–29; Barbara G. Myerhoff, "Balancing Between Worlds: The Shaman's Calling," *Parabola* 1, no. 2 (1976): 6–13; and Nathaniel Tarn and Martin Prechtel, *Scandals in the House of Birds: Shamans and Priests on Lake Atitlán* (New York: Marsilio Publishers, 1979), 279.

103. See John Bierhorst, ed., intro., and commentary, *Cantares Mexicanos: Songs of the Aztecs* (Stanford, CA: Stanford University Press, 1985); and John Bierhorst, transcription and trans., *Ballads of the Lords of New Spain: The Codex Romances de los Señores de la Nueva España* (Austin: University of Texas Press, 2009).

104. *Cantares Mexicanos*, fol. 17r, trans. León-Portilla, *Fifteen Poets*, 80. Bierhorst's translation is not significantly different and therefore has no impact upon my argument (Bierhorst, *Cantares Mexicanos*).

105. *Romances de los señores*, fol. 35r–36r, trans. León-Portilla, *Fifteen Poets*, 80–81. Bierhorst's translation is not significantly different and so has no impact upon my argument (Bierhorst, *Ballads of the Lords of New Spain*).

106. León-Portilla, *Fifteen Poets*, 80, 81–98; see also León-Portilla, *Aztec Thought and Culture*, 7.

107. León-Portilla, *Fifteen Poets*, 82; see also León-Portilla, *Aztec Thought and Culture*, 71–76.

108. León-Portilla, *Aztec Thought and Culture*, 71–72; León-Portilla, *Fifteen Poets*, 153; Bierhorst, *Cantares Mexicanos*, 49.

109. *Cantares mexicanos*, fol. 14 v, trans. León-Portilla, *Fifteen Poets*, 153, numbering mine. León-Portilla (*Aztec Thought and Culture*, 72) offers a slightly different translation of the crucial, first five lines: "It is not true, it is not true, That we come to this earth to live. We come only to sleep. Only to dream." Bierhorst translates the passage similarly: "We merely come to stand sleeping, we merely come to dream. It is not true, not true that we come to live on earth" (Bierhorst, *Cantares Mexicanos*, 175).

110. León-Portilla, *Fifteen Poets*, 152.

111. León-Portilla, *Aztec Thought and Culture*, 71.

112. Ibid.; see also Bierhorst; *Cantares Mexicanos*, 49.

113. Bierhorst, *Cantares Mexicanos*. Bierhorst's interpretation that the *Cantares Mexicanos* consist of post-Conquest "ghost songs" has met with severe criticism at the pens of León-Portilla (*Fifteen Poets*, 16–34, and "¿Hay composiciones de origen prehispánico en el manuscrito de cantares Mexicanos?," *Estudios de cultura náhuatl* 33 [2002]: 141–47) and James Lockhart (*Nahuas and Spaniards: Postconquest Central Mexican History and Philology*, UCLA Latin American Studies, vol. 76, Nahuatl Studies Series 3 [Stanford, CA: Stanford University Press, 1991], 141–57).

114. León-Portilla interprets Nezahualcoyotl and other authors of song-poems as Socrates-like figures who skeptically challenged the religious views of their day (León-Portilla, *Aztec Thought and Culture*; and León-Portilla, *Fifteen Poets*).

115. Quoted in and trans. Sandstrom, *Corn Is Our Blood*, 229.

116. Serge Gruzinski, *Man-Gods in the Mexican Highlands: Indian Power and Colonial Society, 1520–1800*, trans. Eileen Corrigan (Stanford, CA: Stanford University Press, 1989), 181.

117. See Read, *Time and Sacrifice*, 86, 130, 202; Frances Karttunen, *An Analytical Dictionary of Nahuatl* (Norman: University of Oklahoma Press, 1983), 121; R. Joe Campbell, *A Morphological Dictionary of Classical Nahuatl: A Morpheme Index to the Vocabulario en lengua mexicana y castellana of Fray Alonso de Molina* (Madison: Hispanic Seminary of Medieval Studies, 1985), 143–53; and León-Portilla, *Aztec Thought and Culture*, 12–13. The most insightful treatment of *ixtli* is López Austin, *Human Body and Ideology*, I:195–96, II:158, 200.

118. López Austin, *Human Body and Ideology*, II:200.

119. Barbara Tedlock, *Time and the Highland Maya*, rev. ed. (Albuquerque: University of New Mexico Press, 1992 [1982]), 2, 108, 110.

120. Ibid., 2.

121. Miguel León-Portilla, *Time and Reality in the Thought of the Maya*, 2nd enlarged ed. (Norman: University of Oklahoma Press, 1988), 16–17.

122. Ibid., 24; see also 33, 49.

123. Ibid., 54.

124. Monaghan, *Covenants with Earth and Rain*, 98–99.

125. Ibid., 127.

126. Ibid., 98–112, 137–38.

127. Lloyd, *Spinoza and the Ethics*, 6–7. See also Lloyd, *Part of Nature*; and Scharfstein, *Comparative History of World Philosophy*.

128. Jaegwon Kim, *Philosophy of Mind* (Boulder, CO: Westview Press, 1996), 51.

129. Jullien, *Vital Nourishment*, 76.

130. David Hume, *Enquiries Concerning Human Understanding and Concerning the Principles of Morals*, ed. L. A. Selby-Bigge (Oxford: Clarendon Press, 1902).

131. Brian P. McLaughlin, "Philosophy of Mind," in *The Cambridge Dictionary of Philosophy*, gen. ed. Robert Audi (Cambridge: Cambridge University Press, 1995), 597–606.

132. Alfredo López Austin, "The Natural World," in *Aztecs*, ed. Eduardo Matos Moctezuma and Felipe Solís Olguín (London: Royal Academy of the Arts, 2002), 270. See also Alfredo López Austin, *The Myths of the Opossum: Pathways of Mesoamerican Mythology*, trans. Bernard R. Ortiz de Montellano and Thelma Ortiz de Montellano (Albuquerque: University of New Mexico Press, 1993), 126–27; López Austin, *Tamoanchan, Tlalocan*, 12–13, 28–31; and López Austin, "Cosmovision," trans. Scott Sessions, in *The Oxford Encyclopedia of Mesoamerican Cultures: The Civilizations of Mexico and Central America*, ed. Davíd Carrasco (Oxford: Oxford University Press, 2001), 1: 268–74.

133. López Austin, *Myths of the Opossum*, 126–27; López Austin, *Tamoanchan, Tlalocan*, 12–13; López Austin, "The Natural World," 270.

134. López Austin, "The Natural World," 270.

135. See W.V.O. Quine, *Word and Object* (Cambridge, MA: MIT Press, 1960); W.V.O. Quine, *From a Logical Point of View*, 2nd rev. ed. (New York: Harper & Row, 1961); Philip Kitcher, *Abusing Science: The Case against Scientific Creationism* (Cambridge, MA: MIT Press, 1982); and W. H. Newton-Smith, ed., *A Companion to the Philosophy of Science* (Oxford: Blackwell, 2000).

136. López Austin, *Tamoanchan, Tlalocan*, 22–23.

137. See López Austin, "The Natural World," 270. López Austin, *Human Body and Ideology*, I: 57–59, 208–9; López Austin, *Rabbit on the Face of the Moon*, 112; López Austin, *Tamoanchan, Tlalocan*. 3, 40, 101–20; and León-Portilla, *Aztec Thought and Culture*, 52–53, 80–103.

138. López Austin, *Tamoanchan, Tlalocan*, 84–122, 46–47n9.

139. *Popol Vuh: The Definitive Edition of the Mayan Book of the Dawn of Life and the Glories of Gods and Kings*, intro., trans., and commentary by Dennis Tedlock (New York: Simon and Schuster, 1985), 160–67, italics mine.

140. López Austin's earlier interpretation of the Quiché myth of human creation appears to contradict this interpretation of the myth of Tamoanchan. He argues the Quiché myth "indicates that the southern Maya perceived the supernatural *more* as a condition brought about by a reduction in man's perception than as a characteristic, distinct sector of the universe" (López Austin, *Human Body and Ideology*, I: 383, emphasis mine. The "supernatural" – which I assume is equivalent to "light matter" – surrounds us but we simply cannot see it. Similarly, for the Aztecs the supernatural is "remote . . . because of man's limitations" – what I would call epistemologically remote – not because it is physically removed and existing in a sui generis realm. James Dow defends a view similar to mine when writing of indigenous Mesoamerican animism: "People believe that an animating force is contained within all living things and moving objects . . .

Animating forces are the essence of life . . . [T]he forces are part of the present world [but] the average person is just insensitive to them" (James W. Dow, "Central and North Mexican Shamans," in *Mesoamerican Healers*, ed. Brad R. Huber and Alan R. Sandstrom [Austin: University of Texas Press, 2001], 71). Shamans are able to perceive and manipulate these invisible powers.

141. Despite its obvious discordance with commonsense and ordinary sense perception, ontological monisms have been defended by philosophers as varied as Lao Tzu, Spinoza, Parmenides, and Śaṃkara. For discussion, see Scharfstein, *Comparative History of World Philosophy*; Lloyd, *Part of Nature*; Lloyd, *Spinoza and the Ethics*; Ames and Rosemont, *The Analects of Confucius*; Eliot Deutsch, *Advaita Vedānta: A Philosophical Reconstruction* (Honolulu: East-West Center Press, 1969); David Loy, *Nondualism: A Study in Comparative Philosophy* (Amherst, NY: Humanities Books, 1988); and Jonathan Barnes, *The Presocratic Philosophers* (London: Routledge, 1979).

142. Plato, *Plato: The Collected Dialogues*. For discussion, see Plato, *The Republic*; and Richard Lewis Nettleship, *Lectures on the Republic of Plato*, 2nd ed. (London: MacMillan & Co., 1963). Plato assigns less is-ness to illusion than to appearances. I ignore this difference for present purposes. I believe it is this sort of Platonic thinking about appearance (illusion) versus reality that underwrites Bierhorst's and León-Portilla's interpretations of the song-poems discussed above.

143. My understanding is indebted to Deutsch, *Advaita Vedānta*; Scharfstein, *Comparative History of World Philosophy*; and Loy, *Nondualism*. Advaita Vedānta claims there is only one thing: Brahman. Everything else that exists is identical with Brahman. Brahman is a single unified state of Being. It is unitary, whole, plain, formless, seamless, undivided and indivisible, without parts, without shape or structure, infinite, permanent, immutable, eternal, unmoving, omnipresent, unborn and undying, within everything, constant, and the self of everything. It lacks all differences, including those that depend upon space and time. Advaita Vedānta treats the following intuition as axiomatic: reality (or the real) is that which is permanent, eternal, immutable, and infinite. That which is real is characterized by, and is identical with *being* as such. It is that which *is*. Conversely, it claims that that which becomes, changes, moves, and divides is not real. Thus despite their other differences, Śaṃkara and Plato both embrace a metaphysics of Being, sharing the axiomatic intuition that that which is real does not change, and that which does change is not real. In this important respect, both differ fundamentally from Aztec philosophy's metaphysics of Becoming.

144. See Deutsch, *Advaita Vedānta*, 33.

145. Quoted in T. P. Kasulis, "Truth and Zen," *Philosophy East and West* 30 (1980): 460.

146. For discussion, see Julian Hochberg, "Gestalt Theory," in *The Oxford Companion to the Mind*, ed. Richard L. Gregory (Oxford: Oxford University Press, 1987), 288–91.

147. Tedlock, *Popol Vuh*, 167, emphasis mine.

148. Clifton Wolters, trans., *The Cloud of Unknowing* (Baltimore: Penguin Books, 1961).

149. *Cantares Mexicanos*, fol. 14 v, trans. Bierhorst (*Cantares Mexicanos*, 175). A thorough analysis of this song-poem would require examining the concept of *ahnelli*. I argue that ahnelli is best understood as untrue in the sense of being unrooted and inauthentic (Maffie, "Why Care about Nezahualcoyotl? Veritism and Nahua Philosophy," *Philosophy of the Social Sciences* 32, no. 1 [2002]: 71–91).

150. *Cantares Mexicanos*, fol. 5v, trans. Bierhorst (Bierhorst, *Cantares Mexicanos*, 149).

151. León-Portilla, *Aztec Thought and Culture*, 71–72; León-Portilla, *Fifteen Poets*, 153. León-Portilla advances this interpretation in the course of arguing that Aztec culture contained philosophers and philosophical inquiry commensurate with pre-Socratic Greece. Here he attributes to Tochihuitzin Coyolchiuhqui a Cartesian-like skeptical doubt about the reality of existence based upon the possibility that we are dreaming. Bierhorst (*Cantares Mexicanos*, 49–50) raises the possibility of Christian influence in these song-poems and urges caution in interpreting their metaphysical significance.

152. It is still possible, of course, that Tochihuitzin Coyolchiuhqui subscribes to premise 1 and that he is breaking away from the Aztec philosophical mainstream. León-Portilla however gives no reasons for thinking this is so.

153. López Austin, *Human Body and Ideology*, I:chapter 6.

154. López Austin, *Human Body and Ideology*, I:222–23; see also Jill Leslie McKeever Furst, *The Natural History of the Soul in Ancient Mexico* (New Haven: Yale University Press, 1995), chapter 16; and Timothy J. Knab, *A War of Witches: A Journey into the Underworld of the Contemporary Aztecs* (Boulder, CO: Westview Press, 1995).

155. López Austin, *Human Body and Ideology*, I:224.

156. Ibid. Molina translates *cochitlehua* as "for someone who has been sleeping to leap out of bed" (Alonso de Molina, *Vocabulario en lengua castellana y mexicana y mexicana y castellana*, 4th ed. [Mexico City: Porrúa, 2001], 2:23r.). The word's root verbs are *cochi*, "to dream" (Molina, *Vocabulario*, 2:23r), and *ēhua*, "to get up, to get out of bed" (Frances Karttunen, *An Analytical Dictionary of Nahuatl* [Norman: University of Oklahoma Press, 1983], 36, 76). Because the sections are paginated differently, scholars cite the Spanish-to-Nahuatl section of Molina's dictionary as Part 1 and the Nahuatl-to-Spanish section as Part 2.

157. For the former see Bernardino de Sahagún, *Florentine Codex: General History of the Things of New Spain*, ed. and trans. Arthur J.O. Anderson and Charles Dibble (Santa Fe, NM: School of American Research and University of Utah, 1953–82), VI:82; for the latter, Sahagún, *Florentine Codex*, VI:8, 25, 44, 45, 47, 49, 52, 61, 64, 138.

158. Molina, *Vocabulario*, 2:97v; see also Karttunen, *Analytical Dictionary*, 223. Molina (*Vocabulario*, 2:97v) translates *temiquiliztli* as "dream."

159. See Sahagún, *Florentine Codex*, VI:8, 25, 44, 45, 47, 49, 52 61, 64, 138.

160. For example, see Sahagún, *Florentine Codex*, VI:25, 44, 45, 47, 49, 52, 61, 64, 138.).

161. Sahagún, *Florentine Codex*, VI: 9.

162. *"sueño vano y no verdadero"* (Molina, *Vocabulario*, 2:49v).

163. *"sueño verdadero"* (Molina, *Vocabulario*, 2:55r).

164. Sahagún, *Florentine Codex*, VI:9; see also 8, 181. My discussion of dreams is indebted to R. Joe Campbell's unpublished concordance of instances of *temiqui* in the *Florentine Codex* (Campbell, personal correspondence, 8/4/2005).

165. Campbell, *Morphological Dictionary*, 307.

166. Timothy J. Knab, *The Dialogue of Earth and Sky: Dreams, Souls, Curing and the Modern Aztec Underworld* (Tucson: University of Arizona Press, 2004), 55.

167. Sahagún, *Florentine Codex*, X:168.

168. Ibid., X:191.

169. Bernardino de Sahagún, *Primeros memoriales*. Paleography of Nahuatl Text and English Translation by Thelma Sullivan (Norman: University of Oklahoma Press, 1997), fol. 85v.

170. The view that dreams are real and epistemological probative is upheld by contemporary Nahuatl-speakers and other indigenous peoples in Mexico. See Knab, *Dialogue of Earth and Sky*; Sandstrom, *Corn Is Our Blood*; and Brad R. Huber and Alan R. Sandstrom, eds., *Mesoamerican Healers* (Austin: University of Texas Press, 2001).

Aztec metaphysics' conception of teotl constitutes a form of pantheism. Section 2.1 presents my evidence for this claim. I argue Aztec metaphysics is neither polytheistic nor pan*en*theistic. Sections 2.2, 2.3, and 2.4 explore how Aztec pantheism understands such notions as sacredness, *neltiliztli, ixiptla,* and *teixiptla.* Section 2.5 argues Aztec pantheism entails animism. Section 2.6 anticipates and responds to several possible objections against this interpretation.

2.1. PANTHEISM

Aztec metaphysics' understanding of teotl constitutes a form of pantheism. Definitions of pantheism vary. I adopt the definition proposed by Michael Levine in *Pantheism: A Nontheistic Concept of Deity.*[1] To say that Aztec metaphysics is pantheistic is to say the following. First, the cosmos and all its contents constitute a single, all-inclusive, interconnected, and mutually interrelated unity. Second, this single, all inclusive unity is *substantively* constituted by teotl. (This merely restates constitutional monism.) Teotl is metaphysically immanent within the cosmos. Third, this single all-inclusive unity is *ontologically* identical with teotl. Teotl is thus ontologically immanent in the cosmos. (This merely restates ontological monism.) Fourth, the fact that everything constitutes an all-inclusive, interconnected, and mutually interrelated unity is *explained* by the fact that this unity is ontologically identical with teotl. "The unifying powers and principles" of teotl are "immanent and operative in the all-inclusive whole. They are a part of the unity in which there is no longer a distinction between the natural and supernatural, and they govern intrinsically rather than extrinsically."[2]

DOI: 10.5876_9781607322238.c002

Fifth, this unity is genealogically unified by teotl since it unfolds from teotl. Teotl does not create the cosmos ex nihilo; rather, the cosmos emerges *from* teotl as teotl's self-transformation. Teotl therefore is not the "creator" ex nihilo of the cosmos in a theistic sense but rather the immanent engenderer of the cosmos. The cosmos burgeons forth from teotl.[3] The history of the cosmos is simply the *self-unfolding* and *self-transforming* of teotl.

Sixth, this unity is ordered and arranged by teotl in the process of teotl's own self-unfolding. The order and structure of the cosmos are expressions of how teotl unfolds, that is, expressions of its modus operandi. Teotl is self-ordering and self-arranging, and its self-ordering is immanent. Nothing exists prior to or outside of teotl that imposes order or structure upon teotl. Teotl's self-arranging is a work-in-progress: a "story unfolding itself" rather than a "story already written."[4]

Seventh, this unity is the self-presentation – not self-*re*presentation – of teotl. The distinction between representation and represented suggests an ontological dualism incompatible with the ontological monism of Aztec metaphysics. Eighth, this unity is sacred because teotl is sacred. And lastly, teotl is not a minded, intellectual, or willful person, being, or agent. Teotl lacks intentional states (such as purposes, desires, and plans) along with such capacities as the ability to deliberate, punish, reward, believe, and make decisions. Teotl is not a god, deity, or legislative being who enacts laws of nature or laws of human conduct. In short, teotl is not anthropomorphic in any way. If we define *theism* as the belief in a minded or personal god with whom one might have a personal relationship and who in some sense transcends the world, then Aztec metaphysics is *non*-theistic.[5]

SUPPORTING SCHOLARSHIP

Pantheistic interpretations of Aztec metaphysics are not novel. Hermann Beyer defended a pantheistic interpretation of pre-Columbian Mesoamerica religions nearly a century ago. He writes, "the blatant polytheism which appears to be so characteristic of ancient Mexico is simply a symbolic reference to natural phenomena. The two thousand gods . . . were . . . only so many manifestations of the *One*. In the figure of Tonacatecuhtli we find a substitute for monotheism. . . . In order to express the idea that the cosmic forces were emanations of the divine principle . . . the gods of nature were called children of Tonacatecuhtli."[6] Burr Brundage interprets the numinous godhead of Aztec religion as a "pantheistic essence [that] splits and assumes various masks, each identifiable and unmistakable."[7] The various deities of the Aztec pantheon are one and all mere "transfigurations" of this single, undifferentiated divine force; "not so much substantial entities as qualities." The divine is fluid, endlessly self-transforming, and malleable: "a continuum . . . of activity." It possesses "a wholeness of quality and singleness of essence" that resists articulation as distinct substantive deities.[8] This fact, according to Brundage, explains the deities' widely recognized ability to blur into and absorb one another as well as their ability to incorporate seemingly opposite qualities. For example, despite the fact that Tlaloc was seen as predominantly cold, watery, and dark, Aztec artists routinely depicted Tlaloc holding a lightning bolt, thereby associating him with the opposing power of fire and light. In short, although its "masks were many, the divine . . . was one."[9]

One finds an eloquent exponent of Aztec pantheism in Richard Townsend who in *State and Cosmos in the Art of Tenochtitlan* writes, "there is a rainbowlike quality to these supposed gods of Mesoamerica; the closer one searches for a personal identity . . . the more evanescent and immaterial they become, dissolved into mists of allusion and allegory with which Mexica poets and sculptors expressed their sense of the miraculous in the world about them."[10] It is reasonable, Townsend concludes, to view Aztec religion as an "essentially nontheistic" way of regarding the cosmos as sacred. The Aztecs employed an array of highly condensed and extended metaphoric cult names – what Townsend calls *kennings* – to refer to natural phenomena or aspects of natural phenomena. For example, they used "she of the jade skirt" to refer to lake water and "heart of the earth" to refer to the earth's life force. The first Spanish missionaries interpreted these as the proper names of distinct gods or goddesses, and as a result found themselves faced with an ever-multiplying number of interrelated and interpenetrating gods and goddesses. Looking for a reference point in Occidental history in terms of which to comprehend Aztec religion, the Spaniards found one in the religious mythologies of ancient Greece and Rome. They consequently fashioned their understanding of Aztec religion upon the pantheons of Greek and Roman religions. In reality, however, what we find according to Townsend is a simply litany of kennings used for describing the various rainbowlike aspects of a single reality, teotl.

Eva Hunt offers one of the clearest and most insightful articulations of Mesoamerican pantheism:

Mesoamerican cultures were neither polytheistic nor monotheistic. . . . [R]eality, nature, and experience were nothing but multiple manifestations of a single unity of being. God was *both* the one and the many. Thus the deities were but his multiple personifications, his partial unfoldings into perceptible experience. The partition of this experience into discrete units such as god A or god B is an artifice of iconography and analysis, not part of the core conception of the divinity. Since the divine reality was multiple, fluid, encompassing of the whole, its aspects were changing images, dynamic, never frozen, but constantly being recreated, redefined. This fluidity was a culturally defined mystery of the nature of divinity itself. Therefore, it was expressed in the dynamic, ever-changing aspects of the multiple "deities" that embodied it. For didactic, artistic, and ritual purposes, however, these fluid images were carved in stone, painted into frescoes, described in prayer. It is here, at this reduced level of visualization, that the transient images of a sacralized universe became "gods," with names attached to them, with anthropomorphic attributes, and so on.[11]

Sacred reality was conceived as "simultaneously complex, ultimately unknowable, ever-changing, and unitary." Interpreting Contact-era indigenous religions as pantheistic, Hunt adds, helps explain their quick incorporation of Christian religion. "Because reality is one and many," she writes, "the addition of new images such as the Christian saints or Jesus simply expands the repertoire of sacred 'words.'"[12] As pantheists, indigenous people saw no conflict. Pantheism easily accommodates syncretism.

Striking a similar note, Irene Nicholson writes, "The multiplicity of gods' was simply "the divinity already separated, as it were, by the *prism* of human sight, into its many attributes." The many gods were "depictions of [Ometeotl's] attributes, personifications of his manifold talents, or fragments of his corporeal form."[13] They were merely "manifestations of one-and-the-same powerful deity."[14] In this way "the many existed in the One."[15] Using similar imagery, Mercedes de la Garza describes "the world of the gods" as "a *kaleidoscope*: each god existing in relation with the others and all in motion, creating diverse images."[16]

Louise Burkhart characterizes Aztec metaphysics as "a polytheistic monism' that sees a "single divine principle – *teotl* – [that] manifested itself in multiple forms" and that was "responsible for the nature of the cosmos," including both its deleterious and beneficial aspects.[17]

Recent scholarship suggests contemporary indigenous peoples in Mexico continue to embrace pantheism. In their study of papermaking and cut-paper figures among contemporary Nahua, Otomí, and Tepehua peoples of Mexico, Alan Sandstrom and Pamela Effrein Sandstrom write:

[D]ivinity is expressed in the workings of the universe as a whole, including the sun, the earth, water, growing crops, and human beings... [T]he universe ... is deified, and the spirits . . . are nothing more than temporary manifestations of a great unity. The nature of the unity is such that everything is related, and what appears to be separate and even opposite is actually the same thing. . . . The earth, for example, is not a unitary spirit that makes crops grow; rather it is an aspect of a deified universe that is connected to everything else and that contains within it all of the complexity and contradictions of the universe at large.[18]

They argue shamans carve up the single sacred unity into "manageable segments" such as seeds, earth, hills, disease-causing spirits, clouds, and water for ritual purposes only. During rituals shamans treat the segments as single separate spirits. Yet shamans see no essential distinction between seed, water, and earth, and view the multiplicity of ritual paper images as portraying the same sacred reality "in different guises."[19] The segments are only temporarily abstracted from the unified whole. They meld back into the unified whole upon the ritual's conclusion. Shamans' tendency to anthropomorphize various aspects of reality by representing them as human-like figures – a practice López Austin argues is rooted in pre-Hispanic thought and ritual practice – does not, therefore, entail polytheism.[20] Sandstrom and Sandstrom contend Nahuatl-speakers view the existence of discrete, independently existing things as illusory. There exists only one thing. What is illusory is the appearance of a multitude of discrete, independently existing things. One and all exist as guises or aspects of the single cosmic whole. Finally, Sandstrom and Sandstrom see the pantheism of Contact-era indigenous peoples as helping explain their easy syncretic absorption of Christian ideas.

Alan Sandstrom's ethnography of contemporary Nahuatl-speakers in Northern Veracruz defends the same thesis:

[E]verything is an aspect of a grand, single, and overriding unity. Separate beings and objects do not exist – that is an illusion peculiar to human beings. In daily life we divide up our environment into discrete units so that we can talk about it and manipulate it for our benefit. But it is an error to assume that the diversity we create in our lives is the way reality is actually structured. . . . [E]verything is connected at a deeper level, part of the same basic substratum of being. . . . The universe is a deified, seamless totality.[21]

The apparent multiplicity of discrete, independently existing spirits, humans, and physical objects, therefore, is an illusion. One and all exist as "aspects of a great unity, a unity that transcends all apparent diversity."[22] One and all exist as "part of the same basic substratum of being."[23] As we saw above, what is illusory is the appearance of a multitude of discrete, independently existing individual things. What is not illusory is their existence per se since one and all exist as aspects of the single sacred unity. What the Nahuas call *totiotsij*, "our honored deity,"[24] Sandstrom interprets as a modern version of teotl.[25] Here again we find the idea that reality consists of a single sacred unity and that the division of this sacred unity into discrete, independently existing particulars is an artifice of human conception rooted in human practices. In the course of their ritual – and in this work Sandstrom adds their daily practical activities – humans carve up the single unity into various segments they deem useful. Here too, the tendency to anthropomorphize the various aspects of the single unity by itself does not entail polytheism. Lastly, Sandstrom finds the foregoing views shared by the Nahuas' Otomí, Tepehua, Totonac, and Huastec neighbors.

Sandstrom's more recent article, "The Cave-Pyramid Complex among the Contemporary Nahua of Northern Veracruz," further elaborates and defends this interpretation. He writes, "the cosmos itself is the deity, and all apparent diversity and separation among objects and beings is illusory."[26] A single, sacred animating principle occupies the center of existence. The various spirits in the Nahua pantheon "personify" different facets of this single sacred principle.[27] Here, again, contemporary Nahuas continue the pre-Hispanic practice of using the human body as a central metaphor for thinking about the cosmos. And here again, shamans continue the pre-Hispanic practice of using anthropomorphic paper-cut figures to represent spirit entities in rituals. Contemporary Nahuas simultaneously conceive these spirits in two, not wholly compatible, ways: as sentient beings with their own human-like personalities and foibles, and as "impersonal energy fields."[28]

Sandstrom insightfully contends that it is precisely the pantheistic – as opposed to polytheistic – nature of Mesoamerican religions that helps explain why the Mesoamerican pantheon of spirits appear to undergo constant "fusion," "fission," and "remixing" (as López Austin acutely puts it regarding the pre-Hispanic Aztec pantheon[29]), why their properties and guises constantly change, and why humans are always reinterpreting and reconceiving them. "The apparent fluidity of the Mesoamerican pantheon of spirits is problematic and confusing only to people socialized to think in a monotheistic or polytheistic tradition."[30] Sandstrom's conclusion clearly applies to the multitude of deities traditionally assigned to the Aztec religious pantheon.

Some scholars suggest the ancient Maya embraced pantheism. León-Portilla, for example, characterizes ancient Maya philosophico-religious thought as an unusual type of pantheism: one that he calls "pan-chronotheism."[31] León-Portilla contends the ancient Maya notion of kinh refers to the primordial, limitless, and divine reality of sun-day-time. Kinh is neither abstract nor shapeless; rather, it is distinguishable into innumerable moments, each bearing its own face, personality, or burden of attributes. Included among these faces are the many faces of the solar deity (in all its forms) as well as the faces of the gods and goddesses of earth, moon, rain, corn, death, sacrifice, and hunting. In short, kinh (sun-day-time) is the single, sacred reality of which everything is but a mere face. Kinh appears to function in Maya metaphysics analogously to teotl. Nancy Farriss similarly writes, "the pre-Hispanic Maya, in common with the rest of Mesoamerica . . . possessed a concept of an all-encompassing divinity of whom their lesser deities were refractions or manifestations."[32]

What does the foregoing show? In his recent survey of Mesoamerica religions, Monaghan writes, "the Mesoamerican concept of deity is best viewed as 'pantheistic.'"[33] This is certainly true of Contact-era Aztec religion and its metaphysics. I submit that Sandstrom's analyses of the metaphysical views and of the ritual and artistic practices of contemporary Nahuas, Otomís, Tepehuas, Totonacs, and Huastecs apply mutatis mutandis to Aztec metaphysics as well as to Aztec ritual and artistic practices. The fact that Aztec artists depicted the various aspects of teotl anthropomorphically does not mean they believed these representations stood for distinct deities. And the fact that elite and commoner Aztec rituals singled out and abstracted from the single unity of teotl various "manageable segments" – such as sun, earth, maize, water, and wind – and treated these segments as single spirits or "deities" with highly condensed and extended metaphoric cult names or kennings – such as Tonatiuh, Chalchiuhtlicue, and Centeotl – does not entail that they embraced polytheism. In short, neither anthropomorphism in art nor multiplicity in ritual activity entails polytheism. Aztec metaphysics sees no essential metaphysical distinction between these various guises. It regards the multiplicity of artistic images as portraying different faces or aspects of teotl, and the various kennings as referring to different aspects of teotl.

Borrowing from Hunt, I contend teotl is a single, sacred, energy-in-motion that is "multiple, fluid, encompassing of the whole." Its many facets are "changing images, dynamic, never frozen, but constantly recreated, redefined." The alleged manifold deities of Aztec religion are merely unfoldings, aspects, and faces of teotl. Like Hunt, I believe Aztec metaphysics conceives teotl as "simultaneously complex, ultimately unknowable, ever-changing, and unitary." Although the Aztecs divided their experiences of teotl's single continually circulating power into discrete clusters of attributes, their doing so was an artifice of ritual, divination, pedagogy, art, iconography, and analysis. The cosmos is teotl's ever-changing, kaleidoscopic self-transformation.

Before continuing, let's briefly look at two of pantheism's more paradoxical consequences. First, there is no metaphysical distinction between individual selves or souls, on the one hand, and teotl on the other. The former are merely facets of teotl and are ultimately identical with teotl. What is illusory is their apparently discrete independence, not their existence per se. As Monaghan writes, "in the pantheistic cosmologies of Mesoamerica, the human soul . . . is regularly viewed as part of a universal life force that is substantively, spatially and temporally continuous."[34] There is no metaphysical distinction between teotl and individual human self (soul, spirit), just as there is no distinction between teotl and individual sandals, bushes, and valleys. And because there is no substantive distinction between human self (soul, spirit) and teotl, it follows there is no substantive distinction (and hence dichotomy) between individual human self and cosmos (including sun, earth, wind, trees, and other human selves).

Second, given that individual human self and teotl are identical, it follows that there is no distinction between the experiences of the self and teotl. As Hunt mentions in the quoted passage above, "reality, nature and experience were nothing but multiple manifestations of a single unity." Given the identity of humans and teotl, it follows that human perception – both veridical *and* illusory – consists of teotl perceiving itself! Veridical perception consists of teotl perceiving itself, illusory perception, of teotl misperceiving itself.

The identity of self and teotl as well as the identity of human perceptual processes as instances of teotl's processing constitute two further motivations for pursuing the epistemological strategy for handling the distinction between illusion and reality discussed in chapter 1.

Pantheism, Process, and Polytheism

Beginning with the initial contact between Europeans and Aztecs, sixteenth-century Aztec metaphysics has routinely been characterized as polytheistic.[35] What light does pantheism shed on this issue?

The Aztecs singled out and emphasized certain facets, aspects, or qualities of teotl for ritual, practical, pedagogical, and artistic purposes (these being often indistinct). The different deities of the Aztec "pantheon" represent different clusters of these aspects or qualities and hence different clusters of specific forces or energies. The Tlaloc cluster differs from the Ehecatl-Quetzalcoatl cluster and the Xiuhtecuhtli cluster, for example. Tlaloc, Ehecatl-Quetzalcoatl, and Xiuhtecuhtli are not distinct, independently existing substantive deities, personages, or beings in their own right. The word *Tlaloc* simply names a specific cluster of energies. Although each deity cluster possesses its own distinct "personality," this personality is a function of the powers clustered together by human artifice, and not a function of a distinct metaphysical essence. In keeping

with the metaphysical principle *esse sequitar operari* ("being follows from operation"), the personality of each deity cluster is thus defined by what it does. The
partitioning of teotl into these various clusters is a matter of human contrivance and not a matter of trying to cut reality at the seams (to borrow Plato's
famous phrase).[36] After all, teotl has no seams! These clusters overlap with one
another, interact with one another, merge with one another, and flow in and
out of one another.[37] This makes sense since sacred reality is dynamic, multiple,
ever-changing, and fluid. The merging and overlapping of these constellations
does not, as Hunt remarks, "reflect an 'impoverished' or 'unfinished' religious
pantheon. It was in fact the pantheon's very nature."[38] The Aztecs referred to
these energy-clusters using metaphoric names or kennings, and depicted them
artistically by means of semantically charged colors, vestments, insignia, para-
phernalia, body postures, and human shapes.[39] Specific activities are commonly
associated with specific deities or patrons-patronesses. For example, spinning
and weaving are associated with Tlazolteotl-Ixcuina. What does the relationship amount to? I suggest the activity in question is materially constituted
by the powers and forces associated with the relevant deity-cluster. Weaving
involves the kind of powers and energies identified with Tlazolteotl-Ixcuina.

And what about so-called divine possession? I suggest "divine possession"
actually consists of the relevant "god's" powers or energies saturating the affected
person. For example, a person's becoming intoxicated from drinking excessive
octli (pulque or fermented maguey sap) does not consist of his being possessed
by the Tzenton Totochtin ("Four Hundred Rabbits") agricultural fertility "gods"
and members of the Ometochtli ("God Two Rabbit") complex.[40] Rather, it consists of the person's being infused by the kind of energies named by the four
hundred rabbits, Ometochtli, and so on. To become intoxicated was to "rabbit
yourself."[41] Texts on drunkenness use phrases such as *itech quinehua* ("it takes
possession of him") and *itech quiza* ("it comes out in him"). This indicates the
Aztecs believed that the forces present in fermented maguey sap entered the
individual and caused the effects of drunkenness.

Aztec philosophy, as we saw in chapter 1, embraces a process metaphysics.
Processes, rather than perduring entities or substances, are ontologically fundamental. According to this view, teotl is a complex, all-encompassing unified
macroprocess that consists of a myriad of coordinated microprocesses. These
processes are systematically interrelated, interconnected, interdependent, interpenetrating, overlapping, and covariant. They are mutually affecting and mutually arising. They are interwoven with one another like threads in a cloth, where
the total woven cloth is teotl. Switching metaphors, the processes are interrelated like the various processes in a biological organism or ecosystem.

What light does this shed on the question of Aztec polytheism? I believe the Aztecs singled out and emphasized specific processes and constellations of processes for ritual, practical, pedagogical, and artistic purposes. The various gods and goddesses of the Aztec pantheon are nothing more than these specific constellations of processes. Gods' and goddesses' names – *Tlazolteotl* and *Xiuhtecuhtli*, for example – serve as conventional, shorthand handles or tags for specific constellations of processes. The use of these names no more entails that the Aztecs considered their referents to be perduring substantive entities than our calling a hurricane "Sandy" commits us to the view that hurricanes are substantive entities rather than processes. Names, after all, may refer to entities or to processes. Contemporary speakers of English, for example, commonly assign names to processes: for example, "the Bradley effect" and "the Macy's Thanksgiving Day Parade." Aztecs did so as well.

Let's briefly flesh out this view borrowing from H. B. Nicholson's excellent analysis of pre-Hispanic religion in central Mexico. Nicholson proposes that the deities of the Mesoamerican pantheon be organized around several fundamental "cult themes," each of which, in turn, may be analyzed into smaller subthemes that are expressed by what Nicholson calls "deity complexes."[42] Three cult themes stand out according to Nicholson: "Celestial Creativity-Divine Paternalism," "Rain, Moisture, and Agricultural Fertility," and "War-Sacrifice-Sanguinary Nourishment of the Sun and the Earth."[43]

I suggest each of these three major themes (along with its respective subthemes) refers to a complex constellation of macroprocesses along with its respective, organically nested microprocesses. Each constellation is essentially interrelated and interwoven with the other two. None is completely autonomous or discrete. Each constellation possesses the power to bring about changes in things outside itself through external mechanical-style causation as well as the power to bring about changes within itself through organic-style, immanent causation. Many of the changes occurring within one constellation are covariant or co-related with changes occurring in another constellation in the same way that we consider the myriad changes constituting a change in the seasons to be covariant or co-related with one another.

"Celestial Creativity-Divine Paternalism" refers to the vast constellation of processes involved in "primordial creative origins" including creativity, generation and regeneration, renewal, sustenance, and transformation. It includes three deity complexes: Ometeotl, Tezcatlipoca, and Xiuhtecuhtli. The Ometeotl complex, for example, includes a cluster of deities that Nicholson writes "were in effect only aspects of a single, fundamental creative, celestial, paternal deity." Ometeotl stands out among the deities of this theme as "a sexually dualistic, primordial generative power."[44] I suggest Ometeotl and the other deities that constitute this cluster – Ometecuhtli and Omecihuatl, Tonacatecuhtli and Tonacacihuatl – are nothing more than specific constellations of processes concerned with never-ending generation, renewal, and sustenance. And likewise for Tezcatlipoca and Xiuhtecuhtli: the name *Xiuhtecuhtli*, for example, refers not to a substantive entity but to a specific manifold of powerful processes including fire, solar heat, and life-giving warmth.[45]

The same holds true for the "Rain, Moisture, and Agricultural Fertility" and "War-Sacrifice-Sanguinary Nourishment of the Sun and the Earth" themes and their respective deities complexes. "Rain, Moisture, and Agricultural Fertility" refers to a complex constellation of water- and fertility-related processes: for example, rain, clouds, wind, thunder, lightning, streams, rivers, flooding, food cultivation, crop irrigation, decomposition, sexuality, and birth. This theme, as Nicholson sees it, includes the Tlaloc, Centeotl-Xochipilli, Teteoinnan, Ometochtli, and Xipe Totec deity complexes. These deities are specific subsets of the above-mentioned processes.[46]

"War-Sacrifice-Sanguinary Nourishment of the Sun and the Earth" picks out a complex constellation of processes united by the Aztecs' belief that the fertility, well-being, and continued existence of the Fifth Age (or Sun-Earth Ordering) depends on the gods' being nourished "by their preferred sustenance, human hearts and blood, sustenance which was made available to them primarily by constant war."[47] This theme includes the Tonatiuh, Huitzilopochtli, Mixcoatl Tlahuizcalpantecuhtli, and Mictlantecuhtli deity complexes. These deities represent specific subsets of the above processes.

Let's take a closer look, for instance, at the word *Tonatiuh*, which names the Sun. J. Richard Andrews and Ross Hassig translate *Tonatiuh* as a present-agentive noun meaning, "he-goes-becoming-warm."[48] Tonatiuh is defined by what he customarily does. His nature is dictated by his operation. Tonatiuh is "he who goes-becoming-warm." This accords with the processive interpretation of the gods defended here. As a constellation of processes, the deities of the Aztec pantheon consist of what they do, that is, their powers and capacities.

These three broad constellations of processes not only causally interact with one another but also interpenetrate, crosscut, and overlap with one another. Scholars commonly point out that at some point the various Aztec deities eventually blur one into the other due to their extensive interrelationships. Andrews and Hassig remark, for example, that "Although heuristically useful, [Nicholson's categories] do not separate the gods into discrete, non-overlapping categories. Rather, the gods may share in all of them to varying degrees."[49] And this, I believe, is as it should be, since it helps explain the irreducible ambiguity of all things (which is one of key intuitions of Aztec metaphysics discussed in chapter 1). For example, the constellation of water processes includes lightning, drowning, and flooding, thereby connecting the constellation of water-related forces to the constellations of fire and death. Hence artistic depictions of Tlaloc often have him carrying a lightning bolt, a symbol of fire.

Certain activities are typically associated with a specific deity or patron/patroness: for example, spinning and weaving with Tlazolteotl-Ixcuina. What does the relationship amount to? I suggest the relevant activity is constituted by the same forces and processes as are denoted by the deity's name. For example, *Tlazolteotl-Ixcuina* denotes the forces and processes involved in spinning and weaving. Tlazolteotl-Ixcuina and spinning and weaving consist of one and the same forces and processes. Tlazolteotl-Ixcuina is *not* the *goddess of* spinning and weaving. *Chalchiuhtlicue* ("she of the jade skirt") similarly denotes the forces and processes comprising springs, rivers, lakes, and sea. Chalchiuhtlicue is *not* the *goddess of* springs, rivers, lakes, and sea.

The foregoing pantheistic interpretation of Aztec deities as clusters of powers and constellations of processes (rather as individual substantive gods) has several additional theoretical virtues. First, it enables us to capture López Austin's insight that the gods of the Aztec pantheon undergo "fusion," "fission," and "remixing."[50] Fusion occurs when two or more gods combine with one another to form a new god; fission, when a single god divides into two or more distinct gods sharing some of the original god's attributes. Tlalchitonatiuh ("the setting sun") for example, represents a fusion of Tonatiuh and Tlaloc.[51] If we imagine Aztec deities as clusters of powers, then we can also easily imagine these clusters of powers fusing, fissioning, and remixing in various ways. If we imagine the gods as constellations of processes, we can easily imagine the same. The various powers and processes of the gods combine and divide in various ways. In so doing they embody and constitute the changes in the cosmos and therefore help explain the various processes of and changes in the cosmos. The various manifold processes and forces of the cosmos fluidly combine and divide like so many kaleidoscopic colored threads in a woven fabric.

Second, the foregoing interpretation supports the claim that the Aztecs' tendency to anthropomorphize the various aspects of teotl by depicting them as human-like figures does not entail polytheism. Third, the forgoing helps us understand that the alleged deities are in fact identical with the forces they name; they are not the gods *of* those forces and processes. Tonatiuh ("He who goes-becoming-warm") names the forces and processes comprising the sun. Tonatiuh is identical with these forces and processes, and is not the god *of* the sun. Lastly, as Hunt and Sandstrom point out, pantheism helps explain the quick incorporation of Christianity into indigenous religions after the conquest.

SEVERAL QUESTIONS

Interpreting Aztec metaphysics as a form of pantheism raises a host of questions. Why is there something rather than nothing? And given that there is something, why are things the way they are rather than some *other* way? This pair of questions may be interpreted in two ways. First, why is there teotl rather than nothing at all, and given that teotl does exist, why is teotl the way it is rather than some *other* way? Second, why is there a cosmos rather than no cosmos, and given that there is a cosmos, why is it the way it is rather than some *other* way?

Aztec metaphysics' response to the first question is that teotl simply exists and has always existed. Teotl's existence is a brute fact, a given. No explanation is possible. It is a mystery. And why is teotl the way it is rather than some other way? This, too, is a mystery. There is no explanation for why teotl is the way it is; it simply *is* that way. Aztec metaphysics' answer to the second question is accordingly that teotl simply unfolds the way it does, generating and regenerating the cosmos out of itself the way it does. Humans will never know the ultimate why and how of the cosmos. Moreover, everything that happens does so without reason, purpose, or goal. There is no grand *telos* or final destiny toward which the cosmos strives and that gives meaning to human existence. Aztec metaphysics is noneschatological in this respect.

Levine notes that this sort of response is typical among pantheists. Baruch Spinoza, for example, argues that God acts without plans, goals, or intentions. Everything that happens does so without design, forethought, or purpose; it simply emanates from God's nature. God's intellect does not precede his will, meaning that he does not think out what he is doing before doing it.[52] According to Lao Tzu, "the myriad things" emanate from a nonpersonified dao that lacks desires, intentions, and designs.[53] More generally, because the divine and creation (the cosmos) are identical, and because there is no creation ex nihilo of the cosmos by a transcendent divinity, pantheists do not typically advance cosmogonies (i.e., stories about the beginning of the cosmos) the way theists do. Levine writes, "Pantheism rejects the theistic creation storyline in its entirety because it rejects so much of what it is based on – like the theistic God."[54] Chapter 7 argues that Aztec metaphysics does not offer a conventional, theistic-style cosmogony although it does offer a nontheistic, pantheistic storyline of its own. Aztec metaphysics accordingly emphasizes regeneration over generation, rebirth over birth, and recreation (renewal) over creation.

Pantheism raises a third question. Does pantheism commit the Aztecs to either animism (i.e., the view that all things are animated) or to panpsychism (i.e., the view that all things, both animate and inanimate have mental properties)? Although both views are logically compatible with pantheism, Levine cogently argues that neither is logically entailed by pantheism.[55] Aztec philosophy is therefore not logically committed to either.

Fourth, why think that Aztec metaphysics is pantheistic rather than pan*en*theistic? *Panentheism*, according to Peter Forrest, maintains that the cosmos and God are neither identical nor fully coextensional with one another.[56] God overlaps with the cosmos but is not exhausted by the cosmos. Part of God exists outside of, apart from, and independently of the cosmos. Pantheism, by contrast, identifies God with the cosmos. A. P. Martinich argues pantheism claims that God is identical with everything, whereas panentheism claims that God merely *saturates* everything in the way that water saturates a sponge without being identical with the sponge.[57] H. P. Owen defines panentheism as the thesis that "the world is a self-expression of God . . . [but] there is an aspect of God's life which is entirely separate from and independent of the world."[58] Finally, Genevieve Lloyd argues that panentheism refuses to identify God with the cosmos and hence refuses to collapse the cosmos into God and God into the cosmos.[59] In short, panentheism is thus committed to an ontological dualism. Furthermore, it leaves conceptual room both for constitutional dualism and for thinking of God as a person or agent.

Panentheism does not therefore adequately capture the relationship between teotl and the cosmos. Teotl and cosmos are identical and hence wholly coextensional. They are one and the same. There is no element or aspect of teotl that transcends or exists outside of the cosmos (and conversely).

2.2. THE SACRED

Why did the Aztecs consider teotl sacred? Teotl and the cosmos form a single unity, but why is this unity sacred rather than merely ontological, as Monaghan asks?[60] What is it about teotl that *makes* it sacred? Robert Solomon poses the question nicely: what is the difference between the atheist who believes the cosmos exists, and the pantheist who believes the cosmos exists *and* that it is sacred?[61] The answer lies in the metaphysical makeup of teotl – not in humans' attitudes or feelings toward teotl or their attitudes toward certain propositions about teotl. Sacredness is a matter of teotl's objective nature. Teotl is sacred not because humans regard or experience it as sacred; rather, humans regard and experience teotl as sacred because it is objectively sacred.

But what is it about teotl that makes it sacred and that elicits the kinds of human responses that we customarily associate with the sacred? I suggest the *brute fact* of power is the starting point of the Aztecs' understanding of the sacred: creative, destructive, transformative power. As the all-encompassing power that vitalizes and makes happen all things in the cosmos, teotl is the power of lightning strikes, drifting clouds, torrential rains, howling winds, scorching solar heat and droughts, and the fiery liquid of human blood. It is the power of fertility, nourishment, and growth; the power that gives and nurtures life, cripples and destroys life, and circulates life throughout the cosmos. This power, as Burkhart remarks, is manifest in the "bursting and blossoming of shimmering, radiant color" as well as "shimmering light, precious stones, brightly colored birds and flowers, fragrant scents, and pleasing music."[62] Serge Gruzinski writes, "There exists a physical presence to power – a visual, auditory, palpable, olfactory dimension perceptible in incense and flowers."[63]

Of indigenous North American conceptions of the sacred, Laguna Pueblo poet-philosopher Paula Gunn Allen writes: "The word *sacred*, like . . . *power* . . . has a very different meaning to tribal people than to members of technological societies. It does not signify something of religious significance and therefore believed in with deep emotional fervor – 'venerable, consecrated or sacrosanct' as the *Random House Dictionary* has it – but something that is filled with an intangible but very real power or force."[64] Sacred things do not represent power; they *are* power. Healing, harvest, and purification songs, for example, have power and thus are sacred. Peggy V. Beck, Anna Lee Walters, and Nia Francisco add that indigenous North Americans consider feathers, thunderstones, obsidian, dreams, and visions as sacred because they are powerful.[65] The Sioux, according to Weaver, maintain that it is wakan-tanka's power to create and destroy that makes it sacred.[66] Reverence, wonder, fear, admiration, and awe are consequently its due.

The Aztec response to Monaghan's and Solomon's questions is therefore this: sacredness is an objective property that consists of being powerful. The sacredness of teotl consists of its all-encompassing and magnificent power. This conception of sacredness generally and of teotl's sacredness specifically is compatible with the distinct claim that the Aztecs *attributed* sacredness to teotl on the basis of *the immediate felt presence* of power or perhaps even *the immediate felt presence* of sacredness itself. Indeed, such experiences would help explain *why* the Aztecs experienced teotl as powerful and as sacred. They experienced teotl as powerful because teotl is objectively powerful; and they experienced teotl as sacred because it is objectively sacred. As Vine Deloria Jr. averred, the immediate felt-presence of energy and power is the starting point of indigenous understandings of the cosmos.[67] I suggest that for the Aztecs the experiences of power and sacredness were "givens" in the sense of not being analyzable in terms of anything more basic (just as we understand the sensations of redness and sweetness to be "givens"). The Aztecs sensed power and sacredness in the everyday things, occurrences, and rhythms of the cosmos.

Sahagún and Durán offer additional insight into the nature of the sacred. Sahagún's informants in the *Florentine Codex* refer to the sea as *teuatl* ("sacred or divine water").[68] They characterize *teuat* as simultaneously *mahuiztic* ("marvelous, worthy of esteem"),[69] *tlamauizolli* ("miraculous, marvelous),[70] and *temauhti* ("frightening").[71] Sahagún's *Colloquios* further reveals the Aztecs' attitude toward *in teteo* ("the gods") and the sacred. In responding to the Franciscans' denunciation of their gods as false, a group of indigenous rulers and priests from Tenochtitlan and Tlatelolco spoke: "Verily [our ancestors], gave us their way of life (*intlamanitiliz*). They followed them as true (*quineltocatihui*), they served them (*quintlayecoltitihui*), they honored them (*quimmahuiztililitihuij*), the gods (*in teteo*). They taught us all their ways of serving (*intlayecoltiloca*), their modes of honoring (*immahuiztililoca*); thus before them we eat earth, thus we bleed ourselves, thus we discharge our debts. . . . Verily, it was the gods by whom we live."[72]

This passage illuminates several attitudes. First, consider *quintlayecoltitihui*. William Bright and Jorge Klor de Alva translate this as "they served."[73] The ancestors served the gods. *Quintlayecoltitihui* derives from the verb "*tlayecoltiā*," which, according to Karttunen, means in its reflexive form "to provide for oneself, to earn one's living," and in its transitive form means "to serve others."[74] Karttunen refers us to *yecoā* ("to finish or conclude something").[75] Serving and providing for others suggest the idea of completing a gift cycle, reciprocating, and discharging one's debt. The passage later enumerates some of the ways by which humans provide for while simultaneously discharging their debt to the gods: bleeding themselves, sacrifice, and burning incense. These activities provide for the gods by feeding, nourishing, and re-energizing them. Such activities are an integral part of the circulation of energy through the cosmos. The word *intlayecoltiloca* occurs later in the passage. Klor de Alva translates it as "their ways of serving them." The Aztecs regarded the sacred as that which humans serve and provide for.

Consider next *quimmahuiztilitihui en teteo*. Bright translates this as "they reverenced the gods," and Klor de Alva as "they honored the gods." *Immahuiztiloloca* occurs later in the passage, which Bright translates as "their ways of doing reverence," and Klor de Alva as "their modes of honoring." Both Nahuatl words participate in a conceptual cluster including *mahui* ("to be frightened"), *mahuitzi* ("to be held in esteem"), *mahuiztli* ("awe, or person worthy of awe and respect"), *mahuizoā* ("to marvel at something; to observe something"), *mahuiztiliā* ("to honor, respect someone; to hold someone in awe; to adore someone"), and *mahuiztiliztli* ("adoration").[76] In her entry for *mahuiztli*, Karttunen refers us to *mahui* ("to be frightened"), from which is derived *mahuiliā* ("to fear someone or something") and *mahuini* ("someone fearful, frightened").[77] Among the related constructions recorded by Molina are *ixmauhtia* ("to become frightened at seeing large things or a big crowd, or to become dizzy from looking into deep things"), *mauhcamiquini* ("one who has fainted in this way"), *mahuiz icac* ("to attend or be in the presence great people"), and *tlateomahuiztiliztli* ("spiritual ceremony of adoration and honor of God").[78] The *Florentine Codex* reports that the individual selected to be a Quetzalcoatl priest (*teopixqui*) was said to "have awe in his heart" (*imauhqui yiollo*) and to be "god-fearing" (*teuimacacini*).[79] Why did the Aztecs believe humans are indebted to the sacred, to the gods? In short, it is they "by whom we live." The passage from the *Colloquois* above continues: "it is they who give us our evening meal, our food, and everything that we eat, that we drink, our flesh, the corn, the beans, the amaranth, the chia; it is they from whom we request the water, the rain, by which they grow on earth."[80] Humans must provide for the gods as the gods provide for humans.

Diego Durán reports in the *History of the Indies of New Spain* that the Aztecs regarded the crossing red and blue streams that marked the sacred spot where Tenochtitlan was to be founded as *espanto*, that is "frightening, terrifying, astonishing, awesome."[81] Lastly, León-Portilla argues the Aztecs regarded teotl's sacred power as incomprehensible and ultimately mysterious.[82] Existence is itself fundamentally mysterious. There is a brute givenness to existence – to the continuing transformation of all things – that eludes human comprehension. It appears that this feature, too, should be included in the Aztecs' understanding of the sacred.

In sum, teotl is sacred because teotl is power. The Aztecs experienced teotl's power as a brute fact. They experienced teotl's power as irresistible, indefatigable, all-encompassing, all-creating, all-nurturing, all-destroying, and in the end profoundly mysterious. Because they experienced teotl in this way, they experienced teotl as sacred. And because they experienced teotl in this way, they experienced teotl and the sacred as simultaneously miraculous, awesome, terrifying, dizzying, humbling, mysterious, and deserving of human respect, admiration, veneration, and reciprocity.

Let's tease out several consequences of the foregoing. First, because teotl is sacred and the cosmos is identical with teotl, it follows that the cosmos is sacred. Everything – rocks, centipedes, birds, tortillas, springs, humans, and so on – consists of teotl's power and is thus sacred. Second, the sacred is not confined to the extraordinary, exceptional, or unusual. It includes the commonplace and quotidian.[83] The Aztecs did not "split the sacred from any aspect of life," as Cherokee scholar Andrea Smith writes when characterizing indigenous North American views of the sacred.[84] Barbara Myerhoff likewise argues the Huichol make no distinction between sacred and profane and between sacred and secular.[85]

Third, Aztec philosophy's constitutional monism logically precludes it from making a metaphysical distinction between two, essentially distinct kinds of reality or stuff: the sacred versus the profane. It does not balkanize reality into a transcendent sacred realm and an immanent profane realm. *Pace* Mircea Eliade and Davíd Carrasco, Aztec metaphysics does not bifurcate reality into "two modes of being in the world" – sacred and profane – divided by "an abyss."[86] *Pace* Émile Durkheim, the sacred is not "set apart and forbidden"[87] but immanent, immediate, and concrete. Everything is sacred – including the ephemeral, dreamlike, bodily, sexual, filthy, and earthly (mundane). Indeed, the sacred versus profane distinction, so central to Western understandings of religion, appears to rest upon a Platonic-style constitutional dualism that equates the sacred with the transcendent, eternal, perfect, and immutable, on the one hand, and the profane with the mundane, ephemeral, imperfect, and mutable, on the other. A different set of metaphysical intuitions guides Aztec metaphysics and religion.

Fourth, attempts to define the sacred nonmetaphysically in terms of humans' attitudes toward certain linguistic expressions likewise prove inadequate. Roy Rappaport, for example, defines the sacred in terms of sanctity, that is, "*the quality of unquestionableness imputed by congregations to postulates in their nature objectively unverifiable and absolutely unfalsifiable.*"[88] Sanctity is a property of discourse, not of experience, time, place, or deities. All religions according to Rappaport accept one or more discursive expressions that function as their "Ultimate Sacred Postulates" and as their creed.[89] To these postulates or "doxologies" they attribute self-evident and unquestionable truthfulness.[90] The postulates are absolutely unfalsifiable and unverifiable. The rituals of all religions presuppose such doxologies, even those that explicitly espouse no creed or postulate no divinities.

Rappaport's theory fails to capture the Aztecs' understanding of the sacred on several scores. First, it remains steadfastly dualistic. By Rappaport's definition, the lion's share of reality is not sanctified or sacred. Yet Aztec metaphysics maintains all of reality is sacred. Second, his account is anthropocentric. Sanctity is a defined wholly in terms of human beings' epistemological attitudes toward certain propositions. Were there no humans, then, there would be no sacred. However for the Aztecs, teotl's sacredness no more depends upon humans' attitudes toward teotl or toward certain propositions regarding teotl than does teotl's existence. Third, Rappaport's definition is logocentric. Sanctity is defined as a property of propositional discourse. However this puts the cart before the horse. If there is special class of expressions regarding teotl (to wit, those that I describe as "well-rooted" below), they are special because of their objective relationship with teotl qua sacred reality, not vice versa. Fourth, Rappaport's theory is intellectualistic. Aztec religion focused upon practice – not belief or acceptance. It stressed orthopraxy, not orthodoxy. I argue elsewhere that Aztec philosophy and religion are what Angus Graham, David Hall, and Roger Ames (in their work on pre-Han Daoism and Confucianism) character-ize as "way-centered" as opposed to "truth-centered" endeavors.[91] This distinc-tion cuts deeply, including how each conceives belief, mind, wisdom, language, truth, behavior, ethics, and so on. Fifth, Rappaport's definition of sanctity relies upon what I regard as outmoded, positivist notions of verifiability, falsifiability, science, and religion.[92]

The fact that the Aztecs excluded nothing from the sacred is compellingly illustrated by the cluster of teotl aspects or powers dubbed *Tlazolteotl*, literally "Sacred Filth" (although standardly translated theistically as "Goddess of Filth"). The word *tlazolteotl* combines *tlazolli* ("filth, rubbish, garbage") with teotl ("sacred" or "deity"). Filth, rubbish, and garbage are sacred. *Tlazolli* derives from the prefix *tlah-* ("thing") and the suffix *–zolli* ("old, dirty, worn out, exhausted, deteriorated").[93] *Tlazolli* refers to that which is rotten, worn out, used up, decom-posed, disintegrated, deranged, and decayed: for example, excrement, vomit, nasal mucus, dirt, muck, slime, rags, and random bits of straw or hair. It refers, in short, to *stuff out of place* (*or improperly placed*).[94] That which is characterized by *tlazolli* is disordered, deranged, and displaced. As such, it exists at the oppo-site end of a continuum from that which is clean, well-ordered, well-arranged, well-integrated – that is, *stuff in place* (*well placed or in its place*). The sacredness of tlazolli is further demonstrated by its association with Tezcatlipoca, one of two major Aztec deity complexes along with Quetzalcoatl.[95]

The Aztecs associated Tlazolteotl with excess, sexual perversion and way-wardness, and inappropriate lovemaking. Tlazolli (filth and disorder) was seen as both cause and consequence of human misbehavior. It induced humans to slip into excessive, licentious, and perverse sexual behavior that sullied and besmirched both actors and those around them. Tlazolli-causing behavior ren-dered humans dirtied, damaged, imbalanced, and deranged. This could result in disease – both physical and mental, individual and communal – and even death. Yet the Aztecs nevertheless regarded Tlazolteotl and tlazolli as sacred.

The Aztecs also associated Tlazolteotl with the tremendously powerful creative and nurturing powers of the Earth. Tlazolteotl also forms part of Tlazolteotl-Ixcuina, the Mother-Goddess complex, the great genetrix and parturient of all things. Tlazolteotl thus possesses profound generative, regenerative and transformative powers. Another aspect of Tlazolteotl is Tlaelquani ("Eater of Ordure").[96] Those who transgress moral norms – who murder, steal, lie, and commit adultery, for example – besmirch themselves with ordure; turn themselves into ordure. By confessing their transgressions to Tlazolteotl-Tlaelquani, Sullivan explains, they transfer their ordure to Tlazolteotl-Tlaelquani, who then eats it. By eating their ordure, she cleanses, purifies and thusly regenerates them. Tlazolteotl-Tlaelquani was also the goddess (deity complex) of the fertile earth who "receives all organic wastes – human and animal excrement, vegetables and fruit leavings, fish and animal bones and so forth – which when decomposed are transformed into humus."[97] By eating excrement, she transforms excrement into humus, which in turn fertilizes and revitalizes the soil that, in turn, nourishes the corn that feeds humans. Humans thus arise from humus. Aztec metaphysics has a keen appreciation of ecology or the circulation of energy in the life-death-eating cycle.[98] An Aztec sculpture represents this idea by depicting Tlazolteotl giving birth to the god of maize, Cinteotl.[99] Corn arises from filth. The statue's green color suggests sacredness, fertility, renewal, balance, and life-energy. The sacred power of filth is further demonstrated by the fact that the Aztecs commonly used excrement and urine in curing and purifying practices.[100]

Aztec artists standardly depicted Tlazolteotl wearing raw, unspun cotton in her headdress. Burkhart argues the cotton's rawness is highly significant. Raw cotton is unstructured, unordered, and unformed yet it nevertheless possesses the creative potential to become something well-ordered and well-arranged: namely, woven fabric. Unspun cotton is characterized by tlazolli.[101] The ubiquity of the sacred is further illustrated by the Aztec conception of precious minerals as excrement. The Aztecs called gold *coztic teocuitlatl* ("yellow sacred excrement") and *tonatiuh icuitl* ("excrement of Tonatiuh"), and called silver *iztac teocuitlatl* ("white sacred excrement").[102] Sahagún tells us that because gold and silver were viewed as excrement of Tonatiuh, they were held to be highly sacred, precious, and desirable. Furthermore, like other forms of excrement (human and divine), gold possessed curative and restorative powers. As Cecelia Klein points out, Aztec philosophy's attitude toward excrement and filth contrasts dramatically with Euro-American popular and Christian religious discourses that conceive excrement and filth as paradigmatically profane and polluting. It also contrasts profoundly with the Christian view that pollution and sacredness are mutually exclusive.[103]

The Aztecs thus regarded tlazolli as a powerful, sacred, vital, and essential aspect of the cosmos and teotl. From tlazolli emerge order, purity, and life in a cosmic metaphysics of ever-circulating and recycling energies. As Burkhart stresses, human life comes from undifferentiated sexual secretions, cooked food comes from the raw and uncooked, and woven fabric comes from undifferentiated bunches of grass or cotton.[104] In this respect, purity and impurity, order and disorder, generation and degeneration, and well-arranged and deranged are akin to life and death: mutually arising and mutually interdependent, complementary polarities. As a consequence, the Aztecs did not try to eliminate tlazolli from the cosmos any more than they tried to eliminate death. Instead, their efforts focused on displacing tlazolli to its proper place: the periphery.

In sum, excrement and filth are powerful, transformative, and ambiguous. They participate in processes resulting in disease and death as well as processes resulting in fertility and rebirth. They transform the living into the dead, and the dead into the living. Excrement and filth are sacred: hence the moniker, *Tlazolteotl*, "sacred filth or excrement."

Burkhart argues the concept of tlazolli serves as the basic pollution concept in Aztec thought.[105] Tlazolli is impure. This role is not surprising, given tlazolli's association with filth, dirt, and licentious behavior. What is surprising, however, is that even though tlazolli (filth, excrement) is impure and polluting, it is nevertheless seen as sacred. Sacredness includes both the pure *and* the impure, the clean *and* the polluted, and the well-placed *and* the out-of-place. Pollution and sacredness are not mutually exclusive. This consequence gives us better insight into the name *Tlazolteotl* and into the processes to which the name applies.

The Aztecs' nonhierarchical metaphysics requires that it conceptualize purity and impurity nonhierarchically. The distinction between purity and impurity accordingly consists of *how* things are arranged, not *what* things consist of. Things become more pure by becoming better arranged or ordered – not by becoming closer to a higher, transcendent sacred realm. And things become more impure by becoming more deranged or disordered – not by becoming closer to a lower, profane realm. That which is pure is that which is well-ordered, well-arranged, and well-integrated, whereas that which is impure is that which disordered, disarrayed, and displaced. Pure and impure exist at opposite ends of a single *nonhierarchical* continuum. Contemporary Huichol, for example, similarly deny any principled, hierarchical distinction between sacred and profane. Rather, they distinguish things nonhierarchically in terms of their "degrees of religious intensity."[106]

The Aztecs' conception of sacrifice likewise invokes ideas of nonhierarchical ordering and stuff in place. The Nahuatl word *uemana* ("to make an offering"),

standardly translated as "to sacrifice," means literally "to spread out an offering."
Read parses *uemana* as a combination of the noun *uentli* ("offering") and the
verb *mana* ("to spread or pat something out, as a tortilla is patted out").[107] R. Joe
Campbell claims it combines *uentli* with the causative form of the verb *mani*
("for something flat to cover a surface, as water in a shallow pan") to mean "to
put something flat on the ground or to make tortillas, before they cook them
on the *comal*."[108]

Finally, the Aztecs' idea of the sacred does not ex hypothesi guarantee human
knowledge of the sacred. That is, from the fact the sacred (teotl) is metaphysically immanent, it does not follow that the sacred is therefore epistemologically
immanent in the sense of being humanly knowable either easily or even in
principle. Being and knowing are two different matters. Even though humans
may directly experience the sacred in such ordinary events as childbirth and
the seasonal cycles, this does not mean such prosaic experiences enable them to
comprehend fully the sacred.

2.3. *NELTILIZTLI*, SELF-PRESENTATION, AND NONHIERARCHICAL WELL-ORDERING

Aztec philosophy makes two key distinctions that appear inconsistent with a
pantheistic interpretation of Aztec metaphysics since both distinctions seemingly presuppose constitutional dualism and a hierarchical metaphysics. Can
my interpretation preserve these two distinctions or must it abandon them? In
what follows, I show how they may be preserved.

First, Aztec philosophy distinguishes between objects, humans, activities,
behaviors, utterances, and processes in terms of how fully, truly, and authentically they present, disclose, and unconceal teotl. The conventional strategy for
understanding this distinction appeals to notions such as hierophany and special presence, and unpacks these in terms of a hierarchical metaphysics and
constitutional dualism of sacred versus profane. Eliade, Carrasco, and Eduardo
Matos Moctezuma argue sacred and profane constitute two essentially distinct
realms and that these two realms are bridged by what they call *hierophany*, that
is, by the appearance, revelation, or manifestation of the sacred (or divine) in a
special object, place, or occasion in the profane realm.[109] Hierophanies are "the
quintessential meeting places of the supernatural and natural realms," writes
Carrasco.[110] Cultures commonly characterize these places as an *axis mundi* – the
stabilizing center or navel of their cosmos – and Aztec culture is no exception.
Carrasco, Matos Moctezuma, and Leonardo López Luján contend the Templo
Mayor served as an axis mundi. Hierophanies are accordingly viewed as sacred,

powerful, valuable, meaningful, and revealing of the nature of the sacred (or divine).[111] Such objects, places, and occasions are also described by scholars as enjoying what Ninian Smart calls "special presence," that is, a localized spatio-temporal manifestation and revelation of God or the divine that by definition transcends time, space, and cosmos. According to Smart, sacred and profane constitute two distinct metaphysical realms that are bridged only by special presence. The sacred does *not* reveal itself in those places or objects that are not hierophanies and that do not enjoy sacred presence. The profane neither reveals nor manifests the sacred.[112]

Both these proposals for understanding the distinction between things that present, disclose, and unconceal the sacred as opposed to those that do not are *not* available to Aztec metaphysics as I interpret it since both presuppose a hierarchical and dualistic metaphysics. Is it possible to preserve this distinction in a manner compatible with Aztec philosophy's nonhierarchical metaphysics and constitutional monism? I offer the following.

First, the distinction needs to be understood in quantitative rather than qualitative terms. Created things exist along a nonhierarchical continuum ranging from those that more fully present, disclose, and unconceal teotl (the sacred), at one end, to those things that less fully present, disclose, and unconceal teotl, at the other. But what accounts for this difference if not a hierarchically and dualistically conceived metaphysics?

Aztec metaphysics characterizes persons, objects, activities, behavior, processes, and utterances equally and without equivocation in terms of *neltiliztli*, and understands neltiliztli in terms of well-rootedness in teotl. That which is well-rooted − or *nelli* in Nahuatl − in teotl is true in the sense of being genuine, authentic, and well-balanced as well as true in the sense of being non-referentially disclosing and unconcealing of teotl. Among the created things that fall on this end of the continuum are the Huey Teocalli (Templo Mayor) of Tenochtitlan; a *yolteotl* ("teotlized human heart"); fine pieces of jade and turquoise; fine quetzal plumes; and well-crafted works of art (*in xochitl in cuicatl*). Such things are clearly deemed precious and thus special by Aztec lights. Falling on the opposite end of the continuum is that which is poorly rooted − or *ahnelli* − in teotl and hence that which does not fully present, disclose, or unconceal teotl. Among the things that fall at this end of the continuum are disordered, deranged, and disintegrated things such as excrement, unspun cotton, vomit, straw, and rags.

Let's examine more closely the notion of neltiliztli. León-Portilla writes, "the word 'truth' in Nahuatl, *neltiliztli*, is derived from the same radical as *tla-nel-huatl*, 'root,' from which in turn derives *nelhuayotl*, 'base' or 'foundation.' The stem syllable *nel* connotes originally 'solid firmness or deep rootedness.' With this we may say that etymologically the word 'truth' in the abstract for the Nahuas, *neltiliztli*, was to be identified with the quality of well-grounded stability, well-foundedness, or rootedness."[113]

According to León-Portilla, the Aztecs possessed a concept of truth and defined truth in terms of neltiliztli or well-grounded stability, well-foundedness, and well-rootedness (henceforth "well-rootedness" for short). A person cognizes truly if and only if she cognizes well-rootedly. Willard Gingerich upholds León-Portilla's translation and etymological reconstruction of *neltiliztli* and cites as additional confirmation Friar Mijango's translation of the Nahuatl sentence, *nitlanelhuayotocac uel ynelhuayocan onacic*, as "I discovered the truth of something." According to Gingerich, the original Nahuatl sentence borrows the imagery of "a tree whose roots have been dug up and revealed" and literally says, "I sought out the root of the matter; I reached completely down to the place where the roots were." Gingerich also points out that *truth* occurs in the early post-Conquest sources more often in its adverbial form, *nelli*, meaning "truly" or "with truth" (which I believe reflects the Aztecs' process metaphysics).[114] Gingerich's analysis suggests the following: nelli cognizing (cognizing truly) is cognizing that reaches completely down to the place where the roots are; ahnelli cognizing (cognizing untruly) does not.

Gingerich goes on to argue that well-rootedness does not exhaust the full meaning of neltiliztli. Its meaning includes an ineliminable Heideggerian component, namely, nonreferential *aletheia* – "disclosure," "clearing and lighting,"[115] "unconcealedness,"[116] "self-deconcealing,"[117] and "unhiddenness."[118] Following Gingerich, I propose we understand neltiliztli *as well-rootedness-cum-aletheia*. Aztec philosophy, in other words, conceives truth in *ontological* terms. *Truth is a way of being and doing*, a way of living, conducting one's life, and so on. It is in such an ontological sense that we commonly speak of true north, true friend, and truing a bicycle rim. Aztec philosophy does not conceive truth in *semantic* terms, that is, in terms of correspondence, reference, signification, representation, and aboutness. Truth is not defined, for example, as a relationship between the content of a sentence or proposition, on the one hand, and some fact or state of affairs, on the other.[119]

I suggest that that which is well-rooted in teotl and thus more fully disclosing of teotl is at the same time that which is well-ordered, well-integrated, and well-balanced. It is that which is truly or rightly ordered, arranged, and so forth. It is true in the sense of being authentic, right, and genuine. It is stuff-in-place. Conversely, that which is poorly rooted in teotl and thus less fully disclosing of teotl is that which is ill-centered, imbalanced, deranged, decomposing, disintegrated, and disordered. It is stuff-out-of-place. In short, Aztec metaphysics expresses the distinction between the more disclosing and the less disclosing nonhierarchically and monistically in terms of *how* the single stuff of teotl is organized and arranged.

Those things that are poorly rooted in teotl do certainly disclose an aspect of teotl. After all, all things are self-presentations of teotl. Yet they are less disclosing of the complete and full nature of teotl in the sense that they present merely one specific aspect out of the manifold aspects of teotl, and what's more, fail to show how that aspect is integrated and interrelated with the rest of the totality that is teotl. They present disconnected fragments or frozen snapshots of teotl's total nature and power. As we saw in our discussion of Tlazolteotl and tlazolli, that which is disordered and disintegrated is a vital and essential aspect of teotl. But that is not the entire story. Such things do not fully disclose teotl.

An obvious question arises at this point. That which is well-rooted, well-ordered, and well-balanced more fully discloses the nature of teotl. In what sense, exactly, does it do this? I submit it does so by disclosing teotl's diachronic balancing, ordering, and unifying of complementary polarities, such as order and disorder, male and female, and fire and water, as well as teotl's processiveness and continuing self-generation, self-regeneration, and self-transformation.

Thus, while all created things are self-presentations of teotl and hence self-presentations of the sacred, some self-presentations are more disclosing and unconcealing of teotl and the sacred than others. The former are better rooted in teotl than the latter, and are certainly special in this regard. The former are also more well-centered, well-ordered, and well-balanced than the latter, and are very special in this regard, too. They are simply *not* special in the sense of presencing a qualitatively distinct, transcendent sacred substance in the way that Carrasco and others maintain. After all, that which makes something special need not be the presence of a transcendent and ontologically different substance. Understanding the distinction between those things that present, disclose, and unconceal the sacred (teotl) as opposed to those that do not in terms of neltiliztli-cum-aletheia and well-orderedness captures the distinction nonhierarchically and monistically in terms of how the single stuff of teotl is ordered, organized, and arranged. As we will see below, some disclosing, well-ordered things are created by teotl without human ritual participation (e.g., jade and quetzal plumage) while others are created by teotl only with human ritual participation (e.g., the Templo Mayor and flower and song).

Aztec philosophy recognizes a second distinction that appears incompatible with its nonhierarchicalism and constitutional monism. It distinguishes between power that is cosmically balancing, ordering, stabilizing, and immediately beneficial to human beings, on the one hand, and power that is cosmically imbalancing, disordering, deranging, unstabilizing, and immediately detrimental to human beings, on the other. One common way of understanding this distinction by scholars introduces a hierarchical metaphysics and a constitutional dualism. It holds there are two constitutionally and hence essentially different kinds of power: sacred (which is higher and transcendent) and profane (which is lower and mundane). The profane may become beneficially powerful only by acquiring beneficial, transcendent sacred power through sacred or special presence.[120]

However, this way of thinking about things is *not* available to Aztec philosophy since it is logically incompatible with its nonhierarchicalism, constitutional monism, and claim that the entire cosmos is sacred. Is it possible to preserve a distinction between ordering power and disordering power without invoking a hierarchical metaphysics and constitutional dualism of sacred versus profane? Aztec metaphysics underwrites the distinction as follows. Since all things are equally constituted by and ultimately identical with the single, uniform, and sacred power of teotl, it follows that all things are equally constituted by sacred power. This notwithstanding, some things are characterized by power that is balancing, ordering, stabilizing, and beneficial to human beings, while other things are characterized by power that is imbalancing, disordering, unstabilizing, and detrimental to human beings. But what explains this difference if not the existence of two essentially distinct, hierarchally graded kinds of power?

For philosophies embracing constitutional monism and nonhierarchical metaphysics, the explanation proceeds in terms of *how* stuff is nonhierarchically arranged – rather than in terms of *what kind* of hierarchically graded stuff they consist of. Those things that possess power that is balancing, ordering, stabilizing, and beneficial to humans do so by virtue of being well-ordered, well-composed, well-centered, and well-balanced – both internally (in terms of the interrelationships between their constituent elements) as well as externally (in terms of their interrelationships with the things in their environment). (Indeed, each is a necessary condition of the other. After all, the boundaries between individual things and their surroundings are porous if not ultimately nonexistent since individual things are merely momentary condensations of teotl's energy-in-motion.) In short, they constitute stuff-in-place. By this way of thinking, *to create is to order, compose, integrate, and arrange that which already exists.*[121] As though attuned to the law of the conservation of energy, Aztec metaphysics denies creation from nothing.

By contrast, those things that possess power that is imbalancing, disordering, destabilizing, and harmful to humans do so by virtue of being disordered, deranged, decentered, and unbalanced – both internally in terms of the interrelationships between their constituent elements as well as externally in terms of their interrelationships with their surroundings. They represent stuff-out-of-place. The Nahuatl word *aompayotl* nicely conveys this. Although commonly translated as "misfortune," it means literally "condition of something out of its place."[122] Only when occupying their proper place can humans, for example, find well-being. By this way of thinking, *to destroy is to disintegrate, disorder, decompose, and derange things.* As though attuned to the law of the conservation of energy, Aztec metaphysics denies destruction into nothing.

The Templo Mayor, for example, possesses power that is balancing, ordering, stabilizing, and beneficial to humans by virtue of its internal formal and material ordering as well as its external ordering vis-à-vis the cosmos, that is, its location at the earth's navel and the cosmos' axis mundi.[123] And so likewise with the properly constructed Aztec *altepetl.* James Lockhart argues that the Aztecs structured the altepetl (a social, political, and economic unit or "city-state" plus adjoining agricultural land) in a "cellular or modular as opposed to *hierarchical*" manner.[124] He writes, "The Nahua manner of creating larger constructs, whether in politics, society, economy or art, tended to place emphasis on a series of relatively equal, relatively separate and self-contained constituent parts of the whole, the unity of which consisted in the symmetrical numerical arrangement of the parts, their identical relationships to a common reference point, and their orderly, cyclical rotation."[125] Indeed, Lockhart asserts the cellular-modular arrangement functioned as *"the most general Nahua model for constructing anything whatever."*[126] The altepetl consisted of four smaller neighborhoods or *calpultin* (pl., *calpulli* sing.), arranged in this manner. Its four-part arrangement mirrored the four-petaled flower arrangement of the cosmos and aligned with the four cardinal directions (see Figure 4.6).[127] At a smaller level, Aztecs arranged their houses, areas of cultivation, and individual *milpas* both internally and externally so as to enhance their beneficial powers.[128] Altepetl, calpolli, milpa, and household are ordered by "elaborate schemes of numerical symmetry and strict rotational order."[129] Lastly, I submit Aztecs also sought to order their lives – psychologically, socially, politically, economically, and cosmologically – in a nonhierarchical fashion so as to balance themselves and enhance their beneficial powers.[130] In sum, *nonhierarchical ordering is key.*

Aztec emphasis upon nonhierarchical ordering is further illustrated by a speech delivered by the indigenous rulers and priests of Tenochtitlan and Tlatelolco recorded in the *Colloquios.* Of their high priests and sages, the *tlatolmatinime* ("they who are wise in words"), they say, "they are the ones who put in order (*quitecpana*) how a year falls, how the day count (*tonalpohualli*) follows its path (*otlatoca*), and the complete twenty day periods."[131] The key verb here is *tecpana*, meaning "to arrange or put in order, to line up, to arrange in a sequence."[132] Molina lists several related words that shed further light on the activity of tecpana: *nauatiltecpana* ("to establish laws"), *nemiliztecpanilia* ("to lay down a line of conduct for someone"), *netecpantlaliliztli* ("order or arrangement of those who are seated in their places"), *tecpancapoa* ("to count something in order"), and *quauhtecpantli* ("wooden lattice or grating").[133] Ordering the tonalpohualli's sequence of days involves arranging or laying them out on a flat surface: the flat surface of the tonalamatl, the book of days. Ordering a way of life for human beings involves arranging them on a nonhierarchical surface, tlalticpac (the surface of the earth). A wooden lattice or grating is likewise a nonhierarchical ordering of motifs – one, moreover, that nicely illustrates Lockhart's notion of cellular-modular organization as consisting of self-contained motifs that repeat in a symmetrical sequence.[134] Lockhart adds that *tecpana* is also used to refer to the composing of poetry and sometimes to a testator's ordering his will.[135]

The foregoing claim in the *Colloquios* about ordering the days of the tonalpohualli is made in the context of listing a plethora of services the tlatolmatinime perform: they "guide," "carry," "govern," "make offerings," "offer incense," "let blood," "read the books of red and black ink," and "cause the path to speak."[136] The tlatolmatinime, in short, organize a complete *way of life*. And they do so with the aim of enabling humans to live in balance, to live truly, authentically, and well-rootedly in teotl. What's more, given the Aztecs' beliefs that human actions affect the cosmos and that the cosmos is open to human participation, Aztec tlatolmatinime do so with the aim of actively participating in and contributing to the balance of the cosmos of the Fifth Sun. Aztec ritual does not seek simply to mirror the ordering of the cosmos but rather seeks to participate, contribute to, and thereby sustain, enhance, and regenerate the well-orderedness of the cosmos.[137]

In sum, as a consequence of their being properly arranged, temples, *altepemeh* (pl., *altepetl*, sing.), calpultin, households, milpas, and human lives acquire power that is balancing, ordering, stabilizing, and beneficial. In contrast, things possessing power that is imbalancing, disordering, deranging, unstabilizing, and hence detrimental to humans possess such power by virtue of their being disordered, decomposed, disintegrated, and imbalanced. Ordering and disordering power do not represent two constitutionally different kinds of power – sacred versus profane – but two different nonhierarchical orderings of the single, constitutionally uniform sacred power of teotl. Both ordering and disordering power are sacred. What we saw to be the case with tlazolli is likewise the case with disordering and unstabilizing power generally. It is sacred.

How do the preceding two distinctions relate to one another? I submit that that which is more well-rooted in teotl, more true, and more fully disclosing of teotl is coextensional with that which possesses power that is more ordering, stabilizing, centering, and beneficial to humans; and that which is more poorly rooted in teotl, less true, and which fails to disclose teotl is coextensional with that which possesses power that is more disordering, unstabilizing, peripheral-izing, and detrimental to human beings. The two sets of properties are there-fore also isomorphic. Aztec metaphysics maps things on a nonhierarchical continuum combining both sets of properties. At one end of the continuum are things that enjoy well-rootedness-cum-aletheia (i.e., that are well-rooted in teotl and disclose and unconceal the nature of teotl) as well as enjoy power that is ordering, stabilizing, centering, creative, and beneficial to humans. Some of the things occurring at this end of the continuum are:

- The color green (blue-green). According to López Austin, the Nahuatl-speak-ing inhabitants of the High Central Plateau of Mexico regarded green (blue-green) as the color of "order and equilibrium" (*orden y equilibrio*).[138] The Aztecs imagined the surface of the earth to be a four-petaled flat disk surrounded by water. In the center of the flower-shaped disk, they imagined a pierced, precious green stone. Each of the five directions – east, north, west, south, and center – had its own color. Blue-green was the color of the center and navel (*xictli*) of the cosmos as well as the balanced synthesis of the other four colors. It was associated with vegetation, maize, blood, water, earth, and sky, and asso-ciated more broadly with fertility, renewal, and ultimately life-energy itself.[139] Sahagún identifies the place where according to myth Nanahuatzin immolates himself and is reborn as the Fifth Sun as *teutlecuilco in xiuhtetzaqualco* ("the god's hearth, the turquoise enclosure").[140] Sahagún later refers to the turquoise enclosure as the earth's "navel" (*tlalxicco*).[141] *Codex Borbonicus*, plate 34 pictures as turquoise blue the fiery hearth at the center of the New Fire ceremony (see Figure 4.8).[142]

- *Teuxiuitl* (*teoxihuitl*; "turquoise, sacred green stone") and *chalchiuitl* (*chal-chihuitl*; "jade, sacred green stone").[143] In Book XI of the *Florentine Codex*, Sahagún states that *teuxihuitl* derives from *teutl* (*teotl*) and *xiuitl* (*xihuitl*), meaning that this stone "is his property, the tonalli of the god (*itonal in teutl*)."[144] I propose either leaving *teotl* untranslated or translating it as "sacred"; hence, "teotl's or sacred green stone." Sahagún's informants describe these as *cenca mahuizio* ("highly estimable"), *tlazoctli* ("precious, beloved"), and *tecpieli* ("noble").[145] *Mahuizio* participates in the conceptual cluster rooted in the verb *mahui* and connotes something awesome, dizzying, marvelous, venerated, astonishing, esteemed, and fearful.[146] Jade and turquoise are considered special and uncommon because highly precious, awesome, dizzying, astonishing, marvelous, and venerable.

Presumably by virtue of their color, jade and turquoise were also associated throughout Mesoamerica with maize and hence with life-energy. Jade, turquoise, and maize convey the ordering and balancing life-energy of teotl. I suggest the Aztecs viewed jade and turquoise as well-rooted in teotl, as disclosing the nature of teotl, and as possessing sacred power that is balancing, ordering, centering, and beneficial to humans. According to McKeever Furst, the inhabitants of Central Mexico commonly regarded gemstones as manifestations of gods' and high-ranking humans' power.[147]

The Aztecs imagined the center of the earth to be a pierced, precious green stone or a *chalchihuitl*. They identified the chalchihuitl with maize, water, sky, vegetation, the earth, and more broadly fertility, generation, regeneration, and life.[148] They also believed these sacred greenstones possess curative powers, especially for ailments of the spleen, liver, and kidneys.[149]

- The *quetzalli* or iridescent, shimmering blue-green tail feathers of the quetzal bird. Like other Mesoamericans, the Aztecs associated quetzal plumes with maize, life, and hence considered them precious. Taube reports the Middle Formative Olmec considered jade and quetzal plumes to be rarefied forms of maize.[150]

- The *yolteotl*. León-Portilla translates *yolteotl* as "heart rooted in God" and "deified heart."[151] I prefer "sacred heart," "heart rooted in teotl," and "teotlized heart." The individual possessing a yolteotl was said to "have teotl in his/her heart" (*teotl yiollo*).[152] According to Sahagún's informants, "The good scribe-painter [*qualli tlacuilo*] is wise [*mimati*]; God is in his heart [*iolteutl*]. He puts divinity into things [*tlaiolteuuiani*]."[153] The good scribe-painter possesses a yolteotl and customarily applies his teotlized heart to things (*tlayolteohuiani*). Sahagún's informants also reported that the individual who was selected as Quetzalcoatl priest was of "godly of heart" (*in mjtoa teutl yiollo*) – that is, "has teotl or the sacred in his heart" – and was *tlateumatini* ("wise in or knowledgeable of the things of teotl or the sacred").[154] They also characterize the beloved and esteemed noble (*tlazopilli*) as "a precious green stone [chalchihuitl], a bracelet of fine turquoise [*maquiztli teoxihuitl*], a precious feather [*quetzalli tlazotli*]."[155]

- Well-crafted in xochitl in cuicatl ("flower and song"), that is, well-rooted in the teotlized heart of its artistic creator and thus ultimately well-rooted in teotl itself. "Flower and song" refers generally to creative activities such composing and performing song-poems, composing and playing music, writing-painting, weaving, goldsmithing, and featherworking. Aztec poets commonly characterized song-poems as pieces of jade, and the composing-performing of song-poems as drilling and carving turquoise beads.[156] Sahagún's informants characterize the products of good artisans as well-prepared, well-arranged, well-measured, well-fitted, well-matched, and well-designed.[157]

Frances Karttunen and James Lockhart contend Aztec song-poems, like Aztec altepemeh, are characterized by a specific pattern of nonhierarchical cellular-modular ordering.[158] Song-poems are distinguished from other forms of linguistic expression by their structure. They ideally form coherent wholes by numerically and symmetrically arranging an even number of independent cellular parts that Karttunen and Lockhart call "verses." Two self-standing verses form a verse pair most commonly by dint of shared content (less commonly, by subtle parallels or complementarity).

Lockhart claims the Aztecs also regularly used two different words to refer to activity of composing new song-poems or rearranging already existing ones: *tecpana* and *tlalia*.[159] *Tecpana*, as we saw, means "to arrange or put in order, to line up, to arrange in a sequence."[160] It also refers to the arranging of laws, customs, and a way of life for people. *Tlalia* means "to set down, to provide, to issue under one's responsibility, to compose, to sit down, to settle, to put something down, to set things in order, to set down statutes and ordinances."[161] Like tecpana activities, tlalia activities are metaphysically nonhierarchical in the sense of arranging things on a nonhierarchical surface such as tlalticpac (the surface of the earth). Arranging human conduct likewise consists of ordering how humans live their lives on the nonhierarchical surface of the earth as well. Here again, we also see a parallel between the nonhierarchical ordering of spoken words by means of cellular-modular symmetry into a song-poem, and the nonhierarchical ordering of human conduct and living arrangements by means of statutes and ordinances into a way of life. One of the songs collected in the *Cantares mexicanos* delcares, *noncuicamanaco* ("I come spreading song"). According to Karttunen, the verb *mana* suggests the singer's spreading out smooth and flat, arranging, and offering of sung words.[162]

The foregoing has the following consequence. If teotl is the consummate cosmic artist and the cosmos of the Fifth Age is teotl's "flower and song," then it follows that the cosmos of the Fifth Age must be ordered and arranged in the same manner as poetry. The proper arrangement of the cosmos and the proper arrangement of song-poems (along with altepemeh, households, and milpas) are homologous.

- *Teotlahtolli* ("sacred or teotlized words or language") spoken by those with a teotlized, sacred heart and by those through whom the gods speak. These included the speeches made by the *tlatoani* ("ruler") and high priest. Among the figures of speech recorded by Sahagún in Book VI of the *Florentine Codex*, two stand out. The first is *uel chalchiuhtic, uel teuxiuhtic, uel acatic, uel oloiuhqui* ("fine jade, rich turquoise, long as reeds and very round"). Of a royal orator who wisely counseled others, the people said, "He spoke magnificently – with jades, turquoises – and his words sounded as precious stones, long as reeds and very round."[163] The second is *ontetepeoac, onchachayaoac,* which Sullivan glosses as "there has been a sowing, there has been a scattering of precious jades, etc."[164] The Aztecs viewed such spoken words as beneficial, nourishing, renewing, life-sustaining, and conveying life-energy.

- The Templo Mayor (*Huey Teocalli*) together with the ceremonial precinct of Tenochtitlan. These were well-rooted in teotl and hence true to teotl in the sense of disclosing and presenting the nature of teotl. They were also potent with ordering, centering, and stabilizing power. They were well-rooted by virtue of their cosmic location and their architectural composition and arrangement. First, they were located at the overlapping centers of the earth (its navel) and of the cosmos, as well as the overlapping meeting points of the earth's surface (*tlalticpac*), heaven (*ilhuicatl*), and underworld (*mictlan*), or of the four directions. Here was the axis mundi, where the various forces energizing the cosmos converged: the procreative forces from the heavens, the generative forces from the underworld, and the vitalizing forces from the four corners of the cosmos. However I submit Aztec metaphysics conceived the axis mundi nonhierarchically (*pace* Johanna Broda, Carrasco, and Matos Moctezuma).[165] Second, as Broda, Matos Moctezuma, López Luján, and others have shown, the very architectural (formal and material) arrangement of the Templo Mayor and ceremonial precinct gathered together, properly arranged, and presented all of the major features of the Aztec cosmos.[166] Both were homologous with the cosmos. Because of this, claims Carrasco, the Templo Mayor and ceremonial precinct jointly functioned as an *imago mundi*, or "image, living screenfold, in its own time and space" of Aztec cosmology.[167] They functioned, in other words, as large three-dimensional cosmograms in the manner of *Codex Fejérváry-Mayer* plate 1 (see Figure 4.3).[168] In light of this, I suggest the Templo Mayor and ceremonial precinct jointly constituted a grand altar (or *mesa*) as well as microcosm (i.e., a scaled-down presentation of the Fifth Sun-Earth Ordering).[169] The Templo Mayor and ceremonial precinct were more than physical backdrops or stage-settings for Aztec ritual. As vivified objects empowered with teotl's ordering and centering energy, they actively participated in and contributed to the success of rituals taking place within them. They helped arrange, order, and center ritual energy. Like beacons, they radiated ordered and ordering energy, and centered and centering energy. In this way, too, the Templo Mayor and ceremonial precinct authentically disclosed and presented the nature of teotl. Finally, in keeping with Aztec philosophy's metaphysical nonhierarchicalism and constitutional monism, these features of the Templo Mayor and ceremonial precinct did *not* set them apart as some sui generis "sacred" space distinct in kind from the "profane" space surrounding them (*pace* Broda, Matos Moctezuma, and Carrasco).[170]

The aforementioned items enjoy well-rootedness-cum-aletheia as well as enjoy power that is ordering, stabilizing, centering, and beneficial to humans. The Aztecs accordingly regarded these things as particularly awesome, marvelous, fearsome, astonishing, dizzying, worthy of veneration, esteem, and adoration, and hence sacred. There was indeed something extremely special about these things – but it was not the presence of a metaphysically distinct sacred substance. Teotl more genuinely presented and disclosed itself in them.

At the other end of this nonhierarchical continuum are things that are poorly rooted in teotl, that partially or inauthentically present teotl, and that possess power that is disordering, deranging, and detrimental to humans. Some items located at this end of the continuum are rags, straw, cobwebs, excrement, coagulated sperm, slime, dust, and clumps of unspun cotton. Here, too, are individuals the Aztecs characterized as the "big mossy-haired one, the big excrement-ashed one" (*tzonpachpul, cuitlanexpul*),[171] the "deranged one" (*yolpoliuhqui*),[172] "the madman" (*yollotlahueliloc*),[173] and the "lump of flesh, a lump of flesh with two eyes" (*tlacamimil, tlacamimilli*).[174] Here, too, are the "bad" (*amo qualli*), "villanous" (*tlahueliloc*), "bad-impure-unclean-crooked" (*amo yectli*), and "stupid" (*xolopitli*) artisan, carpenter, featherworker, esteemed noble, person of noble lineage, wiseman, and soothsayer who Sahagún's informants characterize as individuals who "deceive," "confound," "beguile," "disturb," "damage," "waste," "form crooked objects," "create disorder," and "destroy things or people."[175] Sahagún's informants describe the speech of the "bad-impure-unclean esteemed lord" (*amo yectli tlazopilli*), for example, as "crooked, incoherent, disorganized, stupid."[176] They characterize the products of bad tailors, spinners, and weavers as "knotted," "tangled," "crooked," "uneven," "gouged," "loose," and "resembling a corn cob."[177] Lastly, in the middle range of the continuum between those two endpoints fall those things that are somewhat well-rooted, that somewhat present and disclose teotl, and that possess some ordering power.

Before proceeding, two points require making. First, those things that enjoy well-rootedness-cum-aletheia and that possess ordering, centering, and stabilizing power do *not* represent, signify, or symbolize teotl. Nor, for that matter, are they images, pictures, copies, substitutes, containers, or impersonators of teotl. Why not? Because such relationships suggest an intolerable ontological dualism of represented versus representation, symbolized versus symbol, original versus substitute, and signified versus signifier. If Aztec metaphysics embraces ontological monism, these distinctions cannot obtain. Teotl is ontologically identical with that which discloses teotl – as well as that which conceals teotl – since in the final analysis both are self-presentations of teotl. In the end, signified and signifier, symbolized and symbolic, and so on cannot be otherwise than identical. In short: teotl's medium of presentation and self-disclosure – like its medium of self-concealment – is itself.[178] The distinction between that which discloses teotl and that which conceals teotl is not an ontological distinction consisting of teotl's being identical with the former but not the latter. Rather, it is a distinction between *how* the energy of teotl is organized and arranged. The former is well-ordered and well-arranged; the latter is not.

Equally unacceptable is characterizing the relationship between teotl and that which discloses teotl in terms of such concepts as containment, embodiment, receptacle, and envelopment.[179] These concepts likewise suggest an ontological dualism of container versus contained, embodiment versus embodied, receptacle versus received, and envelope versus enveloped that is inconsistent with Aztec monism. They imply that teotl is *in* things but *not identical with* them. But for Aztec metaphysics, the distinction between that which discloses teotl and that which conceals teotl is not an ontological distinction between teotl's inhabiting, occupying, or being enveloped by the former but not the latter. Rather, it is a distinction between *how* the single uniform energy of teotl is organized and arranged.

Second, in the process of becoming increasingly well-ordered and well-rooted in teotl, a thing increasingly discloses and unconceals teotl more authentically and truly. How did the Aztecs understand this process? Exactly how do such disclosing and unconcealing happen? Let's return to the *Popol Vuh*'s metaphor of breath on the mirror. Under normal conditions humans perceive teotl as though looking into a befogged mirror. However, it now appears that there is an exception to this: namely, things that are well-ordered and well-rooted. These things – jade, quetzal plumes, and flower and song, for example – enable humans to perceive teotl more clearly, as though the breath on the mirror has dissipated. The *Popol Vuh*'s metaphor suggests the Aztecs conceived the process of, say, a work of art's gradually coming to disclose and unconceal teotl more truly and authentically in terms of the dissipating of the breath on the mirror that obscures our perception of teotl. Less metaphorically, the artist orders, centers, arranges, and balances her raw materials, transforming them from stuff-out-of-place into stuff-in-place, and hence from stuff that conceals teotl into stuff that discloses teotl.

As the good (*qualli*) goldworker, featherworker, and poet, for example, labor upon their work of art, the breath on the mirror surrounding the raw materials increasingly dissipates, and the work of art increasingly unconceals and discloses teotl. Sahagún's informants report, for example, that the "good artisan" (*qualli toltecatl*) "works with care . . . constructs [*tlatlalia*], prepares [*tlahimati*], arranges [*tlayocoya*], orders [*tlahuipani*], fits, matches."[180] In contrast, the "stupid or foolish" (*xolopitli*) artisan "is careless – a mocker, a petty thief. He acts without consideration; he deceives, he steals."[181] The bad feather worker is "a destroyer of good work . . . he harms, damages, wastes." The bad coppercaster lets the work "disintegrate." The bad lapidary "scrapes, roughens, shatters, pulverizes, ruins, damages" gemstones.[182] The bad scribe "paints askew" while the bad stone mason is a "crooked cutter, a crooked builder . . . a builder of curved leaning [walls]."[183] In short, the bad craftsperson pushes his/her raw materials (gems, feathers, etc.) toward the tlazolli end of the continuum. At the hands of the "stupid or foolish" artisan, teotl becomes more obscured by the breath on the mirror.

2.4. *IXIPTLA* AND *TEIXIPTLA*

Consistency requires that we understand the relationship between teotl, on the one hand, and those ritual objects, figures, and persons called an *ixiptla* or *teixiptla*, on the other hand, in terms of a nonhierarchical metaphysics and ontological and constitutional monism. The Aztecs, according to Arild Hvidtfeldt, used the terms *ixiptla* and *teixiptla* to refer to physical manifestations of deities ranging from humans dressed in special ritual attire, ritually dressed and painted wood or stone figures, and effigies made of amaranth dough to any arrangement of ritual attire mounted on a wooden frame and provided with a mask.[184] *Teixiptla* and *ixiptla* are commonly translated as "impersonator," "image," "substitute," "stand-in," and "representative."[185] Both combine *ix(tli)* ("face, surface") with *xip-* ("peeling, flaying"). López Austin concludes that an ixiptla served as a "container" or "envelope" of the divine.[186]

However, these standard ways of understanding the relationship between teotl and ixiptla seem to require a deity versus nondeity ontological dualism and/or a sacred versus profane constitutional dualism, and hence a hierarchical metaphysics.[187] I propose we understand the distinction between ixiptla and nonixiptla both nonhierarchically and nondualistically in terms of how teotl's single energy is ordered and arranged. An ixiptla consists of materials that are properly ordered so as to unconceal teotl or some aspect of teotl. The proper organization of the various elements composing an ixiptla along with the requisite accompanying ritual activities enable the assemblage to disclose specific clusters of teotl's aspects, such as those associated with Tlazolteotl or Xipe Totec, for example. The assemblage is thus able to serve as a medium through which ritual participants can focus upon and engage with specific aspects of teotl. What's more, the assemblage also becomes metaphysically (not just symbolically) potent itself since it becomes empowered with a concentration of the specific forces associated with and constituting the relevant cluster of teotl aspects. The assemblage ceases being an ixiptla and loses its potency upon disassembly. A nonixiptla is simply not properly arranged. That which becomes an ixiptla or teixiptla, in short, does so by virtue of becoming properly arranged and well-ordered as well as incorporated into relevant ritual activities. The Aztecs' ritual construction and use of an ixiptla and teixiptla appears cut from the same cloth as contemporary Nahuas', Otomís', and Tepehuas' ritual construction and use of cut-paper figures. In both cases, ritual specialists temporarily single out and abstract from the sacred whole various manageable segments for ritual attention. In both cases, there is no essential metaphysical distinction between ritual object and totality.[188]

The metaphysical relationship between teotl and teotl's ixiptla, therefore, is one of strict *identity*. Ixiptla and teotl are numerically one and the same. Teotl's medium of presentation is itself. There is neither ontological nor constitutional distinction between representation (signifier) and represented (signified). There is only teotl presenting itself. And teotl presents itself in a variety of ways, some of which disguise and conceal its nature, others of which disclose and unconceal its nature. A well-made teixiptla discloses and unconceals certain aspects teotl. It is well-rooted in teotl, enjoys well-rootedness-cum-aletheia, and therefore possesses power that is ordering, stabilizing, centering, and beneficial to humans. Yet remember that the relationship between teotl and that which is not an ixiptla is also one of identity.

2.5. ANIMISM

Since the cosmos and all its inhabitants are not only constituted by but also identical with teotl, it follows that all things are empowered and vivified by teotl's energy. If we think of animism as the thesis that all things are empowered and vivified, then Aztec metaphysics clearly embraces animism. Aztec animism appears to be underwritten by the following ideas. First, to exist (to be) is to be alive (or animated) in the sense of being energized, vitalized, or empowered.

Second, to exist and to be alive is to move, act, change, transform, affect, and be affected. Things change, move, and affect both themselves and other things by dint of their animating energy. Since all things possess power to make things happen, all things may be said to possess agency. The ongoing agency of all things contributes to the ongoing transformation of the cosmos.

From this it follows that everything – from rocks, mountains, earth, water, fire, wind, sun, buildings, works of art, weapons, tools, games, and musical instruments to insects, plants, incense, tobacco, pulque, animals, and humans – is literally animated, empowered, and vivified.[189] James Dow writes, "Uncontaminated animistic philosophy is relatively simple. All things move and act because their animating force gives them the power to do so."[190] Kay Read adds, "All Mesoamericans lived in a world in which everything was alive. All lived and moved because all were imbued with many kinds of powers."[191] To the foregoing list of items Guilhem Olivier, López Austin, Doris Heyden, and McKeever Furst add music and spoken words including song-poems, incantations, prayers, and names.[192] As we saw above, the energy of buildings, song-poems, and works of art can be well-balanced, well-ordered, and beneficial to humans or it can be disordered, ill-balanced, and harmful to humans. Furthermore, since all things are alive, adds Read, it follows that all things are born, mature, and eventually die. All things, in other words, have life cycles; all undergo change and transformation.[193]

From this it follows that what we in the West call "nature" is by Aztec lights thoroughly alive. Nature is neither dead matter nor lifeless machine. Indeed, Aztec animism is grounded in the immediate perception that all things are empowered. Aztec metaphysics does not start from a lifeless world and only later attribute animating energy to it. Reality is not divided into two essentially different kinds of stuff: animate versus inanimate, mind versus matter, or spirit versus body. Once again quoting Monaghan, "If the division between spirit and matter is axiomatic in Judeo-Christian thought, Nuyootecos begin in a different place, assuming that everything in existence is endowed with a life principle. . . . [A] single sacred force animates all of existence."[194] Furthermore, as Dow argues, there is no distinction between "symbolic and physical effects or between psychological and medicinal causality. All significant actions are the result of animating forces at work."[195] López Austin and Dow also contend the omnipresence of vivifying energy in the cosmos helps us understand shamanism. The shaman, according to Dow, is able to see and manipulate these forces, being "a specialist in manipulating the unseen, living animating forces."[196] According to López Austin, the shaman is able to communicate with the hidden nature of things using *nahuallatolli* ("the language of the occult").[197]

Arturo Gómez Martínez argues contemporary Nahuatl-speakers in the municipality of Chicontepec in the Huasteca region of Veracruz embrace a form of animism according to which "all existing things on earth and in the cosmos possess '*una fuerza*,' an energy, vigor or force, that provides them with life, but not a life like that of humans, but an eternal life that only comes to an end with the destruction of the universe."[198] According to Alan Sandstrom, Nahuatl-speakers in Amatlán likewise embrace animism. They believe all things have a *yolotl* ("life force") by virtue of partaking in the larger life force of the cosmos, and therefore all things may be said to be alive.[199] They cite as evidence of the vitality of mountains, lakes, and stars, for example, the fact they "impinge on human thoughts and actions."[200]

2.6. OBJECTIONS AND REPLIES

In what follows I consider several objections against interpreting Aztec metaphysics as an instance of pantheism.

Objection 1

León-Portilla opposes interpreting Aztec metaphysics as a form of pantheism on three grounds. Although he does so in the context of rejecting Hermann Beyer's attribution of pantheism to the Aztecs, his reasons are fully general. First, he argues that the concept is too vague to be useful in explicating Aztec thought.[201]

Levine's exhaustive survey of pantheism, however, reveals a remarkably high degree of consensus regarding the concept of pantheism.[202] Levine offers a definition of pantheism that captures this consensus, and it is this definition that I adopt here. León-Portilla's claim, therefore, simply does not ring true. I believe that by stating precisely one's definition of pantheism at the outset one may avoid the confusion about which he worries. Furthermore, the concept of pantheism does not appear any less vague than other etic concepts that theorists including León-Portilla employ such as religion, theology, truth, mysticism, skepticism, metaphysics, and philosophy. Moreover, the concept of pantheism seems less burdened by the sorts of derogatory connotations borne by such Enlightenment concepts as magic, divination, and sorcery.

León-Portilla's subsequent discussion interweaves two very different kinds of reasons: metaphysical and epistemological.[203] The fact that he evaluates the merits of pantheism in terms of Ometeotl rather than teotl does not matter for present purposes. I accordingly treat teotl and Ometeotl as interchangeable.

Some of the time León-Portilla argues that pantheism cannot be the correct interpretation of Aztec metaphysics because the Aztecs believed the cosmos to be ultimately unknowable by human beings and hence fundamentally mysterious. Ometeotl, he tells us, was commonly referred to by the paired-metaphoric difrasismo *Yohualli-ehécatl,* literally "night and wind" but meaning more broadly "he who is invisible (like the night) and intangible (like the wind)."[204] The "supreme principle," he writes, "is an invisible and impalpable reality. His transcendent nature goes beyond that world of experience so graphically conceived by the Nahuas as the visible and tangible."[205] Consequently human beings are guaranteed epistemological access and knowledge of Ometeotl neither in fact nor even in principle. Hence Ometeotl is transcendent: "*Yohualli-ehécatl* is, then, the title that most clearly implies the transcendent character of Ometéotl."[206] León-Portilla concludes, "In the face of the acknowledged transcendency of Ometeotl, pantheism would make little sense."[207]

Unfortunately, León-Portilla's argument is unsound. First, it seeks to draw a metaphysical conclusion about the ways things are from epistemological premises about what humans can know. But one is not logically entitled to infer such a metaphysical conclusion from epistemological premises. Doing so confounds what medieval European philosophers called the "order of being" (*ordo essendi*) and "the order of knowing" (*ordo cognoscendi*). Nothing follows about the nature of reality from facts about human cognitive abilities. Second, in drawing his conclusion, León-Portilla assumes without argument that epistemological transcendence logically entails metaphysical transcendence (or equivalently, that epistemological transcendence precludes metaphysical immanence). But this inference is invalid as well. His premise states that Ometeotl is what Western philosophers call "epistemologically transcendent," that is, that human beings are not guaranteed epistemological access and hence knowledge of Ometeotl. But this *epistemological* fact does not logically entail the *metaphysical* fact that Ometeotl must therefore be metaphysically transcendent. León-Portilla mistakenly believes that from the fact that Ometeotl is "invisible and intangible" it necessarily follows that Ometeotl cannot be metaphysically immanent (as required by pantheism). But there is no relationship of logical entailment between metaphysical immanence and epistemological immanence. Neither position logically entails the other. Hence from the fact that Ometeotl is metaphysically immanent it does not follow that humans must a fortiori have epistemological access to Ometeotl.

Levine argues pantheists are committed to the metaphysical immanence of the sacred but not necessarily to the epistemological immanence of the sacred (i.e., to the thesis that the sacred is easily or in principle knowable by humans).

Spinoza, for example, embraces pantheism yet explicitly rejects the epistemological immanence of the sacred. Similarly, for Lao Tzu the dao is metaphysically immanent yet mysterious and unknowable.[208]

I dispute neither León-Portilla's assertion that Ometeotl is correctly called *in Tloque in Nahuaque* nor his assertion that this difrasismo correctly means "He who has everything inside himself," "The one who is near to everything and to whom everything is near," and "Lord of the Close Vicinity."[209] Nor do I not dispute the appropriateness of Fray Alonso de Molina's remark that the name "applies to him who is the very being of all things, preserving them and sustaining them."[210] Lastly, I do not dispute León-Portilla's claim that these names suggest that Ometeotl is "multipresent" and "omnipresent."[211] What I do dispute, however, is León-Portilla's presumed logical connection between Ometeotl's "multipresence" and "omnipresence," on the one hand, and Ometeotl's necessary knowability, on the other. Humans may simply be unable to come to know or understand – via the senses, reason, or mystical awareness – that which is metaphysically speaking all about them and intimately within them.

Third, León-Portilla appears to oppose pantheistic interpretations of Aztec metaphysics on the grounds that Aztec metaphysics is ontologically dualistic whereas pantheism is ontologically monistic. He reasons that since Ometeotl is "invisible like the night and intangible like the wind," it follows necessarily that Ometeotl must be metaphysically distinct from (i.e., metaphysically transcendent of) that which is visible and tangible. He concludes, "In the face of the acknowledged transcendency of Ometeotl, pantheism would make little sense."[212] His argument runs as follows:

1. That which is perceptible is ontologically distinct from that which is imperceptible.
2. Ometeotl is imperceptible.
3. Therefore Ometeotl is ontologically distinct from the perceptible world.
4. Therefore Aztec metaphysics is committed to ontological dualism.
5. Pantheism is committed to ontological monism.
6. Therefore Aztec metaphysics cannot be pantheistic.

Unfortunately León-Portilla's argument is unsound. I simply see no reason to accept the first premise. The epistemological transcendence of Ometeotl does not entail Ometeotl's nonidentity with the epistemologically immanent. One and the same reality (process or entity) may possess both perceptible and imperceptible, and occult and nonoccult aspects.

The current interpretation is guilty of imposing a nonautochthonous, Judeo-Christian-style, Mediterranean monotheism upon Aztec thinking. Richard Haly, for one, contends the notion of Aztec monotheism is the post-Conquest invention of scholars such as Alfonso Caso and León-Portilla. Caso, according to Haly, misinterprets the Nahuatl appellation Tloque Nahuaque ("one who is near to everything and to whom everything is near") as a product of the Aztec elite's "philosophical zeal for unity."[213] León-Portilla, in turn, misconstrues Ometeotl as a transcendent, imperceptible supreme being and unifying cosmic principle.[214] Because both scholars are sympathetic to the Aztecs, Haly argues Caso and León-Portilla set out to make the Aztecs more palatable to their modern audience, which means making the Aztecs more like *us*. And what are *we* like? We are monotheists according to Haly. Caso and León-Portilla consequently characterize Aztec thought favorably so as "to imply an evolution [in Aztec thought] from polytheism to monotheism."[215] But Haly denies there exists such a deity as Ometeotl and that León-Portilla confuses the deity Omitecuhtli ("Bone Lord") as Ometecuhtli ("Two Lord").[216]

Is the present interpretation of Aztec metaphysics guilty of this error? If we accept Levine's conceptual mapping of these issues, then the present interpretation is monotheistic in the sense that it posits the existence of a single sacred force in the cosmos: teotl. However, as Levine argues, pantheism is a very strange kind of monotheism – "a non-theistic or non-personal type of monotheism" that embraces "a non-theistic conception of deity."[217] Pantheism rejects the idea that the sacred must be a personal or conscious being and as such represents a "de-anthropomorphised theism."[218]

Aztec metaphysics is therefore not theistic if one understands theism as entailing belief in the existence of a personal, conscious god. Indeed, the likes of Thomas Hobbes and Samuel Taylor Coleridge argued pantheism is a form of atheism for this very reason. The elders of the Sephardic synagogue in Spinoza's own Amsterdam excommunicated Spinoza for his "abominable heresies" and "monstrous deeds" that prominently included his pantheism.[219] Although my pantheistic interpretation may be construed as monotheistic in the sense that it speaks of the existence of a single sacred power or force, pantheism is a far cry from the brand of monotheism that dominates Judeo-Christian theology and thus the kind of monotheism that Haly believes Aztec sympathizers and contemporary Christians find palatable. In fact, pantheism has long been condemned by the Catholic Church as atheistic, false, and heretical. As Edward Pace writes in *The Catholic Encyclopedia*, "pantheism eliminates every characteristic that religion presupposes."[220] In short, it would appear there's nothing comforting about a pantheistic interpretation to traditionally minded Christians. The differences between the two views are not only legion but profound. If teotl can be likened to any nonautochthonous notion, it would be the Melanesian notion of mana, Taoist notion of dao, Chinese notion of qi, Jicarilla Apache notion of usen, Sioux notion of wakan orenda, and Mixtec notion of *yii*.

Objection 3

Jongsoo Lee takes a hard look at the arguments of chroniclers and historians such as Fernando de Alva Ixtlilxochitl, Juan Bautista Pomar, Fray Juan de Torquemada, Alfonso Caso, and Miguel León-Portilla who portray Nezahualcoyotl as a peace-loving, sacrifice-rejecting poet-philosopher-king who discovered the idea of a single, unknown god of gods, whom he worshipped in a special temple in Texcoco.[221] Lee argues Nezahualcoyotl's unknown god is the product of these chroniclers' and historians' attempt to "Westernize" Nahua religion. Although I find Lee's argument compelling, I do not think it applies to my interpretation of Aztec metaphysics. I claim neither that Nezahualcoyotl worshipped an unknown god of gods nor that teotl was that unknown god of gods.

Objection 4

Teotl does not appear in any descriptions or pictorial depictions of Aztec rituals and ceremonies offered by early chroniclers such as Sahagún, Durán, and Toribio de Benavente Motolinía. The Aztecs fashioned no images of teotl and addressed no specific rituals or ceremonies to it. Doesn't this gainsay pantheism as well as ontological and constitutional monism?

In many respects, teotl's absence resembles that of other "deities" comprising Nicholson's "Ometeotl complex": Ometeotl, Ometecuhtli and Omecihuatl, and Tonacatecuhtli and Tonacacihuatl. Eloise Quiñones Keber explains the absence of images of and rituals devoted to Tonacatecuhtli-Tonacacihuatl, for example, by the fact that Tonacatecuhtli-Tonacacihuatl was not a calendar god. References are confined to cosmological or cosmogonic texts.[222] Yet no one argues this gainsays Tonacatecuhtli-Tonacacihuatl's existence.

My response takes a page from Quiñones Keber. Like Tonacatecuhtli-Tonacacihuatl – along with Ometeotl and Ometecuhtli-Omecihuatl – teotl was not a calendar "god." Aztec rituals and ceremonies singled out and focused upon specific workable segments of teotl with specific practical purposes in mind such as releasing the forces of agricultural fertility, revitalizing the forces of human fertility and sustenance, cleansing and recirculating tlazolli, and renewing and revitalizing the Fifth Sun. I maintain that teotl unifies these into a coherent ritual cycle – rather than leaving them as an arbitrary sequence of disconnected activities. The sequence of rituals along with the specific rationale behind each ritual makes sense in terms of the cyclical unfolding of teotl. Scholars customarily understand the ritual cycle in terms of the two sacred calendars, the xiuhpohualli and tonalpohualli. Chapter 7 argues that the tonalpohualli and xiuhpohualli are properly understood as *modi operandi* of teotl.

2.7. CONCLUSION

Aztec metaphysics embraces pantheism and consequently is neither polytheistic nor panentheistic. It recognizes no distinction between sacred and profane since teotl is sacred and everything is identical with, constituted by, and vivified by teotl. Teotl is sacred because teotl is power.

NOTES

1. Michael Levine, *Pantheism: A Non-Theistic Concept of Deity* (London: Routledge, 1994).

2. Levine (*Pantheism*, 39). Aztec metaphysics falls in line with Levine's interpretation of the metaphysics of Lao Tzu, Spinoza, Plotinus, and Hegel. Pace Benjamin Keen (*The Aztec Image in Western Thought* [New Brunswick, NJ: Rutgers University Press, 1971]), it also falls in line with the metaphysical views of ancient Greek philosophers such as Parmenides.

3. See Levine, *Pantheism*, 195.

4. I borrow this distinction from Boyd and Williams's discussion of Shinto metaphysics (Richard Boyd and Ron Williams, "The Art of Ritual in Comparative Context," in *Zoroastrian Rituals in Context: Proceedings of the Conference at the Internationales Wissenschaftsforum*, University of Heidelberg, April 2002, ed. Michael Stausberg [Leiden: Brill, 2004], 140).

5. See Levine, *Pantheism*, 2; and Vine Deloria Jr., *God Is Red: A Native View of Religion* (Golden, CO: Fulcrum Publishing, 1994), 79, 95n1.

6. Quoted in Miguel León-Portilla, *Aztec Thought and Culture: A Study of the Ancient Nahuatl Mind*, trans. Jack Emory Davis (Norman: University of Oklahoma Press, 1963), 212. Alfonso Caso (Caso, *The Aztecs: People of the Sun*, trans. Lowell Dunham [Norman: University of Oklahoma Press, 1958], 7–8) advances a view that clearly looks more monotheistic than pantheistic. He locates three strains in Aztec thought: popular, priestly, and philosophical. He contrasts "the exaggerated polytheism" of the uneducated classes with

"the efforts of the Aztec priests to reduce the multitude divinities to different aspects of the same god." Aztec priests viewed the numerous deities of popular religion as "aspects" and "manifestations or attributions of one god." He also finds a genuinely philosophical strain: "a very ancient school of philosophy" that located the creative origin of all things – gods, cosmos, and humankind – in a single dual masculine-feminine principle called Tloque Nahuaque or Ipalnemohuani ("God of the immediate vicinity," "the one through whom all live"). These philosophers were motivated by the "philosophical desire for unity" and sought "a single cause to explain all other causes." However, they never appear to embrace pantheism. Caso alleges that Nezahualcoyotl, the most renowned of these philosophers, built a temple in Texcoco devoted to the invisible Tloque Nahuaque. Caso's Nezahualcoyotl remains a monotheist.

7. Burr Cartwright Brundage, *The Fifth Sun: Aztec Gods, Aztec World* (Austin: University of Texas Press, 1979), 51.

8. Ibid., 55–56.

9. Ibid., 55.

10. Richard F. Townsend, *State and Cosmos in the Art of Tenochtitlan* (Washington, DC: Dumbarton Oaks, 1979), 30–31; see also 28–29.

11. Eva Hunt, *The Transformation of the Hummingbird: Cultural Roots of a Zinacatecan Mythical Poem* (Ithaca, NY: Cornell University Press, 1977), 55–56; see also 148–149.

12. Ibid., 56.

13. Irene Nicholson, *Firefly in the Night: A Study of Ancient Mexican Poetry and Symbolism* (London: Faber and Faber, 1959), 63–64, emphasis mine.

14. Ibid., 60.

15. Ibid., 61.

16. Mercedes de la Garza, *El universo sagrado de la serpiente entre los mayas* (México, DF: Universidad Nacional Autónoma de México, 1984), 48, translation and emphasis mine.

17. Louise M. Burkhart, *The Slippery Earth: Nahua-Christian Dialogue in Sixteenth-Century Mexico* (Tucson: University of Arizona Press, 1989), 37.

18. Alan Sandstrom and Pamela Effrein Sandstrom, *Traditional Papermaking and Paper Cult Figures of Mexico* (Norman: University of Oklahoma Press, 1986), 275–77. See also Alan R. Sandstrom, "Sacred Mountains and Miniature Worlds: Altar Design among the Nahua of Northern Veracruz, Mexico," in *Mesas and Cosmologies in Mesoamerica*, ed. Douglas Sharon, San Diego Museum of Man Papers 42 (San Diego: San Diego Museum of Man, 2003), 56.

19. Sandstrom and Sandstrom, *Traditional Papermaking*, 277.

20. Alfredo López Austin, *The Human Body and Ideology: Concepts of the Ancient Nahuas*, trans. Thelma Ortiz de Montellano and Bernard R. Ortiz de Montellano (Salt Lake City: University of Utah Press, 1988).

21. Alan R. Sandstrom, *Corn Is Our Blood: Culture and Ethnic Identity in a Contemporary Aztec Indian Village* (Norman: University of Oklahoma Press, 1991), 238.

22. Ibid., 239.

23. Ibid., 238.

24. Alan R. Sandstrom, "Sacred Mountains and Miniature Worlds," 56.

25. Sandstrom, personal correspondence, August 20, 2011.

26. Alan R. Sandstrom, "The Cave-Pyramid Complex among the Contemporary Nahua of Northern Veracruz," in *In the Maw of the Earth Monster: Mesoamerican Ritual Cave Use*, ed. James E. Brady and Keith M. Prufer (Austin: University of Texas Press, 2005), 42–43.

27. Ibid., 42–43.

28. Ibid., 44.

29. Alfredo López Austin, *The Rabbit on the Face of the Moon: Mythology in the Mesoamerican Tradition*, trans. Bernard R. Ortiz de Montellano and Thelma Ortiz de Montellano (Salt Lake City: University of Utah Press, 1996); Alfredo López Austin, *Tamoanchan, Tlalocan: Places of Mist*, trans. Bernard R. Ortiz de Montellano and Thelma Ortiz de Montellano (Niwot: University Press of Colorado, 1997); Alfredo López Austin, "Cosmovision," trans. Scott Sessions, in *The Oxford Encyclopedia of Mesoamerican Cultures: The Civilizations of Mexico and Central America*, ed. Davíd Carrasco (Oxford: Oxford University Press, 2001), 1:268–74.

30. Sandstrom, "The Cave-Pyramid Complex," 43.

31. Miguel León-Portilla, *Time and Reality in the Thought of the Maya*, 2nd enlarged ed., trans. Charles Boiles, Fernanado Horcasitas, and Miguel León-Portilla (Norman: University of Oklahoma Press, 1988), 55.

32. Nancy M. Farriss, *Maya Society under Colonial Rule: The Collective Enterprise of Survival* (Princeton, NJ: Princeton University Press, 1984), 301.

33. John D. Monaghan, "Theology and History in the Study of Mesoamerican Religions," in *Supplement to the Handbook of Middle American Indians*, vol. 6, ed. John D. Monaghan (Austin: University of Texas Press, 2000), 27.

34. John D. Monaghan, "The Person, Destiny, and the Construction of Difference in Mesoamerica," *RES* 33 (Spring 1998): 141.

35. See, for example, Fray Diego Durán, *Book of the Gods and Rites* and *The Ancient Calendar*, trans. and ed. Fernando Horcasitas and Doris Heyden (Norman: University of Oklahoma Press, 1971); Bernardino de Sahagún, *Florentine Codex: General History of the Things of New Spain*, ed. Arthur J. O. Anderson and Charles Dibble, 12 vols. (Santa Fe, NM: School of American Research; Salt Lake City: University of Utah, 1953–1982); George Clapp Vaillant, *Aztecs of Mexico*, ed. Suzannah B. Vaillant (New York: Penguin Books, 1944); Jacques Soustelle, *Daily Life of the Aztecs on the Eve of the Spanish Conquest*, trans. Patrick O'Brien (Stanford, CA: Stanford University Press, 1970).

36. *Plato: The Collected Dialogues Including the Letters,* ed. Edith Hamilton and Huntington Cairns (Princeton, NJ: Princeton University Press, 1961), 265d–266a.

37. Inga Clendinnen writes, "[T]he Mexica . . . thought . . . in terms of sacred forces, with associated qualities and ranges of manifestations, moving in constant complex interaction: more clusters of possibilities invoked by a range of names than specific deities with specific zones of influence" (Clendinnen, *Aztecs: An Interpretation* [Cambridge: Cambridge University Press, 1991], 248). Although he does not share my views about teotl and pantheism, López Austin makes many of the same points about the "gods" in terms of their "essences" (López Austin, *Tamoanchan, Tlalocan,* 22–26).

38. Eva Hunt, *Transformation of the Hummingbird,* 55.

39. See Townsend, *State and Cosmos in the Art of Tenochtitlan*; Henry B. Nicholson, "Religion in Pre-Hispanic Central Mexico," in *Handbook of Middle American Indians,* vol. 10, ed. Robert Wauchope, Gordon F. Elkholm, and Ignacio Bernal (Austin: University of Texas Press, 1971); and Elizabeth Hill Boone, *Stories in Red and Black: Pictorial Histories of the Aztecs and Mixtecs* (Austin: University of Texas Press, 2000).

40. See Bernard R. Ortiz de Montellano, *Aztec Medicine, Health, and Nutrition* (New Brunswick, NJ: Rutgers University Press, 1990), 59; and López Austin, *Human Body and Ideology,* 1:355–356.

41. Ortiz de Montellano, *Aztec Medicine, Health, and Nutrition,* 59.

42. Nicholson, "Religion," 408.

43. Ibid., 410, 414, 424.

44. Given Ometeotl's "sexual dualism," one wonders why Nicholson characterizes this complex as "paternal."

45. Nicholson, "Religion," 410–12.

46. Ibid., 415–22.

47. Ibid., 424.

48. J. Richard Andrews and Ross Hassig, trans. and eds, *Treatise on the Heathen Superstitions That Today Live among the Indians Native to This New Spain,* by Hernando Ruiz de Alarcón (Norman: University of Oklahoma Press, 1984), 240.

49. Ibid., 11. See also López Austin, *Tamoanchan, Tlalocan*; and Hunt, *Transformation of the Hummingbird.*

50. López Austin, *Rabbit on the Face of the Moon*; López Austin, *Tamoanchan, Tlalocan.*

51. López Austin, *Tamoanchan, Tlalocan,* 213.

52. See Levine, *Pantheism,* 179–96; Stuart Hampshire, *Spinoza* (Harmondsworth, UK: Penguin Books, 1951), 40–45; Derek Pereboom, "Early Modern Philosophical Theology," in *A Companion to Philosophy of Religion,* ed. Philip L. Quinn and Charles Taliaferro (Oxford: Blackwell, 1997), 105.

53. Ku-ying Ch'en, *Lao Tzu: Text, Notes, and Comments,* trans. Rhett Y.W. Young and Roger T. Ames (San Francisco: Chinese Materials Center, 1977), 45, 142–46, 177–79.

54. Levine, *Pantheism*, 179.

55. Levine, *Pantheism*, 113–17.

56. Peter Forrest, "Pantheism and Science," *The Monist* 80, no. 2 (1997): 308.

57. A. P. Martinich, "Pantheism," in *The Cambridge Dictionary of Philosophy*, ed. Robert Audi (Oxford: Cambridge University Press, 1995), 556.

58. Quoted in Levine, *Pantheism*, 11.

59. Genevieve Lloyd, *Spinoza and the Ethics* (London: Routledge, 1996), 40.

60. Monaghan, "Theology and History in the Study of Mesoamerican Religions," 27.

61. Robert C. Solomon, *The Big Questions: A Short Introduction to Philosophy*, 5th ed. (New York: Harcourt Brace College Publishers, 1998), 78–80; see also Levine, *Pantheism*, 40–72.

62. Louise M. Burkhart, "The Amanuenses Have Appropriated the Text: Interpreting a Nahuatl Song of Santiago," in *On the Translation of Native American Literatures*, ed. Brian Swann (Washington, DC: Smithsonian Institute Press, 1992), 345.

63. Serge Gruzinski, *Man-Gods in the Mexican Highlands: Indian Power and Colonial Society, 1520–1800*, trans. Eileen Corrigan (Stanford, CA: Stanford University Press, 1989), 19. See also John D. Monaghan, *The Covenants with Earth and Rain: Exchange, Sacrifice and Revelation in Mixtec Sociality* (Norman: University of Oklahoma Press, 1995), chapter 4; Barbara Tedlock, *The Woman in the Shaman's Body: Reclaiming the Feminine in Religion and Medicine* (New York: Bantam Books, 2005); Brundage, *The Fifth Sun*; and Barbara Deloria, Kristen Foehner, and Sam Scinta, eds., *Spirit and Reason: The Vine Deloria Jr. Reader* (Golden, CO: Fulcrum Publishers, 1999), 356.

64. Paula Gunn Allen, *The Sacred Hoop: Recovering the Feminine in American Indian Traditions* (Boston: Beacon Press, 1986), 72.

65. Peggy V. Beck, Anna Lee Walters, and Nia Francisco, *The Sacred: Ways of Knowledge, Sources of Life*, redesigned ed. (Tsaile, AZ: Navajo Community College Press, 1992), 10.

66. Jace Weaver, "Introduction: Notes from a Miner's Canary," in *Defending Mother Earth: Native American Perspectives on Environmental Justice*, ed. Jace Weaver (Maryknoll, NY: Orbis Books, 1996), 11. See also B. Deloria et al., *Spirit and Reason*, 356–57; George Tinker, "Religion," in *Encyclopedia of North American Indians*, ed. Frederick E. Hoxie (Boston: Houghton Mifflin, 1996), 54; and Mercedes de la Garza, "The Harmony between People and Animals in the Aztec World," in *The Aztec Empire*, ed. Felipe Solís (New York: Solomon Guggenheim Foundation, 2004), 70–75.

67. B. Deloria et al., *Spirit and Reason*, 356. See also Levine, *Pantheism*.

68. Sahagún, *Florentine Codex*, XI:247.

69. Alonso de Molina, *Vocabulario en lengua castellana y mexicana y mexicana y castellana*, 4th ed. (Mexico City: Porrúa, [1571] 2001), 2:54v. See also Frances Karttunen,

An Analytical Dictionary of Nahuatl (Norman: University of Oklahoma Press, 1983), 132–33.

70. Molina, *Vocabulario*, 2:126r.

71. Karttunen, *Analytical Dictionary*, 222.

72. Bernardino de Sahagún, *Colloquios y doctrina christiana con los doce de San Francisco*, 946–60, trans. Jorge Klor de Alva ("The Aztec-Spanish Dialogue of 1524," *Alcheringa/ Ethnopoetics* 4 [1980]: 121–22); William Bright ("'With One Lip, with Two Lips': Parallelism in Nahuatl," *Language* 66, no. 3 [1990], 437–52); and the author. See also Sahagún, *Florentine Codex*, III:69.

73. Klor de Alva, ed. and trans., "Aztec-Spanish Dialogue of 1524," 121; Bright, "'With One Lip, with Two Lips,'" 447.

74. Karttunen, *Analytical Dictionary*, 304.

75. Ibid., 337.

76. Ibid., 132–33.

77. Ibid.

78. Quoted in R. Joe Campbell, *A Morphological Dictionary of Classical Nahuatl: A Morpheme Index to the* Vocabulario en lengua mexicana y castellana *of Fray Alonso de Molina* (Madison, WI: Hispanic Seminary of Medieval Studies, 1985), 181–83.

79. Sahagún, *Florentine Codex*, II:69.

80. Sahagún, *Colloquios y doctrina christiana*, 964–71, translated by Bright, "'With One Lip, with Two Lips,'" 447. For further discussion of the *Colloquois* see Miguel León-Portilla, *Bernardino de Sahagún: First Anthropologist*, trans. Mauricio J. Mixco (Norman: University of Oklahoma Press, 2002).

81. Fray Diego Durán, *Historia de las Indias de Nueva España e islas de tierra firme*, 2nd ed., ed. Angél María Garibay K. (México, DF: Editorial Porrúa, 1984), 2:48.

82. León-Portilla, *Aztec Thought and Culture*.

83. Peter T. Furst, Doris Heyden, and Kay A. Read also propound this view. See Furst, "Shamanistic Survivals in Mesoamerican Religion," *Actas del XLI Congreso Internacional de Americanistas*, vol. 3 (Mexico: Instituto Nacional de Antropología e Historia, 1976); Heyden, "Sand in Ritual and History," in *Representing Aztec Ritual: Performance, Text, and Image in the Work of Sahagún*, ed. Eloise Quiñones Keber (Boulder: University Press of Colorado, 2002); Read, *Time and Sacrifice in the Aztec Cosmos* (Bloomington: Indiana University Press, 1998), 32–43. I arrived at this view independently by teasing out the logical consequences of Aztec metaphysics' ontological and constitutional monism and nonhierarchical metaphysics.

84. Andrea Smith, "Walking in Balance: The Spiritual-Liberation Praxis of Native Women," in *Native American Religious Identity: Unforgotten Gods*, ed. Jace Weaver (Maryknoll, NY: Orbis Books, 1998), 178. See also Jace Weaver, "Preface," in *Native*

American Religious Identity: Unforgotten Gods, ed. Jace Weaver (Maryknoll, NY: Orbis Books, 1988), ix–x.

85. Barbara G. Myerhoff, *Peyote Hunt: The Sacred Journey of the Huichol Indians* (Ithaca, NY: Cornell University Press, 1974), 74.

86. Mircea Eliade quoted in Brian Morris, *Anthropological Studies of Religion: An Introductory Text* (Cambridge: Cambridge University Press, 1987), 178; see also Davíd Carrasco, *Quetzalcoatl and the Irony of Empire: Myths and Prophecies in the Aztec Tradition* (Chicago: University of Chicago Press, 1982); Davíd Carrasco, *Religions of Mesoamerica: Cosmovision and Ceremonial Centers* (San Francisco: Harper and Row, 1990); and Davíd Carrasco, "The Sacrifice of Tezcatlipoca: To Change Place," in *To Change Place: Aztec Ceremonial Landscapes*, ed. Davíd Carrasco (Niwot: University Press of Colorado, 1991). Read (*Time and Sacrifice*, 29–43) likewise argues that Aztec religion rejects the sacred-versus-profane dichotomy.

87. Quoted in Morris, *Anthropological Studies of Religion*, 115. See also John Bowker, ed., *The Oxford Dictionary of World Religions* (Oxford: Oxford University Press, 1997), 832.

88. Roy A. Rappaport, *Ritual and Religion in the Making of Humanity* (Cambridge: Cambridge University Press, 1999), 281, emphasis mine.

89. Ibid., 277.

90. Ibid., 281.

91. Angus Graham, *Disputers of the Tao: Philosophical Argument in Ancient China* (LaSalle, IL: Open Court, 1989); David L. Hall, "Just How Provincial *Is* Western Philosophy? 'Truth' in Comparative Context," *Social Epistemology* 15, no. 4 (2001): 285–97; David L. Hall and Roger T. Ames, *Thinking through Confucius* (Albany: State University of New York Press, 1987); David L. Hall and Roger T. Ames, *Thinking from the Han: Self, Truth and Transcendence in Chinese and Western Culture* (Albany: SUNY Press, 1998). See also Talal Asad, *Genealogies of Religion: Discipline and Reasons of Power in Christianity and Islam* (Baltimore: Johns Hopkins University Press, 1993). I defend these differences in James Maffie, "*In Huehue Tlamanitiliztli* and *la Verdad*: Nahua and European Philosophies in Fray Bernardino de Sahagún's *Colloquios y doctrina cristiana*" (*Inter-American Journal of Philosophy* 3 [2012]: 1–33).

92. For supporting discussion, see W.V.O. Quine, *From a Logical Point of View*, 2nd rev. ed. (New York: Harper & Row, 1961); Philip Kitcher, *Abusing Science: The Case against Scientific Creationism* (Cambridge, MA: MIT Press, 1982); and W. H. Newton-Smith, ed., *A Companion to the Philosophy of Science* (Oxford: Blackwell, 2000).

93. For further discussion, see Molina, *Vocabulario*, 2:118v; Karttunen, *Analytical Dictionary*, 271, 348; Thelma D. Sullivan, "Tlazolteotl-Ixcuina: The Great Spinner and Weaver," in *The Art and Iconography of Late Post-Classic Central Mexico*, ed. Elizabeth Hill Boone (Washington, DC: Dumbarton Oaks, 1982), 7; Burkhart, *Slippery Earth*, 88;

and Cecelia Klein, "*Teocuitlatl*, 'Divine Excrement': The Significance of 'Holy Shit' in Ancient Mexico," *Art Journal* (1993). Following scholarly convention, I use *tlazolli* rather than *tlahzolli*.

94. See Burkhart, *Slippery Earth*, 88. Molina defines the kindred concept of *itlacauhtica* as "for something to be out of place or badly put (*estar malpuesta*)" (Molina, *Vocabulario*, 2:37r).

95. Burkhart, *Slippery Earth*, 91–92; see also Nicholson "Religion"; and Guilhem Olivier, *Mockeries and Metamorphoses of an Aztec God: Tezcatlipoca, "Lord of the Smoking Mirror,"* trans. Michel Besson (Niwot: University Press of Colorado, 2003). I confine my discussion to Tlazolteotl.

96. Sullivan, "Tlazolteotl-Ixcuina," 15.

97. Ibid.

98. Philip P. Arnold and Kay A. Read also make this observation. See Arnold, *Eating Landscape: Aztec and European Occupation of Tlalocan* (Niwot: University Press of Colorado, 1999); Read, *Time and Sacrifice*.

99. Frances F. Berdan, *The Aztecs* (New York: Chelsea House Publications, 1989), 82.

100. See Klein, "*Teocuitlatl*"; Ortiz de Montellano, *Aztec Medicine, Health, and Nutrition*.

101. See Burkhart, *Slippery Earth*, 93.

102. Sahagún, *Florentine Codex*, XI:233.

103. See Sahagún, *Florentine Codex*, XI:234; and Klein, "*Teocuitlatl*," 25–26.

104. Louise M. Burkhart, "Mexica Women on the Home Front: Housework and Religion in Aztec Mexico," in *Indian Women of Early Mexico*, ed. Susan Schroeder, Stephanie Wood, and Robert Haskett (Norman: University of Oklahoma Press, 1997), 35.

105. Burkhart, *Slippery Earth*, 89–90. See also Klein, "*Teocuitlatl*."

106. Myerhoff, *Peyote Hunt*, 73–74 and note 2. See also B. Deloria et al., *Spirit and Reason*, 357; Cordova, "European Concept of Usen"; and Beck, Walters, and Francisco, *The Sacred*.

107. Read, *Time and Sacrifice*, 144–45, 249.

108. Campbell, *Morphological Dictionary*, 397, 172. See also Karttunen, *Analytical Dictionary*, 136.

109. Mircea Eliade, *The Myth of the Eternal Return, or Cosmos and History* (Princeton, NJ: Princeton University Press, 1954); Mircea Eliade, *Patterns of Comparative Religion*, trans. Rosemary Sheed (Lincoln: University of Nebraska Press, 1996); Carrasco, *Quetzalcoatl and the Irony of Empire*; Carrasco, "Myth, Cosmic Terror, and the Templo Mayor," in *The Great Temple of Tenochtitlan: Center and Periphery in the Aztec World*, ed. Johanna Broda, Davíd Carrasco, and Eduardo Matos Moctezuma (Berkeley: University of California Press, 1987); Carrasco, *City of Sacrifice: The Aztec Empire and the Role of*

Violence in Civilization (Boston: Beacon Press, 1999); and Eduardo Matos Moctezuma, *Life and Death in the Templo Mayor*, trans. Bernard R. Ortiz de Montellano and Thelma Ortiz de Montellano (Niwot: University Press of Colorado, 1995). For related discussion, see Read, *Time and Sacrifice in the Aztec Cosmos*, 33–35.

110. Carrasco, *Quetzalcoatl and the Irony of Empire*, 5; Matos Moctezuma, *Life and Death in the Templo Mayor*; and Leonardo López Luján, *The Offerings of the Templo Mayor of Tenochtitlan*, rev. ed., trans. Thelma Ortiz de Montellano and Bernard Ortiz de Montellano (Albuquerque: University of New Mexico Press, 2005).

111. Carrasco, *Quetzalcoatl and the Irony of Empire*, 79.

112. Ninian Smart, "Myth and Transcendence," *The Monist* 50, no. 4 (1966). See also Levine, *Pantheism*, 105–11.

113. Miguel León-Portilla, *La filosofía náhuatl: Estudiada en sus fuentes con un nuevo apéndice*, new ed., prologue by Angel María Garibay K. (México, DF: Universidad Nacional Autónoma de México, 2001 [1956]), 61, translation mine.

114. Willard Gingerich, "Heidegger and the Aztecs: The Poetics of Knowing in Pre-Hispanic Nahuatl Poetry," in *Recovering the Word: Essays on Native American Literature*, ed. Brian Swann and Arnold Krupat (Berkeley: University of California Press, 1987), 102–3.

115. Gingerich, "Heidegger and the Aztecs," 104.

116. Ibid., 102.

117. Ibid., 105.

118. Ibid.

119. For supporting argument, see James Maffie, "Why Care about Nezahualcoyotl? Veritism and Nahua Philosophy," *Philosophy of the Social Sciences* 32 (2002); Maffie, "*In Huehue Tlamanitiliztli*" (2012); and Gordon Brotherston, "Native Numeracy in Tropical America," *Social Epistemology* 15, no. 4 (2001). Eliot Deutsch advances a full-fledged ontological theory of truth in Deutsch, *On Truth: An Ontological Theory* (Honolulu: University of Hawaii Press, 1979).

120. See Carrasco, *Quetzalcoatl and the Irony of Empire*; Carrasco, "Myth, Cosmic Terror, and the Templo Mayor"; Carrasco, *City of Sacrifice*; and Matos Moctezuma, *Life and Death*.

121. The Maya verb *tz'akah* means both "to bring into existence" and "to put in order" (David Freidel, Linda Schele, and Joy Parker, *Maya Cosmos: Three Thousand Years on the Shaman's Path* [New York: William Morrow, 1993], 68). Freidel, Schele, and Parker point out that Alfredo Barrera Vásquez glosses the Yucatec verb *tz'akah* as *hacer existente* ("to make or create existing or being"). It is also glossed as "grade, step, degrees of relatedness, and knots (as on a string)" and "measure of a milpa." Charles Wisdom glosses the Chorti verb *tz'akse* as "to regulate arrange or adjust, put in order." The verb connotes both "to put in order" and "to bring into existence" (Freidel, Schele, and Parker, *Maya Cosmos*, 416–17n11).

122. López Austin, *Human Body and Ideology*, I:347.

123. See Matos Moctezuma, *Life and Death*, 61–65; Heyden, "Sand in Ritual and History"; Davíd Carrasco, "Introduction," in *The Great Temple of Tenochtitlan: Center and Periphery in the Aztec World*, ed. Johanna Broda, Davíd Carrasco, and Eduardo Matos Moctezuma (Berkeley: University of California Press, 1987), 1–14; Carrasco, "Myth, Cosmic Terror, and the Templo Mayor"; López Luján, *Offerings*; Johanna Broda, "Templo Mayor as Ritual Space," in *The Great Temple of Tenochtitlan: Center and Periphery in the Aztec World*, ed. Johanna Broda, Davíd Carrasco, and Eduardo Matos Moctezuma (Berkeley: University of California Press, 1987), 61–123; and Richard F. Townsend, "Pyramid and Sacred Mountain," in *Ethnoastronomy and Archaeoastronomy in the American Tropics*, ed. Anthony Aveni and Gary Urton, Annals of the New York Academy of Sciences, no. 38 (New York: New York Academy of Sciences, 1982), 371–410.

124. James Lockhart, *The Nahuas after the Conquest: A Social and Cultural History of the Indians of Central Mexico, Sixteenth through Eighteenth Centuries* (Stanford, CA: Stanford University Press, 1992), 151, fig. 10.1, emphasis mine. See also Rudolph van Zantwijk, *The Aztec Arrangement: The Social History of Pre-Spanish Mexico* (Norman: University of Oklahoma Press, 1985).

125. Lockhart, *Nahuas after the Conquest*, 15.

126. Ibid., 440, emphasis mine.

127. See Lockhart, *Nahuas after the Conquest*, 14–28, 436–38, 440–42; Michael E. Smith, *Aztec City-State Capitals* (Gainesville: University Press of Florida 2008), 89–93, 158, 175–76; and Zantwijk, *Aztec Arrangement*.

128. See Lockhart, *Nahuas after the Conquest*, 59–72, 436–37, 440; and Smith, *Aztec City-State Capitals*, 163–70. See also the description of the good farmer in Sahagún, *Florentine Codex*, X:41. The same motivates contemporary Mesoamericans according to Rossana Lok, "The House as a Microcosm," in *The Leiden Tradition in Structural Anthropology: Essays in Honor of P. E. de Josselin de Jong*, ed. R. De Ridder and J.A.J. Karremans (Leiden: Brill, 1987); Sandstrom, *Corn Is Our Blood*; Sandstrom, "Sacred Mountains and Miniature Worlds"; López Austin, *Rabbit on the Face of the Moon*; and Barbara Tedlock and Dennis Tedlock, "Text and Textile: Language and Technology in the Arts of the Quiché Maya," *Journal of Anthropological Research* 41, no. 2 (1985): 121–46.

129. Lockhart, *Nahuas after the Conquest*, 436.

130. See ibid., 437. See also James Maffie, "To Walk in Balance: An Encounter between Contemporary Western Science and Pre-Conquest Nahua Philosophy," in *Science and Other Cultures: Philosophy of Science and Technology Issues*, ed. Robert Figueroa and Sandra Harding (New York: Routledge, 2003), 70–91; and Maffie, "*In Huehue Tlamanitiliztli*."

131. Sahagún, *Colloquios*, 794–97, translation mine.

132. Karttunen, *Analytical Dictionary*, 217; see also Lockhart, *The Nahuas after the Conquest*, 398.

133. Quoted in Campbell, *Morphological Dictionary*, 303.

134. Lockhart, *Nahuas after the Conquest*, 437, fig. 10.1.

135. Ibid., 398.

136. Sahagún, *Colloquios*, 769–97.

137. See Sandstrom, *Corn Is Our Blood*; Sandstrom, "Sacred Mountains and Miniature Worlds"; Sandstrom, "The Cave-Pyramid Complex"; Read, *Time and Sacrifice*; Arnold, *Eating Landscape*; and Maffie, "*In Huehue Tlamanitiliztli.*"

138. Alfredo López Austin, *Cuerpo humano e ideología: Las concepciones de los antiguos Nahuas*, 2 vols., 2nd ed. (México, DF: Universidad Autónoma de México, 1984), 2:65; López Austin, *Human Body and Ideology*, 1:58–59. See also Wayne Elzey, "Some Remarks on the Space and Time of the 'Center' in Aztec Religion," *Estudios de cultura náhuatl* 12 (1976): 315–34; and León-Portilla, *Aztec Thought and Culture*, 32.

139. Mary Miller and Karl Taube, *An Illustrated Dictionary of the Gods and Symbols of Ancient Mexico and the Maya* (London: Thames and Hudson, 1993), 101–3. See also Joyce Marcus, Kent V. Flannery, and Ronald Spores, "The Cultural Legacy of the Oaxacan Preceramic," in *The Cloud People: Divergent Evolution of the Zapotec and Mixtec Civilizations*, ed. Kent Flannery and Joyce Marcus (New York: Academic Press, 1983), 36–39; Hunt, *Transformation of the Hummingbird*, 77; and Karl Taube, "The Turquoise Hearth: Fire, Self Sacrifice, and the Central Mexican Cult of War," in *Mesoamerica's Classic Heritage*, ed. Davíd Carrasco, Lindsay Jones, and Scott Sessions (Niwot: University Press of Colorado, 2000), 269–340; and Karl Taube, "Maize: Iconography and Cosmological Significance," in *The Oxford Encyclopedia of Mesoamerican Cultures: The Civilizations of Mexico and Central America*, ed. Davíd Carrasco (Oxford: Oxford University Press, 2001), 2:150–52.

140. Sahagún, *Florentine Codex*, I:84.

141. Sahagún, *Florentine Codex*, VI:88–89.

142. *Codex Borbonicus* (Loubat: Bibliothéque du Palais Bourbon, 1899), plate 34.

143. Sahagún, *Florentine Codex*, VI:113–14, 248; XI:223–24; see also XI:222–23 where Sahagún discusses two other greenstones, *quetzalitzltli* and *quetzalchalchiuitl*.

144. Sahagún, *Florentine Codex*, XI:224.

145. Ibid., XI:223–24; see also Karttunen, *Analytical Dictionary*, 306; and Campbell, *Morphological Dictionary*, 359–60.

146. See Karttunen, *Analytical Dictionary*, 132; and Campbell, *Morphological Dictionary*, 181–83.

147. Jill Leslie McKeever Furst, *The Natural History of the Soul in Ancient Mexico* (New Haven, CT: Yale University Press, 1995), 71–73.

148. Miller and Taube, *Illustrated Dictionary*, 101–2; see also Read, *Time and Sacrifice*; and Taube, "The Turquoise Hearth."

149. Ortiz de Montellano, *Aztec Medicine, Health, and Nutrition*, 176–77; see also Miller and Taube, *Illustrated Dictionary*, 102.

150. Taube, "Maize," 150; see also Sahagún, *Florentine Codex*, VI:241.

151. León-Portilla, *Aztec Thought and Culture*, 172 and 181–82, respectively.

152. Sahagún, *Florentine Codex*, X:69, see also VI: 92. León-Portilla (*Aztec Thought and Culture*, 143) translates *teotl yiollo* as "he had God in his heart," while Dibble and Anderson translate it as "godly of heart."

153. Quoted in León-Portilla, *Aztec Thought and Culture*, 172, 180–81, brackets mine; see Sahagún, *Florentine Codex*, X:28.

154. Sahagún, *Florentine Codex*, II:69. I believe this analysis also applies to López Austin's (*Human Body and Ideology*) and Gruzinski's (*Man-Gods*) "*hombre-dios*" and "*mujer-diosa*."

155. Sahagún, *Florentine Codex*, X:16, brackets mine.

156. See, for example, John Bierhorst, *Cantares Mexicanos: Songs of the Aztecs* (Stanford, CA: Stanford University Press, 1985), fols. 9v, 15, 18v, 22, 23, 28; and Matos Moctezuma, *Life and Death*, 107.

157. Sahagún, *Florentine Codex*, X:25–30, 35–36.

158. Frances Karttunen and James Lockhart, "La estructura de la poesía náhuatl vista por sus variantes," *Estudios de cultura náhuatl* 14 (1980): 15–64. See also Lockhart, *Nahuas after the Conquest*, 15, 394–97, 440; and William Bright, "'With One Lip, with Two Lips,' 437–52.

159. Lockhart, *Nahuas after the Conquest*, 398. Writing-painting likewise involves ordering and spreading out things on a horizontal surface. See Boone, *Stories in Red and Black*.

160. See Karttunen, *Analytical Dictionary*, 217; and Lockhart, *Nahuas after the Conquest*, 398.

161. See Lockhart, *Nahuas after the Conquest*, 398; and Karttunen, *Analytical Dictionary*, 275.

162. Bierhorst, *Cantares mexicanos*, fol. 67r.; Kartunnen, *Analytical Dictionary*, 135.

163. Sahagún, *Florentine Codex*, VI:248; Thelma Sullivan, *A Scattering of Jades: Stories, Poems and Prayers of the Aztecs*, ed. Timothy Knab (New York: Simon and Schuster, 1994), 211.

164. Sahagún, *Florentine Codex*, VI:248; Sullivan, *A Scattering of Jades*, 212.

165. See Carrasco, "Introduction"; Carrasco, "Myth, Cosmic Terror, and the Templo Mayor"; Matos Moctezuma, *Life and Death*; and Broda, "Templo Mayor as Ritual Space."

166. See Broda, "Templo Mayor as Ritual Space"; Matos Moctezuma, *Life and Death*, 61–65; López Luján, *Offerings*; Carrasco "Introduction"; Carrasco, "Myth, Cosmic Terror, and the Templo Mayor"; and Heyden, "Sand in Ritual and History."

167. Carrasco, "Introduction," 5.

168. I adapt this idea from James E. Brady, "In My Hill, in My Mountain: The Importance of Place in Ancient Maya Ritual," in *Mesas and Cosmologies in Mesoamerica*,

ed. Douglas Sharon, San Diego Museum of Man Papers 42 (San Diego: San Diego Museum of Man, 2003), 87.

169. See Sandstrom, "Sacred Mountains and Miniature Worlds," 58; and Félix Báez-Jorge and Arturo Gómez Martínez, "Los equilibrios del cielo y de la tierra: Cosmovisión de los nahuas de Chicontepec," *Desacatos*, Invierno 5 (2000). Altars are commonly referred to as *mesas* by contemporary indigenous peoples in Mexico. See the articles in Sharon, ed., *Mesas and Cosmologies in Mesoamerica*, for discussion.

170. See Matos Moctezuma, *Life and Death*, 60; Broda, "Templo Mayor as Ritual Space"; Carrasco, "Introduction"; Carrasco, "Myth, Cosmic Terror, and the Templo Mayor."

171. Burkhart, *Slippery Earth*, 90–91.

172. Sahagún, *Florentine Codex*, VI:37.

173. Ibid.

174. Ibid., X:11, see also 3.

175. Ibid., X:17, 19, 22, 24, 30, 31; see also Karttunen, *Analytical Dictionary*.

176. Sahagún, *Florentine Codex*, X:17.

177. Ibid., X:35–36.

178. Clendinnen (*Aztecs*, 253), David Stuart ("Kings of Stone: A Consideration of Stelae in Ancient Maya Ritual and Representation," *RES* 29/30 [Spring/Autumn 1996], 147–71), and Monaghan ("Theology and History in the Study of Mesoamerican Religions," 26) advance similar accounts. Gruzinski (*Man-Gods*, 22, 149) proposes a deceptively similar view when observing that well into the eighteenth century the Nahuas' view "circumvented the dichotomy of the signifier and the signified [since] symbol and symbolized were inextricably confused [and since] the sign combined with its reference, the image merged with the god." However, Gruzinski's understanding of the *hombre-dios* presupposes an ontological dualism since he believes this identity between image and god is *exceptional*. This contrasts with all other times during which image and god are metaphysically distinct. Mircea Eliade states that in such circumstances "one becomes what one displays," yet his view is also dualistic and hierarchical (Eliade, *Shamanism*, 179).

179. See, for example, David Carrasco, "The Sacrifice of Women in the *Florentine Codex*: The Hearts of Plants and the Players in War Games," in *Representing Aztec Ritual: Performance, Text, and Image in the Work of Sahagún*, ed. Eloise Quiñones Keber (Niwot: University Press of Colorado, 2002), 202–3, 206–8; Gruzinski, *Man-Gods*; López Austin, *Tamoanchan, Tlalocan*, 153; and López Austin, *Hombre-dios*, 119–20.

180. Sahagún, *Florentine Codex*, X:25, brackets mine; see 25–30 for similar characterizations of other occupation holders.

181. Ibid., X:25.

182. Ibid., X:25–26.

183. Ibid., X:28.

184. Arild Hvidtfeldt, *Teotl and *Ixiptatli: Some Religious Conceptions in Ancient Mexico* (Copenhagen: Munksgaard, 1958), 76–100.

185. See Elizabeth Hill Boone, *Incarnations of the Aztec Supernatural: The Image of Huiztilopochtli in Mexico and Europe* (Philadelphia: American Philosophical Society, 1989); Johanna Broda de Casas, "Tlacaxipehualiztli: A Reconstruction of an Aztec Calendar Festival from 16th Century Sources," *Revista española de antropología Americana* 5 (1970), 197–274; Carrasco, *Religions of Mesoamerica*, 17; Hvidtfeldt, *Teotl and *Ixiptatli*, 76–100; Townsend, *State and Cosmos in the Art of Tenochtitlan*; and Stuart, "Kings of Stone."

186. López Austin (*Human Body and Ideology*, I:119–20); López Austin (*Tamoanchan, Tlalocan*, 153). Carrasco ("Sacrifice of Women in the *Florentine Codex,*" 202–3, 206–8) and Gruzinski (*Man-Gods*, 22, 212) adopt López Austin's view. For etymology, see Karttunen, *Analytical Dictionary*, 115.

187. Townsend's proposal (in *State and Cosmos*, 28) that we understand teixiptla as a "talismanic token of the sacred" fares little better. While he captures the idea of teotl's truly presenting and disclosing itself as a particular object, his talk of tokens suggests an ideal type that is metaphysically distinct from its token instances and thus also suggests ontological dualism.

188. See Sandstrom and Sandstrom, *Traditional Papermaking*; Sandstrom, *Corn Is Our Blood*; and Hunt, *Transformation of the Hummingbird*.

189. See Doris Heyden, "Caves, Gods, and Myths: World-View and Planning in Teotihuacan," in *Mesoamerican Sites and World-Views*, ed. Elizabeth P. Benson (Washington, DC: Dumbarton Oaks, 1981, 1–35); Doris Heyden, *The Eagle, the Cactus, the Rock: The Roots of Mexico-Tenochtitlan's Foundation Myth and Symbol*, BAR International Series 484 (Oxford: BAR, 1989); Olivier, *Mockeries and Metamorphoses*; López Austin, *Tamoanchan, Tlalocan*; Read, *Time and Sacrifice*; Levine, *Pantheism*; James W. Dow, "Central and North Mexican Shamans," in *Mesoamerican Healers*, ed. Brad R. Huber and Alan R. Sandstrom (Austin: University of Texas Press, 2001), 71; Furst, "Shamanistic Survivals in Mesoamerican Religion"; Guy Stresser-Péan, *The Sun God and the Savior: The Christianization of the Nahua and Totonac in the Sierra Norte de Puebla, Mexico* (Boulder: University Press of Colorado, 2009); Townsend, *State and Cosmos*; and Richard F. Townsend, "Coronation at Tenochtitlan," in *The Aztec Templo Mayor*, ed. Elizabeth Hill Boone (Washington, DC: Dumbarton Oaks, 1987, 371–410).

190. Dow, "Central and North Mexican Shamans," 71.

191. Read, *Time and Sacrifice*, 8. See also Burkhart, *Slippery Earth*, 48.

192. Olivier, *Mockeries and Metamorphoses*; López Austin, *Tamoanchan, Tlalocan*, 30; McKeever Furst, *Natural History of the Soul*. For related understanding of ritual speech and song according to indigenous North American philosophy, see David Norton-

Smith, *The Dance of Person and Place: One Interpretation of American Indian Philosophy* (Albany: State University of New York Press, 2010), chapter 6.

193. Read, *Time and Sacrifice*. In similar vein, Paula Gunn Allen (*The Sacred Hoop*, 183) writes, "Things are not perceived as inert but as viable, as alive; and living things are subject to processes of growth and change as a necessary component of their existence." See also Beck, Walters, and Franciso, *The Sacred*, 10.

194. Monaghan, *Covenants with Earth and Rain*, 98–99; see also B. Deloria et al., *Spirit and Reason*, 356.

195. Dow, "Central and North Mexican Shamans," 71.

196. Ibid., 90. The manipulation of unseen forces may strike some readers as "magic." Indeed, Carrasco characterizes the Aztecs' worldview as a "cosmo-magical *cosmovisión*" (Carrasco, *Quetzalcoatl and the Irony of Empire*; Carrasco, *Religions of Mesoamerica*; Carrasco, "The Sacrifice of Women in the *Florentine Codex*"). See also Alfredo López Austin, "Los ritos: Un juego de definiciones," *Arqueología Mexicana* 6, no. 34 (1988), 4–37. Asad, in *Genealogies of Religion*, argues that concepts such as magic and animism carry a host of unintended and undesirable philosophical assumptions including Enlightenment assumptions concerning the nature of reality, reason, and science that portray magic as childlike and irrational. The concepts also include Judeo-Christian assumptions regarding the evolutionary primitiveness of animism compared to monotheism. I suggest we refrain from using *magic* and *cosmo-magical*. Allen (*Sacred Hoop*, 68–69) argues the magical is not "the childish sort" discussed by anthropologists but

> an enduring sense of the fluidity and malleability, or creative flux, of things. The tribal person perceives things not as inert but as viable and alive . . . [L]iving things are subject to processes of growth and change as a necessary component of their aliveness. Since all that exists is alive, and since all that is alive must grow and change, all existence can be manipulated under certain conditions and according to certain laws. These conditions and laws, called "ritual" or "magic" in the West, are known to native Americans variously. The Sioux refer to them as "walking in a sacred manner," the Navajo as "standing in the center of the world," and the Pomo as "having a tradition."

197. López Austin, *Tamoanchan, Tlalocan*, 30.

198. Arturo Gómez Martínez, *Tlaneltokilli: La espiritualidad de los nahuas chicotepecanos* (México, DF: Ediciones del Programa de Desarrollo Cultural de la Huasteca, 2002), 77, translation mine.

199. Sandstrom, *Corn Is Our Blood*, 258, see also p. 239; and Sandstrom, "The Cave-Pyramid Complex." Monaghan (*Covenants with Earth and Rain*, 98–99) attributes animism to contemporary Nuyootecos.

200. Sandstrom, *Corn Is Our Blood*, 258. See also Norton-Smith, *Dance of Person and Place*, chapters 5 and 6; and B. Deloria et al., *Spirit and Reason*.

201. León-Portilla, *Aztec Thought and Culture*, 96.

202. Levine, *Pantheism*. This is corroborated by Forrest, "Pantheism and Science"; Martinich, "Pantheism," 556; and Alasdair MacIntyre, "Pantheism," in *Encyclopedia of Philosophy*, ed. Paul Edwards (New York: Macmillan, 1967), VI: 31–35.

203. León-Portilla, *Aztec Thought and Culture*, 94–103.

204. Ibid., 92.

205. Ibid.

206. Ibid.

207. Ibid., 102.

208. Levine, *Pantheism*, 102.

209. León-Portilla, *Aztec Thought and Culture*, 93 passim.

210. Quoted in ibid., 93.

211. Ibid., 93 and 102, respectively.

212. Ibid., 102.

213. Caso, quoted in Richard Haly, "Bare Bones: Rethinking Mesoamerican Divinity," *History of Religions* 31, no. 3 (February 1992): 271.

214. Haly, "Bare Bones," 272.

215. Ibid., 270, 297; see also 271–73, brackets mine.

216. León-Portilla responds to Haly in León-Portilla, "Ometeotl, el supremo díos Dual, y Tezcatlipoca," *Estudios de cultural náhuatl* 30 (1999), 133–52.

217. Levine, *Pantheism*, 147.

218. Ibid., 149; Deloria (in *God Is Red*, 79, 95n1) writes, "The overwhelming majority of American Indian tribal religions refused to represent deity anthropomorphically."

219. See Levine, *Pantheism*, 147ff.

220. Edward Pace, "Pantheism," *The Catholic Encyclopedia*, vol. 11 (New York: Robert Appleton Company, 1911); http://www.newadvent.org/cathen/11447b.htm (accessed 4/8/2013).

221. Jongsoo Lee, "Westernization of Nahuatl Religion: Nezahualcoyotl's Unknown God," *Latin American Indian Literatures Journal* 19, no. 1 (2003), 19–48.

222. *Codex Telleriano-Remensis: Ritual, Divination, and History in a Pictorial Aztec Manuscript*, ed. Eloise Quiñones Keber (Austin: University of Texas Press, 1995), 162–63. Farriss (*Maya Society under Colonial Rule*, 301) defends a pantheistic interpretation of elite Maya theology yet concedes the Maya godhead did not "figure prominently, in his unitary aspect, in Maya ritual."

3

Aztec metaphysics claims teotl's ceaseless becoming is characterized by the cyclical struggle between paired complementary polarities such as life and death. Sections 3.1–3.3 explore this claim. Section 3.4 looks at how Mesoamerican artists represented this notion of polar duality. Section 3.5 focuses upon several more abstract dualities such as being and nonbeing. Section 3.6 argues that balance and imbalance and center and periphery are *not* among teotl's dual aspects. Section 3.7 discusses Ometeotl's relationship to polar duality. I conclude in section 3.8.

3.1. AGONISTIC *INAMIC* UNITY

Teotl's process of continual and continuous self-transformation is defined by what I call *agonistic inamic unity*, that is, the continual and continuous cyclical struggle (*agon*) of paired opposites, polarities, or dualities. Agonistic inamic unity refers to a brute fact about the nature of teotl and hence brute fact about the nature of reality per se. It accordingly serves as a fundamental premise of Aztec metaphysics. Teotl's ceaseless self-becoming, self-presenting, and self-unfolding, and therefore its ceaseless generating and regenerating of the cosmos, are defined by agonistic inamic unity. The cosmos and all its inhabitants are accordingly defined by it. Aztec metaphysics sees these paired opposites as interdependent, interrelated, mutually engendering, and mutually complementary *while at the same time* mutually competitive and antagonistic. Neither opposite is *conceptually* or *temporally* prior to the other. Neither is morally or metaphysically superior to the other. Consistent with ontological and constitutional

DOI: 10.5876_9781607322238.c003

monism, these paired opposites are *dual aspects or facets of teotl.* They are *not* two metaphysically distinct essences or kinds of stuff (as this would entail constitutional dualism).

Teotl's dual aspects include life and death, day and night, fire and water, and male and female. Day and night, for example, are simultaneously mutually competitive as well as mutually arising, mutually dependent, and mutually complementary. Day is always becoming night, and night is always becoming day. Day temporarily vanquishes night yet emerges from night. Night temporarily vanquishes day yet emerges from day. Each contains within itself the seed of its opposite. Neither excludes nor can exist without the other. The Nahuatl term for this relationship is *inamic.* Day and night, for example, are each other's inamic. Day and night constitute an inamic pair, or set of inamic partners. Day and night may also be characterized as inamic partners. Day is the inamic of night, night the inamic of day. Generally speaking, an inamic is a power, force, or influence that is necessarily matched, partnered, or paired with a second power, force, or influence. Each is conceived as the complementary polar opposite of the other. In what follows I mark this relationship using the tilde ("~"), for example, day~night, life~death, and male~female.[1]

The cyclical, back-and-forth tug-of-war between inamic partners combined with the alternating, temporary dominance of one inamic over its partner constitutes and hence explains the genesis, diversity, movement, and momentary ordering of the cosmos. Each moment in this back-and-forth, cosmic tug-of-war consists of the temporary dominance of one or the other inamic within a pair, and therefore represents a temporary imbalance between the two. As López Austin points out, the continuing agonistic interaction between inamic partners produces a *continuo desajuste* ("continuous imbalance or maladjustment") in the cosmos.[2] This notwithstanding, teotl's long-term cosmic self-unfolding exhibits an overarching *diachronic* balance and equilibrium. Although each moment in the cosmic tug-of-war consists of the temporary dominance of one or the other of inamic partners, and therefore a moment of imbalance, *over the long run* their alternating yields a *diachronic* and *dynamic* balance. Short-term imbalances are woven together into long-term balance.

As a prosaic example of this, consider the kind of balancing involved in walking. Walking is a process, not an event. It is diachronic, not static. Walking requires being able to achieve an overarching, diachronic balance between a repeating series of momentary imbalances (or maladjustments). Starting from standing position, one extends one's left leg forward, shifts one's weight left-forwardly, and in so doing puts oneself off balance. But before falling leftwards too far and crashing to the ground, one quickly extends one's right leg and shifts one's weight rightwards. This, of course, creates a right-leaning imbalance that counterbalances the first, left-leaning imbalance. However, before falling rightwards too far and tumbling to the ground, one quickly extends one's left leg, thereby shifting one's weight leftwards. The process of walking involves repeating these imbalancing and counterbalancing actions over and over again. One does not try to achieve a static middle or mean point of balancedness. Rather one passes through such a point in the constant "to and fro" of walking. Indeed, one cannot walk without embracing alternating momentary imbalances. One walks straightforwardly by walking crookedly. One walks in balance by walking imbalancedly. One walks in balance by walking middlingly – not by walking in the middle. Balance is attained dialectically, diachronically, and dynamically. Individual moments of short-term imbalance are woven together to yield a diachronic process of long-term balancing. Viewed kinesiologically, walking is a complex balancing act. In sum, long-term balancing consists of and is achieved by a rhythmic series of mutually interdependent and reciprocally influencing individual acts of short-term imbalance. This is precisely the sort of balancing struck by teotl. Although devoid of any stable, permanent created structure, teotl's ceaseless becoming – and hence the becoming of the cosmos and all its contents – are nevertheless characterized by an enduring, *immanent* rhythm or pattern; namely, agonistic inamic unity.

But if this is so, then isn't Aztec metaphysics guilty of logical inconsistency? After all, on the one hand it claims that everything changes, yet on the other, claims these changes exhibit a pattern or rhythm that does *not* change. The contradiction is merely apparent. Agonistic inamic unity is an *unchanging* pattern of change according to which everything changes; an *uncreated* pattern of creating and destroying according to which neither creation nor destruction is stable or lasting; and an ungenerated pattern of generating and degenerating according to which neither generation nor degeneration is stable or lasting. Agonistic inamic unity is an *orderly* pattern of ordering and disordering according to which neither order nor disorder is stable or enduring. Borrowing terminology from Western philosophy, we might say agonistic inamic unity is a stable, *second-order* pattern of *first-order* orderings and disorderings according to which first-order orderings and disorderings are unstable, short-lived, and impermanent. It is a stable *second-order* pattern of being and nonbeing according to which neither being nor nonbeing is stable or lasting. In sum, agonistic inamic unity is an enduring rhythmic reiterative pattern in the becoming, changing, and processing of teotl and hence in the becoming, changing and processing of reality, cosmos, and all things.

This answer, however, yields a further question: what is a pattern? Isn't a pattern a thing, and if so, aren't we then still faced with an internal inconsistency?

I believe not. Agonistic inamic unity is *not a thing*, no less a *created* thing, and this fact absolves Aztec metaphysics of internal inconsistency. Agonistic inamic unity is a *how*, not a *what*. It is *how* teotl transforms, becomes, and processes; it is *how* teotl presents and discloses itself. It is *how* teotl's energy circulates about the cosmos. Agonistic inamic unity is, in short, teotl's *modus operandi*. It is a *patterning*, and a patterning is not a thing but a *way: a how*, not a *what*. As a patterning, agonistic inamic unity characterizes *how* teotl – and hence *how* reality, cosmos, and all things – become and unfold; it is the *way* teotl, reality, cosmos, and all things become and unfold. And because it is not a thing, it follows that agonistic inamic unity is not an unchanging thing. Chapter 1 suggested we treat the word *teotl* as a verb. I suggest now we treat the phrase *agonistic inamic unity* as an adverb, one that modifies the verb *teotl*. We must therefore resist reifying not only teotl but also agonistic inamic unity. Aztec metaphysics is a process metaphysics. Chapter 1 also argued that Aztec metaphysics claims that nature follows function. Since agonistic inamic unity defines how teotl functions, it defines the kind of process teotl is and hence the nature of teotl.

Since teotl is self-transforming, it follows that teotl is self-patterning. Agonistic inamic unity is generated *by* teotl *from within* teotl, and as a result, it is metaphysically immanent and nonhierarchical. It is not, in other words, a pre-existing, transcendent Platonic-style law, norm, or principle that is imposed upon teotl's self-becoming and that governs teotl's self-becoming from above or outside. Nor is it a transcendent matrix to which teotl's self-unfolding must conform. Rather, agonistic inamic unity *emerges* in the course of teotl's self-transforming, just as the pattern of rings in a tree trunk *emerges* in the course of a tree's growing. A tree's ring pattern is adverbial in the sense that it discloses *how* the tree grows. It is a *how*, not a *what*.[3]

3.2. AGONISTIC INAMIC UNITY AS A PATTERN IN THE WEAVING OF THE COSMOS

Agonistic inamic unity may also be characterized as emerging from teotl in the same manner that a pattern emerges and discloses itself in the process of weaving a textile. A weaving pattern characterizes *how* a textile is woven. It, too, is a *how*, not a *what*. Conceiving agonistic inamic unity as a pattern that emerges in the process of weaving of a fabric is especially apposite in light of the larger significance of weaving in Aztec philosophy. What is this larger significance? First, chapter 1 argued that Aztec metaphysics conceives teotl as a consummate cosmic artist, and conceives the cosmos as teotl's grand, ongoing work of performance art. Since the Aztecs viewed weaving as a creative-artistic process, it is fitting that they viewed teotl as a consummate weaver, the cosmos as teotl's grand work of weaving in progress, and agonistic inamic unity as a defining pattern in teotl's cosmic weaving. Agonistic inamic unity functions as the pattern *by* which and *in* which teotl weaves itself, reality, the cosmos, and all existing things. The patterns and designs woven by teotl into itself as sacred textile parallel the pictures painted-written by teotl on itself as sacred *amoxtli* (paper, book). Both processes consist of teotl's continual self-configuration.[4]

Second, weaving functions as an organizing principle and root metaphor in Aztec metaphysics. The work of Cecelia Klein, Barbara Tedlock, Dennis Tedlock, Kay Read, Peter Furst, and Stacy Schaefer suggests the Aztec cosmos is, in Klein's words, a "weaver's paradigm."[5] But what does it mean to say that weaving functions as a root or organizing metaphor? Stephen Pepper argues philosophical systems – what he calls "world hypotheses" – are generated from, determined by, and organized around "root metaphors" or "basic analogies." He writes:

> A man desiring to understand the world looks about for a clue to its comprehension. He pitches upon some area of commonsense fact and tries if he cannot understand other areas in terms of this one. This original area becomes . . . his *basic analogy* or *root metaphor*. He describes as best he can the characteristics of this area, or if you will, discriminates its structure. A list of its structural characteristics becomes his basic concepts of explanation and description. We call them a set of categories. In terms of these categories he proceeds to study all other areas of fact . . . He undertakes to understand all facts in terms of these.[6]

López Austin's notion of *cosmovisión* with its "unifying nucleus" closely resembles Pepper's notion of world hypothesis with its root metaphor.[7]

George Lakoff and Mark Johnson argue in *Metaphors We Live By* that conceptual systems play a central role in defining our cognitive processes, belief systems, affective-motivational processes, value systems, and everyday practices, and that these conceptual systems are "fundamentally metaphorical."[8] "[T]he way we think, what we experience, and what we do every day is very much a matter of metaphor."[9] A culture's most fundamental values and value system "cohere with the metaphorical structure of the most fundamental concepts of that culture."[10] And what is a metaphor? "The essence of a metaphor is understanding and experiencing one kind of thing in terms of another."[11] Metaphors are not solely a linguistic matter or an aesthetic matter of artistic-literary embellishment. They are fundamental to how we think, value, and act.[12]

Victor Turner likewise claims cultures are characterized by "root paradigms"; that is, "certain consciously recognized (though not consciously grasped) cultural *models*" that "have reference to" social relationships, "cultural goals, means ideas, outlooks, currents of thought [and] patterns of belief."[13] Charles Taylor similarly defends the existence of a set of basic conceptualizations or assumptions regarding nature, society, and humanity that function as the "constitutive meanings" of a social group's *form of life*."[14]

Timothy Knab argues the notion of a "basic," "organizing metaphor" sheds light upon Aztec thought, culture, and society.[15] He interprets an organizing metaphor as an "essential" part of a conceptual system that "relates broad areas of human experience to one another in a concrete manner on the basis of a single prototypical class of metaphor."[16] It "touches on almost all aspects of life."[17] Like Pepper, Knab believes a culture's organizing metaphor "is to be found in the features of human culture and the experiences of everyday life."[18] Organizing metaphors are "pervasive" in Aztec thought, culture, and society, each organizing one or more aspects of the Aztecs' conceptual system.[19] More than one root metaphor may thus be at work in organizing a culture's philosophical system. Knab's own work focuses upon one such metaphor: the biological metaphor expressed by the statement, "Man is plant."

Building on the groundbreaking work of Klein and others, I argue weaving functions as an organizing principle and root metaphor for Aztec metaphysics. This metaphor may be expressed succinctly by the statement, "The cosmos is a woven fabric," or perhaps more aptly, "The cosmos is a grand weaving in progress." Since weaving broadly construed includes spinning raw fiber into thread, we might amend the foregoing: "The cosmos is a grand spinning and weaving in progress." This metaphor organizes Aztec thinking about the structure of cosmos and reality in terms of weaving. It not only construes the entire cosmos as a grand weaving in progress, it also construes the various aspects of the cosmos as different aspects of spinning and weaving.

Weaving serves as an especially powerful and illuminating heuristic for our understanding of Aztec metaphysics. Weaving functions as an organizing principle of Aztec metaphysics and also concretely instantiates agonistic inamic unity. Weaving is an agonistic activity that treats warp and weft fibers as inamic partners to be united into a single fabric. It interlaces warp and weft into agonistic inamic unity. Weaving describes the *way* in which warp and weft are brought together to form a fabric. It characterizes *how* a textile is engendered. Weaving, like agonistic inamic unity, is a *how*, not a *what*.

Chapters 4 through 8 argue that weaving functions as a root metaphor and organizing principle of Aztec metaphysics and that the Aztecs interpreted the cosmos as a grand weaving in progress. Sexual commingling and military combat/hunting (Aztec metaphysics treats combat and hunting as roughly equivalent) represent two additional root metaphors in Aztec philosophy. Weaving, sexual commingling, and combat/hunting are instances of agonistic inamic unity. All three offer us ways of understanding agonistic inamic unity and hence the unfolding of teotl, reality, and cosmos.

3.3. EXAMINING AGONISTIC INAMIC UNITY

Teotl's self-emerging and self-transforming are configured by agonistic inamic unity. The unceasing struggle between the inamic partners constitutes as well as explains the genesis, diversity, movement, and momentary ordering of the cosmos. Various scholars have commented upon this feature of Aztec and Mesoamerican metaphysics. Alfredo López Austin refers to it as the "dual opposition of contrary elements."[20] Barbara Tedlock contrasts what she calls the "dialectical or complementary dualism" of Mesoamerica with the "analytical or oppositional dualism" of European philosophy and theology.[21] Dennis Tedlock characterizes Mesoamerican dualities as "complementary rather than oppositional . . . contemporaneous rather than sequential."[22] Dualities are "interpenetrating rather than mutually exclusive. Instead of being in logical opposition to one another, [they] are joined by mutual attraction."[23] Nigel Davies contrasts the "dialectical dualism" of Mesoamerican philosophy with the eschatological, "radical dualism" of Zoroastrianism.[24] Jill McKeever Furst emphasizes the dynamic and fluid nature of Mesoamerican duality, which she describes as a "fundamental organizing principle in Mesoamerican cultures."[25]

UNDERSTANDING INAMIC PAIRS

Inamic pairs are standardly characterized as dualities, polarities, or contraries that are coexisting, mutually arising, compatible, complementary, interdependent, competitive, and locked in a continual process of agonistic, dialectical alternation with one another. But are terms such as *contrary*, *duality*, or *polarity* adequate translations? Do they faithfully convey the nature of the inamic relationship? In what follows, I examine first the Aztec concept of an inamic pair and then examine the concept of their agonistic interrelationship. While doing so, we must be mindful that both concepts function within the larger conceptual context of ontological and constitutional monism.

Alfredo López Austin defines *inamic* as "*su complemento*" ("its complement"), "*su contrario*" ("its opposite"), and "*su correspondiente*" ("its correspondent").[26] These translations, however, add little to the aforementioned. In what sense is an inamic an opposite, complementary, and correspondent? Fray Alonso de

Molina translates *inamic* as *"su igual, o cosa que viene bien y cuadra con otra"* ("its equal or something that goes well and fits, adjusts, or balances with another."[27] R. Joe Campbell translates it as "its match."[28] Siméon translates it as *"igual, que va bien y concuerda con alguna cosa"* ("equal, that which goes well and agrees with some thing").[29]

After endorsing what he calls Molina's "literal" translation, Miguel León-Portilla proposes we translate *inamic* as *"su comparte* para indicar así la relación en que se halla el *nelli téotl* con 'su igual o lo que con él embona'" ("his consort or sharer in order to so indicate the relation in which the true teotl exists with 'his equal or that which fits, suits or joins with him'").[30] We might also gloss *comparte* as "associate, companion, accompanist, mate, comrade, or one who shares one's destiny or lot." The English edition of León-Portilla's text reads slightly differently. It defines *inamic* as "'consort,' in order to indicate that the *nelli téotl,* the 'true god,' is related to or complemented by 'his equal,' or 'that which improves him or makes him more complete.'"[31] This adds the idea that one's inamic not only suits or joins one but also improves or completes one.

The word *inamic* combines the singular possessive *i-* ("its, his, her") with the verb *namiqui* and the locative suffix *−c* ("on, in, among").[32] Molina lists two separate entries for *namiqui: "salir a recibir al que viene, o encontrar con alguno, o contender con otros"* ("to go out to receive someone who is coming, to encounter something, to quarrel with others"), and *"incurrir en pena puesta por la ley"* ("to incur a punishment under the law").[33] Campbell suggests *namiqui* has the sense of "to find, meet, join."[34] León-Portilla defines *namiqui* as *"encontrar, ayudar"* ("to find, to help").[35] The word *tenamic* combines the possessive *te* ("someone's") with *namic* to yield "husband, wife, or companion, or an enemy competitor against someone in a game."[36]

Molina lists other *namiqui*-derived words that help shed light on the concept of namiqui and by extension the concept of inamic. This will give us a more concrete sense of *namiqui* as "its equal, its match, or something that goes well and fits, adjusts, or balances with another." The verb *ixnamiqui,* for example, combines the noun *ix(tli)* ("face, surface, eyes") with *namiqui* to mean "to look at each other face to face."[37] The verb *moquanamiqui* combines the reflexive *mo,* the noun *qua(itl)* ("tree, wood, stick, staff, beam"), and *namiqui* to mean "for two ends to join together."[38] *Quinamiqui* means "to fit or for one thing to go together right with another." Molina also lists *teixnamiqui* ("opposite [*contrario*], competitor, or adversary" [literally, "to bring eyes or face to someone"?]), *tenamiquini* ("adversary of a player in a game" or "one who customarily brings eyes to someone"), *tlanamiquini* ("one who suffers a punishment"), *qualli onnenamictliliztli* ("fortunate encounter"), *tlananamiquini* ("one who helps"), *mixnamicticate* ("for

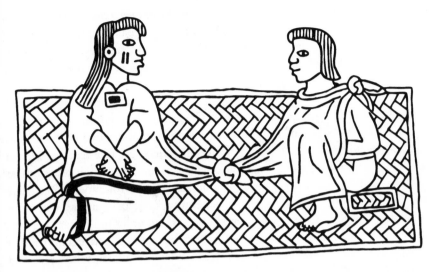

FIGURE 3.1. *Newlyweds. (*Codex Mendoza *[1997: fol. 61r]; courtesy of Frances F. Berdan and Patricia Rieff Anawalt.)*

several people to live together"), *motlatolnamiquini* ("to agree on what is said"), *tlatennamictli* ("kissed on the mouth"), and *tepan namiqui* ("for one's field to share a boundary [a stone wall (*tetl* + *pantli*)] with someone else's").

Molina translates *namictia*, the causative form of *namiqui*, as "to marry someone; to get married; to argue or quarrel with someone; to join two things together or interpret dreams." The illustration of the Aztec wedding ceremony in *Codex Mendoza*'s folio 61r depicts bride and groom as inamic partners in two ways: they sit face-to-face across from one another, and their clothes are knotted together (see Figure 3.1). A host of words are constructed using *namictia*, including *cuicanamictia* ("to get singers in tune" or "to cause singing to fit, match, or come together"), *ixnamictia* ("to fight or quarrel with others; to line or cover something or to put one thing against another one" [literally, "to cause faces, surfaces, or eyes to match or fit"?]), *nanamictia* ("to set something in order or to arrange it"), *tlaixnamictiliztli* ("act of putting things together"), *tlanamictilli* ("something that is evened up"), *tlatlatolnamictiani* ("mediator or advocate" [literally, "one who customarily brings together speech"]), *nequa-namictliliztli* ("joint between two extremities"), *tlanamictia* ("to trade one thing for another, or to recompense someone"), *tlanamictiqui* ("one who evens some things up with other things"), and *tlanamictia* ("to trade one thing for another, or to recompense someone").

In sum, *namiqui*-based words suggest bringing things together, putting things against or next to one another, and aligning, arranging, matching, fitting, or evening up things vis-à-vis one another: face to face, eye to eye, spoken word to spoken word, song to song, lips to lips, side by side, or top to bottom. That which may be brought together in this fashion includes concrete things such as mouths, faces, songs, fields, strips of land, and quarreling people as well as more abstract things such as the content of spoken words; criminal and punishment; and a needy person and help. Processes of bringing things together in this fashion include arranging things; making things even; matching things with or against one another; fitting things; making them face one another; setting them in tune with one another; punishing (matching punishment with misdeed); helping (matching help with need); matching goods in trade or commerce; matching words by agreement or mediation (what we would call "seeing eye to eye"); and matching opponents and adversaries against or with one another. Thus X's inamic, Y, is that with which X is inamically arranged or ordered. And if Y is X's inamic, then X is Y's inamic. X is that with which Y is inamically arranged or ordered. Here again, we observe Aztec metaphysics' emphasis upon arranging and ordering things. Bringing together things *inamically* consists of ordering and arranging them in a specific way.

How then shall we translate *inamic*? Following Campbell, I propose "its match," as I believe "match" best captures in English the foregoing ways in which things are brought together. We commonly speak of soccer, bridge, wrestling, debating, and tennis matches; being matched up with an opponent or antagonist; meeting one's match; one's spouse as one's match; those who make wedding matches as matchmakers; colors, patterns, or articles of clothing (socks and shirts) as being well- or ill-matched; a person's being unmatched in her accomplishments or abilities; matching aid with need; and people (e.g., adversaries, teams, bridge and groom) as well- or ill-matched. One's match is that which one encounters or faces. In short, X's inamic, Y, is that with which X is matched. And if Y is X's match, then X is Y's match.

The concept of being a match shares the ambiguity of the Nahuatl concept of inamic. One's match is simultaneously creative and destructive of oneself. Well-matched opponents (those worthy of one another's abilities; each other's equal) in a tennis match, for example, challenge, antagonize, provoke, frustrate, and aim to dominate each other. In so doing they simultaneously stimulate, improve, and engender one another. Tennis partners thus contribute to the fulfillment and completion of one another qua tennis players. Indeed, at a very basic level each partner needs the other in order to become a tennis player at all. One cannot become a tennis player solely by hitting a ball against a wall. One needs a partner, opponent, or match. In this sense, too, one's partner completes oneself. Playing tennis is a relational activity and being a tennis player requires someone with whom to play tennis. (Similarly, one cannot become a boxer, for example, solely by shadow boxing. One needs a sparring partner.) In this sense, then, one's tennis partner completes oneself as a tennis player. Tennis partners define themselves as well as define one another in the process of playing tennis *against* one another. They antagonize and compete with one another: one's strength and triumph is one's partner's weakness and loss. Finally, although tennis partners antagonize one another, they do not aim to exterminate one another as doing so would spell the end of the game and the demise of the victor's existence as a tennis player. One aims to triumph momentarily over one's opponent in a way that allows her to return another day and resume the contest.

An inamic relationship consists of matching of two things. Why do inamic partners come in twos rather than threes? Twoness signifies *completeness* and *wholeness* in Aztec thought.[39] This is an irreducible brute fact about teotl and reality. It simply admits of no further explanation. Teotl unfolds and presents itself in two aspects or guises. Twoness captures both aspects of teotl and hence captures teotl as a unified whole. The fact that twoness signifies completeness and wholeness in Aztec metaphysics is therefore grounded in Aztec metaphysics' dual-aspect monism. Consonant with ontological and constitutional monism, these inamic partners are *dual aspects* or *facets* of teotl. They do *not* represent two metaphysically distinct essences or substances but two aspects of one and the same thing. When brought together, X and Y not only complete one another but also form a single complete whole.

Inamic partners share the following additional characteristics. First, they are symmetrically related to one another (like spouses or twins). Second, they are correlated with one another in the sense that they are mutually dependent, mutually conditioning, and mutually engendering. Life emerges from death, and death from life. Life depends upon death, and death upon life. What's more, life can exist neither apart from death nor apart from the life~death unity of which life forms an essential component. Analogously, the sun's daytime light alternates with its nighttime darkness on pain of earthly things' burning up. Rain alternates with drought on pain of catastrophic flooding. Third, inamic partners are inversely correlated with one another in the sense that one's triumph and strength is the other's defeat and weakness. Although this does not logically preclude them from reaching moments of equilibrium, such moments are evanescent. Fourth, inamic partners are mutually defining. Life is defined by death; death, by life. Each can only be understood in terms of its match. The idea of an isolated inamic, like that of an unmarried husband, is logically incomplete and conceptually ill-defined. One cannot be a husband without being matched with a wife (and conversely). Fifth, being an inamic is a relational property. An inamic has no independent status apart from its inamic partner, just as a husband has no status qua husband apart from his wife. Inamic partners thus require one another as necessary conditions of being what they are (e.g., as day requires night, male requires female, and up requires down). Sixth, inamic partners are mutually nurturing. Life feeds death, for example, and death feeds life. Eighth, inamic pairs are complementary; that is, they complete and fulfill one another and in so doing form a single unit or whole.

Metaphysical relationalism is consequently central to the Aztecs' concept of inamic. Inamic partners are defined by their interrelationship with one another rather than independently of one another (in terms, for example, of their possessing distinct Platonic- or Aristotelian-style essences). Talk of inamic partners describes the way things are arranged in their dynamic and ever-changing interrelationships and interdependencies with other things. The vocabulary of inamic partners does not describe reified, Platonic- or Aristotelian-style essences such as maleness per se. Furthermore, because inamic partners are aspects of teotl's energy-in-motion, they are properly understood as forces or powers rather than as static states of being, conditions, or things. They entail neither constitutional dualism nor ontological dualism. Understanding inamic relationships is vital to understanding the nature of teotl and hence reality; that is, *how* things become, move, and change the way they do.

Inamic partners are continually struggling back and forth with one another, creating a single, inamic unity. This unity is processive rather than substantive. Struggling tennis partners, for example, create a tennis game – that is, a process in which both participate and to which both contribute; a dyadic process in which both are at once subsumed, conserved, antagonized, transformed, and completed. Both inamic partners become something otherwise unattainable apart from the process. Similarly, from the interacting of marriage partners emerges a single, male~female process. "It takes two to tango," as the popular saying goes, and when two do tango, something new emerges: a single, tangoing couple.

Inamic Pairs, Relationalism, Holism, and the Fabric of the Cosmos

López Austin contends everything in the Aztec cosmos has an inamic. A wife is the inamic of her husband; a warrior, the inamic of his enemy; the player of a game, the inamic of his opponent.[40] The *Florentine Codex* characterizes certain medicines as inamic partners of certain illnesses (e.g., an infusion of *teouaxin* with chili and salt is the inamic of a constant cough).[41] The *Primeros memoriales* describes certain foodstuffs as inamic partners of other foodstuffs (e.g., large folded tortillas and hot chili sauce).[42] The sacred clusters of specific powers picked out by the alleged deities of the Aztec pantheon are also inamically interrelated with one another. Quetzalcoatl, for example, is the inamic of Mictlantecuhtli and Tezcatlipoca; Ometecuhtli, the inamic of Omecihuatl; and Tonacacihuatl, the inamic of Tonacatecuhtli.

At any given moment, any particular thing simultaneously participates in a web of different inamic relationships and simultaneously interacts with a web of different inamic partners. An individual man, for example, simultaneously participates in inamic relationships with his wife, his enemy in combat, his adversary in the ballgame, and so on. He is simultaneously the inamic of each of these. And each of his inamic partners, in turn, operates within its own web of inamic interrelationships, and these latter with theirs, and so on without end. In other words, if López Austin is correct and everything in the cosmos has an inamic and therefore *is* an inamic, then it appears everything in the cosmos is ultimately interrelated and interdependent with everything else. It appears teotl, reality, and cosmos consist of a grand, all-inclusive web of dynamic inamic interrelationships.

Upon realizing that a given man's inamic status as husband is influenced by his inamic status as player, partner, warrior, and so on, we come to realize in addition that the fabric of cosmic interrelatedness and interdependency is more complexly woven than we had thought. This fabric becomes even more complexly woven once we realize that each individual's inamic status becomes increasingly ambiguous as it enters into more and more inamic relationships. For example, as a warrior of Tenochtitlan, a given man is inamically male in relation to his Tlaxcalteca enemy, who is inamically female. Yet the same Aztec warrior is by the same token also inamically female from the perspective of his Tlaxcalteca adversary. In short, one and the same individual may be inamically male in relation to some things, and inamically female in relation to others. Similarly, according to William Madsen, among contemporary Nahuatl-speakers in San Francisco Tecospa, a fair skinned man is warm in relation to a woman but cold in relation to a dark skinned man.[43] One and the same individual is both male and female, hot and cold, dry and wet, and so on, and therefore irreducibly ambiguous.

Inamic partners are not only interrelated and interdependent with one another, they are also mutually *defining*. If things are defined by what they do (since "being follows function"), then everything is defined at least partially in terms of its inamic relationships. So, in addition to being influenced by the fabric of his inamic relationships, a given man is also *defined* by the fabric of his inamic relationships with his wife, ballgame partner, and enemy in combat, for example. And his inamic partners are, in turn, defined by their respective fabrics of inamic interrelationships, and so on with their inamic partners. In short, everything appears to be ultimately defined in terms of its fabric of inamic interrelationships and interdependencies, and this eventually includes the entire cosmos.

If everything in the cosmos has an inamic and everything operates within a fabric of inamic interrelationships that eventually extends throughout the entire cosmos, if everything is defined by what it does, and lastly, if inamic partners are defined in terms of one another, then it follows that everything in the cosmos is defined in terms of a fabric of inamic interrelationships and interdependencies that eventually includes the entire cosmos. Everything in the cosmos is not only ultimately interrelated and interdependent with everything else but also defined in terms of its relationships with everything else. Upon reaching this conclusion we return to chapter 1's claim that Aztec metaphysics conceives reality holistically. Reality consists of a special kind of unity, namely, one in which every individual component is *essentially* interrelated, interdependent, co-related, interactive, and ultimately defined in terms of every other component.

Upon reaching this conclusion we also return to metaphysical relationalism. Individual things are defined in terms of their inamic relationships with other things. Things differ from one another not in terms of their intrinsic, Aristotelian-style essences but in terms of their inamic relationships as well as their inamic proportions (i.e., how much masculinity as opposed to femininity, heat as opposed to cold, and so on that they possess). And we also return to the nonhierarchical nature of Aztec metaphysics. Things are understood without appeal to transcendent Platonic-style principles, laws, or essences. If this is correct, then understanding inamic relationships is essential to understanding the nature of teotl, reality, and cosmos; that is, how things become and change the way they do. As these interrelationships spread across the fabric of reality, one witnesses the interrelatedness and interdependency of all things. In the final analysis, teotl, reality and cosmos are not only constituted but also defined by this patterned fabric of dynamic inamic interrelationships and interdependencies. If nature follows function and teotl is as teotl does, then teotl *is* this dynamic fabric of inamic interactions.

Inamic patterning is universal in scope. Everything in the cosmos is characterized in terms of inamic relationships. Everything is an inamic and thus has an inamic. What's more, everything is inherently inamically mixed and therefore inherently ambiguous. Nothing is purely ordered or purely disordered, purely male or purely female, and so on. Inamic partners are inseparable from one another both *internally* or *within* individual things (e.g., within Tonacacihuatl or with an individual woman) as well *externally* or *between* two things (e.g. between Tonacatecuhtli and Tonacacihuatl or between male and female). The fact that all created things are inamically mixed reflects the deeper metaphysical fact that teotl and reality are inamically mixed and hence inherently and irreducibly ambiguous. This notwithstanding, López Austin tells us any created thing in the cosmos falls into one or the other inamic, and that it does so by virtue of whichever inamic predominates in its makeup.[44]

Lastly, teotl has always been characterized by agonistic inamic unity. Chapter 7 argues Aztec metaphysics lacks a cosmogony in the strict sense of positing an original beginning and ex nihilo creation. Teotl has always existed. This befits Aztec metaphysics seeing as inamic relationships have no beginning. Neither inamic is conceptually or temporally prior to the other. "To claim otherwise," as David Hall points out, "would be to provide some concept of initiation and, thus, to give priority to one of the elements in the creative relationship."[45] Aztec metaphysics thus appears to subscribe to the principle *ex nihilo nihil fit* ("from nothing, nothing comes"). The centrality of inamic relationships in Aztec metaphysics encourages understanding creativity in terms of rhythmic self-transformation and self-regeneration. It reminds us that there are no absolute beginnings or absolute endings – only continuations and transformations. Death, for example, is not an ending but a change of status, as that which dies flows into and nourishes the living. Everything that exists is enmeshed within an endless process of regeneration, recycling, and transformation

Finally, agonistic inamic unity is nonteleological and noneschatological. The cosmic process consisting of the cyclical agonistic alternation of inamic partners has no final goal, purpose, or destiny toward which it strives. And this is fitting, seeing as the processing of teotl is nonteleological and noneschatological. Although the Fifth Era – like the preceding four Eras and all individual created things in all five Eras – is destined to disintegrate and come to an end, teotl is not. And since teotl is identical with both reality per se and the cosmos per se, neither reality nor cosmos per se is destined to come to an end. Briefly put, while there is an end to the Fifth Era, there is no end to teotl. Any moment of cosmic disintegration is inevitably succeeded by an alternating inamic moment of cosmic integration. Teotl, reality, and cosmos both precede and succeed the Fifth Era.

What so gravely concerned the Aztecs and accordingly dominated their ritual activities was the continued existence of the Fifth Era – not the cosmos per se. Thinking otherwise, I believe, rests upon a failure to distinguish *the cosmos* per se from the Fifth Era or *Sun-Earth Ordering*. However the demise of the latter does not entail the demise of the former. The demise of the Fifth Sun-Earth Ordering is not good news to humans, obviously, but this is an entirely different matter. Many scholars commonly use the word *cosmos* indiscriminately to refer to both the cosmos per se and the cosmos of the Fifth Sun-Earth Ordering, resulting in serious confusion. The history of the cosmos includes – but is not exhausted by – the succession of five Sun-Earth Orderings. Humans currently live in the Fifth and apparently last. Like its four predecessors, it too will eventually succumb to catastrophic imbalance and come to an end. Aztec tlamatinime confessed ignorance regarding the nature of the cosmos after the unraveling and disintegration of the Fifth Sun-Earth Ordering.[46]

UNDERSTANDING AGONISM

A second essential component of agonistic inamic unity is agon, that is, the cyclical back-and-forth struggle between inamic partners. Gary Gossen writes that conflict is a "creative and life-sustaining force" that is "primordial" and "ubiquitous." Conflict is "the genesis and precondition for order."[47] Tranquil coexistence is fundamentally alien to agonistic inamic unity and hence alien to teotl and the cosmos. Inamic partners struggle tirelessly against one another like sparring partners. They aim to dominate one another yet never eliminate one another. A momentarily overpowered inamic always reasserts itself to dominates its inamic. Consider life and death. Life struggles against death, yet life does not aim to eliminate death; death in turn struggles against life, yet does not aim to eliminate life; and so on without end. Each depends vitally upon the other. Neither seeks total victory. Their struggle is neither eschatological nor teleological.

Paradoxically, perhaps, inamic partners complement one another in the process of competing with one another. Indeed, these two processes are ultimately one and the same. Inamic partners are simultaneously complementary *and* competitive. Equally paradoxical perhaps, their struggle creates an overarching balance or equilibrium. Although each moment in their tug-of-war consists of the temporary dominance of one or the other inamic and therefore a temporary imbalance, in the long run their back-and-forth tug-of-war creates an overarching *diachronic* and *dynamic* balance. Their back-and-forth tug-of-war weaves together short-term imbalances into long-term balance. Balance and equilibrium are thus the products of struggle – not peaceful cooperation and coexistence.

In sum, struggle (agon) is an ineliminable and indeed essential aspect of the processing of teotl, reality, cosmos, and all things. It plays an essential role in agonistic inamic unity. One attempts to eliminate struggle on pain of folly. Like weaving and biological transmutation, agonism is dynamic and processive. Warfare, hunting, childbirth, sexual intercourse, weaving, and the ballgame are paradigmatic instances of agonism as each involves a back-and-forth struggle between inamic partners.[48]

Understanding Unity

Agonistic inamic partners unite to form ambiguous dual-aspect singularities. As Viviana Jímenez Estrada writes, "duality engenders unity as opposed to division."[49] From the agonistic struggling of tennis partners, for example, emerges a tennis match: a dyadic process in which both partners participate and to which both contribute; a process in which both partners are simultaneously subsumed, conserved, transformed, and completed. From the agonistic struggling of marriage partners emerges a single, male–female processive unity. Through interacting dance partners emerges a single, two-person tangoing unity. In short, dual-aspect oneness signifies wholeness in Aztec metaphysics. What's more, agonistic inamic unity is dynamic and diachronic. It is not a static condition or state of being.

Parallel Aligned Inamic Pairs

Aztec metaphysics' inamic pairs include death~life, darkness~light, night~day, below~above, feminine (female)~masculine (male), ascending influence~descending influence, humidity~drought, cold~hot, passive~active, flint stone~flower, ocelot~eagle, wind~fire, rainy season~dry season, agriculture~war/hunting, east~west, and north~south. Garibay also includes east-west~south-north.[50] (Single inamic pairs commonly multiply into twofold paired inamic pairs, reflecting Aztec metaphysics' and Aztec numerology's preference for twoness and its multiples.) In addition to these routinely mentioned inamic pairs I propose being~nonbeing, generation~degeneration, order~disorder, and arrangement~derangement.

In keeping with process metaphysics, I suggest we understand inamic pairs dynamically as forces, influences, or energies-in-motion – not as static things, properties, or states of being. (We might think of them as gerunds or adverbs that modify teotl.) Feminine and masculine, for example, are kinds of energy – not things, states of affairs, or static properties. Order and disorder are properly understood as ordering and disordering energies or influences – not as static conditions or states of affairs. So construed, agonistic inamic unity consists of the ceaseless tug-of-war between feminine and masculine forces, and so on. López Austin aligns inamic pairs into two opposing columns.

MOTHER female	male FATHER
night	day
death	life
ascending influence	descending influence
ocelot	eagle
wind	fire
underworld	heaven
below	above
9	13
darkness	light
weakness	strength
water	large fire
minor	major
night stream (death)	stream of blood (life)
humidity	drought
flint stone	flower
foul smell	perfume[51]

Nonbeing, disorder, and derangement would appear to fall on the "Mother" side of this alignment; being, order, and arrangement, on the "Father" side.

López Austin's arrangement of inamic pairs sheds important light upon the nature of what it is to be an inamic as well as upon the analogies and correlations between what I call *parallel aligned inamic pairs*. First, it graphically illustrates a defining pattern in the unfolding of teotl (hence reality and cosmos). Second, it suggests the availability in Aztec metaphysics of a wealth of analogies and correlations for more fully understanding inamic pairs (and hence reality and teotl). We are now better able to see, for example, that life is to death as generation is to degeneration, light is to darkness, and male is to female. These parallels give us deeper insight into the inamic interrelationship between life and death itself as well as into the inamic relationships between male and female, and so on. Third, López Austin's alignment offers us deeper insight into each individual inamic by showing its corresponding fellow aligned inamic pairs. We gain a richer understanding of life, for example, upon realizing that life is parallel-aligned with being, generation, order, male, hot, and dry. Aztec metaphysics understands life in terms of ordering, generating, arranging, descending forces, and so on. (Descending forces are those descending from the heavens, while ascending forces are those ascending from below the surface of the earth.) Expressed processively, life energy is simultaneously ordering, generating, arranging, and masculine. And we better understand death upon realizing that death is parallel-aligned with nonbeing, derangement, ascending influence, feminine, and cold. Aztec metaphysics understands death in terms of nonbeing, disorder, derangement, female, and cold. Death energy is at the same time disordering, degenerating, deranging, cold, and feminine.

In sum, López Austin's presentation suggests new avenues for understanding Aztec metaphysics. Teotl is grand work of weaving in progress – a ceaseless interweaving of inamic interrelationships and parallel inamic interrelationships; a grand woven fabric patterned by inamic interrelationships and analogous parallel inamic interrelationships. Agonistic inamic unity is an immanent pattern in the cosmic self-weaving of teotl. The Aztecs had at their disposal a wealth of inamic interrelationships and analogous parallel inamic interrelationships for understanding the processive unfolding of teotl, reality, and cosmos.[52]

Noticeably absent from the above list of inamic pairs is good versus evil.[53] Aztec metaphysics conceives neither reality nor human existence in terms of a struggle between good and evil. Indeed, good and evil as such simply do not exist. Teotl is thoroughly *amoral*. Agonistic inamic unity thus differs strikingly from the Zoroastrian- and Manichean-style dualisms that have exercised so much influence upon Western religious and philosophical thought.[54] Generally speaking, the latter commonly view goodness, life, order, or light, on the one hand, and evil, death, chaos, or darkness, on the other, as contradictories. They see history as the zero-sum, either/or struggle between these contradictories. At the end of history, one will, or ought to, defeat and completely eliminate its contradictory. By contrast, Aztec metaphysics claims that darkness~light, nonbeing~being, and death~life alternate endlessly without resolution. The unfolding of teotl and hence the unfolding of the cosmos are *amoral*. Aztec tlamatinime rejected the idea that life (light, etc.) is intrinsically good while death (darkness, etc.) is intrinsically evil – as well as the notion that life will or ought to triumph over death. Aztec wisdom accordingly rejects as folly the quest for eternal life. Life without death is metaphysically impossible. Aztec religion, accordingly, is nonsalvific. And while the demise of the Fifth Era is obviously undesirable from the standpoint of humans, it is not intrinsically evil. Although space does not allow me to tease out its consequences here, noticeably absent from the Aztecs' list of inamic pairs are also such prominent Western binaries as mind (spirit, soul) versus body and reason versus emotion.

INAMIC PAIRS VERSUS CONTRARIES AND CONTRADICTORIES

Inamic pairs differ in important ways from contraries and contradictories as these are standardly defined by Western philosophy.[55] Western philosophy defines contrary properties as follows:

Properties *X* and *Y* are contraries if and only if:

    (i)   it is not the case that both *X* and *Y* simultaneously obtain;

    (ii) not-*X* does not entail *Y*; and

    (iii) not-*Y* does not entail *X*.

Contraries are *mutually exclusive*. Nothing may be both *X* and *Y* (at the same time and in the same sense). However, they are *not jointly exhaustive*. It is possible for something to be neither *X* nor *Y*. The relationship of contraries allows for a tertium quid: a property *Z*. The colors red and blue, for example, are contraries. While nothing may be both red and blue at the same time and in the same place, it is possible for something to be neither red nor blue. It may be green, for example. Something's being not-blue does not entail its being red, and conversely.

Inamic pairs differ from contraries since inamic partners are not mutually exclusive. Something may be both male and female at the same time. In fact, inamic partners simultaneously characterize all things. Inamic partners are, however, mutually exhaustive. Everything is *both X* and *Y*; nothing is *neither X nor Y*. There is no tertium quid, no property *Z* (like green in the example above) that is neither *X* nor *Y*. Contraries also differ from inamic partners in that contraries neither define, complement, condition, nor mutually engender one another. In conclusion, we should avoid translating *inamic* as "contrary" and avoid thinking of inamic pairs as contraries in this sense.

Western philosophy defines contradictory properties as follows:

Properties X and Y are contradictories if and only if:

    (i)   everything is either X or Y; and

    (ii) nothing is both X and Y.

Hence, if something is *X*, then it is not-*Y*, and if something is *Y*, then it is not-*X*; and if something is not-*X*, then it is *Y*, and if something is not-*Y*, then it is *X*. *X* and *Y* are *mutually exclusive*: nothing can be both *X* and *Y* (at the same time in the same sense). In addition, *X* and *Y* are also *jointly exhaustive*: that is, everything is *either X or Y but not both*. (Nothing can be both *X* and *Y*, and nothing can be neither *X* nor *Y*.) Consider, for example, the semantic properties true and false. According to the leading way of thinking about true and false in Western philosophy of language, true and false are contradictories. Every unequivocal, meaningful sentence is either true or false. It cannot be both true and false (for then it would be self-contradictory and hence meaningless), and it cannot be neither true nor false (for then it would assert nothing and so be meaningless). If the sentence is true, then it is not false; if it is false, then it is not true.

Inamic pairs differ from contradictories since inamic partners are not mutually exclusive. Everything is both male and female, hot and cold, and so on. Indeed, as we've seen, inamic pairs jointly characterize all things. We should therefore avoid translating *inamic* as "contradictory" and avoid thinking of inamic pairs as contradictories in this sense.

THE INELIMINABLE AMBIGUITY OF THINGS

Agonistic inamic unity entails the fundamental, ineliminable ambiguity of all things. Reality is ineliminably ambiguous. All things consist simultaneously of *both* male *and* female, being *and* nonbeing, hot *and* cold, and ordering *and* disordering inamic forces. Nothing is characterized *exclusively* by heat or masculinity; nothing *exclusively* by cold or femininity. Nothing is wholly ordered; nothing wholly disordered. The entire constellation of aligned inamic forces complement, complete, and compete with one another within the cosmos and within every individual entity in the cosmos. Of course not everything is constituted by these forces in equal proportions, and the inamic proportions characterizing individual things is always changing.

Consider Tlaloc, for example, the figurehead and most prominent "deity" of Nicholson's Rain-Moisture-and-Agricultural-Fertility constellation of processes and powers. Aztec artists standardly depicted Tlaloc carrying a lightning bolt. Lightning bolts symbolize fire along with fire's parallel aligned inamic partners: heat, male, and drought. Why? Because Aztec metaphysics conceives Tlaloc and the Rain-Moisture-and-Agricultural-Fertility constellation as consisting of both aqueous and fiery, feminine and masculine, wet and dry forces. The Rain-Moisture-and-Agricultural-Fertility constellation (together with all its associated aspects and microprocesses including Tlaloc, the Tlaloque-Tepictoton, and Chalchiuhtlicue) is therefore ex hypothesi irreducibly inamically mixed and ambiguous since it consists of the inamic forces of both water and fire, female and male, humidity and drought, foul smell and perfume, and so on. The constellation is accordingly both beneficial and detrimental to humans.

Contemporary Nahuatl-speakers in San Martín Zinacapan in the Sierra Norte de Puebla continue to conceive reality in these terms. Timothy Knab writes, "*Taloc* [lord of the underworld] and *talocan* [the underworld]. . . . are both male and female at the same time, source of life and place of death, father and mother."[56] Depending upon a complex juxtaposition of relationships and circumstances, Taloc may be either beneficial or harmful to humans.

Let's look more closely at death~life. Life is both creative and destructive; death, both destructive and creative. Life and death are mutually arising, dependent, complementary, and completing as well as mutually competitive forces interwoven with one another within a single cyclical process. Life struggles against death, yet at the same time arises from death. Death struggles against life, yet at the same time arises from life. Life is constantly flowing into death; death, constantly flowing into life. The two are continually creating, nurturing, competing, and overcoming one another; continually transmuting into one another; and continually enabling one another. Life completes death, and death completes life. Only together do they constitute completeness and wholeness. What's more, neither life nor death is wholly positive or negative. Life feeds off the death of other living things, and so has a negative aspect. Death makes life possible and so has a positive aspect. Each needs the other. Life contains within itself the fatal, disordering germ of death while death contains within itself the fertile, ordering seed of life.

Since life and death are not mutually exclusive it follows that life and death are neither contraries nor contradictories. Nothing is characterized exclusively by life; nothing exclusively by death. Nothing is wholly alive; nothing wholly dead. Rather, everything is characterized by both life and death (in one degree or another). Everything consists of an ineliminable mixture of life and death forces and is therefore ineliminably ambiguous.[57]

The artists of Tlatilco and Soyaltepec depicted the agonistic inamic unity of life~death by fashioning a split-faced mask, one half with flesh and alive, the other half, fleshless, skeletal, and dead. Each mask is intentionally ambiguous seeing as each unifies within a single figure both life and death. Each portrays the agonistic inamic unity and inamic ambiguity of life~death forces fused together within a single process that is simultaneously creative of life and destructive of life. Each figure is simultaneously *neither* alive *nor* dead yet *both* alive *and* dead. Each is *neither* completely alive (fleshed) *nor* completely dead (skeletal). Yet each is also *both* alive *and* dead since each presents both life and death as two aspects of a single figure. (See Figure 3.2.)

Yet the inamic ambiguity of these pieces does not end with this. Each half-face is by itself also ambiguous. On the one hand, skulls symbolize death and life. McKeever Furst argues skeletonization – skulls, fleshless jaws, and bones generally – symbolizes life-giving and life-sustaining energy, generation, rebirth, and fertility because life springs from the bones of the dead. "Skeletal remains were – and in fact continue to be – regarded as the seat of the essential life force and the metaphorical seed from which the individual, whether human or animal or plant, is reborn."[58] The *Legend of the Suns* nicely illustrates this point. Quetzalcoatl travels to Mictlan (Land of the Dead) to retrieve the bones of the humans from the preceding Era in order to generate humans for the current

FIGURE 3.2. *Soyaltepec life~death mask. (Author's photo.)*

Fifth Era.⁵⁹ Peter Furst claims Mesoamericans commonly believe the essential life force of animals and humans resides in their bones and in particular the bones of their heads.⁶⁰ Lastly, semen is produced within the bones. Fleshy faces, on the other hand, simultaneously symbolize life and death. Living flesh obviously symbolizes life, yet, since it also nourishes death, it also symbolizes evanescence, expiry, and death. (See Figure 3.3.)

3.4. ARTISTIC PRESENTATIONS OF AGONISTIC INAMIC UNITY

Mesoamerican artists depicted agonistic inamic unity in a variety of additional ways including spirals, butterflies, olin figures, quincunxes, and face-to-face anthropomorphic figures. To this list Elizabeth Brumfiel adds squiggles, step-frets, zigzags, the *coliuhqui* ("a curved hill"), the *xicalcoliuhqui* (step-fret spiral), and ribbons,⁶¹ while Esther Pasztory adds undulating figures (such as

FIGURE 3.3. *Aztec life~death sculpture.*
(Author's photo.)

serpents), bicephalous figures,[62] and figures involving "opposition, pairing, and intertwining."[63]

Painter-scribes standardly depicted agonistic inamic unity by means of face-to-face marriage partners and face-to-face binomial deity pairs. *Codex Mendoza* (fol. 61r) portrays bride and groom sitting face-to-face (see Figure 3.1). *Codex Borbonicus* (pl. 21) depicts the married couple, Cipactonal~Oxomoco, in the same fashion.[64] The post-Conquest pictorial censuses of Tepetlaoztoc found in the *Códice de Santa María Asunción* and *Codex Vergara* depict household heads and wives facing one another.[65] *Codex Borbonicus* (pl. 22) depicts the inamic deities Quetzalcoatl~Tezcatlipoca face-to-face (see Figure 3.4).[66] *Codex Fejérváry-Mayer* depicts a number of binomial deity pairs in this fashion, including Chicomecoatl~Cinteotl (pl. 36), Tonacacihuatl~Tonacatecuhtli (pl. 24), Red Tezcatlipoca~Blue Tezcatlipoca (pl. 25), and Xochiquetzal~Xochipilli (pl. 35).[67] *Codex Borgia* (pl. 56) depicts Quetzalcoatl~Mictlantecuhtli matched back-to-back as though sharing a common spine, much in the way two fields share a common stone-wall boundary (see Figure 3.5).[68]

Aztec artists also depicted agonistic inamic unity by means of intertwining, pairing, and opposition motifs that Brumfiel calls "oscillating motion or recipro-cal motifs."[69] The motifs adorn woven fabric, spinning whorls, ceramic flat and cylindrical stamps, plates and bowls, codices, and architectural constructions. They include spirals, S-spirals (*xonecuilli*), the olin, zigzags, step-frets, the coli-uhqui (a curved hill), the xicalcoliuhqui (a step-fret spiral), cutaway shells, the

FIGURE 3.4. *Quetzalcoatl~Tezcatlipoca.* (Codex Borbonicus *[Loubat 1899: pl. 22]; courtesy of Foundation for the Advancement of Mesoamerican Studies, Inc.)*

patolli (board game), quincunx (cruciform), and squiggles. These motifs depict simultaneous inward-and-outward, coming-and-going, and back-and-forth reciprocal motion and hence the ambiguous motion of agonistic inamic unity. Many of these motifs exhibit the figure-ground phenomenon of alternating perceived images exhibited by Gestalt figures such as Rubin's vase, the Necker cube, and the duck/rabbit (see Figure 1.1).[70] Both Gestalt figures and agonistic inamic unity motifs are ambiguous. Consider the xicalcoliuhqui motif (see Figures 3.6 and 3.7). By visually switching from white figure and black ground to black figure and white ground, one perceives the motif's undulating motion moving either from left to right or from right to left. One also perceives the reciprocal interlocking or spinning together of downward-hanging white frets and upward-rising black frets. This creates a dynamic tension and dynamic unity.

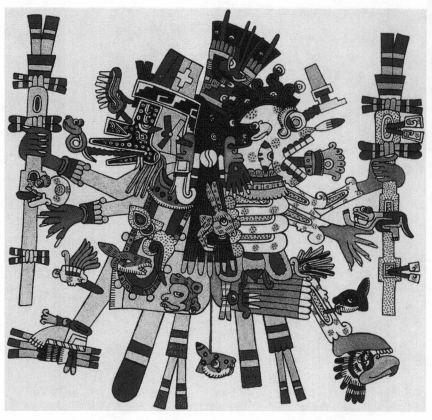

Figure 3.5. *Mictlantecuhtli~Quetzalcoatl (*Codex Borgia *[1993: pl. 73]; courtesy of Dover Press.)*

Spiral motifs function the same way. They are ambiguous since they simultaneously exhibit inward and outward motion. Like the xicalcoliuhqui, they express the mutual spinning together and hence unifying of white and black agonistic inamic partners (see Figure 3.8). The same may be said of the cutaway shell motif displayed most prominently by Quetzalcoatl and the *almenas* (crenellated battlements) atop the *calmecac* (the temple school where young people were trained to become priests) of Tenochtitlan (see Figure 3.9).[71]

Aztec sculptors presented the ambiguity of inamic unified twoness using bicephalous figures such as the statue of Coatlicue ("Skirt of Serpents").[72] Coatlicue's single face is formed by two facing snakes. When looking at the statue, one experiences a Gestalt figure-ground effect, the statue alternating

FIGURE 3.6. *Xicalcoliuhqui. (Enciso [1953: 32, fig. iii]; courtesy of Dover Press.)*

FIGURE 3.7. *Xicalcoliuhqui. (Enciso [1953: 21, fig. i]; courtesy of Dover Press.)*

FIGURE 3.8. *Spiral. (Enciso [1953: 13, fig. ii]; courtesy of Dover Press.)*

between perceiving a forward-facing, two-eyed Coatlicue, and two single-eyed, face-to-face snakes. The statue unites in dynamic reciprocal tension female~male, death~life, and so on. It not only symbolizes but also embodies agonistic inamic unity.

FIGURE 3.9. *Cutaway shell. (Enciso [1974: Figure 166]; courtesy of Dover Press.)*

Turning to architecture, Johanna Broda, Davíd Carrasco, and Eduardo Matos Moctezuma argue the combination of the Templo Mayor's architectural design, twin temples to Tlaloc and Huitzilopochtli, directional orientation, adornments, and ritual objects captured continuous and simultaneous ascending and descending reciprocal motion and influence as well as continuous and simultaneous centering and peripheral reciprocal motion and influence.[73] The Templo Mayor not only depicted but also embodied agonistic inamic unity in all its aspects: death~life, agriculture~war, and so on.

3.5. ABSTRACT INAMIC PAIRS

Agonistic inamic unity includes more abstract notions such as being~nonbeing, order~disorder, arrangement~derangement, regeneration~degeneration, creation~ destruction, and integration~disintegration. These are parallel aligned with male~female, life~death, hot~cold, dry~wet, and so on. Nonbeing, disorder, and derangement fall on the "Mother" side of López Austin's alignment, while being, order, and arrangement fall on the "Father" side. Let's examine two of these: being~nonbeing and order~disorder. What is true of these two is true mutatis mutandis of the others.

Being and nonbeing (existence~nonexistence) are inamically matched and inseparably bound to one another both *metaphysically* and *conceptually*. They are neither contraries nor contradictories; nor are they *conceptually*, *metaphysically*, or *temporally* prior to one another. Neither can exist without the other. They are mutually arising, dependent, and complementary while at the same time mutually agonistic. Each complements, completes, and competes with the other. Each nourishes and engenders the other while also struggling to undermine and dominate the other. Yet neither struggles to extinguish the other. Each continually flows and transmutes into as well as emerges from the other.

The agonistic unity of being~nonbeing characterizes all things. Consequently all things are ineliminably ambiguous with being *and* nonbeing. Nothing is exclusively being *or* nonbeing; nothing is characterized by pure being or pure nonbeing. Teotl, reality, and the entire cosmos are at bottom metaphysically ambiguous. Agonistic inamic unity therefore rejects the fundamental metaphysical intuition shaping Western philosophy since Plato that maintains that that which is real is by definition pure, unambiguous, and unmixed. Only appearances are ambiguous. According to this view, the apparent ambiguity of reality is therefore by necessity eliminated upon correctly understanding reality. For Aztec metaphysics, by contrast, both being *and* nonbeing are ineliminable aspects of teotl and reality. What's more, being and nonbeing are both positive and negative. Since being feeds off nonbeing, it may be said to have a negative aspect. Since nonbeing nurtures and engenders being, it may be said to have a positive aspect. Since all things are characterized by both being and nonbeing, all things have both positive and negative aspects in this respect.

The continuous agonism of being~nonbeing results in a tertium quid: continuous *becoming*. Everything is defined by continuous becoming. The continuing agonism of being~nonbeing results in a *second* tertium quid: continuous *transformation*. Everything is simultaneously defined by continuous transforming. Becoming and transforming are nothing other than the continuous self-becoming and self-transforming of teotl. The cosmos and all its inhabitants are defined by continuous becoming and transformation. As a consequence, reality contains no immutable or permanent entities, structures, or arrangements. Everything that teotl generates out of itself is by nature dynamic, unstable, and transient.

Becoming and transformation are simultaneously creative and destructive. Just as life emerges from death (and conversely), creation emerges from destruction (and conversely). Creation and destruction are inamically bound together. Creating something necessarily involves destroying something. Beginning to be something new necessarily involves ceasing to be something previous. Transformation from one thing into another likewise necessarily involves destroying some previous thing. Creation and transformation do not arise from nothing.

Although each moment in the agonistic tug-of-war between being and nonbeing consists of the temporary dominance of one or other inamic and therefore an imbalance, in the long run their tug-of-war creates an overarching *diachronic* and *dynamic* balance. By weaving together being and nonbeing, teotl generates itself and all things. The pattern of teotl's weaving is nothing other than agonistic inamic unity. It is immanent and nonhierarchical.

In sum, the ceaseless becoming and transformation of teotl consists of the ceaseless agonism of being~nonbeing. Teotl's self-becoming and self-transforming – that is, its self-creating, -destroying, and -recreating – consists of the continual weaving together and commingling of being and nonbeing. Like the life~death masks discussed earlier, teotl is *neither* being *nor* nonbeing yet it is simultaneously *both* being *and* nonbeing. It neither *is* nor *is not* – yet it both *is* and *is not*. As David Hall explains regarding the dao, "only becoming (coming into being which illustrates some mixture of being and nonbeing) is; not-becoming (either being or nonbeing abstracted away from its polar relation with its opposite) is not."[74]

Consider next order~disorder (ordering energy~disordering energy). As inamic partners order and disorder are bound together in an endless back-and-forth struggle. Neither is *conceptually, metaphysically,* or *temporally* prior to the other. They are mutually competitive, complementary, and completing. Order competes with disorder yet emerges from disorder, just as disorder competes with order yet emerges from order. Each continually flows into the other and transmutes into the other. As Burkhart writes, "Entropic forces [erode] order, but [are] themselves fertile and energizing, providing the substance for new establishments of order."[75] The agonistic unity of order~disorder characterizes teotl, reality, and all things in the cosmos. Teotl, reality, and all things are thus irreducibly ambiguous with order *and* disorder. Nothing is wholly orderly *or* wholly disorderly. Like the life~death masks above, teotl is *neither* orderly *nor* disorderly yet it is at the same time *both* orderly *and* disorderly. Order and disorder are ineliminable features of teotl, reality, and cosmos.

The continuous dialectical struggle of order~disorder, like that of being~nonbeing, results in its own tertium quid: an overarching *second-order* pattern or ordering of *first-order* ordering~disordering. This second-order pattern or ordering is immanent. Unfortunately we have no word in English like *becoming* that refers to such a tertium quid. Although *unorder* looks promising, it is too close in meaning to *disorder*. The metaphysics of ordinary English gets in our way. In what follows I therefore use *order* and *disorder* simpliciter to refer to first-order order and first-order disorder, respectively. It is first-order order and first-order disorder that constitute an inamic pair. When it becomes necessary to write of second-order order, I explicitly indicate it as such.

Order and being are unstable, short-lived, and impermanent. And thus we arrive yet again at the ineluctable evanescence and instability of all ordered things, from trees, houses, and humans to cosmic eras. Disorder is constantly subverting order. Disordering, degenerating, disintegrating, deranging, and decomposing forces are metaphysically fundamental and ineliminable. This fact gives rise to one of the defining characteristics of human existence: the Fifth Sun-Earth Ordering is a perilous habitat for humans. It is "slippery," as a Nahua proverb recorded by Sahagún puts it.[76] Life on earth is slippery because order and being are always sliding into disorder and nonbeing. The existence and well-orderedness of the things upon which humans depend slip away from under their feet, causing them to lose their balance and suffer pain, hunger, thirst, sorrow, disease, and death.

This fact contributes to a second defining characteristic of human existence: the *epistemological* inability of humans to fully comprehend reality (teotl).[77] Although the agonism of order~disorder, being~nonbeing, and so on is rhythmically patterned, humans are nevertheless unable to *know with certainty* at any given locus in time and place whether or not – and if so, to what extent – order and being will collapse into disorder and nonbeing. It is impossible to know precisely when disorder and nonbeing will erupt and undermine order and being. This epistemological shortcoming contributes to the peril of human existence. When undertaking any kind of project – be it planting corn, getting married, going to war, or embarking upon a trading expedition – it is impossible to know one's exact location in the periodic, pendulum-like swinging of cosmic inamic partners. Is one embarking on the cusp of order and generation or that of disorder and degeneration? Are ordering or disordering forces in ebb or in flow? Reality is ultimately unknowable and hence unpredictable.

I refer to the ineliminable uncertainty and unpredictability of reality as the *Tezcatlipoca factor*. The inamic "deity" pair Quetzalcoatl~Tezcatlipoca represents the creative~destructive and generative~degenerative forces whose continuing agon defines the becoming of reality.[78] The Aztecs saw the becoming of the cosmos as the product of the ongoing inamic struggle between the generative, ordering forces of Quetzalcoatl, on the one hand, and the degenerative, disordering forces of Tezcatlipoca, on the other. Quetzalcoatl represents the forces of generation, creation, being, ordering, arrangement, and hence creative transformation. Tezcatlipoca represents the forces of degeneration, destruction, nonbeing, disorder, derangement, and hence destructive transformation. Tezcatlipoca represents forces that at any moment erupt in our lives, subverting being and order and so sabotaging our endeavors. "Tezcatlipoca, " writes McKeever Furst, "introduced random and unexpected occurrences into the universe."[79] Tezcatlipoca is also associated with dust, filth, pollution, and tlazolli.

To be in Tezcatlipoca's presence is to be in a dangerously slippery place.[80] And humans are always in his presence!

Tezcatlipoca is accordingly said to mock, ridicule, laugh at, and play sport with humans. Tezcatlipoca thus reminds us of the role of chance in our lives and of the consequent "slipperiness" of life on the surface of the earth. I interpret this as the upshot of the following passage from Book VI of the *Florentine Codex*: "Our Master, the Lord of the Close Vicinity, thinks and does what He wishes; He determines, He amuses himself. As He wishes, so will it be. In the palm of His hand He has us; at His will He shifts us around. We shift around, like marbles we roll; He rolls us around endlessly. We are but toys to Him; He laughs at us."[81] Chance, uncertainty, and unpredictability are ineliminable elements of our lives.

3.6. BALANCE AND IMBALANCE, AND CENTER AND PERIPHERY ARE *NOT* INAMIC PAIRS

Balance and imbalance (equilibrium and disequilibrium) do not constitute an inamic pair. They are *not* inamic pairs and hence not inamic partners. The importance of this fact cannot be overstressed. Balance and imbalance are *not* mutually competitive, complementary, or completing. Rather, balance – or more precisely, *balancing* – is generated by the ceaseless back-and-forth alternating of two *imbalances* – excess and deprivation, or excessive indulgence and excessive deprivation – just as becoming is generated by the back-and-forth alternating of being~nonbeing (life~death, etc.). The relevant agonistic inamic partners here are the two imbalances: excess and deprivation. Balancing occurs by middling these two extremes; it occurs in the middle of two extremes. Balancing is a *triadic* relationship, whereas an agonistic inamic pair is a *dyadic* relationship. Balancing, therefore, belongs alongside becoming, second-order ordering, and transformation as a tertium quid. Balancing is not *subject to* agonistic inamic unity but rather is a *consequence of* agonistic inamic unity. As our earlier discussion of walking showed, balancing is *an overarching macroprocess* consisting of a rhythmic series of mutually interdependent and reciprocally influencing imbalancing *microprocesses*. Balancing is *dynamic* and *diachronic*. It is not a static state of affairs or condition. Willard Gingerich and Barbara Myerhoff argue that what I am here calling agonistic inamic unity has its roots in Mesoamerican shamanism. The process of agonistic inamic unity yields what Myerhoff calls "shamanic balance," which she describes as follows: "Shamanic balance is . . . not a balance achieved by synthesis, nor a static condition achieved by resolving oppositions. It is not a compromise. Rather, it is a state of acute tension, the kind of tension which exists . . . when two unqualified forces encounter each other, meeting headlong, and are not reconciled but held teetering on the verge of chaos."[82]

Western theologies and philosophies overwhelmingly equate balance and equilibrium with peace, serenity, and harmony. Aztec metaphysics *does not*. The unity of agonistic inamic pairs is neither peaceful, serene, nor harmonious. Inamic partners make war upon one another and subdue one another. Since agonistic inamic unity defines reality, it follows that agonistic tension is built into the very fabric of reality. Although the cosmos has always consisted of balancing agonistic inamic partners, it has never enjoyed peace, serenity, and harmony.

Center and periphery are *not* agonistic inamic partners, either. This fact is also of paramount importance. Center – or more precisely, *centering* or *well-centeredness* – is defined in relationship to two (or more) peripheries. Well-centeredness in the Fifth Era, for example, is defined in relation to the four directional inamic pairs: east~west, south~north, east-west~south-north, and above~below. Center is generated by the back-and-forth alternating of inamically defined peripheries – just as balancing is generated by the back-and-forth alternating of inamically defined imbalances. Like the balanced needle of a scale, center is situated equidistantly from peripheries. The relevant agonistic inamic partners here are the matched peripheries. Centering occurs by middling these peripheries; it is defined as the midpoint of these peripheries. Centering is a *triadic* relationship and as such belongs alongside balancing, becoming, second-order ordering, and transformation as a tertium quid.

3.7. OMETEOTL

The concepts of dual-aspect monism and agonistic inamic unity as well as their centrality in Aztec metaphysics find perhaps their sharpest expression in Ometeotl.[83] *Ometeotl* is commonly translated as "God of Duality" or "Two God," and commonly parsed as combining *ome* ("two") or *omeyotl* ("twoness"), and *teotl* ("god," "deity").[84] Since Aztec metaphysics is pantheistic, however, Ometeotl cannot be a god, no less one distinct from teotl. I suggest we gloss *Ometeotl* as "two sacred energy" or "two sacred power." Talk about Ometeotl represents another way of talking about teotl: one that focuses upon teotl's agonistic inamic unity. Ometeotl – or what Nicholson calls the "Ometeotl complex"[85] – is a single, all-encompassing cluster of energies consisting of the agonistic unity of all inamic pairs: male~female, dry~wet, being~nonbeing, order~disorder, and so on. Neither Ometeotl's male and ordering aspects nor Omteotl's female and disordering aspects are logically, metaphysically, or temporally prior to the other. Like *teotl*, we should treat *Ometeotl* as a gerund, not a noun.

Ometeotl is the primordial agonistic inamic unity from which everything – including all other "gods" – emerges, upon which the continuing existence of everything depends, and to which everything returns. It is the primordial agonistic inamic unity of which everything is a manifestation, and in which everything participates. Ometeotl's continual and continuous agonistic unifying of male~female together with the entire panoply of inamic pairs parallel aligned with male~female – e.g. life~death, dry~wet, being~nonbeing, order~disorder, and generation~degeneration, and so on – results in the ceaseless becoming, transforming, second-order ordering, and balancing of the cosmos. Ometeotl's becoming and transforming are thus simultaneously creative and destructive, ordering and disordering, and so forth. Ometeotl is therefore also irreducibly ambiguous. Agonistic inamic unity and dual-aspect monism accordingly define primordiality and all things created.

According to Fray Gerónimo de Mendieta, this primordial, male~female creative unity was also called *moyucoyatzin áyac oquiyocux, áyac oquipic* ("no one formed him or gave him existence").[86] This appellation suggests Ometeotl is self-generating and has always existed. Fray Juan de Torquemada reports that the "Indians" understood "divine nature to be divided into two gods, a man and a woman."[87] This primordial male~female creative force was also called *Ometecuhtli-Omecihuatl* ("Two Lord-Two Lady"), *Tonacatecuhtli-Tonacacihuatl* ("Lord of Our Flesh or Sustenance-Lady of Our Flesh or Sustenance), *in Tonan, in Tota* ("our mother, our father"), *in teteuinan, in teteu ita, Huehueteotl* ("father~mother of the gods, old or ancient god"), and *Ipalnemohuani* ("He~She through Whom One Lives").[88] Sahagún's informants tell us that Ometecuhtli and his "inamic," Omecihuatl, ruled the twelve heavens. "It was said that there were we, the common people, created; thence came our souls."[89]

León-Portilla, Michel Graulich, H. B. Nicholson, and Rafael Tena (among others) contend the following two appellations also apply to Ometeotl: *in Tloque in Nahuaque* ("Lord of the Near and the Nigh" or "Lord of the Everywhere") and *Yoalli Ehecatl* ("Night, Wind").[90] The former suggests Ometeotl is not only metaphysically omnipresent but also *metaphysically immanent*. The latter suggests Ometeotl is invisible and intangible, that is, imperceptible by the senses under normal circumstances. As we saw in chapters 1 and 2, however, imperceptibility entails neither metaphysical transcendence nor metaphysical dualism (*pace* León-Portilla and López Austin). Several scholars identify the male~female figure depicted in *Codex Borgia* (fol. 61) as Ometeotl.[91] Ometeotl wears a female skirt and a male *maxtlatl* (breach cloth). He~she poses in the childbearing position, suggesting endless generation and regeneration.

Ometeotl (Ometecuhtli~Omecihuatl, Tonacatecuhtli~Tonacacihuatl) consists of the continuing agonism of male and female inamic partners. Paramount among these agonistic interactions is sexual commingling. Ometeotl's two inamic aspects engage in a single, never-ending process of back-and-forth interweaving, commingling, and intercoursing with one another – a process that is simultaneously creative and destructive and hence transformative. From this ceaseless commingling comes the cosmos and all its inhabitants.

Ometeotl dwells in *omeyocan* ("two time-place" or "time-place of duality") – the time-place of continual agonistic inamic unity; the time-place of continual generation, regeneration, and transformation; the birth time-place of all things; and the highest fold or layer of the cosmos.[92] León-Portilla describes Omeyocan as "The source of generation and life, the ultimate metaphysical region, the primordial dwelling of Ometeotl."[93] Omeyocan is defined by the irreducible ontological ambiguity of agonistic inamic unity. Although it is a time-place of balance, it is not – nor has it ever been – a time-place of stasis, peace, serenity, and harmony.

John Monaghan writes, "Throughout Mesoamerica, 'twoness' is an abstract image of wholeness."[94] Nathaniel Tarn and Martin Prechtel note similarly, "nothing complete, nothing fully fulfilling its function in the world, can be other than [both male and female]."[95] Ometeotl and Omeyocan dramatically illustrate these ideas. The notion of *unified twoness* contained in the concepts of Ometeotl and Omeyocan entails completion and wholeness. What's more, this is a special kind of completion and wholeness; namely, one resulting from the agonistic interaction of inamic partners. It is a dynamic, diachronic, and processive wholeness – not a static one. It is a wholeness characterized by continual struggle, tension, becoming, transformation, and diachronic balancing. When properly unified, two things constitute a balanced and stable singularity.

Ometeotl and Omeyocan also suggest *twofold oneness*. Although single, they are constituted by the agonistic interaction of inamic pairs that are by definition mutually dependent, related, and arising. This, too, is a special kind of wholeness and completion; namely, one consisting of the agonism of inamic pairs. We must not, therefore, think of Ometeotl and Omeyocan as constituted by two metaphysically distinct and independently existing entities (or dualities) that are merely contingently fused together by means of agonistic interaction. There was no time-place when either inamic existed without the other. Inamic oneness and wholeness are indissoluble.

In sum, the centrality of agonistic inamic unity, unified twoness, and twofold oneness in conjunction with their equation with completeness, wholeness, and well-balancedness highlight Aztec metaphysics' fundamental orientation toward twoness. Singles do not exist, only pairs do. Single things are not only internally composed of inamic pairs, they are always externally paired with inamic partners. As a result Aztec metaphysics conceives apparently single things (such as Ometeotl and Omeyocan) as inherently and irreducibly ambiguous.

3.8. CONCLUSION

The ceaseless becoming and transforming of teotl, reality, and cosmos are the products of the ceaseless agon between being and nonbeing, creation and destruction, order and disorder, and the constellation of their aligned inamic pairs. Aztec metaphysics claims the unifying struggle of inamic partners is characterized by three distinct principal patterns: *olin*, *malinalli*, and *nepantla*. These three patterns define the dynamics of reality and of the Aztec cosmos. Olin unifies inamic partners through simple up-and-down movement or through more complex up-and-over and down-and-under movement. Malinalli unifies inamic partners by spinning and twisting them together. Nepantla unifies them by middling them and weaving them together. Since inamic partners are defined in terms of one another, one can therefore fully understand them only by understanding *how* they complement, complete, and compete with one another. Olin, malinalli, and nepantla also characterize three different ways inamic partners complement, complete, and compete with one another. Chapters 4, 5, and 6 examine these three in turn.

NOTES

1. I borrow this convention from J. A. Scott Kelso and David A. Engstrøm, *The Complementary Nature* (Cambridge, MA: MIT Press, 2006).

2. Alfredo López Austin, "Complementos y composiciones," *Ojarasca* 5 (1992): 40, translation mine.

3. The relationship between inamic partners resembles the relationship between yin and yang according to classical East Asian metaphysics. For a discussion of yin and yang, see Roger T. Ames, "Images of Reason in Chinese Culture," in *Introduction to World Philosophies*, ed. Eliot Deutsch (Upper Saddle River, NJ: Prentice-Hall, 1997), 254–59; Ames, "Yin and Yang," in *Encyclopedia of Chinese Philosophy*, ed. Antonio S. Cua (New York: Routledge, 2003), 846–47; Roger T. Ames and Henry Rosemont Jr., *The Analects of Confucius: A Philosophical Translation* (New York: Ballantine Books, 1998); David L. Hall and Roger T. Ames, *Thinking through Confucius* (Albany: State University of New York Press, 1987); Hall and Ames, "Understanding Order: The Chi-

nese Perspective," in *From Africa to Zen*, eds. Robert Solomon and Kathleen Higgins (Lanham, MD: Rowman and Littlefield, 1993), 1–23; and Hall and Ames, *Anticipating China: Thinking through the Narratives of Chinese and Western Culture* (Albany: SUNY Press, 1995).

4. For parallels between weaving and painting-writing, see Barbara Tedlock and Dennis Tedlock, "Text and Textile: Language and Technology in the Arts of the Quiché Maya," *Journal of Anthropological Research* 41, no. 2 (1985): 121–46.

5. Cecelia Klein, "Woven Heaven, Tangled Earth: The Weaver's Paradigm of the Mesoamerican Cosmos," in *Ethnoastronomy and Archaeoastronomy in the American Tropics*, eds. Anthony Aveni and Gary Urton, Annals of the New York Academy of Sciences, No. 38 (New York: New York Academy of Sciences, 1982), 1. See also Tedlock and Tedlock, "Text and Textile"; Peter T. Furst, "The Thread of Life: Some Parallels in the Symbolism of Aztec, Huichol and Puebla Earth Goddesses," in *Balance y perspectiva de la antropolgía de Mesoamerica y del centro de México*, Mesa Redonda 13th, 1973 (México, DF: La Sociedad Mexicana de Antropolgía, 1975), 235–45; Stacy B. Schaefer, *To Think with a Good Heart: Wixárika Women, Weavers, and Shamans* (Salt Lake City: University of Utah Press, 2002); Kay A. Read, *Time and Sacrifice in the Aztec Cosmos* (Bloomington: Indiana University Press, 1998); and Louise M. Burkhart, "Mexica Women on the Home Front: Housework and Religion in Aztec Mexico," in *Indian Women of Early Mexico*, eds. Susan Schroeder, Stephanie Wood, and Robert Haskett (Norman: University of Oklahoma Press, 1997), 25–54. Gerardo Reichel-Dolmatoff argues weaving functions as an "organizational principle" for the Kogi of the Sierra Nevada de Santa Marta in northern Columbia (Reichel-Dolmatoff, "The Loom of Life: A Kogi Principle of Integration," *Journal of Latin American Lore* 4, no. 1 [1978]: 10).

6. Stephen Pepper, *World Hypotheses: A Study in Evidence* (Berkeley: University of California Press, 1970), 91, emphasis mine.

7. Alfredo López Austin, *Tamoanchan, Tlalocan: Places of Mist*, trans. Bernard R. Ortiz de Montellano and Thelma Ortiz de Montellano (Niwot: University Press of Colorado, 1997), 8.

8. George Lakoff and Mark Johnson, *Metaphors We Live By* (Chicago: University of Chicago Press, 1980), 3.

9. Ibid.

10. Ibid., 22.

11. Ibid., 5

12. If Pepper and Lakoff and Johnson are correct, metaphors shape all of human thinking, rational and otherwise, scientific and otherwise, elite and commoner. Metaphorical thinking is not confined to so-called prelogical, primitive, emotional-affective, mythopoeic, or prescientific modes of thought as many scholars argue. And so I contend the organizing concepts and root metaphors employed by Aztec philosophers in

speculating about the nature of things derived from everyday ways of thinking and speaking about commonplace activities such as weaving, sexual reproduction, hunting, and warfare. While certainly philosophers had more opportunity to reflect upon, refine, and articulate their metaphysical views than did ordinary folk, their views nevertheless differed in degree of refinement rather than in kind. For further discussion, see Brian Morris, *Anthropological Studies of Religion: An Introductory Text* (Cambridge: Cambridge University Press, 1987); Hall and Ames, *Thinking through Confucius*; and David L. Hall and Roger T. Ames, *Thinking from the Han: Self, Truth and Transcendence in Chinese and Western Culture* (Albany: SUNY Press, 1998).

13. Victor Turner, *Dramas, Fields and Metaphors: Symbolic Action in Human Society* (Ithaca, NY: Cornell University Press, 1974), 64, emphasis mine.

14. Quoted in Brian Fay, *Contemporary Philosophy of Social Science* (Oxford: Blackwell, 1996), 115, emphasis mine.

15. Timothy J. Knab, "Metaphors, Concepts, and Coherence in Aztec," in *Symbol and Meaning beyond the Closed Community: Essays in Mesoamerican Ideas*, ed. Gary H. Gossen (Albany: Institute for Mesoamerican Studies, SUNY Press, 1986), 45.

16. Ibid., 45, 55.

17. Ibid., 46.

18. Ibid., 45.

19. Ibid.

20. Alfredo López Austin, *The Human Body and Ideology: Concepts of the Ancient Nahuas*, 2 vols., trans. Thelma Ortiz de Montellano and Bernard R. Ortiz de Montellano (Salt Lake City: University of Utah Press, 1988), 1:52. See also Alfredo López Austin, *The Rabbit on the Face of the Moon: Mythology in the Mesoamerican Tradition*, trans. Bernard R. Ortiz de Montellano and Thelma Ortiz de Montellano (Salt Lake City: University of Utah Press, 1996); Alfredo López Austin, "*Complementos y composiciones,*" 40–42; Alfredo López Austin, *The Myths of the Opossum: Pathways of Mesoamerican Mythology*, trans. Bernard R. Ortiz de Montellano and Thelma Ortiz de Montellano (Albuquerque: University of New Mexico Press, 1993); and Alfredo López Austin, *Tamoanchan y Tlalocan* (México: Fondo de Cultura Económica, 2004). For discussion of duality in Mesoamerican philosophy, see Mercedes de la Garza, *El universo sagrado de la serpiente entre los mayas* (México, DF: Universidad Nacional Autónoma de México, 1984); Cecelia Klein, "None of the Above: Gender Ambiguity in Nahua Ideology," in *Gender in Pre-Hispanic America*, ed. Cecelia Klein (Washington, DC: Dumbarton Oaks, 2001), 183–254; Timothy J. Knab, *A War of Witches: A Journey into the Underworld of the Contemporary Aztecs* (Boulder: Westview Press, 1995); Timothy J. Knab, *The Dialogue of Earth and Sky: Dreams, Souls, Curing and the Modern Aztec Underworld* (Tucson: University of Arizona Press, 2004); Eduardo Matos Moctezuma, *Muerte a filo de obsidiana: Los nahuas frente a la muerte* (México, DF: Fondo de Cultura Económica, 2008); John D. Monaghan,

The Covenants with Earth and Rain: Exchange, Sacrifice and Revelation in Mixtec Social-ity (Norman: University of Oklahoma Press, 1995); John D. Monaghan, "The Person, Destiny, and the Construction of Difference in Mesoamerica," *RES* 33 (Spring 1998): 137–46; John D. Monaghan, "Theology and History in the Study of Mesoamerican Reli-gions," in *Supplement to the Handbook of Middle American Indians*, vol. 6, ed. John D. Monaghan (Austin: University of Texas Press, 2000), 24–49; Noemí Quezada, "Cre-encias tradicionales sobre embarazo y parto," *Anales de antropología* 14 (1977): 307–26; James M. Taggart, *Nahuat Myth and Social Structure* (Austin: University of Texas Press, 1983); Nathaniel Tarn and Martin Prechtel, "Constant Inconstancy: The Feminine Prin-ciple in Atiteco Mythology," in *Symbol and Meaning: Beyond the Closed Community*, ed. Gary Gossen (Albany: SUNY Press, Institute for Mesoamerican Studies, 1986), 173–84; and Susan Kellogg, "From Parallel and Equivalent to Separate but Unequal: Tenocha Mexica Women, 1500–1700," in *Indian Women of Early Mexico*, ed. Susan Schroeder, Ste-phen Wood, and Robert Haskett (Norman: University of Oklahoma Press, 1997), 123–43. For discussion of closely similar conceptions of duality in native North American philosophies, see Anne Waters, "Language Matters: Nondiscrete Nonbinary Dualism," in *American Indian Thought: Philosophical Essays*, ed. Anne Waters (Oxford: Blackwell, 2004), 97–115; and George Tinker, "Religion" in *Encyclopedia of North American Indians*, ed. Frederick E. Hoxie (Boston: Houghton Mifflin 1996), 537–40.

21. Barbara Tedlock, *Time and the Highland Maya*, rev. ed. (Albuquerque: University of New Mexico Press, 1992 [1982]), 42–44.

22. Dennis Tedlock, "Creation in the Popol Vuh: A Hermeneutical Approach," in *Symbol and Meaning beyond the Closed Community: Essays in Mesoamerican Ideas*, ed. Gary H. Gossen (Albany, NY: Institute for Mesoamerican Studies, SUNY Press, 1986), 81.

23. Dennis Tedlock, "Introduction," in *Popol Vuh: The Definitive Edition of the Mayan Book of the Dawn of Life and the Glories of Gods and Kings*, trans. Dennis Tedlock (New York: Simon and Schuster, 1985), 63.

24. Nigel Davies, "Dualism as a Universal Concept: Its Relevance to Mesoamerica," in *Mesoamerican Dualism/Dualismo Mesoamericano*, ed. R. van Zantwijk, R. de Ridder, and E. Braahuis (Utrecht: RUU-ISOR, 1990), 9.

25. Jill Leslie McKeever Furst, "Duality," in *The Oxford Encyclopedia of Mesoamerican Cultures: The Civilizations of Mexico and Central America*, ed. Davíd Carrasco (Oxford: Oxford University Press, 2001), 1:344.

26. López Austin, "Complementos y composiciones," 40.

27. Fray Alonso de Molina, *Vocabulario en lengua castellana y mexicana y mexicana y castellana*, 4th ed. (Mexico City: Porrúa, 2001), 2:38v, translation mine.

28. R. Joe Campbell, *A Morphological Dictionary of Classical Nahuatl: A Morpheme Index to the* Vocabulario en lengua mexicana y castellana *of Fray Alonso de Molina* (Madi-son: Hispanic Seminary of Medieval Studies, 1985), 197.

29. Rémi Siméon, *Diccionario de la lengua náhuatl o mexicana*, trans. Josefina Olivia de Coll (México, DF: Siglo Veintiuno Editores, 1977), 191, translation mine.

30. Miguel León-Portilla, *La filosofía náhuatl: Estudiada en sus fuentes con un nuevo apéndice*, new ed., prologue by Angel María Garibay K. (México, DF: Universidad Nacional Autónoma de México, 2001 [1956]), 152, translation mine. See also Miguel León-Portilla, "*El Tonalámatl de los Pochtecas (Códice Fejérváry-Mayer): Estudio introductorio y comentarios*," *Arqueología Mexicana, Edición especial* 18 (2005): 90.

31. Miguel León-Portilla, *Aztec Thought and Culture: A Study of the Ancient Nahuatl Mind* (Norman: University of Oklahoma Press, 1963): 82, trans. Jack Emory Davis.

32. Frances Karttunen, *An Analytical Dictionary of Nahuatl* (Norman: University of Oklahoma Press, 1983), 35; R. Joe Campbell and Frances Karttunen, *Foundation Course in Nahuatl Grammar*, 2 vols. (Missoula: University of Montana, 1989), 1:41.

33. Molina, *Vocabulario*, 2: 62v, translation mine.

34. Campbell, *Morphological Dictionary*, 197.

35. León-Portilla, *La filosofía náhuatl*, 152, translation mine.

36. Campbell, *Morphological Dictionary*, 198.

37. Ibid., 197. The following translations are taken from or based on ibid., 197–99.

38. Karttunen, *Analytical Dictionary*, 58.

39. See Monaghan, "The Person, Destiny, and the Construction of Difference," 142–43.

40. López Austin, *Rabbit on the Face of the Moon*, 116.

41. Bernardino de Sahagún, *Florentine Codex: General History of the Things of New Spain*, ed. and trans. Arthur J.O. Anderson and Charles Dibble (Santa Fe, NM: School of American Research; Salt Lake City: University of Utah, 1953–1982), 10:153; see also 156–59.

42. Bernardino de Sahagún, *Primeros memoriales*. Paleography of Nahuatl Text and English Translation by Thelma D. Sullivan (Norman: University of Oklahoma Press, 1997), 200–1.

43. See López Austin, *Myth of the Opossum*, 172.

44. López Austin, *Rabbit on the Face of the Moon*, 118–19; see also López Austin, *Hombre-dios: religión y política en el mundo náhuatl*, 3rd ed. (México, DF: Universidad Autónoma de México, 1998 [1973]); López Austin, "Cosmovision," in *The Oxford Encyclopedia of Mesoamerican Cultures: The Civilizations of Mexico and Central America*, ed. by Davíd Carrasco (Oxford: Oxford University Press, 2001), 1: 270.

45. Quoted in Roger T. Ames, "Putting the *Te* Back into Taoism," in *Nature in Asian Traditions of Thought: Essays in Environmental Philosophy*, ed. J. Baird Callicott and Roger T. Ames (Albany: State University Press of New York, 1989), 137. See also Gordon Brotherston and Dawn Ades, "Mesoamerican Description of Space, I: Myths, Stars and Maps, and Architecture," *Ibero-Amerikanisches Archiv* 1, no. 4 (1975): 228–89.

46. See Fray Diego Durán, *The History of the Indies of New Spain*, trans., annotation, and intro. Doris Heyden (New York: Orion Books, 1994); Sahagún, *General History of the Things of New Spain*; and León-Portilla, *Aztec Thought and Culture*.

47. Gary H. Gossen, "Mesoamerican Ideas as a Foundation for Regional Synthesis," in *Symbol and Meaning beyond the Closed Community: Essays in Mesoamerican Ideas*, ed. Gary H. Gossen (Albany: SUNY Press, 1986), 6. See also Gary H. Gossen, "The Religious Traditions of Mesoamerica," in *The Legacy of Mesoamerica: History and Culture of a Native American Civilization*, ed. Robert Carmack, Janine Gasco, and Gary H. Gossen (Upper Saddle River, NJ: Prentice Hall, 1996), 315.

48. See Philip P. Arnold, *Eating Landscape: Aztec and European Occupation of Tlalocan* (Niwot: University Press of Colorado, 1999); Davies, "Dualism as a Universal Concept"; Enrique Florescano, *Memory, Myth, and Time in Mexico: From the Aztecs to Independence*, trans. Albert G. Bork with the assistance of Kathryn R. Bork (Austin: University of Texas Press, 1994); Read, *Time and Sacrifice*; López Austin, *Human Body and Ideology*; López Austin, *Myths of the Opossum*; López Austin, *Rabbit on the Face of the Moon*; Gossen, *Symbol and Meaning*; Gossen, "Religious Traditions of Mesoamerica"; Eva Hunt, *The Transformation of the Hummingbird: Cultural Roots of a Zinacatecan Mythical Poem* (Ithaca, NY: Cornell University Press, 1977); Linda A. Curcio-Nagy, "Faith and Morals in Colonial Mexico," in *The Oxford History of Mexico*, ed. Michael C. Meyer and William H. Beezly (Oxford: Oxford University Press, 2000), 151–82; and Knab, *War of Witches*.

49. Vivian M. Jímenez Estrada, "The Tree of Life as a Research Methodology," *Australian Journal of Indigenous Education* 34 (2005): 47.

50. Reported in López Austin, *Human Body and Ideology*, I:58. This points to the fact that twofold inamic relations multiply into fourfold paired inamic relations such as the four Tezcatlipocas, four colors, and four elements. For discussion, see López Austin, *Human Body and Ideology*, I; López Austin "Los ritos: Un juego de definiciones," *Arqueología Mexicana* 6, no. 34 (1988): 4–37; López Austin, *Rabbit on the Face of the Moon*; Louise M. Burkhart, "Mexica Women on the Home Front: Housework and Religion in Aztec Mexico," in *Indian Women of Early Mexico*, ed. Susan Schroeder, Stephanie Wood, and Robert Haskett (Norman: University of Oklahoma Press, 1997), 35; Davíd Carrasco, "Uttered from the Heart: Guilty Rhetoric among the Aztecs," *History of Religions* 39 (1999): 1–31; Carrasco, *City of Sacrifice: The Aztec Empire and the Role of Violence in Civilization* (Boston: Beacon Press, 1999); Curcio-Nagy, "Faith and Morals"; Michel Graulich, "Creator Deities," in *The Oxford Encyclopedia of Mesoamerican Cultures: The Civilizations of Mexico and Central America*, ed. Davíd Carrasco (Oxford: Oxford University Press, 2001), I:284–86; Knab, *War of Witches*; Knab, *Dialogue of Earth and Sky*; McKeever Furst, "Duality"; Quezada, "*Creencias tradicionales*"; Read, *Time and Sacrifice*; Sandstrom, "Center and Periphery in the Social Organization of Contemporary Nahuas of Mexico," *Eth-*

nology 35, no. 3 (1996): 161–80; Sandstrom, "Sacred Mountains and Miniature Worlds: Altar Design among the Nahua of Northern Veracruz, Mexico," in *Mesas and Cosmologies in Mesoamerica*, ed. Douglas Sharon, 51–70, San Diego Museum of Man Papers 42 (San Diego: San Diego Museum of Man, 2003); and Taggart, *Nahuat Myth and Social Structure.*

51. López Austin, *Human Body and Ideology*, I: 53. See also Quezada, "*Creencias tradicionales.*"

52. Hall and Ames call thinking in terms of inamic analogies "correlative thinking," which they contrast with the "causal thinking" of Western philosophy and science. Correlative thinking relies upon analogies, images, and metaphors rather than transcendent principles, categories, and mechanical causal laws (Hall and Ames, *Anticipating China*).

53. See Davies "Dualism as a Universal Concept"; McKeever Furst, "Duality"; Peter T. Furst, "Shamanistic Survivals in Mesoamerican Religion," *Actas del XLI Congreso Internacional de Americanistas*, vol. 3 (Mexico: Instituto Nacional de Antropología e Historia, 1976); Peter T. Furst, "Introduction: An Overview of Shamanism," in *Ancient Traditions: Shamanism in Central Asia and the Americas*, ed. Gary Seaman and Jane S. Day (Niwot: Denver Museum of Natural History and University Press of Colorado, 1994); López Austin, *Human Body and Ideology*; López Austin, *Rabbit on the Face of the Moon*; Burkhart, "Mexica Women"; Curcio-Nagy, "Faith and Morals"; Alan R. Sandstrom, *Corn Is Our Blood: Culture and Ethnic Identity in a Contemporary Aztec Indian Village* (Norman: University of Oklahoma Press, 1991); and Read, *Time and Sacrifice*. Peggy V. Beck, Anna Lee Walters, and Nia Francisco (*The Sacred: Ways of Knowledge, Sources of Life*, redesigned ed. [Tsaile, AZ: Navajo Community College Press, 1992], 15) and Clara Sue Kidwell, Homer Noley, and George E. "Tink" Tinker (*A Native American Theology* [Maryknoll, NY: Orbis, 2002]) argue that abstract notions of good and evil play little if any role in indigenous North American metaphysics and ethics.

54. See Homayoon Sepasi-Tehrani and Janet Flesch, "Persian Philosophy," in *From Africa to Zen: An Invitation to World Philosophy*, eds. Robert C. Solomon and Kathleen Higgins (Lanham, MA: Roman and Littlefield, 1993), 151–186.

55. See Robert Audi, gen. ed., *The Cambridge Dictionary of Philosophy* (Cambridge: Cambridge University Press, 1995).

56. Knab, *Dialogue of Earth and Sky*, 77, brackets mine.

57. The death~life inamic relationship instantiates the biological root metaphor of Aztec metaphysics. It captures biological themes of life, death, generation, decay, feeding, eating, transformation, the ecological interdependence of all things, and the continual circulation of life-energy. See Read, *Time and Sacrifice*; Arnold, *Eating Landscape*; Matos Moctezuma, *Muerte a filo de obsidiana*; Knab, "Metaphors, Concepts, and Coherence in Aztec"; Cecelia Klein, "Post-Classic Mexican Death Imagery as a Sign of Cyclic

Completion," in *Death and Afterlife in Pre-Columbian America*, ed. Elizabeth P. Benson (Washington, DC: Dumbarton Oaks, 1975), 69–84; and López Austin, *Tamoanchan, Tlalocan*, 10–12.

58. Jill Leslie McKeever Furst, *Codex Vindobonesis Mexicanus: A Commentary* (Albany: SUNY and Institute for Mesoamerican Studies, 1978), 318; see also Jill Leslie McKeever Furst, "Skeletonization in Mixtec Art: A Revaluation," in *The Art of Iconography of Late Post-Classic Central Mexico*, eds. Elizabeth P. Benson and Elizabeth H. Boone (Washington, DC: Dumbarton Oaks, 1982), 207–25; McKeever Furst, *The Natural History of the Soul in Ancient Mexico* (New Haven, CT: Yale University Press, 1995), 59–61.

59. John Bierhorst, trans.,"Legend of the Suns," in *History and Mythology of the Aztecs* (Tucson: University of Arizona Press, 1992) 145.

60. Furst, "Shamanistic Survivals," 152.

61. Elizabeth M. Brumfiel, "Domestic Politics in Early-Middle Postclassic Mexico: Variability and Standardization in Decorative Motifs," paper presented in Estudios de género en el México antiguo, coordinated by M. Rodríguez-Shadow and R. García Valgañon (Congreso Internacional de Americanistas, México, DF, 2009), 4.

62. Esther Pasztory, *Aztec Art* (Norman: University of Oklahoma Press, 1983), 80–83, 160–61, 233–34.

63. Ibid., 88.

64. *Codex Borbonicus* (Loubat: Bibliothéque du Palais Bourbon, 1899), plate 21; http://www.famsi.org/index.html, accessed 4/14/2013.

65. See Herbert R. Harvey, "Household and Family Structure in Early Colonial Tepetlaoztoc: An Analysis of the *Códice de Santa María Asunción*," *Estudios de cultura nahuátl* 18 (1986): 275–94. Thanks to an anonymous referee for bringing this to my attention.

66. *Codex Borbonicus*, plate 22.

67. *Codex Fejérváry Mayer* (Loubat: Bibliothéque Du Palais Bourbon, 1901); http://www.famsi.org/index.html, accessed 4/14/2013. For discussion see León-Portilla, "*El Tonalámatl de los Pochtecas*"; and Ferdinand Anders, Maarten Jansen, and Luis Reyes García, *El Libro de Tezcatlipoca, Señor del Tiempo, libro explicative del llamado Códice Fejérváry-Mayer* (Austria: Akademische Druck- und Verlagsanstalt, 1994).

68. Gisele Díaz and Alan Rodgers, *Codex Borgia: A Full Color Restoration of the Ancient Mexican Manuscript*, with introduction and commentary by Bruce E. Byland (New York: Dover Publications, 1993), plate 56. See also plate 73.

69. Brumfiel,"Domestic Politics," 4; see also Constanza Vega Sosa, "El Curso del sol en los glifos de la cerámica azteca tarde," *Estudios de cultura náhuatl* 17 (1984): 125–70.

70. See Julian Hochberg, "Gestalt Theory," in *The Oxford Companion to the Mind*, ed. Richard L. Gregory (Oxford: Oxford University Press, 1987), 288–91; R. L. Gregory, *Eye*

and Brain: the Psychology of Seeing, 3rd ed., revised and updated (New York: McGraw-Hill, 1978), 9–14. Mauricio Orozpe Enríquez, *El código oculto de le greca escalonada: Tloque Nahuaque* (México, DF: UNAM, 2010), offers a thought-provoking treatment of the xicalcoliuhqui motif. Katherine Seibold ("Textiles and Cosmology in Choquecancha, Cuzco, Peru," in *Andean Cosmologies through Time: Persistence and Emergence*. ed. Robert V. H. Dover, John McDowell, and Katherine E. Seibold [Bloomington: Indiana Univerity Press, 1992], 186) discusses the same dynamic interplay between background and figure to create positive and negative images in Andean weaving. She writes, "[T]he two sides unite (the light and the dark, the foreground and the background) to form one whole." Such figures illustrate what I am calling in the Aztec context agonistic inamic unity.

71. See Blas Castellón Huerta, "Cúmulo de símbolos: la serpiente emplumada," *Arqueología Mexicana* 9, no. 53 (2002): 28–35; and Raúl Barrera Rodríguez and Gabino López Arenas, "Hallazgos en el recinto ceremonial de Tenochtitlan," *Arqueología Mexicana* 16, no. 93 (2008): 18–25.

72. For discussion, see Pasztory, *Aztec Art*, 157–159, and Elizabeth Baquedano, "Aspects of Death Symbolism in Aztec Tlaltecuhtli," in *The Symbolism in the Plastic and Pictorial Representations of Ancient Mexico*, ed. Jacqueline de Durand-Forest and Marc Eisinger, Bonner Amerikanistische Studien, vol. 21 (Bonn: Bonner Amerikanistische Studien, 1993), 157–80.

73. Johanna Broda, "Templo Mayor as Ritual Space," in *The Great Temple of Tenochtitlan: Center and Periphery in the Aztec World*, ed. Johanna Broda, Davíd Carrasco, and Eduardo Matos Moctezuma (Berkeley: University of California Press, 1987), 61–123; Davíd Carrasco, "Introduction" and "Myth, Cosmic Terror, and the Templo Mayor" in *The Great Temple of Tenochtitlan: Center and Periphery in the Aztec World*, ed. Johanna Broda, Davíd Carrasco, and Eduardo Matos Moctezuma (Berkeley: University of California Press, 1987), 1–14, 124–62; Eduardo Matos Moctezuma, "The Templo Mayor of Tenochtitlan: History and Interpretation," in *The Great Temple of Tenochtitlan: Center and Periphery in the Aztec World*, ed. Johanna Broda, Davíd Carrasco, and Eduardo Matos Moctezuma (Berkeley: University California Press, 1987), 15–60; and Matos Moctezuma, *Life and Death in the Templo Mayor*, trans. Bernard R. Ortiz de Montellano and Thelma Ortiz de Montellano (Niwot: University Press of Colorado, 1995). We should expect Aztec "flower and song," dance, and music to express agonistic inamic unity in similar ways.

74. David L. Hall, "Process and Anarchy: A Taoist View of Creativity," *Philosophy East and West* 28 (1978): 276.

75. Burkhart, *The Slippery Earth: Nahua-Christian Dialogue in Sixteenth-Century Mexico* (Tucson: University of Arizona Press, 1989), 37. See also Curcio-Nagy, "Faith and Morals"; Read, *Time and Sacrifice*; and McKeever Furst, "Duality."

76. *Tlaalahui, tlapetzcahui in tlalticpac* ("It is slippery, it is slick on the earth") was said of a person who had lived a proper life only to lose her balance and fall into impropriety, as if slipping in slick mud (Sahagún, *General History of the Things of New Spain*, VI: 228), trans. Louise M. Burkhart, *The Slippery Earth*, 58.

77. See León-Portilla, *Aztec Thought and Culture*, for supporting argument.

78. See Guilhem Olivier, *Mockeries and Metamorphoses of an Aztec God: Tezcatlipoca, "Lord of the Smoking Mirror,"* trans. Michel Besson (Boulder: University Press of Colorado, 2003), 277.

79. McKeever Furst, *Natural History of the Soul*, 95.

80. Burkhart, *Slippery Earth*, 92.

81. Translation from the Nahuatl by León-Portilla, *Aztec Thought and Culture*, 121.

82. Barbara G. Myerhoff, "Balancing between Worlds: The Shaman's Calling," *Parabola* 1, no. 2 (1976): 10; see also Barbara G. Myerhoff, *Peyote Hunt: The Sacred Journey of the Huichol Indians* (Ithaca, NY: Cornell University Press, 1974); and Barbara G. Myerhoff, "The Huichol and the Quest for Paradise," *Parabola* 1, no. 1 (1976): 22–29. Gingerich's insightful discussion occurs in Willard Gingerich, "Chipahuacanemiliztli, 'the Purified Life,' in the Discourses of Book VI, Florentine Codex," in *Smoke and Mist: Mesoamerican Studies in Memory of Thelma D. Sullivan*, Part 2, ed. J. Kathryn Josserand and Karen Dakin (Oxford: British Archaeological Reports, 1988), 517–43. Others scholars tracing the roots of what I call agonistic inamic unity in shamanism include Furst ("Shamanistic Survivals" and "Introduction"), Gossen ("Religious Traditions of Mesoamerica), McKeever Furst ("Skeletonization in Mixtec Art" and "Duality"), Bernard R. Ortiz de Montellano (*Aztec Medicine, Health, and Nutrition* [New Brunswick, NJ: Rutgers University Press, 1990]), Nicholas J. Saunders ("Shamanism: Pre-Hispanic Cultures," in *The Oxford Encyclopedia of Mesoamerican Cultures: The Civilizations of Mexico and Central America*, ed. Davíd Carrasco [Oxford: Oxford University Press, 2001], 3:141–2), Michael Ripinsky-Naxon ("Shamanistic Knowledge and Cosmology," in *Tribal Epistemologies: Essays in the Philosophy of Anthropology*, ed. Helmut Wautischer [Aldershot: Ashgate, 1998], 119–61), and Mircea Eliade (*Shamanism: Archaic Techniques of Ecstasy* [Princeton, NJ: Princeton University Press, 1964]).

83. The following draws from Alfonso Caso, *The Aztecs: People of the Sun*, trans. Lowell Dunham (Norman: University of Oklahoma Press, 1958); León-Portilla, *Aztec Thought and Culture*; León-Portilla, "Ometeotl, el Supremo Díos Dual, y Tezcatlipoca," *Estudios de cultural náhuatl* 30 (1999): 133–52; León-Portilla, *La filosofía náhuatl*; León-Portilla, "Mitos de los Orígenes en Mesoamerica," *Arqueología Mexicana* 10, no. 56 (2002): 20–53; Michel Graulich, *Myths of Ancient Mexico*, trans. Bernard R. Ortiz de Montellano and Thelma Ortiz de Montellano (Norman: University of Oklahoma Press, 1997); Graulich, "Creator Deities"; López Austin, *Human Body and Ideology*, I: 208; H. B. Nicholson, "Religion in Pre-Hispanic Central Mexico," in *Handbook of Middle American Indians*, vol.

10, eds. Robert Wauchope, Gordon F. Elkholm, and Ignacio Bernal (Austin: University of Texas Press, 1971), 395–446; Laurette Séjourné, *Burning Water: Thought and Religion in Ancient Mexico* (New York: Grove Press, 1960), 99–111; Barbara Tedlock, *Time and the Highland Maya*, rev. ed. (Albuquerque: University of New Mexico Press, 1992 [1982]); Dennis Tedlock "Introduction"; and Dennis Tedlock, "Creation in the Popol Vuh."

84. See León-Portilla, *La filosofía náhuatl*, 386.

85. Nicholson, "Religion," 410.

86. Quoted in León-Portilla, *Aztec Thought and Culture*, 95.

87. Juan de Torquemada, *Monarquía indiana*, 3rd ed. (México, DF: Universidad Nacional Autónoma de México, 1975–1983), 3: 67.

88. See Sahagún, *Florentine Codex*: VI: 41, 175; X: 169; León-Portilla, *Aztec Thought and Culture*, 31–32, 80–103; León-Portilla, *La filosofía náhuatl*, 380, 382; Caso, *The Aztecs*, 9; Graulich, *Myths of Ancient Mexico*; and Graulich, "Creator Deities."

89. Sahagún, *Florentine Codex*: X: 169.

90. León-Portilla, *Aztec Thought and Culture*, 91, 93; Graulich, *Myths of Ancient Mexico*, 47); H. B. Nicholson, "Religion"; Caso, *The Aztecs*, 8; Rafael Tena, "La Religión Mexica: Catálogo de dioses," *Arqueología Mexicana*, Edición especial 30 (2009), 26. Other scholars contend they apply to Tezcatlipoca, not Ometeotl. See Olivier, *Mockeries and Metamorphoses*, for discussion.

91. See Graulich (*Myths of Ancient Mexico*, 48); Miguel León-Portilla ("Three Forms of Thought in Ancient Mexico," in *Studies in Symbolism and Cultural Communication*, ed. F. Allen Hanson [Lawrence: University of Kansas Press, 1982], 9–24); León-Portilla, (Mitos de los Orígenes en Mesoamerica); and Tena ("La Religión Mexica," 26). Graulich ("Creator Deities," 285) identifies it as Ometeotl-Tonacatecuhtli. Libura identifies it as Tonacatecuhtli, who she equates with Ometeotl (Krystyna M. Libura, *Los días y los dioses del Códice Borgia* [México, DF: Ediciones Tecolote, 2000], 25).

92. See *Annals of Cuauhtitlan*, in John Bierhorst, trans., *History and Mythology of the Aztecs: The Codex Chimalpopoca* (Tucson: University of Arizona Press, 1992), 30; and Sahagún, *Florentine Codex:* VI: 175. Sources differ over the number of celestial folds, some saying nine, others twelve. See León-Portilla, *Aztec Thought and Culture*; López Austin, *Tamoanchan, Tlalocan*; Graulich, "Creator Deities"; Monaghan, "The Person, Destiny, and the Construction of Difference"; Bodo Spranz, *Los dioses en los códices mexicanos del grupo Borgia: Una investigacion iconográfica*, trans. María Martínez Peñaloza (México, DF: Fondo de Cultura Económica, 1973); and Cecelia Klein, "None of the Above: Gender Ambiguity in Nahua Ideology," in *Gender in Pre-Hispanic America*, ed. Cecelia Klein (Washington, DC: Dumbarton Oaks, 2001), 183–254. I use *time-place* to indicate that time and place (space) are fused into a single seamless dimension according to Aztec metaphysics. They are not two distinct dimensions as asserted by Isaac Newton's philosophy of space and time.

93. León-Portilla, *Aztec Thought and Culture*, 52.

94. Monaghan, "The Person, Destiny, and the Construction of Difference," 142–43. See also Klein, "None of the Above," 187–89.

95. Tarn and Prechtel, "Constant Inconstancy," 173. Tinker ("Religion") attributes the metaphysical principle of unity through duality to indigenous North American religions.

Teotl as Olin

Aztec metaphysics conceives teotl as a single, all-encompassing macroprocess that consists of a complex constellation of systematically interrelated and interpenetrating microprocesses. As a process, teotl is defined by *how it moves*.[1] And how does it move? Teotl moves in three principal ways: olin, malinalli, and nepantla. Each of these constitutes a different modus operandi of teotl; a different *path* of energy circulation and conveyance; a different *pattern* of causation, interaction, interrelation; and hence a different *pattern* of change, becoming, and transformation. Each is immanent within the unfolding of reality like the pattern of a woven fabric or rings of a tree trunk. Together, olin, malinalli, and nepantla configure the *dynamics* of reality, cosmos, and all things. Along with the two sacred calendars – the tonalpohualli and xiuhpohualli – olin, malinalli, and nepantla engender the "shape and rhythm,"[2] the "eurhythmy,"[3] and "the current and cadence"[4] of reality, cosmos, and all things. The three work together to order teotl's agonistic inamic forces and in so doing arrange reality, cosmos, and all things.

Aztec metaphysics, like ancient Greek and pre-Han East Asian metaphysics, conceives change, becoming, and transformation as species of motion or movement. Motion includes both *physical* and *qualitative* change.[5] Talk about motion refers not only to change of physical position or posture (e.g., walking or crossing one's legs) but also to qualitative change (e.g., one's birth and subsequent transformations from infancy to youth, adult, old age, and death). The Fifth Sun's daily and nightly journey, for example, involves change in both *position* and *attributes*. Aztec metaphysics views the

DOI: 10.5876_9781607322238.c004

agonism of inamic partners – the wet~dry cycle of the seasons, the life~death cycle of all things, for example – as kinds of *motion*. Since change in quality counts as a species of motion, we therefore misunderstand Aztec metaphysics if we construe motion narrowly as physical change only. In order to avoid such misunderstanding, I adopt the phrase *motion-change* to remind us that motion means both physical and qualitative change. When appropriate, I use *qualitative change* to refer exclusively to qualitative change, and *physical motion* to refer exclusively to change of position. Olin, malinalli, and nepantla represent three kinds of motion-change.

I approach the nature of olin, malinalli, and nepantla motion-change via three evidential avenues: linguistic, literary, and graphic.[6] The linguistic avenue looks for the nature of olin motion-change in the concept of olin, and looks for the concept of olin in the various linguistic constructions and uses of the word *olin*. Doing so sheds light on how sixteenth-century Nahuatl-speakers used *olin*, what they meant by *olin*, the content of the concept of olin, and ultimately the nature of olin motion-change itself. This approach is variously called linguistic, conceptual, or ordinary language analysis by twentieth-century Anglo-American philosophy.[7]

4.1. OLIN

Olin constitutes one of teotl's three principal patterns of change, becoming, and transformation, and one of teotl's three principal modi operandi or *how's*. Olin motion-change constitutes a specific kind of motion-change: one defined by a specific pattern and one implicated in specific kinds of processes. *Olin* and *ollin* are commonly translated in the historical sources and in contemporary scholarship as both "motion" or "movement" *and* as "rubber, rubber ball." John Sullivan contends this is fundamentally mistaken. He maintains that the appropriate words are *olin* and *olli* (respectively) and that they are linguistically unrelated. In contemporary Huastecan Nahuatl, for example, *olli* means "rubber, rubber ball," while *olin* means "the agent of the movement exhibited by an earthquake or a building's settling." Such settling movement may be singular or repetitive.[8] In what follows I observe Sullivan's distinction by using the *olli* linguistic family to refer to items related to rubber or rubber balls, and the *olin* linguistic family to refer to items related to movement. However, I also follow the linguistically imprecise scholarly convention of using *olin* to refer to a specific kind of movement (rather than to the agent of this movement). Since I believe olin includes both physical and qualitative change, I use the phrase *olin motion-change*.

Fray Diego Durán tells us ollin is a tree resin greatly prized by the native peoples of Mexico as a potable medicine, as a religious offering (splattered on pieces of paper), and as the material from which the bouncing balls of the Mesoamerican ballgame are made. Native peoples cook the liquid resin, causing it to become "stringy." When formed into a ball, "Jumping and bouncing are its qualities, upward and downward, to and fro."[9] The word "ollin," reports Durán, means "something that moves or goes about, Motion, and is identified with the sun."[10]

Durán's remarks offer us some early insights into the nature of olin motion-change since they highlight key characteristics of the stuff, ollin, and of olin motion-change. First, the stuff, ollin, is a tree resin. This is significant because the Aztecs viewed tree resin as a tree's blood. The stuff, ollin, and blood are conceptually related. Second, ollin resin possesses medicinal and sacred properties. Third, ollin resin is also used to make the bouncing balls that are both the literal and symbolic heart of the Mesoamerican ballgame. Fourth, olin motion-change consists of a specific pattern: up and down, back and forth, to and fro – in short, the pattern exhibited by bouncing rubber balls. Last, Durán explicitly identifies olin with the Sun of the Fifth Era. In sum, his remarks suggest an association between ollin resin, blood, heart, life-energy on the one hand, and the olin-defined up-and-down, back-and-forth, to-and-fro movement of bouncing balls and of the life-sustaining Fifth Sun, on the other.

4.2. LINGUISTIC EVIDENCE

What insights into the nature of olin motion-change do the lexicologies of *ollin* offer? Fray Alonso de Molina translates *olli* as "a gum from medicinal trees from which is made balls for playing."[11] Molina's dictionary of classical Nahuatl (the language of the Aztecs), the *Vocabulario en lengua castella y mexicana y mexicana y castellana*, includes the following related words: *ollama* ("to play ball with one's hips"), *ollamaliztli* ("rubber ball game"), *ulli* ("tree gum which is medicinal gum from trees and is used for making balls for playing"), and *ollo* ("something which has medicinal gum from trees"). Molina's *Vocabulario* places *olin* within a family of words that derives from the verb *olini* ("to move"). Other family members include *olinia* ("to move, stir, swing, or shake, or to move oneself"), *molinia* ("for something to move from side to side, swing, sway, or wiggle, or to boil something"), *moliniani* ("something that moves or stirs, sways from side to side"), *neoliniliztli* ("movement, shaking, stirring or swaying"), *oolin* ("aborted, born before time"), *tlalolini* ("for the earth to tremble, shake, or quiver"), *tlaolinilia* ([intransitive] "for a baby to be born prematurely because of a mishap"), *tlaolinilia* ([transitive] "to induce the birth of a woman's baby"), and *tlaoliniliztli* ("stirring, shaking, swaying something or act of stirring, swaying, shaking or moving something").

What do these tell us about the nature of *olin* motion-change? For starters, it strongly indicates that in classical Nahuatl, the kind of movement designated by *olin* is both more complex and more varied than the simple kind of movement designated by *olin* in contemporary Huastecan Nahuatl (according to John Sullivan). In classical Nahuatl, olin motion-change includes moving up and down, stirring, swaying from side to side, boiling, trembling, quivering, and shaking back and forth. These tend to consist of two parts: up-and-down, back-and-forth, to-and-fro. By contrast, settling involves a single process of dropping or descending (but not subsequently ascending).[12]

Andrés de Olmos's *Arte de la lengua mexicana y vocabulario* contains the following entries: *ol[l]ama*, n[i]- ("to play ball"), *olini* ("to abort without violence"), *olinia, nitla-* ("the moving of the fetus or newborn"), *olinilia, nin[o]* ("to move, to abort when taking something for it, to move without cause"), and *olinilia, nonotal-* ("to abort without cause").[13] Rémi Siméon states *olli* (*ulli*) refers to an elastic gum that comes from the *olquauitl* tree. He lists *olin* and *ollin* as stylistic alternatives of one another and glosses both as "motion." He translates *olinia* as "to move, to stir, to boil, to tremble." Lastly, Siméon claims *olin* and *ollin* as well as *olinia* derive from *olini*, which he glosses as "to go, to move to stir, to follow its path."[14]

Eduard Seler defines *olin* as "*movimiento rodante*" ("rolling movement"),[15] or as I prefer, "rolling motion-change." Seler contends *olin* derives from the primitive radical *ol*, suggesting something round or circling like a bouncing rubber ball.[16] Eva Hunt claims the Nahuatl word for rubber, *oli* or *olli*, as well as the verb *olini* (which Angel Garibay K. translates as "to agitate or move")[17] both derive from *ol*.[18] Doris Heyden maintains *ollin* or *olin* ("rubber") means "motion" because rubber "jumps around as if it were alive."[19] Consequently, reasons Caso, we frequently find *ollin* in words for things that move.[20] Ollin also describes the path and motion-change of the Fifth Sun as it bounces up and down like a rubber ball above and below the earth's surface. Ulrich Köhler summarizes the understandings of *olin* in the sixteenth- and seventeenth-century sources as including movement; earthquake; object that hurries, runs, or moves; sun; tremor; tremble, shiver; and path or way. *Ol* is sometimes translated as "4 Olin" (the Fifth Sun) and other times as "earthquake."[21] Thelma Sullivan derives *yollotl* ("heart"), *yoli* ("to be born, to revive, to quicken"), and *tlaolli* ("the dried kernels of corn that sustain life") from *ollin*.[22]

Hunt glosses *olin* as "something that can be stretched or extended from one place to another or across a given space" as well as "undulant circling, rocking, oscillating or rolling movement."²³ This understanding fits comfortably with the Aztecs' process metaphysics, with the idea that olin describes a modus operandi of teotl's processing, and with the idea that olin characterizes one dynamic in the continuing processing of reality, cosmos, and all things. Processes, after all, stretch across and extend through time-place. The same holds for Hunt's understanding of *olin* as "undulant circling, rocking, oscillating or rolling movement." By Aztec lights, change, becoming, and transformation are literally *shaped; they have a shape. There is a shape to how things change.* This strikes us as odd, for although we are accustomed to thinking of physical motion as having a shape (e.g., elliptical), we are not accustomed to thinking of qualitative change as having a shape. We do not, for example, think of a human being's transformation from birth, adolescence, adulthood, old age, and death as being shaped. The Aztecs, however, did. And what is that shape? It appears to be the shape of a bouncing ball. Olin-shaped motion-change, becoming, and transformation bounce back and forth; they oscillate and undulate.

Alfredo López Austin agues that *olin* derives from the primitive radical, *ol*, which he glosses as "line, curved surface, or volume."²⁴ From *ol* he derives *ol*, meaning "ball, plump body," from which, in turn, he constructs a four-branched philological tree. The first branch consists of *ol* ("rubber ball"), *ol* ("rubber"), and *olin* ("movement"). López Austin, like Eva Hunt, thus claims that *olli* (rubber, rubber ball) and *olin* both derive from *ol* and that the two are in fact linguistically related pace John Sullivan. The second branch consists of *olo* ("corncob"). The Aztecs apparently conceived the corn kernels as curving around a corncob's center or central axis point. The kernels carve out a volume. This pattern is apparent upon examining the widthwise cross-section of a corncob. The third branch consists of *olol* ("roundness, reunion, covering, heap") from which derives *ololoa* ("roundabout"). The fourth and largest branch consists of *yol* or *yul* ("something round, ball") from which derives *yol* or *yul* ("the ball," "heart") and *yol* ("life"). Five sub-branches split off from *yol* ("life"): (1) *yol* ("one of the animistic entities") and *teyolia* ("one of the animistic entities"), (2) *yolca* ("life"), (3) *yoyo* ("disgusting animal or insect"), (4) *yolqui* ("animal"), and (5) *yollo* ("vitality," "heart"). From this fifth sub-branch, López Austin further derives *yollo* (one of the three energies animating not only human beings but also animals, plants, mountains, wind, rivers, and lakes), *yollo* ("center for a volume, like that of the heart"), and *yollo* ("axis").

The foregoing analyses suggest that *olin* motion-change has a specific shape: it moves up and down and to and fro; it follows an arced, rounded, or curved path; it carves out a volume; it revolves around a central axis; and it has centered. It includes the more simple rising and falling motion of an earthquake and the more complex pulsating motion of a beating heart or curving motion of stirring a liquid. Olin-defined processes of becoming and transformation are curvaceous and rounded like a ball, a cross-sectioned corncob, and a plump body. Olin-defined transformational processes unify inamic partners such as life~death, day~night, and male~female by curving, rounding, oscillating, and centering them into a single process. Indeed, this shape would seem to be an essential element of what it means to describe these processes as *cyclical*. Olin motion-change is also vitalizing. It is the shape of the life-sustaining energy of corn and the shape of the vitalizing energy of a fetus's stirring and coming into life. In short, olin defines the *shape of coming-into-life, of cyclical completion, of life-energy* generally. Indeed, it defines *the shape of life or living* per se. Olin life-energy rises and falls. It swings back-and-forth. It pulsates.

The largest branch of *ol*-rooted words according to López Austin's etymology consists of *yol*-derived words. Let's examine some of Molina's entries. Molina translates *yol* as "life,"[25] and its derivation *yoli* as "to live, to be born, to revive, to enliven, to quicken, to come to life, to give life, and to hatch."[26] (To the latter Rémi Siméon adds "for flowers to open.")[27] Other *yol* derivations include[28] *noyolca* ("my nourishment," "my substance"), *toyolca* ("our life," "our sustenance," "our nourishment"), *yoliliztli* ("life" [Siméon adds "breath" and "respiration"][29]), *yolihuani* ("something that sustains life"), *yolihuitia* ("to revive, resuscitate someone"), *yoltinemi* ("to have life"), *yoltoc* ("someone alive, among the living"),[30] *altepeyolloco* ("center [or heart] of the city"), *aoquich yullo* ("coward or of little spirit"), *iuhquin iza noyollo* ("to recover consciousness"), *yoatl* ("drink made from raw corn for those who faint"), and *yuliuani atl* and *yuliliz atl* ("spring water"; literally, "life-giving water" and "water that will give life," respectively).

One of the most important *yol* derivations is *teyolia*. Molina translates it as "*el alma, o anima*" ("soul or spirit"),[31] Miguel León-Portilla as "*lo que confiere vida a alguien*" ("that which confers life upon someone"),[32] and López Austin as "he who animates."[33] *Teyolia* combines *te* (indefinite human object) with the causative form of *yoli* to mean "that which causes someone to live." López Austin sometimes construes *teyolia* as an "animating entity," other times as a "vital force."[34] I prefer "vital force" in light of Aztec philosophy's process metaphysics. Teyolia is one of three kinds of vitalizing and animating energies in the cosmos (along with *tonalli* and *ihiyotl*). It is present in humans, animals, and plants as well as mountains, wind, rivers, and towns. Although it suffuses the entire body, teyolia in humans is concentrated primarily in the heart.[35] It is sensed in the pulse and in breath. Upon death, teyolia loses its association with a specific body. When the human heart is extracted from the body its ollin-patterned life force travels to the sky. Every town (*altepetl*) has an *altepeyollotl* ("heart of the town") or living force.[36] *Tepe yiollo* ("mountain heart") and *tlalli yiollo* ("earth heart") function as metaphors for the life-generative potency of the earth.[37] Also related to *teyolia* is *teyolitia* ("to give life to another").[38] Lastly, there is *yollotl* ("heart, life, spirit, pith of dried fruit").[39] Jill McKeever Furst parses *yollotl* as *y-ōll-otl*, which she glosses as "its movement, or the reason for its movement."[40] León-Portilla maintains *yollotl* derives from *yoli*, which means in its abstract form "*vitalidad*," that is, vitality, liveliness, animation, having to do with life, or sustaining, empowering, and maintaining life.[41] In sum, the life-empowering, -conferring, and -sustaining energies of teyolia and yollotl instantiate olin motion-change. They are olin-shaped; that is, rounded, arced, and centered. They move back and forth; they undulate and oscillate.

Contemporary Nahuatl-speakers in Amatlán, according to Alan Sandstrom, believe humans possess two basic souls: *yolotl* and *tonali*. Although literally "heart," *yolotl* is better translated as "life force," argues Sandstrom.[42] Yolotl is the "heart or essence" of an "object, being, or spirit."[43] Everything in the cosmos (whether living or not, by Western lights) has "a yolotl by virtue of being part of the pantheistic universe. The yolotl is a piece of the universal deity that inheres in everything in existence. Thus, even objects partake of an animate universe, and they can be said to be alive in this sense."[44] The beating human heart is merely an aspect or fragment of this universal vitalizing force. For the Aztecs, too, everything in the cosmos – sun, earth, mountains, rivers, towns, trees, animals, humans, and insects – is vivified since everything partakes of teyolia and thus I submit teotl's olin-shaped motion-change.

Timothy Knab argues contemporary Nahuatl-speakers in San Martín Zinacapan view the yollo as one of three aspects of the soul. They equate the yollo with the heart, "seed," and "core of life." Yollo is that from which "life sprouts"[45] and "the internal life force that gives the body movement and life."[46] In *The Dialogue of Earth and Sky*, Knab adds that the *iyollo* (the possessed form of *yollo*) is an internal "animic" force that gives life to the body. Although centered in the heart, iyollo is distributed throughout the entire body. Although associated with the heart, it is not identical with the heart. And although distributed throughout the body in a way analogous to blood, iyollo it is not identical with blood. Blood is the iyollo's "outward manifestation." Iyollo is so closely associated with the heart and blood that "life of the body and the iyollo are . . . synonymous." Breath, too, is associated with iyollo. Lastly, the heart is also called *yoltagolli* ("the seed of life or grain of corn").[47] The rhythmic undulating motion of heart, blood (pulse), and breath defines iyollo. The shape of iyollo is that of olin motion-change, for iyollo is an instance of olin motion-change.

Heart, corn, blood, breath, life, and nourishment are conceptually as well as materially unified by olin motion-change.

Let's examine further the nature of the heart. Sahagún's informants tell us the human heart is "round" (*ololtic*) and "hot" (*totonqui*).[48] It "beats" (*tecuini*), "it jumps" (*chocholoa*), and "it beats repeatedly" (*motlatlamotla*). They characterize the heart as "life" (*yoliliztli*), "that by which there is existence" (*nemoani*), "it makes one live" (*teyolitia*), "it sustains one" (*tenemitia*), and "it lives" (*yoli*). Let's examine several of these. Frances Karttunen translates *tecuini* as "for a fire to flare up or for one's heart to pound."[49] Related entries in Molina likewise suggest a conceptual association between the heart's beating, pounding, and jumping, on the one hand, and a fire's flaring up, throwing off flame, and making noise, and also the wind's making noise, on the other.[50] The Aztecs associated the motion and sound of a beating heart with the motion and sound of fire and wind. Indeed, McKeever Furst contends the Aztecs (and other Mesoamericans) associated the heart (*yolia*) with breath and life generally.[51] Durán claims the goddess *tlalli iyolli* ("heart of the earth") was so called because "when she so desired, she made the earth tremble."[52] The Aztecs also associated the motion and sound of a beating heart with that of earthquakes.

Second, *chocholoa* derives from *choloa* ("to flee"). Other derivatives include *chocholotia* ("to bounce a ball") and *tlachochololtiliztli* ("bounce of a ball").[53] Thus we have additional linguistic evidence of a conceptual link between the beating of a heart and the bouncing of a ball, or more precisely, the pattern of motion exhibited by beating hearts and bouncing balls.

Third, *motlatlamotla* derives from *motla*, which carries meanings of throwing, bumping, hunting, throwing a stone or rock at someone, something knocking against another thing, and bowling.[54] The beating heart knocks and bumps against the wall of the chest. The presence of balls and their motion is not accidental. The Aztecs likened the heart to a rounded bumping ball or stone; they associated hearts with stones[55] and viewed the heart as a stone. The rounded shape of a heart resembles the rounded shape of a stone or pebble. Indeed, the Nahuatl word, *teyollotl* ("pebble") combines *tetl* ("stone") and *yollotl* ("heart").[56] Sahagún relates the funerary custom of placing in the deceased's mouth a green or greenish stone that would eventually serve as a substitute for her heart (*iniollo* or *yolia*).[57]

What insight into the nature of olin does the preceding offer? Olin identifies a specific kind, shape, or pattern of motion-change. Olin motion-change bounces, stirs, swings, oscillates, sways, pulsates, circles, rounds, curves, and arcs. What's more, it does so in a manner that is orderly, rhythmic, cyclical, centering, and generally speaking reliable and predictable (within the limits of the Tezcatlipoca factor). Olin's pattern of motion-change is instantiated by the up-and-down and back-and-forth bouncing of a rubber ball (as during the ballgame); the pulsating of a human heart and a breathing human chest; the oscillating of the Fifth Sun as it follows its path *over and above* Tlalticpac and *down and under* Tlalticpac; the stirring of a fetus in the womb; and the contractions of birth and trembling motion of earthquakes. Therefore, on the one hand, even if *olli* and *olin* are linguistically unrelated as John Sullivan maintains, I nevertheless see the movement of rubber balls as contingently instantiating the kind of movement referred to by *olin*. And if, on the other hand, López Austin and Hunt are correct in deriving *olin* and *olli* from the single root *ol*, then so much the better. The movement of rubber balls is then conceptually related to the kind of movement referred to by *olin*. Olin's pattern simultaneously constitutes a specific rhythm and shape of qualitative change, becoming, and transformation. The stirring of a fetus, the human life cycle, the Fifth Sun's diurnal-nocturnal back-and-forth journey between east and west and up-and-down journey above and below Tlalticpac, and the Fifth Sun's seasonal back-and-forth coursing between winter and summer solstices are both physical and transformational.

Olin motion-change is both orderly and actively *ordering*. It orders and arranges the processing and becoming of things in a cyclical, oscillating pattern. Olin motion-change is both centered and actively *centering*. It centers the processing and becoming of things. I contend olin orders and centers the processing and becoming of the Fifth Sun – hence the name *Fifth Sun-Earth Ordering* – and therefore creates the shape of the Fifth Sun's existence. Since the Fifth Sun orders and centers the Fifth Age and all its inhabitants, it follows that olin motion-change defines the shape of the existence *of* the Fifth Age and the shape of existence *in* the Fifth Age. It is the defining pattern *of* the Fifth Age. In the history of the five Suns and five Eras, olin motion-change uniquely defines the Fifth Sun, Fifth Era, and all the latter's inhabitants. It defines *how* things process and hence how they live~die in the Fifth Era. Because olin motion-change defines *how* the Fifth Sun, the Fifth Era, and all the latter's inhabitants become and transform, olin constitutes their "heart" or "essence."

In keeping with Aztec metaphysics' animism, olin motion-change defines the processing of what *we* regard as animate ("living") and inanimate ("nonliving") things. When we speak of life and of living things, we must always remember that we are speaking of all existing things, from the Fifth Sun and Fifth Era to mountains, lakes, humans, spindle rods, flutes, and jewelry. To exist is to move-change, to be animated, and so to be alive. All things consist of energy-in-motion, and olin motion-change defines *how* things in the Fifth Era move-change and process. All things have life~death cycles and olin motion-change defines the shape of their life~death cycles: they oscillate, pulsate, and move around a center.

Teyolia is a vitalizing energy present in humans, animals, and plants as well as mountains, wind, rivers, and towns. Teyolia is defined by olin motion-change. Olin motion-change is therefore tied substantively as well as conceptually to the becoming, transforming, and moving-changing that constitutes living and existing. It is the pattern of energy involved in sprouting, blooming, hatching, and coming alive. It is the shape of the life-giving energy of corn. The Aztecs used liquid rubber, itself condensed olin motion-change, as a life-preserving medicine for humans and as life-giving ritual food for teotl (the cosmos). They likewise ritually also offered human blood, another form of condensed olin motion-change, as nourishing energy to the cosmos.

The foregoing linguistic evidence also supports the idea that olin motion-change is irreducibly ambiguous. Olin motion-change moves back and forth between life and death, male and female, and being and nonbeing, for example, and in so doing unifies them into the inamic pairs life~death, male~female, and being~nonbeing (respectively). It creates and destroys. From the standpoint of humans, it is both positive and negative. It defines the creative motion-change involved in renewal, birth, vitality, sustenance, and well-being, yet it also defines the destructive motion-change involved in fatal miscarriages, aging, and lethal earthquakes. It is also olin motion-change that will eventually disorder and destroy the Fifth Age and all humankind.

In sum, olin motion-change constitutes the *biorhythm* of the Fifth Sun, Fifth Age, and all inhabitants of the Fifth Age. It defines cyclical generation and degeneration in the Fifth Age. As León-Portilla remarks, "The profound significance of movement" to the Aztecs "can be deduced from the common Nahuatl root of the words movement, heart and soul."[58]

4.3. LITERARY EVIDENCE

What do the written sources tell us about the nature of olin?

OLIN, TEYOLIA, AND HEART SACRIFICE

Teyolia is a vivifying energy essential to both humans and the cosmos, the shape and pattern of which are defined by olin motion-change. Teyolia is present in humans, animals, and plants as well as mountains, wind, rivers, and towns. In humans, teyolia is concentrated in the heart, which is likewise defined by olin motion-change. Although not separable from a living human body (as is tonalli), teyolia separates from the body upon death.

The ritual excising of human hearts involves seizing the heart's teyolia and transmitting its life-nourishing energy to the Fifth Sun and Fifth Era (since the life of the latter depends upon that of the former).[59] The Fifth Sun is one of the principal recipients of the olin-defined energy of excised hearts. In this way the Aztecs energized the Fifth Sun so that it might continue moving and hence continue ordering and centering the Fifth Age. The heart donor's teyolia helped the Sun ascend each morning and reach its zenith at noon (while the teyolia of women dying in childbirth helped the Sun descend every afternoon). Heart excision thus involved an energy transfusion between humans and the Fifth Sun much in the way we think of a blood transfusion between humans. In this way humans contributed their own teyolia to help renew the teyolia of the Fifth Sun and so sustain the life of the Fifth Age. Heart excision recycled humans' vital teyolia energy back into the larger ecology of the Fifth Sun-Earth Ordering. This transmission of olin-defined energy makes perfect sense, seeing as the energy of Fifth Sun is itself defined by olin motion-change. The rhythmic, oscillating energy of olin motion-change fuels the becoming and processing of humans, Fifth Sun, and Fifth Age. The Aztecs also saw this process of energy transmission as a process of transformation. It transformed the death of the heart donor into the life of the Fifth Sun and life of the Fifth Age.

When the energy of the Fifth Sun ran down at the end of its 52-year cycle, the Fifth Sun needed to be re-energized and renewed by means of the New Fire Ceremony – on pain of its dying (i.e., ceasing to move-change) and the Fifth Age's coming to an end. The New Fire Ceremony transfused the energy of the sacrificial victim's teyolia-rich beating heart (and of his teyolia-rich and tonalli-rich blood) to the Fifth Sun. In this way humans participated in the cosmic circulation and recycling of teyolia and other energies. The victim's teyolia was fed to the fire, which in turn transmitted it to the cosmos. As Kay Read argues, the Aztecs understood this process in terms of feeding or consuming.[60] This understanding held true for less-dramatic occasions of heart sacrifice, too. Their raison d'être consisted of recycling the sacred, vitalizing, and ordering teyolia energy temporarily housed in human hearts to the Fifth Sun and Fifth Era.

The conceptual as well as material centrality of olin motion-change in ritual heart-sacrifice and energy transfusion is evidenced by the prominence of the olin glyph on ritual objects associated with and participating in this transfusion. The olin glyph stood for olin motion-change as well as for the Fifth Sun, the Fifth Era, and existence in the Fifth Era. For example, a bas-relief of the date 4 Olin adorns the side of what Felipe Solís calls the "Nahua [*Olin*] *Téchcatl*."[61] A *techcatl* is a rectangular, prism-shaped stone upon which sacrificial victims were splayed – a process involving no fewer than five priests, four of whom held the unwilling donor's arms and legs, and one of whom excised the donor's heart with surgical precision. Illustrations of techcatls are found throughout surviving codices' illustrations of heart sacrifice. The presence of the olin glyph indicates the destination of the victim's teyolia (and tonalli). After plucking them from the splayed victims' chests, Aztec priests placed the teyolia-rich hearts in a *cuauhxicalli* ("eagle vessel"). Aztec sculptors commonly decorated these flat-bottomed, bowl-shaped vessels with the glyph 4 Olin Tonatiuh, standing for the Fifth Sun, Fifth Era, and life in the Fifth Era. In so doing they signaled the intended purpose and recipient of the teyolia-rich (and tonalli-rich) food deposited there: aiding the Fifth Sun in the completion of its life-cycle.[62] In this manner Aztec sculptors brought together the concept of olin motion-change with the concepts of human heart, teyolia, energy-transfusion, feeding, transformation, and cyclical completion.

Olli, Olin, Medicine, and Ritual

Molina, we've seen, translates *olli* as "a kind of medicinal gum from trees," and *ulli* as "tree gum that is medicinal and is used for making balls for playing." Molina also mentions *oolli* ("a kind of medicinal gum from trees, from which they make balls") and *ollo* ("something which has medicinal gum from trees").[63] Motolinía likewise tells us that olli is the gum of a tree and that from the tapped tree come drops of white liquid, which upon coagulating turn "black as pitch." He adds, "This *ollin* [*olli*] the Indians were much accustomed to offer to demons. They placed some of it on pieces of paper and when the paper was set aflame black drops fell on other pieces of paper. These papers with drops of *ollin* [*olli*] and other pieces of paper with drops of blood they offered to the demon. They also pasted some of this *ollin* [*olli*] on the cheeks of their idols."[64] Durán also reports the native peoples of Mexico greatly prized this *olli* as medicine and as a religious offering.

The Aztecs used this milky tree sap in treating a variety of ills including stomachaches, colic, ear injuries, lip sores, and tongue ailments.[65] These medicinal uses indicate a strong association between olin-defined energy and motion-change, on the one hand, and health, well-being, life, and completion of the life-cycle, on the other. I suggest rubber's medicinal properties were seen as a function of its intrinsic, olin-defined energy – energy that is beneficial because ordered and ordering as well as centered and centering. The medicinal application of liquid rubber communicates olin-shaped energy to patients and in so doing promotes health, well-being, and life. Although we have no direct evidence in this regard, one would expect drinking liquid rubber, for example, to promote regular heart beat, pulse, and regular breathing. Conversely, one would expect irregular pulse and irregular breathing to be expressions of heart troubles and general ill-health.

The Aztecs likened the flowing of liquid rubber within the tree to the flowing of human blood and the flowing of water, and conceived liquid rubber as a precious, life-giving and life-sustaining fluid alongside blood and water.[66] Thus in yet another way we see olin motion-change being equated with the vitalizing energy of growth, health, fertility, transformation, and life. During rituals liquid rubber was splattered on pieces of paper that were then burned, transmitting liquid rubber's vitalizing, olin-patterned energy to water deities such as the *tlaloque* (assistants to Tlaloc). During one such ritual, *I-Atl cahualo*, priests sacrificed children to the tlaloque with the aim of feeding, nourishing, and re-energizing the forces of rain, renewal, agricultural fertility, and thus human nourishment with the children's precious teyolia.[67] The children wore liquid rubber on their faces, feet, and paper costumes. People also raised poles decorated with paper banners spattered with liquid rubber.

Aztec priests routinely smeared rubber on the faces of Tlaloc's statues. Sahagún's informants also state Tlaloc was adorned with black liquid rubber.[68] The Aztecs also used liquid rubber to make balls: smaller ones in rituals, larger ones in the ballgame. The smaller balls, called *ulteloltli*, were burned, buried in offerings, or deposited in springs or lakes with the aim of transmitting their olin-shaped, life-giving energy.[69] The Aztecs likened rubber balls to human hearts, conceiving both as consisting of highly condensed, olin-shaped life-energy.

In sum, rubber and its ritual use bring together olin motion-change, the human heart, teyolia, energy transfusion, feeding, nourishing, fertility, renewal, and cyclical transformation and completion.

OLIN AND THE BALLGAME

The Aztecs used larger rubber balls in the playing of the *ollama,* or "hip ballgame."[70] The ballgame was played in a narrow, I-shaped enclosure called *tlachco* or *tlachtli* in Nahuatl (see Figure 4.11).[71] The game took place within the lengthwise alley formed by the structure. Ballcourts standardly possessed two stone rings, one on each lengthwise side. The rings were commonly adorned with solar discs and rays. The *teotlachtli* or sacred ballcourt located within the sacred precinct of Tenochtitlan was constructed so that its end walls faced the rising sun in the east and setting sun in the west. This aligned the game's play with the east-west diurnal and west-east nocturnal course of the Fifth Sun and with the male~female direction of the Fifth Age.[72]

Scholars as varied as Felipe Solís, Hermann Beyer, Burr Brundage, and Walter Krickeberg believe the ballgame serves as a model of the Fifth Sun-Earth Ordering.[73] Solís refers to the ballcourt as the "mirror of the sky" since it "recreated the celestial vault to mirror the path and movement of the sun."[74] Here again I believe the movement of rubber balls in the ballgame instantiates the movement referred to by *olin*, even if *olli* and *olin* are linguistically unrelated as John Sullivan maintains. If López Austin and Eva Hunt are correct in deriving both from a single root, *ol*, then the two notions are conceptually related. The rubber ball's moving up-and-down and back-and-forth between the ballcourt's two sets of inimically partnered facing walls as well as the ballcourt's I-structured four corners not only manifests olin motion-change but also imitates the olin-patterned motion-change of the Fifth Sun as it travels daily from east to west, nightly from west to east, and annually from winter solstice to summer solstice and then back again. The ballcourt's two inimically partnered, opposing rings represent the two holes through which the Fifth Sun must pass at each dawn and dusk. The I-shaped court's eastern corners represent winter and summer sunrise solstice endpoints while its western corners represent winter and summer solstice sunset endpoints in the Sun's annual cyclical journey up-and-over and down-and-under Tlalticpac. The Sun does not simply rise and fall. It rises and falls in an arced and rounded way. As it moves over and under Tlalticpac, it also oscillates back and forth between winter and summer solstice points. Solís and Brundage claim the ballgame re-creates the Fifth Sun's nocturnal west-east journey through Mictlan, Region of the Dead, a journey of great peril and uncertain outcome. Heather Orr argues that the ballgame portrayed in the *Popol Vuh* functions as "a metaphor for the life cycle of birth, death, and regeneration."[75]

The ballgame symbolizes the cyclical completion and renewal of the Fifth Sun and Fifth Age, and thus the cyclical completion and renewal per se. It brings together at an abstract philosophical level a cluster of olin-related concepts: life-energy; the back-and-forth bouncing movement of rubber balls; cyclical transformation, completion, and renewal; and the oscillating movement of the Fifth Sun. The playing of the ballgame activates these concepts symbolically *and* metaphysically. The rhythmic, oscillating pattern of olin motion-change lies at the heart of these concepts and processes.

Gordon Brotherston remarks that the ballgame's rubber ball is "suggestive in its unique elasticity of one of the most sophisticated philosophies of chance."[76] Unfortunately Brotherston doesn't explain what he means by this remark. However I read him as saying that at any given moment order may collapse into disorder, and that this is an inherent and ineliminable aspect of reality. Although typically orderly, regular, and predictable, the olin-patterned movement of rubber balls is in the final instance chance-like, potentially disorderly, and unpredictable. A ball's regular bouncing can quickly and quite unexpectedly become chaotic upon hitting an uneven surface. The ball takes "a bad bounce," as we say. Similarly, at any given moment a regularly beating human heart can unexpectedly degenerate into chaotic fibrillating, just as the regular oscillating contractions of childbirth can unexpectedly become irregular and fatal.[77] Analogously, at any given moment the life-sustaining, orderly olin motion-change of the Fifth Sun may quickly become disorderly and destructive. And at any moment disorderly earth-shaking motion may erupt, destroying the entire Fifth Age and with it, humankind.

The rubber ball's elasticity reminds us of the ineliminable presence of chance and hence ineliminable potential for disorder in the unfolding of human affairs and in the unfolding of the Fifth Era. What accounts for this? The Tezcatlipoca factor – that is, Tezcatlipoca, the inamic antagonist of Quetzalcoatl; Tezcatlipoca, destroyer of the Fifth Age.[78] Tezcatlipoca represents the ineliminable presence of disordering and disintegrative motion-change in the cosmos generally and in the Fifth Age in particular – disorderly motion that struggles against the orderly and ordering motion-change of olin; disorderly motion that will eventually derange and destroy the Fifth Sun-Earth Ordering. The rubber ball's elasticity, too, therefore reminds us that olin motion-change is metaphysically ambiguous since it is associated with both Quetzalcoatl and Tezcatlipoca as co-creators of the Fifth Era.

Finally, because the olin-patterned motion-change of rubber balls is ineliminably ambiguous, disorderly, chance-like, and unpredictable, the outcome of the ballgame depends upon more than skillful human participation. It also depends upon raw chance. Analogously, the continuing existence of the Fifth Sun and humankind rests upon more than human wisdom and skillful ritual participation. It, too, depends upon the fancy of Tezcatlipoca: "He who mocks us and laughs at us," "He who works arbitrarily."[79]

OLIN AND PATOLLI

Playing *patolli* (a board game resembling parcheesi) imitates and symbolizes the olin motion-change of the Fifth Sun (see Figure 4.1). According to Durán the Aztecs played patolli using an X-shaped pattern of squares painted upon a mat or scratched upon a floor. They divided the four arms of the X into squares

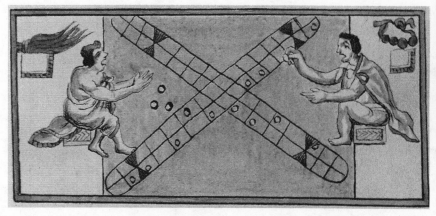

FIGURE 4.1. *Patolli board. (Durán [1971:354, pl. 32]; courtesy of University of Oklahoma Press.)*

using liquid rubber (when available). Twelve pebbles (six red, six blue) were divided between two players. Five or six black beans with numbers painted on their sides served as dice. The object of the game was to move one's pebbles through the entire circuit of the X, returning them to where they began. The player who did so first, won.[80]

Patolli mirrors the structure and dynamics of the Fifth Age in several respects. Patolli board and Fifth Age are homologous. Both are formed by two inter-crossing arms forming an X. Both are defined by five orientations: four cardinal directions (east, west, north, and south) plus center (or, alternatively, four inter-cardinals, defined by the Fifth Sun's eastward rising and westward setting at winter and summer solstices, plus center) (see Figures 4.2 and 4.3). Both form quincunxes. The quincunx is further reproduced in the matrix of squares that forms the board's center. The centers of the patolli board and the Fifth Sun-Earth Ordering are both formed by the crossing paths of the four directions.

Players appear to have oriented the board's four arms to the four cardinal (or intercardinal) directions, thereby aligning the game literally and symbolically with the cosmological ordering of the Fifth Age. The patolli's X-shaped board was divided into a total of 52 spaces mirroring the 52-year cycle created by combining the 360+5-day solar calendar (*xiuhpohualli*) and 260-day ritual calendar (*tonalpohualli*). The 104 spaces represented by the movements of the two players coincide with the 104 years represented by 65 cycles of the planet Venus.

With the patolli board arranged and oriented in this manner, the path followed by a player's pebbles through the board's spaces reproduced and

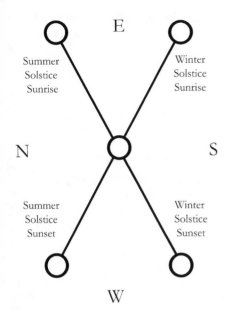

E

N

S

W

Summer
Solstice
Sunrise

Winter
Solstice
Sunrise

Summer
Solstice
Sunset

Winter
Solstice
Sunset

FIGURE 4.2. *Quincunx formed by rising and setting solstice points. (Author's drawing.)*

symbolized the diurnal and annual path of the Fifth Sun. Playing patolli thus mirrored the olin-shaped moving of the Fifth Sun. Winning the game consisted of symbolically moving the Fifth Sun through a complete cycle.[81] The path of the pebbles reproduced the path of the Fifth Sun in yet another respect. As each moved from an arm's end to the center and then back toward another end, both pebbles and Fifth Sun oscillated and pulsated between center and periphery. Their motion was none other than the rhythmic oscillating and pulsating of olin motion-change. It is also not coincidental that the patolli figure itself was painted using liquid rubber, which itself contained and symbolized olin-patterned energy. Playing patolli thus instantiates as well as symbolizes a specific pattern of motion: oscillating motion-change between center and periphery through a fourfold-ordered cosmos and through fourfold-ordered time-place.

The analogy between patolli and the Fifth Sun is not exact, however. Whereas the path of the players' beans is fixed in advance by the X-shaped format of the patolli board, the path of the Fifth Sun is not fixed in advance by the format of the cosmos. The Fifth Sun fashions its X-shaped path in the course of its olin-patterned processing, becoming, and transforming. The quincunx is a consequence and a record of how the Fifth Sun move-changes and it is an instrument for predicting how it will move-change in the future.

FIGURE 4.3. *Quincunx-quatrefoil cosmogram.* (Codex Fejérváry-Mayer *[Loubat 1901: pl. 1]; courtesy of Werner-Forman Archive.)*

Finally, the Aztecs viewed patolli as a game of chance (one commonly accompanied by betting). This aspect mirrors the ineliminable element of chance in the processing of the Fifth Sun, the unfolding of the Fifth Age, and the becoming of human life. Whether or not the Fifth Sun completes its cycle and is reborn every morning depends partly upon chance. Analogously, whether or not a human completes the four phases of her life cycle also depends partly upon chance. Timothy Kendall and León-Portilla argue the Aztecs likened traveling through life from birth to death to playing patolli.[82] The throwing of dice, like the bouncing of a rubber ball, reflects the Tezcatlipoca factor in Aztec metaphysics.

Olin as Day Sign of the Tonalpohualli

Durán reports that *olin* names the seventeenth day of the twenty days that comprise (along with thirteen numerals) the tonalpohualli or 260-day ritual count. On this day olin's unique pattern of energy saturates and influences the entire cosmos. Olin-patterned energy influences in an especially profound way those processes initiated on this day: for example, human life-processes, rituals, military and mercantile expeditions, and most significantly and dramatically, the Fifth Sun itself. Olin thus names a pattern of cosmic motion-change that *precedes* the birth of Fifth Sun, 4 Olin Tonatiuh, on the day 4 Olin.[83] Durán also claims the Aztecs believed males born on the day, Olin, were destined to become men "who would shine like the sun," while females were destined to become "stupid, foolish, limited in their intelligence, obtuse, and confused" and yet nevertheless "rich, prosperous, and as powerful as the men."[84]

Olin and East

Each of the twenty day signs of the tonalpohualli is conceptually and meta-physically associated with one of the four cardinal directions. Olin is one of five day signs associated with East. East is the time-place of light from whence emerges the renewed radiance, heat, and life-energy of the Fifth Sun. The Sun has successfully completed its nocturnal journey through the Land of the Dead and now dawns, reborn and revitalized. It has completed its daily – and on the first day after the winter equinox, its annual – life~death cycle. The Aztecs accordingly conceived East as a time-place of life-energy, fertility, abundance, wealth, creation, regeneration, and cyclical completion and renewal. They associated East with the color red – the color of blood and human hearts; of life and sacrifice; of fertility, nourishment, and feeding; and of cyclical transformation, renewal and completion.[85] Sahagún's version of *The Legend of the Suns* describes the Sun as rising in the "Place of Light," "spreading like red dye" and "spreading in an undulating way."[86] The Sun's "spreading in an undulating way" is fitting, seeing as the Sun is defined by the undulating motion-change of olin. East is also the time-place of the ascending, strengthening, and youthful masculine Sun (as opposed to West, the time-place of the descending, weakening, aging, and eventually dying feminine Sun).

East is thus metaphysically constituted and defined by a special pattern of energy. It is the place-time happening of this energy. And what kind of energy is this? What is its shape? The association of olin with East suggests this energy is the oscillating motion-change of olin. The energy of olin motion-change is an

Eastern energy: an energy of cyclical renewal as well as of abundance, fertility, and potency.

OLIN AND XOLOTL

Xolotl is commonly described as the "patron" or "governing deity" of the day sign, Olin. *Xolotl* names a specific cluster of sacred processes and energies involved in transforming death into life by way of gestation, renewal, and rebirth. Reinterpreted processively and pantheistically, the foregoing patronage claim states that the cluster of forces dubbed Xolotl dominate the days named by the day sign Olin. The codices standardly depict Xolotl as a dog, as dog-headed, or with doglike features (such as paws). He is said to be Quetzalcoatl's twin, counterpart, or *nahualli*.[87] Xolotl commonly wears the accoutrements of Quetzalcoatl such as Quetzalcoatl's spiraling, conch-shell breastplate, *epcololli* (curved-shell ear pendants), and Huastec conical hat.[88]

Xolotl is also patron of the ballgame; twins, doubled things, and conjoined things; and abnormal births, dwarves, hunchbacks, deforming diseases, and all things monstrous. The word *xolotl* refers to twinned or doubled things. It also means "page, servant, or slave."[89] Hunchbacks and dwarves (*xilome*) often served as courtly pages in Mesoamerica.[90] Read points out that *xolotl* also refers to maize leaves, particularly the tender green leaves of the sprouting maize plant.[91]

Sahagún's informants describe dogs as both "constant companions" and creatures who eat "maize, raw meat, cooked meat . . . the flesh of the dead, the spoiled . . . the revolting, the stinking, the rotting."[92] Dogs were known for eating human excrement and for their sexual promiscuity.[93] Their willingness to eat the rotting, the fecal, and the dead suggests dogs' role as transformers of the dead and disordered (*tlazolli*) into the living and well-ordered. By consuming death as a nourishing foodstuff, they create life. Their sexual promiscuity likewise suggests fertility, continual regeneration, and transformation. Dogs' tendency to eat filth explains the depiction in *Codex Telleriano-Remensis* (fol. 19) of Xolotl wearing a headdress of cotton with a cotton-tassel insert – an accoutrement standardly associated with Tlazolteotl (Eater of Filth and Ordure) and Tlazolteotl-Ixcuina (Spinner and Weaver of Life from Raw Fiber). This affirms Xolotl's role as the one who helps the Fifth Sun return reborn each morning from Mictlan (the Underworld and Region of the Dead). The Aztecs assigned these characteristics to Xolotl (Xolotl cluster).

Eduard Seler associates Xolotl's portrayal as a dog with the belief that dogs accompany the souls of the dead to Mictlan.[94] He finds further evidence of the association between Xolotl, dogs, death, and Mictlan in the fact that

Mesoamericans viewed twins as unnatural monstrosities and consequently commonly killed one of two twins shortly after birth. Seler speculates that Xolotl represents the murdered twin who dwells in the darkness of Mictlan, while Quetzalcoatl ("The Precious Twin") represents the surviving twin who dwells in the light of the sun. As Quetzalcoatl's twin and inamic partner, Xolotl carries out in the nighttime darkness below Tlalticpac activities that are inimically partnered with Quetzalcotl's daytime activities above Tlalticpac.

Xolotl and Quetzalcoatl constitute an inamic pair. They constitute inimically partnered phases in the olin-shaped life~death cycle of the Fifth Sun: Xolotl, the phase occurring below Tlalticpac in the Underworld during nighttime, and Quetzalcoatl, the phase upon and above Tlalticpac during daytime. Quetzalcoatl forces govern how things are born so that they may die properly; Xolotl governs how things die so that they may be reborn properly. Quetzalcoatl helps the Fifth Sun follow its diurnal path, while Xolotl helps it follow its nocturnal path. Together they ensure olin-defined cyclical completion, renewal, and transformation.

Because Xolotl and Quetzalcoatl constitute inamically partnered phases in the olin-shaped life~death cycle of the Fifth Sun, they constitute a fortiori inamically partnered phases in the life~death cycle of the Fifth Era and all things in it. Xolotl forces and Quetzalcoatl forces are brought together into agonistic inamic unity by means of olin-shaped motion-change. It is by means of olin motion-change that they complement, compete with, and complete one another. Quetzalcoatl's male, dry, light, vivifying, and ordering energies are complemented, challenged, and completed by, as well as unified with Xolotl's female, wet, dark, enervating, and disordering energies through olin-shaped motion change. Here we thus see the connection between agonistic inamic unity and olin. Olin is one way of agonistically ordering inamic pairs into an agonistic unity. Similarly, we can now see that if Solís's, Brundage's, and Orr's interpretations of the ballgame are correct, then the ballgame actualizes the olin-defined agonistic struggle of inamic partners in the Fifth Era. Olin is the shape of their inamic interrelationship, their struggle, and their unity.

Quetzalcoatl and Xolotl also constitute the twin phases of Venus as the morning star and evening star, respectively. In their respective roles as morning star and evening star Quetzalcoatl and Xolotl constitute inamically paired phases of Venus. Just as Quetzalcoatl qua morning star acts as the harbinger of the Sun's rising (rebirth) every dawn, so Xolotl qua evening star acts as the harbinger the Sun's setting (dying) every dusk.[95] In this way the morning star and evening star complement and complete one another. In this way they divide the single life~death process of cyclical transformation into its two inimically partnered constitutive phases: the one leading from birth to death, the other from death to birth. Together they accomplish what neither could accomplish alone: the completion and reinitiation of the Fifth Sun's life~death cycle. Xolotl does Quetzalcoatl's bidding, as he is Quetzalcoatl's inamic partner below the earth in Mictlan, just as Quetzalcoatl does Xolotl's bidding, as he is Xolotl's inamic partner above the earth in the sky. Xolotl helps the Sun return to life from its journey in the region of the dead.[96]

Seler characterizes Nanahuatzin ("Little Pustule Covered One"), who is deformed by syphilis, as an aspect of Xolotl in his capacity as god of monsters, deforming diseases, and deformities.[97] In Aztec creation stories, Nanahuatzin transforms himself into the Fifth Sun by immolating himself in the great fire at Teotihuacan. His self-sacrificial destruction initiates the life~death cycle of the Fifth Sun.[98] Nanahuatzin is an aspect or alter-ego of Quetzalcoatl. *Codex Borgia* (pl. 10) depicts a deformed Nanahuatzin and a self-immolating figure facing one another alongside the glyph for the day sign, Olin. In so doing the image connects olin with sacrificial motion-change and transformation; that is, sacrificial endings that nourish new life cycle beginnings.

According to the creation account recounted in the *Florentine Codex*, after the Fifth Sun was initially created, it did not move. Ehecatl ("God" of Wind) consequently began slaying all the other "gods" to induce the newly created Sun into movement. Xolotl, however, was unwilling to die in order to give movement to the new Sun. Xolotl transformed himself into a young green maize plant with two stalks (*xolotl*), a doubled maguey plant (*mexolotl*), and an amphibious animal (*axolotl*).[99] Xolotl is thus a master transformer. In the end, Ehecatl nevertheless succeeded in finding and killing Xolotl. It is perhaps Xolotl's unwillingness to die for the Fifth Sun that explains his residence in the dark Underworld. Its involuntariness notwithstanding, Xolotl's death is part of the mass sacrifice of the gods whose deaths lead to the new Sun's moving. According to other accounts, Xolotl leads the mass sacrifice. Xolotl also travels (alone or with Quetzalcoatl) to Mictlan to gather the remains of previous humans to create the new race of humans of the Fifth Sun.[100] Quetzalcoatl enlists Xolotl's help since Xolotl knows how to operate within the Underworld. Without Xolotl there would be no current race of human beings. Once again, the combined inimically partnered activities of Quetzalcoatl and Xolotl make for a successfully completed and renewed life~death cycle.

The Aztecs divided the 260-day tonalpohualli into twenty 13-day periods (called *trecenas* by the Spaniards). Each trecena reflected the influence of its patron deity and the kind of divinatory ritual for which the trecena was consulted. Xolotl governed the sixteenth trecena, 1 Cozcacuauhtli ("One Vulture").[101] *Codex Borbonicus* (pl. 16) depicts this trecena with Xolotl facing Tlalchitonatiuh ("The

Sun Going into the Earth" or "Sun Close to the Earth").[102] Tlalchitonatiuh is Xolotl's partner and the secondary or subsidiary patron of this trecena. He represents an aspect of Xolotl.

Nowotny believes the scene depicts Xolotl singing a song of stone knives and flowers (i.e., a sacrificial song) and holding a sacrificial knife. Xolotl wears various trappings of Quetzalcoatl: bent earrings, conch-shell pendant, and a loincloth with rounded ends. The scene includes various sacrificial gifts: an eagle foot and wing in a bowl, a vessel of foaming liquid, a red pepper-pod, and mortification utensils inserted into a grass ball.[103] Facing Xolotl, Tlalchitonatiuh consists of a mummy-bundle-wrapped dead Fifth Sun (the Sun's death indicated by the arrow sticking in its mouth) that is descending into the devouring jaws of the Earth monster. Xolotl and Tlalchitonatiuh thus have mortuary aspects, both being associated with the levels under the Earth. This mortuary aspect is further highlighted by the reigning bird of the trecena, the vulture Cozacauauhtli. Vultures eat dead flesh or carrion, transforming death into life.

Quiñones Keber characterizes the similar depiction of Tlalchitonatiuh in *Codex Telleriano Remensis* (fol. 20r) as a "rare personification of the Aztec belief that the setting sun, swallowed by the earth (monster), remained in the underworld until its reemergence at dawn."[104] By combining attributes of Tlaloc, Quetzalcoatl, and Tlaltecuhtli ("Lord of Earth"), the depiction of Tlalchitonatiuh suggests the transformative interrelationship between the processes of decay, death, germination, fertility, renewal, and rebirth. The emphasis, once again, is upon cyclical completion and renewal.

Under his guise as Tlalchitonatiuh, Xolotl accompanies the Sun into death each dusk. Xolotl's role does not end there, however. Given his special knowledge of the Underworld, Xolotl guides the nighttime Sun along its eastward journey through the Underworld so that it may exit the Underworld and be reborn each morning. Xolotl is able to help in the Sun's rebirth since Xolotl possesses the power not only to enter but also exit the Underworld. The life~death cycle is completed and renewed.[105] Matos Moctezuma interprets this process as consisting of the dying Sun's penetration and impregnation of the dark, wet, female womb of Coatlicue ("Goddess of Earth"). There the Sun gestates until ready to leave the earth's womb each morning, born anew.[106] A statue of a skeletal Xolotl carrying a solar disc bearing an image of the Sun on his back (called "the Night Traveler") succinctly portrays Xolotl's role in assisting the Sun through the process of death, gestation, and rebirth.[107]

Finally, Xolotl is patron of the ballgame. Some scholars argue the ballgame symbolizes the Sun's perilous and uncertain nighttime journey through the Underworld. The nighttime Sun must do battle with the female nocturnal forces of the terrestrial Underworld represented by the Moon, stars, and night.[108] Xolotl thus helps the Fifth Sun not only complete its life~death cycle but also gestate and reinitiate a new life~death cycle.

In sum, *Xolotl* names a specific cluster of processes that serves cyclical completion, renewal, and hence transformation. These processes help complete existing life~death cycles and help initiate new life~death cycles, and thus aid the transformation of death into life. Susan Gillespie and Kay Read correctly argue the Aztecs were obsessed with beginnings and endings.[109] To put a finer point on it, they were obsessed with cyclical completions and renewals and hence cyclical transformations. How cycles end prefigures whether or not, and if so how, they will begin anew. Proper completions promote proper gestations that, in turn, promote proper renewals. Xolotl's association with olin motion-change underscores Aztec metaphysics' obsession with completions and their role in renewals. Xolotl's association with olin motion-change suggests proper completions and gestations must instantiate olin motion-change. Olin-shaped decomposition and disintegration (i.e., death) promote olin-shaped composition and integration (i.e., rebirth and renewal). The orderly completion of a cycle serves the orderly renewal of that cycle, where completions and renewals are bound together by olin motion-change.

OLIN AND TLAZOLTEOTL-IXCUINA

Tlazolteotl-Ixcuina is the governing cluster of energies or "patroness" of the thirteenth trecena of the tonalpohualli, whose day sign is Olin.[110] Who is Tlazolteotl-Ixcuina, and what does her association with olin tell us about olin motion-change? Tlazolteotl-Ixcuina, according to Thelma Sullivan, "was the Mother-Goddess, the genetrix of all living things . . . [S]he was . . . the Great Spinner of the Thread and Weaver of the Fabric of Life . . . [S]he was the Great Conceiver and the Great Parturient."[111] Her many monikers include *Teteoinnan* ("Mother of the Gods"), *Toci* ("Our Grandmother"), *Tonantzin* ("Our Mother"), *Tlalli iyollo* ("Heart of the Earth"), *Tlazolteotl* ("Goddess of Filth"), *Temazcalteci* ("Grandmother of the Bathhouse"), *Itzapapalotl* ("Obsidian Butterfly"), *Xochiquetzal* ("Flowery Queztal Feather"), *Cihuacoatl* ("Serpent Woman"), and *Quilaztli* ("Plant Generator").[112] Nicholson situates Tlazolteotl-Ixcuina in the "Teteoinnan complex" of deities that he treats as a version of the earth-mother concept. He classifies the Teteoinnan complex under the more general theme of "Rain-Moisture-Agricultural Fertility."[113]

Sahagún reports that Teteoinnan was worshipped by midwives and those who administer abortions; physicians who cure hemorrhoids and eye ailments;

physicians who purge people; physicians who remove worms from the teeth and eyes; owners of sweathouses; those who read-count the future (*tlapouhque*); those who cast auguries by looking into water or by casting grains of maize; and those who read-count tied knots (*mecatlapouhque*).[114] As Xochiquetzal, Teteoinnan was patroness of weavers, embroiderers, sculptors, painters, silversmiths, and "all those whose profession it was to imitate nature in crafts and in drawing."[115]

The Aztecs associated Tlazolteotl-Ixcuina with the Huastecans who revered her as a Mother Goddess and whom the Aztecs viewed as a people of lavish dress, overconsumption, and excessive sexuality. They considered the Huastec region to be a land of fertile, abundant vegetation. The Aztecs extended this association to Tlazolteotl-Ixcuina. They identified Tlazolteotl-Ixcuina processes with the creativity, generation, fertility, and potency of mother-earth. They considered Tlazolteotl-Ixcuina processes to be overwhelmingly female, dark, cold, and wet. Cotton was grown in the Huastec region, and the Aztecs ranked Huastecs as expert weavers. They accordingly associated Tlazolteotl-Ixcuina with spinning and weaving. Sullivan believes *Ixcuina* is a Huastec word meaning "Lady Cotton" or "Goddess of Cotton."[116]

The array of Teteoinnan according to the *Primeros memoriales* includes lips painted with rubber, a round patch of rubber painted on her face, and a head-dress of unspun cotton.[117] Rubber is associated with: olin motion-change; olin-shaped cyclical completion, renewal, and transformation; blood as liquid, life-nourishing energy; pulsating human hearts; and the dynamics of the Fifth Sun. Both the *Codex Telleriano-Remensis* (folio 12r) and the *Florentine Codex* depict Tlazolteotl-Ixcuina with rubber-painted lips, mouth, and chin.[118] Eloise Quiñones Keber suggests this alludes to her role as eater of dirt or filth, and to her role as Tlaelquani ("Eater of Ordure").[119] I believe it also alludes to the fact that Tlazolteotl-Ixcuina's (and Tlaelquani's) consumption of tlazolli (filth, disorder) constitutes an indispensable contribution to olin-patterned transformation into rebirth and olin-patterned renewal of order. The successful completion of olin-shaped life~death cycles requires that the disordered be transformed into the well-ordered. Eating filth does precisely this.

Tlazolteotl-Tlaelquani processes are involved in the earth's recycling and transforming of waste (e.g., human and animal excrement; decaying flesh, fruit, and vegetables) into the nourishment-rich humus needed for renewing life.[120] As H. B. Nicholson writes, "the earth is at one and the same time the great womb and tomb of all life."[121] Tlazolteotl-Tlaelquani's consumption of tlazolli is an essential stage in the olin-shaped recycling and transformation of the disorderly into the orderly, garbage into food, and death into life. Thus we return to agonistic inamic unity: life and death are mutually arising, interdependent, and interrelated. In order for new things to come to life, other living things must die and be properly recycled. And in order for new things to come into life from dead things, new things must unified with dead things through olin-defined motion-change. Life~death must ordered and unified in an olin-defined manner.

Tlazolteotl-Tlaelquani-Ixcuina's association with olin, like Xolotl's, suggests that successful creations, completions, endings, and recreations are defined and shaped by olin motion-change. Controlled and orderly, olin-shaped decomposition and disintegration (death) promotes orderly recomposition and reintegration (rebirth and renewal). The orderly completion of a cycle aids the orderly renewal of a cycle. Olin motion-change defines the transformational processes associated with the earth's fertility and fecundity.

Tlazolteotl-Ixcuina processes are also involved in cleansing, healing, midwifery, and medicines used for inducing menses and abortion. Uterine contractions and premature delivery involve olin-patterned and olin-ordered motion-change. Pregnant women and postpartum mothers, the sick and infirm, and illicit lovers and sexual deviates partook of the cleansing and healing Tlazolteotl-Ixcuina processes found in bathhouses. The effect of these cleansing and healing powers for the pregnant woman was to help stabilize her olin-defined gestation process and help guide the unborn child to its birth day – just as Xolotl helps guide the unborn Sun gestating within the dark, wet womb of the Earth to its birth day (dawn). Codical depictions of Tlazolteotl-Ixcuina standardly emphasize the connection between sacrifice, fertility, and regeneration and thus the role of Tlazolteotl-Ixcuina processes in cyclical completion and renewal. *Codex Borgia* (pl. 12 and 23) and *Codex Telleriano-Remensis* (fol. 12r) depict Tlazolteotl-Ixcuina with spindles and spindle whorls along with headbands, ear ornaments, and hanging tassels made of raw, unspun cotton. They depict Tlazolteotl-Ixcuina as the great spinner and weaver. Like ordure and filth, raw cotton is disordered and characterized by tlazolli. Like ordure and filth, raw cotton is transformed into something well-ordered, namely, woven fabric. Tlazolteotl-Ixcuina processes are thus transformational since they transform disordered stuff into well-ordered stuff. Their significance is accordingly profound in Aztec metaphysics. Sullivan writes, "Weaving and spinning represent life, death, and rebirth in a continuing cycle that characterizes the essential nature of the Mother Goddess."[122] Thus we return to chapter 3's claim that weaving and weaving-related activities serve as an organizing metaphor in Aztec metaphysics and that Aztec metaphysics conceives the cosmos as a grand weaving in progress.

A spindle rod undergoes four phases of expanding and shrinking in the course of its life and in so doing exhibits dramatically the in-and-out, undulating pattern of olin motion-change.[123] A spindle rod begins as an empty stick. As spinning commences, it gradually expands with thread until it can hold no more. During the subsequent process of weaving, the spindle gradually shrinks in size as its thread contributes to the fabric. It completes its life~death cycle as an empty stick again, only to begin anew. The expanding and contracting volume of the thread on the spindle resembles the expanding and contracting of a pulsating human heart and of a prepartum and postpartum mother's abdomen. The spindle's physical motion also constitutes a qualitative change just as the woman's physical change constitutes a qualitative change. The spindle becomes pregnant with thread, as a woman becomes pregnant with child. Spindle, human heart, and child-bearing woman all instantiate oscillating, rising and falling, and pulsating olin motion-change. Spinning thus evokes olin motion-change and sexual pregnancy.

Sahagún's informants report that Ixcuina consists of four women: Tiacapan, Teicu, Tlaco, and Xocotzin.[124] Sullivan interprets Tlazolteotl-Ixcuina's quadruplicity as a metaphor for the four phases of the life~death cycle: "Her fourfold character represents the growth and decline of all living things that, like the spindle, pass through four stages: youth, fecundity, middle age, and old age and death."[125] Tlazolteotl-Ixcuina processes possess four phases and consequently both incorporate and symbolize cyclical beginning, completion, renewal, and transformation. Those things whose life~death cycles are ordered into four phases include most prominently the Fifth Sun, human beings, and maize.

The association of four-phased Tlazolteotl-Ixcuina processes with olin motion-change suggests the following. First, Tlazolteotl-Ixcuina processes undulate, pulsate, and oscillate. Second, cyclical completion and renewal are olin-shaped since they are olin-ordered processes. Indeed, it would appear the Aztecs conceived existence in the Fifth Age itself in terms of four-phased olin-style motion-change and transformation. Third, olin motion-change is four-fold ordered. It consists of a succession of four phases that renews itself upon completion. As such it is cyclical.[126] Fourth, four-phased olin motion-change represents one of the ways in which agonistic inamichuan are united. Not only life~death but also light~darkness and order~disorder, for example, cyclically alternate and oscillate in a four-phased, olin-patterned way. Each inamic unity undergoes the same four phases of birth and infancy, youth, adulthood and matrimony, and old age and death. Fifth, the fact that the Aztecs equated olin motion-change with cyclical oscillation, together with the fact that they divided olin motion-change into four phases, suggests they distinguished four phases in the period of an oscillatory cycle. In the case of the oscillating motion-change of the Fifth Sun, for example, the four consist of the Sun's ascent from its midnight nadir below the earth until almost dawn; its dawning and subsequent rising above and over the earth until it reaches its noontime zenith above the earth; its descent from its noontime zenith to dusk; and its subsequent descent down and under the earth until it reaches its midnight nadir again. These four phases also represent the waxing and waning influences of the paired inamic forces constituting the Sun. Noon is that fleeting moment when the hot, male, dry, light, and descending inamic forces constituting the Sun dominate, while midnight is the fleeting moment when the cold, female, wet, dark, and ascending inamic forces constituting the Sun dominate. From midnight to noon the former forces gain increasing power over the latter forces, while from noon until midnight the latter gain increasing power over the former. Sixth, olin motion-change achieves a dynamic and diachronic balance of agonistic inamic partners by uniting them in four-phased cyclical oscillatory processes.

In sum, olin defines the motion-change involved in cyclical completion and renewal, and thus defines metaphysical transformation *within* cycles as well as *across* cycles.

4 OLIN AS DAY NAME OF THE FIFTH SUN AND FIFTH AGE

The *Annals of Cuauhtitlan* states that the name of the Fifth Sun and name of the Fifth cosmic era is Nahui Ollin [Olin] Tonatiuh, or "Four Movement Sun":

> Like so is the Fifth Sun.
> 4-Movement is its day sign (*itonal*) [its day name; i.e., its heat, light, *tonalli*].
> It is called Moving-Sun because
> It moves.
> It follows a path.
> The old ones say that,
> On 4-Movement, it will be done like so.
> The earth will quake.
> They will be hungry.
> Like so, we will perish.[127]

The *Legend of the Suns* states the Fifth Sun "is named 4 Movement. We who live today [have] this one, it's our sun."[128]

The name *Nahui Olin Tonatiuh* consists of three components: (1) *Tonatiuh*, variously translated as "He goes forth shining,"[129] "He-goes-becoming-warm,"[130] "He who produces heat and light – that is, the day,"[131] and "He who goes forth radiating *tonalli* (tonalli being an impersonal animating energy circulating throughout the cosmos and one of three animating energies possessed by humans); (2) the day sign *olin* ("movement" or "motion-change"); and (3) the day number *nahui* ("four"). I discuss each component since each offers insight into the nature of the Fifth Sun and Fifth Age. Combining the three components to form *Nahui Olin Tonatiuh* we get "4 Motion-Change Sun" or "4 Motion-Change, He who radiates light, heat, the day, and tonalli." Given the connection between the energy of heat and light and the energy of life we also get "4 Motion, He who goes forth vivifying, sustaining, and creating life."

The name *4 Olin Tonatiuh* states the metaphysical essence of the Fifth Sun. According to the Mesoamerican naming practices, the name of a thing indicates its nature, power, and essence. The Fifth Sun along with the preceding four Suns "were named according to what they did or what was attributed to them" according to the *Historia de los mexicanos por sus pinturas*.[132] The name *4 Olin Tonatiuh* is therefore neither arbitrary nor the product of human contrivance. It discloses the heart and essence of the Fifth Sun; it declares the essence of the Fifth Sun to be 4 olin motion-change; and since the Fifth Sun is the essence of the Fifth Age, it identifies olin motion-change as the essence of the Fifth Age. Also, 4 Olin defines the nature of the Fifth Sun's motion-change and its continual four-phased transformation. It specifies the shape and pattern of the Fifth Sun's processing. The *Annals* also states that *4 Olin* refers to the Fifth Sun's mode of destruction. The Fifth Sun and Fifth Age will disintegrate due to violent earthquakes (i.e., olin motion-change). The Fifth Sun and Fifth Age thus live and die by olin motion-change.

The Fifth Sun's heart and essence is therefore to move-change, shine, warm, vitalize, energize, create the day, and emit tonalli energy *in an olin-ordered way*. And since the Fifth Sun is the heart and essence of the Fifth Era, it follows that the Fifth Era is also defined by 4 olin motion-change. Although there are other patterns of motion-change and other energizing forces operating in the Fifth Era, olin motion-change alone *defines* the Fifth Era. The olin-defined motion-change of 4 Olin Tonatiuh functions as the biorhythm of and reference point for the Fifth Age and all its inhabitants. This is nicely illustrated by several adages collected by Sahagún: "The sun hath fallen, or set" and "The sun hath darkened" were said upon a person's growing very old; "He moveth the sun forward a little," upon an infant's growing into childhood; and "I discover my sun; I set out my sun," by a woman upon marrying.[133] As its defining attribute, olin motion-change is unique to the Fifth Sun and sets the Fifth Sun apart from the preceding four Suns and their Eras. Both the *Annals* and the *Legend* state the Fifth Sun is unique among the five Suns since it is the only Sun named, defined, and destroyed by olin motion-change.

Olin motion-change is therefore essential to existence in the Fifth Age. All things are processes, and processes by nature move-change. All things are animated, and animated things by nature move-change. In the Fifth Age all things exist so long as they continue to become and move-change in an olin-defined way. The life processes of the Fifth Sun, the Fifth Age and all things in the Fifth Age *follow a path*: the oscillating path of olin motion-change. Olin-motion-change constitutes their biorhythm.

The *Annals* states *4 Olin* is the day name and tonalli of the Fifth Sun. Things acquire their day name and tonalli on the day of their birth, suggesting the Fifth Sun was born on the calendrical day, 4 Olin. Tonalli includes solar heat, energy, or power; solar radiation; life force sensed and transmitted as heat; day; day sign; day name; a person's fate, destiny, or birth-merit (*mahcehualli*)[134] as determined by her day sign; personal and calendrical name; animating energy, soul, spirit; and vigor, character, or temperament.[135] Although it is one among many components of its overall tonalli, the Fifth Sun's day name is hugely influential. The day sign 4 Olin means the Fifth Sun's personality, vigor, birth-merit, and destiny are characterized by 4 olin motion-change. The other component of the Fifth Sun's name, *Tonatiuh*, tells us that it goes forth shining, warming, making the day, and radiating tonalli (in the above senses). Combining this fact with its day sign, 4 Olin, we see that the Fifth Sun goes forth shining, warming, making the day, and radiating tonalli in an olin-patterned way. It follows a pulsating, olin-shaped path during its diurnal and nocturnal journey and life~death cycle. In short, *Tonatiuh* tells us *that* the Fifth Sun radiates heat, light, life-energy, and tonalli energy, while *4 Olin* tells us *how* it does these things.

Tonalli also includes destiny or birth-merit. The Fifth Sun's 4 Olin tonalli-destiny indicates how and when it will perish. The *Annals* and *Legend* suggest the names of the five Suns indicate the manner and day of their destruction. The Fifth Sun is destined to be destroyed by violent earthquake (*tlalollin*) on the day 4 Olin.[136] Its life-giving, orderly motion-change will become disorderly and deadly, just as an orderly human heartbeat becomes disorderly and deadly upon fibrillating.

In sum, the fact that the Fifth Sun is both ordered and disordered by olin motion-change highlights the inherent ambiguity of olin motion-change and hence inherent ambiguity in the make-up of all things vivified by the Fifth Sun. Olin's cyclical oscillating motion-change unites agonistic inamic partners and therefore possesses both ordering and disordering (male and female, hot and cold, etc.) aspects or phases. Orderly olin motion-change is life-giving; disorderly olin motion-change is life-destroying.

The Significance of the Number Four

Although the day-sign component of a day name carries greater weight than the day-number component in dictating the kind of personality and hence kind of influence a specific day enjoys, the day number does contribute its own distinct personality and influence, and therefore needs to be examined. What is the upshot of four (*nahui*) in the name *4 Olin Tonatiuh*?

Aztec numerology maintains numbers possess both quantitative and qualitative properties.[137] Numbers have specific essences or personalities. As Geraldo Aldana remarks concerning Maya numerology, numbers "have personality along with computational functionality" and it is their personalities rather than their purely quantitative properties that "determined the working of the cosmos."[138] Numbers are concrete metaphysical forces that shape the unfolding of the cosmos. Frank Lipp reports that contemporary Mixe of Oaxaca regard numbers as "spiritual" forces associated with specific deities. These forces may be coaxed to protect humans, or as in the case with number 11 (which is associated with Mikhu', the devil), they may be coaxed through sorcery to harm humans.[139] So, while the *numeral* 4 refers to the serial order of the day (occurring between 3 and 5), the *number* four signifies much, much more. The number four contributes a specific quality to the day named *4 Olin* as well as to those processes it influences. The combination of four plus olin represents a conjuncture of two distinct personalities. So what exactly is the essence of the number four, and what does it contribute to the nature of the day, 4 Olin, and hence the nature of the Fifth Sun and Fifth Age?

Aztec *tonalpouhqui* (those who read-counted-measured-interpreted the significance of the days) characterized the personalities of day numbers as auspicious, inauspicious, or indifferent. They viewed the number thirteen, for example, as auspicious since it reflects or symbolizes cosmic order.[140] Thirteen is the number of heavenly layers above the earth; the number of "Day Lords" who "carried" the tonalli burden of each day and modified the significance of any given day; and the total number of the day-number count, one through thirteen, forming the 260-day tonalpohualli. Seler and Nicholson maintain the Aztecs counted thirteen daylight hours in each day. López Austin places thirteen in the "Father" column of aligned inamic pairs along with light, heat, day, strength, life, and therefore, I argue, order, being, and arrangement. The number thirteen thus symbolizes order because it is *itself* a metaphysically ordering force. The metaphysical value of thirteen grounds the prognosticatory value of thirteen. Numbers name metaphysical forces and these forces have personalities.

By contrast, Aztec tonalpouhque considered the number nine to be inauspicious since it reflects the disordering forces of night and the Underworld.[141]

Nine is the number of layers of Mictlan and the number of "Night Lords" who "accompanied" the tonalli of any given day. Seler argues the Aztecs assigned nine hours to night. The Aztecs associated nine with witchcraft and sorcery, apparently because witches and sorcerers employed cycles of nine in their nefarious dealings. López Austin aligns the number nine alongside death, darkness, night, weakness, and hence, I argue, disorder, nonbeing, and derangement. The number nine thus symbolizes disorder because it is a metaphysically disordering force.

What is the essence of the number four, and how does it influence the nature of the day, 4 Olin, and hence the nature of the Fifth Sun and Fifth Age? Is it ordering or disordering, stabilizing or destabilizing, auspicious or inauspicious? Seler interprets *4* to mean "all kinds of" or "nothing but." For example, *4 Acatl (Reed)* means "all kinds of darts"; *4 Atl (Water)*, "nothing but water"; and *4 Olin*, "all kinds of rolling motion."[142] Elsewhere Seler suggests *4 Olin* means "*todo se mueve, todo se tambelea*" ("everything moves, everything shakes").[143] Everything born on the day 4 Olin moves. Apparently, *4* means "everything."

Sahagún tells us that for the male born on the day 4 Olin "in two ways it might fall."[144] He will nourish the Fifth Sun with the hearts of captives or with his own heart in the field of battle. At the level of the individual human, this prognostication is mixed. Nourishing the Fifth Sun requires that someone dies. Death on the battlefield or on the sacrificial stone was simultaneously glorious and unfortunate.[145] At the level of the Fifth Age, this individual prognostication appears auspicious since the Fifth Sun will be nourished by such deaths and the Fifth Age will continue.

The Aztecs honored the Fifth Sun every 260 days on the day 4 Olin with the Feast of 4 Olin or Feast of the Sun.[146] They approached the day with great fear and consternation since 4 Olin is both the Fifth Sun's birthday *and* its death-day. The day 4 Olin thus possesses the potential for cataclysmic destruction. People accordingly fasted for the four preceding days. On the day of the feast, they offered the Sun nourishing gifts of slain quail, incense, and blood drawn from their ears. This they did four times. At noon they slew human captives in the Sun's honor, offering these nourishing gifts with eyes raised to the Sun. During his ascent to the top of the Templo Mayor, the sacrificial victim carried items intended as gifts for the Sun such as a "shield with five cotton tufts on it" and "an elaborate staff with bows and ties and white feathers attached to it." Both walking stick and shield would help the Sun complete its daily journey and nocturnal struggle in the Underworld. The victim ascended the Templo Mayor's steps slowly and pausing with each step, imitating the motion of the ascending Sun each morning. At high noon four priests splayed him upon the sacrificial stone while a fifth slit his throat and fed his blood and heart to the Sun. Widespread feasting followed. The Fifth Sun had been nourished.

The number four orders the Aztec cosmos before, during, and between each of the five Suns and their respective Eras.[147] Long before the generation of the first Sun and its Era, the *Historia de los mexicanos por sus pinturas* tells us the primordial male~female progenitor~progenetrix, Tonacatecuhtli~Tonacacihuatl, engendered four sons: Tlatlauhqui Tezcatlipoca, Yayauhqui Tezcatlipoca, Quetzalcoatl (Yohualli Ehecatl), and Omitecuhtli or Maquizcoatl (called Huitzilopochtli by the Aztecs).[148] The four sons represent an iteration of Tonacatecuhtli~Tonacacihuatl's unified twoness and twofold oneness. Four is an iteration of two and hence an iteration of metaphysical completeness, wholeness, and the stability of twoness. Other process clusters ("deities") such as Tlaloc and Tlazolteotl-Ixcuina also iterate into four aspects. As we've seen, four also arranges Tlazolteotl-Ixcuina's olin motion-change into four phases.

Four arranges reality and cosmos in other fundamental ways. It is the number of elemental cosmic forces – fire, water, wind, and earth – and the number of basic colors – red, black, white, and blue (or yellow, red, blue-green, and white).[149] Four orders time-place. It is the number of 65-day ritual quarters of the 260-day ritual calendar, the tonalpohualli. These four quarters correspond with the four "growth" periods of the calendar: birth and infancy, youth, adulthood and matrimony, and old age and death. The 20-day cycle divides into four sequences of 5 days each (which the Aztecs used for scheduling market days). Four groups of 13 years make up the xiuhmolpilli or 52-year bundle of years. There are four year signs: House (*Calli*), Reed (*Acatl*), Flint Knife (*Tecpatl*), and Rabbit (*Tochtli*).

If the cosmos prior to the unfolding of the five Sun-Earth Orderings has sides, quadrants, regions, corners, and cardinal (or intercardinal) directions, then these features are also four in number: namely, East, North, West, and South.[150] There are four different Suns, Eras, and earths before the present one, the Fifth. Four orders each of these four Suns and their respective Eras. Each bears *4* in its day name. The First Sun, Ocelotonatiuh ("4 Ocelotl Sun"), was associated with and destroyed by telluric forces. The Second Sun, Ehecatonatiuh ("4 Wind Sun"), was associated with and destroyed by wind forces. The Third Sun, 4 Tletonatiuh ("4 Fire Sun"), was associated with and destroyed by igneous forces. The Fourth Sun, 4 Atonatiuh ("4 Water Sun"), was associated with and destroyed by aqueous forces.[151]

The number four arranges the Fifth Sun (4 Olin Tonatiuh) and the Fifth Sun-Earth Ordering. The Fifth Sun-Earth Ordering has four sides, intercardinal and cardinal directions, and corners. Four is the number of sacred trees (and their respective sacred volutes) that stand at each of the four corners (see Figure 4.3). One of Tlaloc's fourfold aspects, the four tlaloques, resides in each corner of the Fifth Sun-Earth Ordering. Four is the number of forces ("deities") that support the lowest layer of heaven at each of the four cosmic points. The twenty day-signs of the tonalpohualli divide into four groups, one affiliated with each of four cardinal directions. The four year-signs likewise map onto the four cardinal directions. Four is the number of middle level (or lower skies) of the Fifth Age. And lastly, a complete, functioning human heart has four chambers.

Jacinto de la Serna argues the Fifth Sun's olin motion-change incorporates "four motions," one each for the four points of the cosmos.[152] Hence 4 Olin motion-change extends literally everywhere, that is, to all four corners of the cosmos. It includes all kinds of solar motion-change: east-west, south-north, west-east, and north-south. José Corona Núñez claims the people of ancient Mexico believed the sun had two houses in the east and two houses in the west – one for each of the solstitial points that mark both the rising and the setting of the Sun at both the winter and the summer solstices (see Figure 4.2) – and that for this reason they called the Fifth Sun *naollin*, or "Four Motion."[153]

The Fifth Sun move-changes through four phases in its *diurnal* life~death cycle. Sahagún's informants suggest the four phases are dawn, noon, afternoon, and dusk.[154] These four map onto the four stages of the Sun's diurnal life cycle: birth and infancy, youth, adulthood and matrimony, and old age and death.[155] And as the Fifth Sun olin move-changes through these four phases, it engenders the four (inter)cardinal directions and four regions of the Fifth cosmos. The same four phases arrange the olin-defined teyolia life-energy and olin-defined life~death cycle of all living things in the Fifth Age: humans, plants, towns, mountains, tools (such as spindles), and processes (such as the weaving of cloth).[156] The heart's motion-change undergoes four-phases corresponding to its four chambers. The life cycle of corn divides into four phases: *xilotl* (the green ear of corn with kernels just beginning to form), *elotl* (the mature ear of corn with kernels fully formed), *cintli* or *centli* (the dried ear of corn with kernels ready for harvesting), and *tlaolli* (the dried corn kernels removed from the cob, ready for grinding and human consumption or for reseeding another generation of corn).[157] And finally four phases characterize Tlazolteotl-Ixcuina, the great genetrix, the great spinner-weaver of the Fifth Sun-Earth Age. In sum, quadruplicity is woven into the very fabric of the cosmos and Fifth Age.

The Aztecs' belief in the ordering and completing power of four is evidenced in countless other ways. They performed many of the ritual processes comprising the feast of 4 Olin four times. They organized their capital city, Tenochtitlan, into four wards (calpultin) and their empire into four regions (see Figure 4.10).

They distinguished four priestly age grades.[158] Their *tlatoani* ("speaker-ruler") had four advisers. And they demanded labor and cotton tribute be paid in four-phased cycles.[159]

Finally, the number four orders Aztec arithmetic. Twenty (*cempohualli*) serves as the base number in the Aztec vigesimal counting system. *Cempohualli* means "one full or whole count" or "one counted group."[160] Twenty things constitute a single complete unit, and the number twenty accordingly symbolizes a whole count and wholeness. Four orders five counts into a complete count of twenty. Twenty also symbolizes the complete human being consisting of four parts (two hands and two feet), each composed of five appendages.

In conclusion, what does the foregoing tell us about the personality of the number four? The number four operates as an ordering force in the cosmos. It arranges things into four-phased life~death cycles and fourfold patterns of completion. Four reiterates the number two and hence reiterates the number two's agonistic inamic unity and its metaphysical wholeness and completion. Four is the power of fourfold oneness and fourfold wholeness. It is the number of the final phase of a well-ordered whole cycle and therefore the number of well-ordered, cyclical completion and wholeness per se. That the Fifth Sun is named *4 Olin Tonatiuh* tells us that the Fifth Sun and the Fifth Age are four-fold, well-ordered, and whole.

COSMOS, COSMIC ERAS, AND SUN-EARTH ORDERINGS

Before continuing our examination of olin, we need to address an important terminological issue. How are the five Ages or Eras best characterized? Are they cosmic, solar, world, or earth Eras? Scholars routinely characterize them in all these ways.[161] Moreover, how do the five Ages differ from one another? What changes, and what, if anything, remains the same across Ages? Scholars standardly claim the Fifth Age is divided vertically into three basic layers: upper, middle, and lower,[162] and all five apparently share this tripartite division. The nine layers (the nine upper skies or heavens) above the earthly layer, and the nine layers (the nine places of death) below the earthly layer appear to remain unchanged across all five Ages. The two calendars – the tonalpohualli and xiuh-pohualli – likewise remain constant.

What does vary across Ages is the nature of the Sun, the nature of the four lower skies (if they even exist), the nature of the earthly layer, and the nature of the earth's inhabitants.[163] A change in Age thus consists of a change in the middle layer of the cosmos *only*. In light of this, I suggest it is imprecise and consequently misleading to characterize the succession of five Ages as "cosmic" changes and these Ages as "cosmic Ages" when in fact the *entire* cosmos does *not* undergo destruction and recreation. *Only the middle level undergoes destruction and recreation.* The appellation *Earth Age* is equally unacceptable, since it makes no mention of the changes in Suns across Ages. *World Era* is likewise unacceptable, since the English word *world* may mean "the earth," "the universe," "all that exists," or "the time and place of human existence."[164]

Since sun and earth are the principal things that change across the five Ages, I suggest referring to the five as *Sun-Earth Ages* or *Eras*. Susan Gillespie uses the term *sky-earth* to refer to what she calls "the conflation of earth and sky" depicted by the face at the center of the Sun Stone with its display of characteristics of both Tlaltecuhtli and Tonatiuh.[165] Barbara and Dennis Tedlock claim the Maya use the term *skyearth* in this way.[166] I propose *Sun-Earth Ordering* since it highlights the role of each Sun in ordering the Sun-Earth fusion that defines each respective Age.

The terms *cosmos* and *cosmovision* ("*cosmovisión*")[167] are also problematic. It is unclear whether *cosmos* refers to (1) the cosmos per se – that is, the universe or totality of everything that has existed, currently exists, and will ever exist, including the time before, in between, and during the five Ages, and upper, middle, and lower layers; (2) the Fifth Sun-Earth Ordering *only* – that is, its particular middle layer (Sun, Earth, and Earthly inhabitants); or (3) the cosmos *of* the Fifth Sun-Earth Ordering, that is, the intermediate layer unique to the current Fifth Sun-Earth Ordering *plus* the unchanging nine upper and nine lower layers. These are obviously not equivalent. Sense (1) includes (2) and (3), but not conversely. Sense (2) is the narrowest; (1), the broadest. When discussing Aztec metaphysics we therefore need to specify which of the three we mean.

4 Olin Tonatiuh, Olin Motion-Change, and the Fifth Sun-Earth Ordering

Olin motion-change is the pulse, heart, defining motion-change, and essence of the Fifth Sun and Fifth Sun-Earth Ordering. The power of 4 Olin Tonatiuh is defined by olin motion-change, and its olin-defined power vivifies and sustains the Fifth Age and its inhabitants. With the creation of the Fifth Sun come heat and light, two essential ingredients of life. Yet without motion-change, heat and light are fatal. Without olin motion-change, there can be no life in the Fifth Age. Enrique Florescano writes, "It is clear that what matters about the sun is not just that it illuminate, but that it is put into motion, because the birth of day, the sequence of the seasons, and the incessant flow of time depend on its journey through the cosmos."[168]

Therefore 4 Olin Tonatiuh does not bring just any kind of motion-change, life, and transformation to the Fifth Age. It brings 4 Olin–patterned and four-phased oscillating motion-change, life, and transformation. By means of its olin-defined motion-change, the Fifth Sun *orders* and *arranges* the Fifth Era and Tlalticpac, resulting in the Fifth Sun-Earth Ordering.[169] Thus 4 Olin Tonatiuh lays out and arranges Tlaltipac into four (inter)cardinal orientations, four sides, four corners, and four regions. The Fifth Sun creates these orientations, corners, and regions in the course of its olin motion-change. East *just is* where-when the Sun rises; West *just is* where-when the Sun sets. One of the Nahuatl words for *east* is thus appropriately *tonalquizayampa* ("the place from which the sun habitually emerges"), and for *west*, *tonalpolihuiyampa* ("the place where [or towards which] the sun habitually perishes").[170] As regions East and West are spread out and defined by the oscillating motion of the Sun's risings and settings between winter and summer solstices.[171] North and South, by contrast, appear to be differently defined. While East and West are defined in terms of the actual path of the Sun, South and North appear to be conceived derivatively in relation to the Sun's path. South (*huitzlampa*, "place of the thorns") is where-when to the left of the Sun's moving-changing,[172] while North (*mictlampa*, "region of the dead") is where-when to the right of the Sun's moving-changing. Indeed, it appears *our* geometrical directional concepts of North and South have no equivalents in Nahuatl.[173] East-West thus appears axial and far more significant ritually, astronomically, and philosophically than North-South.[174]

This view survives among contemporary Nahuat-speakers residing in the Sierra Norte de Puebla, who according to James Taggart, define east as "the place where the sun comes out of the water" (*tonal kisayampa*) and west as "the place where the sun goes [into the water]" (*tonal kalakiyampa*).[175] Félix Báez-Jorge and Arturo Martínez likewise report that contemporary Nahuatl-speakers in Chicontepec define east as *inesca tonatih* ("the place where the sun comes out") and west as *ilhuetzica tonatih* ("the place where the sun becomes hidden"). North (*inesca xopanatl*) is "the place from where rain emerges"; south (*Mihcaohtli*), "the path of the dead."[176]

Consonant with Aztec philosophy's process metaphysics, the orientations and regions of the Fifth Sun-Earth Ordering are defined processively in terms of the Fifth Sun's olin moving-changing (rather than substantively in terms of a perduring space-time framework).[177] East, West, North, and South are not *fixed* geometrical directions or "compass points frozen in space" (as Barbara Tedlock puts it).[178] Indeed, Gordon Brotherston and Dawn Ades contend there are no indigenous Mesoamerican words or glyphs that have the directional significance equivalent to European geometrically defined, fixed cardinal directions or points.[179] Consequently, the Sun does not rise "in" the East, as though East were a permanent direction or place existing *before* the Fifth Sun's rising. Rather, East is *by definition* identical with *wherever* the Fifth Sun does in fact rise. East is defined in terms of the Sun's rising – the Sun's rising is not defined in terms of East. Finally, prior to the Fifth Sun's moving-changing, Tlalticpac and the Fifth Era lacked regions, directions, and orientations.

4 Olin Tonatiuh's four-phased olin-shaped, rubber ball–like bouncing above and below Tlalticpac *creates* as well as *defines* the four intercardinal orientations and four corners of the earth in the same manner. The earth's four intercardinal orientations and corners are identical with the Sun's four solstice points, that is, with its inamically paired extreme risings and settings.[180] These solstice points do not precede the Fifth Sun's moving-changing, and may not be described as fixed compass points frozen in space or as fixed intercardinal points as understood by Old World astronomy. Evon Vogt reports that Zinacanteco Mayas call the summer solstice *snatil* (literally, "[the sun's] longest path or point") and the winter solstice *skomol* (literally, "[the sun's] shortest point or path").[181] The intercardinal orientations are defined by the where-when's of the Fifth Sun's longest and shortest paths.

The Sun's diurnal olin-shaped path above Tlalticpac creates in addition a *fifth* orientation: the center.[182] The Sun's zenith at midday defines the horizontal center of the earthly plane. Like the other orientations and regions, the center does not precede the Fifth Sun's moving-changing. It is not a preexisting, geometrically defined, fixed point or direction. The lexicology of *olin* supports this idea. We saw in section 4.2 that olin motion is centered and centering; it moves around a center; it is motion in a volume. *Yollo* means (among other things) "center of a volume" and "axis." At the cosmological level, this means that the Fifth Sun's centering motion creates a center and that there is a center only as long as there is solar moving-changing. In the process of creating a horizontal center, the Sun also creates a horizontal periphery. Both center and periphery are thus engendered processively by the continual processing of the Fifth Sun.

The Quincunx as Graphic Rendering of the Fifth Sun's Earth-Ordering

By creating a central orientation, the Fifth Sun's olin motion-change distinguishes the Fifth Age from its predecessors. The Fifth Age, as Laurette Séjourné puts it, is "the Era of the Centre."[183] The Sun's olin motion-change centers the Fifth Age and in so doing creates something apparently unique in the history of the cosmos: the center as a fifth time-place and orientation. The first four Ages lacked a center as well as other cardinal orientations – at least as these are currently defined by the Fifth Sun and thus understood by us, the inhabitants of the Fifth Age.[184]

The Sun's olin motion-change orders the horizontal dimensions of the earth.[185] As it olin move-changes through its four-phased life~death cycle, the Fifth Sun creates as well as centers the four horizontal orientations, corners, and regions – pace León-Portilla, who writes, "In abstract terms, motion appeared as a consequence of the spatialization of time and of the orientation of the years and the days toward the four directions."[186] By my way of thinking, the earth's spatialization appears as a consequence of the Fifth Sun's motion-change – not conversely. Consistent with process metaphysics, process and motion-change logically precede spatialization. Spatialization is a function of process and motion-change, not conversely.

The oscillating motion-change of the Fifth Sun unites East and West, and North and South as inamic pairs. East-defining motion-change and West-defining motion-change are aspects of one and the same oscillating pattern and as such are mutually arising and mutually interdependent. The Fifth Sun's daily olin motion-change across the sky horizontally distributes, arranges, and unites in agonistic tension the various inamic partners of the cosmos: male~female, being~nonbeing, day~night, and so on.

Finally, the essential ordering and centering effects of the Fifth Sun helps us better understand the Aztecs' profound anxiety over the continuing motion-change of the Fifth Sun, since without it the earth and humankind would quite literally be stripped of all order, stability, centeredness, and orientation. It is the Sun's moving-changing that keeps us stable, centered, and oriented – not some preexisting, permanent space-time framework.

The Fifth Sun's creating and ordering of four (inter)cardinal and central orientations is shown by the quincunx in Figure 4.2. Figure 4.3 illustrates how Aztec artists depicted the Fifth Sun's olin-shaped path and olin-shaped, horizontal laying out and arranging of the earthly plane. This quincunxial cosmogram records the four cardinal orientations, intercardinal orientations, regions, sides, and corners of the Fifth Sun-Earth Ordering not as preexisting, fixed compass points but rather as products of the Fifth Sun's olin motion-change. Its four larger leaves depict the four cardinal orientations and regions; its four smaller leaves, the four intercardinal orientations and corners. The central square depicts the center.[187] It also serves as a prognosticatory map of the future moving-changing of the Fifth Sun (within the limits of the Tezcatlipoca factor) and as an action-guide for human ritual participation in and shaping of the life of the Fifth Sun and Fifth Sun-Earth Ordering.[188]

THE AMBIGUITY OF A FIFTH ORIENTATION

The addition of the center as a fifth orientation is a mixed blessing. It hardwires the metaphysical constitution of the Fifth Era with an ineliminable and ultimately fatal ambiguity and tension.[189] It contributes a stabilizing, sustaining, umbilical cord–like center, yet it also defines the Fifth Age as one of metaphysical excess, overripeness, and exhausted fullness and completion, and as one inexorably poised for imminent decay and doom. The Fifth Age is consequently an extremely anxious time-place in which to live – a time-place demanding constant human ritual attention, participation, and intervention. Let's examine this ambiguity more closely.

On the one hand, the fact that the Fifth Age is centered contributes to its vitality, sustenance, well-balancedness, well-orderedness, and stability. As León-Portilla, López Austin, Davíd Carrasco, Louise Burkhart, Wayne Elzey, and others stress regarding Postclassic Aztec thought – and as Alan Sandstrom and James Taggart stress regarding contemporary Nahua thought – the center is a time-place of safety, stability, support, familiarity, balance, and well-orderedness.[190] The center is a fifth time-place created by the Sun's oscillating, olin motion-change – one constituted by the Sun's olin-defined mutual binding together and balancing of the four elemental forces (fire, water, earth, and wind), four regions, four cardinal and four intercardinal orientations, and their manifold parallel aligned inamic pairs.

The Aztecs defined the center *qualitatively* rather than *geometrically* as *in tlalxicco* ("navel of the earth" or "place of the navel of the earth")[191] and *xicco* ("place of the navel").[192] Durán's informants refer to the earth's center as "the root, the navel, and the heart of this whole earthly mechanism."[193] I submit the Aztecs regarded the center *specifically* as the navel *of the Fifth Age only*. The preceding four Ages lacked centers.[194] López Austin contends the Aztecs regarded the human navel as one of the most important areas of human beings since the navel lies at the very center of the human organism. It was, as López Austin puts it, "the center of [human] dignity."[195] If so, then it would appear that by giving the Fifth Age a navel, the Fifth Sun gives the Fifth Age and its inhabitants a dignity that the other four Ages and their inhabitants lacked. Contemporary Nahuatl-speakers in Chicontepec continue to refer to the center as Tlalxictli, or "earth's navel."[196]

The Aztecs conceived the center, tlalxicco, in terms of order, purity, wellbeing, and safety, and conceived the periphery in terms of disorder, pollution, ill-being and danger.[197] The emphasis is qualitative, not geometric. According to Taggart, contemporary Nahuas conceive the center in terms of words "standing for the human community – house (-čan), community (*pueblo*), or place where one finds Christians from the earth (*tlaltikpak cristianos*)." They conceive the periphery in terms such as *kwowta* ("forest") or other geographical terms for the forest connoting wildness and danger such as *tepet* ("mountain"), *tepekonko* ("abyss"), *atawit* ("canyon"), and *owikan* ("a dangerous and ugly place").[198] Sandstrom finds a nearly identical view among the residents of Amatlán who define the center in terms of *nocalpixcahuaj* ("the members of our household or consumptive unit"; literally, "our house stewards"), and who identify the periphery with the forest, the wild, and the savage, dangerous, and disordering things that reside in them.[199]

The Aztecs' understanding of the center in terms of the human navel was neither arbitrary nor merely symbolic. As López Austin has shown, the Fifth Sun-Earth Ordering and the human body are homologous.[200] Just as the human navel sits at the center of the human body and its four outstretched limbs, so likewise tlalxicco sits at the center of the earth's surface and four outstretched intercardinal solar paths. More importantly, just as the human navel is the site of the umbilical cord (*xicmecayotl*) through which the human fetus receives life-sustaining energies from its mother, so likewise tlalxicco is the site of the cosmic umbilical cord through which the earthly layer and its inhabitants receive life-sustaining energies from the cosmic layers above and below the earth. Like the human fetus, Tlalticpac and earthly beings receive life-sustaining sacred energy from the upper layers of the Fifth Age through malinalli-shaped pathways, that is, helicoidal, intertwining bicolored cords that resemble the bicolored intertwining arteries and veins of the umbilical cord.[201] The cosmic umbilicus permits energy transmission between earthly and nonearthly layers in both directions. Humans recycle the energy contained within blood and hearts to the Sun and to other clusters of powers through the cosmic umbilicus at the earth's navel. In this manner humans sustain the Fifth Sun-Earth Ordering.[202]

Sahagún's informants state that "the navel of the earth" is a "circle of turquoise" wherein dwells Huehueteotl ("the old god"), Ipalnemohuani ("Giver of Life," "the one through whom one lives"), and Ometeotl.[203] Because it is where Xiuhtecuhtli ("Lord of fire and time") resides, the earth's navel is also called "navel of fire" (*in tlexicco*).[204] Here Xiuhtecuhtli pumps sacred energy to the four quadrants of the Fifth Sun-Earth Ordering. In this respect, the earth's navel doubles as the *tlalli yyolloco* ("the place of the earth's heart"). The Spanish side of Molina's *Vocabulario*, for example, translates "*centro de la tierra*" as *tlalli yyolloco* ("the place of the earth's heart").[205] And hearts and heart–motion are (as we've seen) conceived in terms of olin motion-change. The color of the navel ("place of the earth's heart") and of the human heart (*yollo*) are thus not surprisingly both blue-green.[206] As we saw in chapter 2, the Aztecs regarded blue-green as the color of order, equilibrium, fertility, renewal, and life-energy.

On the other hand, the addition of a fifth orientation defines the Fifth Age as one of metaphysical excess, overripeness, and exhausted completion, and as one staged for imminent doom. Nicholson asserts the number five signifies excess.[207] The Nahuatl word for five, *macuilli*, suggests the full grasp or take (*cui*) of all five fingers of a human hand (*maitl*).[208] A hand can hold no more. Although a symbol of wholeness like the number four, the number five connotes a surfeit or condition of being surfeited. With five, Burkhart writes, "wholeness passes into completion, fullness, and excess."[209] Five thus connotes a sense of inexorable and imminent demise. According to Lipp, Mesoamericans commonly associate the number five with aged gods, aged humans, and old age per se.[210] Thus, whereas the number four is the well-ordered energy of wholeness, the number five is the about-to-become-disordering energy of wearied agedness, excess, and expiry.

Deities representing feasting, youthful pleasure, and excess as well as chance and gaming such as *Macuilxochitl* ("Five Flower") contain the number five in their calendrical names. According to the *Annals of Cuauhtitlan*, Tezcatlipoca tricked Quetzalcoatl into drinking a fifth cup of pulque (*octli*), which caused his downfall.[211] Sahagún reports that drinking four cups of pulque is acceptable while drinking five is not since five results in drunkenness and improper behavior.[212] Five is the mark of overindulgence. In short, with five comes one's downfall and demise.

Five is also associated with chance or luck and hence uncertain outcomes. The patolli board, for example, has the shape of a quincunx. Five grains of corn were commonly used in divination. Five is the number of the dangerous, unlucky *nemontemi* ("uncounted" or "unnamed" days) occurring at the completion of every 360+5–day cycle. Before being renewed, the solar year must pass through these five days of dangerous uncertainty.[213] The number five thus invokes Tezcatlipoca.

How does this bear upon the nature of Fifth Age? The addition of a fifth orientation introduces an ineliminable element of chance in its metaphysical makeup. Tezcatlipoca cocreates the Fifth Age with Quetzalcoatl and he constantly tricks and torments its human inhabitants. The addition of a fifth orientation surfeits the Fifth Age, making it analogous to an overly ripe piece of fruit ready to fall from the tree, its rotting and decay imminent because immanent. The Aztecs knew the Fifth Age was destined to expire, but they did not know precisely when. And there was no way they would ever know. This explains why they approached the day 4 Olin and the completion of the xiuhmolpilli, or 52-year bundle, with profound fear and consternation. On these dates the Fifth Sun might very easily *not* be reborn. These ambiguous deathdays-birthdays thus held the potential for cataclysmic destruction of humankind. The Aztecs saw this as a consequence of the Fifth Sun's and Fifth Age's being defined by the power or personality of the number five (not the number four). Immanent within the number five's energy *is* inexorable and imminent demise. The Fifth Age will be the last. There are no further Suns or Ages in the offing. Five is all the hand of the cosmos can hold.[214]

Skywatching, Olin, and the Fifth Sun

What insights into the nature of olin does observing the path traveled by the Fifth Sun offer? Given that the Fifth Sun is named 4 Olin Tonatiuh and that olin motion-change defines the essence of the Fifth Sun, it necessarily follows that *how* the Fifth Sun moves-changes *paradigmatically* exemplifies olin motion-change. Let's turn to Anthony Aveni's discussion of Mesoamerican "skywatching" for help.[215] Aztec skywatchers practiced what Aveni calls "horizon astronomy." Their astronomical observations concentrated primarily upon astronomical events occurring at the eastern and western horizons where earth meets sky. If one traces the path of the Sun at the horizon, one observes the following phenomena. Each day the Sun rises in the east and sets in the west. Over the course of each solar year (xiuhpohualli or 360+5–day year) the Sun's risings and settings move back-and-forth across the horizon between two endpoints: summer solstice in the north and winter solstice in the south. One observes the "rhythmic oscillation"[216] of sunrise and sunset solstice points along the eastern and western horizons (see Figure 4.4). At each horizon, one observes the Sun oscillating and bouncing back-and-forth like a rubber ball between solstice points.

One also observes over the course of the solar year that the Sun rises and sets at a different spot on the horizon every day, and that the Sun does not set directly opposite from where it rises except for two days, the fall and spring equinoxes.[217] Watching both the path of the Sun overhead and its rising and setting points along the horizon between solstice points, one sees the Sun tracing out a back-and-forth, oscillating path as 4 Olin Tonatiuh undulates and oscillates. (See Figure 4.5.)[218]

The Sun's diurnal oscillation *above* Tlalticpac is completed by its nocturnal oscillation *below* Tlalticpac. Conjoining these two in a single path, the Sun

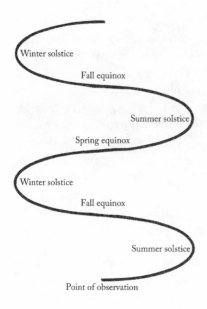

Winter solstice

Fall equinox

Summer solstice

Spring equinox

Winter solstice

Fall equinox

Summer solstice

Point of observation

FIGURE 4.4. *The Fifth Sun's rhythmic oscillations between winter and summer solstices. (Author's drawing.)*

traces out a single, back-and-forth, oscillating path over and above, and down and under Tlalticpac. This is the shape of olin motion-change. If one watches the daily path of the Sun above the earth, one sees it following a rubber ball to-and-fro, and up-and-down-shaped path.

The Fifth Sun behaves in a number of other ways that offer insight into the shape of olin motion-change. Its combined diurnal-nocturnal motion above and below the earth is a circular and centering motion in a volume (with its zenith marking the center point). Its combined vertical undulating and horizontal oscillating path is a centering or centered motion that resembles the growing and shrinking of fiber upon a spindle, and that resembles the undulating path of the weaver's wefting batten as it passes over and under the vertical warp fibers of a weaving. The Sun appears larger at the horizons and smaller at midday and so appears to pulsate. Furthermore, the Sun exhibits four-phased motion-change in several ways: (1) its motion-change from spring equinox-summer solstice, summer solstice-fall equinox, fall equinox-winter solstice, and winter solstice-spring equinox; (2) its ascension above the earth to zenith (midday), descent from zenith to setting, setting to nadir (at midnight), and ascent from nadir to dawn; and (3) its dawning, morning youth, afternoon maturity, and old age and death (at dusk).[219]

In sum, solar skywatching supports the conclusion of our lexicological examination. Olin motion-change is defined by a specific shape or pattern. It

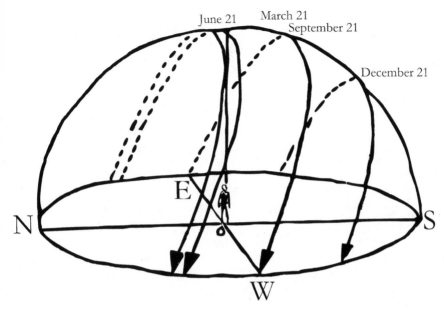

FIGURE 4.5. *The Fifth Sun's rhythmic oscillations between rising and setting points on the horizon. (Redrawn after Aveni [2001:63, Figure 26].)*

is oscillating, pulsating, and centered. Interestingly, the rhythmic oscillation and undulation of the Sun's olin motion-change instantiates simple harmonic motion represented by a sine wave.[220] Finally, skywatching supports the thesis that olin motion-change orders and arranges things in a four-phased pattern.

Summary

The foregoing textual evidence supports understanding olin motion-change as the motion-change that carries things through their four-phased life cycles and hence as the motion-change of cyclical completion and renewal. Olin defines the *shape* of a thing's path through its four-phased life~death cycle. In this respect it resembles the contemporary Tzutujil Maya notion of *jal*, which, according to Robert Carlsen and Martín Prechtel, denotes "the change manifested in the transition to life through birth, through youth and old age, and finally back to death."[221] Olin, too, is the change manifested in the transition to life through birth, through youth and old age, and finally back to death. Since beginnings are simultaneously renewals, olin also defines the shape of cyclical renewal. Olin defines the shape of metaphysical transformation within life~death cycles as well as across life~death cycles.

4.4. GRAPHIC EVIDENCE

What does olin motion-change look like? How did Aztec artists graphically depict it? Aztec artist-scribes depicted olin motion-change as well as conveyed the concept of olin motion-change by means of a variety of ideograms. An ideogram is a motif or figure used to communicate abstract ideas or concepts. Unlike logograms that convey a specific word, ideograms convey an abstract idea, concept, or semantic root "behind the word."[222] Aztec artist-scribes conveyed the idea of olin motion-change – as well as depicted, manifested, and transmitted olin-shaped energy – using a variety of ideograms. They created these not only with the intention of symbolizing and depicting olin motion-change but also with the intention of *causally transmitting* olin-defined energy to their work, other humans, and the cosmos at large. In so doing they sought to participate in and contribute to the ongoing olin-defined processing of the Fifth Age.[223]

When discussing ideograms, it behooves us to acknowledge what Arthur Miller calls "visual simultaneity of meaning."[224] Aztec artist-scribes standardly used ideograms to convey more than one idea and to depict more than one kind of motion-change. Indeed, polysemy runs throughout Aztec visual art as well as Aztec poetry and speech. It is the norm.[225] Any given flower motif, for example, may convey one, several, or all of the following: blood, preciousness, transformative power, creation, life, language, song, nobility, government, the Fifth Sun, an era of the calendar, joy, love, games, sexual pleasure, female sexuality and genitalia, venereal diseases, and the four orientations of the cosmos.[226]

Quatrefoils and Quincunxes

Quatrefoils and quincunxes are symbolically rich figures. Séjourné calls the quincunx a "seed of a revealed cosmology."[227] Quincunxes are standardly thought as X shaped, like a St. Andrew's cross, while quatrefoils are standardly thought of as + shaped, like a Greek cross. Some figures combine the two. What is important is that both possess four points (or regions) and a center. Aztec artists employed quatrefoils and quincunxes to convey the idea of olin motion-change as four-phased and centered; the idea of the Fifth Sun's four-phased olin motion-change; and the idea of the Fifth Sun's olin-defined arranging of Tlalticpac and time-place into four orientations plus center. Both quincunx

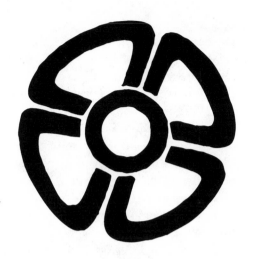

FIGURE 4.6. *Flat stamp of four-petaled flower, from Azcapotzalco, DF. (Enciso [1974]; courtesy of Dover Press.)*

and quatrefoil also serve as cosmograms and cosmographs that trace the olin-defined path of the Fifth Sun upon the surface of Tlalticpac and mark the horizontal ordering of Tlalticpac and the Fifth Age. I include within this motif set less-abstract ideograms such as the four-winged butterfly, patolli game board, ballcourt, and four-petaled flower.[228]

The figure of a four-petaled flower with a circular center such as the "heart flower" (*yolloxochitl*) functions as an ideogram for olin, for four-phased centered motion, for motion-change undulating between center and periphery, for motion in a volume, for the Fifth Sun, and for the Fifth Age. It also serves as a cosmogram that simultaneously traces the olin-defined path of the Sun upon Tlalticpac and sketches the horizontal ordering of Tlalticpac and the Fifth Age (see Figure 4.6). The four-petaled blossom of the heart flower unfolds from a bud that resembles a human heart, suggesting that the four-petaled surface of the earth similarly unfolds from the heart of the earth monster, Tlaltecuhtli (Tlalteotl).[229] Durán's *Historia* (pl. 25) portrays Xochiquetzal wearing a dress adorned with four-petaled flowers.[230]

"The Aztecs conceived of horizontal space as a cross or four-petaled flower with a jade bead in the middle," writes Davíd Carrasco.[231] Each petal represents one of four cardinal regions, while the bead represents the fifth direction, the center. The center bead was a chalchihuitl or precious green stone. Tlalticpac was thus horizontally arranged like a four-petaled flower with Tenochtitlan at its center (or alternatively, splayed in four directions like a sacrificial victim with Tenochtitlan as his heart). The Fifth Sun moved along the perimeter of the flower, oscillating toward the center and then back again toward the periphery, all the while encircling the center. Eric Thompson claims the Maya also depicted *kinh* ("sun-day-time") as a four-petaled flower.[232]

Using a four-petaled flower as a single ideogram for olin motion-change, the Fifth Sun, and the Fifth Age is highly appropriate, given the larger symbolism of flowers in Aztec metaphysics. Flowers symbolize life, death, creativity, sun, light, heat, the womb, the navel, caves, living blood, sacrificial blood, things that radiate tonalli energy, the four directions, the center, centeredness, and the essence or heart of something.[233] The four-petaled flower ideogram thus also identifies olin motion-change as the heart, essence, pulse, life-energy, and biorhythm of the Fifth Sun, the Fifth Age, and all inhabitants of the Fifth Age.

Aztec artists also commonly treated butterflies as ideograms for olin motion-change and the Fifth Sun, as mappings of the Sun's four-phased, olin-defined path, and as cosmograms of Tlalticpac and the horizontal dimension of the Fifth Sun-Earth Ordering. They depicted such butterflies with four wings and a center circle. Durán tells us the Aztecs used both the day sign (olin) and the Fifth Sun (4 Olin Tonatiuh) to depict butterflies.[234] Butterfly ideograms adorned the attire and quarters of the military order called "warriors of the sun." The Cuacuauhtinchan ("House of the Eagles") contained a large painting of the image of the Sun on a piece of cloth. Durán writes, "This figure was in the form of a butterfly with wings and around it a golden circle emitting radiant beams and glowing [undulating?] lines."[235] Eagle and Jaguar Warriors, to whom the House of Eagles was dedicated, devoted themselves to maintaining the olin motion-change of the Sun.[236] The tribute list of the *Codex Mendoza* includes three different kinds of butterfly (*papalotl*) back-devices worn by Aztec warriors in battle (see Figure 4.7).[237]

What do butterflies share in common with olin motion-change, the oscillating path of the Sun, pulsating hearts, respiring chests, and bouncing balls? The association seems based at least in part on the perception that the in-and-out flapping of butterfly wings instantiates the rhythmic pulsating of olin. McKeever Furst adds that when cut open, the arrangement of the four chambers of the human heart resembles a butterfly.[238] Butterflies are also associated with transformation within and across life cycles and are therefore ideally suited as ideograms of olin motion-change.[239] Furthermore, butterflies are connected with the youthful solar-fertility god, Xochipilli ("Flower Prince"). This connection, in turn, associates butterflies and olin with flowers, solar warmth, fertility, generative power, feasting, painting, and pleasure.[240] Hunt associates olin with Itzpapalotl ("Obsidian or Clawed Butterfly"), who is an aspect of the mother-goddess and of Tlazolteotl-Ixcuina.[241] Itzpapalotl includes the generative and regenerative powers of darkness, nighttime, and the obsidian sacrificial knife.[242]

FIGURE 4.7. *Butterfly motif.* (Codex Magliabechiano *[1903: 8v].)*

Finally, butterflies serve as symbols of the human heart, human soul, and humans' animating energy.[243] Sahagún's informants report that the soul (*yolia*) of a warrior who perished in the killing fields or on the killing stone is transformed into a butterfly (and hummingbird) after four years' service accompanying the Sun from sunrise to noon.[244]

More abstract quincunxes and quatrefoils served as ideograms for the concept of ollin motion-change as well as cosmograms representing the horizontal time-place layout of Tlalticpac and the Fifth Age. One finds quincunxes and quatrefoils in a variety of contexts. Antonio Serrato-Combe reconstructs Tenochtitlan's sacred precinct as a quincunx with the Templo Mayor as its center.[245] The sacred precinct served as a large-scale architectural ideogram of olin and large-scale architectural cosmogram of the Fifth Age. Such constructions also depicted, manifested, and radiated olin motion-change. According to Sahagún, the Aztecs arranged gardens as physical instantiations and ideograms of olin.[246] Quincunx motifs adorn the temple walls in the depiction in the *Codex Borbonicus* (pl. 34) of the New Fire Ceremony (see Figure 4.8). A quincunx also forms the center of a relief of Tlaltecuhtli (see Figure 4.9).

Codex Fejérváry-Mayer (pl.1) depicts what is perhaps the most famous Aztec quincunx-quatrefoil (see Figure 4.3). Aveni describes the figure as consisting of "a floral symbol with two sets of four petals: a 'Maltese Cross' with large trapezoidal petals and a 'St. Andrew's Cross' consisting of four smaller, rounded petals between the trapezoidal petals of the Maltese Cross. A square design forms

FIGURE 4.8. *New Fire Ceremony. (Redrawn from* Codex Borbonicus *[Loubat 1899: pl. 34]; courtesy of Foundation for the Advancement of Mesoamerican Studies, Inc.)*

the center of the pattern."[247] It serves as an ideogram conveying the concept of olin motion-change as well as a cosmogram depicting the path and shape of the Fifth Sun's olin-defined ordering of Tlalticpac and time-place in the Fifth Age. *Codex Mendoza* (fol. 2r) depicts a quincunx with Tenochtitlan at the center of two intersecting lines (see Figure 4.10). According to legend, these lines depict the two spring-fed, intersecting streams that emerged from a cave. Upon this site Tenochtitlan was founded. The water of one stream was said to be dark blue, the other, yellow.[248] The spot was identified as *matlalatl-tozpalatl* ("blue water-yellow water").[249] The two streams divided the city into four parts. The Templo Mayor was built at their intersection.

Ballcourts also instantiate the quatrefoil-quincunx motif and function as ideograms and cosmograms. They have four corners representing the four quarters of the 360+5–day year, the four quadrants of the Fifth Age, and the four solstice points. The codices commonly depict them with four colors or two sets of opposing colors.[250] Heyden proposes the ballcourt represents a stylized olin glyph (see Figure 4.11).[251]

FIGURE 4.9. *Quincunx in a relief of Tlaltecuhtli. (Author's photo.)*

The patolli game board similarly serves as an ideogram for olin motion-change and solar motion, and cosmogram of the olin-defined path of the Fifth Sun and horizontal structure of the Fifth Sun-Earth Ordering (see Figure 4.1). León-Portilla suggests playing patolli served as a dynamic ideogram for the four-phased olin-motion of human life.[252]

Finally, Elizabeth Brumfiel has recently brought our attention to spindle whorls from Postclassic Central Mexico on which are painted the four cardinal and intercardinal orientations.[253] They combine quincunxes and quatrefoils in a manner resembling *Codex Fejérváry-Mayer* (pl. 1). The hole at the whorl's center represents the fifth direction (see Figure 4.12).

Early Postclassic spindle whorls in Cholula were often painted using black, rubber-based paint. The use of liquid rubber, as Brumfiel notes, connects the whorls with Tlazolteotl-Ixcuina, hence weaving, spinning, childbirth, female fertility, reproduction, purification, healing, and ultimately olin. Tlazolteotl-Ixcuina is commonly depicted in the codices with mouth, chin, and lower jaw painted with liquid rubber, which is closely associated with ollin.

FIGURE 4.10. *Tenochtitlan as quincunx. (*Codex Mendoza *[1997: fol. 2r]; courtesy of* Frances F. Berdan and Patricia Rieff Anawalt.)

THE OLIN GLYPH

Solís describes the olin glyph as one of the most constantly used Aztec calendrical symbols and as the Aztecs' "favorite emblem."[254] It adorns countless objects including the sides of buildings, monumental statuary (such as the *temalacatl* known as "the Sun Stone" and the sculpture known as "the teocalli

FIGURE 4.11. *Ballcourt. (*Codex Magliabechiano *[1903: pl. 80].)*

FIGURE 4.12. *Spindle whorl with quincunx design. (Redrawn after Brumfiel [2001:73].)*

of sacred war"), gold rattles, fabric, clay vessels and plates, the sacrificial stone (*techcatl*), the eagle vessel (*cuauhxicalli*) used to contain excised hearts and drawn blood, vertical wooden drums, and clay stamps.[255] Several scholars argue the olin glyph predates the Aztecs. Köhler, for example, believes the olin glyph derives from Olmec times.[256] Both Heyden and Séjourné trace the olin glyph to Teotihuacan.[257] Heyden identifies various clay stamps from Teotihuacan as bearing the olin shape.[258]

The olin glyph functions as an ideogram for the concepts of olin motion-change, the Fifth Sun, and the Fifth Age. It also dramatically illustrates the shape given to the Fifth Age and to Tlalticpac by the Sun's olin-defined motion-change. Seler, Köhler, Heyden, and Broda (among others) contend the figure's four arms or trapezoidal extensions depict the Fifth Sun's path between the four solstice points.[259] The glyph closely resembles the quincunx, quatrefoil, ballcourt, patolli, and four-petaled flower designs above. And as Durán remarks, it resembles a butterfly.[260]

Graphic depictions of the olin glyph vary. The depiction most commonly appearing in extant Late Classic codices consists of either:

1. Two arcs or curves sharing a common vertex so as to create four rays. The two are adjoined back-to-back to one another (as in Figure 3.5, which depicts Quetzalcoatl and Mictlantecuhtli as back to back but not intertwined with one another).

2. Four oblong curves or trapezoidal blades with a common vertex arranged so as to form an X-shaped quincunx or quatrefoil (see Figures 4.13a–c).

Séjourné characterizes the glyph as "two divergent lines forming four poles in opposition and uniting in the centre."[261] The central vertex in both motifs is commonly a circle. The circle may be empty, colored, a chalchihuitl (precious jade), or a wide-open or half-open stellar eye.[262] The glyphs typically include two main colors or two opposing sets of four colors. Some olin glyphs include a thorn (e.g., *Codex Telleriano-Remensis* [pl. 13v]). Köhler believes the thorn represents an arrow indicating the principal orientation of Aztec ritual: East. When the figure includes a second arrow, it points toward East's inamic.[263] Olin glyphs appear in a variety of codices, including *Codex Fejérváry-Mayer* (pl. 1; Figure 4.3), *Primeros memoriales* (fol. 302v),[264] and *Codex Tonalamatl Aubin* (fol.11).[265] (See Figures 4.13a–c.)

A similar design adorns the centers of the so-called Aztec Sun Stone, Tizoc Stone, and Moctezuma's cuauhxicalli (see Figure 4.14).[266] Occupying the olin's central circular vertex in Figure 4.14 – which some argue represents the figure's navel (xictli) – is the face of Tonatiuh (the Fifth Sun).[267] Tonatiuh is the heart, essence, and center of the Fifth Age. Matos Moctezuma interprets the four trapezoidal blades surrounding the face of Tonatiuh as the four Suns or Ages preceding the Fifth. Seler, César Sáenz, and Hermann Beyer interpret them as the four cardinal directions.[268] They may well be both. Lastly, a single thorn extends from the vertex. Unlike Köhler who sees such thorns as pointing to the

Figures 4.13A–C. *Olin glyphs. (*a, Codex Borgia *[1993: pl. 25]; courtesy of Dover Press;* b, Codex Magliabechiano *[1903: pl. 13];* c, *redrawn from* Codex Borbonicus *[Loubat 1899: pl. 6, see also pl. 9].)*

East, Solís interprets the thorn as "pointing up or down, depending on whether [the sun] is rising or setting."[269]

A second, less common olin glyph consists of an X formed by two interlocking curves (see Figure 4.15). This glyph occurs mostly in the *Codex Borgia*, and even there, it appears alongside the noninterlocking olin glyphs just discussed. Köhler sees it as a "stylistic variant" of the more common noninterlocking glyph (found in the Valley of Mexico) and considers it confined to the Cholula region.[270] López Austin and López Luján, however, argue the interlocking glyph demonstrates that olin motion-change is merely an iteration or instance of malinalli motion-change. López Austin writes, "in some of its graphic representations, [olin] is a segment of malinalli."[271] López Luján writes, the olin glyph is "a partial representation of the *malinalli* or 'twisted herb'" and "a section of the malinalli."[272] I find this claim puzzling. First, if olin were merely a segment or iteration of malinalli, then it would seem to follow that olin and malinalli could not be two distinct day signs. And yet clearly they are. Second, olin is overwhelmingly depicted by figures such as butterflies, four-petaled flowers, patolli boards, ballcourts, quincunxes, and quatrefoils that do not involve twisting. Third, in support of his view, López Luján cites Köhler's 1979 conference paper, "On the Significance of the Aztec Day Sign 'Olin.'" Yet Köhler published a revised paper by the same title in 1982 that makes no such claim. Apparently, upon further reflection, Köhler retracted the claim. What's more, the 1982 paper claims the interlocking glyph of the *Codex Borgia* is an "artistic variation" of the Central Mexican noninterlocking glyph (and not conversely).[273] In closing, I believe characterizing the *Borgia* interlocking olin glyph in terms of malinalli-twisting *confounds* olin motion-change with malinalli

FIGURE 4.14. *Olin glyph at the heart of the Sun Stone. (Redrawn from Séjourné [2003: Figure 59h].)*

motion-change. Like Köhler, I interpret the *Borgia* interlocking glyph as a stylistic variant of the more frequent noninterlocking glyph. Chapter 8 argues the interlocking olin glyph depicts the Fifth Sun's wefting over and under the warp threads of the Fifth Age in the course of its weaving the Fifth Age.

Finally, olin motifs and glyphs demonstrate how Aztec artists used such figures to convey and illustrate the shape and kind of agonistic inamic unity created by olin motion-change. Olin glyphs and motifs join together paired and opposing arcs, curves, trapezoidal blades, and colors. Olin motion-change joins together inamic partners (e.g., life~death, male~female, and order~disorder) within the swirling and curving of quatrefoils, quincunxes, flower petals, and butterfly wings.

FIGURE 4.15. *Interlocking olin glyph.*
(Redrawn after Codex Borgia *[1993: pl.*
10]; courtesy of Dover Press.)

4.5. CONCLUSION

Olin is one of three principal shapes or patterns of teotl's vivifying energies – not a distinct kind of life-energy. Olin is a "how," not a "what." The
foregoing examination of linguistic, literary, and graphic evidence shows that
olin motion-change consists of four-phased pulsating; enlarging and shrinking; bouncing back-and-forth, up-and-over, and down-and-under; oscillating;
undulating; and centering motion-change. It is exemplified by the oscillating
of the Fifth Sun, the pulsating of a human heart, the bouncing of a rubber ball,
the growing and shrinking of a spindle rod with thread, and (as we will see in
chapter 8) the undulating of a weaver's bobbin.

Cyclical initiation, completion, and renewal – in short, transformation *within*
cycles and *across* cycles – are defined by olin motion-change. Olin motion-
change constitutes the *biorhythm* of the Fifth Sun, the Fifth Era, and all inhabitants of the Fifth Era. It constitutes their essence or heart. It orders, shapes,
and centers their existence. It defines the pattern of the existence *of* the Fifth
Age as well as the pattern of existence *in* the Fifth Age. All things in the Fifth
Age are processes, and all processes move-change according to a specific pattern.
This pattern is their *ohtli*, their *path*. Olin shapes the paths of all things in the
Fifth Sun-Earth Ordering as they move through their four-phased life~death
cycle. Aztec metaphysics identifies the shape of olin motion-change with the
quatrefoil, quincunx, four-petaled flower, four-winged butterfly, and olin glyph.
Lastly, olin motion-change unites paired inamic forces – life~death, east~west,
descending influence~ascending influence, and order~disorder – within the
well-ordered shape of curving, swirling, and oscillating quatrefoils, quincunxes,
flower petals, and butterfly wings. This is the shape of olin-generated agonistic inamic unity. This is the shape of olin-generated cyclical completion and
renewal. Olin motion-change bounces, curves, swirls, oscillates, and pulsates
inamic partners into a single, unified process.

NOTES

1. Processes are not all the same. Digesting differs from respiring; hurricanes differ from tornadoes. Each is defined by its own pattern or regularity. For discussion see Nicholas Rescher, "Process Philosophy," in *A Companion to Metaphysics*, ed. Jaegwon Kim and Ernest Sosa (Oxford: Blackwell, 1995), 417–19; Nicholas Rescher, *Process Metaphysics: An Introduction to Process Philosophy* (Albany: State University of New York Press, 1996); and Dorothy Emmet, *The Passage of Nature* (Philadelphia: Temple University Press, 1992).

2. I borrow this from Linda Schele and Julia Guernsey Kappelman, "What the Heck's Coatepec? The Formative Roots of an Enduring Mythology," in *Landscape and Power in Ancient Mesoamerica*, ed. Rex Koontz, Kathryn Reese-Taylor, and Annabeth Headrick (Boulder: Westview Press, 2001), 29.

3. I borrow this from Eloise Quiñones Keber, *Codex Telleriano-Remensis: Ritual, Divination, and History in a Pictorial Aztec Manuscript*, ed. Eloise Quiñones Keber (Austin: University of Texas Press, 1995), 242.

4. I borrow this from Roger T. Ames, "Putting the *Te* Back into Taoism," in *Nature in Asian Traditions of Thought: Essays in Environmental Philosophy*, ed. J. Baird Callicott and Roger T. Ames (Albany: State University Press of New York, 1989), 121.

5. For classical Greek metaphysics, see Philp Turetzky, *Time* (London: Routledge, 1998). For pre-Han East Asian metaphysics, see David L. Hall and Roger T. Ames, *Thinking through Confucius* (Albany: State University of New York Press, 1987); David L. Hall and Roger T. Ames, *Anticipating China: Thinking through the Narratives of Chinese and Western Culture* (Albany: SUNY Press, 1995). Contemporary Western thought tends to construe motion narrowly in terms of change of place. *The Shorter Oxford English Dictionary* (1990: 773) defines *motion* as "the act or process of moving or changing position" and defines *move* as "to change one's position or posture, or to cause to do this" (1990:775). This reflects the hegemony of modern post-Galilean physics.

6. This resembles Alfredo López Austin's approach in López Austin, *Tamoanchan, Tlalocan: Places of Mist*, trans. Bernard R. Ortiz de Montellano and Thelma Ortiz de Montellano (Niwot: University Press of Colorado, 1997); and David Carrasco's "ensemble approach" in Carrasco, *Religions of Mesoamerica: Cosmovision and Ceremonial Centers* (San Francisco: Harper and Row, 1990).

7. See Robert Audi, *The Cambridge Dictionary of Philosophy*, ed. Robert Audi (Cambridge: Cambridge University Press, 1995); and Michael Beaney, "Analysis," in *The Stanford Encyclopedia of Philosophy* (*Summer 2011 Edition*), ed. Edward N. Zalta, 2011, http://plato.stanford.edu/archives/sum2011/entries/analysis/; accessed 4/18/2013.

8. John Sullivan (personal communication, 5/16/13).

9. Fray Diego Durán, *Book of the Gods and Rites* and *The Ancient Calendar*, trans. and ed. Fernando Horcasitas and Doris Heyden (Norman: University of Oklahoma Press, 1971), 316.

10. Durán, *Book of the Gods and Rites*, 402.

11. Fray Alonso de Molina, *Vocabulario en lengua castellana y mexicana y mexicana y castellana*, 4th ed. (Mexico City: Porrúa, 2001), 2:76r; unless otherwise indicated, all translations are by R. Joe Campbell, *A Morphological Dictionary of Classical Nahuatl: A Morpheme Index to the* Vocabulario en lengua mexicana y castellana *of Fray Alonso de Molina* (Madison: Hispanic Seminary of Medieval Studies, 1985), 222.

12. Translations from the Spanish mine.

13. Andrés de Olmos, *Arte de la lengua mexicana y vocabulario*, ed. René Acuña (México, DF: Universidad Autónoma de México, 1985), 150–51, translation mine.

14. Rémi Siméon, *Diccionario de la lengua náhuatl o mexicana*, trans. Josefina Olivia de Coll (México, DF: Siglo Veintiuno Editores, 1977), 354–55.

15. Eduard Seler, *Commentarios al Códice Borgia* (México, DF: Fondo de Cultural Económica, 1963 [1904]), 1:16.

16. Seler, *Commentarios al Códice Borgia*, 1:143.

17. Quoted in Eva Hunt, *The Transformation of the Hummingbird: Cultural Roots of a Zinacatecan Mythical Poem* (Ithaca, NY: Cornell University Press, 1977), 59.

18. Ibid.

19. Doris Heyden, *The Eagle, the Cactus, the Rock: The Roots of Mexico-Tenochtitlan's Foundation Myth and Symbol*, BAR International Series 484 (Oxford: BAR, 1989), 68. See also Diego Dúran, *The History of the Indies of New Spain*, trans. Doris Heyden (New York: Orion Books, 1994), 83n9.

20. Alfonso Caso, *Los calendarios prehispánicos* (México, DF: Universidad Nacional Autónoma de México, Instituto de Investigaciones Históricas, 1967), 13. See also Miguel León-Portilla, *La filosofía náhuatl: Estudiada en sus fuentes con un nuevo apéndice*, new ed., prologue by Angel María Garibay K. (México, DF: Universidad Nacional Autónoma de México, 2001 [1956]), 120–23, 386.

21. Ulrich Köhler, "On the Significance of the Aztec Day Sign 'Olin,'" in *Proceedings of the Symposium [on] Space and Time in the Cosmovisión of Mesoamerica*, ed. Franz Tichy (Munich: Wilhelm Fink, 1982), 111–12.

22. Thelma D. Sullivan, "Tlazolteotl-Ixcuina: The Great Spinner and Weaver," in *The Art and Iconography of Late Post-Classic Central Mexico*, ed. Elizabeth Hill Boone (Washington, DC: Dumbarton Oaks, 1982), 29.

23. Hunt, *The Transformation of the Hummingbird*, 59.

24. Alfredo López Austin, *The Human Body and Ideology: Concepts of the Ancient Nahuas*, trans. Thelma Ortiz de Montellano and Bernard R. Ortiz de Montellano (Salt Lake City: University of Utah Press, 1988), II:211–12.

25. Quoted in López Austin, *The Human Body and Ideology*, I:230.

26. Campbell, *Morphological Dictionary*, 430–31. See also Sullivan, "Tlazolteotl-Ixcuina," 29; Jill Leslie McKeever Furst, *The Natural History of the Soul in Ancient Mexico*

(New Haven, CT: Yale University Press, 1995), 18; and Frances Karttunen, *An Analytical Dictionary of Nahuatl* (Norman: University of Oklahoma Press, 1983), 341.

27. Siméon, *Diccionario*, 195.

28. Campbell, *Morphological Dictionary*, 222, 430–31. Unless otherwise indicated, all translations are by Campbell.

29. Siméon, *Diccionario*, 195.

30. Karttunen, *Analytical Dictionary*, 343.

31. Molina, *Vocabulario*, 2:95r.

32. León-Portilla, *La filosofía náhuatl*, 396.

33. López Austin, *Human Body and Ideology*, I:230.

34. López Austin, *Human Body and Ideology*, I:chapters 5 and 6. See also McKeever Furst, *Natural History of the Soul*.

35. López Austin, *Human Body and Ideology*, I:chapters 5 and 6.

36. López Austin, *Human Body and Ideology*, I:230, 232. See also Davíd Carrasco with Scott Sessions, *Daily Life of the Aztecs: People of the Sun and Earth* (Westport, CT: Greenwood Press, 1998), 55; and McKeever Furst, *Natural History of the Soul*.

37. Richard F. Townsend, "Malinalco and the Lords of Tenochtitlan," in *The Art and Iconography of Late Postclassic Central Mexico*, ed. Elizabeth H. Boone (Washington, DC: Dumbarton Oaks, 1982), 59.

38. Molina, *Vocabulario*, 2:95r.

39. Karttunen, *Analytical Dictionary*, 342; Sullivan, "Tlazolteotl-Ixcuina," 29; León-Portilla, *La filosofía náhuatl*, 122, 396; and Campbell, *Morphological Dictionary*, 435.

40. McKeever Furst, *Natural History of the Soul*, 17–18.

41. León-Portilla, *La filosofía náhuatl*, 122, 396.

42. Alan R. Sandstrom, *Corn Is Our Blood: Culture and Ethnic Identity in a Contemporary Aztec Indian Village* (Norman: University of Oklahoma Press, 1991), 258.

43. Ibid.

44. Ibid.

45. Timothy J. Knab, *A War of Witches: A Journey into the Underworld of the Contemporary Aztecs* (Boulder, CO: Westview Press, 1995), 30, 42.

46. Ibid., 219.

47. Timothy J. Knab, *The Dialogue of Earth and Sky: Dreams, Souls, Curing and the Modern Aztec Underworld* (Tucson: University of Arizona Press, 2004), 29–31.

48. Bernardino de Sahagún, *Florentine Codex: General History of the Things of New Spain*, ed. and trans. Arthur J.O. Anderson and Charles Dibble (Santa Fe, NM: School of American Research; Salt Lake City: University of Utah, 1953–1982), X:130–31.

49. Karttunen, *Analytical Dictionary*, 218.

50. See Campbell, *Morphological Dictionary*, 304.

51. McKeever Furst, *Natural History of the Soul*, 42–47.

52. Durán, *Book of the Gods and Rites*, 232.

53. Campbell, *Morphological Dictionary*, 72.

54. Ibid., 193; and Karttunen, *Analytical Dictionary*, 153.

55. McKeever Furst, *Natural History of the Soul*, chapter 8.

56. Karttunen, *Analytical Dictionary*, 239.

57. Sahagún, *Florentine Codex*, III: appendix, 45. See McKeever Furst, *Natural History of the Soul*, chapter 8.

58. Miguel León-Portilla, *Aztec Thought and Culture: A Study of the Ancient Nahuatl Mind*, trans. Jack Emory Davis (Norman: University of Oklahoma Press, 1963), 56.

59. Hence, as Eduardo Matos Moctezuma argues, the two claws gripping hearts depicted on the Aztec Sun Stone belong to Tonatiuh (Matos Moctezuma, "The Aztec Calendar," in *The Aztec Calendar and Other Solar Monuments*, by Eduardo Matos Moctezuma and Felipe R. Solís [México, DF: Conaculta-Instituto Nacional de Antropología e Historia, 2004], 64).

60. Kay A. Read, *Time and Sacrifice in the Aztec Cosmos* (Bloomington: Indiana University Press, 1998). See also McKeever Furst, *Natural History of the Soul*, 178f; and Philip P. Arnold, *Eating Landscape: Aztec and European Occupation of Tlalocan* (Niwot: University Press of Colorado, 1999).

61. Felipe R. Solís with Roberto Velasco Alonso, "Monuments of Sun Worship," 127, fig. 116, brackets mine.

62. Ibid., 128–31; see also figs. F118–F123.

63. Campbell, *Morphological Dictionary*, 22. For a description of rubber, rubber balls, and the rubber seller, see Sahagún, *Florentine Codex*, X:87.

64. Toribio de Benavente Motolinía, *Motolinía's History of the Indians of New Spain*, trans. Francis Borgia Steck (Washington, DC: Academy of American Franciscan History, 1951), 119, brackets mine.

65. Laura Filloy, "Rubber," trans. Scott Sessions, in *The Oxford Encyclopedia of Mesoamerican Cultures: The Civilizations of Mexico and Central America*, ed. Davíd Carrasco (Oxford: Oxford University Press, 2001), 3:92–93.

66. Ibid. See also Arnold, *Eating Landscape*, 159; and Mary Miller and Karl Taube, *An Illustrated Dictionary of the Gods and Symbols of Ancient Mexico and the Maya* (London: Thames and Hudson, 1993), 46.

67. Sahagún, *Florentine Codex*, II:42–46; see Arnold, *Eating Landscape*, 78–81, 159–61.

68. Sahagún, *Florentine Codex*, I:7, 37, 47–49.

69. Filloy, "Rubber."

70. Molina, *Vocabulario*, 2:76r; Molina also translates *tlachtli* as "hip ballgame," (Molina, *Vocabulario*, 2:117v); Durán discusses the ballgame in Durán, *Book of the Gods and Rites*, chapter 23.

71. See Molina, *Vocabulario*, 2:117v; and Siméon, *Diccionario de la lengua náhuatl o mexicana*, 566.

72. Felipe R. Solís with Roberto Velasco Alonso, "Monuments of Sun Worship," in *The Aztec Calendar and Other Solar Monuments*, Eduardo Matos Moctezuma and Felipe R. Solís (México, DF: Conaculta-Instituto Nacional de Antropología e Historia, 2004), 143, 151n116. According to Solís, the *Códice Matritense del Palacio Real de Madrid* (fol. 269r) depicts Tenochtitlan's teotlachtli in this manner. In an earlier phase in its construction, the ends faced north and south. See Bernardino de Sahagún, *Primeros memoriales: Facsimile Edition* (Norman: University of Oklahoma Press, 1993), fol. 269r.

73. Hermann Beyer, "El origen, desarollo y significado de la greca escalonada," *El México Antiguo* 10 (1965): 53–104; Walter Krickeberg, *Las Antiguas cultural mexicanas* (México: Fondo de Cultura Económica, 1961), as reported in Heyden, "The Skin and Hair of Tlaltecuhtli," 68; Burr Cartwright Brundage, *The Fifth Sun: Aztec Gods, Aztec World* (Austin: University of Texas Press, 1979); and Solís, *The Aztec Empire*, 139, 143–46.

74. Solís with Velasco Alonso, "Monuments," 139; see also 143–46. For an archaeological discussion of Aztec ballcourts, see Michael E. Smith, *Aztec City-State Capitals* (Gainesville: University of Florida Press, 2008), 106–8.

75. Solís with Velasco Alonso, "Monuments," 141; Brundage, *The Fifth Sun*, 8–12; and Heather S. Orr, "Ballgame," in *Oxford Encyclopedia of Mesoamerican Cultures: The Civilizations of Mexico and Central America*, ed. Davíd Carrasco (Oxford: Oxford University Press, 2001), 1:77.

76. Gordon Brotherston, *Feather Crown: The Eighteen Feasts of the Mexican Year* (London: The British Museum, 2005), 53.

77. This sort of disordered and disorderly motion is also manifested by uncentered creatures that reside in the periphery such as rabbits and deer. See Louise M. Burkhart, "Moral Deviance in Sixteenth-Century Nahua and Christian Thought: The Rabbit and the Deer," *Journal of Latin American Lore* 12, no. 2 (1986): 107–39.

78. See Eduardo Matos Moctezuma, *Life and Death in the Templo Mayor*, trans. Bernard R. Ortiz de Montellano and Thelma Ortiz de Montellano (Niwot: University Press of Colorado, 1995), 46.

79. Guilhem Olivier, *Mockeries and Metamorphoses of an Aztec God: Tezcatlipoca, "Lord of the Smoking Mirror,"* trans. Michel Besson (Niwot: University Press of Colorado, 2003), 17.

80. Durán, *Book of the Gods and Rites*, 302–3. For a general discussion of patolli, see Timothy Kendall, *Patolli: A Game of Ancient Mexico* (Newton, MA: Whitehall Games, 1983).

81. The foregoing draws from Joseph B. Mountjoy, "Patolli," in *The Oxford Encyclopedia of Mesoamerican Cultures: The Civilizations of Mexico and Central America*, ed. Davíd Carrasco (Oxford: Oxford University Press, 2001), 2:224.

82. Miguel León-Portilla, *The Aztec Image of Self and Society: An Introduction to Nahua Culture*, ed. J. Jorge Klor de Alva (Salt Lake City: University of Utah Press, 1992), 208–9; Kendall, *Patolli*.

83. See Durán, *Book of the Gods and Rites*, 402–3; and Sahagún, *Florentine Codex*, IV:6.

84. Durán, *Book of the Gods and Rites*, 402–3. Durán neglects to specify the requisite numerical coefficient.

85. See Jacques Soustelle, *El universo de los aztecas*, trans. José Luis Martinez and Juan José Utrilla (México, DF: Fondo de Cultura Económica, 1982), 170–71; Miguel León-Portilla, "*El Tonalámatl de los Pochtecas (Códice Fejérváry-Mayer): Estudio introductorio y comentarios,*" *Arqueología Mexicana, Edición especial* 18 (2005): 18–20; Alfonso Caso, *The Aztecs: People of the Sun*, trans. Lowell Dunham (Norman: University of Oklahoma Press, 1958); López Austin, *The Human Body and Ideology*; and Carrasco, *Daily Life of the Aztecs*, 60–61.

86. Translation from the Nahuatl by Read, *Time and Sacrifice*, 55.

87. My discussion of Xolotl draws from Karl Anton Nowotny, *Tlacuilolli: Style and Contents of the Mexican Pictorial Manuscripts with a Catalog of the Borgia Group*, ed. and trans. George A. Everett Jr. and Edward Sisson (Norman: University of Oklahoma Press, 2005), 385; Eduard Seler, *Codex Fejérváry-Mayer: An Old Mexican Picture Manuscript in the Liverpool Free Public Museums (12011/M), Published at the Expense of His Excellency the Duke of Loubat* (Berlin: T. and A. Constable, 1901–1902); Seler, *Commentarios al Códice Borgia*, 1:144–48; Solís, "Monuments," 141, 163; Eloise Quiñones Keber, *Codex Telleriano-Remensis: Ritual, Divination, and History in a Pictorial Aztec Manuscript* (Austin: University of Texas Press, 1995), 183–84; Elizabeth Hill Boone, *Cycles of Time and Meaning in the Mexican Books of Fate* (Austin: University of Texas Press, 2007); Brundage, *The Fifth Sun*, 119–21; and Miller and Taube, *Illustrated Dictionary*, 190.

88. See Seler, *Commentarios al Códice Borgia*; Boone, *Cycles of Time and Meaning*, 41, 47; Solís, "Monuments," 141; Eloise Quiñones Keber, "Xolotl: Dogs, Death, and Deities in Aztec Myth," *Latin American Indian Literatures* 7, no. 2 (1991): 229–39; Eloise Quiñones Keber, *Codex Telleriano-Remensis*, 183; and Miller and Taube, *Illustrated Dictionary*, 190.

89. Campbell, *Morphological Dictionary*, 416.

90. For discussion of dwarves, see Rosemary A. Joyce, *Gender and Power in Prehispanic Mesoamerica* (Austin: University of Texas Press, 2000), 192–97.

91. Read, *Time and Sacrifice*, 250n55.

92. Sahagún, *Florentine Codex*, XI:16.

93. Sullivan, "Tlazolteotl-Ixcuina," 18.

94. Seler, *Commentarios al Códice Borgia*, I:144ff.

95. See Seler, *Codex Fejérváry-Mayer*; Seler, *Commentarios al Códice Borgia*.

96. See Seler, *Commentarios al Códice Borgia*, I:144–48.

97. Ibid., I:55, 155; II:45–47.

98. See Sahagún, *Florentine Codex*, VII:5–6, 48; and John Bierhorst, trans., "Legend of the Suns," in *History and Mythology of the Aztecs* (Tucson: University of Arizona Press, 1992), 147–48. The latter text says that before the Fifth Sun was the sun, it was Nanahuatl.

99. Sahagún, *Florentine Codex*, VII:8, 56.

100. See Fray Gerónimo de Mendieta, *Historia ecclesiástica indiana*, 2nd ed. (Mexico City: Editorial Porrúa, 1971), 78–79; and Bierhorst, *The Legend of the Suns*, 145–46. The latter does not mention Xolotl by name but speaks of Quetzalcoatl's nahualli.

101. See Boone, *Cycles of Time and Meaning*, 48; Quiñones Keber, *Codex Telleriano-Remensis*, 184–85, 286, 293; and Nowotny, *Tlacuilolli*, 56.

102. *Codex Borbonicus* (Loubat: Bibliothéque Du Palais Bourbon, 1899), 16.

103. See Nowotny, *Tlacuilolli*, 56, 184; and López Austin, *Tamoanchan, Tlalocan*, 213. Aztec priests and nobles inserted their bloody autosacrificial utensils (e.g., maguey or coral spines) into grass balls called *zacatapayolli* ("grass rounded into the shape of a ball"). The geometric shape of these balls suggests rubber balls, the Fifth Sun, and olin-motion-change. Nanahuatzin's zacatapayolli was made of reed, which is another day sign (along with Olin) associated with East.

104. Quiñones Keber, *Codex Telleriano-Remensis*, 184.

105. See Solís, "Monuments," 141; Seler, *Commentarios al Códice Borgia*, I:147–48; and Nowotny, *Tlacuilolli*, 32.

106. Matos Moctezuma, "The Aztec Calendar," 42, 63.

107. See Solís, "Monuments," 140 (figs. 144 and 145) and 141.

108. Matos Moctezuma, "The Aztec Calendar," 42, 63.

109. See Susan Gillespie, *The Aztec Kings: The Construction of Rulership in Mexica History* (Tucson: University of Arizona Press, 1989); and Read, *Time and Sacrifice*.

110. Boone, *Cycles of Time and Meaning*, 48, table 6.

111. Sullivan, "Tlazolteotl-Ixcuina," 14.

112. Sahagún, *Florentine Codex*, I:15–16, 23; and Sullivan, "Tlazolteotl-Ixcuina," 7.

113. Henry B. Nicholson, "Religion in Pre-Hispanic Central Mexico," in *Handbook of Middle American Indians*, ed. Robert Wauchope, Gordon F. Elkholm, and Ignacio Bernal (Austin: University of Texas Press, 1971), 10:414, 420. See also Sahagún, *Florentine Codex*, I:23–27; VI:29–34.

114. Sahagún, *Florentine Codex*, I:15.

115. Durán, *Book of the Gods and Rites*, 239.

116. Sullivan, "Tlazolteotl-Ixcuina," 12.

117. Bernardino de Sahagún, *Primeros memoriales*. Paleography of Nahuatl Text and English Translation by Thelma D. Sullivan (Norman: University of Oklahoma Press, 1997), 103.

118. Sahagún, *Florentine Codex*, I:fig. 8.

119. Quiñones Keber, *Codex Telleriano-Remensis*, 179. See also Sullivan, "Tlazolteotl-Ixcuina," 15.

120. See Sullivan, "Tlazolteotl-Ixcuina," 15. Sullivan notes that the Nahuatl word for "humus" is *tlazollalli* ("earth garbage" or "earth filth").

121. Nicholson, "Religion in Pre-Hispanic Central Mexico," 422.

122. Sullivan, "Tlazolteotl-Ixcuina," 14. Sullivan ("Tlazolteotl-Ixcuina," 19–21) claims the bark of the cotton plant was used to induce uterine contractions and menstruation, and pulverized cotton seeds were used to induce lactation.

123. Sullivan (ibid., 14) makes a similar point but takes it in a different direction.

124. Sahagún, *Florentine Codex*, I:23.

125. Sullivan, "Tlazolteotl-Ixcuina," 30.

126. See Alan Isaacs, John Daintith, and Elizabeth Martin, eds., *A Dictionary of Science* (Oxford: Oxford University Press, 1999), 208, 720–21.

127. "Annals of Cuauhtitlan," in *Codex Chimalpopoca: The Text in Nahuatl with a Glossary and Grammatical Notes*, John Bierhorst (Tucson: University of Arizona Press, 1992), side 2:42–45; translation by Read, *Time and Sacrifice*, 83–84 (bracketed insertions mine). Following Boone (*Cycles of Time and Meaning*, 38–39), I distinguish day sign from day name. Day names combine a day sign (e.g., olin) and a day number (e.g., 4). Hence, "olin" is a day sign and "4 olin," a day name.

128. "Legend of the Suns," in *History and Mythology of the Aztecs: The Codex Chimalpopoca*, trans. John Bierhorst (Tucson: University of Arizona Press, 1992), 142. The word *tonatiuh* ("sun") is also used to refer to cosmic Ages or Eras. In order to avoid confusion, I refer to the five Suns by the word *Sun* and to the five ages by the words *Age, Era,* or *Sun-Earth Ordering*.

129. Brundage, *The Fifth Sun*, 37.

130. Andrews and Hassig in Hernando Ruiz de Alarcón, *Treatise on the Heathen Superstitions that Today Live among the Indians Native to This New Spain*, trans., ed., intro. J. Richard Andrews and Ross Hassig (Norman: University of Oklahoma Press, 1984), 240.

131. León-Portilla, *La filosofía náhuatl*, 394, translation mine.

132. *Historia de los mexicanos por sus pinturas*, in *Teogonía e historia de los Mexicanos: Tres opúsculos del siglo XVI*, ed. Angel María Garibay K. (México: Editorial Porrúa, 1965), 24.

133. Sahagún, *Florentine Codex*, I:81–82.

134. Karttunen, *Analytical Dictionary*, 130.

135. The preceding draws from López Austin, *Human Body and Ideology*, I:58–60, 205–7; and McKeever Furst, *Natural History of the Soul*, 135–37.

136. Seler believes this claim appeared later in history. Seler writes, "*Pero comprendemos asimismo que en el fondo ollin es el Sol mismo: es muy probable que la palabra Ollin-*

tonatiuh hay significado primordialmente "Sol rodeante" y que sólo por una nueva y posterior interpretación haya adquirido el significado del Sol destinado a perecer por terremotos" (Seler, *Commentarios al Códice Borgia*, I:150).

137. On Mesoamerican numerology, see Gerardo Aldana, *The Apotheosis of Janaab' Pakal: Science, History, and Religion at Classic Maya Palenque* (Boulder: University Press of Colorado, 2007); Boone, *Cycles of Time and Meaning*, 101; Ross Hassig, *Time, History and Belief in Aztec and Colonial Mexico* (Austin: University of Texas Press, 2001); Hunt, *Transformation of the Hummingbird*, chapter 6; León-Portilla, *Time and Reality in the Thought of the Maya*, 2nd ed., trans. Charles Boiles, Fernanado Horcasitas, and Miguel León-Portilla (Norman: University of Oklahoma Press, 1988), 35–37; López Austin, *Tamoanchan, Tlalocan*, 27–28; Barbara Tedlock, *Time and the Highland Maya*, rev. ed. (Albuquerque: University of New Mexico Press, 1992 [1982]); Stanley E. Payne and Michael Closs, "A Survey of Aztec Numbers and Their Uses," in *Native-American Mathematics*, ed. Michael P. Closs (Austin: University of Texas Press, 1986), 215–35. Day numbers, for example, are also associated with the Thirteen Lords of the Day, which further determines their personalities.

138. Aldana, *The Apotheosis of Janaab' Pakal*, 196–97.

139. Frank J. Lipp, *The Mixe of Oaxaca: Religion, Ritual, and Healing* (Austin: University of Texas Press, 1991), 86, 114.

140. See Hunt, *Transformation of the Hummingbird*, 187, 192–94; López Austin, *Human Body and Ideology*, I:53; López Austin, *Tamoanchan, Tlalocan*, 27; Nicholson, "Religion in Pre-Hispanic Central Mexico"; and Louise M. Burkhart, "Mexica Women on the Home Front: Housework and Religion in Aztec Mexico," in *Indian Women of Early Mexico*, ed. Susan Schroeder, Stephanie Wood, and Robert Haskett (Norman: University of Oklahoma Press, 1997), 48. This way of reckoning counts nine upper skies and four lower skies. See López Austin, *Tamoanchan, Tlalocan*, 17, figure 2.

141. See Hunt, *Transformation of the Hummingbird*, 194–95; López Austin, *Human Body and Ideology*, I:53; López Austin, *Tamoanchan, Tlalocan*, 27; Jacques Soustelle, *Daily Life of the Aztecs on the Eve of the Spanish Conquest*, trans. Patrick O'Brien (Stanford, CA: Stanford University Press, 1970), 111; Nicholson, "Religion in Pre-Hispanic Central Mexico"; and Burkhart, "Mexica Women," 48.

142. Seler, *Codex Fejérváry-Mayer*, 71.

143. Seler, *Commentarios al Códice Borgia*, I:17.

144. Sahagún, *Florentine Codex*, IV:6; see also VII:1.

145. Guilhem Olivier, "Aztec Human Sacrifice as Expiation," in *The Strange World of Human Sacrifice*, ed. Jan N. Bremmer (Leuven: Peeters, 2007), 24.

146. Durán, *Book of the Gods and Rites*, 186–93, 414. What follows also draws from Sahagún, *Florentine Codex*, II:35, IV:6, and VII:1.

147. The following draws from Hunt, *Transformation of the Hummingbird*, 195–95; León-Portilla, *Aztec Thought and Culture*; Nicholson, "Religion"; Michel Graulich, *Myths*

of Ancient Mexico, trans. Bernard R. Ortiz de Montellano and Thelma Ortiz de Montellano (Norman: University of Oklahoma Press, 1997); Graulich, "Creation Myths," in *The Oxford Encyclopedia of Mesoamerican Cultures: The Civilizations of Mexico and Central America*, ed. Davíd Carrasco (Oxford: Oxford University Press, 2001), 1:281–84; Graulich, "Creator Deities," in *The Oxford Encyclopedia of Mesoamerican Cultures: The Civilizations of Mexico and Central America*, ed. Davíd Carrasco (Oxford: Oxford University Press, 2001), 1:284–86.

148. *Historia de los mexicanos por sus pinturas*, 24.

149. The four basic colors varied across Mesoamerica. Red, blue, black, and white were the most common among the cultures of Mexico's Central High Plateau (López Austin, *Human Body and Ideology*, I:58). For a different assignment, see Carrasco, *Religions of Mesoamerica*, 71.

150. Gordon Brotherston and Dawn Ades, "Mesoamerican Description of Space, I: Myths; Stars and Maps; Architecture," *Ibero-Amerikanisches Archiv* 1, no. 4 (1975), maintain we have no evidence for thinking the cosmos was initially divided into four geometrical quarters and cardinal directions pace León-Portilla (*Aztec Thought and Culture*) and Aveni (*Skywatchers: A Revised and Updated Version of Skywatchers of Ancient Mexico* [Austin: University of Texas Press, 2001]). I discuss this issue in chapter 7.

151. "Annals of Cuauhtitlan," in *History and Mythology of the Aztecs: The Codex Chimalpopoca*, trans. John Bierhorst (Tucson: University of Arizona Press, 1992), 26. For discussion, see Graulich, *Myths of Ancient Mexico*, 64; León-Portilla, *Aztec Thought and Culture*, 36–38; and Nicholson, "Religion in Pre-Hispanic Central Mexico," 398–99.

152. Quoted in Heyden, *Eagle, Cactus, Rock*, 68.

153. Quoted in ibid., 72n9. Xolotl is standardly depicted as having has two sets of ears: two human and two canine. The two canine ears appear to be torn, suggesting the dying Sun's two solstitial entrances into the Underworld. See also Quiñones Keber, "Xolotl."

154. Sahagún, *Florentine Codex*, VII:1.

155. See Matos Moctezuma, "The Aztec Calendar," 64; Hunt, *The Transformation of the Hummingbird*, 111, 196; Sullivan, "Tlazolteotl-Ixcuina," 30; and Graulich, *Myths of Ancient Mexico*, 266.

156. Sullivan, "Tlazolteotl-Ixcuina," 30.

157. Ibid., 29.

158. Hunt, *Transformation of the Hummingbird*, 196–97.

159. See ibid.; Enrique Florescano, *Memory, Myth, and Time in Mexico: From the Aztecs to Independence*, trans. Albert G. Bork (Austin: University of Texas Press, 1994), 13–14; and Rudolph van Zantwijk, *The Aztec Arrangement: The Social History of Pre-Spanish Mexico* (Norman: University of Oklahoma Press, 1985).

160. See J. Richard Andrews, *Introduction to Classic Nahuatl*, rev. ed. (Norman: University of Oklahoma Press, 2003), 311; Boone, *Cycles of Time and Meaning*, 14–15; and Payne and Closs, "A Survey of Aztec Numbers," 216.

161. See López Austin, *Human Body and Ideology*; León-Portilla, *Aztec Thought and Culture*; León-Portilla, *El Tonalámatl de los Pochtecas* (*Códice Fejérváry-Mayer*); Carrasco, *Daily Life of the Aztecs*; Florescano, *Memory, Myth, and Time*; Miller and Taube, *Illustrated Dictionary*; and Graulich, *Myths of Ancient Mexico*.

162. See López Austin, *Tamoanchan, Tlalocan*, 17, figure 2.

163. See López Austin, *Tamoanchan, Tlalocan*, 16.

164. *The Shorter Oxford English Dictionary* (1990: 1413).

165. Susan Gillespie, "Different Ways of Seeing: Modes of Social Consciousness in Mesoamerican Two-Dimensional Artworks," *Baesler-Archiv* 55 (2007): 128.

166. Barbara Tedlock and Dennis Tedlock, "Text and Textile: Language and Technology in the Arts of the Quiché Maya," *Journal of Anthropological Research* 41, no. 2 (1985): 125; see also Dennis Tedlock, "Introduction," in *Popol Vuh: The Definitive Edition of the Mayan Book of the Dawn of Life and the Glories of Gods and Kings* (New York: Simon and Schuster, 1985), 32.

167. See Johanna Broda, "Astronomy, *Cosmovisión*, and Ideology in Pre-Hispanic Mesoamerica," in *Ethnoastronomy and Archaeoastronomy in the American Tropics*, ed. Anthony Aveni and Gary Urton, Annals of the New York Academy of Sciences, No. 38 (New York: New York Academy of Sciences, 1982), 81–110; Johanna Broda, "Astronomical Knowledge, Calendrics, and Sacred Geography in Ancient Mesoamerica," in *Astronomies and Cultures*, ed. Clive N. Ruggles and Nicholas J. Saunders (Niwot: University Press of Colorado, 1993), 253–95; López Austin, *Human Body and Ideology*; López Austin, *Tamoanchan, Tlalocan*; Alfredo López Austin, "Cosmovision," trans. Scott Sessions, in *The Oxford Encyclopedia of Mesoamerican Cultures: The Civilizations of Mexico and Central America*, ed. Davíd Carrasco (Oxford: Oxford University Press, 2001), 268–74; Carrasco, *Religions of Mesoamerica*; Carrasco, *City of Sacrifice: The Aztec Empire and the Role of Violence in Civilization* (Boston: Beacon Press, 1999).

168. Florescano, *Memory, Myth, and Time*, 17.

169. Although Wayne Elzey is correct in claiming olin motion is ordering, he is mistaken in claiming it consists of "well-defined elements," (Elzey, "Some Remarks on the Space and Time of the 'Center' in Aztec Religion," *Estudios de cultura náhuatl* 12 [1976]: 325). Chapter 3 argued there are no well-defined elements in Aztec metaphysics since everything is mixed and ambiguous.

170. See Karttunen, *Analytical Dictionary*, 246.

171. By contrast, Enrique Florescano and Miguel León-Portilla argue East and West are defined in terms of where the sun rises and sets on its summer and fall equinoxes

(Florescano, *Memory, Myth, and Time*; and Miguel León-Portilla, "Appendix B: Recent Contributions on the Theme of this Book," in *Time and Reality in the Thought of the Maya*, 161–205). See also Aveni, *Skywatchers*.

172. Molina, *Vocabulario*, 2:157v. For discussion, see León-Portilla, *Aztec Thought and Culture*, 46–47; Alfonso Villa Rojas, "Appendix A: The Concepts of Space and Time among the Contemporary Maya," in *Time and Reality in the Thought of the Maya*, 2nd ed., by Miguel León-Portilla (Norman: University of Oklahoma Press, 1988); and Gordon Brotherston, "Mesoamerican Description of Space, II: Signs for Directions," *Ibero-Amerikanisches Archiv* 2, no. 1 (1976): 41, 45.

173. See the Spanish side of Molina, *Vocabulario*, 1:89; León-Portilla, *Aztec Thought and Culture*, 46–47; and Brotherston, "Mesoamerican Description of Space II," 41, 45. Brotherston and Ades ("Mesoamerican Description of Space I," 289) write, "Nothing indicates that Mesoamerican astronomy used as primary scientific terms anything other than the east and west horizons, with their solstitial, equinoctial and other rising and setting positions."

174. As Brotherston ("Mesoamerican Description of Space II," 49) notes, east and west are commonly associated with red and black: the colors associated with writing, wisdom, and right living.

175. James M. Taggart, *Nahuat Myth and Social Structure* (Austin: University of Texas Press, 1983), 57. John M. Watanabe's discussion of directional terms in the Mam language of western Guatemala and Quiché language of the Guatemalan central highlands suggests the same (Watanabe, "In the World of the Sun: A Cognitive Model of Mayan Cosmology," *Man* 18, no. 4 [1983]: 713, 720). For a study of Zinacanteco Maya, see Evon Z. Vogt, "Cardinal Directions and Ceremonial Circuits in Mayan and Southwestern Cosmology," *National Geographic Society Research Reports* 2 (1985): 487–96.

176. Félix Báez-Jorge and Arturo Gómez Martínez, *Tlacatecolotl y el Diablo: La cosmovisión de los nahuas de Chicontepec* (Xalapa, Veracruz, Mexico: Gobierno del Estado de Veracruz, 1998), 23, translation mine.

177. Chapter 7 defends this claim. Process metaphysics thus *explains* why there are no *fixed* cardinal or intercardinal directions or fixed compass points that precede the movement of the Fifth Sun, and thus provides a metaphysical explanation for the claims of Brotherston and Ades ("Mesoamerican Description of Space II") and Brotherston ("Mesoamerican Description of Space II"). See also Gillespie, "Different Ways of Seeing."

178. B. Tedlock, *Time and the Highland Maya*, 178.

179. Brotherston and Ades, "Mesoamerican Description of Space," 300. See also Clemency Coggins, "The Shape of Time: Some Political Implications of a Four-Part Figure," *American Antiquity* 45, no. 4 (1980): 727–39; Watanabe, "In the World of the Sun"; and Vogt, "Cardinal Directions and Ceremonial," 487–96.

180. See Aveni, *Skywatchers*; and Florescano, *Memory, Myth, and Time*, 18. Brotherston and Ades ("Mesoamerican Description of Space") argue the notion of intercardinality makes no sense if the notion of cardinality makes no sense. Köhler ("Significance of the Aztec Day Sign") and Broda ("Astronomical Knowledge," 258) argue the four intercardinal directions or solstice points were more important to Aztec astronomy and ritual than were the four cardinal directions. For related discussion, see Clemency Coggins, "New Fire Drill at Chichen Itza," in *Memorias del Primer Coloquio Internacional de Mayistas* (México: UNAM, 1987), 427–44.

181. Vogt, "Cardinal Directions," 488.

182. The *Relación de Michoacán* states that the sun possesses two houses in the east, two in the west, and a fifth in the middle of the sky, that is, the zenith (Heyden, *Eagle, Cactus, Rock*, 72). Regarding Classic Maya cosmology, Karen Bassie-Sweet writes: "The deities *gave* structure and order to time by *creating* the diurnal and annual passage of the sun. The corners of the world square were formed by the four solstice rise and set points; the center was defined by the zenith passage of the sun at noon" (Bassie-Sweet, *At the Edge of the World: Caves and Late Classic Maya World View* [Norman: Oklahoma University Press, 1996], 61), emphasis mine; see also Coggins, "New Fire Drill." The Fifth Sun's motion-change does not, however, create the vertical layering of the Fifth Age.

183. Laurette Séjourné, *Burning Water: Thought and Religion in Ancient Mexico* (New York: Grove Press, 1960), 91.

184. Caso (*The Aztecs*, 10–11) writes, "the grouping of all beings according to the four cardinal points of the compass and the central direction" is one of the fundamental organizing principles of Aztec metaphysics. If my view is correct, Caso's remark is true of the Fifth Sun-Earth Ordering but *not* any of the other four Sun-Earth Orderings or of the cosmos per se. I believe Caso confounds the Fifth Sun-Earth Ordering and the cosmos per se.

185. Elzey ("Some Remarks," 319) claims the cosmological or spatial focus of olin motion-change is "principally horizontal." Read (*Time and Sacrifice*, 139, 248n30, 249n40) emphasizes the horizontal nature of the Fifth Sun's spreading.

186. León-Portilla, *Aztec Thought and Culture*, 54. Elzey ("Some Remarks") apparently shares León Portilla's view.

187. For further discussion, see León-Portilla, *El Tonalámatl de los Pochtecas (Códice Fejérváry-Mayer)*; Aveni, *Skywatchers*, 148–52; Brotherston, "Mesoamerican Description of Space II"; Florescano, *Memory, Myth, and Time*; Constanza Vega Sosa, "El Curso del sol en los glifos de la cerámica Azteca tarde," *Estudios de cultura náhuatl* 17 (1984): 125–70; and Gillespie, "Different Ways of Seeing."

188. For discussion of how figure 4.3 and other cosmograms functioned as a prognosticatory maps and action-guides, see León-Portilla, *El Tonalámatl de los Pochtecas (Códice*

Fejérváry-Mayer); Quiñones Keber, *Codex Telleriano-Remensis*; Boone, *Cycles of Time and Meaning*; and Hassig, *Time, History and Belief.*

189. See Elzey ("Some Remarks") for an excellent although different analysis of the center.

190. See León-Portilla, *Aztec Thought and Culture*; López Austin, *Human Body and Ideology*; Davíd Carrasco, *Quetzalcoatl and the Irony of Empire: Myths and Prophecies in the Aztec Tradition* (Chicago: University of Chicago Press, 1982), 162; Carrasco, *Religions of Mesoamerica*, 52; Louise M. Burkhart, *The Slippery Earth: Nahua-Christian Dialogue in Sixteenth-Century Mexico* (Tucson: University of Arizona Press, 1989), 59; Elzey, "Some Remarks"; Florescano, *Memory, Myth, and Time*; Alan R. Sandstrom, "Center and Periphery in the Social Organization of Contemporary Nahuas of Mexico," *Ethnology* 35, no. 3 (1996): 161–80; and Taggart, *Nahuat Myth and Social Structure*, 55–56.

191. *Tlal-* derives from *tlalli* ("earth") while *xic-* derives from *xictli* ("navel"). See Karttunen, *Analytical Dictionary*, 324; Elzey, "Some Remarks," 320; López Austin, *Human Body and Ideology*, I:17; and León-Portilla, *Aztec Thought and Culture*, 32.

192. López Austin, *Human Body and Ideology*, I:425n37. Vogt ("Cardinal Directions," 490) reports Zinacantecos similarly call the center *mishik' balamil* or "navel of the universe."

193. Quoted in Elzey, "Some Remarks," 319; and in Carrasco, *Quetzalcoatl and the Irony of Empire*, 162. See also Brotherston and Ades, "Mesoamerican Description of Space I," 286.

194. Carrasco (*Quetzalcoatl and the Irony of Empire*, 162) proposes "the navel of the cosmos" and "sacred center of cosmological space" as translations. I maintain *tlalxicco* is the navel or center of the Fifth Age's earth *only*. It did not exist in the preceding four Ages. Carrasco confounds the cosmos per se and the cosmos of the Fifth Age.

195. López Austin, *Human Body and Ideology*, I:200; see also 173, 197–98.

196. Félix Báez-Jorge and Arturo Gómez Martínez, "Los equilibrios del cielo y de la tierra: Cosmovisión de los nahuas de Chicontepec," *Desacatos*, Invierno 5 (2000): 23, translation mine.

197. See Taggart, *Nahuat Myth*; Elzey, "Some Remarks," 320–22; and Burkhart, "Moral Deviance," 59–65.

198. Taggart, *Nahuat Myth*, 55–56, 161.

199. Sandstrom, "Center and Periphery," 163–65.

200. López Austin, *Human Body and Ideology*.

201. I owe this observation to Arthur G. Miller, "The Iconography of the Painting in the Temple of the Diving God, Tulum, Quintana Roo, Mexico: The Twisted Cords," in *Mesoamerican Archaeology: New Approaches*, ed. Norman Hammond (Austin: University of Texas Press, 1974), 167–86.

202. Following Eliade, Davíd Carrasco interprets the center as an axis mundi (Carrasco, *Quetzalcoatl and the Irony of Empire*; Carrasco, *Religions of Mesoamerica: Cosmovision and Ceremonial Centers* [San Francisco: Harper and Row, 1990], 52). Read, in *Time and Sacrifice*, rightly objects to the metaphysical dualism of sacred and profane inherent in Eliade's and Carrasco's notion of axis mundi, and objects to the permanence and stability the two thinkers attribute to it. Although I agree with Read, chapter 3 argued we may characterize the navel as a time-place of special powers without committing ourselves to a Platonic-style metaphysical dualism and without attributing permanent stability to the navel.

203. See Elzey, "Some Remarks," 320; León-Portilla, *Aztec Thought and Culture*, 31–33, 93–95. For further discussion, see Heyden, *Eagle, Cactus, Rock*; Florescano, *Memory, Myth, and Time*; Carrasco, *Quetzalcoatl and the Irony of Empire*; and López Austin, *Human Body and Ideology*.

204. León-Portilla, *Aztec Thought and Culture*, 31–33, 90.

205. Molina, *Vocabulario en lengua castellana*, 1:341.

206. López Austin, *Human Body and Ideology*, I:59; León-Portilla, *Aztec Thought and Culture*; and McKeever Furst, *Natural History of the Soul*.

207. Nicholson, "Religion," 418. What follows also draws from Seler, *Commentarios al Códice Borgia*, I:109; II:76–77; Hunt, *Transformation of the Hummingbird*, 197–98; and Burkhart, *Slippery Earth*, 74.

208. Campbell, *Morphological Dictionary*, 87, 165.

209. Burkhart, *Slippery Earth*, 74.

210. Lipp, *Mixe of Oaxaca*, 86.

211. "Annals of Cuauhtitlan" in Bierhorst, *History and Mythology of the Aztecs*, 34. See also Sahagún, *Florentine Codex*, III:18.

212. Sahagún, *Florentine Codex*, X:193. See also Sahagún, *Primeros memoriales: Paleography*, 82, 82n11.

213. The 260-day tonalpohualli is divided into five periods of 52 days. The tonalpohualli and xiuhmolpilli counts coincide every 52 years, ending a "century." This is a time of extreme uncertainty and anxiety since there is no guarantee that a new cycle will commence. The New Fire ritual aims at jump-starting anew the 52-year cycle.

214. Chapter 7 argues this fact does not, however, mean that the cosmos per se will come to an end.

215. Aveni, *Skywatchers*. See also Broda, "Astronomy"; Broda, "Astronomical Knowledge"; and Carrasco, *City of Sacrifice*, chapter 3.

216. Aveni, *Skywatchers*, 63.

217. Vogt ("Cardinal Directions," 489–90) reports there are no words in Tzotzil for "equinox" and that Zinacantecos seem unaware of the zenith passages of the sun.

218. Aveni, *Skywatchers*, 62.

219. Sahagún (*Florentine Codex*, VII:1) configures these four phases slightly differently as dawn, midday, late afternoon, and dusk.

220. See Michel Graulich, "Quetzalcoatl-Ehecatl, the Bringer of Life," in *Ancient America: Contributions to New World Archaeology*, ed. Nicholas J. Saunders (Oxford: Oxbow Books, 1992), 267, figure 25; and Isaacs, Daintith, and Martin, *A Dictionary of Science*, 721.

221. Robert S. Carlsen and Martin Prechtel, "The Flowering of the Dead: An Interpretation of Highland Maya Culture," *Man* 26, no. 1 (1991): 26.

222. James Lockhart, *The Nahuas after the Conquest: A Social and Cultural History of the Indians of Central Mexico, Sixteenth through Eighteenth Centuries* (Stanford, CA: Stanford University Press, 1992), 576n5. See also Lockhart, *Nahuas*, chapters 8 and 9; León-Portilla, *Aztec Image of Self and Society*, 45–46, 52–53; and Elizabeth Hill Boone, *Stories in Red and Black: Pictorial Histories of the Aztecs and Mixtecs* (Austin: University of Texas Press, 2000), 34, 253n10.

223. According to Peter T. Furst, Huichol weavers incorporate snake designs into their belts as prayers in order to induce rain (Furst, "The Thread of Life: Some Parallels in the Symbolism of Aztec, Huichol and Puebla Earth Goddesses," in *Balance y perspectiva de la antropolgía de Mesoamerica y del centro de México*, Mesa Redonda 13th, 1973 [México, DF: La Sociedad Mexicana de Antropolgía, 1975], 237). Elizabeth M. Brumfiel also attributes causal potency to design motifs (Brumfiel, "Cloth, Gender, Continuity and Change: Fabricating Unity in Anthropology," *American Anthropologist* 108, no. 4 [2006]: 868; and Brumfiel, "Aztec Women: Capable Partners and Cosmic Enemies," in *The Aztec World*, ed. Elizabeth M. Brumfiel and Gary M. Feinman [New York: Harry N. Abrams, 2008], 90).

224. Miller, "The Iconography of the Painting," 183.

225. Ibid., 181.

226. See Doris Heyden, *Mitología y simbolismo de la flora en el México prehispánico* (México: UNAM, Instituto de Investigaciones Antropológicas, 1983); Doris Heyden, "Las Cuevas de Teotihuacán," *Arqueología Mexicana* 6, no. 34 (1998): 18–27; Jane H. Hill, "The Flower World of Old Uto-Aztecan," *Journal of Anthropological Research* 48, no. 2 (1992): 117–44; Hunt, *Transformation of the Hummingbird*; Cecelia Klein, "The Shield Women: Resolution of a Gender Paradox," in *Current Topics in Aztec Studies: Essays in Honor of Dr. H. B. Nicholson*, ed. Alana Cory and Douglas Sharon, San Diego Museum of Man Papers 30 (San Diego: San Diego Museum of Man, 1993), 39–64; and Ana María Velasco Lozana and Debra Nagao, "Mitología y simbolismo de las flores," *Arqueología Mexicana* 13, no. 78 (2006): 28–35; Louise Burkhart (1991).

227. Séjourné, *Burning Water*, 94.

228. Heyden (*Eagle, Cactus, Rock*, 68) calls this the "X-cross-ollin-quincunx" motif. She also includes the *atl-tlachinolli* ideogram. I believe the atl-tlachinolli depicts malinalli, not olin, and therefore do not discuss it here.

229. Jeanette Favrot Peterson states the Aztecs appreciated the heart flower for its beauty, aroma, and medicinal properties (Peterson, *The Paradise Garden Murals of Malinalco: Utopia and Empire in Sixteenth-Century Mexico* [Austin: University of Texas Press, 1993], 85). For an illustration, see Sahagún's *Florentine Codex*, XI:201; for a description of the heart flower, see *Florentine Codex*, XI:figure 681.

230. Durán, *Book of the Gods and Rites*, 347.

231. Carrasco, *Quetzalcoatl and the Irony of Empire*, 162. See also López Austin, *Human Body and Ideology*, I:58; Heyden, *Mitología y simbolismo de la flora*; and Vega Sosa, "El Curso del Sol."

232. J. Eric S. Thompson, *Maya Hieroglyphic Writing: An Introduction* (Norman: University of Oklahoma Press, 1960), 142. I employ León-Portilla's (*Time and Reality*) translation of *kinh* as "sun-day-time."

233. See Hunt, *Transformation of the Hummingbird*, 92; Hill, "The Flower World"; Solís, "Monuments," 127; Heyden, "The Skin and Hair," 213; Doris Heyden, "Rites of Passage and Other Ceremonies in Caves," in *In the Maw of the Earth Monster*, ed. James E. Brady and Keith M. Prufer (Austin: University of Texas Press, 2005), 22; Elizabeth Brumfiel, "Towards a Middle Range Theory of Household Politics: The Standardization of Decorative Motifs in Middle Postclassic Mexico," in *The Archaeology of Politics: The Materiality of Political Practice and Action in the Past*, ed. Peter Johansen and Andrew Bauer (Newcastle upon Tyne: Cambridge Scholars Press, 2011), 245–82; Velasco Lozano and Nagao, "Mitología y simbolismo de las flores."

234. Durán, *Book of the Gods and Rites*, 187–88.

235. Ibid., 188, brackets mine.

236. Karl Taube, "The Turquoise Hearth: Fire, Self Sacrifice, and the Central Mexican Cult of War," in *Mesoamerica's Classic Heritage*, ed. Davíd Carrasco, Lindsay Jones, and Scott Sessions (Niwot: University Press of Colorado, 2000), 323.

237. *The Codex Mendoza*, 4 vols., by Frances F. Berdan and Patricia Rieff Anawalt (Berkeley: University of California Press, 1992), 20v, 22r, 23v. For discussion, see Patricia Rieff Anawalt, "A Comparative Analysis of the Costumes and Accoutrements of the *Codex Mendoza*," in *The Essential Codex Mendoza*, ed. Frances Berdan and Patricia Rieff Anawalt (Berkeley: University of California Press, 1992), 118.

238. McKeever Furst, *Natural History of the Soul*, 39.

239. See Taube, "The Turquoise Hearth," 323.

240. Anawalt, "A Comparative Analysis," 118; Nicholson, "Religion in Pre-Hispanic Central Mexico," 417; and Miller and Taube, *An Illustrated Dictionary*, 190.

241. Hunt, *Transformation of the Hummingbird*, 59; see also Sullivan, "Tlazolteotl-Ixcuina"; and Miller and Taube, *Illustrated Dictionary*, 100.

242. Heyden in Durán, *The History of the Indies of New Spain*, 289n7.

243. See McKeever Furst, *Natural History of the Soul*; Taube, "The Turquoise Hearth"; and Hunt, *Transformation of the Hummingbird*, 59.

244. Sahagún, *Florentine Codex*, III:appendix, 49.

245. Antonio Serrato-Combe, *The Aztec Templo Mayor: A Visualization* (Salt Lake City: University of Utah Press, 2007), 11. See also Zantwijk, *The Aztec Arrangement*.

246. See Sahagún, *Florentine Codex*, XI:figure 679; for description of gardens, see page 200.

247. Aveni, *Skywatchers*, 150. See also León-Portilla, *El Tonalámatl de los Pochtecas (Códice Fejérváry-Mayer)*; Boone, *Cycles of Time and Meaning*; Read, *Time and Sacrifice*, 216; Seler, *Codex Fejérváry-Mayer*; Köhler, "Significance of the Aztec Day Sign"; Villa Rojas, "Appendix A"; Brotherston, "Mesoamerican Description of Space II"; Broda, "Astronomy"; Broda, "Astronomical Knowledge." Various "corporeal almanacs" (as Boone calls them) assume the form of quincunxes. These include the deerskin almanacs in the *Codex Borgia* and *Codex Vaticanus 3773* B as well as the human-body almanac, *Codex Vaticanus 3738* A, and Quetzalcoatl-Mictlantecuhtli almanac, *Codex Borgia*. See also Gisele Diaz and Alan Rodgers, *Codex Borgia: A Full Color Restoration of the Ancient Mexican Manuscript*, intro. Bruce E. Byland (New York: Dover Publications, 1993), pl. 53, 56; *Codex Vaticanus 3773* B (Graz: Akademische Druck - u. Verlagsanstalt, 1972), pl. 96; and *Codex Vaticanus 3738* A (*Codex Rios*) (Graz: Akademische Druck - u. Verlagsanstalt, 1979), 54r.

248. Heyden, *Eagle, Cactus, Rock*, 53–54, 68. See also Berdan and Anawalt, eds., *The Essential Codex Mendoza*, 7; and Serrato-Combe, *The Aztec Templo Mayor*.

249. Leonardo López Luján, *The Offerings of the Templo Mayor of Tenochtitlan*, rev. ed., trans. Bernard R. Ortiz Montellano and Thelma Ortiz de Montellano (Albuquerque: University of New Mexico Press, 2005), 65. See also Zantwijk, *The Aztec Arrangement*.

250. See Brundage, *The Fifth Sun*; Solís, *The Aztec Empire*, 139, 143–46; Brotherston, *Feather Crown*, 53; and Heyden, *Eagle, Cactus, Rock*, 68.

251. Heyden, *Eagle, Cactus, Rock*, 68.

252. León-Portilla, *Aztec Image of Self and Society*, 208–9. See also Kendall, *Patolli*.

253. Elizabeth M. Brumfiel, "Asking about Gender: The Historical and Archaeological Evidence," in *Gender in Prehispanic America*, ed. Cecelia Klein (Washington, DC: Dumbarton Oaks, 2001), 71–73.

254. Solís, "Monuments," 100.

255. Ibid., chapter 4, figures 47–57, 65, 66, 85, 100–105, 112, 116, 122, 123, and 138; and Jorge Enciso, *Design Motifs of Ancient Mexico* (New York: Dover Publications, 1953), 145–46.

256. Köhler, "Significance of the Aztec Day Sign."

257. Séjourné, *Burning Water*; and Doris Heyden, "Sellos con el símbolo ollin," *Boletín del INAH* 25 (1966): 39.

258. Heyden, *Eagle, Cactus, Rock*, 133, fig. 35.

259. Köhler, "Significance of the Aztec Day Sign"; Heyden, *Eagle, Cactus, Rock*, 67; Seler, *Commentarios al Códice Borgia*, I: 16–17, 149–50; Broda, "Astronomy"; Broda, "Astronomical Knowledge." Others scholars include Alfredo Chavero, Francisco del Paso y Troncoso, and Antonio León y Gama (see Köhler, "Significance of the Aztec Day Sign"; Vega Sosa, "El Curso del Sol," 153, 160). Seler (*Commentarios al Códice Borgia*, I: 149) claims the olin symbol depicts "the path traveled by . . . the sun" (*el camino que recorre . . . el Sol*). Köhler ("Significance of the Aztec Day Sign," 119) also characterizes the olin motif as a "stylistic expression of the annual course of the sun around the earth."

260. Durán, *Book of the Gods and Rites*, 187.

261. Séjourné, *Burning Water*, 93–94.

262. Seler, *Commentarios al Códice Borgia*, I: 16–17; Solís, *The Aztec Empire*, 100. Heyden (*Eagle, Cactus, Rock*, 69) claims chalchihuitl circles symbolize preciousness, jade, water, flowers, plants, and seeds – that is, generative and regenerative power.

263. Köhler, "Significance of the Aztec Day Sign," 122.

264. Bernardino de Sahagún, *Primeros memoriales: Facsimile Edition*, Códice Matritense de la Biblioteca del Real Palacio, *Historia de las cosas de Nueva España por Fr. Bernardino de Sahagún*, ed. Francisco del Paso y Troncoso, vol. 6 (Norman: University of Oklahoma Press, 1993), fol. 302v.

265. *Codex Tonalamatl Aubin* (Loubat, 1901), fol. 11.

266. Solís, "Monuments," chapter 4, figures 58–64, 110–24.

267. Matos Moctezuma, "The Aztec Calendar," 64.

268. As reported in Taube, "The Turquoise Hearth," 321.

269. Solís, "Monuments," 100.

270. Köhler, "Significance of the Aztec Day Sign," 133. Séjourné (*Burning Water*, 97, fig. a) presents an example of what she interprets as an interlocking olin glyph from Teotihuacan. Vega Sosa ("El Curso del Sol," 148, lam. 13; 150, lam. 15) presents examples from Late Aztec ceramics of what she regards as interlocking olin glyphs. Chapter 5 argues her examples are malinalli glyphs.

271. López Austin, *Human Body and Ideology*, II:glossary, 292; see also I:60.

272. López Luján, *Offerings*, 198. McKeever Furst (*Natural History of the Soul*, 18) writes: "In Postclassic symbolism throughout Mexico, motion – especially in a spiraling trajectory – forms a distinct category. Motion appears as two twisted bands and was sufficiently important to be incorporated into the calendar as the day sign olin." McKeever Furst makes two errors: she confounds twisting with olin and confounds olin with malinalli. Vega Sosa ("El Curso del Sol") also misidentifies olin with twisting. The motifs she discusses depict malinalli, not olin.

273. Köhler, "Significance of the Aztec Day Sign," 113.

Malinalli represents a second kind of motion-change, a second principal pattern in teotl's ceaseless becoming and transforming, and a second way of unifying agonistic inamic partners.

5.1. LINGUISTIC EVIDENCE

According to Jeanette Peterson, the word *malinalli* refers to a family of botanically related, native perennial wild grasses today called *zacaton* or *zacate de casa* by residents of the area surrounding Malinalco ("Place of Malinalli").[1] The grasses share several physical characteristics: feathery, seed-bearing flowers that grow in tuftlike bunches; bunches of single compound flower shafts; rough, sharp-edged leaves; and stalks that grow in tuftlike clusters. They also share certain functional features. The flower stalks are used as brooms and as drinking straws; the leaves are used for roofing, cords, ropes, nets, baskets, and mats; and the roots are used as brushes. *Codex Cruz* (fol. 12v) depicts a malinalli plant.[2] Bernardino de Sahagún describes a grass he calls *zacamamaztli* or *teocalzacatl* that appears to be this plant.[3]

Some scholars translate malinalli as "wild grass"[4] or "grass,"[5] others as "twisted grass"[6] or "twisted herb."[7] The glyph for the day sign, Malinalli, is commonly translated as "wild grass,"[8] "twisted grass,"[9] "twisted thing, herb rope, broom,"[10] or "'twisted' or an herb of this name."[11] Why is this family of grasses called *malinalli* ("twisted")? Perhaps the meaning of *malinalli* holds the key. *Malinalli* is formed from the verb, *malina*, meaning "to twist." The addition of the suffix, *-lli*, transforms the verb into a resultant-state deverbative noun that

DOI: 10.5876_9781607322238.c005

refers to something that has undergone the action of the verb *malina*. *Malinalli* thus means "that which has been twisted" or "twisted thing."[12]

What additional clues does the linguistic record hold concerning the nature of malinalli motion-change? Alonso de Molina lists the following entries:[13] *malina* ("to twist a cord on one's thigh"), *malinqui* ("something twisted, like a cord"), *malintiuetzi* ("for two persons to fall on the ground"), *mecamalina* ("to make, to twist cords"), *tepitzmalina* ("to twist a cord, rope or thread hard"),[14] *tlammalintli* ("twisted cord or rope or something similar"), *tlateteuhmalintli* ("something twisted tightly"), and *xomalina* ("to cross one's legs").

Rémi Siméon defines *malina* as "to twist something on one's thigh,"[15] Andrés de Olmos translates it as "to twist thread (or something similar)."[16] Alfredo López Austin defines *malina* as "to twist over itself, like a rope."[17] Peterson translates *malina* as "to twist or braid" and *malinalli* as "twisted or woven thing."[18] Frances Karttunen claims *malina* functions as a reflexive or transitive verb that means "to wind, twist; to wind, to twist, to sprain something." When "fused with the prefix '*tla-*', this means 'to make rope.'"[19] She also lists *tlamalintli* ("rope"), *tlamalinqui* ("rope maker"), and *tlamalina* ("to make rope").[20] Siméon translates *malinalli* as "twined or twisted around itself; twisting climbing plant, plaided without doubt for the construction of houses; broom."[21] Siméon's translation is illuminating since it makes explicit the perceived similarity between the naturally occurring twisting of malinalli grass and spiraling of shoots, vines, and tendrils, on the one hand, and the twisting of grass into rope by humans, on the other. He translates *malinqui as* "twisted, retwisted like a rope" and *malintiuh* as "to be twisted, to be doubled [upon itself], to be folded or creased."[22]

In the process of making rope, cordage, and thread, one seizes raw, disorderly, and disheveled fiber – be it malinalli grass, cotton, or maguey – and twists it. In so twisting one *transforms disordered fiber into ordered thread, rope, or cordage.* One gives that which has been twisted a power that it did not previously possess. By "twisting handfuls of short, weak plant fibre," writes Patricia Anawalt, one creates "long, strong string."[23] The direction may be a Z-twist or an S-twist. And if desired, single threads may be retwisted in the opposite direction so as to create plies (or strands) of two or more single threads.

Spinning is "the operation by which continuous threads are made by stretching and twisting the fibers."[24] This is accomplished by using a spindle, a straight wooden stick (shaft) with tapered ends. The spinning and gyrating of the spindle shaft are steadied by the spindle whorl, which is typically circular or disk-shaped. Rough fiber is twisted into thread or rope by means of a combination of gyrating spindle (shaft and whorl) together with the seizing and twisting of the fiber by hand. It is the human who contributes the actual twisting of the fiber; the spindle simply facilitates the process. One may twist fiber without a spindle by rubbing the fiber against one's thigh. One similarly makes rope, twining, and cordage directly from grass by twisting bunches of cut grass and gradually adding more grass to what has already been twisted. One makes stronger rope by retwisting in the opposite direction the threads one has already created. The pattern repeats that of twisting thread for clothing. In short, twisting transforms grass into something useful, strong, and well-ordered.

Twisting transforms something disorderly and deranged into something orderly and well arranged; something weak into something strong; something useless into something useful. Twisting is therefore a species of ordering and transformative motion-change that is in a very important sense positive, beneficial, and desirable from the standpoint of human beings. It would therefore be a mistake to equate being malinalli-twisted per se with tlazolli or with being disheveled, unbalanced, messy, polluted, deranged, disordered, and negative.[25] Being twisted carries positive connotative force in classical Nahuatl discourse (unlike contemporary popular North American discourse).

The Aztecs conceived vines, tendrils, and climbing plants as twisted or twisting. Because they grow (move-change) in a twisting manner, they are conceptually associated with malinalli. For example, *mouicoma xocomecatl* means "vine or something similar that climbs up a tree" and *xocomecamaitl* means "vine or tendril."[26] Vines and tendrils move-change in the same pattern of motion-change involved in making of rope, cordage, thread, and twining.

In sum, the verb *malina* and the noun *malinalli* are conceptually associated with twisting and that which is (or has been) twisted. Malinalli motion-change is twisting motion-change. Malinalli twisting is a species of *transformational* motion-change: it transforms that which is weak into that which is powerful; that which is useless into that which is useful; and that which is disordered into that which is well ordered. Malinalli twisting thus transforms one *kind* of thing (wild grass) into another *kind* of thing (thread and rope); transforms something in one *condition* (disorderly) into something in another *condition* (well ordered); and transforms one state or way of being into another state or way of being. This, after all, is what happens when one twists wild grass into thread and rope. In what follows I refer to this process as *malinalli motion-change* in order to distinguish it from malinalli grass and the day sign Malinalli. When speaking of the latter two, I use *malinalli grass* and *Malinalli day sign*, respectively.

In his entry for *malina* R. Joe Campbell refers us to *malacatl*, which he translates as "*huso*" or "spindle."[27] Siméon derives *malacatl* from *malinalli* ("to twist") and *acatl* ("*caña*," "reed").[28] Karttunen adds "bobbin, spiral."[29] What is the basis of Campbell's referral? One twists raw fiber into thread with the help of a spindle, and a spindle is an object that one spins and twists. Let's look then at *malacatl*. Molina contains the following *malacatl*-related constructions:[30] *cemmalacatentli* ("a spindle [or corncob] of thread"),[31] *ecamalacotl* ("whirlwind"; literally, "wind spindle"), *malacachiuhcayotl* ("roundness of a shield or table"), *malacachoa* ("to revolve, to turn around, to walk around; to turn or spin something around"), *mamalacachoa* ("to go in a circle"), *malacachihui* ("to spin, revolve"), *tlamalacachiuhcatectli* ("something rounded and trimmed"), and *tonacatzon mamalacachuiuhca* ("curls behind the ears"). Revealing post-Contact entries include *amalacachtli* ("irrigating wheel"), *quauhtemalaca* ("axle of a cart"), and *quauhtemalacatl* ("wheel of a cart or barrow"). Olmos translates *malacachotinemi* as "to spin or turn around something."[32] Karttunen lists *malacaehecatl* ("whirlwind") and *malacachtic* ("something round, circular").[33]

James Lockhart suggests *malacatl* is not an arbitrary name for a spindle.[34] *Malacatl* and its related constructions derive from *ilaca*, meaning "to twist" and "thus would inherently have had something to do with revolving."[35] Related constructions include *ilcatzihui* ("to twist, entwine"), *ilacatzoa* ("to turn one's body in order not to see or look at someone that one hates; for a snake to wrap itself around a tree; to roll up a blanket, mat, piece of paper or to wind up thread or string on one's finger"), *ilacatztic* ("something twisted"), *quauilacatzoa* ("to twist and join plants together"), and *teteuilacachtic* ("whirlwind or something similar").[36]

In sum, central to the concept of a malacatl are processes of spinning, whirling, revolving, and gyrating as well as the shape of roundedness and circularity. *Malacatl* refers to things that spin, gyrate, or revolve (such as spindles, curls of hair, whirlwinds, axles, wheels, and pulleys), and to things that have been rounded or made circular (such as shields, tables, grindstones, wheels, and pulleys). *Malacachoa* functions both as a transitive verb meaning "to spin or turn something around" and a reflexive verb meaning "to turn or revolve." *Mamalacachoa* means "to go around in a circle."

In making thread, one seizes and spins disorderly wild fiber. In so doing one transforms the disorderly into the orderly. This may involve twisting the fibers by rolling them over and over against one's thigh or using a spindle set consisting of spindle shaft, spindle whorl, and spinning bowl (*tzaoalcaxitl*).[37] Hereafter I refer to the spindle set as the "spindle" (*malacatl*). When it matters I will specify whether I am talking about the shaft, whorl, or bowl.[38] The complete spindle unit is constructed by inserting the tapered end of the spindle shaft into the hole at the whorl's center. During spinning, the whorl sits inside a bowl and

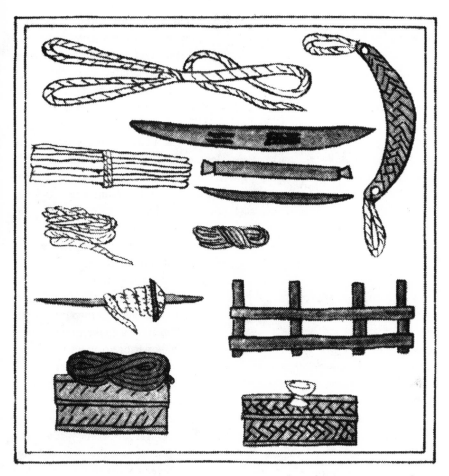

FIGURE 5.1. *Weaving and spinning equipment. (Sahagún [1953–1982, VIII: Figure 75]; courtesy of University of Utah Press.)*

acts as a flywheel for the shaft. Together, whorl and bowl center and stabilize the spindle's gyrating. This makes possible the efficient twisting of disordered fiber into well-ordered thread (rope, cordage, or twine), that is, into tight, even thread without lumps or knots (see Figure 5.1).[39]

Thelma Sullivan observes that spinning and spinning instruments are highly charged with sexual symbolism. The insertion of the spindle shaft into the whorl's center hole suggests sexual intercourse.[40] Bernardino de Sahagún records several sexually suggestive riddles: "What are those things which, at their dancing place, they give stomachs, they make pregnant? They are spindles [*malacatl*],"[41] and "What is it that becomes pregnant in only one day? The spindle [*malacatl*]."[42] The spindle was said to "dance" in the bowl or "dancing place." As for the child, it is the spindle pregnant with a load of thread.

Tzahua also means "to spin thread (*hilar*)."[43] The association between spinning and a spindle's becoming laden with thread, on the one hand, and sexual intercourse and pregnancy on the other, is further suggested by other *tzahua*-related constructions: *axixtetzaualiztli* ("something thick which appears in one's urine, like threads"), *tetzactic* ("something thick or congealed like gum or porridge"), and *tetzaua* ("for a liquid to thicken or congeal"). The Aztecs saw the development of the *in utero* fetus as a coagulating that resembles the coagulating of thread upon a spindle rod.

What, then, is the relationship between the malina-malinalli conceptual cluster, on the one hand, and the malacachoa-malacatl conceptual cluster on the other? What is the relationship between twisting, twining, and winding, on the one hand, and spinning, gyrating, whirling, and revolving on the other? The foregoing suggests Aztec metaphysics regards the two clusters as equivalent and consequently regards twisting, spiraling, spinning, gyrating, curling, revolving, and whirling as one and the same kind of transformative motion-change. In what follows I treat twisting-spinning as a single pattern of motion: what I call *malinalli-twisting-spinning*, or *malinalli-twisting* for short.

The foregoing also suggests twisting and spinning are transformative patterns of motion-change. They transform one kind of thing (wild grass or cotton) into another kind of thing (thread or rope); something in one condition (disorderly, wild, and peripheral) into something in another condition (well ordered and centered); and one state of being into another. Indeed, in light of the centrality of twisting and spinning in weaving, and the role of weaving as organizing metaphor in Aztec metaphysics, I submit twisting-spinning plays a central role in Aztec metaphysics' conception of how reality is ordered, how it processes, and how it is transformed.

Finally, the foregoing offers us a glimpse into how malinalli motion-change differs from olin motion-change. Olin motion-change involves transformation *within and across* life~death cycles. By contrast, malinalli motion-change involves transformation *between* different kinds of things (cotton into thread), *between* different conditions of the same thing (disorderly into orderly), and (as we will see shortly) *between* vertical layers of the cosmos. Not coincidentally, the spinner of thread holds her spindle rod vertically when spinning fiber into thread, and the thread moves up and down the vertical spindle rod in the course of its transformation from fiber into thread.

Figures 5.2A–B. *Tlaltecuhtli's head and disheveled hair. (a, author's photo; b, redrawn from Peterson [1983:142, Figure 11].)*

5.2. LITERARY EVIDENCE

Malinalli Grass and Malinalli Motion-Change

Malinalli Grass as Tlaltecuhtli's Hair

What do the written sources tell us about the nature of malinalli and its role in Aztec metaphysics? The Aztecs considered malinalli grass to be the hair of Tlaltecuhtli ("Earth Lord~Lady"). As such, it both symbolized and manifested Tlaltecuhtli's fertility, fecundity, comestible abundance, vigor, regenerative and restorative powers, and life-energy.[44] The *Histoyre du Mechique* describes Tlaltecuhtli as the source of life: from her hair come the trees, flowers, and plants; from her skin, the smaller plants and flowers; from her many eyes, the springs, fountains, and small caves; and from her mouth, the caverns from which rivers emerge.[45] Aztec artists standardly depicted Tlaltecuhtli with hair consisting of malinalli-grass leaves and spikelike, featherlike flowers at the end of their long, narrow stalks (see Figures 5.2, 5.3, and 5.4).

Aztecs artists often depicted Tlaltecuhtli's grass/hair as well groomed into neatly twisting swirls, curves, and curls with loose spirals at their base (Figures 5.3, 5.4). These symbolized Tlaltecuhtli's ordering, centering, and ever-burgeoning life-energy as well as ever-rejuvenating fecundity, potency, and growth. Yet other times they depicted Tlaltecuhtli's grass/hair as ill-kempt, disheveled, and entangled with spiders, centipedes, and scorpions (Figure 5.2). The Aztecs associated these creatures with darkness, night, death, and the underworld. Spiders, centipedes, and scorpions symbolized tlazolli (i.e., that which is rotten, used up, disintegrated, and decayed – in short, matter out of place), hence impurity and pollution, and hence the dangerously disordering forces of the

FIGURE 5.3. *Tlaltecuhtli's head and well-groomed hair. (Redrawn from Peterson [1983:142, Figure 12].)*

FIGURE 5.4. *Tlaltecuhtli's head and well-groomed hair. (Redrawn from Matos Moctezuma and López Luján [2007:22].)*

earth-mother-goddess complex.[46] Figure 5.2 depicts raw cotton balls between the flower stalks of Tlaltecuhtli's malinalli grass/hair, connecting both Him~Her and malinalli grass with sacrifice.[47] Persons associated with or intended for sacrifice customarily wore raw cotton balls. The Aztecs treated sacrificial victims – or more precisely, the energies they contained – as raw material to be ordered by spinning and subsequently fed into the ongoing weaving of the cosmos. Unspun balls of cotton fiber symbolize disorder and derangement.[48]

These depictions suggest Tlaltecuhtli is ontologically ambiguous. As H. B. Nicholson remarks, Tlaltecuhtli is the great "womb and tomb of all life."[49] How Tlaltecuhtli is depicted on any given occasion therefore depends upon which aspect the artist wished to emphasize. Ill-kempt, tangled hair emphasizes the mortuary aspects of Tlaltecuhtli and hence degenerative, disordering transformation. Well-groomed hair that is carefully twisted and braided into curves and spirals emphasizes the parturient aspects of Tlaltecuhtli and hence generative, ordering transformation. This fact further supports the claim that it is a mistake to equate that which is twisted or twistedness per se with that which is disheveled, entangled, and mossy haired; hence that which is disordered as well as deranged, and hence that which is dangerous, impure, and polluted – that is, in short, with tlazolli. Twisting involves ordering and arranging. It transforms the raw, disordered, and deranged into something well-ordered and arranged. It gives its object a shape conducive to the transmission of energy; a shape that allows energy to flow freely; a shape without crimps, pinches, or kinks that obstruct energy flow. Twisting transforms chaotic clumps of cotton, malinalli

FIGURE 5.5. *Drunkard. (Sahagún [1953–1982, IV: Figure 8]; courtesy of the University of Utah Press.)*

grass, or maguey fiber into orderly strands of thread ready for fashioning into fabric or cordage. Twisting Tlaltecuhtli's hair orders it and makes it useful to human purposes.

Compare the well-coiffed hairstyles of Tlaltecuhtli in Figures 5.3 and 5.4 with the hairstyles of the drunkard (see Figure 5.5) and the *tzonpachpul* ("the big mossy-haired one";[50] see Figure 5.6) portrayed in the *Florentine Codex*. The hair of the latter two is disheveled, entangled, and disordered. The Nahuatl word for disheveled person, *quaichpol*, combines *quaitl* ("head"), *icthli* ("a tow of maguey fiber"),[51] and *pol* (a compounding derogative implying large size or degree).[52]

FIGURE 5.6. *Tzonpachpul ("the big mossy-haired one"). (Sahagún [1953–1982, VI: Figure 42]; courtesy of the University of Utah Press.)*

Tow in this context suggests a loose, coarse, and unkempt bunch of fibers or strands prepared for spinning but not yet spun. Once again, disheveled differs from twisted and spun. Sahagún's informants describe the drunkard as having *quapopolpol* ("a lot or high degree of mussed up hair") and *quatzomapol* ("a lot or high degree of matted hair"). They do *not* describe the drunkard's hair as twisted or braided.[53]

During the seventeenth veintena, *Tititl*, the Aztecs sacrificed a person who impersonated Ilamatecuhtli ("Old Woman"), the most venerable of the earth deities and an aspect of the genetrix complex of the great spinner-weaver Tlazolteotl-Ixcuina.[54] The deity impersonator wore a headdress (*tzompilinalli*) consisting of eagle feathers "twisted, ordered, arrayed" (*tlamalatini, tlahuipantli, tlahuipanalli*) with one another. This juxtaposition of twisted with ordered and arrayed further suggests twistedness is *not* to be equated with disorderliness and tlazolli.

Malinalli Grass as Tonalli-Bearing

The Aztecs believed hair to be one of the primary repositories of tonalli, that is, vitality, heat, strength, and animating life-force received primarily from the Sun. As Tlaltecuhtli's hair, malinalli grass is rich in tonalli. López Austin argues the concept of tonalli centers around the concept of heat-light energy that radiates throughout the Fifth Era from the Fifth Sun and the four tlaloque or sacred trees rooted at the four corners of the earthly plane.[55] Jill McKeever Furst maintains the concept of tonalli is united by "a series of ideas and metaphors that radiate from the central quality [of tonalli] as heat."[56] Tonalli diffuses over the earth's surface, "bathing" and "infiltrating" and thereby energizing and influencing all things.[57] However, tonalli's energy and influence are not uniform. They vary *qualitatively* from day to day with the passing of the 260-day tonalpohualli. There appear to be 260 qualitatively different kinds of tonalli, one for each day of the 260-day cycle, and hence 260 different kinds of tonalli-defined influence bathing the earthly plane. What's more, any given day's specific tonalli changes *quantitatively* over the course of the day with the intensity of the sun: growing stronger as the day waxes, weaker as it wanes. The more tonalli something possesses, the "hotter" it is; the less tonalli, the "colder."

Humans derive their tonalli primarily from the Sun. The kind of tonalli one possesses depends primarily upon one's birthday. A person's tonalli functions as her inner vigor, power, energy, and character. Willard Gingerich writes, "Tonalli is the quality of force that determines the level of animating vitality in the individual."[58] It permeates the entire human mind-body fusion. The vitality of a person's tonalli is manifested in her pulse and body heat, and growth rate of her body, hair, and nails. The highest concentration of tonalli occurs in the head, especially the crown, forehead, and face. Other areas of high concentration include the joints, blood, nails, and hair. The Aztecs valued hair in particular for its capacity to contain and convey tonalli.[59]

Tonalli may be transferred between people, and one of the principal means of doing so involves transferring hair. By seizing an enemy's topknot, a warrior seized the tonalli held therein. In this way he added the captive's tonalli to his own and to his altepetl's tonalli, rejuvenating and fortifying them (see Figure 5.7). Aztec priests cut the hair from prisoners' heads before sacrificing them. Both priests and captors valued these topknots as powerful, tonalli-charged objects, and employed them in various rituals. Warriors preferred capturing courageous rather than cowardly enemy warriors since they possessed superior tonalli. In this way, Sahagún's informants add, the captive's life force, valor, and renown would perish not in vain.[60]

Human blood is also rich in tonalli and consequently possesses the power to generate, rejuvenate, and fortify. Ritual heart and blood sacrifice amounted to a tonalli transfusion from victim to intended recipient (e.g., Tonatiuh). McKeever Furst suggests the Aztecs regarded the captured warrior as a precious, tonalli-filled "sponge" from whom to squeeze, drain, and transfer energy.[61]

Tonalli is a fully general and impersonal force. It is unique neither to individual humans nor to human beings as such. It resides only temporarily in any

FIGURE 5.7. *Warrior seizing a captive's topknot. (*Codex Mendoza *[1997: folio 64r]; courtesy of Frances F. Berdan and Patricia Rieff Anawalt.)*

given human and upon death recycles into the cosmos. Tonalli is absorbed by animals and plants as well as fire, statues, gemstones, brilliantly colored bird feathers, animal skins, and warriors' costumes. Humans are able to perceive (e.g., by sight and touch) the tonalli contained within things.[62] In sum, tonalli diffuses over the earth's surface and its inhabitants, and in so doing energizes and influences them.

Tlaltecuhtli is constantly bathed and infused with heat-light energy coming from Tonatiuh and the four corners, and consequently contains a vast reserve of tonalli. The vigor and potency of Tlaltecuhtli's tonalli is manifested in the growth of grasses, plants, and trees. Tlaltecuhtli's tonalli is highly concentrated in her hair, that is, in malinalli grass. Indeed, the recurring efflorescence of malinalli grasses on the earth's surface expresses Tlaltecuhtli's generative vitality and power. Aztec artists accordingly depicted Tlaltecuhtli's tonalli by grasses growing atop her head. Tlaltecuhtli is also subject to quantitative variations in tonalli due to the Sun's diurnal motion-change as well as qualitative variations in tonalli due to the passing of the 260 days of the tonalpohualli. This helps explain the variation in the Earth's quantities and qualities of agricultural potency and fertility over the course of the day and year. It also helps explain the timing of Aztec ritual sacrifices to Tlaltecuhtli. These rituals would seem appropriately timed to correspond to times when Tlaltecuhtli is in need of tonalli transfusions in order to boost and fortify Her~His tonalli due to seasonal tonalli poverty.

As Tlaltecuhtli's hair, malinalli grass is thus tonalli-bearing. Just as the Aztecs valued human hair for its role in holding, conveying, and transmitting tonalli, so they valued malinallli grass for its role in holding, conveying, and transferring tonalli. Malinalli grass does not therefore merely symbolize or metaphorically signify Tlaltecuhtli's life force. Malinalli grass and those things fabricated from it – for example, rope, nets, mats, roofs, divining cords, autosacrificial cords, brooms, and medicine – contain and convey Tlaltecuhtli's vital energy. Their properties and powers reflect the quality and quantity of tonalli possessed by the malinalli grass from which they are made.

The same holds for cotton. According to the *Histoyre du Mechique*, cotton grew from the hair (corn silk) of Cinteotl ("Dried Corn God" or "Sacred Dried Corn").[63] Cotton is a tonalli-bearing substance like human hair and malinalli grass. The Aztecs valued cotton for its role in holding, conveying, and transmitting tonalli. Cotton and those things fabricated from it (e.g., woven clothing) accordingly symbolize, embody, and convey Cinteotl's tonalli and regenerative potency. This fact (along with its greater comfort) helps explain the Aztec nobility's preference for cotton over maguey clothing and their claim to its exclusive use.

Several consequences follow from the foregoing. First, malinalli-fabricated products possess Tlaltecuhtli's tonalli-fueled vitalizing and ordering power to make things happen. The vigor of this power is explained at least partially in terms of the potency of the tonalli these products contain. Second, the success of divining, curing, carrying, ensnaring, and sweeping depends partly upon the potency of the tonalli contained by the malinalli grass from which their respective instruments are fabricated. Third, humans acquire a tonalli boost from wearing, handling, and using malinalli-fabricated items, just as they do from wearing, possessing, or displaying avian feathers and captive's topknots. Fourth, malinalli grasses have flowers and these must be viewed in the same way the Aztecs viewed all flowers, namely, as especially rich in life-energy. Fifth, the fact that the Aztecs characterized malinalli flowers as feathers and likened feathers to hair suggests they saw malinalli grass flowers as especially potent with tonalli.

The Aztecs equated well-ordered hair with strong, healthy tonalli and equated disordered hair with weak and unhealthy tonalli.[64] They saw caring for one's hair as a way of protecting and fortifying one's tonalli, which in turn protected one's well-being.[65] One way to accomplish this was to keep one's hair well ordered. The same holds for malinalli grass and its tonalli. Just as braiding or plaiting hair is a way of preserving, protecting, and fortifying its tonalli, so braiding, plaiting, or twisting malinalli grass is a way of preserving, protecting, and fortifying its tonalli. And just as braiding hair is one way of ordering it, so malinalli-twisting

Tlaltecuhtli's hair is one way of ordering it. Twisting and braiding are thus ways of acquiring some measure of control over the tonalli power contained within grass. Malinalli twisting enables humans to tap into and utilize this energy in their activities or to transfer it to themselves or others. Peterson suggests the Aztecs extended the properties of malinalli grass to other species of grass (*zacatl*) since all grasses were regarded as Tlaltecuhtli's hair and hence tonalli-bearing. Thus it does not often matter whether an item is fabricated from malinalli or some other species of grass.[66] Let's examine some of the ways the Aztecs used the tonalli contained within malinalli grass.

Using the Tonalli within Malinalli Grass

Malinalli grass played a vital role in Aztec life. One of the principal and most important uses of malinalli grass was twisting it into rope, cordage, and twining.[67] The Nahuatl word *mecatl* means "cord or rope, whip made out of knotted cords, vine."[68] Mecatl is at the center of a rich cluster of concepts. The twisted shape of rope and cordage is attested by the related word *xocomecamaitl* ("vine or tendril").[69] *Zacamecatl* means "rope of feather-grass, or of something similar."[70] The Aztecs employed malinalli-grass ropes in a variety of capacities. They fashioned tumplines (*mecapalli*) for carrying loads on one's back.[71] They depicted the year bearers as porters carrying their burdens with tumplines made of twisted rope.[72] Backstrap weavers employed cordage (*mecamaxalli*) to secure the loom to a post or tree and a braided backstrap (*neanoni*) to bind the weaver to the loom.[73] They constructed baskets, bundling, and boxes from malinalli grass.[74] Antonio Peñafiel states malinalli grass was woven into carrying sacks.[75]

The Aztecs employed malinalli grass in fabricating traps and snares (*mazamecatl*) for hunting and transporting wild game such as deer.[76] Fishermen used twisted malinalli grass in making fish nets and fishing lines (*michmecatl*).[77] Hunters, reports Hernando Ruiz de Alarcón, sang incantations to their ropes in order enlist the cooperation of the ropes' energies in completing their task. They addressed their ropes as *nohueltiuh cenmalinalli* ("my older sister, one twisted grass")[78] and as Cihuacoatl ("Woman-snake").[79] Cihuacoatl is a member of the female genetrix and earth-goddess complex along with Teteoinnan, Tlazolteotl-Ixcuina, and Toci.[80] These incantations suggest hunters viewed their ropes as vivified by Tlaltecuhtli's tonalli. More generally, artisans, hunters, and farmers addressed the vivifying energies in their tools with *nahuallatolli* ("secret or hidden words") in order to solicit their cooperation and effective performance.[81] Presumably other workers adopted the same attitude toward tumplines, brooms, baskets, drinking straws, measuring cords, and mats.

Malinalli-twisted ropes played an essential role in the ordering of things. During the Binding of the Years Ceremony (*xiuhmolpilli*) that occurred every 52 years, Aztec priests bound together 52 wooden poles (each symbolizing one year) by means of four twisted ropes. [82] In light of the metaphysical and symbolic importance of malinalli grass, it is reasonable to suppose that the ropes were made by twisting malinalli grass. The ropes bound together and kept well ordered the 52 years of the Aztec "century" and hence bound together and kept well ordered time-place itself during the Fifth Age. In this way the Aztecs attempted to order the passing of time, bind together past and future, and guarantee the continuity of time between 52-year cycles. The Aztecs accordingly also employed twisted rope as *mecatlapoa* ("counting-reading rope") that is, for divining the future by means of cords.[83] After all, if time-place is bound together and ordered by ropes, then counting-reading ropes is an obvious way to divine the significance of time-place. When ordering and arranging their milpas, the Aztecs measured land using a malinalli-twisted cord called a *tlalmecatl*.[84] Contemporary Quiché Maya continue to use the ancient unit of land measurement called a *c'a'm* ("cord").[85]

Slaves, war captives, criminals, and sacrificial victims were bound using ropes that ordered them and bound them to their destiny. *Tepuzmecayotia*, for example, means "to chain someone."[86] To set someone free is "to cut their rope" (*tlatequililli iuic imecapal*).[87] Codical depictions of sacrificial victims standardly include ropes.[88] The Aztecs used ropes in corporeal punishment such as whipping and garroting.[89] Lastly, funerary bundles and effigies were bound and so ordered with ropes that appear to have been made from malinalli grass.[90]

Aztec artisans braided and wove mats, seats, and thrones for persons of authority from palm leaves, reeds, and malinalli grass. These objects symbolized royal authority. The Aztecs commonly used the word *petlatl* ("mat") to refer to authority and government, equating the mat with the throne. The Aztecs invested their rulers on woven reed thrones.[91] Sahagún's informants report that boys of noble birth were trained to "assume the reed mat, assume the reed seat of authority." The sacred ancestors and founders of Tenochtitlán and its four calpoltin were called *petlacontzitzquique* ("keepers of the mat and the urns").[92] When carefully braided, woven mats contained Tlaltecuthli's tonalli-energy that was conveyed to their occupants. They functioned as ordered and ordering time-places ideally suited for conducting important religious, ritual, judicial, epistemological, and political activities. They transmitted their accumulated tonalli power to those who sat or stood upon them – rulers, judges, diviners, and midwives, for example – heating and empowering them with tonalli-power.

Codex Mendoza (fol. 61r) depicts a wedding ceremony conducted on a woven mat.[93] Woven mats symbolized fertility and sexuality for the Mixtecs, for example. Sexual intercourse occurred on mats. Women gave birth on mats.[94] Weavers also sat upon woven malinalli grass mats. Sahagún's illustration of spinning and weaving equipment includes a mat (see Figure 5.1).

The Aztecs performed various rituals *upon* grass in a special time-place called *zacapan* ("on [the] grass"). According to Durán, this consisted of layers of special mountain grass spread upon the ground (if outdoors) or floor (if indoors).[95] Angel Garibay K. identifies the grass as a species related to malinalli.[96] An outdoor zacapan functioned as a makeshift ritual space. Of an indoor zacapan, Durán writes: "Truly the entire floor was covered with dry grass, resembling the way in which floors are covered today to receive guests and envoys."[97] During the festival of Tlacaxipehualiztli, freshly excised hearts dedicated to Xipe were "cast into a place called Zacapan which means On the Straw, where the sacrificer of the gods stood."[98]

What made a zacapan special? First, it constituted a well-ordered, tonalli-rich time-place that reproduced Tlaltecuhtli's tonalli-rich grassy hills and that was consequently well suited for transmitting power. It constituted a time-place of malinalli-defined transformation. One created this potent time-place by spreading grass upon the ground or floor. The grass had to be arrayed carefully on pain of the zacapan's being a disorderly tlazolli dump. Contemporary Wixáritari, for example, transport a ritually hunted, captured, and slain deer to a temple wherein the deer is placed upon a bed of grass. They liken this bed of grass to the bed of grass upon which human babies are born. The deer's dying is equivalent to the bringing of new life into the world.[99] In short, properly arranged beds of grass function as time-places of malinalli-enabled and -defined transformation.

Malinalli mats, seats, thrones, and zacapans operated as effective time-places of malinalli-defined transformation and energy transmission. They did this by creating a tonalli-rich time-place in which to conduct important functions and ritual performances. They supercharged their occupants with the tonalli-power stored in the grass from which they were made. And they operated as bidirectional conduits for transmitting power. They enabled humans to download and make use of cosmic power in their ritual proceedings as well as upload and transfuse to the cosmos power acquired from the grass and blood sacrifice. The association between malinalli grass and blood sacrifice suggests a further association between malinalli grass and death, nourishment, and rebirth. The bidirectionality of these artifacts evokes the "nurturing and devouring aspects of the earth."[100]

Aztec priests and nobles used hollow grass stalks and twisted cords (called *nezahualmecameh* or "cords of penance") as implements of autosacrifice.[101] These most likely consisted of malinalli grass. *Codex Telleriano Remensis* (fol. 9r) depicts a penitent male priest forcing what appears to be a bundle of malinalli grass through his tongue.[102] As penitents pulled them through holes cut in their tongues and calves, the grass cords and shafts amassed the tonalli-power contained in the penitents' blood, which was then transmitted to the cosmos. Penitents also pierced their tongues, calves, and ears with sharpened bones and maguey thorns. When sufficiently bloodied, they inserted the bones and thorns into grass balls called *zacatapayolli*. Sculptural and graphic depictions suggest the balls were carefully woven.[103] Sahagún's informants describe the grass balls as having "interlaced edges" (*tlatenxinepanolli*).[104] Interlacing the edges created well-ordered balls. The zacatapayolli with inserted thorns also resemble balls of spun thread with embroiderers' needles inserted. Peterson believes the balls were likely fabricated from malinalli grass.[105]

By transmitting their blood-based tonalli-power to the cosmos, humans aimed to revitalize the regenerative powers of the cosmos. They also hoped the cosmos would reciprocate by recycling this tonalli-energy into human and agricultural vitality and fertility.[106] Cecelia Klein argues the Aztecs treated such ritual bloodletting as "a symbolic death substituted for the real thing and as such a debt-payment."[107] I suggest it was a key component in the Aztecs' ethics of reciprocity and well balancedness.[108] The Aztecs named their religious school *calmecac* (*calli* ["house"] plus *mecatl* ["cords, ropes, whips"]), that is, "house of whips or penitence." Aztec priests also used grass shafts to feed the tonalli-rich blood of sacrificial victims to selected aspects of the cosmos. This involved dipping the shafts into the victims' blood and brushing them upon the relevant statues.[109] Here again we see malinalli grass linked with death, feeding, and rebirth.

The Aztecs topped many of their temples with carefully thatched, malinalli grass roofs. It is not implausible to suppose that the grass they used was the grass Sahagún identifies as *teocalzacatl* ("temple grass"), which appears to be malinalli grass.[110] The grass Sahagún's informants call zacamamaztli also fits the descriptions of malinalli. López Austin speculates the Nahuatl word *tzontli* ("hair of the head") gave rise to the verb *tzoma*, which means "to sew" and "to cover the hut with straw" as though "to give it [the hut] long hair."[111] Thatched malinalli grass roofs served as "hair" atop the "heads" of temples and in so doing topped the temples with Tlaltecuhtli's tonalli-rich energy. The conical roof of the famous circular Temple 1 at Malinalco, for example, consisted of thatched grass.[112] *Codex Telleriano-Remensis* (pl. 40r, 41v, and 42r) depicts temples with triple-thatched grass roofs.[113] Such roofs served several functions. First, they heated the interior of the temple with the tonalli energy-power stored in the malinalli grass and supercharged the temple's interior, occupants, and activities with this energy. Second, they served as a two-way cosmic conduit for power-energy conveyance. This enabled humans to download energy from the cosmos for ritual purposes as well as upload to the cosmos energy accumulated through blood sacrifice. Aztec scribe-artists standardly signified the capture of enemy towns by depicting the thatched roofs of the temples ablaze.[114]

Klein argues houses were woven, braided, and twisted together using ropes and cords of malinalli grass.[115] Siméon states malinalli was plaited or braided "without doubt for the construction of houses" (*"trenjada sin duda para la construcción de casas"*).[116] Contemporary Maya, for example, characterize the walls of their houses "as woven or braided" or "interwoven as in a braid or mat."[117]

Lastly, Juan de Torquemada writes of the medicinal uses of malinalli grass.[118] Noemí Quezada claims a concoction of malinalli mixed with other herbs was administered by midwives to pregnant women in order to prevent miscarriages. The drink was thought to energize the pregnant woman.[119] It may also have helped the fetus coagulate properly as well as pass more easily through the malinalli-shaped birth canal. *Codex Vaticanus* 3738 A (fol. 54r) suggests a connection between malinalli and those parts of the human body the Aztecs conceived as twisted like cords and ropes. It depicts a naked man surrounded by the twenty day signs of the tonalpohualli, each connected to a different part of the body. The text's commentator offers this interpretation: "Based on [the association of the twenty day signs with parts of the body], they cured men when they became ill or when some part of the body was truly in pain. . . . *malinalli* [had influence] on the intestines."[120] The text does not indicate whether malinalli grass was administered to cure intestinal disorder but it does associate both the Malinalli day sign and malinalli motion-change with the intestines (*cuitlaxcolli*, literally "twisted excrement") which the Aztecs conceived as twisted.[121] The intestines are twisted like rope.

Healing, curing, and midwifery commonly relied upon information obtained through divination, and one important method of divination was *mecatlapoa* ("to predict the future by means of cords").[122] A *mecatlapouhqui* was "one who counts the ropes."[123] The word *pohua* means "to count, to reckon, to read, to recount, to relate, to give account of, to assign something."[124] According to Torquemada, this involved interpreting the medical significance of knots tied in a rope by the diviner in the patient's presence. If upon tugging on both ends of the rope, the knots loosened and became untied, the patient would recover.[125] If they tightened, the patient would perish.[126]

In sum, malinalli grass abounds with tonalli power. Spinning, twisting, and plaiting malinalli grass locks in, orders, and fortifies this power, and makes it available for use in two-way transmissions between the cosmos and humans.

Grass Brooms, Sweeping, and Malinalli Motion-Change

Malinalli flower shafts (*pototes*) and their feathery flower tops become stiff when dried. The Aztecs bound together the stalks to make straw brooms, and the roots and flowers to make brushes. One of the Nahuatl words for broom and straw is *popotl*.[127] The Spanish side of Molina, the *Codex Borbonicus*, and Toribio de Benavente Motolinía all offer *escoba* or *escobilla* ("broom" or "little broom") as translations for the day sign Malinalli.[128] The Nahuatl word for "broom" is *tlachpanhuaztli* and for "sweeping," *tlachpanaliztli*.[129] Both derive from *tlachpana* ("to sweep something"), which derives from *ichpana* ("to sweep something").[130] Karttunen suggests *ichpana* may be related by metathesis to *chipahua* ("for something to become clean or pure").[131]

Sweeping with malinalli-grass brooms is a powerful and cosmically important metaphysical process in both ritual and nonritual contexts. Sweeping displaces and transmits the disorderly forces of tlazolli from the center to the periphery. In so doing it cleanses and purifies as well as orders, arranges, stabilizes, and balances the local time-place swept and the Fifth Sun-Earth Ordering at large. In so doing, as Thelma Sullivan observes, sweeping "marks the beginning, the inception."[132] Sweeping advances the recycling and transformation of tlazolli into a fertile, regenerating force. It is therefore not an insignificant quotidian chore but rather a causally potent, cosmically consequential, and metaphysically transformative activity. This is particularly true of sweeping temples and the sacred precinct of Tenochtitlan.

What explains the metaphysical potency and cosmic significance of sweeping? Sweeping combines two key metaphysical components: ordered malinalli-grass straw and sweeping motion. First, straw brooms are fashioned from bunches of cut malinalli-grass shafts that are ordered by being bound together with small cordage at the end opposite the feathery flower tops.[133]

As Tlaltecuhtli's hair, malinalli dried grass (or any other kind of grass) is alive with Tlaltecuhtli's regenerative, earthy-female tonalli-power. Binding the straws orders and arranges the straws, thereby securing and fortifying their power. This enables humans to use their power in various endeavors. Brooms are thus tonalli-charged *power tools*. In this respect they resemble other tools such as nets and ropes. Sweeping taps into the broom's power and discharges it. As brooms wear out, they loose their potency and well-orderedness. They become frayed, tattered, and infested with tlazolli. The Aztecs consequently stored their brooms outside of the home and disposed of them with extreme caution.[134] Children were forbidden to play with brooms – new and old – due to brooms' power and the need to direct their power properly. Sweeping with brooms is therefore metaphysically potent partly because brooms are metaphysically potent. They contain tonalli-power and discharge this power in sweeping.[135]

Second, sweeping consists of a specific pattern of motion-change: a whirling or spiraling movement that instantiates the pattern we identified earlier with the malinalli-malacachoa cluster of twisting, spinning, and gyrating. This pattern transforms the disorderly and degenerative into the orderly and generative. Just as spinning orders and transforms raw fiber into thread, so sweeping orders and transforms tlazolli (dirt, pollution) into fertile energy. Sweeping also creates small yet nevertheless perceptible whirlwinds, and thus imitates the sweeping of Ehecatl-Quetzalcoatl. Sweeping with brooms is thus metaphysically potent partly because sweeping involves spiraling and whirling, transformative motion-change.

Sweeping serves as one of humans' principal weapons in their struggle against tlazolli.[136] It operates as an ordering force that displaces the disorderly forces of tlazolli toward the periphery. In so doing, it transforms them into fertilizing and regenerative ordering forces. When one sweeps, one engages in inamic combat with the forces of tlazolli. Tlazolli, we learned in chapter 2, refers to that which is worn out, rotten, decomposed, deranged, disordered, and decayed such as excrement, vomit, dirt, muck, rags, and random bits of straw or hair – in short, stuff out of place. As such, it exists at the opposite end of a continuum with stuff in place, that is, that which is clean, well ordered, well arranged, and well integrated. Tlazolli is contagious like disease; it infects and adversely affects everything with which it comes into contact. Tlazolli is thus not only disordered but also disordering; corrupted but also corrupting. Tlazolli subverts the orderly arrangement of things.

I propose we view tlazolli dynamically as a force much like what we call entropy. Rags, potsherds, and so on represent mere snapshots in larger processes of entropic degeneration and moments in even larger processes of life~death-cycle generation and degeneration. Like entropic forces, tlazolli forces are disordering, deranging, corrupting, and degenerative, and as such are locked in inamic struggle with ordering forces. The fact that tlazolli is reversed by sweeping together with the fact that sweeping involves malinalli-spinning and -whirling suggests that tlazolli and malinalli-twisting are agonistic inamichuan. Tlazolli forces disorder by unraveling, fraying, ripping, shredding, and frazzling; malinalli forces order by spinning, twisting, and gyrating.

Aztec metaphysicians had a keen appreciation of the fact that things fall apart, that things become unraveled, imbalanced, and disordered, and that everything – including the Fifth Sun and Fifth Era – tends toward tlazolli (disorder, entropy). Thus we see another expression of the Tezcatlipoca factor, since tlazolli is associated with Tezcatlipoca. Sahagún includes dust (*teuhtli*) and filth (*tlazolli*) among Tezcatlipoca's attributes.[137] "When he used to go about on the earth, he would bring to life dust and filth."[138] Tlazolli threatens the order, balance, centeredness, and hence very existence of individuals, homes, temples, communities, and the Fifth Era. Aztec philosophers consequently believed the Fifth Era requires tireless and uninterrupted maintaining, attending to, arranging, and purifying. Humans must prevent the forces of tlazolli from accumulating, and sweeping is one of the principal ways of doing so. Brooms stand out as one of the principal weapons in humans' struggle against this threat. When carefully executed, sweeping enables humans to defuse (if only temporarily) the destructive forces of tlazolli and transform them into something creative.

Sweeping orders and arranges tlazolli by moving tlazolli to its proper place: the periphery. The periphery is where tlazolli belongs; where it is recycled and integrated into processes of regeneration, renewal, and rebirth. By swirling and spinning tlazolli, sweeping transforms tlazolli. As Burkhart points out, sweeping is a female-gendered activity (although one not confined to females since male priests and Ehecatl-Quetzalcoatl sweep).[139] Females must sweep their homes daily. Sweeping thus falls into the family of female activities along with spinning thread, weaving fabric, cooking, and procreating. All these are ordering, regenerative, and transformative processes. Finally, sweeping preserves an orderly center and thereby upholds the balance between ordering and disordering forces in the cosmos.

Tlazolli is a vital and indispensable aspect of the cosmos. As we saw in chapter 2, the Aztecs honored tlazolli as a deity or force named Tlazolteotl ("Sacred Humus-Filth-Refuse"). The *Florentine Codex* depicts Tlazolteotl holding a broom.[140] When removed to the periphery, tlazolli gives rise to order and new life in a grand cosmic process of ever-recycling energy. The Aztecs therefore did not aim to eliminate tlazolli from the cosmos. After all, tlazolli and order-purity are inamic partners. The Aztecs' efforts focused instead upon displacing tlazolli to the periphery where it nourished the four Tlaloque, the four rain-helpers of Tlaloc.[141]

Since sweeping represents the active recycling of tlazolli by human beings, and since tlazolli is associated with Tezcatlipoca, it is not surprisingly to learn that sweeping is associated with Quetzalcoatl (Ehecatl-Quetzalcoatl). Quetzalcoatl and Tezcatlipoca are inamic partners. Hence in the apparently inconsequential, quotidian activity of sweeping, we see a confrontation of cosmic proportions between Quetzalcoatl and Tezcatlipoca. Quetzalcoatl energies and processes are ordering, centering, generative, and regenerative; Tezcatlipoca energies and processes are disordering, decentering, corruptive, and degenerative.

In sum, sweeping is a malinalli-defined process and so offers insight into the nature of malinalli motion-change. The combination of well-ordered, tonalli-rich malinalli-grass broom and malinalli-spinning-whirling motion-change makes sweeping a metaphysically potent activity that helps transform degenerative, corruptive, and disorderly energy into fertile, orderly, and regenerative energy.

OCHPANIZTLI: SWEEPING AND MALINALLI MOTION-CHANGE

Sweeping plays an essential role in Aztec religious rituals ranging from daily temple rites to seasonal large-scale festivals and ceremonies.[142] Sullivan claims the concept of *sweeping the way* is related to the idea of initiating and preparing the way for that which follows.[143] Sweeping initiates and prepares the way by sweeping away tlazolli and thus purifying the way to regenerative transformation. Sweeping occurred every morning before daylight in Aztec temples, purifying them and so initiating their activities. Preparation for ballgames, for example, included sweeping the ballcourt.[144] Sweeping played an essential role in the New Fire Ceremony.[145] It initiated, guided, and prepared the path for the successful rebirth of a stable and well-ordered 52-year cycle by removing the tlazolli that would otherwise result in the cycle's being afflicted at birth by filth, disarray, and disorder.

Sweeping holds center place in the ritual ceremony of the eleventh month, Ochpaniztli ("Sweeping the Path or Way").[146] Ochpaniztli focuses specifically upon Chicomecoatl ("Seven Snake"), the fundamental goddess of maize in her guise as Xilonen (goddess of the young maize plant, human sustenance, and fertility). It focuses generally upon the earth-mother genetrix complex of Teteoinnan-Toci ("Mother of the Gods"-"Our Grandmother") and Tlazolteotl-Ixcuina.[147] Sahagún, Durán, the *Codex Borbonicus*, the *Codex Telleriano-Remensis*, and the *Codex Magliabechiano* depict Toci, Teteoinnan, or Tlazolteotl holding a grass broom.[148] Peterson argues the "Song of Cihuacoatl" indicates the brooms consisted of malinalli-grass.[149] Both the *Tovar Calendar* and Jacinto de la Serna represent Ochpaniztli by a broom depicted as a bunch of malinalli-grass.[150]

Ochpaniztli began with the predawn sweeping (and washing) of houses, baths, lots, roads, highways, ditches, streams, springs, temples, and buildings.[151] Priests selected a middle-aged woman to serve as a Toci teixiptla. The woman spun and wove garments from maguey. She was later decapitated and flayed in a temple decorated with large maize cobs. A male priest donned her flayed skin and assumed the role of Toci teixiptla. He donned the blouse and skirt she had woven, her spindle whorls, and garlands of raw cotton, and he carried double ears of corn. He was accompanied by an entourage of corn priestesses – eight Huastec companions (all of whom carried brooms and phallic poles) – and her son, Cinteotl, God of Corn (especially mature corn) and Growth (from whom issues corn, edible plants, and cotton).[152] Together, Toci and her companions waged combat against a group of male warriors. The combat was called "They fight with grass"[153] because they attacked the warriors with grass brooms. As they struck their opponents, their brooms became increasingly bloodied. With brooms as their weapons, Toci, Cinteotl, and their companions attempted to sweep away their opponents who symbolized tlazolli. Like Ehecatl-Quetzalcoatl, they swept away the tlazolli that obstructs the path of the earth's vegetative rejuvenation and renewal (and hence the path of human sustenance). Ochpaniztli sought to initiate, guide, and prepare the way for earthly regeneration.

QUETZALCOATL AND MALINALLI MOTION-CHANGE

Nicholson claims Quetzalcoatl cuts across the major cult themes and deity complexes that organize pre-Hispanic religion in central Mexico.[154] Given their role in primordial generation, sustenance, and renewal, Quetzalcoatl processes and forces express the theme of "Celestial Creativity-Divine Paternalism" and fall within the Ometeotl Complex. Those processes associated with Ehecatl, the wind "deity," express the major theme of "Rain, Moisture, and Agricultural Fertility" – a constellation of water- and fertility-related processes and forces including rain, wind, lightning, rivers, food cultivation, crop irrigation, decomposition, sexuality, and birth. Ehecatl-Quetzalcoatl processes overlap with many Tlaloc processes. As plumed serpent, Quetzalcoatl bridged upper, middle, and lower layers of the cosmos.

López Austin believes the various aspects of Quetzalcoatl are unified by the theme of "*beginning*, or of *extraction*," that is, "the emergence of light before sunrise; the emergence of earthly things beneath that light; the emergence of rain after the wind that sweeps a path for it; the beginning of human life."[155] Graulich similarly characterizes Quetzalcoatl as "the bringer of life."[156] He is the creator twin. After the destruction of the Fourth Era, according to the *Histoyre du Mechique*, Quetzalcoatl and Tezcatlipoca jointly revive the earth at the beginning of the Fifth Era.[157] Quetzalcoatl travels to Mictlan with Xolotl, his double (nahualli), to gather the bones of the humans from the previous Eras so that he may create a new race of humans for the Fifth Era. After obtaining the bones he sprinkles them with blood drawn from his virile member.[158] According to the *Legend of the Suns*, Quetzalcoatl later transforms himself into a black ant and travels to "Food Mountain" from which he extracts food (corn) for the newly created humans.[159] As *Tlahuizcalpantecuhtli* ("Day's Dawning"), Quetzalcoatl brings light to the earth each day before the sun rises. As the morning star, he helps the Sun struggle to remerge from Mictlan. In sum, Quetzalcoatl is associated with beginnings, nourishing energy, renewal, vertical energy transmission, and therefore malinalli motion-change.

Ehecatl-Quetzalcoatl, Sweeping, Blowing, Drilling, and Malinalli Motion-Change

Aztec metaphysics conceives various cosmic processes in terms of sweeping. Although sweeping is perhaps most commonly associated with female-gendered forces included within the Tlazolteotl-Ixcuina complex, the most famous sweeper of all is Quetzalcoatl in his aspect as Ehecatl. The *Florentine Codex* states Quetzalcoatl is "*in ehecatl*" ("the wind"), master of the winds, and "*in tlachpancauh in tlaloque*" ("road-sweeper of the rain gods"), who sweeps the earth's surface (especially the agricultural fields and paths) by blowing-breathing upon it.[160] He cleanses and purifies the earth's surface of tlazolli and so prepares the path for the precious rains that energize and sustain the earth's vegetative renewal and regeneration. Ehecatl-Quetzalcoatl's blowing whirls, twists, and swirls, and thus instantiates malinalli motion-change. His malinalli-defined blowing transforms tlazolli from polluting to fertilizing energy, from disordering to ordering energy, and from degenerate to regenerative energy. By sweeping, Ehecatl-Quetzalcoatl struggles with Tezcatlipoca's tlazolli forces, his inamic. Sahagún also characterizes Ehecatl-Quetzalcoatl as "*in teiacancauh*" ("the guide").[161] By sweeping, Ehecatl-Quetzalcoatl guides the rains that nourish the earth's vegetative rebirth and renewal.

The *Primeros memoriales* states Ehecatl-Quetzalcoatl "blows [wind], he makes the whirlwinds, he blows, he is something that moves in spirals" ("*Ehecca, hecamalacutl quichiva, tlapitza, tlamamally*").[162] Let's examine this description. First, Ehecatl-Quetzalcoatl "blows [wind]" (*ehecca*). Second, he "makes or begets" (*quichihua*) "whirl wind" (*hecamalacutl*). *Hecamalac[a]tl* combines *ehecatl* ("wind") and *malacatl* ("spindle, bobbin") to mean literally "spindle wind." Ehecatl-Quetzalcoatl [Ehecatl-Quetzalcoatl's blowing] twists, whirls, gyrates, spins, and spirals. Twisters and whirlwinds are associated with Ehecatl-Quetzalcoatl, since both gyrate and spin. Not coincidentally, this is the same pattern of motion-change as instantiated by sweeping. As wind-sweeper and wind-blower, Ehecatl-Quetzalcoatl instantiates malinalli motion-change. Aztec artists commonly used depictions of spiraling cross-sections of seashells as ideograms of Ehecatl-Quetzalcoatl's malinalli motion-change. Ehecatl-Quetzalcoatl's malinalli-shaped blowing and sweeping transforms tlazolli from polluting to fertilizing energy, from disorderly to orderly energy, and from degenerative to regenerative energy. What *explains* the transformative power of malinalli-twisting-spinning motion-change? The gyrating motion of twisting and spinning orders and orients its object. It also exposes its object to the cosmic energies flowing from the four corners of the Fifth Era toward the Fifth Era's center (navel), causing the object to absorb and become empowered by these energies. This, in turn, helps fuel its transformation.

Third, the *Primeros* states Ehecatl-Quetzalcoatl "blows things" (*tlapitza*). Tlapitza combines *tla* (nonhuman, nonspecific object prefix) and *pitza* ("to huff and puff with anger; to blow something [*soplar*], to play a wind instrument"[163] and "to blow"[164]). Related words include *tlapitzaliztli* ("the act of playing a wind instrument or forging metals using a bellows"),[165] *piptza* ("to blow on something with bellows, to blow on something repeatedly"),[166] *tlepitza* ("to blow on the fire so that it will burn"), and *tototlapitza* ("to give calls in hunting birds").[167] A metaphor collected by Andrés de Olmos describes a newborn baby as *tlapitzalli* ("blown, smelted").[168] Midwives addressed newborns by stating that they had been "cast" before birth by Ometecuhtli~Omecihuatl as though metal (*otipitzaloc*).[169] Equally telling is *tototlapitza* ("to give calls in hunting birds"). Ehecatl-Quetzalcoatl's blowing is conceptually akin to the measured blowing of a hunter's bird calls. Bird calling prepares the way for one's prey to emerge and be captured, cooked, eaten, and digested. In sum, all of the aforementioned are malinalli-defined processes of transformation. All are associated with Ehecatl-Quetzalcoatl.

Ehecatl-Quetzalcoatl's blowing is a very specific kind of blowing (breathing). It is the kind of rhythmic blowing involved in bringing forth and begetting something new and it is thus involved in emergence and transformation. It is the kind of measured blowing involved in creating music from wind instruments, creating metals through smelting, and creating fire. In creating fire, blowing involves creative destruction, that is creating something new by destroying something prior. Creating fire by blowing thus returns us to agonistic inamic unity. Wind and fire are inamic partners. The proper malinalli-twisting-spinning together of wind and fire results in a healthy fire.

Fourth, the *Primeros* states Ehecatl-Quetzalcoatl is "drilled through or perforated" (*tlamamalli*). Tlamamalli derives from *mamali* ("to drill a hole through something").[170] Drilling is a twisting, whirling, and spiraling motion, and thus an instance of malinalli motion-change. Ehecatl-Quetzalcoatl "moves in spirals." He is "a thing in circles," writes López Austin.[171] As the wind, Ehecatl-Quetzalcoatl twists, gyrates, spins, and spirals. Another metaphor collected by Olmos describes a newborn baby as *tlamamalli* ("drilled, engraved").[172] Midwives addressed newborns by stating that they had been drilled (*otimamalioac*) by Ometecuhtli~Omecihuatl before birth.[173]

Ehecatl-Quetzalcoatl, Wind-Breath-Air, Creating, Blowing, Speaking, Kindling Fire, and Malinalli Motion-Change

The Fifth Sun, according to Sahagún's creation account, was created by the self-sacrifice of Nanahuatzin. After rising, however, the sun refused to move. The gods then realized they must give their hearts – that is, their teyolia and olin motion-defined life force – to the Sun to make it move. Ehecatl was the one who killed them. Yet even after their deaths the Sun refused to move and follow its path. At this point Ehecatl "arose and exerted himself fiercely and violently as he blew," finally causing the Sun to move.[174] Ehecatl "made him move so that he might go on his way."[175] By blowing malinalli-shaped energy into the Sun, Ehecatl-Quetzalcoatl blew life into the Sun and prepared the way for the Sun to follow its path. As though performing mouth-to-mouth resuscitation, Ehecatl-Quetzalcoatl breathed life-giving, malinalli-defined motion-change into the Fifth Sun and Fifth Age.[176]

Guilhem Olivier believes Sahagún's account illustrates the "double nature" of the creative process.[177] Creation involves both breath and self-sacrifice. And the transmission of energy by means of breath and self-sacrifice, I maintain, involves malinalli motion-change. The commentary accompanying *Codex Telleriano-Remensis* (fol. 8v) states that Quetzalcoatl was engendered by Tonacatecuhtli's breath.[178] Ometecuhtli~Omecihuatl breathes life into newborns in the course of drilling and casting them.[179] The malinalli-defined motion-change of Ehecatl-Quetzalcoatl's blowing jumpstarts the Fifth Sun along its olin-defined life~death path, just as Ometecuhtli~Omecihuatl's blowing jumpstarts newborns along their olin-defined life~death paths. By juxtaposing olin and malinalli motion-change in this manner, the preceding accounts highlight their fundamental difference. Whereas olin-defined motion-change consists of motion-change along a life path and within a life cycle, malinalli-defined motion-change initiates and nourishes life-paths and life cycles.

Olivier also maintains that Sahagún's account highlights the "creative capacity of speech-breath" as well as the importance of sung prayer and invocation in the relationship between humans and gods.[180] Breath is a causally powerful force, especially in the form of ritualized – that is, well arranged – spoken and sung word. Noble speech and song involve measured breathing. *Florentine Codex* (Book VI) demonstrates the importance the Aztecs placed upon proper speaking. The composers of the *Cantares mexicanos*, folio 15r and folio 23r, sing of "smelting gold" (*teocuitlatl nicpitza*) song-poems. Smelting consists of well-ordered and measured blowing.[181] Well-ordered speech and song transmit creative and transformative energy from humans to the cosmos and hence *vertically* from earthly to upper and lower layers of the cosmos. Humans do so with an eye toward creating, sustaining, or renewing order and balance in the Fifth Age. Indeed, this appears to be one of the principal aims of ritualized speech, which the Aztecs conceived first and foremost in performative, regulative, and enactive (rather than descriptive) terms. Speaking properly also possessed the causal power of *neyolmelahualiztli* ("heart-straightening"), or power to straighten one's heart. Admitting one's tlazolli-creating actions (such as adultery) in the presence of Tezcatlipoca removed the tlazolli that

FIGURE 5.8. *Flanged song scroll. (Redrawn from* Codex Borbonicus *[Loubat 1899: 70r].)*

tied one's heart in knots and thereby deranged and disordered it. By verbalizing one's misdeeds, one cleansed and purified oneself of one's tlazolli by sending it to the periphery where tlazolli belongs.[182] And as we saw above, hunters, artisans, musicians, and farmers addressed their instruments with nahuallatolli ("secret or hidden words") in order to induce their cooperation and better ensure effective performance.[183]

The life-initiating and transformative malinalli-defined power of Ehecatl-Quetzalcoatl's wind-breath-air is also manifested in playing wind instruments. Aztec artists standardly depicted speaking and singing using volutes, or "speech-scrolls" (resembling unfolding fiddlehead ferns), that emerge from speakers' mouths. In doing so they made explicit the idea that speaking and singing, like spinning, gyrating, and coiling, instantiate malinalli motion-change (see Figures 5.8 and 5.9).

Breath's power is further demonstrated by the kindling of fire. One breathes life-energy into fire when kindling it. Like the breath involved in singing and

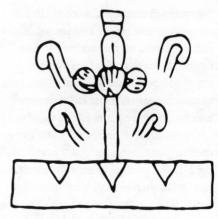

FIGURE 5.9. *Speech scrolls.* (Codex
Mendoza *[1997: folio 70r]; courtesy of
Frances F. Berdan and Patricia Rieff
Anawalt.)*

FIGURE 5.10. *Fire drill with volutes.*
(Codex Mendoza *[1997: folio 15v]; courtesy
of Frances F. Berdan and Patricia Rieff
Anawalt.)*

speaking, kindling breath is carefully measured. Like singing and speaking
breath, kindling breath is more powerful when ritually arranged. Nowhere is
the power of ritualized kindling breath more dramatically illustrated than in
the New Fire Ceremony. During this ritual a priest breathes life into a fire
drilled in the chest of a splayed sacrificial victim. Kindling the fire initiates a
new 52-year cycle. Aztec artists depicted fire using spiraling volutes (see Figure
5.10).

Karl Taube argues Mesoamerican artist-scribes standardly used the "twisted-
cord motif" to designate fire-making. The fires of burning braziers and torches
in the *Codex Dresden*, for example, are "rendered as tightly twisted cords, quite
possibly alluding to the swirling, twisting nature of rising flames."[184] Fire and
speech volutes resemble the swirls of hair atop some depictions of Tlaltecuhtli.
Fire itself is a malinalli-defined motion-change.

Lastly, the power of well-ordered breathing is demonstrated by the playing of
musical wind instruments such as the flute (*tlapitzalli*) and the marine-conch
trumpet (*tecciztli*). First, by breathing into wind instruments one breathes
malinalli-shaped energy into them. As a result they become nourished and
powerful. Second, by breathing into wind instruments one creates music that
"communicates" with the gods according to Guilhem Olivier. Expressed less
theistically, music activates various aspects of teotl by conveying to them bits
of malinalli-shaped energy. Humans and gods communicate with one another

using conch shells.[185] Conch shells are spiral-shaped, and blowing through them creates air that swirls and spirals. The conch's ability to communicate between vertical layers of the cosmos is suggested by its spiral shape. Spiraling is the shape of such vertical energy transmission and transformation between layers of the cosmos. The Aztecs associated the conch with Ehecatl-Quetzalcoatl, and Aztec artists standardly depicted Ehecatl-Quetzalcoatl wearing spiralling adornments (see Figures 3.4, 3.5, and 5.18).

Quetzalcoatl's association with conches and malinalli motion-change goes deeper. According to the *Legend of the Suns*, Quetzalcoatl descends to the land of the dead in search of bones from which to make humans of the Fifth Era.[186] Mictlantecuhtli demands that Quetzalcoatl first blow through a conch shell. This is a trick since the conch lacks holes. With the help of worms (who malinalli-drill wind holes in the conch) and bees (who malinalli-swirl about the shell's interior, sweeping, cleansing, and circulating air within it), Quetzalcoatl blows through the conch and creates music. He later ascends (vertical motion-change) to the earthly layer with the bones.

The conch shell is an appropriate adornment for Quetzalcoatl in his capacity as progenitor of human beings. Conch shells symbolize the womb and hence fertility, birth, regeneration, and new life. The *Codex Vaticanus A* states, "just as the snail comes forth from the folds of this bone or conch, so man goes and comes forth from his mother's uterus."[187] The sectioned shell reveals an interior spiral, indicating its creative-transformative power. The Aztecs also regarded shells as the bones of shellfish, and regarded bones as the seeds of life.[188] They also conceived the female womb, the birth canal, and the process of creative generation as spiral-shaped. Quetzalcoatl's generative and transformative energy and motion-change are spiral-shaped and instances of malinalli motion-change.

Quetzalcoatl as Venus and Malinalli Motion-Change

Quetzalcoatl is associated with Venus and its appearance as Morning and Evening Stars. As Venus, Quetzalcoatl sweeps the way for the Sun's morning reappearance (rebirth) and evening disappearance (death). Quetzalcoatl thus aids the Sun's vertical path between the sky, earthly, and underworld layers of the Fifth Age. By sweeping, cleansing, blowing, and preparing a path for the Sun, Quetzalcoatl makes life possible in the Fifth Age. By sweeping, cleansing, blowing, and creating paths throughout the cosmos, Quetzalcoatl helps make possible the continuing circulation and recycling of energies throughout the cosmos.

Although associated with both Evening and Morning Stars, Quetzalcoatl is more closely associated with the Morning Star, while Xolotl is more closely

FIGURE 5.11. *Sign of Venus. (Redrawn from Castellón Huerta [2002:32].)*

associated with the Evening Star. By helping the Sun die at dusk, Xolotl helps the Sun properly complete its life cycle and in so doing helps Quetzalcoatl reinitiate a new solar life~death cycle the following dawn. Aztec artists standardly depicted Venus as a spiral (that also resembles the cutaway-shell motif commonly adorning Quetzalcoatl and the *almenas* atop the calmecac of Tenochtitlan (see figure 5.11; see also Figures 3.4, 3.5, and 5.18). As Morning and Evening Stars, Quetzalcoatl and Xolotl spiral and gyrate in ways that resemble the malinalli-shaped dancing of a spindle rod in its spindle bowl. Their malinalli-shaped dancing helps complete and reinitiate the Sun's transformation through its olin-defined life~death cycle. In sum, Quetzalcoatl is associated with beginnings, life-initiating, life-sustaining energy, and energy transmission and transformation between vertical layers of the cosmos. His malinalli-defined motion-change initiates and nourishes olin-defined life~death cycles in the Fifth Age.[189]

FIRE AND MALINALLI MOTION-CHANGE

Drilling, Fire Drilling, and Malinalli Motion-Change

Drilling is a creative and transformative process that instantiates malinalli twisting and spinning. Humans drill ceremonial and hearth fires as well as gemstones. The composer of the *Cantares mexicanos* (folio 23v, stanza 26) sings of "drilling jade" (*nicchalchiuhmamali*) song-poems.[190] The Nahuatl word for drilling fire, *tlemamali*, combines *tletl* ("fire") and *mamali* ("to pierce, introduce, or drill a hole through something").[191] Molina translates *tlemamali* as "to make fire with a certain wooden instrument."[192] *Mamali* refers both to the process of grinding, polishing, and perforating gemstones (lapidary drilling) and to the process of igniting fires (fire drilling). Nahuatl words for "fire drill" (*mamalhuaztli*) and "drill" (*tlamamaliualoni*) derive from *mamali*.[193]

Drilling involves rapidly spinning an upright wooden stick on a flat, horizontal base. In the case of lapidary drilling, the base is a gemstone; in the case of fire drilling, a wooden fire board. The wooden stick used in making fire, the *tlequauitl*, combines the words for fire and wood.[194] The horizontal base used in fire drilling is called *teoquauitl* ("sacred wood").[195] The upright stick is the male component of the drill set; the horizontal board, the female. They are related as inamic partners. Drilling malinalli-twists together and in so doing agonistically unites male and female in an obviously sexual manner.

Gyrating the upright stick causes the stick to pierce and penetrate the wooden base, making a hollow resembling a navel and a hearth. It creates heat, igniting a spark that in turn ignites the kindling. The fire maker blows upon – adds spiraling air-breath to – the spark while continuing to spin the fire stick. The *Historia de los mexicanos por sus pinturas* characterizes Mixcoatl's fire drilling as "[drawing] fire from the sticks."[196] This characterization suggests that the combination of drilling, blowing, and fire board enables one to draw the fiery energy already existing within the fire board and transform it into an actual fire. The Aztecs must have seen fire boards as akin to flint (*tecpatl*), which they also used to ignite fires and which they described as "having fire" (*inin tleyo*).[197] Flint is created when lightning strikes the earth, which charges the stone with fiery energy.[198] (Flint knives of course also play an essential role in the transformative process of heart excision.) The Aztecs apparently believed fire boards contain fire. The foregoing also suggests they regarded fire sticks and fire boards as causally powerful objects since they possess the energy necessary for creating fire.

FIGURE 5.12. *Fire drilling. (Redrawn from Codex Laud [Graz 1966: pl. 8].)*

The Aztecs appear to have spun their fire sticks between their open palms. "With his hands he proceeded to bore continuously his fire drill" is how Sahagún's informants describe the fire priest during the New Fire Ceremony. The codices also portray fire drilling in this manner (see Figure 5.12).[199] *Codex Borgia* (pl. 46) depicts Quetzalcoatl drilling a fire upon what appears to be the navel of Xiuhtecuhtli.[200]

If a bow or pump drill were used in making fire, then there would be an additional conceptual association between hunting, fire drilling, and malinalli motion-change by way of the twisted cord of the bow and pump cord.[201] This association fits, seeing as Mixcoatl is both the first creator of fire and the patron of hunting. Taube accordingly suggests that in many instances the twisted cords accompanying fire drills double as the twisted rope of the bow or pump drill (as well as umbilical cords).[202] Fire making thus combines three malinalli processes: spinning the fire stick, drilling the fire stick into the fire board, and blowing.

Making fire dramatically illustrates the shape of malinalli motion-change as well as the transformative power of malinalli motion-change.

The Spanish side of Molina offers two Nahuatl translations for "to start fire" (*encender huego* [*fuego*]): *tletlalia* and *tlepitz*.[203] *Tletlalia* combines *tletl* ("fire") and *tlalia* ("to set down, to put down, to put things in order").[204] Starting a fire involves the ordering and putting down of fire. In her entry for *tlalia* Karttunen refers us to *tlalli* ("earth"), suggesting that *tlalia* involves ordering or putting things down on earth. Following this line of reasoning, *tletlalia* ("starting a fire") involves ordering and preparing things for fire. This is significant for three reasons. First, starting a fire involves ordering, which accords with our conception of malinalli-twisting as a process of ordering of things. Second, drilling fire illustrates the ability of malinalli-twisting to channel energy between vertical layers of the cosmos. Fire drilling transmits fiery energy to the upper layers of the cosmos from Tlalticpac.[205] The vertical posture of the fire stick also suggests this. (Starting a fire with flint similarly involves using fire that originated in the heavens.) Third, starting a fire illustrates the transformative power of malinalli-twisting. This is borne out by another Nahuatl term for drilling fire, *uetzi in tlequauhuitl* ("the fire drill falls").[206] The fire drill falls upon the board just as fiery energy descends from the Sun, and as fiery lightning and meteors fall from the sky. This, too, suggests drilling fire involves bringing fiery energy down from the heavens and hence the vertical transmission of energy.

Taube claims the fire board resembles worm-eaten wood, and that worms were seen as drilling creatures.[207] This accords with the incident recounted earlier from the *Legend of the Suns* in which Quetzalcoatl summons the help of worms to drill holes in a solid conch shell given to him by Mictlantecuhtli, thus enabling him to blow the shell.[208]

The analogies between twisting-spinning and drilling run deep. The fire-drill stick resembles the spinning spindle. Fire stick and spindle are both held vertically. Fire stick and spindle pierce fire board and spindle whorl (respectively). Both twisting-spinning thread and drilling fire processes are conceived in sexual terms. The vertical spindle shaft and drill stick are masculine; the horizontal spindle whorl and fire board are feminine. The same holds *mutatis mutandis* for drilling song-poems. Drilling and spinning agonistically unite male and female inamic partners (and hence hot and cold, dry and wet, and so on). Most significantly, drilling fire, gemstones, and song-poems, on the one hand, and twisting-spinning thread, on the other, are metaphysically transformative processes. Drilling fire and song-poems also conveys energy vertically between the various layers of the cosmos.

Drilling New Beginnings: Drilling Tonalli into in Utero Humans

Drilling initiates new beginnings and new olin-defined life~death cycles by conveying heat-fire energy from one thing to another. Mixtec supernaturals and culture heroes, for example, carried fire sticks and fire boards along with their sacred bundles and staffs of authority. They founded new kingdoms by fire drilling.[209] The Nahuatl word *teocalmamali* conveys the same idea. It combines *teocalli* ("temple") and *mamali* ("to pierce, to drill a hole in something") to mean "to inaugurate or dedicate a church [or temple]."[210]

As we've seen, Ometecuhtli~Omecihuatl implants tonalli into the *in utero* child. Sahagún reports that upon the occasion of the newborn's first ritual bathing, the midwife stated, "You were breathed into [*otipitzaloc*], thou were drilled into [*otimamaliuac*] your house."[211] Tonalli enters the child from the heavens by means of two processes. The first, *pitza*, means "blowing, blowing into a wind instrument, huffing and puffing like a bellows when casting metals." The second, *mamali*, means "to drill, or to drill through something." Creating a new life, like creating a new fire, involves drilling and breathing. Ometecuhtli~Omecihuatl drills a child's tonalli (i.e., heat-fire energy) in the way one drills a new fire. Furthermore, both verbs carry connotations of piercing, perforating, and penetrating. A person's tonalli serves as her umbilical connection to the cosmos. And umbilical cords are malinalli-shaped.

Drilling New Beginnings: The New Fire Ceremony

Malinalli-shaped energy transmission and transformation play essential roles in a variety of Aztec rituals and festivals including Xocotl Huetzi and Izcalli (two veintenas devoted to Xiuhtecuhtli-related processes and fire), the New Fire Ceremony, and Tlacaxipehualiztli. In what follows I examine the latter two.

Arguably the single most important instance of fire drilling occurred during the "New Fire Ceremony" or "Binding of the Years" (*toxiuhmolpilia*).[212] The Aztecs performed the ceremony every 52 years (18,980 days) upon the completion of the calendrical cycle defined by the intermeshing 260-day ritual count (tonalpohualli) and 360+5–day solar count (xiuhpohualli). They called the complete calendar round the *xiuhmolpilli* ("bundle of years"). As the moment of completion approached, Sahagún reports, it was said the years were "piled up, added one to another, and brought together" and "tied and bound."[213] The ceremony repeated the original creation of fire by Mixcoatl and by Nanahuatzin's original creation of the Fifth Sun by self-immolation. Yet the ceremony was not merely a symbolic reenactment. The moment between the expiration of one 52-year cycle and the birth of a new cycle was one of cosmic free-fall and therefore a moment of profound anxiety. There was no metaphysical guarantee that a new 52-year cycle would emerge. A new calendrical cycle therefore needed to be jump-started and the onus of this monumental task fell upon the shoulders of human beings. If they should fail to give birth a new cycle, the Fifth Era would unravel and disintegrate.

Humans jump-started a new 52-year cycle by drilling it into existence, that is, by seizing energy from a sacrificed donor and transmitting it to the Sun via malinalli-drilling. The central part of the ceremony occurred in a temple devoted to Xiuhtecuhtli located atop the sacred hill of Uixachtlan (now called "Hill of the Star"). This was the very spot where Mixcoatl drilled the very first fire. The Aztecs required that the victim be a captive warrior of high status and to have a name that included the word *xiuitl*. As Kay Read notes, the fact that the victim was a captive warrior links drilling a new calendrical cycle to waging war (and hunting).[214] War involves seizing an enemy's disorderly and peripheral female energy and ordering and centering it. The captive warrior provided the birthing of the new calendrical cycle with female energy while the capturing warrior and participating priests provided the male energy. The captive functioned as the female-gendered horizontal drilling board for the male-gendered vertical drilling stick.

Priests stretched the victim upon the sacrificial stone and excised his heart. Another priest, skilled in the art of fire drilling, then placed his sacred fire board and drill into the empty chest cavity where the victim's heart once beat. And "with his hands he proceeded to bore continuously his fire drill."[215] The newly created fiery energy was conveyed to a large pile of wooden faggots. When it had grown into a great bonfire, it was fed the victim's tonalli-rich heart and body. The fire was then transmitted by pine torch (*tlepilli*) to the temple of Huitzilopochtli at the center of Tenochtitlan. Having been centered, the fire was subsequently transmitted to other temples and households throughout Tenochtitlan and its outlying areas. The entire Aztec domain was thus illuminated and energized by this new fire. The ceremony ended with the burning or burying of a bundle of 52 wooden poles, symbolizing the old calendrical cycle. Codical and sculptural representations indicate that the poles were bound using malinalli-twisted cordage. Malinalli-twisted cordage binds together time-place.

The New Fire Ceremony unites a host of malinalli-defined activities: twisting, drilling, blowing, making fire, and binding with cordage. Malinalli-defined activities play a central role in transmitting energy from humans to the cosmos. Malinalli motion-change plays an essential role in initiating and nourishing the olin-defined life~death cycles of the Fifth Age.

Fire and Malinalli Motion-Change

Drilling fire creates a transformative agent in its own right: namely, fire. Fire is a transformative energy process that figures prominently in Aztec metaphysics. It is one of four fundamental forces of the cosmos along with water, wind (air, breath), and earth. Fire went by various names that reflected its various aspects, including Huehueteotl ("Old, Old Teotl," eldest of the gods), Xiuhtecuhtli ("Turquoise Lord," "Fire Lord"), and Chantico ("In the House," "Goddess of the Domestic Hearth Fire").[216] Nicholson gathers these within his "Xiuhtecuhtli Complex," which he subsumes under the "Celestial Creativity-Divine Paternalism" theme alongside the "Ometeotl Complex."[217] The fire god merged with Ometeotl in his capacity as Teteoinnan-Teteointa ("Mother, Father of the Gods") and thus with primordial creation and beginnings. Aztec artists depicted fire with spiraling volutes and malinalli-twisting-spinning ropes, cords, and flames, suggesting they conceived fire as a species of malinalli motion-change.

Fire's malinalli motion-change figures centrally in beginnings, endings, and transformations. The *Legend of the Suns* states fire destroyed the Third Sun and transformed it into the Fourth Sun.[218] According to Sahagún, the Fifth Sun and moon emerged from the fiery self-immolations of Nanahuatzin and Tecuciztecatl in the great fire at Teotihuacan.[219] By immolating themselves, Nanahuatzin and Tecuciztecatl transformed themselves (by cooking) into food so as to initiate a new olin-defined life~death cycle. Their fiery deaths fed new life. Here we return to Quetzalcoatl's role in initiating life by means of malinalli-shaped energy, since Nanahuatzin is an aspect of Xolotl and Quetzalcoatl. Before self-immolating, Nanahuatzin burns as incense the scabs from bloody sores created by his own acts of autosacrifice. Sahagún's informants describe Nanahuatzin as "twisting off" (*concocoleoaia*) his bloody scabs.[220] That is, Nanahuatzin orders the vital energy of his tonalli-rich scabs by malinalli-twisting. He then transmits their life energy through burning (another malinalli-shaped process). Burning transmits energy through the swirling and curving malinalli-shaped energy conduits of smoke. Burning copal incense (tree blood) and human blood and hearts likewise transmits their life-energies to upper layers of the cosmos. Smoke transmits ordered energy from earth to heavens and hence serves as a means of communicating with "the gods."

Fire is simultaneously destructive, creative, and transformative. Its power begins, sustains, and ends life. It initiates life by contributing the vivifying spark of life. It sustains life by contributing life-giving warmth. It supports the growth, health, and survival of newborn children. Sahagún reports that midwives placed newborns near their homes' hearth fires in order to expose them to fire's tonalli.

Aztec metaphysics accordingly conceives igniting a new fire (especially by drilling) in terms of giving birth – hence the connection between fire and umbilical cords, and hence their common malinalli-twisting shape. McKeever Furst writes, it "was probably impossible to make a non-ritual, secular fire using the drill. By nature fire was sacred, whether ignited . . . in the chest at birth or in other ritual and practical contexts."[221] Fire's heat also makes cooking possible. Cooking transforms disordered, inedible foodstuffs into ordered, edible foodstuffs. It prepares foodstuffs for their subsequent transformation by eating, digestion, and defecation. Digestion itself consists of heat-generated cooking.[222] Lastly, burning ends life. Fiery endings, like fiery beginnings, however, are malinalli-defined transformations. Ritual immolation terminates life while also vertically transmitting the terminated life-energy to the nonterrestrial layers of the cosmos.

Xiuhtecuhtli-fire energy concentrates at the confluence point of the Above, the Below, and the Middle, and serves as the central hearth fire of the Fifth Era. From this pivotal time-place Xiuhtecuhtli fire-energy radiates to all three vertical layers and all four corners of the cosmos. *Codex Fejérváry-Mayer* (pl. 1) depicts these fiery forces radiating cyclically and spirally from center to periphery in all four intercardinal directions – in so doing, energizing, renewing, and transforming the Fifth Era and its inhabitants (see Figure 4.3).

Xiuhtecuhtli's fiery cosmic hearth at the Earth's navel is the ideal time-place to situate ritual activities aimed at transmitting energy from the earthly layer to the layers above and below. On this spot the Aztecs accordingly located the Templo Mayor that served as the center of all important religious and political rituals (just as the domestic fire served as the center of all important domestic rituals). The Aztecs also called this fiery center "the Turquoise Hearth." The fiery energy dominating this spot spins, twists, and gyrates. Like the navel of the man depicted by *Codex Vaticanus 3738 A* (pl. 54r), we should expect the spot itself to be spiral-shaped.

Malinalli-shaped fire energy fuels the four-phased olin motion-change and four-phased olin-defined cyclical renewal and completion of the Fifth Sun and all inhabitants of the Fifth Age. Tonatiuh rides on the back of Xiuhcoatl ("the fire serpent") and is fueled by malinalli-shaped fire energy. Tonatiuh, in turn, radiates the fiery heat-energy and tonalli essential to life. This energy fuels – and is thus conceptually associated with – sustenance, ripening, and renewal. It travels down to earth via malinalli-twisting-spinning channels.

Fire, Hunting, and Malinalli Motion-Change

Fire is also associated with hunting. Mixcoatl-Camaxtli (patron of hunters) drilled the first fire. According to the *Historia de los mexicanos por sus pinturas*,

Tezcatlipoca became Mixcoatl, who then, desiring to celebrate the gods, "drew fire from the sticks" ("*sacó lumbre de los palos*") and initiated the festival of making many and large fires.[223] The *Annals of Cuauhtitlan* states Itzpapalotl ("Obsidian or Flint Butterfly" or "Clawed Butterfly")[224] then showed the Chichimecs how to shoot arrows toward the four directions and instructed them to carry wild game they had they killed to the center, where resided the fire. And so began cooking. Given the association between flint and obsidian with fire, shooting arrows in the four directions amounts to shooting fire energy to the four corners of the cosmos. This account thus reveals further associations between fire, fire drilling, hunting, war, and cooking.[225] We also see the role of fire and hunting in centering and ordering that which is peripheral and disordered. Flint and obsidian are associated with fire, war, and hunting. Obsidian is used to make swords and knives. Flint is used to make sparks. Flint knives are used in heart excision. Flint is thus associated with the forces of sacrificial death, transformation, and renewal. Moreover, flint and obsidian are both used in weapon making – further associating fire, war, and transformation. Xiuhtecuhtli has martial aspects that strengthen the association between fire, war, and creative-destructive transformation.[226]

In sum, flint, obsidian, fire, fire drilling, war-making, hunting, cooking, and sacrifice are conceptually interrelated. They arrange, order, center, and prepare energy for vertical transmission *between* different kinds of things (rabbit into edible foodstuff), *between* different conditions of the same thing (disorderly to orderly), and *between* vertical layers of the cosmos. One and all are malinalli-defined transformational processes.

Tlacaxipehualiztli and Malinalli Motion-Change

Malinalli-shaped motion-change, energy transmission, and transformation all figure prominently in the festival of Tlacaxipehualiztli ("Flaying of Men"), which the Aztecs celebrated in honor of Xipe Totec during the second veintena.[227]

Narrative

Tlacaxipehualiztli involved the slaying and flaying of large numbers of captives. The festival's first day was marked by dancing. The people made twisted tortillas called *cocolli* (from *col*, meaning "something twisted" or "twisted bread") and adorned themselves with garlands fashioned from them.[228] Like López Luján, I believe the twisted tortillas symbolize malinalli motion-change.[229] Captives were ritually bathed, purified, and seized by their captors who cut the hair from the crowns of their heads. Captors placed their captives' tonalli-rich hair before the hearth (the fire center, the fire heart) of their calpultin (wards). The captives' hair, heads, and necks were thus malinalli-twisted a second time, the first having occurred when captured on the battlefield. The codices standardly depict captured warriors with their topknots twisted by their captors and their bodies, heads, and necks twisted to one side (see Figure 5.7).

On the second day some captives were dubbed *xipeme* ("skinned ones"), others *tototectin* ("dead in honor of Totec").[230] Priests seized and dragged some by their remaining hair to the sacrificial stone (*techcatl*) atop of the pyramid of Huitzilopochtli. They seized others to die upon the so-called gladiatorial stone. These seizures involved further malinalli twisting-spinning. Five priests took the captives from the former group and stretched them out upon the techcatl. This further ordered and centered their energies since the techcatl was situated at the navel and axis mundi of the Fifth Age. Presumably the priests further arranged the captive's energies by aligning his body with the four directions. A sixth priest cut open his chest and wrenched out his heart. Sahagún tells us they called the victims "eagle men" and their hearts "precious eagle-cactus fruit."[231] "Hence it was said [of the captive]: 'The eagle man is taken upwards because indeed he who died in war went looking, sat resting in the presence of the sun.'"[232] The priest raised the heart and "offered it to him [the Sun]; they nourished him [the Sun]."[233] The priest then placed the victim's heart and blood in the *cuauhxicalli* ("eagle vessel"). Sahagún states they placed blood and heart into a *xicara* ("gourd vessel").[234]

The priests then rolled the victims' bodies down the pyramid's steps, the bodies "bouncing" and "turning over and over" until they reached the bottom terrace.[235] The bodies were then decapitated. The heads were mounted on the *tzompantli* ("skull rack") and headless bodies taken to the captive's *capulco* ("ward") where they were butchered. One thigh was sent to the tlatoani. The rest was cooked in a stew of dried maize called *tlacatlaolli*. A bowl was enjoyed by each member of the captor's family but not the captor. Cooking and eating the captive's flesh transmitted the captive's energy to the captor's family.

Tlahuahuanaliztli ("striping") took place on the second day. Five high-ranking Aztec warriors confronted the captives intended for striping. Each warrior approached the captives, raising and dedicating his war club and shield to the Sun. Each then "turned back; he retreated. He turned to the rear; once again he went back. . . . [And as] they were turning to the rear, at once they were coming forth. They came dancing; they each went turning about."[236] The warriors danced circles around the captives, incorporating further the twisting-spinning of malinalli motion-change into the ritual.

Deity-impersonators of Tonatiuh, Quetzalcoatl, Toci, Huitzilopochtli, Itzpa-palotl, and Xipe (reports Durán)[237] joined the captives and warriors and encir-cled the *temalacatl* ("gladiatorial stone") in a twisting-spinning manner.[238] An incenser circled the temalacatl four times, energizing it with a torch of burning incense called *Xiuhcoatl* (because it resembled a snake).[239] Each captive was led to the temalacatl whereupon he was given a vessel of *teooctli* ("sacred octli").[240] After raising the vessel four times to the sun, he imbibed the octli through a hollow cane. In honor of the captive, a priest wrung the neck and snapped off the head of a quail (*in oconquechcoton zolin*), further incorporating malinalli-twisting into the ritual. The root verb *cotona* means "to cut something, to break something off, to wound something,"[241] and appears related to *cotoni* ("for a cord, thread or rope to snap").[242] The Aztecs apparently regarded the quail's neck (spine) as a cord that snapped upon twisting.

The priests forced the captive to ascend and stand upon the temalacatl, at which point began the striping (*tlahuahuano*) or "gladiatorial combat."[243] The temalacatl was a horizontal circular stone carved precisely for this ritual.[244] Eduardo Matos Moctezuma and Felipe Solís claim the stones were painted entirely or predominantly red: the color of Xipe Totec, the red Tezcatlipoca, and East. The other color was yellow, the color of the Sun.[245] Both the *Codex Magliabechiano* and *Codex Nuttall* depict a rope tied around the captive's waist.[246] Sahagún states the rope was long enough to allow the captive to cir-cumambulate the temalacatl's circumference (see Figure 5.13).[247] The rope's other end was tied to a "socket" (*ojo*) at the temalacatl's center. In some cases, it was tied to a crosspiece on the stone.[248] The crosspiece of the temalacatl known as "Moctezuma's cuauhxicalli," for example, is formed by the sacrificial-knife-shaped tongue of Tonatiuh protruding from a hollow at the stone's center.[249]

The captive then waged combat with the *tlahuahuanqui*. *Tlahuahuanqui* derives from *huahuana* ("to scratch, scrape something, to incise lines on some-thing").[250] Durán glosses tlahuahuanqui as "tanner or scraper of skins,"[251] Dibble and Anderson, as "striper."[252] There were five stripers, each of whom was armed with an obsidian-bladed war club and each of whom moved freely around the temalacatl. The captive was armed with only four wooden balls and a feather-bladed war club. *Codex Magliabechiano* (pl. 30r) depicts him carrying a club covered with unspun balls of cotton (see Figure 5.13). His arms and legs are cov-ered with unspun cotton balls, suggesting his status as raw energy needing to be malinalli spun upon the temalacatl before feeding the Sun. The five warriors sought "to stripe" the captive, that is, cut his thighs, calves, arms, and head caus-ing him to bleed upon the temalacatl. Although the sources do not say, it would make sense for the five to circumambulate the temalacatl counterclockwise,

FIGURE 5.13. *Striping on the temalacatl.* *(*Codex Magliabechiano *[1903: pl. 30r].)*

repeating the path of the Sun and spinning the victim's spilling blood in all four directions. By constraining the captive, the rope forced the captive to spin around the temalacatl. In doing so, he moved in a malinalli twisting-spinning manner and thereby ordered his energies for transmission. Not coincidentally, he spun around like a spindle shaft, while his energies spun around like twisting thread. The striping proceeded until the captive fell upon the temalacatl, his energies ritually prepared for extraction and transfusion to a hungry cosmos.

Let's examine briefly the temalacatl. The temalacatl functioned as a site of energy transmission between vertical layers of the Fifth Age and time-place of human ritual participation in its continuing existence. It operated as *a launching pad* for twisting and spinning energy up into the cosmos. *Temalacatl* derives from *tetl* and *malacatl*, and literally means "stone spindle." Indeed, a temalacatl resembles a large spindle whorl. Like the spindle whorls discussed by Elizabeth Brumfiel, Aztec temalacatl's bore carved images upon their upward-facing horizontal surfaces.[253] These typically consisted of bas-reliefs of sun disks, the face of Tonatiuh, or the glyph 4 Olin.[254] Plate 16 of Durán's *Book of the Gods and Rites* depicts a warrior standing upon a temalacatl with a 4 Olin bas-relief at its center.[255] The temalacatl rests upon a square pedestal with steps on four sides, giving the larger structure the appearance of a quincunx. Above the warrior's head is a 4 Olin glyph, symbolizing Tonatiuh and the Fifth Age, the recipients of his energies. One surviving temalacatl, called "The Stone of Tizoc," displays an elaborate bas-relief of a radiating solar disk on its upper surface. Quincunxes, chalchihuitls, and eagle feathers adorn its rim.[256]

The hole at the center of the temalacatl was called *iyollo* ("its heart").[257] It commonly contained a depiction of Tonatiuh.[258] Like human navels and spindle whorl holes, this hole is the product of piercing, penetrating, and drilling. It symbolizes the human navel; the Earth's navel where the axis mundi pierces the Earth's surface; the hole of a fire board; the hole of a spindle whorl; a woman's vagina; and the empty cavity left in the victim's chest subsequent to heart excision. These are all sites of malinalli-shaped energy transformation. The downward face of another temalacatl displays a bas-relief of Tlaltecuhtli with Tlachitonatiuh (the nighttime phase of Tonatiuh) passing between its open jaws.[259] The energies obtained through sacrifice upon the stone were intended to help Tonatiuh complete its life~death cycle.

The Aztecs called the rope binding the captive to the temalacatl *tonacamecatl* ("sustenance rope or cord").[260] *Tonacamecatl* combines *mecatl* ("rope or cord formed by twisting") and either *tonacayo* ("human body, our flesh") or *tonacayotl* ("human sustenance, produce, fruit of the earth, one's daily nourishment, corn"), or both.[261] Seler glosses it as "rope of corn" (*soga de maíz*) and "rope of fruits" (*soga de frutos*).[262] The tonacamecatl served as an umbilicus binding the captive to the Sun. Umbilical cords bind fetus to mother and ancestors, and transmit tonalli sustenance from mother and ancestors to fetus. The tonacamecatl analogously bound captives to the Sun and transmitted tonalli sustenance from captive to Sun. The ties that bind are ties that nourish. Both a human umbilical cord and the tonacamecatl are malinalli-twisted and possess the shape of a malinalli energy-transmission conduit. Seler's translations are thus apt, seeing as corn is man's sustenance, fruit of the earth, and a metaphor for sustenance. The captive is the Sun's sustenance and a piece of earthly fruit seized to nourish the Sun. When tied around the captive's waist, the tonacamecatl makes contact with the victim's navel. The tonacamecatl thus serves as a sustenance cord for the Sun.

The captive eventually faltered and fell upon the temalacatl. Five priests then seized him and stretched him out at the edge of the temalacatl while a sixth opened his chest and wrenched out his heart.[263] Moctezuma's cuauhxicalli, according to Solís, functioned as both temalacatl and cuauhxicalli in this manner.[264] Durán's *History* states the victim was stretched out and his heart seized upon the same temalacatl. His heart was then taken to a second, large circular stone where it was presented to the Sun.[265] Durán calls this second stone a "cuauhxicalli." He also reports that Axayacatl commissioned the construction of two stones: one for striping that commemorated his victories, and one depicting the symbols of the days and years.[266] Durán however contradicts this account in *Book of the Gods and Rites*, saying the victim was taken to this second stone (also called a "cuauhxicalli") for heart excision.[267] Matos Moctezuma believes the Aztecs used two different circular stones: temalacatl and cuauhxicalli. The "Stone of Tizoc" exemplifies the former, the so-called "Sun Stone," the latter.[268] The *Florentine Codex* (Bk IV, Figure 30) depicts a heart excision on a temalacatl.[269]

Durán also reports that the striping and subsequent seizure and dedication of the captive's heart to the Sun occurred in a "smooth and plastered courtyard measuring seven yards around" that was also called a *cuauhxicalli*.[270] *Cuauhxicalli* ("eagle vessel") typically refers to a stone vessel in which the victim's heart and blood were placed for transmission to the Sun. It was called "eagle vessel" because it contained the "eagle man's" (victim's) heart and blood. Here, however, *cuauhxicalli* apparently refers to a place of sacrifice, to an entire courtyard, that served as a large eagle vessel for the victim's heart and blood. I suggest the courtyard functions as a large spindle bowl, the "dancing place" in which spindle shaft and whorl "dance." Like a spindle stick, the victim danced in the spindle bowl, the cuauhxicalli.

The parallels between tlahuahuanaliztli (striping) and spinning are manifold: upright captive and upright spindle shaft; temalacatl and spindle whorl; and courtyard cuauhxicalli and spinning bowl. Striping a captive and spinning thread both involve malinalli-twisting-spinning and hence malinalli transmission. Both involve the transformation of disordered energy (of wild captive and wild fiber, respectively) into ordered energy (of spun victim and spun thread, respectively). Tlahuahuanaliztli simply represents transformation by malinalli motion-change on a grander scale. The disorderly raw energy of the captive is metaphysically spun, twisted, and transformed into orderly energy before being fed to the cosmos.

Sahagún's informants state the sixth priest "seized his [the victim's] heart."[271] The Nahuatl reads "*conanilia in iyollo*." The verb *ana* means "to grab, take hold, remove, or seize something or someone."[272] Related constructions include *tlaanaliztli* ("act of grabbing something and separating [it] from among other things") and *tlanana* ("to pull someone's tooth").[273] Conceiving heart sacrifice in terms of seizing highlights the fact that the Aztecs understood seizing hearts, captives on the battlefield, the hair of captives, ripe corn from the stalk, and prey in hunting in identical terms. The verb *ana* enters such constructions as *yaoana* ("to seize an enemy") and *tochanqui* ("rabbit hunter" or "one who customarily seizes rabbits").[274] Seizing involves violent twisting and wrenching. In seizing a heart, one forcibly plucks the heart from its attachments to the great vessels within the chest cavity.[275] In seizing a prey or enemy, one violently plucks them from the periphery. Finally, *ana* enters into constructions meaning "to lead, guide, and govern."[276] By seizing captives, hearts, and prey, one initiates them upon and guides them along the path of malinalli-defined vertical transformation.

After wrenching the captive's heart from his chest, the presiding priest "raised [the tonacamecatl] in dedication to the four directions,"[277] conveying to the four directions the vital blood energy that had soaked into the umbilicus. Another priest placed a "hollow eagle cane" in the blood-filled vessel of the victim's chest and raised the cane to the Sun. "It was said: 'Thus he giveth [the Sun] to drink.'"[278] Just as the captive had drunk octli through a hollow straw before striping, so now the Sun drank his blood. Just as the former fortified the captive, so the latter fortified the Sun. It seems likely the drinking tubes were the stiff shafts of malinalli flower stalks or their symbolic equivalents.[279] If so, we see yet another instance of malinalli-defined motion-change involved in energy transmission between earthly and heavenly levels. After this, the sacrificing priest poured the victim's blood into a feather-rimmed, green xicalli (gourd vessel) and placed a feathered hollow cane into the xicalli. The captor carried the blood-filled xicalli to the statues of Tenochtitlan in order to fortify the sacred processes ("deities") they represented with the captive's blood. "On the lips of the stone images, on each one, he placed the blood of his captive. He made them taste it with the hollow cane."[280]

Upon finishing with this, Sahagún reports "they danced (*mitotia*), they went in procession about the round stone of gladiatorial sacrifice (*qujiaoloa in temala-catl*)."[281] *Quijiaoloa* consists of *qui* (indirect object) plus *yahualoa*, meaning "to go around something, to go in procession."²⁸² The participants spun, gyrated, and danced in circles around the temalacatl so as to ensure better the successful ordering and transmission of energy. Later the victim's body was flayed and dismembered in the captive's calpulli. One thigh was offered to the reigning tlatoani. The remainder was cooked and consumed by the captor's family in a stew of dried maize.

On the third day of the festival, associates of the captors donned the skins of the flayed victims and stood "upon grass" (*zacapan*). This was called "Placing [of Xipes] upon Grass."²⁸³ Sahagún writes, "they were in rows upon white earth (*tizapan*) or upon grass (*zacapan*). . . . And wherever in the city grass was shaken out, upon it they placed, set up, exhibited, before all, the *xipeme* who had put on the skins of men."²⁸⁴ *Tizapan* and *zacapan* refer to time-places of sacrificial transformation; portals for transmitting malinalli-shaped energy. White is the color of sacrificial struggle and death. They wore these skins for twenty days. Some were called *xipeme* ("Xipe impersonators") because they wore the skins of sacrificed captives who had personified Xipe. Others were called *tototectin* because they wore the flayed skins of sacrificed captives who had been given the name *Totec*.²⁸⁵ The two inamically paired groups circulated throughout Tenochtitlan, spreading and transmitting the power possessed by the skins. They engaged in mock battles with one another during which they "went turning back, went circling back" ("*hualmocueptihui, hualmomalacachotihui*").²⁸⁶ *Hualmocueptihui* derives from *cuepa*, a reflexive verb meaning "to turn, to turn back, to turn into something, to become something."²⁸⁷ *Hualmomalacachotihui* derives from *malacacho* ("to turn, to revolve").²⁸⁸ The two groups gyrated around one another, spinning, twisting, and thereby transmitting the skins' energies.²⁸⁹

Between nightfall and midnight of the third day, rulers, leaders of youth, mothers, and "pleasure girls" joined together in *cuicoanolo*, a twisting, curving, coiling, curling dance formation with singing.²⁹⁰ Gertrude Kurath and Samuel Martí translate *cuicoanolo* as "serpent dance with song."²⁹¹ *Cuicoanolo* has roots in *coloa* ("to twist, to curve, to change direction; to bend something, to fold something, to detour around something").²⁹² Related to *coloa* is *colihui* ("for something to curve, turn"). Related constructions include *quacocolochoa* ("to curl someone's hair"), *tlacoloa* ("to go somewhere by a roundabout course"), *tlatlacolotiuh* ("to go about in a twisting way"), and *tlaxcalcolli* and *tlaxcalcoltontli* ("spiral bread roll").²⁹³ The serpentine dance was performed by a single line of dancers, joined to one another by holding hands or linking arms. The dancers moved in a serpentine, spiraling path, further incorporating malinalli twisting-spinning into the ritual and contributing to the ritual's successful energy transmission.²⁹⁴

Interpreting Tlacaxipehualiztli: The Centrality of Malinalli Motion-Change

Tlacaxipehualiztli was dedicated to Xipe Totec. Although controversy surrounds the precise meaning of *Xipe Totec*, most scholars gloss it as "Our Lord the Flayed One."[295] Xipe is associated with Tlatauhqui Tezcatlipoca (Red Tezcatlipoca), Camaxtli,[296] and East: the time-place of renewed olin-defined life~death cycles and rebirth. Xipe's array includes malinalli-twisted ropes; vertical, malinalli-twisting rope facial painting; red conical hat; flayed human skin; quail design; and *chicahuaztli* (rattle staff).[297] These symbolize impregnation, fertility, (re)birth, feeding, revitalization, and sacrifice – all of which are conceived in terms of malinalli-twisting-spinning motion-change and vertical energy transmission and transformation.

Xipe Totec and Tlacaxipehualiztli combine agricultural and military processes in a manner that points to the conceptual connection between rain, insemination, agricultural fertility, renewal, and prosperity on the one hand, and blood, sacrifice, war, and military prosperity on the other.[298] Nicholson understands Xipe Totec as "a very special expression" of the Rain-Moisture-Agricultural Fertility theme – namely, one with "a strongly martial flavor."[299] Tlacaxipehualiztli combines elements of Nicholson's "War-Sacrifice-Sanguinary Nourishment of the Sun and the Earth" and his "Rain-Moisture-Agricultural Fertility."[300] As Tlacaxipehualiztli dramatically illustrates, humans participated in the transmission and circulation of energies between the various layers of the Fifth Age via ritually controlled sacrificial feeding that involved seizing, ordering, extracting, and transmitting captives' energies.

Tlacaxipehualiztli is thus concerned most fundamentally with metamorphosis, one involving the vertical transmission of energy between humans, Sun, and Earth.[301] The various activities of Tlacaxipehualiztli aided and abetted this metamorphosis. They seized, spun, gyrated, centered, ordered, extracted, transmitted, and transformed every last drop of disorderly energy of high-value enemy warrior captive-victims with the aim of nourishing and revitalizing Sun and Earth. They recycled into the cosmos the energies that were drilled into humans at birth, that humans had absorbed since birth through sunlight, and that humans had ingested by eating corn. Harvesting human fruit from the battlefield involved twisting their hair, striping them, spinning them, bleeding them, wrenching out their hearts, mounting their heads on the tzompantli, cooking and eating their flesh, and donning and spinning their flayed skins. Tlacaxipehualiztli thus points to one of the defining transformational interrelationships of the Fifth Age. War produces sacrificial victims whose energies revitalize the Earth and Sun. Revitalized Sun and Earth, in turn, yield agricultural abundance that nourishes humans and produces new warriors for war and sacrifice. This malinalli-defined process of agonistic inamic unity nourishes and sustains the Fifth Era.

The Aztecs perceived enemy combatants in terms of what they contained – namely, the precious liquid, blood – and in terms of the needs of Aztec agriculture: the precious liquid, water. [302] They regarded enemy combatants as feminine, disordered, and peripheral and hence as agonistic inamic partners of Aztec eagle and jaguar warriors who they regarded as male, ordered, and centered.[303] Like hunters, Aztec warriors ventured out into the periphery in order to seize, wrench away, and bring home – and thereby center and order – the disorderliness, femaleness, and off-centeredness of enemy combatants. The various activities of Tlacaxipehualiztli spin together captor, priest, and striper (male, dry, etc.) and captive (female, wet, etc.) in transformative agonistic tension. They concretely instantiate as well as nourish the malinalli-defined agonistic inamic unity of military success~agricultural prosperity and parallel inamic unities such as order~disorder, female~male, and death~life.[304]

Malinalli-defined motion-change plays an essential role in each phase of the metamorphic processes of Tlacaxipehualiztli. The captive-victims' energies are centered, ordered, guided, transmitted, and transformed by means of spinning, gyrating, twisting, wrenching, encircling, rolling over, and curving. The latter transforms the captives' energies, just as twisting and spinning transform raw fiber into spun thread. Captives' bodies, hair, heads, and necks are twisted when seized in combat and during Tlacaxipehualiztli. Their hearts are wrenched from their chests. Their corpses spin as they tumble down pyramids. Quail's heads are wrenched from their torsos. Victims, Xipe impersonators, priests, incensors, mothers, harlots, and attackers gyrate, dance, and circle around one another. Captives and attackers circumambulate the temalacatl – a monumental stone spinning whorl and malinalli launching pad for transmitting captives' energies. Victims spin around the whorl like a spindle rod. Spinning and circling orient, order, and center the victims' energies relative to the four directions.[305] Doing so also draws energies from the four directions and adds them to the captive's energies. Captives drink octli, nature's power drink for humans, while deities drink blood, humans' power drink for deities. Both drink through hollow malinalli grass shafts.

In closing, Tlacaxipehualiztli was more than a symbolic or theatrical reenactment of past mythological events; more than a series of formalized standardized, obligatory actions that dramatized central shared values and beliefs regarding the Aztecs' natural and social environments.[306] Tlacaxipehualiztli involved humankind's hands-on causal participation in and contribution to the ongoing cosmic circulation of energy by means of carefully controlled malinalli-defined motion-change. Humans provided teyolia and tonalli to be transformed from one condition (human hearts and blood) to another condition (processes such as rain, fertility, and Sun). They inserted themselves into the cosmic circulation of energy in order to nourish the regenerative powers of the Fifth Sun-Earth Ordering.

MALINALLI AS DAY SIGN OF THE TONALPOHUALLI

Malinalli names the twelfth day of the tonalpohualli. On this day malinalli-defined forces saturate the cosmos, influencing in particular those processes initiated on the day (from human lives to mercantile expeditions). According to Durán, those born under the day sign Malinalli are augured to undergo an annual cycle of grave illness and complete recovery. Their disease, writes Durán, is like annual wild grass that appears suddenly and equally suddenly disappears.[307] Malinalli thus augurs transformative renewal.

Each of the twenty day signs of the tonalpohualli is associated with one of four cardinal directions, and malinalli is associated with South (*huiztlampa* or "Time-place of Thorns").[308] The Aztecs used thorns as bloodletting implements in autosacrifice, linking malinalli with the reinvigorating energies released by autosacrifice. León-Portilla argues South is a direction of danger, unpredictability, and "uncertain character."[309] Since it is the time-place of the nighttime Sun, it raises the deeply troubling question, "Will the Sun complete its nighttime journey and be reborn?" South is also the time-place of the winter Sun and winter solstice, which raises the equally troubling question, "Will the Sun complete its annual journey and be reborn in spring?" It is fitting, therefore, that South is associated with the rabbit, a creature "whose next leap one cannot anticipate."[310] Yet because the rabbit is also a creature of prodigious reproductive power, South is also associated with fertility, reproduction, and life. South is often assigned the color blue: the color of water, fertility, and fecundity. Its inamic is North (*mictlampa*), which is associated with death. The North~South inamic opposition is thus one of death~life as indicated by their respective symbols, flint and rabbit.[311]

Pahtecatl and Malinalli as Day Sign

The set of processes dubbed *Pahtecatl* govern the day sign Malinalli. Pahtecatl is one of the most important *octli* (pulque) fertility-agricultural forces or *centzon totochtin* ("four hundred rabbits").[312] Pahtecatl is said to have discovered the roots with which one ferments octli from the agave's *aguamiel* (honey water), and to have instructed humans in the art. Sahagún's informants write, "the name of the one who discovered the stick, the root, with which wine [octli] was made, was Pahtecatl."[313] *Pahtecatl* combines *pah(tli)* and *tecatl*. Karttunen translates *pah(tli)* as "medicine, potion," adding that it may mean harmful poison or beneficial medicine.[314] Related words include *pahtia* ("to take medicine or poison; to administer medicine or poison to someone") and *pahtiliztli* ("cure, restoration of health").[315] *Teca(tl)* is a suffix meaning "resident of, person from."[316] One of the three annotators of the *Codex Telleriano Remensis* claims Pahtecatl's name refers to the roots added to octli for fermentation.[317] Seler glosses *Pahtecatl* as "he from the land of the medicine used for curing octli."[318] I propose "forces of curing, fermentation, and medicine" or "forces residing in medicine."

Fermenting maguey sap into octli requires the addition of specific roots (or herbs). Motolinía says the roots are called *ocpatli* or "*medicina para pulque*" ("medicine for octli").[319] The *Primeros memoriales* states *ocpatli* is the name of the root (or herb) added to octli to enhance its intoxicating powers.[320] Octli has the power to intoxicate. Ome Tochtli ("Two Rabbit") named this power (or "deity"). According to Sahagún, the effects of drinking octli were explained in terms of the forces that inhabit octli – the "400 Rabbits" (*centzontotochtin*).[321] Unfermented octli acquires these powers by adding "pulque medicine." Fermentation thus transforms powerless sap into a sacred, power-filled liquid. *Pahtecatl* also names this transformative process. Drinking octli enabled humans to communicate with the gods through divine intoxication.

The Aztecs believed octli to possess strong revitalizing and regenerative powers in addition to strong medicinal and curative powers. The *Primeros memoriales* states octli is used in treating venereal diseases.[322] Drinking octli cools down people's tonalli in the event of its overheating. Too much, however, endangers a person's tonalli by cooling it too much and diminishing it.[323] The Aztecs considered octli to be a vital food source with tremendous nourishing power. Drinking octli amounted to drinking the earth's breast milk~semen, blood, and hence life energy. Octli was the Aztecs' power drink.[324] *Pahtecatl* names the nourishing, vitalizing, and regenerative powers of octli specifically and of medicine generally.

Pahtecatl is husband to and hence inamic of Metl or Mayahuel ("Goddess of Maguey"). This is fitting since their union results in the creative transformation of aguamiel into power-charged octli. *Mayahuel* means "powerful flow," a name given to her because of her four hundred breasts and prodigious fecundity.[325] I understand Mayahuel as a constellation of powers associated with the maguey plant. The Aztecs found the maguey plant abundantly useful. They used its sap to induce menstruation. They twisted its fibers into rope and also spun them into thread from which they wove cloth. They fashioned it into sandals. They used maguey thorns as autosacrificial bloodletting implements and maguey leaves in making paper. They ate its roots, leaves, and stalks. By virtue of malinalli's association with Pahtecatl and Pahtecatl's association with Mayahuel, we see a conceptual association between malinalli motion-change, on the one hand, and nourishment, regeneration, and revitalization as well as autosacrifice, healing, medicine, twisting-spinning, and octli, on the other.

Mayahuel's regenerative powers govern the day sign, *Tochtli* ("rabbit"), and rabbits reproduce prodigiously. She is patronness of the eighth trecena, 1 Malinalli.[326] Mayahuel's depiction in the *Codex Borbonicus* contains several telling features.[327] She wears blue clothing (the color of fertility) and a headdress of spindles and unspun maguey fiber (*ixtle*). These symbolize malinalli motion-change and malinalli-defined transformation of disorder into order. In her right hand she holds a pair of twisted cords that symbolize sacrifice, autosacrifice, and regeneration through malinalli-powered transformation. Also present are glyphs for the nighttime sky, octli vessels, cuauhxicalli (eagle vessel for sacrificial blood and hearts), sacrificial banners, a person drinking octli, and a sacrificial victim standing below an arched snake. Quiñones Keber suggests the scene represents a nighttime ritual focusing on sacrifice and octli.[328] One of Xipe Totec's monikers, *Yolometl* ("Heart of Maguey"), places malinalli energy transmission, sacrificial transformation, and regeneration at the heart of Mayahuel's reproductive powers and her olin-defined life cycle.[329] Just as we saw malinalli-generated and -transmitted energy fueling the olin-defined life cycle of the Sun, here we see it doing the same vis-à-vis the olin-defined life cycle of Mayahuel.

Pahtecatl and the pulque gods are further associated with fertility, fecundity, and abundance by virtue of their association with rabbits. Sahagún's informants tell us the sign One Rabbit (*Ce Tochtli*) is one of good fortune. Those born under its influence are destined to be prosperous, wealthy, industrious, diligent, attentive to the future, and successful providers. They will enjoy an abundance of foodstuffs. They will save their wealth and divide it justly between their offspring.[330]

Pahtecatl governed the eleventh trecena which begins with 1 Ozomatli (Monkey).[331] The Aztecs regarded monkeys as licentious and sexually promiscuous. According to *Legend of the Suns*, Quetzalcoatl reigned over the Second Sun, "4 Wind." Upon its destruction, the people of the Second Age were blown away and turned into monkeys.[332] The monkey is associated with Quetzalcoatl under his guise as Ehecatl, and thus with the gyrating motion of whirlwinds. A particularly dynamic statue depicts Ehecatl-Quetzalcoatl as a buccal mask-wearing monkey (Ehecatl Ozomatli) (see Figure 5.14).[333] The monkey appears to be whirling about and dancing, his legs spiraling around one another. He grasps

FIGURE 5.14. *Ehecatl-Ozomatli (Author's photo.)*

an unnaturally long tail that spirals under his left arm, over his left shoulder, and around the right side of his neck. He stands upon a coiled serpent that coils up his right leg. His buccal mask associates Ehecatl-Quetzalcoatl with the malinalli motion-change of blowing, wind, and air, and with ducks. Because ducks fly, walk, swim, and dive beneath surface water they are associated with vertical motion-change that bridges all three layers of the cosmos.[334] Monkeys were also associated with the consumption of octli. A monkey's head adorns a large octli vessel (*octecomatl*) depicted in *Codex Borbonicus* (pl. 11).[335] Pahtecatl-forces are thus associated with Ehecatl-Quetzalcoatl's twisting, spinning, and whirling forces of reproduction, regeneration, and renewed beginnings.

The Aztecs associated Pahtecatl with Ehecatl-Quetzalcoatl. Both hail from the Huasteca. Pahtecatl often wears a half-red, half-blue conical hat (*copilli*), standard Huastecan headgear for Ehecatl-Quetzalcoatl,[336] along with other items associated with Quetzalcoatl, including penitential bone, brown and white head fan, headdress with large bow and extended loops, shell trimmed brown collar, and hooked shell ear ornaments.[337] Elsewhere Pahtecatl wears other items associated with Quetzalcoatl such as penitential bone, brown and white head fan, headdress with large bow and extended loops, shell-trimmed brown collar, and hooked-shell ear ornaments. Finally, both Pahtecatl and Quetzalcoatl are sexual partners with and hence inamic partners of Mayahuel.[338]

What light do the codical depictions of Pahtecatl shed upon his nature? Various codices depict overflowing octli vessels (sometimes adorned with a monkey's head) alongside Pahtecatl, associating him with octli consumption and prodigious regeneration.[339] *Codex Borbonicus* (pl. 11), for example, depicts Pahtecatl accompanied by a sun-night (half-sun–half-night) ideogram.[340] Seler argues the latter ideogram conveys the concept of *crepúsculo* ("dawn" or "twilight"), that is, "the transition between day and night, life and death, and equally, the resurrection or revival of day from night and of life from death."[341] Pahtecatl's half-black, half-red facial painting conveys the concept of *tlilli tlapalli*, that is, of transition, metamorphic change, and waxing and waning.[342] Pahtecatl and the octli gods typically wear malinalli-herb pendants or necklaces.[343] In sum, Pahtecatl (and the octli deities generally) represent the vital energies that nourish the continuing reemergence of life from death, day from night, and order from disorder.

Why is octli associated with war and sacrifice? Quiñones Keber draws our attention to the fact that during the festival of Two Rabbit, octli was imbibed through hollow tubes (malinalli shafts?) from a vessel called "two-rabbit basin."[344] Those allowed to imbibe the octli included the elderly as well as "the intrepid warriors, the bold, the foolish, who paid their debt with their heads and their breasts." By drinking octli, Aztec warriors "went about mocking death" since it was their destiny to nourish the Sun either by feeding captives to the Sun or by being fed to the Sun as captives themselves.[345] Octli is further associated with sacrifice since the Aztecs standardly administered octli to those about to be sacrificed. Doing so initiated and prepared the way for the victim's blood donation to the Sun by cooling and ordering his life energies.

The codices also standardly portray Pahtecatl with implements of autosacrifice such as sharpened bones, knives, and maguey thorns.[346] Seler contends the top right quarter of plate 13 of *Codex Borgia* depicts Pahtecatl sitting opposite "a bunch or sheaf of malinalli" with inserted sacrificial banners.[347] *Codex Telleriano-Remensis* (fol. 15v) depicts Pahtecatl wearing a pendant of malinalli grass.[348] *Codex Borbonicus* (pl. 11) shows him sitting by several receptacles, including one containing a sacrificial knife, sacrificial banner, and twisted rope, the other a cuauhxicalli with human hearts. Twisted rope is associated with sacrifice and sacrificial transformation. Pahtecatl wears a sacrificial knife breastplate (*tecpatl*) in *Codex Vaticanus 3773 B* (pls. 31 and 90) and in *Codex Fejérváry-Mayer* (pl. 14).[349] These connect Pahtecatl with blood obtained through autosacrifice, sacrifice, and war, and thereby connect Pahtecatl with the malinalli-ordered energy with which humans nourish the cosmos.

Depictions of Pahtecatl also standardly include symbols of war. Accompanying Pahtecatl in *Codex Borgia* (pl. 13) is *yaoyoatl* (the sign for war), consisting of a bundle of war implements including a rounded shield (*chimalli*), a bunch of darts (*tlacochtli*), a lance (*atlatl*), a bag of flint points, and a curved axe with studded blades.[350] He holds a curved axe in the *Codex Telleriano-Remensis* (fol. 15v).[351] *Codex Borgia* (pl. 13) and *Codex Borbonicus* (pl. 11) depict him wearing a crescent-moon-shaped nosepiece (*yacametzli*), also symbolizing war.[352]

In sum, the constellation of processes associated with Pahtecatl and Mayahuel demonstrate the metaphysical link between blood, autosacrifice, sacrifice, and war, on the one hand, and nourishment, rebirth, and renewal, on the other. Furthermore, they reveal that this metaphysical connection consists of energy that is prepared, ordered, and transmitted by means of malinalli-twisting-spinning. Pahtecatl and Mayahuel processes demonstrate how reproductive fecundity, renewal, and the metamorphosis of death into life (and life into death) that occurs between olin-defined life~death cycles are powered by malinalli-ordered energies. Malinalli-defined and -transmitted energy fuels the olin motion-change and olin-defined life-cycles of the Fifth Sun, Fifth Era, and all living things in the Fifth Era. Lastly, they make clear that malinalli-twisting-and-spinning represents one of the principal ways by which inamic partners are bound together with one another in agonistic tenstion.

HUNTING, WARRING, HARVESTING, COOKING, AND MALINALLI MOTION-CHANGE

Malinalli is associated with rabbits by way of their common association with Mayahuel, Pahtecatl, octli, and South. Rabbits symbolize great reproductive power and fertility because they possess great reproductive power and fecundity. They are conceptually and metaphysically associated with Tlaltecuhtli's reproductive prowess because they feed on the earth's grasses, feed close to the surface of the earth, and live and breed in the earth. Their reproductive prowess demonstrates Tlaltecuhtli's reproductive prowess because they derive their nourishment and hence their prowess from the energies contained in Tlaltecuhtli's malinalli grasses. This latter energy becomes available to them by means of digestion, a malinalli-defined process.[353] The year One Rabbit was the year sign of the Earth's birth and hence the year sign of Tlaltecuhtli.

The Aztecs also regarded rabbits as restless, anxious, fearful, timid, and lacking in self-discipline and self-control.[354] They move about unpredictably, skittishly, and rapidly. They follow the wild and wayward path of vagabondage – as opposed to the straight and middled path of civilized living. Rabbits also symbolize sexual excess, self-indulgence, profligacy, debauchery, and drunkenness. They dwell in forests or grasslands, that is, in the periphery. In lifestyle, movement, and dwelling, rabbits are therefore disordered and peripheral. The Aztecs viewed these attributes negatively since they contribute to imbalance and disintegration in the self, family, community, and Fifth Age. And yet rabbits are an abundant source of nourishment for humans. The rabbit was a favorite animal of the hunt, and rabbit meat, an important foodstuff. Durán reports that victorious warriors returning from battle were fed rabbit, that Moctezuma II fed his guests rabbit meat, and that rabbits "some uncooked, others in barbecue" were a tribute item.[355]

What does this tell us about malinalli? Like corn, rabbits are a source of earthly nourishment. Rabbits are wild, peripheral, and disorderly creatures whose life-energies require ordering before being transformed into and transmitted as nourishing life-energy for humans. Rabbit-energy is ordered and centered via hunting, capturing, cooking, and digesting – all malinalli-defined processes. The association with hunting implicates rabbits in a conceptual and metaphysical cluster uniting hunting, war, cooking, sacrifice, feeding, nourishment, and malinalli-defined metamorphosis.

Central to this cluster are the Chichimecs, who were renowned as excellent hunters (e.g., of rabbits and deer) and by extension, the Chichimec gods Mixcoatl ("Cloud Serpent") or Camaxtli ("Lord of Hunting"), and his female consort and inamic, Itzpapalotl. According to the *Annals of Cuauhtitlan*, cooking wild game was originally taught to the Chichimecs by Itzpapalotl.[356] Mixcoatl was embraced by Tenochtitlan; Camaxtli, by Huexotzinca and Tlaxcala.[357] As preeminent warriors and hunters, Mixcoatl and Camaxtli are associated with hunting, war, and sacrifice. The link between rabbits and Mixcoatl-Camaxtli further links hunting, war, and sacrifice with malinalli motion-change. Interestingly, the *Historia de los mexicano por sus pinturas* states Camaxtli rather than Pahtecatl discovered how to ferment aguamiel into octli.[358] This ties Camaxtli to octli, sacrifice, rabbits, and the energies fueling renewal. The name *Mixcoatl* ("Cloud Serpent") combines *mixtli* ("cloud)" and *coatl* ("serpent)" and thus refers to gyrating and spinning clouds.[359] Here we see a further link between malinalli twisting-spinning and hunting.

Aztec metaphysics understands hunting and capturing game in the wild, and hunting and capturing humans on the battlefield in identical terms. Both involve venturing forth from the center to seize wild foodstuffs from the periphery and then returning with them to the center. The relevant verb, *ma*, means "to hunt, to catch something, to take captives,"[360] "to capture," and "to fish."[361] Malinalli-twisting wild enemy warriors and wild game is an essential part of centering, ordering, and eventually transmitting their energy. Both occur during the dry winter season named *Tonalco* ("heat time-place") when the Sun is in the south, the time-place of the rabbit, life, and the day sign malinalli. Both provide energy-rich comestibles during the nonagricultural season.

Aztec metaphysics conceives the harvesting of corn and maguey in terms of hunting and capturing and thus also in terms of malinalli-defined transformation.[362] Unharvested corn and maguey are wild and of the periphery. One initiates hunting and harvesting with a variety of malinalli-defined rituals including uttering incantations that prepare the path for extracting energy from prey, foodstuffs, and captives. Uttering incantations enlists the creative powers of Ehecatl-Quetzalcoatl's malinalli-defined wind-speech-breath. One catches rabbits and deer with nets and snares made of twisted malinalli grass. One seizes, twists, and wrenches game, corn from stalks, and enemy hair. One tethers and guides all three using malinalli ropes that bind them to their destiny as food for humans and the Fifth Age (respectively). Finally, one cooks, eats, and digests the three as foodstuffs. Both cooking and digesting consist of malinalli-twisting and hence malinalli-ordering the disordered energies of raw foodstuffs. Both processes employ fire's malinalli-defined, transformative heat energy. Digestion adds a further stage of malinalli motion-change since it occurs in one's malinalli-twisted intestines.[363]

In sum, seizing wild game and corn yields Tlaltecuhtli's food for humans, while seizing enemy combatants yields human food (*tlacatlacualli*) for cosmic processes. As Read notes, the Aztecs regarded these as "reciprocal cosmic processes" of "transformative exchange."[364] This transformative exchange, so absolutely crucial to survival *in* the Fifth Age and survival *of* the Fifth Age, is defined by malinalli motion-change. David Freidel argues that one of the key concepts in Maya metaphysics is *k'awil*, which refers to any precious substance like blood or sap that nourishes gods, plants, animals, and humans. He writes, "K'awil as 'substance' conveys the idea of the magical [sic] transformative cycle that changes food (maize) into the flesh of gods and humans, and then back again into food (blood or its equivalent)."[365] Aztec metaphysics subscribes to such a notion. It conceives this "transformative cycle" in terms of malinalli-twisting-spinning-gyrating.

MALINALLI MOTION-CHANGE AND THE DYNAMICS OF ENERGY TRANSMISSION

Navel Cords and Lineage

The Aztecs used malinalli grass in the malinalli-twisting of *mecatl* (rope or cordage), and mecatl was commonly used to bind things together. Mecatl's twisting and spiraling shape is attested by related words such as *xocomecamaitl* ("vineshoot or tendril").[366] Vines and tendrils twist and spiral.[366] The abstract noun *mecayotl* ("genealogy, family relationship or lineage") combines *mecatl* ("rope") with the suffix *–yotl*, which is added to word stems to form abstract nouns meaning "-ness, -hood, -ship."[367] *Mecayotl* thus conveys the idea of being bound. One is bound to one's ancestors, who are also said "to guide one" (*xotemecayotia*).[368] Ancestral ties are ties that bind as well as ties that guide and that prepare the way. Descendants are bound to their ancestors by invisible (malinalli-twisted) cordage that functions as a conduit for the transmission of tonalli energy from ancestors to descendents.[369] A person's tonalli also links her to various clusters of cosmic powers. The Aztecs conceived this link as an invisible malinalli-twisted thread extending from her head to the sacred.[370]

Mother and unborn child are bound by a malinalli-twisted cord, namely, the umbilical cord (*xicmecayotl*, literally "cord of the navel" or "intestine of the navel").[371] *Xicmecayotl* combines *xictli* and *mecayotl*. Molina translates *xictli* as "navel or hole to shoot straight."[372] López Austin translates *xictli* as "navel: depression, knot, cord; navel region." He contends *xictli* derives from *xic*, meaning both "piercing"[373] and "hollow" (as in *xicalli* [jar] and *xiquipilli* [bag]).[374] The umbilical cord pierces the child's body at the navel, enabling the transmission of tonalli from mother to fetus and from cosmos to fetus. The umbilical cord operates as an energy channel. *Xicmecayotl* also suggests the child's tonalli lineage by way of the navel. The navel is the site of this energy transmission and thus the site of emergence and transformation. The Nahuatl word *axictli* ("whirlpool of water") supports this interpretation.[375] Whirlpools are sites of spiraling malinalli-defined transformation. They are pierced hollows in the skin of Tlaltecuhtli, up through which life energy swirls to the earth's surface. *Codex Vaticanus 3738 A* depicts the human navel as a spiral.[376] The image links various parts of the human body to the twenty days signs of the tonalpohualli, and links the navel to the day sign, Malinalli. We thus see further evidence of the connection between navels, twisting, spirals, spiraling energy, and malinalli motion-change.

López Austin argues the Aztecs modeled the cosmos upon the human body.[377] They believed the Fifth Sun-Earth Ordering possessed a navel and they located the navel at the center of the earth's surface. They called it *in tlalxicco* ("navel of the earth" or "place of the earth navel")[378] and *xicco* ("place of the navel").[379] Just as the human navel is one of the most significant areas of human beings since it lies at the center of their body, so too the earth's navel is one of the most significant areas of the Fifth Sun-Earth Ordering since it lies at the center of the body of the Fifth Age.[380] The Aztecs characterized the earth's center as "the root, the navel, and the heart of this whole earthly mechanism,"[381] and characterized "the navel of the earth" as a "circle of turquoise" wherein dwells Huehueteotl ("the Old God"), Ipalnemohuani ("Giver of Life," "the One through Whom One Lives"), and Ometeotl.[382] The Spanish side of Molina's *Vocabulario* translates *centro de la tierra* as *tlalli yyolloco* ("the place of the earth's heart").[383]

The Aztecs also characterized the earth's navel as the "navel of fire" (*in tlexicco*) since there resides Xiuhtecuhtli (Lord of Fire, the Year, and Time; the Turquoise Lord; who overlaps with the aged fire god, Huehueteotl).[384] From there Xiuhtecuhtli pumps sacred energy to the four quadrants of the Fifth Sun-Earth Ordering. The earth's navel thus doubles as *tlalli yyolloco* ("the place of the earth's heart"). The color of the navel and color of the human heart (yollo) is blue-green (turquoise): the color of order, equilibrium, fertility, rebirth and renewal.[385] The earth's navel-center is also the turquoise hearth, the primordial creative and transformative fire of the Fifth Age. Xiuhtecuhtli occupies the center-hence-navel of the quincunx depicted in *Codex Fejérváry-Mayer* (pl. 1; see Figure 4.3).

The earth's navel is where the *horizontal* and *vertical* centers of the Fifth Sun-Earth Ordering coincide. The navel sits at the solar- and hence olin-defined horizontal center of the Fifth Age's four orientations, four regions, and four corners. It also sits at the vertical center of the grand cosmic malinalli-defined umbilicus or axis mundi that transmits energy vertically between upper, earthly, and lower layers of the Fifth Age.[386] Aztec metaphysics conceives this cosmic axis as a grand cosmic umbilical cord, that is, as a malinalli-twisting and -spiraling, energy-transmitting conduit. Just as the human navel is the site where the umbilical cord pierces the human fetus, supplying it with life-sustaining and transforming energies from its mother, so likewise is tlalxicco the site where the vertical axis pierces the earth, supplying the earth's inhabitants with life-sustaining and transforming energies from the cosmic layers above and below. Like the human fetus, Tlalticpac and earthly beings receive life-sustaining sacred energy from "the Above and the Below" through malinalli-shaped pathways, that is, bicolored, two-ply intertwisted cords that resemble the bicolored intertwining arteries and veins of the umbilical cord.[387]

The vertical cosmic umbilicus conveys energy in two directions: from earthly to nonearthly and from nonearthly to earthly. This enables humans to recycle energy to "the Above and the Below" and thereby contribute to the continuing existence of the Fifth Age. The Aztecs accordingly built the Huey Teocalli, the sacred precinct, and Tenochtitlan upon this very spot. These, in turn, sit in Valley of Mexico: the navel and hollow of the earth's surface.

Finally, according to the creation story presented in the *Histoyre du Mechique*, Ehecatl and Tezcatlipoca met in the heart of Tlalteotl ("Earth Goddess") after entering her body through her navel and mouth (respectively). They then split her in half, forming the earth and the sky with her two halves.[388] It is not accidental that Ehecatl enters Tlalteotl at the navel and that he does so by means of piercing.

Malinalli Channels of Energy Circulation

Vital energies circulate continually between upper, middle, and lower layers of the cosmos, and do so in the form of two-ply spirals or double helices. These vertically flowing energy currents twist around one another like two-ply spun thread. Since they are malinalli-shaped, López Austin and Carrasco refer to them as "the malinalli." The axis mundi is obviously the most prominent of these.[389] Aztec artists commonly depicted the malinalli as two differently colored cords twisting around one another in double helical fashion.

Malinalli-defined twisting, spinning, whirling, drilling, coiling, spiraling, and gyrating therefore *define* the shape of the flowing and transfusing of energy between the vertical layers of the cosmos. Malinalli-twisting-spinning defines the shape of the vital forces that fuel creation, destruction, revitalization, rebirth, regeneration, and transformation. The Kogi of the Sierra Nevada de Santa Marta, for example, conceive the axis mundi as a giant spindle rod.[390] It is highly likely that the Aztecs did so as well, given the role of weaving as organizing metaphor in Aztec metaphysics and the centrality of malinalli-twisting-spinning in vertical energy transmission.

Each of the two intertwisting energy currents consists of one of two agonistic inamic partners: hot~cold, dry~wet, life~death, descending influence~ascending influence, and so on.[391] Hot, dry, and masculine (and so on) forces descending from above Tlalticpac form a double helix with with cold, wet, and feminine (and so on) forces ascending from below Tlalticpac. Through these malinalli-shaped currents travel the nourishing, initiating, and transformative energies that affect all things earthly. The two energy currents, according to López Austin, enabled "communication between the turquoise place (the sky) and the obsidian place (the underworld) to create the center, the place of the precious green stone (the surface of the earth)."[392] Malinalli-twisting-spinning constitutes one of the principal ways by which agonistic inamic partners are unified in the Fifth Age and therefore one of the principal forms of agonistic inamic unity and transformative motion-change in the Fifth Age.

These malinalli-shaped energy currents are bidirectional since they allow humans to convey energy from Tlalticpac to the above and to the below. Humans do so by malinalli-twisting-spinning the energies they wish to convey. Here, then, is the metaphysical rationale behind the centrality of malinalli-twisting-spinning in the Aztec rituals discussed above. By malinalli-twisting-spinning the energies of sacrificial victims and situating them within malinalli-twisting-spinning place-times (such as the zacapan, the temalacatl, and Tenochtitlan's sacred precinct), Aztec priests sought to give these earthbound energies the *shape* required for successful transmission to the above and the below.[393] The bidirectionality of these energy currents is essential to human participation in the continuation of the Fifth Age.

Perhaps the most telling of the cosmic layers is *ilhuicatl mamalhuacoca* ("sky where whirling, gyrating, or drilling occurs").[394] *Mamali*, as we've seen, means "to pierce, introduce, or drill a hole through something." Ilhuicatl mamalhuacoca is the fifth layer above Tlalticpac, the first and lowest layer of the nine genuine heavenly layers.[395] *Codex Vaticanus 3738 A* (fol. IV) depicts Ilhuicatl mamalhuacoca by round disks and arrows, suggesting the malinalli-spinning of a fire drill. Nicholson translates "ilhuicatl mamalhuacoca" as "Heaven of the Fire Drill."[396] López Austin believes the arrows allude to the "irradiation" of celestial forces.[397]

Ilhuicatl mamalhuacoca appears to be the interface between upper and middle realms as well as the place where the malinalli-twisting-spinning of heavenly forces occurs, giving them the shape necessary for drilling through the middle layers and penetrating the earth's surface and its inhabitants (see

Figure 8.7).[398] It is from this layer, for example, that "the gods" malinalli-drill tonalli and malinalli-breathe vital air into babies. Here, then, sacred energies are spun, whirled, twisted, and thus properly ordered for transfusion and transformative efficacy. The fact that the malinalli-defined gyrating, spinning, and twisting together of agonistic inamic forces occurs on ilhuicatl mamalhuacoca and *not* on any higher heavenly layers of the cosmos strongly suggests that malinalli motion-change applies to the middle realm of the cosmos (i.e., the Fifth Sun-Earth Ordering) but *not* the upper realm and hence *not* the cosmos per se.

Lastly, given the role of weaving as organizing metaphor in Aztec metaphysics, it is reasonable to suppose that the Aztecs modeled the vertical malinalli channels upon several aspects of spinning. First, a weaver holds her spindle rod (more or less) vertically when spinning raw fiber into thread. The spindle rod thus spins vertically and exhibits vertical malinalli motion-change. Second, as fiber is malinalli-twisted-spun into thread, it moves up and down the vertically positioned spindle rod. Analogously, the malinalli-twisted energies originating in "the Above, the Below" move both up and down the vertically positioned axis mundi, as do the energies originating in human ritual that are conveyed to "the Above, the Below." In short, the motion-change of malinalli channels and spindle rods is vertical and transformative.[399]

Malinalli Twisting Cosmic Trees

The Aztecs conceived the vertical currents of double-helix-shaped energy as flowing up and down within the trunks of five great ceiba trees rooted in the under, spanning the middle, and holding up the heavenly levels. They are located at the horizontal cum vertical center and four cardinal points of the Fifth Age. *Codex Fejérváry Mayer* (pl. 1) illustrates these trees (see Figures 4.3 and 5.15).[400]

Malinalli Twisting, Cosmos, and the Human Body

López Austin argues the Aztecs believed the interior of the human body to be "a system of intercommunication through multiple canals which allowed fluids to flow with relative ease from one viscera to another,"[401] and believed these canals to be malinalli-shaped. One of the Nahuatl words for blood vessel is *mecatl* ("rope or cordage").[402] Blood vessels are malinalli-shaped tubes through which blood flows. The umbilicus is yet another malinalli-twisted passageway of energy transfusion. The Aztecs correspondingly conceived the Fifth Age as consisting of a widespread system of malinalli-shaped tubes through which energy traveled from one layer to another.

5.3. GRAPHIC EVIDENCE

Aztec artist-scribes communicated the idea of malinalli motion-change and malinalli-defined transformation using a variety of polysemous ideograms and motifs including spirals, double helices, coils, swirls, twisting cords, fiddlehead volutes, and the Malinalli glyph. These not only depict and symbolize malinalli motion-change but also transmit malinalli-defined energy to their works and to the cosmos.

SPIRALS, COILS, AND DOUBLE HELICES

Aztec artists employed spirals, twists, coils, and double helices to convey the concept of malinalli-shaped, vertical transmission and transformation of vital energy. The figures are wonderfully ambiguous since they simultaneously suggest ascending *and* descending motion-change as well as decentering *and* centering motion-change. Double helices emphasize the malinalli-defined unification of agonistic inamichuan.

The Malinalli and Atl Tlachinolli

Artist-scribes depicted the dual malinalli-intertwisting currents of ascending~ descending energies traveling within the great cosmic trees as double helices consisting of two different-colored strands twisted one around another. Each stream represents one of two parallel agonistic inamic partners, and their double helical intertwisting represents their unification through malinalli-twisting-spinning. López Austin claims the ascending cold current is commonly depicted by a stream of water, nocturnal stream, stream of wind, flint stone points, shells, or drops of water, while the descending hot current is commonly depicted by a stream of blood, strand of flowers, or simply flowers (see Figure 5.15).[403]

The malinalli-intertwisting currents of ascending and descending energies that transverse the intermediate realm of the Fifth Age are also commonly depicted by the *atl tlachinolli* (see Figure 5.16). The ideogram consists of the same two streams of inamic forces bound together in agnotics tension by means of malinalli twisting-spinning.

The couplet *atl tlachinolli* consists of *atl* ("water") and *tlachinolli* ("burned thing"). Scholars translate it as "water and fire," "water-burned things," "water-burnt field," or "flaming water."[404] Narrowly construed, couplet and ideogram function respectively as metaphor for and symbol of warfare, where the latter is conceived as a process that twists-spins inamic partners together in agonistic tension with one another. More broadly, they serve as metaphor for and symbol of the malinalli processes that twist-spin together the inamic forces that travel

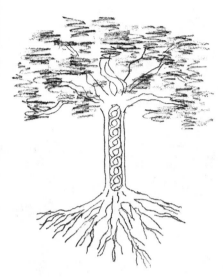

FIGURE 5.15. *Malinalli within the interior of the cosmic tree. (Redrawn from López Austin [1997:117, Figure 14].)*

FIGURE 5.16. *Atl tlachinolli. (Author's drawing, Teocalli of the Sacred War.)*

between layers of the cosmos.[405] Atl tlachinolli also serves as an ideogram for the continuous revitalization and regeneration of olin-defined life~death cycles. Like the life~death figures discussed in chapter 3 (Figures 3.2 and 3.3), atl tlachinolli expresses the irreducible ambiguity of reality.

Many scholars deem the atl tlachinolli to be one of two definitive ideograms of the Fifth Age (the other being the Olin glyph).[406] Its importance to Aztec thought is indicated by the image carved on the back of the Teocalli of the Sacred War. The image depicts an eagle perched upon a nopal cactus holding the atl tlachinolli in its beak.

Finally, an early colonial terra cotta disk from San Juan Teotihuacan shows a Christian cross perched atop a pyramid. Behind the cross sits a solar flower from which radiates malinalli-swirling and -twisting energy beams (see Figure 5.17).

Quetzalcoatl

Aztec artists standardly depicted Quetzalcoatl (including his aspects as Ehecatl and Venus) by means of coiling feathered serpents, a twisting monkey standing atop a coiled serpent, spirals, double helices, coils, and twists (see Figures 3.8, 3.9, 5.11, 5.14). Quetzalcoatl and Ehecatl-Quetzalcoatl commonly

FIGURE 5.17. *Solar flower radiating malinalli energy. (Courtesy of the Field Museum.)*

wear spiralling adornments such as the "twisted wind jewel" pendant (*ehecacoz-catl* or *ecailacatzcozcatl*), "twisted-shell ear ornaments" (*tzicoliuhqui nacochtli* or *epcolloli*), and "golden snail collar" (*teocuitla acuechcozcatl*) (see Figures 3.4, 3.5, and 5.18).⁴⁰⁷

Twisted-wind-jewel adornments represent the cross-sectioned conch shells from which they are commonly made. Conch shells symbolize wombs, fertility, regeneration, and the reinitiation of the life~death cycle. As such they are appropriate adornments for Quetzalcoatl as progenitor of humans. Quetzalcoatl initiates new beginnings, new dawnings, and new cycles – and the shape of this doing is a spiral. The cutaway shell also reveals an interior spiral, indicating its malinalli-shaped power of creative transformation. The Aztecs conceived both the womb and the birth canal as spiral-shaped. Artist-scribes also routinely depicted Quetzalcoatl's and Xolotl's paths as morning and evening stars as spirals (see Figures 3.8. 3.9, and 5.11.).

The Aztecs built Ehecatl-Quetzalcoatl's temples as large life-renewing wombs with conical roofs and spiraling interiors resembling cross-sectioned conches.[408] The codices standardly depict Quetzalcoatl wearing a conical hat (*copilli*). The conical shape appears to be of Huastec origin. Two, non–mutually exclusive interpretations come to mind. First, the conical shape depicts the shape of a spindle

FIGURE 5.18. *Quetzalcoatl's "twisted wind jewel." (Redrawn from Séjourné [2003:51, Figure 49].)*

rod "pregnant" with spun thread (see Figures 3.4, 3.5, 5.1, and 5.19). Both spindle rod and spinning instantiate malinalli motion-change and transformation. Recall the Aztec riddle likening a spindle rod's dancing in the spindle bowl to sexual intercourse and the spindle rod's accumulating spun thread to becoming pregnant. Spinning gives birth to woven cloth. This helps explain why Ehecatl-Quetzalcoatl's temples were regarded as wombs, and why he wears a copilli. The copilli indicates his role as the bringer of life. Second, Jacques Galinier claims contemporary Otomí and ancient Huastec traditions interpret the conical shape as the male glans.[409]

Spirals

Spirals often depict the swirling water of springs and small lakes. As wombs of Chalchiuhtlicue ("She of Jade Skirt," goddess of surface waters), they are places of life, fertility, regeneration, and transformation.[410] The Nahuatl word for whirlpool, *axictli*, combines *atl* with *xictli* and literally means "water navel."[411] Two words for spring water, *yuliuani atl* and *yuliliz atl*, mean "life-giving water" and "water that will give life" (respectively).[412] They combine *atl* ("water") and *yoli* ("life, live, or something that is alive"). *Yoli* is, of course, related to *yollo, teyolia*, and ultimately *olin*. Swirling, spiraling water is conceptually and metaphysically associated with replenishing olin-defined life~death cycles.

The most important shrine to Chalchiuhtlicue was Pantitlan, a spot in the center of Lake Texcoco where, according to Durán, the lake had a great

FIGURE 5.19. *Spindle rod "pregnant" with thread. (Author's drawing.)*

"tremendous whirlpool" that appears "when the water is sucked down." During Huey Tozoztli ("Great Vigil"), priests slit the throat of a young girl and poured her blood into the spiraling water. They then cast her body into the drain, where it disappeared.[413] If Durán's description is correct, Pantitlan functioned as a portal for descending malinalli-shaped energy transmission.

Aztec artist-scribes depicted speaking, singing, song-prayer, playing musical instruments, fire, and smoke using volutes (see Figures 5.8. 5.9., 5.10, and 5.12). Copal smoke nourished the gods and transmitted messages from the human realm to the upper realm.[414] Volutes are fitting since these processes transmit energy and communicate between earthly and nonearthly layers of the cosmos via malinalli-shaped paths.

Constanza Vega Sosa discusses a motif she calls "*la espiral desdoblada*" ("the unfolding spiral").[415] Two spirals unfold in opposite directions, one counterclockwise, the other (its inamic?) clockwise. The motif seems better characterized as an S-shaped, *double unfolding spiral* since it consists of a single curved line with unfolding spirals on each end. *Codex Borbonicus* (pl. 31) depicts a banner decorated with a double unfolding spiral (see Figure 5.20; see also Figure 3.8). This motif is plausibly interpreted as depicting the malinalli-shaped paths of the Sun's rebirth each dawn and death each dusk connected by the Sun's course over and under the earth; the malinalli-shaped paths of Quetzalcoatl and Xolotl as Morning and Evening Stars (respectively) as they accompany the Sun's risings and settings; a swirling rain cloud and by association the constellation of malinalli-defined Ehecatl-Quetzalcoatl wind-, water-, and fertility-processes including rain, wind, thunder, rivers, sexuality, and rebirth; and Mixcoatl ("Cloud Serpent") and hence coiling and gyrating clouds.

Xicalcoliuhqui

One of the most striking Postclassic Aztec and Mesoamerican motifs is the xicalcoliuhqui (see Figures 3.6 and 3.7).[416] *Xicalcoliuhqui* derives from *xicalli* and *colihui*. Molina translates *xicalli* as "*vaso de calabaza*" ("gourd vessel");[417] Durán, as "bowl (*lebrillo*)" or "shallow tray or trough (*batea*) made from large calabazas."[418]

López Austin contends *xicalli* derives from *xic* ("navel, depression, knot"), which means "hollow" in the case of words such as *xicalli* ("*vaso*" or "cup") and *xiquipilli*. Etymologically, *xic* means "piercing."[419] *Colihui* means "for something to curve, turn."[420] *Colihui* refers to curving, coiling, twisting, and turning around something, and so appears to be an instance of malinalli motion-change broadly construed. Combining the two we get "curved or twisted gourd vessel." Sahagún reports that the Aztecs placed the blood and heart of sacrificial victims into a *xicara*

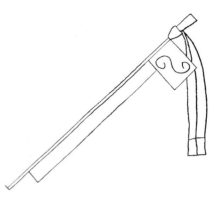

FIGURE 5.20. *Double unfolding spiral on a banner. (Redrawn from* Codex Borbonicus *[Loubat 1899: pl. 31].)*

or "gourd vessel."[421] Guy Stresser-Péan asserts Mesoamericans have long consumed water and pulque from decorated, lacquered xicalli (now called *jícaras*) and regard the bowls as female-gendered objects and symbols of water.[422]

The xicalcoliuhqui conveys the ideas of malinalli-twisted energy, malinalli-generated energy transmission, and malinalli-generated nourishment, regeneration, and transformation. Like spirals and coils, the xicalcoliuhqui is ambiguous since it suggests simultaneous ascending *and* descending, inward *and* outward, and decentering *and* centering motion-change. It also conveys the idea of malinalli-defined sacrificial transformation. During Tlacaxipehualiztli, for example, the pierced, malinalli-twisted-spun body of a captive enemy warrior – or more precisely, his blood-filled chest cavity sans heart – served as a malinalli-twisted, female-gendered gourd vessel (xicalli) from which the gods drank blood (water, nourishing liquid).[423]

THE MALINALLI DAY SIGN GLYPH

The Malinalli day-sign glyph is, as Elizabeth Boone points out, one of the most challenging due to its variability.[424] Aztec codices emphasize grass, while *Borgia* group codices emphasize a defleshed mandible (with an extruded eye sometimes rising from the teeth). Another common glyph consists of a skull or defleshed jawbone from which grows a stand of malinalli grass (see Figures 5.21 and 5.22). Teeth and eyes figure prominently in these. Sometimes the grass bears the distinctive featherlike flowers of malinalli grass (see Figure 5.24). Several instances consist of a toothed mandible with neither extruded eye nor grass

FIGURE 5.22. *Mandible with grass. (Redrawn from* Codex Vaticanus *3773 B [Loubat 1900: pl. 90].)*

FIGURE 5.21. *Skull with grass. (Redrawn from* Vaticanus *3738 A [Loubat 1900: pl. 28r].)*

FIGURE 5.23. *Mandible lacking grass. (Redrawn from* Codex Fejérváry-Mayer *[Loubat 1901: pl. 39].)*

FIGURE 5.24. *Mandible with volute and grass. (*Codex Borgia *[1993: fol. 73]; courtesy of Dover Press.)*

(Figure 5.23). Occasionally, a coiling volute ascends from the jawbone alongside the ascending malinalli grass (Figure 5.24). In several other cases, the malinalli glyph includes an eye extruding from the mandible (Figure 5.25).

Codex Fejérváry-Mayer contains multiple instances (e.g., pl. 20) of an abbreviated malinalli glyph consisting of a half-red, half-white eye extruding from a circle. *Codex Borgia* (pl. 13) includes a malinalli motif that lacks skull and

FIGURE 5.25. *Mandible with extruding eye.*
(Redrawn from Codex Laud *[Graz 1966:*
pl. 9]; see also Codex Fejérváry-Mayer
[Loubat 1901: pl. 23].)

FIGURE 5.26. *Bush with teeth, eyes, and*
*sacrificial flags. (*Codex Borgia *[1993: pl.*
13]; courtesy of Dover Press.)

mandible (see Figure 5.26). According to Seler sacrificial or mortuary paper banners sprout among the malinalli grass leaves and flower-bearing stalks. Two, red, serpentine-tongue-like roots descend in opposite directions from what appears to be a mouth, which bears teeth. A single half-red, half-white eye sits at the image's center above its the mouth.[425]

What do these tell us about malinalli motion-change? First, skulls and mandibles symbolize the life-renewing powers of death and hence renewal and regeneration. The fact that malinalli grass grows from skulls and mandibles further suggests the abundant regenerative power of death to bring into existence new life.

Second, teeth are associated with ritual capturing, killing, eating, and feeding, and thus with the transformative power of life to feed death and death to feed life. Indeed, life and death both consume and feed one another (as is fitting for inamic partners). Teeth alone, but also combined with a skull or mandible, suggest the mouth, which is a location of transformational consumption. One of riddles quoted by Sahagún refers to human teeth as "that which grinds like flint knives."[426] Flint knives, of course, are associated with death, feeding, transformation, and rebirth. Teeth also evoke Tlaltecuhtli, our life-giving and flesh-devouring Earth-Mother. Teeth and mouth figure prominently in depictions of Tlaltecuhtli, as does her obsidian-knife tongue. The latter clearly ties her reproductive ability to the consumption of human energy: that is, sacrificial transformation and the transfusion of vital energy from one state (human beings) to another (earth processes). According to the *Histoyre du Mechique*, the gods decided Tlaltecuhtli would bring forth all the food needed to sustain human life. Yet she is equally linked to human sacrifice because she refuses to bring forth fruit if not fed human hearts.[427] Humans and earth are bound together by mutual eating.

Teeth also figure prominently in depictions of Tlaltecuhtli's open maw. Peterson argues a bony jaw with teeth is "the most consistent denominator of the earth goddess complex."[428] Frances Berdan claims the Nahuatl word for tooth (*tlantli*) may also mean "abundance of,"[429] and that the use of teeth in glyphs may convey the concept of abundance. When included in the malinalli glyph, therefore, teeth may suggest abundant power of the earth manifested by the annual reappearance of malinalli grasses upon the hills. Teeth symbolize the Tlaltecuhtli's prodigious powers of regeneration and transformation. Teeth may also signify a weaver's comb (*tziquaoaztli*).[430] Weavers use combs to beat down and tighten the weft threads in the process of weaving thread into cloth. If so, teeth once more participate in and so symbolize transformation.

Third, Seler contends extruding eyes symbolize sacrificial practices such as bloodletting and mortification.[431] Here, too, we have references to sacrificial transformation, feeding, renewal, and the transmission of energy from humans to "the Above, the Below." Mandibles also convey the idea of sacrificial death, feeding, transformation, rebirth, and life – especially when combined with an extruded eye.[432]

Lastly, there's malinalli grass itself: a wild, annual grass that burgeons from Tlaltecuhtli with the first rains only to die shortly thereafter with the arrival of the hot, dry summer. As an annual, the grass repeats this cycle of birth, death, and renewal yearly. The grass accordingly symbolizes cyclical renewal as well as the earth's boundless power to generate new life from death. The occasional coiled, ascending volute emerging from the jawbone alongside the malinalli grass suggests vertical energy transmission between layers of the cosmos. The malinalli grass sometimes yields tall featherlike flowers that resemble sacrificial banners marking the time-place of transformation. Both flowers and feathers symbolize preciousness and evanescence. Flowers also symbolize the Fifth Sun, heat, tonalli, fire, flower war, human hearts, and human blood spilled in war and sacrifice.[433]

The ideogram on plate 13 of *Codex Borgia* (see Figure 5.26) consists of a malinalli bush with featherlike flowers; two roots consisting of two streams of blood flowing from a teeth-bearing mouth and into the earth; a single eye; and sacrificial or mortuary paper banners. Blood flowing into the earth suggests sacrificial feeding of Tlaltecuhtli. That the two streams of blood resemble common depictions of a snake's forked tongue suggests transformation, as snakes symbolize transformation. The banners symbolize transformation and renewal through ritual sacrifice. The ideogram also suggests the concept of zacapan or time-place of sacrifice. It includes sacrificial banners, the Nahuatl name for which is *pan(tli)*. The root, *pan*, is a homonym with the Nahuatl postposition, -*pan*, meaning "on the surface of, for or at a particular time.⁴³⁴ Such wordplay is in keeping with what Berdan calls the Nahuas' "love of puns."⁴³⁵ This wordplay means "in the time-place of sacrificial transformation."

In sum, the foregoing Malinalli day-sign glyphs emphasize sacrificial transformation and renewal, the regeneration of life from death via eating and digesting, the fructifying and vivifying potency of death, and the transmission of energy between vertical layers of the cosmos (i.e., Upper, Middle, and Lower layers). Spirals, coils, and double helices likewise convey the transmission and transformation – both ascending and descending – of vital forces between vertical layers of the cosmos. Double helices in particular highlight the malinalli-defined, agonistic unification of inamic partners.

5.4. CONCLUSION

Malinalli motion-change plays a vital and indispensable role in the becoming and processing of the Fifth Sun, Fifth Age, and all inhabitants of the Fifth Age. If olin motion-change constitutes the biorhythm of the Fifth Sun, Fifth Age, and all inhabitants of the Fifth Age, then malinalli motion-change constitutes the shape of the conveyance, circulation, and recycling of vital energies that initiate, nourish, fortify, and complete these olin-defined biorhythms. Olin-defined processes need nourishing and malinalli processes supply them with such nourishment. If we think of olin as the beating heart of the Fifth Age, then we should think of malinalli as the twisting arteries, veins, and entrails through which circulates the energy that nourishes that beating heart. These twisting and gyrating paths of circulating energy function as the energy-conveying and life-sustaining bloodstream/foodstream of the Fifth Age. Malinalli motion-change figures prominently in Aztec rituals because it makes possible humankind's active participation in the regeneration and continuation of the Fifth Age.

Like olin motion-change, malinalli motion-change is *not a kind* of life-energy but rather one of three principal *shapes* and *orderings* of life-energy in the cosmos. Like olin, malinalli refers to a specific kind of quantitative and qualitative motion-change. If olin motion-change constitutes the pattern of motion-change involved in the transmission of energy *within* and *across* olin-organized, four-phased life~death cycles, then malinalli motion-change constitutes the pattern of motion-change involved in actively transmitting energy *between* vertical layers of the Fifth Sun–Earth Ordering (e.g., the Above, the Below, and Tlalticpac; humans, Sun, and Earth); *between* the olin-defined life-cycles of different kinds of things (e.g., between Sun and grass, grass and rabbit, rabbit and human, human and Sun, Sun and grass, and so on); and *between* different conditions of the same thing (e.g., disorderly raw cotton and orderly thread; raw foodstuffs and cooked foodstuffs; tlazolli-ridden wrongdoer and purified wrongdoer before and after confessing to Tezcatlipoca; and disorderly captives and orderly foodstuff during Tlacalxipehualiztli). Finally, like olin motion-change, malinalli motion-change binds together inamic partners such as life~death, being~nonbeing, dry~wet, and male~female into agonistic unity. But unlike olin, malinalli does so by twisting, spinning, drilling, and coiling.

NOTES

1. Jeanette Favrot Peterson, "Sacrificial Earth: Iconography and Function of Malinalli Grass in Aztec Culture," in *Flora and Fauna Imagery in Precolumbian Cultures: Iconography and Function*, ed. Jeanette Favrot Peterson, BAR International Series, 171 (Oxford: BAR, 1982), 113–48. These grasses are members of the *Muhlenbergia* family.

2. See Xavier Noguez, "Códice de la Cruz-Badiano," *Arqueología Mexicana* 16, no. 94 (2008): 84–85.

3. Bernardino de Sahagún, *Florentine Codex: General History of the Things of New Spain*, ed. and trans. Arthur J.O. Anderson and Charles Dibble (Santa Fe, NM: School of American Research and University of Utah, 1953–1982), 11:194, see fig. 635b.

4. Fray Diego Durán, *Book of the Gods and Rites* and *The Ancient Calendar*, trans. and ed. Fernando Horcasitas and Doris Heyden (Norman: University of Oklahoma Press, 1971), 401.

5. E.g., Alexander von Humboldt and Aimé Bonpland, *Researches Concerning the Institutions and Monuments of the Ancient Inhabitants of America*, trans. Helen Maria Williams (Amsterdam: Theatrum Orbis Terrarum and Da Capo Press, 1972), 1:313; Elizabeth Hill Boone, *Cycles of Time and Meaning in the Mexican Books of Fate* (Austin: University of Texas Press, 2007), 37; Richard F. Townsend, "Coronation at Tenochtitlan," in *The Aztec Templo Mayor*, ed. Elizabeth Hill Boone (Washington, DC: Dumbarton Oaks, 1987), 371–410; Kay A. Read, *Time and Sacrifice in the Aztec Cosmos* (Bloomington: Indian University Press, 1998); Ross Hassig, *Time, History and Belief in Aztec and Colonial Mexico* (Austin: University of Texas Press, 2001), 9; and Davíd Carrasco with Scott Sessions, *Daily Life of the Aztecs: People of the Sun and Earth* (Westport, CT: Greenwood Press, 1998).

6. Peterson, "Sacrificial Earth," 115.

7. Leonardo López Luján, *The Offerings of the Templo Mayor of Tenochtitlan*, rev. ed., trans. Bernard R. Ortiz de Montellano and Thelma Ortiz de Montellano (Albuquerque: University of New Mexico Press, 2005), 198.

8. Durán, *Book of the Gods*, 401.

9. Peterson, "Sacrificial Earth," 115.

10. *"Malinalli, cosa torcida, soga de hierba, escoba"* (Eduard Seler, *Comentarios al Códice Borgia*, 3 volumes [México, DF: Fondo de Cultura Económica, 1963 (1904)], I:19), translation mine.

11. *"'Torcido' o una hierba de este nombre"* (Alfonso Caso, *Los Calendarios Prehispánicos* [México, DF: Universidad Nacional Autónoma de México, Instituto de Investigaciones Históricas, 1967], 12), translation mine.

12. See R. Joe Campbell, *A Morphological Dictionary of Classical Nahuatl: A Morpheme Index to the* Vocabulario en lengua mexicana y castellana *of Fray Alonso de Molina* (Madison: Hispanic Seminary of Medieval Studies, 1985), 170.

13. All translations are by Campbell (*Morphological Dictionary*, 170) unless otherwise indicated.

14. I have added "thread" to Campbell's translation since it omits Molina's *hilo*.

15. Rémi Siméon, *Diccionario de la lengua náhuatl o mexicana*, trans. Josefina Olivia de Coll (México, DF: Siglo Veintiuno Editores, 1977), 251, translation from the Spanish mine.

16. Andrés de Olmos, *Arte de la lengua mexicana y vocabulario*, ed. René Acuña (México, DF: Universidad Autónoma de México, 1985), 142.

17. Alfredo López Austin, *Tamoanchan, Tlalocan: Places of Mist*, trans. Bernard R. Ortiz de Montellano and Thelma Ortiz de Montellano (Niwot: University Press of Colorado, 1997), 118.

18. Peterson, "Sacrificial Earth," 115.

19. Frances Karttunen, *An Analytical Dictionary of Nahuatl* (Norman: University of Oklahoma Press, 1983), 134.

20. Ibid., 280.

21. Siméon, *Diccionario*, 251, translation mine.

22. Ibid.

23. Patricia Rieff Anawalt, "Weaving," in *The Oxford Encyclopedia of Mesoamerican Cultures: The Civilizations of Mexico and Central America*, ed. Davíd Carrasco (Oxford: Oxford University Press, 2001), 3:324.

24. Alba Guadalupe Mastache, "Weaving in Ancient Mexico," trans. Debra Nagao, *Arqueología Mexicana* Edición especial, 19 (2005): 86.

25. Pace Louise Burkhart, Cecelia Klein, and Jeanette Peterson, who equate twistedness with that which is disheveled, entangled, knotted, and disorderly, and therefore

with that which is undesirable and ought to be avoided. See Louise M. Burkhart, *The Slippery Earth: Nahua-Christian Dialogue in Sixteenth-Century Mexico* (Tucson: University of Arizona Press, 1989), chapter 4; Cecelia Klein, "Woven Heaven, Tangled Earth: The Weaver's Paradigm of the Mesoamerican Cosmos," in *Ethnoastronomy and Archaeoastronomy in the American Tropics*, ed. Anthony Aveni and Gary Urton, Annals of the New York Academy of Sciences, No. 38 (New York: New York Academy of Sciences, 1982), 1–35; and Peterson, "Sacrificial Earth." Molina lists no *malina*-related words that refer to twisted minds, cognitive abilities, emotions, or moral characters (see Campbell, *Morphological Dictionary*, 170).

26. Campbell, *Morphological Dictionary*, 184–85.

27. Ibid., 169–70.

28. Siméon, *Diccionario*, 251.

29. Karttunen, *Analytical Dictionary*, 134.

30. All translations are by Campbell unless otherwise indicated. Campbell, *Morphological Dictionary*, 160–70.

31. Campbell omits *mazorca* from his English translation.

32. Olmos, *Arte de la Lengua*, 141, translation mine.

33. Karttunen, *Analytical Dictionary*, 134.

34. James Lockhart, *The Nahuas after the Conquest: A Social and Cultural History of the Indians of Central Mexico, Sixteenth through Eighteenth Centuries* (Stanford, CA: Stanford University Press, 1992), 557n9.

35. Ibid.

36. The preceding terms are from Karttunen (*Analytical Dictionary*, 193) or Campbell (*Morphological Dictionary*, 122–23).

37. Paso y Troncoso's depiction of a spinner using a spinning wheel is thus anachronistic (see Sahagún, *Florentine Codex*, X:fig. 57).

38. Jonathan Amith reports contemporary Nahuatl-speakers in Guerrero use *malakatl* to refer to the entire spindle and use *malakateyo:hli* or *malakatetl* to refer to the whorl (Amith, personal correspondence, 2/23/09).

39. See the descriptions of good and bad spinners in Sahagún, *Florentine Codex*, X:35, 52.

40. Thelma D. Sullivan, "Tlazolteotl-Ixcuina: The Great Spinner and Weaver," in *The Art and Iconography of Late Post-Classic Central Mexico*, ed. Elizabeth Boone (Washington, DC: Dumbarton Oaks, 1982), 14. According to Stacy Schaefer, Wixáritari believe "spinning yarn is like giving life." The great genetrix Takutsi "breathed" life into all her creations when she spun yarn (Stacy B. Schaefer, *To Think with a Good Heart: Wixárika Women, Weavers, and Shamans* [Salt Lake City: University of Utah Press, 2002], 229).

41. Sahagún, *Florentine Codex*, VI:240.

42. Ibid., VI:239.

43. The following terms are taken from Campbell, *Morphological Dictionary*, 378.

44. See Peterson, "Sacrificial Earth"; Doris Heyden, "The Skin and Hair of Tlaltecuhtli," in *The Imagination of Matter: Religion and Ecology in Mesoamerican Tradition*, ed. Davíd Carrasco, 211–24, BAR International Series 515 (Oxford: BAR, 1989), 211–24; Elizabeth Baquedano, "Aspects of Death Symbolism in Aztec Tlaltecuhtli," in *The Symbolism in the Plastic and Pictorial Representations of Ancient Mexico: A Symposium of the 46th International Congress of Americanists, Amsterdam 1988*, ed. Jacqueline de Durand-Forest and Marc Eisinger, Bonner Amerikanistische Studien, vol. 21 (Bonn: Bonner Amerikanistische Studien, 1993), 157–80; Elizabeth Baquedano, "Earth Deities," in *The Oxford Encyclopedia of Mesoamerican Cultures: The Civilizations of Mexico and Central America*, ed. Davíd Carrasco (Oxford: Oxford University Press, 2001), 1:350–51; and Richard F. Townsend, "Malinalco and the Lords of Tenochtitlán," in *The Art and Iconography of Late Postclassic Central Mexico*, ed. Elizabeth H. Boone (Washington, DC: Dumbarton Oaks, 1982), 111–40.

45. *Histoyre du Mechique*, in *Teogonía e historia de los mexicanos: Tres opúsculos del siglo XVI*, 1st ed., ed. Angel María Garibay K. (México: Editorial Porrúa, 1965), 108.

46. See Peterson, "Sacrificial Earth," 118; Burkhart, *Slippery Earth*, 88 and chapter 2.

47. Peterson, "Sacrificial Earth," 118.

48. See ibid.; Sullivan, "Tlazolteotl-Ixcuina"; and Burkhart, *Slippery Earth*, 93.

49. Henry B. Nicholson, "Religion in Pre-Hispanic Central Mexico," in *Handbook of Middle American Indians*, vol. 10, ed. Robert Wauchope, Gordon F. Elkholm, and Ignacio Bernal (Austin: University of Texas Press, 1971), 422.

50. *Tzonpachpul* consists of *tzontli* ("head of hair"), *pachtli* and *pul* ("big" in a derogatory sense). *Pachtli* refers to parasitic plants such as moss and to plant refuse such as hay (see Karttunen, *Analytical Dictionary of Nahuatl*, 183).

51. Campbell, *Morphological Dictionary*, 115.

52. Karttunen, *Analytical Dictionary*, 202.

53. Sahagún, *Florentine Codex*, IV:11.

54. Ibid., II:155; see also Sahagún, *Primeros memoriales: Paleography*, 66–67.

55. Alfredo López Austin, *The Human Body and Ideology: Concepts of the Ancient Nahuas*, trans. Thelma Ortiz de Montellano and Bernard R. Ortiz de Montellano (Salt Lake City: University of Utah Press, 1988), I:204–29. See also Jill Leslie McKeever Furst, *The Natural History of the Soul in Ancient Mexico* (New Haven, CT: Yale University Press, 1995); John D. Monaghan, "The Person, Destiny, and the Construction of Difference in Mesoamerica," *RES 33* (Spring 1998): 137–46; Davíd Carrasco, *City of Sacrifice: The Aztec Empire and the Role of Violence in Civilization* (Boston: Beacon Press, 1999); and Davíd Carasco, "Uttered from the Heart: Guilty Rhetoric among the Aztecs," *History of Religions* 39 (1999): 1–31.

56. McKeever Furst, *Natural History*, 136, brackets mine.

57. López Austin, *Human Body and Ideology*, 1:205; see also 58–61.

58. Willard Gingerich, "*Chipahuacanemiliztli*, 'the Purified Life,' in the Discourses of Book VI, Florentine Codex," in *Smoke and Mist: Mesoamerican Studies in Memory of Thelma D. Sullivan, Part II*, ed. J. Kathryn Josserand and Karen Dakin (Oxford: British Archaeological Reports, 1988), 527.

59. López Austin, *Human Body and Ideology*, 1:204–29; McKeever Furst, *Natural History*, 126–27.

60. McKeever Furst, *Natural History*, 126.

61. Ibid., 128–30.

62. McKeever Furst, *Natural History*, 176–77; see also López Austin, *Human Body and Ideology*, 1:220–22.

63. Garibay, "Histoyre du Mechique," 110. *Centeotl* combines *cintli* or *centli* ("dried ears of maize") and *teotl* ("sacred"). See Karttunen, *Analytical Dictionary*, 35.

64. Burkhart, *Slippery Earth*, ch. 4.

65. McKeever Furst, *Natural History*, 126.

66. Peterson, "Sacrificial Earth."

67. What follows is indebted to Peterson, "Sacrificial Earth"; Klein, "Woven Heaven"; and Campbell, *Morphological Dictionary*.

68. Karttunen, *Analytical Dictionary*, 142.

69. Campbell, *Morphological Dictionary*, 185.

70. Ibid.

71. For example, see Sahagún, *Florentine Codex*, VIII:fig. 90.

72. Henry B. Nicholson, "The Significance of the 'Looped Cord' Year Symbol in Pre-Hispanic Mexico," *Estudios de cultura náhuatl* 6 (1966): 135–48.

73. Sahagún, *Florentine Codex*, VII:49, fig. 75; X:figs. 3, 21, 58.

74. See *The Essential Codex Mendoza*, ed. Frances F. Berdan and Patricia Rieff Anawalt (Berkeley: University of California Press, 1997), fols. 10v, 52r, 61r, 70r.

75. Reported by Klein, "Woven Heaven," 6.

76. Campbell, *Morphological Dictionary*, 184. See also Hernando Ruiz de Alarcón, *Treatise on the Heathen Superstitions That Today Live among the Indians Native to This New Spain*, trans., ed., and intro. J. Richard Andrews and Ross Hassig (Norman: University of Oklahoma Press, 1984), 94–96.

77. Frances F. Berdan, "Appendix E: The Place-Name, Personal Name, and Title Glyphs of the Codex Mendoza: Translations and Comments," in *The Codex Mendoza*, ed. Frances F. Berdan and Patricia Rieff Anawalt, vol. 1 (Berkeley: University of California Press, 1992), 190.

78. Ruíz de Alarcón, *Treatise*, 95, 96, 104.

79. Ibid., 101, 103.

80. See Nicholson, "Religion," 420–22; Sullivan, "Tlazolteotl-Ixcuina," 7; and Mary Miller and Karl Taube, *An Illustrated Dictionary of the Gods and Symbols of Ancient Mexico and the Maya* (London: Thames and Hudson, 1993), 61.

81. López Austin, *Human Body and Ideology*; Alfredo López Austin, *The Rabbit on the Face of the Moon: Mythology in the Mesoamerican Tradition*, trans. Bernard R. Ortiz de Montellano and Thelma Ortiz de Montellano (Salt Lake City: University of Utah Press, 1996), 27–28.

82. See *Codex Borbonicus*, plate 34. See also Felipe R. Solís Olguín, ed., *The Aztec Empire* (New York: Guggenheim Museum Publications, 2004), fig. 116.

83. Campbell, *Morphological Dictionary*, 184. A *mecatlapouhqui* is one who makes predictions by means of cords.

84. Ibid., 185. Plate XIII of Diego Durán (*The History of the Indies of New Spain*, trans., annot., and intro. Doris Heyden [Norman: University of Oklahoma Press, 1994]) depicts Mexica fieldworkers measuring farmland with a tlalmecatl.

85. Barbara Tedlock and Dennis Tedlock, "Text and Textile: Language and Technology in the Arts of the Quiché Maya," *Journal of Anthropological Research* 41, no. 2 (1985): 127.

86. Campbell, *Morphological Dictionary*, 184.

87. Ibid., 185.

88. For example, see *Codex Borbonicus*, plate 11, and *Codex Vaticanus 3773 B*, plate 51.

89. See Sahagún, *Florentine Codex*, VIII:fig. 86.

90. See ibid., III:figs. 15, 16. See also Berdan, "Appendix E," 190.

91. Sahagún, *Florentine Codex*, VI:61–62.

92. See Sahagún, *Florentine Codex*, VI:214; Doris Heyden, "Metaphors, Nahualtocaitl, and other 'Disguised' Terms among the Aztecs," in *Symbol and Meaning beyond the Closed Community: Essays in Mesoamerican Ideas*, ed. Gary H. Gossen (Institute for Mesoamerican Studies, Albany: SUNY Press, 1986), 35-43; and Rudolph van Zantwijk, *The Aztec Arrangement: The Social History of Pre-Spanish Mexico* (Norman: University of Oklahoma Press, 1985), 20, 202, 220, 298.

93. Berdan and Anawalt, eds., *The Essential Codex Mendoza*, 61r.

94. Kevin Terraciano, *The Mixtecs of Colonial Oaxaca: Ñudzahui History, Sixteenth through Eighteenth Centuries* (Stanford, CA: Stanford University Press, 2001), 169.

95. Durán, *Book of the Gods*, 147, 176, 226. See also Peterson, "Sacrificial Earth," 119.

96. Reported in Peterson, "Sacrificial Earth," 119.

97. Durán, *Book of the Gods*, 226.

98. Ibid., 176.

99. Schaefer, *Think with a Good Heart*, 214.

100. Peterson, "Sacrificial Earth," 119.

101. Durán, *Book of the Gods*, 163. See also Sahagún, *Primeros memoriales: Paleography*, 73; Peterson, "Sacrificial Earth," 120; and Klein, "Woven Heaven," 10.

102. Eloise Quiñones Keber, *Codex Telleriano-Remensis: Ritual, Divination, and History in a Pictorial Aztec Manuscript* (Austin: University of Texas Press, 1995), 166.

103. See Durán, *Book of the Gods*, plate 11, and the two bas-reliefs of a zacatapayolli reproduced in Davíd Carrasco and Eduardo Matos Moctezuma, *Moctezuma's Mexico: Visions of the Aztec World* (Niwot: University Press of Colorado, 1992), 128, 129. A stone zacatapayolli held by Mexico City's Museo Nacional de Antropología has a plaided exterior, suggesting that artisans constructed the balls by braiding grass.

104. Sahagún, *Florentine Codex*, II:61, brackets mine.

105. Peterson, "Sacrificial Earth," 126n14. See also Quiñones Keber, "Ritual and Representation," 189; Klein, "Woven Heaven," 10; and Cecelia Klein, "The Ideology of Autosacrifice at the Templo Mayor," in *The Aztec Templo Mayor*, ed. Elizabeth Hill Boone (Washington, DC: Dumbarton Oaks, 1987), 296.

106. Klein, "Ideology of Autosacrifice," 294.

107. Ibid., 297. See also Miguel León-Portilla, "Those Made Worthy by Divine Sacrifice: The Faith of Ancient Mexico," in *South and Meso-american Spirituality: From the Cult of the Feathered Serpent to the Theology of Liberation*, ed. Gary Gossen and Miguel León-Portilla (New York: Crossroads, 1993), 41–64; and Read, *Time and Sacrifice*.

108. Alan Sandstrom (personal communication, 8/20/11) points out that contemporary Nahua view blood sacrifice in terms of reciprocity.

109. For example see Sahagún, *Florentine Codex*, II:54.

110. Ibid., XI:194. Sahagún states the grass was used in building houses. He does not mention temples.

111. López Austin, *Human Body and Ideology*, II:185. Alonso de Molina (*Vocabulario en lengua castellana y mexicana y mexicana y castellana*, 4th ed. [Mexico City: Porrúa, 2001], 2:153v) translates *tzoma* as "*coser algo, o cubrir de paja el bohio*" ("to sew, to cover a hut in straw"), translation mine.

112. See Townsend, "Coronation at Tenochtitlan," 101–4; Peterson, "Sacrificial Earth," 118, 143, fig. 14; and Klein, "Woven Heaven."

113. Eloise Quiñones Keber, ed., *Codex Telleriano-Remensis: Ritual, Divination, and History in a Pictorial Aztec Manuscript* (Austin: University of Texas Press, 1995).

114. E.g., see ibid., 29r.

115. Klein, "Woven Heaven."

116. Siméon, *Diccionario*, 251, translation mine.

117. Klein, "Woven Heaven," 5–6.

118. Juan de Torquemada, *Monarquía indiana: De los veinte y un libros rituales y monarquía indiana, con el origen y guerras de los indios occidentales, de sus poblazones, descurbrimiento, conquista, conversión y otras cosas maravillosas de la mesma tierra*, 3rd ed., coordinated by Miguel León-Portilla (México, DF: Universidad Nacional Autónoma de

México, 1975–1983), 3:433. Francisco Hernández claims malinalli grass was eaten mixed with other foods (see Berdan, "Appendix E," 190).

119. Noemí Quezada, "Creencias tradicionales sobre embarazo y parto," *Anales de antropología* 14 (1977): 313.

120. Quoted in López Austin, *Human Body and Ideology*, I:349.

121. Karttunen (*Analytical Dictionary*, 74) suggests the second part of the word is related to *coloa* ("to curve, twist").

122. Campbell, *Morphological Dictionary*, 184. See also Alfredo López Austin, "Cuarenta clases de magos del mundo náhuatl," *Arqueología Mexicana* 7 (1967): 106; and Bernard R. Ortiz de Montellano, *Aztec Medicine, Health, and Nutrition* (New Brunswick, NJ: Rutgers University Press, 1990).

123. Campbell, *Morphological Dictionary*, 184.

124. Karttunen, *Analytical Dictionary*, 201.

125. Torquemada, *Monarquía indiana*, 3:131.

126. López Austin, "Cuarenta clases," 106.

127. See Peterson, "Sacrificial Earth," 117; and Karttunen, *Analytical Dictionary*, 203. The following draws from Burkhart, *Slippery Earth*; Louise M. Burkhart, "Mexica Women on the Home Front: Housework and Religion in Aztec Mexico," in *Indian Women of Early Mexico*, ed. Susan Schroeder, Stephanie Wood, and Robert Haskett (Norman: University of Oklahoma Press, 1997), 25–54; and Peterson, "Sacrificial Earth."

128. Toribio de Benavente Motolinía, *History of the Indians of New Spain*, trans. E. A. Foster (Westport, CT: Greenwood Press, 1950), 59; *Codex Borbonicus*, plates 4, 8, 9, 12, 15, 18; and the Spanish side of Molina, *Vocabulario*, 1:57v.

129. See Sahagún, *Primeros memoriales: Paleography*, 75, 127; and Karttunen, *Analytical Dictionary*, 255.

130. Karttunen, *Analytical Dictionary*, 93, 255.

131. Ibid., 93.

132. Thelma Sullivan, "The Mask of Itztlacoliuhqui," in *Actas del XVI Congreso Internacional de Americanistas 1974*, vol. 2 (México: Instituto Nacional de Antropología e Historia, 1976), 257. See also Peterson, "Sacrificial Earth," 117; Burkhart, *Slippery Earth*; and Burkhart, "Mexica Women."

133. Sahagún, *Florentine Codex*, X:87. Sahagún states brooms and besoms came in many lengths and colors. *Codex Mendoza*, folio 57r, depicts a handheld broom. For discussion, see Berdan and Anawalt, *The Essential Codex Mendoza*, 148.

134. Sullivan, "Mask of Itztlacoliuhqui," 257. See also Burkhart, "Mexica Women."

135. Burkhart, *Slippery Earth*, 121. I thus reject Burkhart's (ibid., 121) explanation of the efficacy of brooms in terms of the metaphysical principle "filth wards off filth" together with "the fact that [brooms] were themselves made with *tlazolli* – grass or straw."

136. See Sahagún, *Florentine Codex*, II:199; Sullivan, "Mask of Itztlacoliuhqui," 255–57; and Burkhart, "Mexican Women," 35.

137. Burkhart, *Slippery Earth*, 92. See also Sullivan, "Mask of Itztlacoliuhqui."

138. Sahagún, *Florentine Codex*, I:5, translation by Burkhart, *Slippery Earth*, 92.

139. Burkhart, *Slippery Earth*, 118; Burkhart, "Mexica Women," 35–36.

140. Sahagún, *Florentine Codex*, I:fig. 12.

141. *Codex Laud* (Graz: Bodelian Library, 1966), plate 15, depicts a flayed-skin-wearing Tlazolteotl sitting at the center of a quincunx, suggesting the latter's four corners as the destination of tlazolli.

142. Sahagún, *Primeros memoriales: Paleography*, 126.

143. Sullivan, "Mask of Itztlacoliuhqui," 155–57.

144. Sahagún, *Florentine Codex*, VII:58.

145. Sahagún, *Florentine Codex*, VII:25.

146. *Ochpaniztli* combines *ohtli* ("path, road") with *ichpana* ("to sweep"). See Durán, *Book of the Gods*, 229–37, 447–49; Sahagún, *Florentine Codex*, II:118–26; *Codex Borbonicus* (Loubat: Bibliothéque Du Palais Bourbon, 1899, plates 29–31; and Quiñones Keber, *Codex Telleriano Remensis*, 31. For discussion, see Johanna Broda de Casas, "Tlacaxipehualiztli: A Reconstruction of an Aztec Calendar Festival from 16th Century Sources," *Revista española de antropología Americana* 5 (1970): 197–274; Sullivan, "Mask of Itztlacoliuhqui"; Patricia Anawalt, "Analysis of the Aztec Quechquemitl: An Exercise in Inference," in *The Art and Iconography of Late Post-Classic Central Mexico*, ed. Elizabeth Boone (Washington, DC: Dumbarton Oaks, 1982), 37–72; Peterson, "Sacrificial Earth"; Burkhart, *Slippery Earth*, 120–21; Burkhart, "Mexica Women"; Quiñones Keber, *Codex Telleriano-Remensis*, 143–44; Gordon Brotherston, *Feather Crown: The Eighteen Feasts of the Mexican Year* (London: The British Museum, 2005); and Catherine DiCesare, *Sweeping the Way: Divine Transformation in the Aztec Festival of Ochpaniztli* (Niwot: University Press of Colorado, 2009).

147. See Sahagún, *Florentine Codex*, I:13; Durán, *Book of the Gods*, 229–37; Anawalt, "Analysis," 51; Sullivan, "Mask of Itztlacoliuhqui"; and Sullivan, "Tlazolteotl-Ixcuina."

148. *Codex Borbonicus* (Loubat, 1899), plate 36; Sahagún, *Florentine Codex*, I:fig. 8; Durán, *Book of the Gods*, plate 24; *Codex Telleriano-Remensis* (1995), plate 31; and *Codex Magliabechiano* (*The Book of the Life of the Ancient Mexicans*), facsimile ed. Zelia Nuttall (Berkeley: University of California Press, 1903), plate 39.

149. See Sahagún, *Florentine Codex*, II:236; and Peterson, "Sacrificial Earth."

150. *The Tovar Calendar: An Illustrated Mexican Calendar ca. 1585*, reproduction and comment, G. Kubler and C. Gibson (New Haven, CT: Memoirs of the Connecticut Academy of Arts and Sciences, XI, 1951), plate IX. Serna's depiction is reproduced in *Tovar Calendar* (88, fig. 14). Peñafiel makes an identical claim (reported in Peterson, "Sacrificial Earth," 126n16).

151. Durán, *Book of the Gods*, 448–49.

152. See Sahagún, *Florentine Codex*, II:120; *Codex Borbonicus* (1899), plates 29–31; Sullivan, "Mask of Itztlacoliuhqui," 259; Brotherston, *Feather Crown*; and Anawalt, "Analysis," 54.

153. Sahagún, *Florentine Codex*, II:120.

154. Nicholson, "Religion," 428–29. For further discussion see Gordon Brotherston, *Image of the New World: The American Continent Portrayed in Native Texts* (London: Thames & Hudson, 1979); Carrasco, *Moctezuma's Mexico*; *Histoyre du Mechique*; Enrique Florescano, *The Myth of Quetzalcoatl*, trans. Lisa Hochroth (Baltimore: Johns Hopkins University Press, 1999); Michel Graulich, "Quetzalcoatl-Ehecatl, the Bringer of Life," in *Ancient America: Contributions to New World Archaeology*, ed. Nicholas J. Saunders (Oxford: Oxbow Books, 1992), 33–38; Miguel León-Portilla, "Three Forms of Thought in Ancient Mexico," in *Studies in Symbolism and Cultural Communication*, ed. F. Allen Hanson (Lawrence: University Press of Kansas, 1982), 9–24; and Alfredo López Austin, *The Myths of the Opossum: Pathways of Mesoamerican Mythology*, trans. Bernard R. Ortiz de Montellano and Thelma Ortiz de Montellano (Albuquerque: University of New Mexico Press, 1993). I understand "Ehecatl-Quetzalcoatl" as naming a specific cluster of processes and energies rather than as a substantive deity.

155. López Austin, *Myths of the Opossum*, 126 (emphasis in original); see also 238–41.

156. Graulich, "Quetzalcoatl-Ehecatl," 34. Juan de Torquemada tells us infertile women sought to end their infertility by making sacrifices to Quetzalcoatl (Graulich, "Quetzalcoatl-Ehecatl," 34).

157. *Histoyre du Mechique*, 105.

158. Ibid., 106; and John Bierhorst, trans., "Legend of the Suns," in *History and Mythology of the Aztecs* (Tucson: University of Arizona Press, 1992), 145–46.

159. Bierhorst, "Legend of the Suns," 146–47.

160. Sahagún, *Florentine Codex*, I:9.

161. Ibid.

162. Sahagún, *Primeros memoriales: Paleography*, 121. See López Austin, *Myth of the Opossum*, 241 and 373n6.

163. Sahagún, *Primeros memoriales*, 121.

164. Campbell, *Morphological Dictionary*, 254.

165. Karttunen, *Analytical Dictionary*, 291–92.

166. Karttunen, *Analytical Dictionary*, 197.

167. Campbell, *Morphological Dictionary*, 254.

168. Judith M. Maxwell and Craig A. Hanson, *Of the Manners of Speaking That the Old Ones Had: The Metaphors of Andrés de Olmos in the TULAL Manuscript, Arte para Aprender la Lengua Mexicana, 1547* (Salt Lake City: University of Utah Press, 1992), 83, 170.

169. Sahagún, *Florentine Codex*, VI:202. See also López Austin, *Human Body and Ideology*, I:207–9; and McKeever Furst, *Natural History*.

170. Karttunen, *Analytical Dictionary*, 134.

171. López Austin, *Myths of the Opossum*, 241.

172. Maxwell and Hanson, *Manners of Speaking*, 83, 170.

173. Sahagún, *Florentine Codex*, VI:202. See also López Austin, *Human Body and Ideology*, I:207–9; and McKeever Furst, *Natural History*.

174. Sahagún, *Florentine Codex*, VII:8.

175. Ibid., see also 3–9.

176. According to Graulich ("Quetzalcoatl-Ehecatl," 35), *ihiyotl*, one of three vivifying energies residing in human beings, is an aspect of Ehecatl-Quetzalcoatl's "wind" or "air." Karttunen (*Analytical Dictionary*, 76) also remarks upon the connection between *ehecatl* and *ihiyotl*.

177. Guilhem Olivier, *Mockeries and Metamorphoses of an Aztec God: Tezcatlipoca, "Lord of the Smoking Mirror,"* trans. Michel Besson (Niwot: University of Colorado Press, 2003), 21.

178. Quiñones Keber, *Codex Telleriano-Remensis*, 165.

179. Sahagún, *Florentine Codex*, VI: 202. See also López Austin, *Human Body and Ideology*, 1:207–9; and McKeever Furst, *Natural History*.

180. Olivier, *Mockeries and Metamorphoses*, 21. McKeever Furst (*Natural History*, 155) claims the Aztecs regarded words and breathing as almost identical.

181. *Cantares mexicanos: Songs of the Aztecs*, trans., intro., commentary, John Bierhorst (Stanford, CA: Stanford University Press, 1985), fols. 15r and 23v, translation mine.

182. See Olivier, *Mockeries and Metamorphoses*, 21–22, 24–25, 149; and Burkhart, *Slippery Earth*, 92–93, 181–82.

183. For further discussion of the creative, performative, and enactive role of ritual speech, see Olivier, *Mockeries and Metamorphoses*; Sam Gill, *Native American Religious Action: A Performative Approach to Religion* (Columbia: University of South Carolina Press, 1987); and James Maffie, "*In Huehue Tlamanitiliztli* and *la Verdad*: Nahua and European Philosophies in Fray Bernardino de Sahagún's *Colloquios y doctrina Cristiana*," *Inter-America Journal of Philosophy* 3 (2012): 1–33, and Jane H. Hill, "Today There Is No Respect: Nostalgia, 'Respect,' and Oppositional Discourse in Mexicano (Nahuatl) Language Ideology," in *Language Ideologies: Practice and Theory*, ed. Bambi B. Schieffelin, Kathryn A. Woolard, and Paul Kroskrity (New York: Oxford University Press, 1998), 68–86.

184. Karl Taube, "The Turquoise Hearth: Fire, Self Sacrifice, and the Central Mexican Cult of War," in *Mesomerica's Classic Heritage*, ed. Davíd Carrasco, Lindsay Jones, and Scott Sessions (Niwot: University Press of Colorado, 2000), 292; see figs. 10.14 a–h.

185. Olivier, *Mockeries and Metamorphoses*, 21, 225–26.

186. Bierhorst, "Legend of the Suns," 145. Mictlantecuhtli also demands that Quetzalcoatl circle four times around Mictlan. Circling-spinning motion is essential to vertical transformation.

187. *Codex Vaticanus A*, plate 20, quoted in Graulich, "Quetzalcoatl-Ehecatl," 35.

188. López Luján, *Offerings of the Templo Mayor*, 189; and Graulich, "Quetzalcoatl-Ehecatl," 35–36. See also Laurette Séjourné, *El universo de Quetzalcoatl, prefacio por Mircea Eliade*, 7th ed. (Mexico City: Fondo de Cultural Económica, 2003), 50–53, 63.

189. See Anthony F. Aveni, *Skywatchers: A Revised and Updated Version of Skywatchers of Ancient Mexico* (Austin: University of Texas Press, 2001), 81, fig. 35c; Gordon Brotherston and Dawn Ades, "Mesoamerican Description of Space I: Myths; Stars and Maps; and Architecture," *Ibero-Amerikanisches Archiv* 1, no. 4 (1975): 279–305; Blas Castellón Huerta, "Cúmulo de símbolos: La Serpiente emplumada," *Arqueología Mexicana* 9, no. 53 (2002): 28–35; and Séjourné, *El universo de Quetzalcoatl*.

190. *Cantares mexicanos: Songs of the Aztecs*, trans., intro., commentary, John Bierhorst (Stanford, CA: Stanford University Press, 1985), fol. 23v, translation mine.

191. Karttunen, *Analytical Dictionary*, 134; Campbell, *Morphological Dictionary*, 171.

192. Molina, *Vocabulario*, 2:147r.

193. Campbell, *Morphological Dictionary*, 171.

194. Ibid., 362; Sahagún, *Florentine Codex*, VII:27. See Sahagún, *Florentine Codex*, X:26 for characterization of lapidary drilling.

195. Carrasco, *City of Sacrifice*, 100.

196. *"sacó lumbre de los palos"* (*Historia de los mexicanos por sus pinturas*, in *Teogonía e historia de los mexicanos: Tres opúsculos del siglo XVI*, 1st ed., ed. Angel María Garibay K. [México, DF: Editorial Porrúa, 1965], 33).

197. See Sahagún, *Florentine Codex*, XI:229.

198. Miller and Taube, *Illustrated Dictionary*, 88.

199. See also *Codex Borbonicus* (Loubat, 1899), plate 34, and *Historia Tolteca-Chichimeca*, 33r (Dana Leibsohn, *Script and Glyph: Pre-Hispanic History, Colonial Bookmaking, and the Historia Tolteca-Chichimeca* [Washington, DC: Dumbarton Oaks, 2009], 55, fig. 10).

200. Miller and Taube, *Illustrated Dictionary*, 87. Taube ("Turquoise Hearth") suggests it is a mirror.

201. Taube, "Turquoise Hearth," 292, 305.

202. For relevant images and discussion, see ibid., 292, 305, and Clemency Coggins, "New Fire Drill at Chichen Itza," in *Memorias del Primer Coloquio Internacional de Mayistas* (México, DF: UNAM, 1987), 459.

203. Molina, *Vocabulario*, 1: 52r.

204. Karttunen, *Analytical Dictionary*, 275.

205. Alfredo López Austin, "The Masked God of Fire," in *The Aztec Templo Mayor*, ed. Elizabeth Hill Boone (Washington, DC: Dumbarton Oaks, 1987), 257–92.

206. Taube, "Turquoise Hearth," 294.

207. Ibid.

208. Bierhorst, "Legend of the Suns," 145.

209. Boone, *Cycles of Time*, 207.

210. Campbell, *Morphological Dictionary*, 171, brackets mine.

211. Sahagún, *Florentine Codex*, VI:202; translation by López Austin, *Human Body and Ideology*, I:208. For further discussion, see McKeever Furst, *Natural History*, chapter 9.

212. Sahagún, *Florentine Codex*, VII:25. The following draws upon Sahagún, *Florentine Codex*, VIVI:25–32; Burr Cartwright Brundage, *The Fifth Sun: Aztec Gods, Aztec World* (Austin: University of Texas Press, 1979); Davíd Carrasco, *City of Sacrifice: The Aztec Empire and the Role of Violence in Civilization* (Boston: Beacon Press, 1999), chapter 3; Susan Gillespie, *The Aztec Kings: The Construction of Rulership in Mexica History* (Tucson: University of Arizona Press, 1989); Read, *Time and Sacrifice*, 124–27; and Michiyo Sasao, "New Fire Ceremony," in *The Oxford Encyclopedia of Mesoamerican Cultures: The Civilizations of Mexico and Central America*, ed. Davíd Carrasco (Oxford: Oxford University Press, 2001), 2:366–68.

213. Sahagún, *Florentine Codex*, VII:25.

214. Read, *Time and Sacrifice*, 266n1.

215. Sahagún, *Florentine Codex*, VII:27.

216. Carrasco, *City of Sacrifice*, 103. The following is indebted to Sahagún, *Florentine Codex*, I:29–30; Nicholson, "Religion," 412–14; Brundage, *Fifth Sun*; López Austin, "Masked God of Fire"; Silvia Limón Olvera, "Fire Deities," in *The Oxford Encyclopedia of Mesoamerican Cultures: The Civilizations of Mexico and Central America*, ed. Davíd Carrasco (Oxford: Oxford University Press, 2001), 1:409–10; Leonardo López Luján, "Old Gods," in *The Oxford Encyclopedia of Mesoamerican Cultures: The Civilizations of Mexico and Central America*, ed. Davíd Carrasco (Oxford: Oxford University Press, 2001), 2:403–5; Quiñones Keber, *Codex Telleriano-Remensis*, 151; Taube, "Turquoise Hearth"; Townsend, "Coronation at Tenochtitlan"; and Susan Milbrath, "Sun," in *The Oxford Encyclopedia of Mesoamerican Cultures: The Civilizations of Mexico and Central America*, ed. Davíd Carrasco (Oxford: Oxford University Press, 2001), 3:172–74.

217. Nicholson, "Religion in Pre-Hispanic Central Mexico," 410–14.

218. Bierhorst, "Legend of the Suns," 143.

219. Sahagún, *Florentine Codex*, VII:3–9. See also Bierhorst, "Legend of the Suns," 147–48; and *Historia de los mexicanos*.

220. Sahagún, *Florentine Codex*, VII:4. This derives from *colihui*, meaning "for something to curve or turn." See Karttunen, *Analytical Dictionary*, 39–40; and Campbell, *Morphological Dictionary*, 77–78.

221. McKeever Furst, *Natural History*, 68.

222. For related discussion, see Read, *Time and Sacrifice*; López Austin, *Human Body and Ideology*, I; Philip P. Arnold, *Eating Landscape: Aztec and European Occupation of Tlalocan* (Niwot: University Press of Colorado, 1999); Carrasco, *City of Sacrifice*, chapter 6; Limón Olvera, "Fire Deities"; and John D. Monaghan, *The Covenants with Earth and Rain: Exchange, Sacrifice and Revelation in Mixtec Sociality* (Norman: University of Oklahoma Press, 1995).

223. *Historia de los mexicanos por sus pinturas*, 33. According to the "Legend of the Suns," it was Tezcatlipoca who drilled the first fire (Bierhorst, "Legend of the Suns," 145).

224. *Itzpapalotl* literally means "Obsidian (*itzli*) Butterfly." In light of the iconographic renderings of her wings as flint, Miller and Taube (*Illustrated Dictionary*, 100) prefer "Flint (*tecpatl*) Butterfly." Given the association between olin motion-change and butterflies (discussed in chapter 4), Itzpapalotl's combining of flint and butterfly connects the malinalli-shaped energies of sacrifice with the olin-shaped energies of life~death cycles.

225. See Taube, "Turquoise Hearth"; Miller and Taube, *Illustrated Dictionary*, 100; and Burkhart, "Moral Deviance," 113.

226. Quiñones Keber, *Codex Telleriano-Remensis*, 150.

227. The name derives from *tlacatl* ("man, person"), *xipehua* ("to flay, skin, or peel something"), and the suffix *-liztli* ("the act of doing something") (see Karttunen, *Analytical Dictionary*). My narrative follows Sahagún, *Florentine Codex*, II:3–4, 47–60, appendix B; IX:7; Durán, *Book of the Gods*, 172–85; Broda de Casas, "Tlacaxipehualiztli"; and Johanna Broda de Casas, "Tlacaxipehualiztli, A Reconstruction of an Aztec Calendar Festival from 16th Century Sources," *Revista española de antropología Americana* 5 (1970): 197–274; and Carrasco, *City of Sacrifice*, chapter 5.

228. Durán, *Book of the Gods*, 415–16.

229. López Luján, *Offerings*, 219.

230. Carrasco, *City of Sacrifice*, 142, 156.

231. Sahagún, *Florentine Codex*, II:8.

232. Ibid., II:49.

233. Ibid., II:48, brackets mine.

234. Ibid., II:3. See also Siméon, *Diccionario*, 764.

235. Sahagún, *Florentine Codex*, II:48.

236. Ibid., II:1.

237. Durán, *Book of the Gods*, 175; Durán, *History of the Indies*, 170–71.

238. "*quijiaualo in temalacatl*" (Sahagún, *Florentine Codex*, II:51). The verb here is *yahualoa*, meaning "to go around something, to go in procession" (Karttunen, *Analytical Dictionary*, 334).

239. Quoted in and translated by Eduardo Matos Moctezuma, "The Aztec Calendar," in *The Aztec Calendar and Other Solar Monuments*, Eduardo Matos Moctezuma and

Felipe R. Solís Olguín (México, DF: Conaculta-Instituto Nacional de Antropología e Historia, 2004), 35.

240. Durán, *Book of the Gods*, 178.

241. Karttunen, *Analytical Dictionary*, 42; see also Campbell, *Morphological Dictionary*, 80.

242. Ibid.

243. Sahagún, *Florentine Codex*, II:52, 190; VIII:84. Sahagún (*Florentine Codex*, II:203) gives a general description of *tlahuahuanaliztli* or "the act of striping."

244. Sahagún, *Florentine Codex*, II:52; VIII:84. See also Matos Moctezuma, *Aztec Calendar*, 36.

245. Matos Moctezuma, *Aztec Calendar*, 36; Felipe R. Solís Olguín with Roberto Velasco Alonso, "Monuments of Sun Worship," in Eduardo Matos Moctezuma and Felipe R. Solís, *The Aztec Calendar and other Solar Monuments*, 148.

246. *Codex Magliabechiano*, plate 30r; Zelia Nuttall, *Codex Nuttall* (New York: Dover, 1975), pl. 83. Durán (*History of the Indies*, 171; *Book of the Gods*, 178) states the rope was four yards in length and bound to the captive's ankle.

247. Sahagún, *Florentine Codex*, II:4.

248. Solís with Velasco Alonso, "Monuments," 104.

249. Ibid., 120.

250. Karttunen, *Analytical Dictionary*, 80.

251. Quoted in and translated by Broda de Casas, "Tlacaxipehualiztli," 211n37.

252. Sahagún, *Florentine Codex*, II:53.

253. See Elizabeth M. Brumfiel, "Asking about Gender: The Historical and Archaeological Evidence," in *Gender in Prehispanic America*, ed. Cecelia Klein (Washington, DC: Dumbarton Oaks, 2001), 57–86; and Elizabeth Brumfiel, "Domestic Politics in Early-Middle Postclassic Mexico: Variability and Standardization in Decorative Motifs," paper presented in Estudios de género en el México antiguo, coord. M. Rodríguez-Shadow y R. García Valgaño (México, DF: Congreso International de Americanists, 2009).

254. For excellent descriptions of these stones, see Solís with Velasco Alonso, "Monuments," 104–24; and Taube, "Turquoise Hearth," 321.

255. Durán, *Book of the Gods*, plate 16.

256. See Solís with Velasco Alonso, "Monuments," 110, fig. 86.

257. Sahagún, *Florentine Codex*, II:52.

258. Solís with Velasco Alonso, "Monuments."

259. Ibid., 123. Other examples of the temalactl include the so-called Sun Stone and the ex-Archbishop's Palace Stone. For photographs and discussion, see Solís with Velasco Alonso, "Monuments," 104–24.

260. Sahagún, *Florentine Codex*, II:52.

261. Campbell, *Morphological Dictionary*, 195; Karttunen, *Analytical Dictionary*, 155, 245; Eduard Seler, *Comentarios al Códice Borgia* (México, DF: Fondo de Cultural Económica, 1963), 1:131.

262. Seler, *Comentarios*, 1:131.

263. Sahagún, *Florentine Codex*, II:53.

264. Solís with Velasco Alonso, "Monuments," 120.

265. Durán, *History of the Indies*, 172.

266. Ibid., 264.

267. Durán, *Book of the Gods*, 179. The caption accompanying plate 16 of Durán's *The History of the Indies of New Spain* states that it depicts a heart sacrifice occurring upon such a cuauhxicalli stone.

268. Matos Moctezuma, "Aztec Calendar," 28, 36–37.

269. Sahagún, *Florentine Codex*, IV:fig. 30.

270. Durán, *Book of the Gods*, 177.

271. Sahagún, *Florentine Codex*, II:53.

272. Karttunen, *Analytical Dictionary*, 11; Campbell, *Morphological Dictionary*, 12.

273. Campbell, *Morphological Dictionary*, 12.

274. Translations by Campbell (*Morphological Dictionary*, 13) and the author, respectively.

275. This is precisely what is required to remove a heart from the chest by means of the left anterior intercostal approach according to Robicsek and Hales (Francis Robicsek and Donald Hales, "Maya Heart Sacrifice: Cultural Perspectives and Surgical Technique," in *Ritual Human Sacrifice in Mesoamerica*, ed. Elizabeth H. Boone [Washington, DC: Dumbarton Oaks, 1984], 81).

276. Campbell, *Morphological Dictionary*, 12–13.

277. Sahagún, *Florentine Codex*, II:54, brackets mine.

278. Ibid., II:53.

279. See Peterson "Sacrificial Earth," 117, 120.

280. Sahagún, *Florentine Codex*, II:54.

281. Ibid.

282. Karttunen, *Analytical Dictionary*, 334.

283. Sahagún, *Florentine Codex*, II:204; Sahagún, *Primeros memoriales: Paleography*, 57.

284. Sahagún, *Florentine Codex*, II:50; see also 204.

285. López Luján, *Offerings of the Templo Mayor*, 218.

286. Sahagún, *Florentine Codex*, II:50.

287. Karttunen, *Analytical Dictionary*, 69.

288. Ibid., 134.

289. López Luján (*Offerings*, 219) offers a similar interpretation.

290. Sahagún, *Florentine Codex*, II:55.

291. Gertrude Prokosch Kurath and Samuel Martí, *Dances of Anahuac: The Choreography and Music of Precortesian Dances* (New York: Wenner-Gren Foundation for Anthropological Research, 1964), 146, 224.

292. Kurath and Martí, *Dances of Anahuac*, 224. See Karttunen, *Analytical Dictionary*, 40; and Campbell, *Morphological Dictionary*, 78.

293. Campbell, *Morphological Dictionary*, 78.

294. Kurath and Martí, *Dances of Anahuac*, 149. Matthew Looper ("Dance Performance at *Quiriguá*," in *Landscape and Power in Ancient Mesoamerica*, ed. Rex Koontz, Kathryn Reese-Taylor, and Annabeth Headrick [Boulder: Westview Press, 2001], 113–36) discusses the centrality of spinning and twirling in Maya ritual dance.

295. Sahagún, *Florentine Codex*, I:39; Carrasco, *City of Sacrifice*, 140; Miller and Taube, *Illustrated Dictionary*, 188.

296. Sahagún, *Florentine Codex*, VII:52.

297. Ibid., II:39, fig. 18; Bernardino de Sahagún, *Primeros memoriales*. Facsimile edition (Norman: University of Oklahoma Press, 1993), fol. 263r; Sahagún, *Primeros memoriales: Paleography*, 102.

298. See Broda de Casas, "Tlacaxipehualiztli"; Doris Heyden, "Xipe Totec," in *The Oxford Encyclopedia of Mesoamerican Cultures: The Civilizations of Mexico and Central America*, ed. Davíd Carrasco (Oxford: Oxford University Press, 2001), 3:353–54; Nicholson, "Religion"; Townsend, "Coronation at Tenochtitlan"; López Luján, *Offerings*; and Seler, *Comentarios*, 1:131.

299. Nicholson, "Religion," 424.

300. Ibid., 414–24.

301. Xipe's capacity as the "patron deity" of goldsmiths further confirms Xipe's association with metamorphosis since goldsmithing is essentially a metamorphic process. See Sahagún, *Florentine Codex*, IX:69, X:25; and Cecelia Klein, "The Shield Women: Resolution of a Gender Paradox," in *Current Topics in Aztec Studies: Essays in Honor of Dr. H. B. Nicholson*, ed. Alana Cory and Douglas Sharon, San Diego Museum of Man Papers 30 (San Diego: San Diego Museum of Man, 1993), 26.

302. See Carrasco, *City of Sacrifice*, chapter 5; McKeever Furst, *Natural History*; and Read, *Time and Sacrifice*.

303. See Burkhart, "Moral Deviance," 120; and Read, *Time and Sacrifice*.

304. Kurath and Martí (*Dances of Anahuac*, 68, 70) interpret Tlacaxipehualiztli as involving the struggle of summer against winter, sky against earth, and most poignantly "the struggle for rebirth after death." See also López Luján, *Offerings*, 219–224.

305. Townsend ("Pyramid and Sacred Mountain," 50, 59) writes of the widespread indigenous custom of defining and creating sacred areas by "circular or rectangular processions" and a "circumambulation path." Aveni (*Skywatchers*, 152) argues circling movement is characteristic of directional assignments in native almanacs and in ritual circuits

followed by native pilgrims. William Hanks and Vine Deloria Jr. discuss the role of circling and centering motion in Maya and indigenous North American ritual, respectively. See William F. Hanks, *Referential Practice: Language and Lived Space among the Maya* (Chicago: University of Chicago Press, 1990), 349; and Barbara Deloria, Kristen Foehner, and Sam Scinta, eds., *Spirit and Reason: A Vine Deloria Jr. Reader* (Golden, CO: Fulcrum Publishers, 1999), 55.

306. Following the dominant anthropological paradigm, Isbell defends such a view of ritual (Billie Jean Isbell, *To Defend Ourselves: Ecology and Ritual in an Andean Village* [Prospect Heights, IL: Waveland Press, 1978], 17).

307. Durán, *Book of the Gods*, 401.

308. See Miguel León-Portilla, *El Tonalámatl de los Pochtecas (Códice Fejérváry-Mayer)*, plate 1, page 20; Miguel León-Portilla, *Aztec Thought and Culture: A Study of the Ancient Nahuatl Mind*, trans. Jack Emory Davis (Norman: University of Oklahoma Press, 1963), 47; and Miguel León-Portilla, *La filosofía náhuatl: Estudiada en sus fuentes con un nuevo apéndice*, new ed., prologue by Angel María Garibay K. (México, DF: Universidad Nacional Autónoma de México, 2001[1956]), 122.

309. León-Portilla, *Aztec Thought*, 47. See also López Austin, *Human Body and Ideology*, I:164–65.

310. León-Portilla, *Aztec Thought*, 47.

311. López Austin, *Human Body and Ideology*, I:58.

312. As such they fall within Nicholson's ("Religion") Ometochtli and Tlaloc complexes and under the Rain-Moisture-Agricultural Fertility theme.

313. Sahagún, *Florentine Codex*, X:193; see also Quiñones Keber, *Codex Telleriano-Remensis*, 177, 263.

314. Karttunen, *Analytical Dictionary*, 185.

315. Ibid., 183–84.

316. Ibid., 215.

317. Quiñones Keber, *Codex Telleriano-Remensis*, 177.

318. "*el del país de la medicina [para que pulque] (de aquello con que se cura el [pulque])*" (Seler, *Commentarios*, 1:110).

319. Quoted in Seler, *Comentarios*, 1:109.

320. Sahagún, *Primeros memoriales: Paleography*, 284n19.

321. Sahagún, *Florentine Codex*, IV:15–17. See also López Austin, *Human Body and Ideology*, 1:355–56; and Bernard R. Ortiz de Montellano, *Aztec Medicine, Health, and Nutrition* (New Brunswick, NJ: Rutgers University Press, 1990), 59.

322. Sahagún, *Primeros memoriales: Paleography*, 284.

323. Ortiz de Montellano, *Aztec Medicine*, 111.

324. See Ortiz de Montellano, *Aztec Medicine*, 111, 217; Eloise Quiñones Keber, "Mayahuel and Maguey: Sustenance and Sacrifice in Aztec Myth," *Latin American Indian*

Literatures Journal 5 (1989): 72–83; John D. Monaghan, "Sacrifice, Death, and the Origins of Agriculture in the *Codex Vienna*," *American Antiquity* 55 (1990): 567; and Jill McKeever Furst, "Skeletonization in Mixtec Art: A Revaluation," in *The Art of Iconography of Late Post-Classic Central Mexico*, ed. Elizabeth P. Benson and Elizabeth H. Boone (Washington, DC: Dumbarton Oaks, 1982), 207–26.

325. See Sullivan, "Tlazolteotl-Ixcuina," 24; and Quiñones Keber, "Mayahuel and Maguey," 74–75.

326. Quiñones Keber, *Codex Telleriano-Remensis*, 286.

327. *Codex Borbonicus* (Loubat 1899), plate 8.

328. Quiñones Keber, "Mayahuel and Maguey," 75. See also Jacqueline de Durand-Forest, Françoise Rousseau, Madeleine Cucuel, and Sylvie Szpirglas, *Los elementos anexos del Códice Borbónico*, trans. Dr. Edgar Samuel Morales Sales (México, DF: Universidad Autónoma del Estado de México, 2000), 100–15; and Sullivan, "Tlazolteotl-Ixcuina," 23.

329. Heyden, "Xipe Totec," 353.

330. Sahagún, *Florentine Codex*, IV:127.

331. Sahagún, *Primeros memoriales: Paleography*, 82n9.

332. Bierhorst, "Legend of the Suns," 142.

333. A similar statue held by the *Collection Musée de l'Homme*, Paris, depicts Ehecatl-Quetzalcoatl in an unusual twisting pose. See Graulich, *Myths of Ancient Mexico*, 81, fig. 9. López Austin discusses these and other figures in Alfredo López Austin, *Myths of the Opossum*; and Alfredo López Austin, *Rabbit on the Face of the Moon*, 85–89.

334. Guilhem Olivier and Leonardo López Luján, "Images of Moctezuma and His Symbols of Power," in *Moctezuma: Aztec Ruler*, ed. Colin McEwan and Leonardo López Luján (London: British Museum Press, 2009), 99.

335. *Codex Borbonicus* (1899), plate 11.

336. E.g., *Codex Vaticanus* 3773 B (1900), 90; *Codex Fejérváry-Mayer* (1901), plate 14. See Seler, *Comentarios*, 1:107.

337. E.g., *Codex Telleriano-Remensis* (1995), plate 15v; *Codex Borbonicus* (1899), plate 11. For discussion, see Quiñones Keber, *Codex Telleriano-Remensis*, 177.

338. *Histoyre du Mechique*, 106–7. A mural in the Red Temple of Cacaxtla depicts Ehecatl-Quetzalcoatl wearing a maguey hat and thus depicts him as the inventor of octli. See Román Piña Chan, *Cacaxtla: Fuentes Históricas y Pinturas* (México, DF: Fondo de Cultura Económico, 1998), 46.

339. See *Codex Borgia* (1993), plate 68; *Codex Borbonicus* (1899), 11; and *Codex Tonalamatl Aubin* (1901), plate 11.

340. *Codex Borbonicus* (1899), plate 11; see also *Codex Borgia* (1993), plate 68; *Codex Tonalamatl Aubin* (1901), plate 11.

341. Seler, *Comentarios*, 1:107, translation mine. Seler claims the ideogram conveys the concept of "gloaming," "the twilight hours," and "the parting of day and night" (Eduard

Seler, *Codex Fejérváry-Mayer: An Old Mexican Picture Manuscript in the Liverpool Free Public Museums* [12014/M], German edition [Berlin and London: T. and A. Constable, 1901–1902], 74).

342. Seler, *Comentarios*, 1:107, 2:203. See also *Codex Telleriano-Remensis* (1995), plate 15v; *Codex Borgia* (1993), plate 13; *Codex Tonalamatl Aubin* (1901), plate 11; and *Codex Fejérváry-Mayer* (1901), plate 14.

343. See Seler, *Comentarios*, 1:110; and Quiñones Keber, *Codex Telleriano-Remensis*, 177. I am indebted to Cecelia Klein for bringing this to my attention.

344. Quiñones Keber, *Codex Telleriano-Remensis*, 178.

345. Sahagún, *Florentine Codex*, IV:17. See also Seler, *Comentarios*, 2:203.

346. See *Codex Tonalamatl Aubin* (1901), plate 11; *Codex Fejérváry-Mayer* (1901), plate 14. For discussion, see Seler, *Codex Fejérváry-Mayer*, 72–74; Seler, *Comentarios*, 2:202; and León-Portilla, "*El Tonalámatl de los Pochtecas*," 46–47.

347. "*un haz de hierba*" (Seler, *Comentarios*, 1:107); *Codex Borgia* (1901), plate 14.

348. Quiñones Keber, *Codex Telleriano-Remensis*, 177.

349. *Codex Vaticanus 3773 B* (1900), plates 31, 90; *Codex Fejérváry-Mayer* (1901), plate 14. For discussion, see Seler, *Codex Fejérváry-Mayer*, 73; León-Portilla, "*El Tonalámatl de los Pochtecas*," 46–47; and Durand-Forest et al., *Elementos anexos*, 147–62.

350. *Codex Borgia* (1993), plate 13. See Seler, *Comentarios*, 1:111.

351. *Codex Telleriano-Remensis* (1995), fol. 15v.

352. *Codex Borgia* (1993), plate 13; *Codex Borbonicus* (1899), plate 11. For discussion, see Seler, *Comentarios*, 1:107; and Karl Anton Nowotny, *Tlacuilolli: Style and Contents of the Mexican Pictorial Manuscripts with a Catalog of the Borgia Group*, ed. and trans. George A. Everett Jr. and Edward Sisson (Norman: University of Oklahoma Press, 2005), 20.

353. Sahagún, *Florentine Codex*, XI:13. See also Burkhart, "Moral Deviance"; and Burkhart, *Slippery Earth*.

354. Burkhart, "Moral Deviance"; and Burkhart, *Slippery Earth*, 59, 62.

355. Durán, *History of the Indies*, 166, 406, and 205 (respectively); see also 302, 318.

356. Bierhorst, *History and Mythology*, 23. See Doris Heyden, "La Diosa Madre: Iztpapalotl," *Boletín Instituto Nacional de Antropología e Historia* (1974): 6; Burkhart, "Moral Deviance," 113.

357. Durán, *Book of the Gods*, chapter 7. See also Burkhart, "Moral Deviance"; Nicholson, "Religion," 126; and Miller and Taube, *Illustrated Dictionary*, 115.

358. *Historia de los mexicanos*, 37.

359. Read, *Time and Sacrifice*, 269n17.

360. Karttunen, *Analytical Dictionary*, 126.

361. Campbell, *Morphological Dictionary*, 161.

362. Read, *Time and Sacrifice*, 130–32.

363. Karttunen, *Analytical Dictionary*, 74. Karttunen suggests the word for intestines, *cuitlaxcolli*, derives from *coloa* ("to twist or curve") and *cuitlatl* ("excrement"). According to Sahagún, *coatl* ("snake") was another word for the intestines (Sahagún, *Florentine Codex*, X:131).

364. Read, *Time and Sacrifice*, 130. See also Arnold, *Eating Landscape*; Durán, *Book of the Gods*; Sahagún, *Florentine Codex*, II:chapter 21; and Carrasco, *City of Sacrifice*.

365. David Freidel, Linda Schele, and Joy Parker, *Maya Cosmos: Three Thousand Years on the Shaman's Path* (New York: William Morrow, 1993), 195. I do not endorse Freidel's use of the word *magic*.

366. Campbell, *Morphological Dictionary*, 185.

367. Ibid., 184–85; and Karttunen, *Analytical Dictionary*, 142, 339. See Olmos's metaphors VI and VII (Maxwell and Hanson, *Manners of Speaking*, 80–83, 171).

368. Campbell, *Morphological Dictionary*, 185. Various sources (including the *Colloquois* and *Florentine Codex*) refer to the ancestors as guides who teach people the path, who show people the way. In this manner, they make possible the transmission of the ancient ways (*huehue tlamanitiliztli*) (Sahagún, *Florentine Codex*; Sahagún, *Colloquios y doctrina*). Klein ("Ideology of Autosacrifice," 358) suggests the twisted cords Aztec royalty drew through their tongues (*nezahualmecatl*) symbolized the continuity of royal lineage. See also Arthur G. Miller, "The Iconography of the Painting in the Temple of the Diving God, Tulum, Quintana Roo, Mexico: The Twisted Cords," in *Mesoamerican Archaeology: New Approaches*, ed. Norman Hammond (Austin: University of Texas Press, 1974), 167–84.

369. McKeever Furst, *Natural History*, chapter 12; 125–26.

370. López Austin, *Human Body and Ideology*, I:218.

371. Campbell, *Morphological Dictionary*, 185. Molina's Spanish translation is *la tripa del ombligo* (Molina, *Vocabulario*, 2:159v). According to Miller ("Iconography," 183), "There is impressive array of evidence suggesting that an umbilical cord may be represented by a twisted cord" throughout Mesoamerican mythology and iconography. Taube ("Turquoise Hearth," 292) also claims twisted cords are used refer to umbilical cords and birth ropes.

372. "*ombligo o brújula para tirar derecho*" (Molina, *Vocabulario*, 2:159v). Karttunen (*Analytical Dictionary*, 324) translates it as "navel, peephole."

373. López Austin, *Human Body and Ideology*, II:186. This is supported by Molina's translation: "navel or *brúxula* for shooting." "*Brújula*," writes López Austin, means a "small hole that serves to direct shots of a gun, and which nowadays is called a sight, although the shape is different." The Aztecs gave this name to the Spaniards' gun sights.

374. López Austin, *Human Body and Ideology*, II:209.

375. Molina, *Vocabulario*, 2:10.

376. *Codex Vaticanus 3738 A* (Graz 1979), fol. 54r.

377. López Austin, *Human Body and Ideology*. One might just as easily argue that the Aztecs modeled the human body upon the cosmos. However, if the body was indeed their model, I submit pace Lopez Austin that they modeled the Fifth Age upon it but not the cosmos per se.

378. *Tlal-* derives from *tlalli*, meaning "earth," and *xic-* derives from *xictli*, meaning "navel." See Karttunen, *Analytical Dictionary*, 324; Wayne Elzey, "Some Remarks on the Space and Time of the 'Center' in Aztec Religion," *Estudios de cultura náhuatl* 12 (1976): 320; López Austin, *Human Body and Ideology*, I:173; and León-Portilla, *Aztec Thought*, 32.

379. López Austin, *Human Body and Ideology*, I:425n37. Vogt reports Zinacantecos call the center *mishik' balamil* or "navel of the universe" (Evon Z. Vogt, "Cardinal Directions and Ceremonial Circuits in Mayan and Southwestern Cosmology," *National Geographic Society Research Reports* 2 [1985]: 490).

380. López Austin, *Human Body and Ideology*, I:200; see also I:173, 197–98; II:241–42.

381. Quoted in Elzey, "Some Remarks," 319; Carrasco, *Quetzalcoatl*, 162.

382. Sahagún, *Florentine Codex*, VI:18–19, 88–89. See Elzey, "Some Remarks," 320; León-Portilla, *Aztec Thought*, 31–33, 93–95; Heyden, *Eagle, Cactus, Rock*; Florescano, *Memory, Myth, and Time*; and Carrasco, *Quetzalcoatl*.

383. Molina, *Vocabulario*, I:34r.

384. León-Portilla, *Aztec Thought*, 31–33, 90; and Taube, "Turquoise Hearth," 321. See also López Luján, *Offerings*, 141–47; Miller and Taube, *Illustrated Dictionary*, 189–90.

385. See López Austin, *Human Body and Ideology*, I:58–59; León-Portilla, *Aztec Thought*; McKeever Furst, *Natural History*; Miller and Taube, *Illustrated Dictionary*, 101–2; Eva Hunt, *The Transformation of the Hummingbird: Cultural Roots of a Zinacatecan Mythical Poem* (Ithaca, NY: Cornell University Press, 1977), 77; Taube, "Turquoise Hearth"; and Taube, "Maize."

386. See López Austin, *Human Body and Ideology*, I:58f, 173; Carrasco, *Quetzalcoatl*; Dávid Carrasco, *Religions of Mesoamerica: Cosmovision and Ceremonial Centers* (San Francisco: Harper and Row, 1990); Mircea Eliade, *Rites and Symbols of Initiation: The Mysteries of Birth and Rebirth*, trans. Willard R. Trask (New York: Harper and Row, 1958), 99–100, 375; Elzey, "Some Remarks"; Hunt, *Transformation of the Hummingbird*; Limón Olvera, "Fire Deities," 410; and Taube, "Turquoise Hearth" 305.

387. I owe this observation to Miller, "Iconography."

388. *Historye du Mechique*, 105.

389. See López Austin, *Human Body and Ideology*, I:60, 65; López Austin, *Myths of the Opossum*, 2:290; López Austin, *Rabbit on the Face of the Moon*; López Austin, *Tamoanchan, Tlalocan: Places of Mist*, 98–101; and Carrasco, *Religions of Mesoamerica*, 51; Carrasco, "Uttered from the Heart," 9–10. Referring to these malinalli-shaped energy currents as "the malinalli" runs the risk of reifying them, that is, treating them as permanent passageways that exist independently of the energy they convey. I interpret them as processes

that exist only as long as there is energy constituting them. They are analogous to lightning strikes, the pathway of which is the lightning itself.

390. Gerardo Reichel-Dolmatoff, "The Loom of Life: A Kogi Principle of Integration," *Journal of Latin American Lore* 4, no. 1 (1978): 13.

391. López Austin, *Human Body and Ideology*, I:59–60; López Austin, *Rabbit on the Face*, 85–89; López Austin, *Tamoanchan, Tlalocan: Places of Mist*, 98–101.

392. López Austin, *Human Body and Ideology*, I:60.

393. Malinalli-shaped forces originating from upper and lower realms enter the earthly layer through its navel, springs, mountains, caves, fires, sunlight, stones, animals, and forests. These also serve as portals for recycling energy back to the above and below and thus for influencing the forces originating there. See López Austin, *Human Body and Ideology*, I:57–58; Carrasco, *Daily Life of the Aztecs*, 47; and Carrasco, "Uttered from the Heart," 9–10.

394. See Lopez Austin, *Human Body and Ideology*, I:210; and Carrasco with Sessions, *Daily Life of the Aztecs*, 44.

395. See López Austin, *Human Body and Ideology*, I:54–55, 209–210; López Austin, *Tamoanchan, Tlalocan*, 17, fig. 2.

396. Nicholson, "Religion," 409.

397. López Austin, *Human Body and Ideology*, I:209. The *Historia de los mexicanos por sus pinturas* states that the fifth level is the place of fire serpents that emit meteors: "*En el quinto había culebras de fuego, que hizo el dios de fuego, y de ellas salen los cometas y señales del cielo*" (Garibay, *Historia*, 69).

398. López Austin, *Human Body and Ideology*, I:209–10. See also López Luján, *Offerings of the Templo Mayor*, 224.

399. Reichel-Dolmatoff ("Loom of Life") makes a similar observation about the role of spinning in Kogi metaphysics.

400. See López Austin, *Human Body and Ideology*, I:58–59; López Austin, *Rabbit on the Face*, 85–89; López Austin, *Tamoanchan, Tlalocan*, 97–120.

401. López Austin, *Human Body and Ideology*, I:173.

402. Ibid., I:140.

403. Ibid., I:60, 62; see also López Austin, *Myths of the Opossum*, 60, fig. 3; López Austin, *Rabbit on the Face*, 85; and López Austin, *Tamoanchan, Tlalocan: Places of Mist*, 17, fig. 2; 198, fig. 14; 199, fig. 15.

404. See Heyden, *Eagle, Cactus, Rock*, 67; Olivier, *Mockeries and Metamorphoses*, 264; and Brundage, *Fifth Sun*, 199, 247n6. "Burned things" refers to the incinerated fields, homes, and temples of one's enemy, the funerary cremations of dead warriors, and the cremated hearts of the sacrificed.

405. See Heyden, *Eagle, Cactus, Rock*, 65–66; López Luján, *Offerings of the Templo Mayor*, 198, 225; and Graulich, "Ochpaniztli."

406. See Alfredo López Austin, *Hombre-Dios: Religión y política en el mundo náhuatl* (México: Universidad Nacional Autónoma de México, 1998); López Luján, *Offerings of the Templo Mayor*; Brundage, *Fifth Sun*; and Heyden, *Eagle, Cactus, Rock*.

407. See Graulich, "Quetzalcoatl-Ehecatl," 35; Séjourné, *Universo de Quetzalcoatl*, 50–52; Castellón Huerta, "Cúmulo de Símbolos"; and Raúl Barrera Rodríguez and Gabino López Arenas, "Hallazgos en el recinto ceremonial de Tenochtitlan," *Arqueología mexicana* 16, no. 93 (2008): 18–25. The *yecacozcayo* ("jewel of Ehecatl or wind-ornament design") adorns woven mantles (Berdan and Anawalt, *Essential Codex Mendoza*, 2:189, 192n122). See also the mantles depicted - *Magliabechiano* (1903), plate 3v.

408. Graulich, "Quetzalcoatl-Ehecatl," 35–36.

409. Jacques Galinier, *The World Below: Body and Cosmos in Otomí Indian Ritual* (Boulder: University Press of Colorado, 1997), 170.

410. Heyden, *Eagle, Cactus, Rock*, 64–65. See also Sullivan, "Tlazolteotl-Ixcuina."

411. Campbell, *Morphological Dictionary*, 409.

412. Ibid., 19, 431.

413. Durán, *Book of the Gods*, 164. See also Townsend, "Coronation at Tenochtitlan," 137.

414. See Olivier, *Mockeries and Metamorphoses*, 224–25, 347nn103–4; Heyden, "Metaphors, Nahualtocaitl"; and Doris Heyden, "Trees and Wood in Life and Death," in *Chipping Away on Earth: Studies in Prehispanic and Colonial Mexico in Honor of Arthur J.O. Anderson and Charles Dibble*, ed. Eloise Quiñones Keber (Lancaster, CA: Labyrinthos 1994), 144.

415. Constanza Vega Sosa, "El curso del sol en los glifos de la cerámica azteca tarde," *Estudios de cultura náhuatl* 17 (1984): 156–57, 159.

416. See Mauricio Orozpe Enríquez, *El código oculto de le greca escalonada: Tloque Nahuaque* (México, DF: UNAM, 2010).

417. Molina, *Vocabulario*, 2:158v.

418. Quoted in Broda, "Tlacaxipehualiztli," 208n24.

419. López Austin, *Human Body and Ideology*, II:209. See also Lopez Austin, *Cuerpo Humano*, 2:219.

420. Karttunen, *Analytical Dictionary*, 40. Campbell (*Morphological Dictionary*, 78, 267) lists the following related constructions: *quacocolochoa* ("to curl someone's hair"), *tlacoloa* ("to go somewhere by a roundabout course"), *tlatlacolotiuh* ("to go about in a twisting way"), and *tlaxcalcolli* ("spiral bread roll").

421. Sahagún, *Florentine Codex*, II:3. See also Siméon, *Diccionario de la Lengua*, 764.

422. Guy Stresser-Péan, *The Sun God and the Savior: The Christianization of the Nahua and Totonac in the Sierra Norte de Puebla, Mexico* (Boulder: University Press of Colorado, 2009), 230.

423. Thanks to Joanna Sánchez for sharing this idea with me (personal communication).

424. Boone, *Cycles of Time*, 36. See also Peterson, "Sacrificial Earth"; and Seler, *Comentarios*.

425. Seler, *Comentarios*, 1:15–16.

426. Sahagún, *Florentine Codex*, VI:238.

427. *Histoyre du Mechique*, 108. See Baquedano, "Earth Deities," 351.

428. Peterson, "Sacrificial Earth," 122.

429. Berdan, "Appendix E," 168, 169, 176.

430. Sahagún, *Florentine Codex*, III:43.

431. Seler, *Codex Fejérváry-Mayer*, 83, 90–93, 106.

432. See McKeever Furst, "Skeletonization," 213, 53–54. Schele and Miller argue Maya artists depicted the god of sacrificial death with a human hand gripping his lower jaw. The latter represents a form of Maya sacrifice involving the removal of the living victim's jaw (Linda Schele and Ellen Miller, *The Blood of Kings: Dynasty and Ritual in Maya Art* [Fort Worth, TX: Kimbell Art Museum, 1986]).

433. See Doris Heyden, *Mitología y simbolismo de la flora en el México prehispánico* (México: UNAM, Instituto de Investigaciones Antropológicas, 1983); Jane Hill, "The Flower World of Old Uto-Aztecan," *Journal of Anthropological Research* 48, no. 2 (1992): 117–44; Brumfiel, "Domestic Politics"; Vega Sosa, "Curso del sol"; Ana María Velasco Lozano and Debra Nagao, "Mitología y simbolismo de las flores," *Arqueología Mexicana* 13, no. 78 (2006): 28–35.

434. Karttunen, *Analytical Dictionary*, 186.

435. Berdan, "Appendix E," 168.

6

Nepantla constitutes a third kind of motion-change, a third principal pattern in teotl's ceaseless becoming and transforming, and a third way of unifying inamic partners in agonistic tension. Like olin and malinalli, it represents one of teotl's *hows* or modi operandi.

6.1. LINGUISTIC EVIDENCE

Durán reports interviewing a Nahuatl-speaker regarding the status of the Aztecs' conversion to Christianity. The man characterizes the Aztecs' condition using the concept of *nepantla*. He states, "Father, do not be astonished, we are still *nepantla*."[1] But what exactly does this mean? Durán translates *nepantla* as *"en medios"* ("in the middle" or "betwixt and between") and *neutros* ("neither one nor the other" or "neither fish nor fowl.")[2] Molina glosses *nepantla* as an adverb meaning *"en el medio, o en medio, o por medio"* ("in the middle").[3] Wayne Elzey translates *nepantla* as "center," "middle," or "in between."[4] Frances Karttunen translates it as "in the middle of something." She parses *nepantla* (*"nepantlah"*) as a compound of *nepan-* and *-tlah. Nepan-* occurs only as an element of compounds and derivations. It combines *ne*, a nonspecific reflexive object prefix, with *pan*, a postposition meaning "on the surface of, for or at a particular time." *Nepan* accordingly conveys a sense of mutuality or reciprocity. *Tlah* is a locative compound conveying a sense of abundance. Compounds incorporating *-tlah* include *tetlah* ("rocky place" or "abundant with stones") and *cuauhtlah* ("forest" or "abundant with trees"). *Nepantla*, Karttunen concludes, conveys a sense of abundant reciprocity or mutuality; or more precisely, reciprocity

DOI: 10.5876_9781607322238.c006

or mutuality that consists of a dynamic condition of being abundantly middled, betwixt and between, or centered. It suggests an abundance of middleness or betwixt-and-betweenness.[5]

Let's see what we can learn about nepantla by examining some of Molina's entries for *nepan*-compounded and -derived words.[6] Let's begin with the following verbs: *nenepantlazotlalo* ("to love each other"), *nenepantlazotlaltia* ("to create bonds of friendship between people"), *manepanoa* ("to get married, or to join hands"), *motlatolnepanoa* ("to agree on what is said"), *nepanotl titotlapaloa* ("to greet one another"), *nepan tzatzilia* ("to shout to one another or for those who are working to hurry one another"), *tictonepantlatlaxilia* ("to blame each other for something"), *ixnepoa* ("to line or cover something, or to fold a blanket, or to join one with another"), and *tenepantla moctecani* ("to stir up trouble among others"). Next consider these nouns: *tenepantla moquetzani* ("one who puts himself between those who are quarreling in order to calm them"), *nepantla quiza titlantli* ("messenger between two people"), *nenepantlapaloliztli* ("reciprocal greeting"), *tlatolnepaniuiliztli* ("agreement or conformity of reasons and opinions"), and *nenepantlazoltlaliztli* ("love they have for each other").

The foregoing confirm Karttunen's contention that *nepan-* conveys a sense of abundant mutuality, middlingness, and reciprocity. The verbs designate activities and processes that are interrelational, interactive, transactional, reciprocating, and dialogical. They involve mutual contact, interaction, negotiation, and intercourse between two or more individuals. They bring together two or more things in mutual commerce or transaction. They are social processes occurring in a distinctly *interpersonal* or *social space* that exists betwixt and between or in the middle of the relevant actors. What's more, the processes appear to be simultaneously destructive and constructive. For example, the process of becoming friends, lovers, or marital partners destroys the participants' prior identities as distinct individuals while at the same time creating new relational identities as friends, lovers, or marriage partners. They create an interpersonal space that is "neither fish nor fowl" – that is, neither one person nor the other yet both. When calming down people, when agreeing or communicating with people, and when stirring up people, one interacts with and places oneself in the middle of people. These are essentially social processes involving back-and-forth motion between people. They are processes that create something distinctly social: agreement, discord, harmony, and friendship. The nouns likewise refer to things that are dynamic, reciprocating, transactional, and interactive, such as a "messenger between two people" and "agreement or conformity of reasons and opinions."

Nepanoa figures centrally in many of the above terms. Karttunen glosses *nepanoa* as a reflexive verb meaning "for things to intersect, unite, join together" and as a transitive verb meaning "to join, unite something, to examine something."[7] R. Joe Campbell translates it as "to unite one thing with another, to lay one thing on another." Nepanoa-processes involve the abundantly mutual intersecting, uniting, juxtaposing, conjoining, or superimposing two (or more) things. Molina contains a second entry for *nepanoa*: "to have intercourse with a woman or to push into a group of people." The corresponding noun, *nenepanoliztli*, means "copulation or carnal intercourse." Sexual intercourse involves the mutual communing, joining together, commingling, and intercoursing of sexual partners. It is a quintessentially interpersonal process that creates a quintessentially interpersonal space: a middle space betwixt and between sexual partners; one created by and defined by their reciprocal back-and-forth motion. Sexual commingling is simultaneously destructive and constructive in several ways. First, it destroys the participants' prior identities as independent beings while at the same time constructing a new interdependent or relational identity as sexual partners. The lives and identities of sexual partners become interwoven and transformed. They emerge into a new third, social space betwixt and between their erstwhile single individual spaces. Second, through heterosexual reproduction sexual partners are typically transformed into fathers and mothers. Last, and perhaps most significantly, sexual commingling results in the mixing and shaking together of male and female fluids that results in the creation of a new human being – one who is neither mother nor father yet at the same time both mother and father. Through sexual reproduction sexual partners are therefore further transformed into fathers and mothers.

The related term *manepanoa* means "to get married or join hands." Getting married involved joining together arms and legs, just as holding hands involves the joining together and interlacing of hands and fingers. *Codex Vaticanus 3738A* (pl. 12v) depicts a sexually engaged male~female inamic pair with legs interwoven (see Figure 6.1). Traditional Aztec marriage ritual includes tying together the bride's and groom's woven clothing (see Figure 3.1). *Ixnepanoa* means "to line or cover something, or fold [*doblar*] a blanket, or to join one with another" and also "for a man and woman to unexpectedly meet each other face to face."

Abundantly reciprocating betwixt-and-betweeness characterizes those processes designated by *nenepanoa* ("to join or mix one thing with another"), *cennepanoa* ("to mix some things with others"), *nepan uiuixoa* ("to shake or swing two things together"), and *tlanelpanuiuixoliztli* ("act of shaking and mixing something together"). Mixing and shaking unite and join together things; they situate things in the midst of one another. In the case of preparing foodstuffs, they combine ingredients with one another so as to create something new. In the case of sexual copulation, mixing and shaking together unite female and

male fluids to create new humans. Shaking and mixing together are thus simultaneously creative-destructive and transformative.

Shaking and mixing are middling in several senses. For brevity, let's examine shaking. First, shaking takes place between two endpoints and consists of the back-and-forth motion between these two endpoints. Second, shaking is middling in the sense that it (typically) involves the mutual intermixing of more than one thing. It is thus social in this sense. Third, shaking places the original ingredients in a new physical location, one suspended betwixt and between the two endpoints of its back-and-forth motion. Fourth, shaking is conceptually middling in the sense that it removes the original ingredients from their conceptual categories, X and Y, and transforms them into a new, third conceptual category, Z. This new category, Z, is ambiguous since betwixt and between X and Y; neither X nor Y yet at the same time in some sense still X and Y. Fifth, shaking is metaphysically middling in the sense of being metaphysically destructive-creative and hence metaphysically transformative. Shaking involves the mutual destruction of the original ingredients, X and Y, as well as their interactive transformation into something new, Z, where Z is neither X nor Y *(neutro)*. By shaking things up, by confusing the originals, and by placing them in a process of transition, one creates something new; namely, "something neither fish nor fowl." Shaking together X and Y destroys X and Y yet does so in a manner that preserves them within Z. After all, Z transformatively emerges from both X and Y. Since there is no ex nihilo creation in Aztec metaphysics, new things are generated from old things. In the case of sexual shaking, this results in a new child who is neither parent yet both parents mixed together.

FIGURE 6.1. *Married couple. (*Codex Vaticanus 3738 A *[Loubat 1900: pl.12v]; courtesy of Foundation for the Advancement of Mesoamerican Studies, Inc.)*

Consider next *tlaxinepanoa* ("to weave something"), *tlaxinepanoliztli* ("the act of weaving"), and *xinepanoa* ("to weave something, like mats, fences, or something similar").[8] Since weaving operates as an organizing metaphor in Aztec metaphysics it deserves close attention. Aztec metaphysics conceives the cosmos as a grand weaving in progress, and because it conceives weaving as a nepanoa-process, it follows that Aztec metaphysics conceives the cosmos as a grand nepanoa-process. Weaving illustrates clearly the properties of nepa-noa-processes discussed so far: abundant mutuality, reciprocal middlingness, betwixt-and-betweenness, conceptual and metaphysical ambiguity, and cre-ative-destructive transformation. It therefore follows that the cosmos as grand weaving in progress must also possesses these properties.

Backstrap weaving exhibits middling in several ways. First, it transpires in a time-place middled by (betwixt and between) top and bottom loom bars and opposing sides of the loom. Second, weaving involves the rhythmic, horizontal back-and-forth motion of the weft-carrying shuttle stick as it travels from one side of the loom to the other. What's more, it involves the weaver's rhythmic, forward-and-backward, in-and-out motion as she tightens and loosens the ten-sion of the loom with the backstrap tied around her waist. For this reason the Aztecs associated weaving with sexual intercourse and childbirth. They likened a weaver's rhythmic back-and-forth moving to that of a woman in sexual inter-course and in childbirth. Third, weaving involves the interlacing of warp and weft threads. Weft threads cross over and under alternating strands of warp threads. Fourth, it involves the mutual agonistic interaction of more than one thing. One interlaces warp and weft threads so as to create a dynamic unity of mutual tension. Warp tugs upon weft; weft tugs upon warp. Weaving uni-fies warp and weft in reciprocal, agonistic tension. Weaving thus creates a new, middle space of mutual tension, a space that exists only to the degree that such mutual tension exists, and only to the degree that warp and weft coexist in reciprocal agonistic balance with and against one another. The well-woven fab-ric holds its weave and shape, while the poorly woven one becomes warped, frayed, or unraveled. Well-woven fabric may thus be characterized as *middled*. Finally, the finished fabric, the middled product created by this middling pro-cess, also exists in the middle of the loom. In sum, weaving occurs in the middle, is a middling activity, and produces something that is itself middled and occu-pies the middle. The accomplished weaver (*qualli tlaxinepanoani*) knows how "to middle" the threads, that is, bring warp and weft into a dynamic condition of firm mutual tension. She balances warp and weft to create a good fabric.[9]

Weaving is metaphysically ambiguous in the sense of being simultane-ously destructive and creative. On the one hand, it creates something new and different, a tertium quid; namely, *tlaxinepanolli* ("something woven"). It creates something that is neither warp thread nor weft thread yet nevertheless incorporates both warp and weft. Woven fabric is "neither fish nor fowl." On the other hand, it destroys the prior identities of warp and weft threads as distinct individuals. Weaving transforms individual threads into woven fabrics, just as malinalli-twisting-spinning transforms disordered fiber into ordered thread. More generally, weaving creates an ordered fabric from the *collective* disorder of spun fibers, loom sticks, treadle, heddle rods, shed stick, rolling stick, and batten. It destroys this collective disorder and transforms it into an ordered unity. Furthermore, weaving is an *ordering* as well as *orderly* process (and hence a species of ordering and orderly motion-change). It involves both the correct *spatial* as well as the correct *temporal* arrangement and implementation of the aforementioned components. It requires using the right component at the right time and placing it in the right place.[10] This is essential to weaving's capacity to creatively destroy, destructively create, and thus transform. Weaving transforms disorder into order.

In sum, *nepanoa*-derived verbs designate activities or processes that are middling in several senses. First, they are middling in the intransitive sense of occurring in the middle of, or betwixt and between, two (or more) relata. Second, they are middling in the intransitive sense of involving mutual back-and-forth motion, reciprocal action, and dialogical interaction. Third, they are middling in the transitive sense of doing something to their relata: they middle them. And fourth, they are middling in the sense of creating something new, a tertium quid, that is ontologically speaking betwixt and between the original relata. These processes occupy, use, and apply the middle as well as create a middled product. They are ambiguous since simultaneously destructive and creative. They destroy old identities yet also preserve them by incorporating them in the making of something new. They are metaphysically transformative. Finally, nepanoa-processes represent one way of uniting inamic partners and creating agonistic inamic unity. In weaving, warp and weft inamic partners compete with one another, complement one another, and complete one another. Warp and weft coexist in *dynamic balance* with one another. Analogously, in sexual intercourse male and female inamic partners compete with one another, complement one another, and complete one another. Male and female exist in dynamic, middled balance with one another.

Let's briefly examine some *nepan*-compounded and -derived nouns and adjectives. The referents of these appear to be either creative processes (such as weaving), the products of nepanoa-processes, or things that behave in a middling way. The semantic cluster *tlanepanoani* ("one who compares or verifies something"), *tlanepanoliztli* ("comparison of this sort"), and *tlanepanolli* ("something collated or verified") conveys the sense of reciprocal back-and-forth motion between two things. Although a post-Conquest construction, *peso ynepantla ycac* is nevertheless illuminating. Molina translates it as *"fiel de la balanza"* ("needle or pointer of a balance").[11] The needle of a balance behaves middlingly, swinging back-and-forth between extremes as a consequence of the agonistically interacting forces (weights) of the objects tugging on either end of the balance's arm. The needle moves about in a dynamic middle zone, betwixt and between the two endpoints.

Anepanolli ("joining of waters that flow into some place") combines *atl* ("water") with *-nepanolli*, which Karttunen translates as "something joined, crossed, formed by placing one thing on top of another." Other *–nepanolli* constructions include *calnepanolli* ("two-story house"), *quauhnepanolli* ("wooden cross"), and *tlanepanolli* ("something collated").[12] *Anepanolli* refers to the mutual confluence of waters resulting in their intermixing and commingling. *Inepaniuhca yn ome atoyatl* ("the junction of two rivers") refers to the place where this occurs: their junction, a place of continuous, back-and-forth flowing and mixing together. The confluence is ontologically ambiguous since it lies betwixt and between the two feeder rivers. It is neither river yet both rivers at once. It is creatively destructive, destructively creative, and hence transformative. It destroys the two feeder rivers while simultaneously preserving them in the process of creating a new, third river. A sense of being in the middle or in the midst of is equally expressed by *anepantla* ("gulf, or in the middle of the lake, or the sea").

Onepanco and *onepanolco* are commonly translated as "crossroads" (*"encrucijada de caminos"*). They combine *ohtli* ("path, road"), *nepan* ("mutuality or reciprocity"), and *–co* (a locative suffix meaning "in, on, among"). Elzey treats the crossroads as a paradigmatic instance of nepantla.[13] The Aztecs saw the crossroads as the middle of two conjoining and intersecting paths. The joining together of the two paths creates a new space: an ambiguous space betwixt and between the two. The crossroads is ontologically ambiguous since it is neither one path nor the other yet simultaneously both paths together. Formed mutually by two roads coming together, the crossroads is abundantly middled.

Let's return to *nepantla*. Molina parses *nepantla* as an adverb. This suggests we should translate *nepantla* as "mutually," "reciprocally," "middlingly," "in the middle," or (their inelegance notwithstanding) "betwixt-and-betweenly" or "neither-fish-nor-fowly." As an adverb, *nepantla* modifies primarily activities, processes, becomings, doings, or behavings. It tells us how, when, or where an agent or thing acts, behaves, or does something, or how, when, or where a process proceeds. Nepantla-modified activities and processes transpire middlingly, betwixt-and-betweenly, neither-fish-nor-fowly, reciprocally, and with abundant mutuality. I call such processes and activities *nepantla-processes* and *nepantla-activities*. I have been referring to these as *nepanoa-processes* in the preceding, however given the prominence of nepantla in scholarly discussions, I henceforth use *nepantla-processes*. Nepantla-processes are nepantla-middling or nepantla-reciprocating. They consist of nepantla motion-change.

If this adverbial understanding of nepantla is correct, then we need to resist the temptation to *reify* nepantla that comes with treating *nepantla* as a noun designating (or adjective modifying) a state of being, state of affairs, condition, relationship, arrangement, place, or thing. I worry such common translations of *nepantla* as "the middle" and "the center" support this temptation, and I urge us to eschew them. Similarly, if this adverbial understanding is correct, then we should also stop thinking of *nepantla* as referring to the noun *crossroads*. This, after all, is the job of *onepanco* and *onepanolco*.

Molina lists the related adverb *nepanotl*,[14] which Campbell translates as "one another, reciprocally"[15] and Karttunen as "mutuality, reciprocity."[16] Karttunen states *nepanotl* is used primarily in adverbial constructions suggesting "mutually, reciprocally." Sahagún contains the following: "*nepanotl mococolia, nepanotl momictia, nepanotl motlaxima*," which Charles Dibble and Arthur Anderson translate as "they hated one another, they slew one another, they committed adultery one with another."[17] Nepantla-processes are ex hypothesi correctly modified by the adverbs *nepanotl* and *nepantla* and are characterized by abundant reciprocal middling, and abundant mutual betwixt-and-betweenness. Lastly, Molina contains the related noun *nepantlatli* ("the middle part between two extremes") and adjectives *tenepantla* ("among others") and *tlanepantla* ("in the middle"). Nepantla-processes and -activities suspend people and things in nepantlatli, that is, in the middle, betwixt and between. Those things subjected to nepantla-processes or -activities are aptly described as *tenepantla* or *tlanepantla*.

The nonautochthonous concept most closely resembling nepantla would appear to be liminality. Indeed, many scholars invoke liminality when explicating nepantla.[18] Victor Turner defines the liminal as "a no-man's-land betwixt and between the structural past and the structural future"[19] and as "that which is neither this nor that, and yet is both."[20] The liminal is "transitional," "neutral," and "ambiguous." "Logically antithetical" processes such as death and growth are represented by ambiguous symbols such as serpents since serpents "are neither living nor dead from one aspect, and both living and dead from another."[21] Consequently, argues Turner, the liminal cannot be defined statically: "We are not dealing with structural contradictions ... but with the essentially unstructured (which is at once destructed and prestructured)."[22] The liminal is "interstructural." He writes, "This coincidence of opposite processes and notions in a single representation characterizes the peculiar unity of the liminal: that which is neither this nor that, and yet is both."[23] Liminality is also "a gestational process, a fetation of modes appropriate to postliminal existence."[24] Finally, Turner suggests the liminal be understood in terms of "the subjunctive mood of culture, the mood of maybe, might be, as if, hypothesis, fantasy, conjecture, desire," whereas the ordinary is understood in terms of "the indicative mood, where we expect the invariant operation of cause and effect, of rationality and commonsense."[25]

Their similarities notwithstanding, I argue that nepantla and liminality are fundamentally different concepts and that it is therefore erroneous to equate the two.[26] Simply put, the concept of nepantla flips Turner's notion of liminality on its head. Turner's liminality is temporary and exceptional. It occurs only temporarily in interstitial transitions from one established state of being or permanent structure to another. Structure, order, being, and is-ness are the norm, metaphysically speaking, whereas liminality is the exception. Turner's liminality presupposes a Platonic-style metaphysics of Being. Nepantla, by contrast, is neither temporary nor exceptional but rather the permanent condition of the cosmos, human existence, and indeed reality itself (teotl). Nepantla-processes such as weaving and sexual commingling serve as root or organizing paradigms in Aztec metaphysics. The cosmos is a grand weaving in progress. Nepantla is therefore ordinary – not extraordinary. The ordinary is not interrupted by nepantla; nepantla *is* the ordinary. Becoming and transition are the norm – not being and stasis. Ontological ambiguity is the norm – not ontological unambiguity. For example, nothing is purely being or nonbeing, purely male or female, or purely ordered or disordered. Inamic partners are interdependent, complementary and mutually arising – not logically antithetical and mutually exclusive. In the normal course of things, being, male, and order are always already transitioning back and forth with, intermixing with, arising from, and giving way to nonbeing, female, and disorder (respectively). This is not exceptional. Inamic partnerships are not static, stable, or pure conditions. Furthermore, nepantla is not merely a social, conventional, performative, or ritually induced condition. It defines the processing of the cosmos. Lastly, nepantla is not fruitfully understood in terms of "the subjunctive mood," "fantasy," "maybe," or "as if." Nepantla is a metaphysical condition: one that defines the nature and constitution of teotl and hence the nature and constitution of reality, Fifth Age, and human existence. Nepantla is indeed gestational and fetiferous, but not of some postliminal existence, for there is no postliminal existence available. There is only continuing nepantla-defined processing and motion-change.

In sum, the foregoing linguistic evidence suggests that nepantla-processes (and nepantla motion-change) bring, join, interlace, interlock, or unite two or more things together; that they mix, fuse, shake, or weave things together; and that they do so in a way that is middling, betwixt-and-betweening, and abundant with mutuality and reciprocity. Nepantla-processes bring, join, unite, or interlace together two or more things in a manner that is simultaneously creatively destructive and destructively creative, and therefore transformative. Like weaving, nepantla-processes join inamic partners into a well-balanced albeit agonistic unity. They create and sustain unity through reciprocal action or reciprocity. Nepantla-processes do not, therefore, merely place their participants in the middle. They metaphysically transform fish and fowl into something novel, into a tertium quid – that is, something neither fish nor fowl yet at the same time both fish and fowl. Nepantla-processes destroy their participants' prior status as fish and fowl while simultaneously creating something that is neither fish nor fowl. As we've seen, the confluence of two rivers transforms rivers A and B into a new river, C. By mixing together A and B, the confluence destroys A and B while also creating something both ontologically and conceptually novel: C. Since C incorporates and preserves A and B, it follows that C is neither A nor B yet at the same time both A and B. Thus C is irreducibly ambiguous.

6.2. LITERARY EVIDENCE

OMEYOCAN AND NEPANTLA MOTION-CHANGE

What do the written sources tell us about nepantla? Sahagún records a speech delivered by a midwife upon the ritual bathing of a newborn in which she declares the newborn to have been "bored" in Omeyocan, Chicnauhnepaniuhcan.[27] The speech identifies Chicnauhnepaniuhcan with Omeyocan, the place of duality and double heaven that occupies the twelfth and thirteenth layers of the cosmos, and that (according to López Austin) is frequently identified with Tamoanchan.[28]

What does "Chicnauhnepaniuhcan" mean? Dibble and Anderson translate it as "place of the nine heavens."[29] Josefina García Quintana translates it as "place of the nine confluences."[30] Although he acknowledges the correctness of García Quintana's translation, López Austin prefers "place of the nine levels." He bases this translation on the word's root verb, nepanoa, which he translates as "to throw one thing on top of another."[31] However López Austin proposes we translate nepanoa more narrowly as "placing a long object over another of equal length so that they cross (*de manera tal que queden cruzados*), resulting in the geometric shape of a cross (*aspa*)."[32] López Austin apparently bases this narrower definition of *nepanoa* upon the observation that "the shape of the cross (*aspa*) was very important in [indigenous] ritual symbolism."[33] The Aztecs used terms containing *nepan* to designate articles employed in religious rituals such as the *amanepaniuhqui* ("crossed paper stole"[34] or "cape of plaited paper"[35]) and *epnepaniuhqui* ("crossed mother-of-pearl stole"[36] or "[bands of] gold crossing [bands of] seashells"[37]). Post-Contact Aztecs referred to the Christian cross as a *quauitl nepaniuhtoc* ("wooden cross or wooden planks that are crossed").[38] Since Omeyocan and Chicnauhnepaniuhcan are obviously extremely sacred places, López Austin reasons that they, too, must be cross-shaped. Chicnauhnepaniuhcan must be the place consisting of nine crosses or crossings.

Superimposing these nine crosses so that they are united and continuing, López Austin deduces with the help of geometry and graphic illustrations that they constitute a spiraling "malinalli with nine crossings."[39] He writes, "the result would be a series of nine crossed figures, nine superimpositions. Assuming the figures were united and continuous, the result would be that the two bands or strands [were] in a helical shape, i.e. the shape of *malinalli*. Tamoanchan, under the name of Chicnauhnepaniuhcan, would be the place where the celestial forces and those of the underworld were superimposed nine times, the spiral formed by the hot and cold currents."[40] He further supports his inference by the fact that spirals consisting of paired opposites are "crucial element[s] in creation miracles."[41] He concludes: "Tamoanchan was not only identified with the highest part of the universe, but with the world of the dead, because it was all a process of the marvelous crossing of the celestial and earthly currents, the place of creation where the hot forces of the nine skies and the cold ones of the nine levels of the underworld revolve in a spiral."[42]

A closer examination of López Austin's line of reasoning, however, reveals that it shows something quite different. I submit it shows that nepantla motion-change – *not* malinalli motion-change – defines Chicnauhnepaniuhcan, Tamoanchan, and Omeyocan; that nepantla motion-change – *not* malinalli motion-change – functions as the crucial element in creation miracles; and that nepantla motion-change – *not* malinalli motion-change – defines Tamoanchan's process of "marvelous crossing" and hence the highest level of the cosmos, Omeyocan.

Let's retrace the steps of López Austin's argument. First, he defines *nepanoa* narrowly as "placing a long object over another of equal length so that they cross, resulting in the geometric shape of a cross." My examination of *nepanoa-* and *nepan*-derived words shows that although the linguistic evidence permits such a narrow definition it clearly does not mandate it. *Nepanoa* refers broadly to all kinds of intersectings, joinings together, juxtaposings, and superimposings, including most pertinently weaving and sexual commingling. While some of these processes may involve objects of equal length, they clearly need not. For example, Sahagún's informants say of the mourning dove (*huilotl*) that "its nest is only sticks thrown on top of one another" (*in itapazol zan tlacotl in connepanoa*).⁴³ There is no suggestion that the sticks are of equal length. Nor is there any mention of equal size in weaving, sexual intercourse, holding hands, shaking together things, or the confluence of two rivers. Furthermore, while many of these nepanoa-processes involve throwing or placing one thing on top of another, not all of them involve placing things at right angles to one another. *Calnepanolli* ("top floor of a house"), *ixnepanoa* ("to line or cover something, or fold [*"doblar"*] a blanket, or to join one with another"), and *tlaixnepanolli* ("something lined or covered, or joined together") involve one thing's being superimposed squarely upon another.⁴⁴

Second, López Austin identifies the shape of nepanoa-crossed planks of equal length and of the *quauitl nepaniuhtoc* ("wooden cross") with the saltire, or X-shaped St. Andrew's cross. He contends the shape of a cross is extremely important in Aztec religious symbolism, and then attributes this geometric shape to the nepanoa-arranged levels that comprise Chicnauhnepaniuhcan (and hence Tamoanchan and Omeyocan). However, one wonders why he identifies the relevant Aztec cruciforms as X-shaped St. Andrew's crosses rather than as +-shaped Greek crosses or even olin day signs or quincunxes. López Austin's identification is underdetermined.

Next, "using geometry" López Austin transforms the nine united and continuous *cross-shaped figures* (composed of one plank placed upon another) entailed by the meaning of *chicnauhnepaniuhcan* into nine superimposed, united, and continuous *spirals* (or *double helices*). In so doing, López Austin transforms *crosses* into *spirals*. He reconfigures nepanoa- (what I am calling nepantla-) shaped motion-change into malinalli-shaped motion-change, eliding over the substantial differences between nepantla (nepanoa) and malinalli. In so doing he erases nepantla motion-change from Aztec metaphysics and replaces it with malinalli motion-change. By replacing crosses with spirals and by equating nepantla with malinalli, López Austin *confounds* nepantla motion-change and malinalli motion-change.

Chicnauhnepaniuhcan along with the Nahuatl terms used in the creation miracles reproduced by Alvarado Tezozomoc and cited by López Austin as supporting evidence – *nepaniuhtoc, nepaniuhyan,* and *nepaniuhticac* – are all derived from *nepanoa* – not from *malina* (the verb root of *malinalli*).⁴⁵ Yet López Austin systematically ignores this fact and treats them all as though one and all are *malina*-derived. Yet the verbs *nepanoa* and *malina* are not synonymous and the kinds of motion-change to which they refer are not identical. Nepantla motion-change and malinalli motion-change constitute two distinct kinds or shapes of motion-change. Interlacing, interweaving, and commingling are not the same as twisting, spinning, and coiling.

The family of nepanoa- (nepantla-) processes includes intersecting, joining together, juxtaposing, uniting, intermixing, shaking together, confluencing, interlacing, superimposing, and, most relevantly for present purposes, weaving and sexual commingling. Both weaving and sexual intercourse involve placing things on top of one another – in the former cases, warp and weft fibers; in the latter, the legs and arms of sexual partners. In light of this, I submit the series of nine superimposed, united, and continuous figures suggested by the name *chicnauhnepaniuhcan* is more faithfully interpreted as a series of nine interweavings, comminglings, or confluencings. I further submit that it is nepantla-processes of motion-change that are "crucial element[s] in creation miracles" that define Tamoanchan, Omeyocan, and Chicnauhnepaniuhcan, and that the "process of the marvelous crossing" that defines Tamoanchan is a nepantla – not a malinalli – process. A process of marvelous *interweaving* defines Chicnauhnepaniuhcan. Tamoanchan, Omeyocan, and Chicnauhnepaniuhcan consist of the continuous weaving together – *not* the twisting-spinning together – of inamic partners. The time-place of continuous creation and regeneration is a time-place of continuous nepantla-defined sexual commingling and interweaving. The cross (*aspa*) is a nepantla motif, not a malinalli motif.

In sum, nepantla motion-change defines Chicnauhnepaniuhcan, Tamoanchan, and Omeyocan and functions as the essential component in creation miracles. Nepantla motion-change defines Tamoanchan's process of "marvelous crossing." If, as we saw in chapter 5, Ilhuicatl mamalhuacoca ("Sky Where Gyrating Occurs") is the place where the malinalli twisting-spinning-drilling of sacred forces occurs before being transmitted to the earthly layers of the cosmos, then it would seem to follow that these sacred forces are *not* therefore twisting, gyrating, or spinning in the nine heavenly layers *above* Ilhuicatl mamalhuacoca. Therefore, while malinalli motion-change defines the movement and transmission of energy between upper and earthly realms, it does not define the movement of energy in the layers *above* Ilhuicatl mamalhuacoca. Nepantla motion-change defines the heart and essence of the uppermost realm, Omeyocan (Chicnauhnepaniuhcan or Tamoanchan). Omeyocan ("Two Time-Place" or "Time-Place of Paired Inamic Partners") is defined by nepantla motion-change. Omeyocan is the time-place of continual nepantla-defined agonistic inamic interaction and unification; the time-place of continual nepantla-defined regeneration and transformation; the birth time-place of all other things; and the highest fold of the cosmos.[46] León-Portilla characterizes Omeyocan as "The source of generation and life, the ultimate metaphysical region, the primordial dwelling of Ometeotl."[47] In light of the preceding, León-Portilla's characterization is to be understood in terms of nepantla motion-change.

John Monaghan, we've seen, claims " 'twoness' is an abstract image of wholeness" across Mesoamerica,[48] and Nathaniel Tarn and Martin Prechtel claim "nothing complete, nothing fully fulfilling its function in the world, can be other than [both male and female]."[49] Omeyocan dramatically illustrates these claims. The notion of *unified twoness* contained in the concept of Omeyocan entails wholeness. What's more, this is a special kind of wholeness: one resulting from the nepantla-defined agonistic interweaving and mutual balancing of inamic partners. It is a dynamic, diachronic, and processive wholeness – not a static one. It is a processive wholeness characterized by continual becoming, where becoming takes the form of continuous nepantla-defined weaving or sexual commingling. Omeyocan also suggests *twofold oneness*. It is defined by the agonistic interaction of inamic partners, and inamic partners, as we've seen, cannot by definition exist without one another. They are mutually interdependent, interrelated, and arising. They compete with one another, complement one another, and complete one another. This, then, is also a special kind of wholeness – namely, one produced by the interweaving of inamic partners into agonistic balance. We must not, therefore, think of Omeyocan as constituted by two metaphysically distinct and independently existing entities or substances (dualities) that are merely contingently fused with one another. There was no time when either inamic existed without being agonistically united with its inamic partner.

Ometeotl and Nepantla Motion-Change

Omeyocan is the time-place of Ometeotl ("Two Sacred Energy" or "Two Sacred Power").[50] We saw in chapter 3 that Fray Juan de Torquemada claims the "Indians" understood "divine nature to be divided into two gods, a man and a woman"[51] and that they also called this primordial male~female creative force Ometecuhtli~Omecihuatl ("Two Lord-Two Lady"), Tonacatecuhtli~Tonacacihuatl ("Lord of Our Flesh/Sustenance~Lady of Our Flesh/Sustenance"), *in Tonan, in Tota* ("our Mother, our Father"), *in teteuinan, in teteu ita, Huehueteotl* ("Father~Mother of the Gods, old or ancient God"), and Ipalnemohuani ("He~She through Whom One Lives").[52] This primordial male~female creative force further illustrates Monaghan's and Tarn and Prechtel's claims.

Aztec metaphysics treats Ometeotl, Ometecuhtli~Omecihuatl, et al. as the primordial male~female agonistic unity from which all things – from other gods to humans, animals, and trees – are engendered, sustained, and re-engendered. The becoming and processing of Ometeotl et al. consists of the continual agonistic interacting of male and female inamic partners. The creative-generative as well as destructive-degenerative power of Ometeotl and hence the cosmos springs from its continual unifying of agonistic inamic partners.[53] Creation involves ordering inamic partners; destruction, disordering them. What's more, the unified twoness of Ometeotl, Ometecuhtli~Omecihuatl, et al. is not confined to male~female. Ometeotl is defined equally by the dynamic agonistic unifying of the corresponding parallel-aligned inamic pairs: hot~cold, dry~wet, life~death, being~nonbeing, and so on. Ometeotl embodies what Monaghan calls "plural singularity or unity."[54] Cecelia Klein contends these primordial male~female pairs possess both genders *completely* and hence both gendered powers *completely*, and that they are not, therefore, properly understood as androgynous or just partly male and partly female.[55] Since they are fully male *and* fully female, they are fully "doubled."[56] By combining both genders and their powers, Ometeotl's powers are doubled and therefore fully complete.

Prominent among the processes of agonistic inamic interaction and unification attributed to these primordial male~female creator pairs is sexual intercourse. As Klein points out, although Ometecuhtli~Omecihuatl, Tonacatecuhtli~Tonacacihuatl, et al. are never artistically depicted as sexually engaged, "their role as the mother and father of both gods and all living things implies a pretty constant embrace."[57] Indeed, it implies a *continuous* embrace! Their continuing embrace involves continuous sexual commingling and hence continuous motion-change and reproduction. The philological evidence above strongly suggests the Aztecs conceived sexual intercourse as a nepantla-process and thus one involving the abundant and mutual commingling of agonistic inamic partners. Ometecuhtli~Omecihuatl et al. unite inamic partners within a single, nepantla-process of mutual back-and-forth commingling and overlaying – a process that is simultaneously creative and destructive and hence transformative.[58]

Aztec metaphysics conceives war (military struggle) in analogous terms. Both sexual intercourse and war unify inamic partners in agonistic struggle.[59] Molina, Siméon, Campbell, and Olivier translate the verb *yecoa* as "to test, to taste, to copulate, to strike forcefully in war, to make war."[60] Graulich asserts that sexual intercourse "was as war, and giving birth was compared to a battle during which a captive was made."[61] Although itself not a *nepan*-derived word, *yecoa* nevertheless designates a nepantla-like interpersonal and middling activity that intermixes and unites inamic partners through the reciprocal back-and-forth exchange of thrusts and parries. In *xochiyaoyotl* ("flower war") in particular, one aims to dominate but not kill one's match.[62] The Aztecs conceived the captured enemy warrior as a sexually conquered female with the Aztec warrior's male arrow penetrating the enemy's female shield.[63] Both sexual intercourse and capturing enemy warriors are transformative processes. In both activities male (hot, dry, etc.) and female (cold, wet, etc.) inamic partners compete with one another, complement one another, and complete one another. Inamic combat was not alien to "the gods." The *Historia de los mexicanos* portrays Quetzalcoatl~Tezcatlipoca as inamic partners locked in – and thus united by – continual back-and-forth flower combat with one another, a transformative process resulting in the creation and destruction of the first four Cosmic Ages.[64]

Chapter 3 claimed that sexual intercourse, war, and weaving all function as root or organizing metaphors in Aztec metaphysics. Aztec metaphysics sees these three as mutually consistent and defined by the same kind of motion-change. Weaving, war, and sexual intercourse offer us three mutually consistent and ultimately identical ways of understanding the agonistic inamic unity that defines Ometeotl, Omeyocan, and hence the processing and becoming of the cosmos.

Ometeotl (Ometecuhtli~Omecihuatl, Tonacatecuhtli~Tonacacihuatl) is not merely engaged in a process of never-ending sexual commingling with him~ herself: indeed, he~she *is* sexual commingling.[65] Since sexual commingling is an agonistic process, it follows that Omeyocan is a time-place of never-ending struggle and opposition. And since sexual commingling is a nepantla-process, it follows that Omeyocan is a time-place of ceaseless nepantla-generated inamic unity and balance. Thus, Omeyocan is *neither* a time-place of peace and harmony (if these entail an absence of conflict) *nor* a time-place of inactivity, immutability, and stasis.

Teotl and Nepantla Motion-Change

Talk of an omnipresent, metaphysically immanent, self-generating, and self-regenerating primordial male~female unity – be it Ometeotl, Ometecuhtli~ Omecihuatl, or Tonacatecuhtli~Tonacacihuatl – is simply a way of focusing human consciousness upon certain aspects or characteristics of the grand dynamic unity that is teotl. Ometeotl et al. are identical with teotl. Like Ometeotl, teotl is therefore a single, all-encompassing, grand nepantla-process.

Given the identity of teotl with the cosmos, it follows that the cosmos, too, is a single, grand nepantla-process. And so we return to the proposition that weaving, sexual commingling, and war serve as root or organizing metaphors of Aztec metaphysics. The cosmos is a grand sexual commingling and weaving in progress. Teotl is simultaneously weaver, weaving, and woven product, just as it is simultaneously sexual comminglers, sexual commingling, and sexually commingled product.

In sum, chapter 1 argued that process, movement, change, transformation, and becoming define teotl. We may now be more specific: teotl is defined by nepantla-defined processing, motion-change, becoming, and transformation. Chapter 1 also argued that Aztec metaphysics defines reality in terms of *becoming* rather than *being* (or is-ness). To exist is to become, to move, to change. We may now be more specific: to exist is to nepantla-become, -move-change, and -transform. Reality nepantla move-changes, nepantla-processes, and nepantla-becomes. Nepantla-processing, nepantla-becoming, and nepantla motion-change define the basic working of the cosmos. The concept of nepantla plays a fundamental role in Aztec metaphysics. Reality consists of a never-ending process of nepantla commingling, interweaving, and intersecting – that is, nepantla middling, unifying, and balancing – of inamic partners.

TLAZOLTEOTL-IXCUINA, WEAVING, AND NEPANTLA MOTION-CHANGE

Weaving functions as an organizing metaphor in Aztec metaphysics, and weaving is a nepantla process. Weaving unites warp and weft in agonistic balance, just as sexual commingling unites male and female. In weaving, warp and weft compete with one another, complement one another, and complete one another – as do male and female in sexual commingling. The similarities between weaving and sexual commingling did not escape Aztec thinkers. They considered the rhythmic, back-and-forth motion of weaving as well as the interlacing of threads into a single fabric to imitate sexual commingling. Weavers themselves were said to be charged with excessive sexual energy.

Chapter 3 articulated the role of weaving as an organizing metaphor with the statement, "The cosmos is a grand weaving in progress." I now want to explore the claim that Ometeotl (Ometecuhtli~Omecihuatl, Tonacatecuhtli~Tonacacihuatl) is a grand cosmic weaver, and that the cosmos is Ometeotl's grand weaving in progress. Omeyocan is accordingly the place-time of continuous cosmic weaving. Since weaving involves the interlacing of threads transformed from raw fiber through twisting-spinning, we should revise the foregoing to read: the cosmos is a grand malinalli-twisting-spinning and nepantla-weaving in progress.

Weaving, weaving implements (e.g., spindles, whorls, battens) and woven products (e.g., cloth, fabric, and mats) are thus accorded an extremely powerful place in Aztec metaphysics (as are malinalli-twisting-spinning and malinalli-twisted-spun products). Broadly construed, weaving includes not only the interlacing of warp and weft threads but also the twisting-spinning of raw fiber into thread suitable for weaving.

Xochiquetzal ("Flowery Queztal Feather") is the "patronness" of weaving, embroidery, and spinning (the feminine crafts *par excellence*) as well as of pregnant women and childbirth. Durán states she was patroness of weavers, embroiderers, sculptors, painters, silversmiths, and "all those whose profession it was to imitate nature in crafts and in drawing."[66] The Aztecs associated her with exuberant and youthful female sexuality, desire, fecundity, and generative power along with flowers, feasting, and pleasure generally. The anonymous annotator of the *Codex Vaticanus 3738 A* states the Aztecs believed Xochiquetzal "made the earth bloom."[67] As first wife of Tlaloc, Xochiquetzal is also associated with water. *Codex Fejérváry-Mayer* (pl. 29) depicts a breastfeeding Xochiquetzal wearing a turtle shell on her back.[68] Breastfeeding symbolizes her life-giving powers, while turtle shells invoke the creative energies of water, thunder, music, and the earth.[69] She sits facing a flowering plant springing from a pot that contains two sacrificial flint blades, indicating the contribution of blood sacrifice to the flowering, growth, and renewal of the earth. *Codex Telleriano Remensis* (pl. 22v) depicts her holding a weaving batten, an instrument symbolizing women's weaving skills and women's roles as creators of cloth and life.[70] She is also accompanied by a coral snake and centipede, creatures associated with the regenerative powers of filth, garbage, and the earth. Following the *Historia de los mexicanos*, H. B. Nicholson identifies Xochiquetzal with the female aspect of Ometeotl. He identifies her inamic partner – sometimes the young, male, solar god Chicomexochitl ("Seven Flower"), other times the young, male, solar god Xochipilli ("Flower Prince") – with the male aspect of Ometeotl.[71]

Weaving, spinning, and embroidery are not, however, exclusively associated with Xochiquetzal. As Klein notes, "all Aztec . . . creation and fertility goddesses were described as great weavers."[72] Xochiquetzal is merely the youthful aspect of the great genetrix, spinner, and weaver, Tlazolteotl-Ixcuina ("Filth Goddess-Lady Cotton"). As we saw in chapter 4, Nicholson locates Tlazolteotl-Ixcuina and Xochiquetzal within the "Teteoinnan complex" of deities that he interprets as a creative~destructive earth-mother complex.[73]

Thelma Sullivan argues Tlazolteotl-Ixcuina, like all Mother Goddesses, is "the genetrix of all living things, plant and animal" as well as "the Great Spinner of the Thread and Weaver of the Fabric of Life" and "the Great Conceiver and the Great Parturient."[74] All great genetrixes are great spinners and weavers. She is both the "Goddess of Filth-Lady Cotton" and "the Great Genetrix, that is, the Great Spinner and Weaver."[75] The moniker "Goddess of Filth-Lady Cotton" ties her to degeneration, while "Great Spinner and Weaver" ties her to regeneration. Tlazolteotl-Ixcuina therefore "represents the Mother-Goddess concept in its totality," that is, both generative and degenerative aspects.[76] Both *Codex Telleriano-Remensis* (fol. 12r) and *Florentine Codex* depict Tlazolteotl-Ixcuina with rubber-painted lips, mouth, and chin.[77] Quiñones Keber suggests this points to her role and regenerative powers as Tlaelquani ("Eater of Ordure"), who eats filth and transforms it into life.[78] Tlazolteotl-Ixcuina's eating of tlazolli transforms the disordered into the ordered, just as spinning and weaving transform disordered raw cotton into ordered woven cloth. Tlazolteotl-Tlaelquani processes are implicated in the earth's reception, consumption, and subsequent recycling of waste (human and animal excrement; decaying flesh, fruit, and vegetables) into the nourishing humus needed for renewing earthly life.[79]

Several depictions of Tlazolteotl-Ixcuina emphasize the role of Tlazolteotl-Ixcuina processes in cyclical completion and renewal and thus the connection between sacrifice, fertility, and regeneration. *Codex Telleriano-Remensis* (fol. 17v) depicts her arms and legs covered with the downy white feathers worn by victims about to be sacrificed. From her body hangs the yellowish, flayed skin of a sacrificial victim. From her wrists hang the victim's hands. She wears a headdress of cotton and spindles from which hang cotton tassels. She carries a multilayered feather back-panel adorned by the image of a skull and shell rattles.[80] *Codex Borbonicus* (pl. 13) depicts Tlazolteotl-Ixcuina wearing the flayed skin of a sacrificial victim while simultaneously conceiving a child *and* giving birth to another child. The child emerging from her womb holds two malinalli-twisted cords. The cords together with the flayed skin suggest the interweaving of generation and regeneration through sacrifice. The interweaving of life and death through sacrifice is further symbolized by the items placed around her. Those associated with life include an *ientzommaye petlazolcoatl* (centipede and snake twisted together). Centipedes (*petlazolcoatl*, "frayed mat snake") symbolize (among other things) tlazolli and prolific regeneration. Snakes symbolize generation and transformation. Items associated with sacrifice include maguey thorns, techcatl (sacrificial stone), and tzompantli (skull rack).[81] In short, *Codex Borbonicus* (pl. 13) conveys the idea of Tlazolteotl-Ixcuina as the great genetrix of all things.

Ixcuina, we've seen, consists of four women or aspects,[82] which Sullivan interprets as expressing all four phases of the life~death cycle: "Her fourfold character represents the growth and decline of all living things that, like the spindle, pass through four stages: youth, fecundity, middle age, and old age and death."[83] Spinning and spindle rods, like weaving and woven cloth, are defined by four phases and hence by four-phased life~death cycles. Spindle rods and spinning are therefore polysemous since they are associated with both olin motion-change *and* malinalli motion-change. This fact, adds Sullivan, indicates that Tlazolteotl-Ixcuina processes represent all four stages in the cosmic processing of the Mother Goddess and therefore fully express the concept of the Mother Goddess. All processes – including what *we* think of as things but that are really processes, according to process metaphysics – undergo four-phased life~death cycles.

The fact that Aztec metaphysics conceives Tlazolteotl-Ixcuina as the great spinner and weaver of life and as the great Mother conceiver and parturient of life together with the fact that it regards Tlazolteotl-Ixcuina as an aspect of Ometecuhtli~Omecihuatl, Ometeotl, and ultimately teotl itself, strongly supports the thesis that Aztec metaphysicians conceived the becoming and processing of the cosmos in terms of weaving (and weaving-related processes such as spinning) and therefore in terms of nepantla motion-change (and weaving-related processes such as malinalli-twisting-spinning). Although spinning transforms raw fiber into thread, it is weaving that transforms bunches of thread into well-ordered cloth. Chapter 7 argues that nepantla motion-change subsumes both malinalli and olin motion-change. Both are components of weaving broadly construed. Weaving therefore functions as the fundamental generative-regenerative process of the cosmos as well as the fundamental form taken by agonistic inamic unity in the cosmos.

The preceding together with the fundamental role of weaving in generating and ordering the Fifth Age from the disordered remains of the previous Four Ages helps explain the prominence of quadruplicity in ordering the Fifth Age. It explains, for example, why the Fifth Age is arranged into four sides, corners, and intercardinal and cardinal directions, and why the Sun's daily and nightly paths are arranged into four phases. Ometeotl weaves together the elements of the Fifth Sun-Earth Ordering into four-phased life~death cycles.

Why did Aztec metaphysicians regard weaving as such a highly significant and powerful metaphor? Weaving is fundamentally and thoroughly transformative, and it is precisely *how* weaving transforms that appears to have most impressed Aztec thinkers. Weaving begins with raw fiber that it malinalli twists-spins into ordered thread. It organizes bunches of spun thread into two groups: warp and weft. It arranges the warp fibers on a loom and then interlaces warp and weft. It transforms disordered plant fiber into ordered cloth. Weaving serves as a paradigmatic case of transforming and uniting two things in agonistic balance: for example, male~female, hot~cold, and dry~wet. Warp and weft function as paired inamic forces. Weaving favors neither warp nor weft, nor does it eliminate warp or weft. Rather, it treats the two as mutually necessary and mutually interdependent. It preserves warp and weft while transforming them into something new: woven cloth. It allows inamic partners to compete with one another while also forcing them to complement and complete one another. Warp and weft coexist in balanced mutual tension with one another. Nepantla motion-change intertweaves inamic partners to form an agonistic unity. The term *ixnepanoa* ("for a man and woman to unexpectedly meet each other face to face") nicely expresses the ability of nepantla-processes to bring together inamic partners face to face.

In sum, Aztec metaphysics understands weaving as a cyclical, four-phased transformational process of generation, degeneration, and regeneration. It conceives Ometecuhtli~Omecihuatl as engaged in continuous self-weaving, just as he~she is engaged in continuous sexual intercourse with him~herself. By means of both processes Ometecuhtli~Omecihuatl cyclically generates and regenerates the cosmos. Since both are nepantla-processes, I submit nepantla motion-change defines the fundamental generative and regenerative processes of the cosmos. Given the identity of Ometecuhtli~Omecihuatl with Ometeotl and ultimately teotl, we thus arrive at the Aztecs' vision of teotl as grand nepantla-process that continually generates and regenerates the cosmos.

The Power of Woven (Nepantla-Ordered) Products

Aztec artisans wove floor mats, sleeping mats, pillows, seats, and thrones from reeds, palm leaves, and malinalli grass. Aztec rulers and judges conducted important business sitting on woven seats and thrones. Marriage ceremonies took place on woven mats (see Figure 3.1) as did sexual intercourse. Women gave birth on woven mats. Woven mats symbolized fertility and sexuality in Mixtec thought, for example.[84] Weavers wove while sitting on braided mats, further associating mats with sexual intercourse and parturition since the Aztecs understood weaving in terms of sexual intercourse and in terms of giving birth (to a cloth). Sahagún's illustration of spinning and weaving equipment includes a mat (see Figure 5.1). The *Codex Mendoza* lists four thousand woven seats and four thousand woven mats among Aztec tribute items.[85]

Sahagún's informants report that mats came in a variety of sizes, shapes, degrees of thickness, colors, and designs. They describe the good reed-mat seller as one who "weaves reed mats . . . he lays out [the reeds], arranges them, selects the best ones." The bad mat seller, by contrast, sells "rotten, bruised, frayed mats."[86]

His mats are *itlacauhqui* ("damaged, flawed, harmed, or rotten"). He weaves the reeds improperly, creating mats that are off balanced and warped. The reeds do not fit together properly and are out of place, as suggested by the related terms *cuicaitlacoliztli* ("dissonance in singing"), *itlacauhtica* ("for something to be out of place [*estar malpuesta*] or damaged"), and *iytlacauhca intilmatl* ("flaw or defect in a piece of cloth").[87] The related noun *tlatlacolli* means "something damaged, defective, corrupted, spoiled, displaced, or off balance."[88] This semantic cluster refers to *stuff out of place*, reminding us of our earlier understanding of tlazolli as stuff out of place. It suggests the Aztecs conceived well-woven cloth, by contrast, as *stuff in place, properly placed, or in the right place* – that is, *nepantla-middled and -balanced*. As a nepantla-process, weaving involves middling warp and weft threads, arranging them properly, and putting them in the right place. It also suggests that well-woven things exist at the opposite end of a nonhierarchical continuum from poorly woven, unraveled, and frayed things characterized by tlatlacolli and tlazolli.

The codices contain abundant illustrations of woven mats, seats, and thrones (see Figure 6.2).[89] The diphrase *in petlapan, in icpalpan* ("the mat, the seat") served as a metaphor for the throne.[90] Molina translates *icpalpan petlapan nica* as "to have the duty of ruling and governing."[91] *Codex Mendoza* (fol. 69r) depicts Motecuhzoma Xocoyotzin sitting on a twilled seat that rests upon a twilled mat. It also depicts various buildings in his royal courtyard – including council hall, council hall of war, and guest lodges – with woven floor mats. These provided a well-ordered time-place for important activities. Durán's illustrations of Aztec rulers likewise depict them standing or sitting upon woven mats.[92] The illustrations accompanying Books IV and VI of the *Florentine Codex* depict various activities taking place on woven thrones, seats, and floor mats, including divining by Oxomoco and Cipactonal, making penance, giving thanks to Tezcatlipoca, and arranging a marriage, as well as a ruler's exhorting the people.[93] The diphrase "the eagle mat, the jaguar mat" served as a metaphor for those who are strong and unable to be vanquished. Warriors who single-handedly seized four captives earned the honor of sitting on woven mats and seats in the Jaguar and Eagle warriors' halls.[94]

Many of these mats, seats, and thrones appear to have been fabricated using a weaving technique Alba Guadalupe Mastache calls "twill" (*sarga*) (see Figure 6.3).[95] Twilling produces a complex, multilayered, diagonally ascending and descending stepped pattern that resembles the xicalcoliuhqui motif as well as what Sahagún's informants call a *coapetlatl* or *petlacoatl* ("serpent mat"). The coapetlatl consists of snakes swarming together in a twilled pattern. The snake mat "goes, it travels . . . it runs back and forth; it runs in all directions."[96]

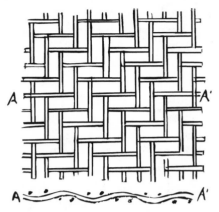

FIGURE 6.2. *Woven seat, throne, and mat.*
(Codex Mendoza [1997: folio 68r]; courtesy
of Frances F. Berdan and Patricia Rieff
Anawalt.)

FIGURE 6.3. *Twilling (*sarga*), top and*
side views. (Redrawn from Mastache, "El
tejido en el México antiguo," Arqueología
Mexicana, *Edición especial, 19 [2005]: 31.)*

As Sahagún's informants' description suggests, twilling produces an ambiguous, back-and-forth pattern whose strands travel seemingly in all directions at once – a pattern, I suggest, that represents the ambiguous, reciprocating motion of nepantla motion-change. Well-twilled mats, seats, and thrones functioned as balanced and *balancing*, ordered and *ordering*, middled and *middling* time-places that empowered their occupants while performing religious, medical, judicial, epistemological, prognosticatory, and political activities. Careful weaving conserves Tlaltecuthli's tonalli-energy and conveys it to the woven objects' occupants. Woven products operate as multidirectional power conduits or portals for energy transmission and transformation. Woven mats, seats, and thrones enabled humans to access power from the upper and lower layers of the cosmos as well as to recycle to those layers power acquired from their grass composition, their occupants, and the ritual activities performed upon them. The ambiguous, motion-in-all-directions-at-once nature of twilled products finally suggests their ability to draw energy from and send energy to all four directions of the Fifth Sun-Earth Ordering.

Nepantla-woven floor mats thus contributed importantly to various rituals and ceremonies. The *Primeros memoriales'* illustrations of Atemoztli ("Descent of Water") and Izcalli ("Growth") depict ritual participants standing on floor mats.[97] Durán's illustrations of Atemoztli, Panquetzaliztli ("Raising of Banners"), and Tititl ("Stretching") depict rituals being conducted on long woven mats.[98]

During Etzalcualiztli ("The Eating of Etzalli") people collected and wove reeds into green-and-white mats and seats with backs.[99] At various points during the festivals they stretched out these mats in the calmecac, sat upon them, laid upon them, and placed sacred objects such as green stones upon them. *Codex Magliabechiano* (pl. 34r) illustrates Etzalcualiztli with Tlaloc standing upon a green-and-white mat.[100]

Numerous illustrations in the *Primeros memoriales* depict temples with cross-hatched roof façades.[101] These play a similar role in providing an empowered and empowering, well-balanced time-place for energy transmission. These façades resemble the walls of the small threshold building (among the complex of buildings called "Group H" at the Preclassic Maya site of Waxaktun in Guatemala) that are "marked with great mats modeled in plaster." Freidel contends these figures indicate the building functioned as a "Popol Nah, a community council house, a ritual space where the king interacted with his people – especially through the performance and teaching of sacred dance."[102] The term *Popol Nah* ("council or meeting house," literally "mat house") derives from *pop* ("mat") and is related to *popol* ("council"). The Maya stored the regalia for dancing and ritual in the Popol Nah. Great mats of mosaic stonework also adorn the sides of a Popol Nah to the west of 18-Rabbit's temple at Copan. Barbara Fash claims the woven mats define the ritual space outside the building as one used for teaching and performing sacred dance.[103] Vogt reports that woven-reed mats continue to play an important role in constructing ritual spaces among contemporary Zinacantecos.[104] I suggest the floor mats in the buildings of Motecuhzoma Xocoyotzin's royal courtyard performed the same function.

The Aztecs nepantla-constructed their immensely fertile agricultural plots called *chinampas* ("on the square made of canes or stalks" or "on the fence of reeds").[105] After driving posts vertically into a shallow lake bed, Aztec farmers wove the posts together into rectangular enclosures using vines and branches. They then placed mud and muck from the lake bottom within these enclosures to form agricultural plots. This seldom-discussed use of weaving was obviously crucial since the chinampas played an indispensable role in growing the food-stuffs needed to feed Tenochtitlan. Here we witness yet another instance of the generative power of nepantla-ordering, -arranging, and -putting stuff in place.

The *huey tzompantli* ("great skull rack or skull banner") of the sacred precinct of Tenochtitlan (the largest of seven such structures in the precinct according to Sahagún) represents perhaps the most unexpected case of Aztec weaving. Dúran describes the structure as consisting of a massive masonry platform some 30 meters long. On top of this structure, writes Rubén Mendoza, "was erected [a] wooden palisade and scaffolding comprised of between 60 to 70 massive uprights or timbers *woven together* with an impressive constellation of horizontal cross beams."[106] The Aztecs impaled upon the horizontal crossbeams the decapitated heads of sacrificial victims. If Mendoza's characterization is correct, then it appears the Aztecs may have conceived the huey tzompantli as a grand, skull-studded woven flag. Embedding the skulls within this woven structure nepantla-ordered the tonalli energy they contained. More than a mere display of human trophies, the tzompantli therefore functioned as a huge, power-charged battery pack that radiated the well-ordered tonalli energy of the woven skulls.

Lastly, key players in rituals commonly wore nepan-cruciform clothing. The Aztecs used terms containing the root *nepan* to designate ritual articles such as the *amanepaniuhqui* ("crossed paper stole"[107] or "cape of plaited paper"[108]) and *epnepaniuhqui* ("crossed mother-of-pearl stole"[109] or "[bands of] gold crossing [bands of] seashells"[110]). The festival of Cuahuitl ehua included sacrificing a child (known as *epcoatl*, or "mother of pearl serpent") who wore an *epnepaniuhqui* vestment. He was transported to a place in the middle of the lake called Pantitlan ("Paper Banner Place") and thrown into a watery vortex at this spot.[111] The *Primeros memoriales'* illustrations of Tlacaxipehualiztli, Toxcatl, Etzalqualiztli, Panquetzaliztli, Atemoztli, and Izcalli include figures wearing white, sacrificial, crossing paper strips (*amaneapanalli*).[112] Finally, Sahagún relates that Moctezuma II sent many precious gifts to Cortés, including the sacred arrays of Quetzalcoatl and Tezcatlipoca. Included in the former's array were a *nenepaniuhqui* ("plaited neck band of greenstone beads") and an *epnepaniuhqui* ("shield with [bands of] gold crossing each other, or with [bands of] gold crossing [bands of] seashells."[113]

The Power of Weaving Activities and Instruments

Weaving activities and instruments figure prominently in Aztec rituals, associating rituals and their participants with nepantla motion-change, and hence with rebirth, regeneration, transformation, and ultimately the Mother Goddess as great genetrix. Martin Prechtel and Robert Carlsen report, for example, that contemporary Tzutujil Maya female shaman-midwives believe the various parts of the loom possess creative power and use them in aiding childbirth.[114]

Weaving battens played a major role in the festival of Tititl ("Stretching") which scholars variously interpret as honoring Tona, Xochiquetzal, Ilamatecuhtli, Cihuacoatl, or Camaxtli.[115] The female figures fall within Nicholson's Teteoinnan complex and are aspects of Tlazolteotl-Ixcuina, the great genetrix, spinner, and weaver. Illustrations of Tititl commonly include a female figure holding a batten and military shield. Battens associate her with weaving, weavers, and Xochiquetzal. Combined with shields, they associate her with hunting, war, death, and thus regeneration and transformation.

Stretching

What is the significance of stretching and battens? Let's first consider stretching. According to one account in the *Histoyre du Mechique*, Quetzalcoatl and Tezcatlipoca formed the earth and lower skies of the Fifth Age by transforming themselves into serpents who then coiled themselves around Tlaltecuhtli (the wild and disorderly giant earth monster, often identified with Cipactli, the great crocodile). One of them seized her by her right hand and left foot, the other, around her left hand and right foot. Constricting their serpentine bodies, Quetzalcoatl and Tezcatlipoca pulled on and stretched Tlaltecuhtli in opposing directions until she split down the middle, the upper half forming the earth, the lower half, the sky.[116] In this manner they ordered her into the shape of an X, 8, or + with her navel at the center. Here we see both the ordering power of stretching as well as the creative power of nepantla-crossing.

Stretching occurred every time Aztec priests centered and arranged someone upon the sacrificial stone. Four priests stretched the victim down over the sacrificial stone by pulling upon his arms and legs in the four intercardinal directions. A fifth priest pulled his head back down toward the cosmic center, the fifth direction. When the victim, his heart, and vital energies were thus properly arranged, a sixth priest removed the heart.[117] Sahagún and Durán tell us that at the conclusion of Ochpaniztli, priests stuffed, mounted, and stretched the skin of the Toci teixiptla on a wooden scaffold at Tocititlan, located at the south causeway of Tenochtitlan.[118] Stretching also figured prominently in *tlacacaliliztli* (so-called arrow sacrifice).[119] The victim (a captured enemy warrior) was well arranged by having his legs and arms stretched out and bound tightly to the four corners of an elevated square scaffolding (*quatzatzatli*). Archers then shot him repeatedly with arrows. After being stretched out and penetrated like a woman in sexual coitus, the victim's heart was removed. The Aztecs oriented the four corners of the scaffolding, and hence the victim's energies, toward the four intercardinal directions. This ordered, fortified, and guided his energies.

The Aztecs also associated stretching with sexual intercourse, parturition, and reproduction. Like the victims of tlacacaliliztli (who were female gendered since enemy captives), women are stretched out and penetrated during sexual coitus. With pregnancy comes the stretching of a woman's abdomen, which causes stretch marks. Seler claims *Codex Borgia* and *Codex Vaticanus B 3773* depict the Cihuateteo (spirits of women who died in childbirth) with the abdominal stretch-marks of pregnancy.[120] In this context other *tititl*-related words become significant: *cuitlatitica* ("for an infected wound or abscess to hurt before bursting"), *netititzaliztli* ("cramp in the abdomen"), and *yollo cuitlatiticaliztli* ("to suffer in this way").[121] Abdominal cramping and suffering, like the suffering involved in an abscess's growing larger and finally bursting, suggest pregnancy, childbirth, and regeneration. Their bodies stretched taut in four directions, one imagines victims of arrow sacrifice suffered similarly before their blood burst from their symbolically vaginal arrow wounds. Stretched to the limit, pregnant women and sacrificial victims are ready to burst forth with their life-giving energies. In sum, the Aztecs associated stretching sacrificial victims with sexual intercourse, parturition, and regeneration

Stretching also plays an essential role in weaving. One stretches and draws out raw fiber when spinning it into thread. Stretching helps the weaver grow the ball of thread that coils around the spindle rod. One stretches the spun threads upon the warp board and then stretches these same warp threads again when mounting them upon the loom. Lastly, stretching helps maintain the proper degree of tension in the mounted warp threads. The backstrap weaver maintains the proper degree of tension for each of the various stages of the weaving process by leaning forward and backward, a motion the Aztecs likened to the motion of sexual intercourse. In sum, stretching plays an essential role in regeneration, renewal, and transformation.

Battens

The batten is a flat stick made of hard wood, usually beveled on both sides and pointed at both ends. Weavers use battens to open (and keep open) the shed (the space between upper and lower threads of the warp) so they may insert the weft threads into the warp, and to beat the weft into place, down into the warp. Sahagún and Molina tell us the Aztecs called the batten a *tzotzopaztli*.[122] Molina defines *tzotzopaztli* as a "broad stick like a knife used to press the cloth being woven."[123] Karttunen defines *tzotzopaztli* as a "weaver's reed, stick to push down and tighten the weft."[124] Sahagún describes it as an instrument "almost like a *machete*."[125] Berdan claims the batten was commonly referred to as a "weaving sword."[126] *Tzotzopaztli* suggests the verbs *tzopa* ("to finish something, like weaving cloth, making a vault, putting wood on a house, or something similar")[127] and *tzopi* ("for a piece of weaving to get finished").[128] The meaning of *tzopa* is particularly apposite. It further supports the idea of the cosmos as a woven fabric (or house), and accords neatly with the notion of the sky (*ilhuicatl*) as vaulted. The Aztecs conceived weaving, sexual intercourse, and housebuilding in essentially identical terms. Finally, the related word *quicentzoptiuh* means "it is arranged perfectly or completely finished."[129] We saw in chapter 4 that olin motion is a specific pattern of ordering motion. In the case of weaving, the olin-style motion-change of the batten, shuttle, and weft threads orders, arranges, and completes the cloth. In the case of the cosmos, the olin-style weft motion-change of the Fifth Sun orders, arranges, and completes the Fifth Era or Sun-Earth Ordering. (I expand on this in chapter 8.)

Both batten and its use in weaving have obvious parallels in sexual inter-course and reproduction. Using the batten to pry open the shed so that the weft may be inserted into the shed (the warp's place) imitates sexual intercourse, as does using the batten to beat down the weft into the warp. With her male batten, the weaver penetrates the stretched female warp threads. The weaver's rhythmic pattern of leaning forward to open the shed and insert the weft, fol-lowed by her holding onto both ends of the batten and leaning backward in order to beat down and tighten the weft into the warp, imitates female motion in sexual coitus and in labor. Contemporary Tzutujil Maya and Huichol con-sider the weaver's forward-and-back motion to be a distinctly female motion, one that simulates the motion of childbirth as well as the motion of grinding corn.[130] Donald and Dorothy Cordry report this pattern of movement functions today as a common gesture indicating sexual intercourse.[131]

The Aztecs regarded battens as male-gendered instruments alongside swords and sacrificial knives. The festival of Atemoztli ("Falling of the Water" or "The Tlalocs Descend") honored the mountain gods in hopes of their releasing rain from within the mountains.[132] Sahagún's informants report that ordinary people made figures called *Tepictotoni* out of amaranth-seed dough. After dressing, feeding, and singing to the figures, the Tlaloc priests sacrificed them with a weaver's batten. Using a weaver's batten they opened the dough figures' breasts, removed their hearts, and cut off their heads. Cordry and Cordry contend the ritual consisted of symbolically opening the mountains so that the water in their hearts would gush forth and give life to the dry valley below.[133]

Battens and battening are thus male gendered and function as symbols of male potency and authority.[134] In this respect they resemble shuttle sticks, weft threads, digging sticks, the warping of thread, and indeed the Fifth Sun itself. Contemporary Nuyoo Mixtec, for example, regard battens as male gendered. They refer to a batten as a *machete* and regard the machete as a preeminently male symbol.[135] Although a female-gendered process, weaving – like sexual commingling – involves both male- and female-gendered components. It is precisely the commingling and uniting of these paired inamic components that gives weaving its creative and transformative power. Holding a batten attests to a woman's ability to wield successfully a preeminently male-gendered instrument and male power symbol, and thus attests to her command of generation and regeneration. *Codex Borbonicus* (pl. 36)[136] and *Codex Magliabechiano* (pl. 44r)[137] depict Cihuacoatl figures holding shields and blue weaving battens. These demonstrate her command of the creative processes of parturition and war as well as her ability to bring these processes to successful fruition.[138] Batten and shield show her ability to bring together, properly orchestrate, and weave together both male and female inamic powers and thus show her creative prowess.

The festival of Ochpaniztli, dedicated to Tlazolteotl-Ixcuina, Teteoinnan-Toci, and the great Earth Mother as genetrix and destroyer-creator, abounds with spinning and weaving activities and symbolism. A central component of the festival consisted of the female teixiptla of Teteoinnan engaging in weaving-related activities. She combed and washed raw maguey fiber, spun it into thread, wove the thread into huipil and skirt, and then displayed and earned money by selling the garments in the marketplace.[139] In this way, Durán tells us, the teixiptla demonstrated Teteoinnan's ability to complete successfully her role as a parturient and provider. After her decapitation, another individual donned both her flayed skin and the cloths she produced. On his head he wore the cotton garland of her spindle whorls and carded cotton. At the conclusion of Ochpaniztli, both skin and clothes were removed from this second teixiptla and stretched over a straw figure at the Cihuateocalli ("Shrine of the Women") located at the gates of Tenochtitlan.[140]

The Power of Nepantla-Middling

The Aztecs sought to nepantla-middle and -balance ritual activities (including speech, song, dance, music, etc.), objects, and participants, both spatially and temporally. (Indeed, they sought to nepantla-middle and -balance every aspect of their lives.) Nepantla-processes weave together and middle agonistic inamic partners into reciprocal balance, order, and unity. That which is properly *nepantlaized* or nepantla-middled (e.g., woven fabric, ritual, or sacrificial victim) is that which is well balanced, well arranged, and well ordered. It is *stuff in place, properly placed, or in the right place*. Keeping processes in balance requires constant vigilance and nepantla-middling. The energy of that which has been nepantla-middled (e.g., the victim of arrow sacrifice) is energy that is well balanced and consequently ideally suited for vertical malinalli-patterned transmission to the cosmos. One feeds the cosmos only well-ordered energy, because balanced and nepantla-middled energy contributes to the well-balancedness of the cosmos. At their most general level, Aztec rituals aim at preserving, sustaining, renewing, and contributing to the balance of the Fifth Age.

Time-places may be nepantla-middled, and these serve as ideal locations for vertical malinalli-defined energy transmission. Middled time-places facilitate energy transmission as well as positively contribute to the well-orderedness of the energy humans seek to transmit. Various ritual activities accordingly took place either at midday (*nepantla tonatiuh*), the middled point in the daytime Sun's journey above, or at midnight (*yohualnepantla*), the middled point in the nighttime Sun's journey below. Given Aztec metaphysics' equation of place and time, midday and midnight refer to specific time-places, not simply times. Midday is the when-where of the Sun's zenith; the middle or center of its journey across the sky; when-where it is directly overhead. In order to enhance their efficacy, the Aztecs synchronized specific rituals with the "middled" time-places of the Sun's life~death cycle.

During the four-day "flower fast" in honor of Macuilxochitl and Xochipilli, participants ate food only at midday (*nepantla tonatiuh*) and drank *atole* only at midnight (*yohualnepantla*).[141] During Huey Tecuilhuitl, people ate at midday.[142] Sahagún also relates that at the local calpulli, noblemen, rulers, and constables fasted every twenty days for a period of five days, which consisted of their abstaining from food except at midday or midnight.[143] At midnight during Etzalqualiztli, the Aztecs sacrificed deity impersonators, excised their hearts, and placed the hearts in a blue, four-sided "cloud vessel" (*mixcomitl*).[144] Dancing and singing took place at midday during the festivals of Tlaxochimaco, Xocotl huetzi, Ochpanitzli, and Teo eco ("the Gods arrive").[145] Ritual skirmishing between participants in the festival of Panquetzaliztli occurred at midday.[146] The Aztecs sacrificed captives at midday in honor of the day sign 4 Olin and during the New Fire Ceremony.[147] New Fire Ceremony priests drilled the new fire at midnight.[148] They beheaded quails in honor of Macuilxochitl and Xochipilli at noon.[149] And at noon on the feast day of Yohualtecuhtli, people drew straws through their flesh, cut the earlobes of their small children, and offered incense.[150] During Etzalqualiztli priests traveled in boats to a powerful place "in the middle of the lake" (*anepantla*), a spiraling vortex called Pantitlan. There they deposited various offerings including a *mixcomitl* ("cloud vessel") containing human hearts.[151] During Cuauhuitl ehua, priests threw a child wearing a nepantla-middled *epnepaniuhqui* ("crossed-mother-of-pearl stole") into Pantitlan.[152]

The Aztecs called the crown of the head *quanepantla* ("the crown of the middle of the head")[153] or *quanepantlatli*.[154] Both terms are *nepan*-related. This nepantla-middled spot on the top of the head is where Aztec captors seized and removed the tonalli-rich hair of their captives,[155] where the "gods" malinalli-drilled tonalli energy into newborns, and where midwives poured tlazolli-cleansing and purifying waters upon newborns.[156] The crown of the head is an important site of ritual activity.

I consider it noteworthy that Aztec midwives in their addresses to newborn males stated, "He belongeth to the battlefield there in the center, in the middle of the plains [*inepantla*],"[157] also saying, "And if [his name were] yaotl, they went saying to him: 'o yaotl, o yaotl, know the interior of the plains, the middle of the plains [*inepantla*], the battlefield.'"[158] Waging combat in the middle of a battle and seizing captives from the middle seems to have been important.

Nepantla-middling, we saw above, figured crucially in heart sacrifice. Priests stretched the victim down over the techcatl (apparently with the stone directly below his navel or center) by pulling his four arms and legs toward the four intercardinal directions. When the victim and his heart and vital energies were properly nepantla-middled, when they were rightly placed vis-à-vis the layout of the Templo Mayor, sacred precinct, and ultimately the Fifth Age, a sixth priest excised his heart. Nepantla-middling obviously figured crucially in the middled stretching of the victim of the arrow sacrifice. The X-shaped figure created by the four bundles of wood being fed to the fire of the turquoise hearth during the New Fire Ceremony suggests a nepantla-middling (see Figure 4.8). A new 52-year xiuhmolpilli emerges at the very heart of the crux of a cruciform or crossroads. The crucible constitutes the flashpoint of inamic unification and hence creative-destructive transformation.

The Aztecs located the Templo Mayor and surrounding sacred precinct – by far the grandest and most powerful nepantla-middled ritual time-place stretched out and put in place by human beings – at *tlallinepantla* ("in the middle of the earth").[159] Tlallinepantla coincided with the center of the earth (*tlalli olloco*),[160] the navel of the earth (*tlalxicco*), the crossroads of the horizontal forces of the Fifth Sun-Earth Ordering, the confluence of vertical malinalli-twisting-spinning forces that ascend from below and descend from above the earth, and the axis mundi. Here is the meeting point of the four roads created by the four sons of Tonacatecuhtli~Tonacacihuatl (each associated with one of four intercardinal directions).[161] In so doing, they arranged the earth into four quadrants and a center. Here, too, is the time-place defined by the crossing of two springs, red and blue (or yellow), on a small island in the middle of Lake Texcoco. Mendieta describes their crossing as *formada a manera de una aspa de san Andrés* ("shaped like a Saint Andrew's cross").[162] Hernando Alvarado Tezozomoc likewise describes a spot defined by two springs intersecting one another. Van Zantwjik, Berdan and Anawalt, and Heyden read Tezozomoc as claiming the two springs are *Tleatl-Atlatlayan* ("Fire Water, Place of Burning Water") and *Matlalatl-Toxpalatl* ("Dark Blue Water, Yellow Water"). The former ran from east to west, the latter, from north to south, and so they crossed one another.[163] López Austin and López Lujan, however, read Tezozomoc as identifying the two intersecting springs as *Matlalatl* ("Dark Blue Water) and *Toxpalatl* ("Yellow Water").[164] Either way, their intersecting divides the island into four quadrants and forms the St. Andrew's cross depicted in *Codex Mendoza*, fol. 2r. Dúran says the Aztecs found the sight of yellow and blue streams *"espanto"* ("frightening, terrifying, astonishing, awesome").[165] Next to this spot was where an eagle perched upon a prickly pear cactus. Lastly, here, too, the Aztecs constructed their Huey Teocalli. After building their first temple at the site, the Aztecs ordered the surrounding area divided into four quarters, with the Huey Teocalli at their intersection. The roads of Tepeyac, Itztapalapa, and Tlacopan, which arranged the city into four quadrants and served as communication routes between the island and the surrounding lake shores, intersected at the Huey Teocalli, forming a grand human-constructed crossroads with the Huey Tecocalli at its center.[166] All of these crossings and intersectings coincided with one another as well as with the center of the earth, the navel of the earth, and the axis mundi. *Codex Mendoza* (fol. 2r) depicts the founding of Tenochtitlan at this nepantla-middled, nepantla-intersecting time-place (see Figure 4.10).

Lastly, Sahagún's informants state the first man and woman, Cipactonal and Oxomoco, invented the tonalpohualli. They describe Cipactonal and Oxomoco as placing the tonalamatl "in the middle" (*inepantla*) when *reading* it and when *painting* it. By middling their male~female (and corresponding parallel-aligned) inamic energies, Cipactonal and Oxomoco become "lords of the day count."[167] Both the *Florentine Codex* and *Codex Borbonicus* depict Cipactonal and Oxomoco "in the middle."[168] Painting as well as interpreting the tonalpohualli requires the middling of both books and readers on woven mats. It also requires that the reader him/herself be individually properly middled.

THE CROSSROADS (ONEPANCO)

The concept of the crossroads is indisputably one of the most significant concepts associated with nepantla. What does the crossroads tell us about the nature of nepantla motion-change? Unfortunately, understanding Aztec metaphysics' conception of the crossroads is not as straightforward as it might seem. Current scholarship tends to emphasize the dangerous, deadly, and destructive aspects of the crossroads. Jacques Soustelle characterizes the crossroads as "the disquieting place of apparitions and omens, the point of encounter with foreign worlds."[169] Elzey sees the crossroads as a "marginal and ill-defined" "no-place" beset by "danger, uncertainty, ambiguity and anomaly" and "anti-structure."[170]

Elizabeth Boone claims the crossroads is a place of "danger, destruction, or conflict."[171] For Klein the crossroads symbolizes "a lack of direction, disorder, and immorality" because it represents "an excessive number of paths or directions."[172] Seler believes the Aztecs associated the crossroads with death, sacrifice, the forces of night and darkness, the downward direction, and the Underworld (the lower region, the realm of darkness, the region of the dead).

The Cihuateteo and the Degenerative Power of Crossroads

Sahagún tell us that at certain times the five Cihuapipiltin ("Noble Women"), who "hate," "mock," and cast spells upon people, descended upon and resided at the crossroads (*omaxac chaneque*). During this time parents kept their children at home and people made offerings to the Cihuapipiltin at the crossroads (*omaxac*).[173] The Cihuapipiltin were also known as Cihuateteo ("Goddesses"): angry, malevolent spirits of women who had died in their first childbirth with child in utero.[174] They were the female counterparts of warriors fallen in battle or on the sacrificial stone; yet, apparently unlike their male counterparts, the Cihuateteo were furious and ill-willed because unfulfilled. The Cihuateteo accompanied the Sun from its zenith at midday to its setting in the west (Cihuatlampa, "The Place of Women"), which was their residence. The *Primeros memoriales* states the Cihuapipiltin "hover over the crossroads (*otlamaxac*)."[175] They descended to Earth on the days 1 Deer, 1 Rain, 1 Monkey, 1 House, and 1 Eagle, inflicting disease and deformities upon children as well as leading adults astray by instigating unbalanced (i.e., immoral, unwise) behavior such as adultery.[176] Those who came in contact with them became diseased, disoriented, disordered, and unbalanced – in short, stuff out of place.

The wombs of women who die in childbirth suffered from an imbalance caused by excessive sexual fluids (semen). This imbalance caused the fetus to stick to the sides of the womb. It also polluted mother and fetus. Postpartum mothers normally required ritual bathing to cleanse themselves of the filth associated with sexual intercourse. Having died in childbirth and never cleansed themselves, however, the Cihuateteo remained permanently polluted and hence *polluting*.[177] Unable to cleanse themselves of their tlazolli, they remained permanently characterized by tlatlacolli. They remained permanently unbalanced and disordered and hence permanently unbalancing and disordering.

Weaving, we've seen, is analogous to sexual commingling, and successfully completing a cloth is analogous to successful parturition. Weavers give birth to cloth, as women give birth to children. Dying during their first childbirth, the Cihuateteo were thus unable to fulfill their womanly role as parturients *and* as weavers. "They were spinners who had woven nothing, the parturients who had brought forth nothing."[178] Unable to fulfill themselves as weavers while alive on earth, the Cihuateteo searched the earth for the weaving instruments (spindles, whorls, battens, etc.) they had left behind at death in hopes of fulfilling themselves after death.[179] The women sacrificed during the festival of Quecholli burned all their weaving instruments so as to make them available after death.[180] Recall that a central component of Ochpaniztli consisted of the female teixiptla's demonstration of Teteoinnan-Toci's ability to fulfill her role qua woman by spinning, weaving, and selling a huipil and skirt. The Cihuateteo also returned to earth in search of the child they never bore so as to fulfill their role as parturients. In this way, they sought to complete and balance themselves as mothers, just as they sought their weaving instruments to complete and balance themselves as weavers. Because they had failed to complete their womanly roles as parturients and weavers, the Cihuateteo were left permanently unbalanced, deranged, polluted and hence angry, frustrated, malevolent, and corrupting. They were forces of unbalance, disorder, and tlatlacolli.

Cordry and Cordry report that contemporary Zoques of Tuxtla Gutiérrez and Tzotzils of San Bartolomé de los Llanos believe in women spirits or *brujas* who spin but do not weave.[181] Zoques consider spinning without weaving – like pregnancy without successful childbirth – to be unproductive, incomplete, and futile. Just as spinning and weaving are necessary for the successful birth of a fabric, so successful sexual intercourse, parturition, and childbirth are necessary for successful reproduction and regeneration. According to Prechtel and Carlsen, the Tzutujil Maya of Santiago Atitlán characterize weaving in terms of sexual intercourse, pregnancy, and parturition. They describe completing a cloth as giving birth to the cloth. "Weavings are not just woven but in fact born."[182] Contemporary Wixárika women likewise speak of giving birth to cloth through weaving.[183]

The depictions of the five Cihuapipiltin in *Codex Borgia* (pl. 47) present a slight variation on this theme. Represented as Tlazolteotl-Ixcuina, they wear headbands made of unspun cotton that lack spindle whorls, which Sullivan argues indicates their inability to spin and transform fiber into thread and hence their inability to produce cloth.[184] They are unproductive and fruitless, and consequently unable to fulfill their womanly roles as producers of cloth and, by analogy, their womanly roles as producers of children. In one of the five depictions, Tlazolteotl-Ixcuina stands before a crossroads (see Figure 6.4). A centipede connects her mouth with the crossroads, suggesting the Cihuateteo's role in eating tlazolli. Centipedes, we've seen, are associated with tlazolli.

During 1 Rain (*ce quiauitl*), according to Book I of the *Florentine Codex*, Cihuateteo energies descended upon earth and inflicted various maladies upon

FIGURE 6.4. *Cihuateteo with centipede at an X-shaped crossroads.* *(*Codex Borgia *[1993: pl. 47]; courtesy of Dover Press.)*

those they encountered outside their houses. People responded by building a shrine (called *cihuateocalli* or *cihuateopan*) to the Cihuateteo in every neighborhood "where there were two streets" ("*donde había dos calles*").[185] During the accompanying festival dedicated to the Cihuateteo, the Aztecs sacrificed individuals convicted of capital offenses (and hence filthy with tlazolli). In Book IV Sahagún's informants state that during the day sign 1 Eagle *(ce quauhtli)*, the dreaded Cihuateteo – whom they describe as "harmful, furious, hateful, hostile, and merciless" – descended and did evil to small children. Mothers kept children inside to protect them from this harm. At this time the people honored the Cihuateteo in their shrines at the crossroads. "Sand was sprinkled on the roads and at street crossings and crossroads – places where roads came together" ("*tlaixalhuilo in otlica, in omaxac, in inepanihuiyan otli*") from midnight until midday.[186]

Book III states the people also made offerings on the roads and at the crossroads (*in momoztli in otlica, omaxac*) to Tezcatlipoca.[187] Indeed, Tezcatlipoca resided at the crossroads, which was accordingly seen as a terrifying place haunted by unpredictable, dangerous forces. The crossroads was where sorcerers conducted their malevolent acts under cover of nightfall. Tezcatlipoca's association with the crossroads is illustrated in *Codex Fejérváry-Mayer* (pl. 2) where, under the guise of Ixtli ("Flint Knife," one of the Nine Lords of the Night), he inserts his foot into the open-mouthed flint knife sitting atop a crossroads. Below this scene are depicted a second crossroads with sacrificial offerings and a sacrificial victim from whose open chest sprays blood.[188] *Codex Fejérváry-Mayer* (pl. 30) depicts Tezcatlipoca once more before a crossroads consisting of two equally lengthed planks (see Figure 6.5).

Seler maintains the codices depict the crossroads almost exclusively alongside Tezcatlipoca, Tlazolteotl, and the Cihuateteo.[189] Others include Mictlantecuhtli and Xolotl of the North.[190] Ideograms of crossroads are standardly accompanied by sacrificial knives, excised hearts, offerings of wood, flowering hearts, and owls. Aztec thought thus associated the crossroads with death, forces of night and darkness, the downward direction, and the Underworld (the lower region, the realm of darkness, the region of the dead). The association between the crossroads and the region of the dead is further suggested by *Codex Laud* (pl. 43).[191] It depicts a crossroads with a sacrificial offering at its center, sacrificial victim suspended above it, and the gaping maw of the earth monster below.

Lastly, among the figures of speech recorded by Sahagún one is especially relevant here: "*nexetepeoalli, otlamaxalli nicnonantia, nicnotatia*," which Dibble and Anderson translate as "I make the ash heap, the crossroads my mother, my father."[192] This was said of someone who made themselves the offspring of the crossroads and ash heap – that is, someone who had made the wrong choices, gone astray, and sullied himself; someone who had strayed from the center into the periphery.[193]

The Regenerative Role of Crossroads

And yet the crossroads also played a vital regenerative and beneficial role in human affairs since it served as a place of purification and renewal,[194] and

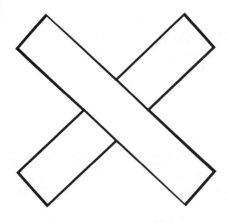

FIGURE 6.5. *Crossroads. (Redrawn from* Codex Fejérváry-Mayer *[Loubat 1900: pl. 30].)*

therefore also played a vital regenerative role in the processing of the cosmos since it facilitated the recycling and transformation of tlazolli.[195] Individuals seeking to cleanse themselves of tlazolli accumulated through acts of wrongdoing confessed their wrongdoings to Tlazolteotl. They then went to the shrine of the Cihuateteo located at the crossroads wearing a paper skirt. By shedding and abandoning this skirt at the shrine, they shed and abandoned their tlazolli.[196] By receiving the tlazolli of wrongdoers, the crossroads enabled their purification. This ritual was associated with Tlazolteotl, Tlazolteotl-Ixcuina, and ultimately the creative~destructive Earth-Mother complex.[197] It contributed tlazolli for recycling and earthly renewal. As Sahagún puts it, Tlazolteotl both "cast" tlazolli upon one and "cleansed" one of tlazolli. Continuing, Sahagún's informants say, "In her hand lay the blue and yellow waters."[198] The crossing of the blue and yellow waters marked the spot on which the Huey Teocalli and Tenochtitlan were constructed. They are waters of purification, creation, and renewal. The tlazolli accumulated at the crossroads was then dispersed to the four corners of the earth (i.e., to the periphery) for cosmic recycling.

Codex Laud (pl. 15) depicts Tlazolteotl confronting an X-shaped crossroads with offering in hand (see Figure 6.6).[199] Codex Fejérváry-Mayer (pl. 4) depicts Tlazolteotl standing before an X-shaped crossroads on top of which sits a human-heart offering.[200] León-Portilla suggests Tlazolteotl holds in her hands straw brooms, presumably for sweeping tlazolli to the four corners of the earth.[201]

The Cihuateteo depicted in Codex Borgia (pl. 47) appears to be regurgitating a centipede onto an X-shaped crossroads (see Figure 6.4). This suggests the roles of all five Cihuateteo in transforming tlazolli into regenerative energy: they eat tlazolli and recycle it to the periphery by placing it upon the crossroads.

Figure 6.6. *Tlazolteotl confronting an X-shaped crossroads.* (Codex Fejérváry-Mayer *[Loubat 1900: pl. 4]; courtesy of the Foundation for the Advancement of Mesoamerican Studies, Inc.)*

The image thus refers to the tlazolli-eating, regenerative powers of Tlazolteotl-Ixcuina and the Earth-Goddess complex. Lastly, the juxtaposition of the crossroads with Xolotl under the guise of Yacatecuhtli-Quetzalcoatl in *Codex*

Fejérváry-Mayer (pl. 37) associates the crossroads with the transition between life and death.[202] Xolotl helps the Fifth Sun journey safely through the region of the dead each night and successfully dawn anew each morning.

Crossing Roads and Forked Roads

The crossroads, like all things, therefore appears to be fundamentally ambiguous. What is it exactly about the metaphysical makeup of the crossroads that explains this ambiguity? What exactly is the nature of the X- or +-shaped space (time-place) created by the intersecting of two paths? What is it about the crossroads that attracts the forces of Tezcatlipoca, Tlazolteotl, and the Cihuateteo?

Beginning with Molina and Sahagún, scholars have standardly translated the Nahuatl words *onepanco, onepanolco, omaxalco, otlamaxalco, otlamaxac, otlimaxac, omaxac,* and *otlamaxalli* as "*encruzijada de caminos,*" or "crossroads."[203] All these begin with *ohtli,* meaning "path, road, way," and may be variously translated as "crosspath," "crossroad," or "crossway." After this the terms fall into *two distinct semantic families*: *nepan*-related words (*onepanco, onepanolco*) and *maxatl*- (or *maxaliui-*) related words (*otlamaxac, omaxac, omaxalco, otlamaxalco,* and *otlamaxalli*). Existing scholarship tends to treat these two families as semantically equivalent.[204] Are they?

Discussions of crossroads in the *Florentine Codex* almost universally employ *maxatl*-related rather than *nepan*-related words, and it is these *maxatl*-based passages on which scholars typically ground their interpretations of the crossroads. The one exception appears to be Book IV, page 107, where Sahagún's informants mention placing sand at *both* the *omaxac* and the *inepanihuiyan otli* ("*tlaixalhuilo in otlica, in omaxac, in inepanihuiyan otli*"). What is the significance of this passage? The fact that the text uses both terms suggests that Sahagún's informants believed the terms to be *non-equivalent* and not coreferential. Similarly, with the exception of Book IV, page 107, all the discussions of crossroads as places of danger, sorcery, tlazolli, and deformity, and as residences of Tezcatlipoca, the Cihuateteo, and Tlazolteotl, use *maxatl*-related words rather than *nepan*-related words. This suggests that it is not *nepan*-defined crossroads that are associated with these things but *maxatl*-defined crossroads. Lastly, both León-Portilla (in his commentary on the *Codex Fejérváry-Mayer*) and Seler (in his commentaries on the *Codex Fejérváry-Mayer* and *Codex Borgia*) refer to the ideogram standardly associated with the crossroads – that is, two planks of equal length, one laid across the other – as an *otlamaxac* (see Figure 6.5).[205] Neither scholar mentions *onepanco* or *onepanolco* in their commentaries. Presumably they do not do so because the chronicles themselves overwhelmingly refer to the crossroads as *otlamaxac* and not as *onepanco*. One wonders, therefore, whether the two semantic families are equivalent or even coreferential. When talking about an otlamaxac, are we talking about the same thing as an onepanco? Let's examine each semantic family.

Crossing Roads. Onepanco and *onepanolco* refer to a space that has been abundantly and reciprocally middled by the crossing or intersecting of two paths. The words' root, *nepanoa*, entails several things joining together, commingling, and intersecting. Nepanoa-processes (what I am calling nepantla-processes) bring together two (or more) things and mutually middle them in a manner that is simultaneously creatively destructive, destructively creative, and transformative. The crossroads (onepanco) is a place of abundant mutuality and reciprocity; an ambiguous place betwixt and between both roads *and the energies these roads convey*. The crossroads closely resembles the anepanolli (joining of waters that flow into some place) – that is, the confluence of two rivers, an ambiguous place created by the dynamic back-and-forth mixing together of two rivers. Like the anepanolli, the crossroads (onepanco) is literally the creative-destructive *contact point* of agonistic inamic partners: for example, the contact point of male~female and dry~wet commingling. Like the anepanolli, the crossroads is the creative-destructive and hence transformative *flash point* of inamic partners. The crossroads commingles and weaves together degenerative and regenerative forces. As such the crossroads (onepanco) literally *embodies* – and because of this *symbolizes* – agonistic inamic unity as well as the ineliminable ambiguity created by agonistic inamic unity. According to Gerardo Reichel-Dolmatoff, the Kogi similarly conceive the intersection of the two cross-poles of their loom (and the intersection of the intercardinal axes) as an ambiguously male~female symbol.[206] This understanding of the crossroads (onepanco) is consistent with its identification as a place of "miraculous" and "marvelous crossing" and of "creation" (as López Austin puts it): the place where the blue and yellow waters crossed to mark the place where the Huey Teocalli was to be built.

Forking Roads. Starting with Molina, scholars have standardly translated *otlamaxac, omaxac,* and *otlamaxalli* as "crossroads."[207] However, these terms appear to refer *not* to the intersecting or crossing of two roads but rather to the *forking, dividing, bifurcating, or branching of a single road into two roads. And the forking of a single road into two roads is not the same as the crossing or intersecting of two distinct roads.* These words combine *ohtli* with the verb *maxaliui* to mean "crotch, fork, or branching of the road." *Maxaliui* means "for the road to divide into a fork, or the river into creeks, or the branches of a tree." The otlamaxac, therefore, is fittingly depicted by a *Y-shaped figure, not an X-shaped figure.* Alan Sandstrom reports that contemporary Nahuatl-speakers in Veracruz use the related word, *ojmaxali*, to refer to a Y-shaped fork in the road, not an X-shaped crossroads.[208] Molina records related words suggesting the same thing: *amaxac* ("place where the river divides into several parts"), *nomaxac* ("crotch of my legs, or between my legs"), and *tomaxac* ("between one's legs or in the crotch").[209] Berdan translates *amaxac* as "where the water divides into many parts."[210] The *Florentine Codex* contains the related words *cuammaxac* ("in the fork of a tree; in the crotch of a tree; tree crotch"),[211] *maxaliuhqui* ("forked; having forked ends"),[212] *maxallotl* ("bifurcation"),[213] *mamaxallo* ("having forks"),[214] and *cuitlapilmaxaltic* ("forked-tailed, having a fork tail").[215] Sahagún's informants describe the cypress tree as *maxallo, mamaxaliuhqui, mamaxaltic* ("it has forked branches, many forks, it is forked").[216] They describe the willow tree as *mamaxalloa* ("it continually forms crotches; it forms crotches; it branches out").[217] They describe the *tecutlacozauhqui* ("a large snake with rattles") as having a *nenepilmaxaliuhqui* ("forked, divided tongued, having a forked tongue") and a *nenepilmaxaltic* ("forked, divided tongued, having a forked tongue").[218] The *Primeros memoriales* describes Xipe Totec's conical headdress (*yopitzontli*) as having "bifurcated" or "forked" (*maxaliuhqui*) ends.[219]

Karttunen's etymology suggests this semantic cluster arose from the word *maxalli*, the Nahuatl word for "earwig."[220] Indeed *otlamaxalli* straightforwardly combines *ohtla* and *maxalli* to mean literally "road earwig." Earwigs possess two forceps-like pincers that form a Y on their rear ends. The word *cuitlapilmaxaltic* ("forked-tailed, having a fork tail") would obviously apply to the earwig with its forked tail. Earwigs are prodigious breeders. They are nocturnal. During the day they prefer dark, cool, moist places. The females build nests in the earth. They also feed on garbage. Like other small creatures who live in the dirt such as scorpions and centipedes, earwigs are associated with the earth and tlazolli. This sheds further light on the association between a Y-shaped fork in the road and tlazolli, purification rites, Tlazolteotl, and the Cihuateteo.

The association between bifurcation, forking, and crotches, on the one hand, and tlazolli, filth, garbage, disorder, and that which is harmful to humans, on the other, is underscored by the following related terms: *maxaloa* ("for someone to betray his or her spouse by having sexual relations with another person; committing adultery"), *ixmaxaliui* ("to stray from the way of righteousness"), *maxaloa* ("to leave a path to follow someone"),[221] and *nenepilmaxal* ("sower of discord, forked-tongue person").[222] Burkhart argues that the idea of otlamaxac as crotch-of-the-road invokes inappropriate and excessive *female* sexuality.[223] Where the female body splits into two is where sexual commingling occurs. As such it is ripe with the potential for error, excess, imbalance, and hence tlazolli. Its Y-shape suggests continual openness, continual sexual intercourse, and hence continual excess-causing imbalance and tlazolli.

Contemporary Huastecan Nahuatl-speakers, according to Eduardo de la Cruz Cruz, call a Y-shaped fork in the road an *ohmaxali*.[224] They consider the ohmaxali to be a dangerous place for several reasons. Shamans (*curanderos*) deposit at the ohmaxali objects they employ in cleansing and curing sick persons (such as cut-paper figures, according to James Dow and Alan Sandstrom) so that the invisible, malevolent airs that the cleansing objects have attracted and absorbed will be swept away (presumably to the periphery where they will be recycled).[225] Accidentally stumbling upon these objects exposes the unwitting passerby to the bad airs they contain, and sickens him. Extreme caution is therefore in order.

Dow adds that the bundle of cleansing attractors used to sweep up the bad airs from a patient's house may be thrown into a canyon. Canyons are conceived as peripheral areas, according to James Taggart, just as they were in pre-Hispanic times, according to Burkhart.[226] The bundle may also be hung in the forest (another peripheral place) on the west side of a mountain so that the descending sun will take the airs it contains down with it into the Underworld (for recycling). Here we see a parallel with the Cihuateteo accompanying the descending Sun. It seems likely the Cihuateteo similarly attracted the filth placed in the otlamaxac and carried it with them to the periphery.

Dow asserts that contemporary ritual cleansings are characterized by words connoting cleaning up, sweeping, and fixing up.[227] Here we see an obvious continuity between contemporary and pre-Hispanic practices and beliefs (as reported by Sahagún) regarding the role of sweeping in cleansing filth as well as the role of the omaxalli (or otlamaxac) in dispersing filth to the periphery for recycling. Dow also claims plant branches are commonly used as brooms to sweep houses and to clean sweat from the skin in sweatbaths. Because of this, "branches symbolize cleaning."[228] Here we see an obvious analogy between the branches in a tree and the branches in a road (omaxalli). Branches in the road sweep away tlazolli just as tree branches do. We also see demonstrated the pre-Hispanic connection between sweeping, sweatbaths, sweathouses, and the cleansing of filth (tlazolli).

In sum, the semantic cluster consisting of *otlamaxac, omaxac*, and *maxaliui* suggests bifurcating and divisive motion-change along with motion-change away from wholeness, completeness, unity, singularity, well-centeredness, and well-middledness. Trees branch out or branch apart; rivers fork; sowers of discord speak with forked tongues and divide people against one another; torsos divide into crotches; and roads fork. Maxaliui motion-change consists of moving energy away from center to periphery and of dividing wholeness, completeness, and unity into multiplicity. The semantic cluster suggests a Y-shaped bifurcating, not an X-shaped intersecting.

And yet ambiguity surrounds splitting, bifurcating, the crotch, the otlamaxac, and the Y-shaped figure. The ritual possessions of women sacrificed during Quecholli included their *imecamaxal* ("her bifurcated malinalli-twisted cord").[229] Their mecamaxalli was burned, as was the mecamaxalli of all women as part of their female funeral bundle. Among the weavers' instruments depicted by Sahagún is a mecamaxalli (see figure 5.1). Weavers use the mecamaxalli to secure a backstrap loom to a post (or tree trunk) by tying the single end around the post and looping each of the bifurcated ends around each end of the top bar of the loom. The mecamaxalli thus creates the crotch of the weaving. It creates a Y-shaped space of bifurcation where creating and birthing a new cloth occur. Analogously, the female crotch is where sexual commingling, parturition, and birthing occur. The crotch therefore appears ambiguous. It is ripe with the potential for excess, inappropriate behavior, and hence tlazolli, disorder, and imbalance. And yet it is also ripe with the potential for regeneration. In short, the forked road is thus ambiguous in the same way Tlazolteotl and tlazolli are ambiguous.

This ambiguity notwithstanding, the concept of the forked road, like the concepts of tlazolli and Tlazolteotl, *emphasizes* the harmful, disorderly, and destructive *aspects of* or *phases in* the circulation of creative and destructive forces. The seemingly permanent openness of a Y-shaped crotch with two legs spread apart – spread apart like the rear pincers of an earwig – suggests uninterrupted and unsatisfied sexual longing, uninterrupted reckless indulgence, and thus excess and imbalance. The Y-shape suggests female inamic without male inamic partner and thus an incomplete inamic pair. By contrast, I suggest *Codex Vaticanus 3738 A* (pl. 12v; see Figure 6.1) conveys the idea of appropriate sexual intercourse with its face-to-face depiction of a married couple with X-shaped interlocking legs. Here is a complete and whole inamic pair. I believe characterizing the continuing sexual intercourse (and weaving) of Ometeotl, Ometecuhtli~Omecihuatl, and so on as an X conveys appropriate sexual intercourse as well. Although also uninterrupted sexual intercourse, it is complete and whole because it is constituted by unified twoness and twofold oneness. It also yields something well middled, well-ordered, and well-balanced. It would seem therefore that X represents a complete inamic pair whereas Y does not. Y is a splitting apart rather than a twofold coming together.

Crossing Roads and Forking Roads Distinguished. The foregoing supports the conclusion that an otlamaxac differs from an onepanco. An otlamaxac is a forking or bifurcating of a single road. It is where a single road splits into two roads. Forks, crotches, and bifurcatings are not the same as crosses, crossings, and intersections. *The former are Y-shaped, the latter are +- or X -shaped.* Moreover, the idea of forking, branching, and bifurcating associated with the otlamaxac suggests movement *away from* singularity, wholeness, unity, and center, and *toward* disorder, derangement, devision, and periphery. As "crotch of, fork in the road," otlamaxac is a place of division, bifurcation, and hence a place where unity and order become frayed, unraveled, and undone. I suggest the fork in the road (otlamaxac) emphasizes the coming apart and bifurcating of erstwhile united agonistic inamichuan.

How do maxaliui motion-change and the otlamaxac compare with nepantla motion-change and the onepanco? Maxaliui motion-change emphasizes branching apart; nepantla motion-change emphasizes coming together. Maxaliui motion-change involves movement away from the center and toward the periphery, while nepantla motion-change involves middling motion that balances and centers peripheries. Maxaliui motion-change involves dividing, coming apart, unravelling, and hence disordering and deranging. Nepantla motion-change involves weaving together, ordering, unifying, middling, making whole, reciprocating, mutualizing, and balancing. The otlamaxac is a place where things come apart, disintegrate, and so become disordered and imbalanced. It is a time-place consisting of movement away from the center and toward the periphery. This is why one performs purification rituals at the otlamaxac. The onepanco, by contrast, is a place of abundantly middled unification and balance: a place where agonistic inamic partners are united and completed through reciprocal intermixing, commingling, and interweaving. It embodies and thus symbolizes well-orderedness and balance.

This understanding of the differences between the *forking* of a single road (otlamaxac) and the *intersecting* of two roads (onepanco) is consistent with the former's association with Tezcatlipoca, Tlazolteotl, the Cihuateteo, and the forces of death, darkness, corruption, filth, and disease. These after all, are generally speaking disordering, deranging, decentering, and imbalancing forces. As women who are condemned to spin but do not weave, the Cihuateteo return to the metaphorical mecamaxalli hoping to finish their weaving; as women who died in childbirth without successfully delivering a baby, the Cihuateteo return to the road's crotch hoping to complete their parturition. Seeing the otlamaxac as involving *centrifugal* motion also explains the placing of tlazolli there for dispersal to the periphery.

The dispersal of energy to the periphery appears to be the significance of the *maxtlatzon* worn by the child victims of Cuauhuitl ehua. Sahagún reports the children "went with their head-bands (*inmaxtlatzon*) . . . crammed with precious feathers" to the places where they died.[230] *Inmaxtlatzon* parses into *in* (plural possessive), *maxtlatl* ("loincloth, breechcloth, or something similar"), and *tzontli* ("head of hair" or "head").[231] *Maxatlatzon* literally means "head breechcloth." The *maxtlatzon* appears to be formed by the Y-shaped forking of two bands across the energy portal formed by the crown of the head.[232] So placed, the maxtlatzon thus guides the energies contained within the victim's head to the periphery. Wearing the maxatlatzon also connected the energies of intended victim with the cycles of the cosmos. Prechtel and Carlsen claim contemporary Tzutujil Maya of Guatemala believe wearing a woven headcloth (called *x' cajcoj zut*) similarly performs such a role.[233]

This understanding of the differences between the *forking* of a single road (otlamaxac) and the *intersecting* of two roads (onepanco) also suggests that we translate the figure of speech *nexetepeoalli, otlamaxalli nicnonantia, nicnotatia* as "I make the ash heap, the *fork in the road* my mother, my father." Such a person lives as though begotten by disordering, peripheralizing, and tlazolli-producing processes. Such a person is the disordered, tlazolli-laden product of such processes. A fork in the road explodes the idea of following the straight path. By placing oneself in the fork of the road, one places oneself at a spot where one can no longer follow a straight path. One pursues one extreme or the other.

The foregoing helps us understand why the Spaniards and their Nahua accomplices chose the *nepan*-derived word *quauitl nepaniuhtoc* ("wooden cross or wooded planks that are crossed") rather than a *maxaliui*-related word, such as *cuammaxac* ("tree crotch"), to refer to the sacred Christian cross.[234] The latter suggests human crotches, forking roads, excessive and socially divisive sexual intercourse, tlazolli, and so on, and would therefore be wholly inappropriate as the name for the sacred Christian symbol. López Austin refers to an X-shaped figure resembling Figure 6.5 as an "X-shaped cross or *nepaniuhtli*."[235] He reminds us that the Christian cross was called a *quauitl nepaniuhtoc* ("wooden cross or wooden planks that are crossed"). The arm of the cross was called *inepaniuhca yn cruz*.[236] Carol Callaway describes the first Christian crosses erected in Mexico as huge, unadorned wooden standards.[237] Diego Muñoz Camargo's *Historia de Tlaxcala* contains a drawing depicting the 1524 arrival of the first twelve Franciscans in Mexico. We see the twelve kneeling at the foot of a large wooden cross consisting of a smaller transverse beam placed over a larger vertical beam.[238] During the sixteenth-century, Carol Callaway writes, the indigenous peoples of New Spain worshipped the cross (known as "La Santa Cruz") as a god. Mendieta reports the Tlaxcaltecas referred to the cross of Tlaxcala as *Tonaca cuauitl* ("wood that gives us sustenance to our lives") and that they worshipped and incensed the cross as an idol.[239] In sum, post-Contact Nahuas regarded the cross as a sacred nepan-constructed object *not* to be confused with the otlamaxac or Y-shaped crotch of the road.

Lastly, and most crucially, the X- and +-shaped crossroads in *Codex Mendoza* (fol. 2r; see Figure 4.10) and *Codex Fejérváry-Mayer* (pl. 1; see Figure 4.3) function as quintessential cosmograms of the Fifth Age. If the crossroads were associated exclusively or even predominantly with death, disorder, immorality, tlazolli, sacrifice, Tezcatlipoca, the Cihuateteo, the forces of night and darkness, and lack of direction (as some scholars maintain), then I submit these X- and +-shaped crossroads would *not* function in this capacity. But they do. The X- and +-shaped crossroad ideograms serve as preeminent sacred cosmograms of the nepantla-generated agonistic inamic unity, completion, balance, and centeredness of the Fifth Age. The crossroads, of course, is ambiguous. It weaves together and middles inamic partners into well-balanced agonistic unity. As such, it possesses both generative *and* degenerative as well as ordering *and* disordering aspects. Its association with Tezcatlipoca, disorder, filth, immorality, and death occurs in specific ritual contexts that emphasize that *one* aspect. The crossroads per se is therefore *not* to be equated one-sidedly with death, tlazolli, danger, and so on. Doing so would be analogous to equating the ocean's tidal movements solely with the ebb tide on the grounds that specific rituals occur only during ebb tide.

In light of the foregoing, it seems one can conclude only that Seler and León-Portilla are guilty of *mis*identifying the X-shaped motif in the pictorial codices as an *otlamaxac*, and that Molina, Seler, León-Portilla, and Dibble and Anderson are guilty of *mis*translating *omaxac* and *otlamaxac* as *encrucijada de caminos* (or "crossroads" in English). Furthermore, given that no pre-Contact pictorial codices depict crossroads as Y-shaped forks, or for that matter even contain Y-shaped motifs, it would seem to follow that the cleansing rituals involving Tlazolteotl, Tezcatlipoca, and the Cihuateteo described by Sahagún's informants using the words *otlamaxac* or *omaxac* are *not* the same rituals as those rituals depicted in the pictorial codices that employ X-shaped motifs.[240]

In sum, the crossroads represents the contact point where agonistic inamic forces are bound together and united. It is where creative forces confront, commingle, and eventually unify with destructive forces. As such, the crossroads is neither creative nor destructive yet both, neither life-enhancing nor life-threatening yet both, and so on. The crossroads is, in other words, a time-place of transformation. The crossroads is charged with ambiguous energy: energy that is creative~destructive, polluting~purifying, and so forth, and hence potentially beneficial and potentially harmful to humans.[241] As the contact point of agonistic inamic partners, the crossroads is unstable and potentially explosive: it requires constant negotiating and balancing of inamic forces. One can never be wholly certain what will occur at the contact point of commingling inamic partners, hence the crossroads' association with Tezcatlipoca and danger. The crossroads must therefore be entered with the utmost preparation, trepidation, skill, and care. This fact explains why it is such a dangerous space for children and hapless travelers. It is a place where people lose their balance and lose their way. It is a slippery place.

Yet if the foregoing analysis of the crossroads is correct, then the crossroads does not appear to be any more inherently dangerous to the wandering child or aimless traveler than any other highly energized and powerful spot, such as the Huey Teocalli. All powerful places are dangerous, awesome, and frightening. Access to places such as the Huey Teocalli and other ritual time-places was accordingly restricted to those who were ritually, epistemologically, and morally qualified to enter such power zones without losing their balance and/or disturbing the fragile balance of power they contained. Ritual activities – from dancing and playing music to sweeping, making amaranth-dough figures, and excising hearts – had to be meticulously orchestrated and precisely executed or else the energies contained in those places and released by those activities would backfire and knock the Fifth Age out of balance.

6.3. GRAPHIC EVIDENCE

Aztec artist-scribes conveyed and depicted the idea of nepantla motion-change – as well as embodied and transmitted nepantla-shaped energy – using a variety of ideograms (many of which are polysemous). Not being a day sign, nepantla has no day-sign glyph. Rather than seeing this as evidence of the metaphysical insignificance of nepantla, I regard it as evidence of its utmost significance. Nepantla is cosmogonically and metaphysically more primordial and fundamental than the tonalpohualli and its twenty day signs.

CROSSROADS AND CROSSES

Cruciform motifs both depict and embody nepantla. *Codex Mendoza* (fol. 2r; see Figure 4.10) and *Codex Fejérváry-Mayer* (pl. 1; see Figure 4.3) do so most dramatically. They suggest the fundamental centrality of nepantla motion-change in the ordering and arranging of the Fifth Sun-Earth Ordering. Both figures form a crossroads (onepanco), portray the center of the cosmos as a crossroads, and declare the fundamental significance of crossroads. Antonio Serrato-

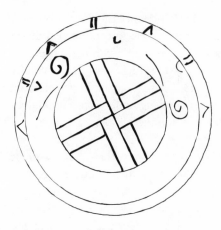

FIGURE 6.7. *Ceramic plate with woven cruciform motif. (Regional Museum of Tlaxcala; author's drawing.)*

Combe reconstructs Tenochtitlan's sacred precinct as a large crossroads with the Templo Mayor as its heart.²⁴² The sacred precinct thus served as a concrete architectural ideogram of nepantla and concrete architectural cosmogram of the nepantla-defined cosmos. Aztec gardens were also constructed to serve as physical embodiments, ideograms, and cosmograms of nepantla.²⁴³ A ceramic vessel held by the Regional Museum of Tlaxcala depicts an interwoven cross (see Figure 6.7).

Cruciforms, quincunxes, quatrefoils, patolli boards, ballcourts, and four-petaled flowers with central circles also serve as ideograms for nepantla-defined agonistic inamic unity. They also express the irreducible ambiguity of crossed figures and crossroads. In this broader sense, cruciforms and quincunxes symbolize the continual transformation born from the interweaving of inamichuan in agonistic tension. *The crossroads is the quintessential ideogram not only of the Fifth Age but of reality (teotl) as such.*

TWILLING

Twilling (sarga) produces a diagonal, stepped pattern that creates the appearance of mutually interdependent and mutually balanced reciprocal motion. Twilled mats embody and express nepantla motion-change (see Figure 6.3).

RECIPROCATING-MOTION MOTIFS

Among the three design motifs Elizabeth Brumfiel finds commonly decorating Early–Middle Postclassic Aztec household ceramic serving-vessels is one she calls the "oscillating motion or reciprocal motif."²⁴⁴ This includes zigzags, squiggles, wavy lines, ribbons, and the xicalcoliuhqui (see Figures 3.6 and 3.7). All of these, she argues, not only refer to reciprocal motion but are themselves "perfect expressions . . . of balance and reciprocity."²⁴⁵ Continuing, she adds the *xicalcoliuhqui* motif "is exemplary in this regard. It is a design composed of interlocking identical elements arranged so that each mirrors the other, resulting in a design where either element may be regarded as foreground and the other as background. The *xicalcoliuhqui* is the epitome of reciprocal action and balance in visual design principles that guided Nahua personal behavior. These concepts are perhaps summarized by the concept of nepantla."[246] Elsewhere she claims the xicalcoliuhqui is "the perfect expression of *nepantla*, since in a horizontal panel a *xicalcoliuhqui* automatically creates an inverted reciprocal *xicalcoliuhqui*," thereby capturing the oscillating, back-and-forth reciprocity, middling mutuality, and balanced reciprocity of weaving and nepantla motion-change.[247] Chapter 3 analyzed this effect in terms of the figure–ground phenomenon of Gestalt theory. By visually switching figure and ground, the motif's undulating motion moves from left to right, and from right to left. Its interlacing also appears to alternate between downward-hanging, moving white frets and upward-arising, moving black frets. As we saw in chapter 3, Katherine Seibold describes the dynamic interplay between background and figure in Andean weaving uniting the two sides "(the light and the dark, the foreground and the background) to form one whole."[248]

The xicalcoliuhqui motif commonly adorns spindle whorls, where it depicts the back-and-forth, balanced, reciprocal nepantla motion-change involved in successful weaving.[249] It also causally contributes to the successful weaving of nepantla-balanced cloth. John Pohl and Mauricio Orozpe Enríquez interpret the xicalcoliuhqui friezes at Mitla as textile designs and identify a number of stamps for applying designs to textiles as xicalcoliuhqui motifs.[250] These nepantla-balance the buildings and the fabrics they adorn as well as radiate nepantla-shaped energy into the cosmos.

6.4. CONCLUSION

Aztec metaphysics conceives the cosmos as a grand nepantla-defined weaving in progress. Teotl is simultaneously weaver of the cosmos, the weaving of the cosmos, and woven cosmic product. Nepantla motion-change, like olin and malinalli, plays an essential role in the becoming and processing of the cosmos and all its inhabitants. Like olin and malinalli, it is a *shape* or *pattern* of energy in the cosmos, not a kind of energy. Like them, it orders, arranges, and puts stuff in place. Nepantla-processes weave together inamic partners into an agonistic yet balanced unity, and do so in a way that is: middling, betwixt-and-betweening, and abundant with mutuality and reciprocity; simultaneously creatively destructive and destructively creative; and hence transformative. That which is nepantla-middled is that which is well balanced, well arranged, and well ordered.

NOTES

1. Fray Diego Durán, *Book of the Gods and Rites* and *The Ancient Calendar*, trans. and eds. Fernando Horcasitas and Doris Heyden (Norman: University of Oklahoma Press, 1971), 410–11. Portions of this chapter first appeared in James Maffie, "The Centrality of Nepantla in Conquest-Era Nahua Philosophy," *The Nahua Newsletter* 44 (2007): 11–31.

2. Quoted in and translated by Wayne Elzey, "Some Remarks on the Space and Time of the 'Center' in Aztec Religion," *Estudios de cultura náhuatl* 12 (1976): 324; Elzey, "Nepantla," in *The Oxford Encyclopedia of Mesoamerican Cultures: The Civilizations of Mexico and Central America*, ed. Davíd Carrasco (Oxford: Oxford University Press, 2001), 2:365.

3. Quoted in R. Joe Campbell, *A Morphological Dictionary of Classical Nahuatl: A Morpheme Index to the Vocabulario en lengua mexicana y castellana of Fray Alonso de Molina* (Madison: Hispanic Seminary of Medieval Studies, 1985), 212–13.

4. Elzey, "Some Remarks on the Space and Time," 324–25.

5. Frances Karttunen, *An Analytical Dictionary of Nahuatl* (Norman: University of Oklahoma Press, 1983), 160, 169, 186, 259.

6. Alonso de Molina, *Vocabulario en lengua castellana y mexicana y mexicana y castellana*, 4th ed., facsimile of 1571 edition (México, DF: Porrúa, 2001). Unless otherwise indicated, the following entries and their translations are from Campbell, *Morphological Dictionary*, 212–13.

7. Karttunen, *Analytical Dictionary*, 169.

8. According to Campbell (*Morphological Dictionary*, 411), these terms combine *xiotl* ("thread for weaving cloth; scabies or mange") with *nepan*. Molina and Sahagún define *iquiti* as "to weave cloth" (Molina, *Vocabulario*, 2:42r; Bernardino de Sahagún, *Florentine Codex: General History of the Things of New Spain*, ed. and trans. Arthur J.O. Anderson and Charles Dibble [Santa Fe, NM: School of American Research; Salt Lake City: University of Utah, 1953–1982], X:36).

9. Sahagún (*Florentine Codex*, X:36, 51) offers descriptions of good and bad weavers. For Kogi descriptions of good and bad weavers, see Gerardo Reichel-Dolmatoff, "The Loom of Life: A Kogi Principle of Integration," *Journal of Latin American Lore* 4, no. 1 (1978): 5–17. In both cases, the descriptions carry moral overtones.

10. See Anni Albers, *On Weaving* (Middletown, CT: Wesleyan University Press, 1965); Patricia Rieff Anawalt, "Weaving," in *The Oxford Encyclopedia of Mesoamerican Cultures: The Civilizations of Mexico and Central America*, ed. Davíd Carrasco (Oxford: Oxford University Press, 2001), 324–28; Marilyn Anderson, *Guatemalan Textiles Today* (New York: Watson-Guptill Publications, 1978); Louise M. Burkhart, "Mexica Women on the Home Front: Housework and Religion in Aztec Mexico," in *Indian Women of Early Mexico*, ed. Susan Schroeder, Stephanie Wood, and Robert Haskett (Norman: University of Oklahoma Press, 1997): 45; Stacy B. Schaefer, *To Think with a Good Heart:*

Wixárika Women, Weavers, and Shamans (Salt Lake City: University of Utah Press, 2002); Guadalupe Mastache, "El tejido en el México antiguo," *Arqueología Mexicana, edición especial* 19 (2005): 20–28; and Alba Guadalupe Mastache, "Téchnicas prehispánicas," *Arqueología Mexicana, edición especial* 19 (2005): 29–32.

11. Molina, *Vocabulario*, 2:81r.

12. Karttunen, *Analytical Dictionary*, 169.

13. Elzey, "Some Remarks on the Space and Time," 324–25.

14. *"unos a otros, o unos con otros, o los a los otros"* (Molina, *Vocabulario*, 2:69r).

15. Campbell, *Morphological Dictionary*, 212.

16. Karttunen, *Analytical Dictionary*, 169.

17. Sahagún, *Florentine Codex*, I:60. I am indebted to Joe Campbell (personal correspondence, 9/7/09) for bringing this passage to my attention.

18. Recent work analyzing nepantla in terms of liminality includes Louise M. Burkhart, *The Slippery Earth: Nahua-Christian Dialogue in Sixteenth-Century Mexico* (Tucson: University of Arizona Press, 1989); Elzey, "Some Remarks on the Space and Time"; Viviana Díaz Balsera, *The Pyramid under the Cross: Franciscan Discourses of Evangelization and the Nahua Christian Subject in Sixteenth-Century Mexico* (Tucson: University of Arizona Press, 2005); Miguel León-Portilla, "Testimonios nahuas sobre la conquista," *Estudios de cultura náhuatl* 11 (1974): 11–36; Miguel León-Portilla, *Endangered Cultures*, trans. Julie Goodson-Lewis (Dallas: Southern Methodist University Press, 1990); J. Jorge Klor de Alva, "Spiritual Conflict and Accommodation in New Spain: Toward a Typology of Aztec Responses to Christianity," in *The Inca and Aztec States: 1400–1800*, ed. George A. Collier, Renato Rosaldo, and John D. Walsh (New York: Academic Press, 1982), 345–66; and Davíd Carrasco and Scott Sessions, "Middle Place, Labyrinth, and Circumambulation: Cholula's Peripatetic Role in the *Mapa de Cuauhtinchan No. 2*," in *Cave, City, Eagle's Nest: An Interpretive Journey through the* Mapa de Cuauhtinchan No. 2, ed. Davíd Carrasco and Scott Sessions (Albuquerque: University of New Mexico Press, 2007), 427–54.

19. Victor Turner, "Dewey, Dilthey, and Drama: An Essay in the Anthropology of Experience," in *The Anthropology of Experience*, ed. Victor Turner and Edward Bruner (Urbana: University of Illinois Press, 1986), 41.

20. Victor Turner, "Betwixt and Between: The Liminal Period in Rites of Passage," in *Reader in Comparative Religion: An Anthropological Approach*, 4th ed., ed. William A. Lessa and Evon Z. Vogt (New York: Harper and Row, 1979), 236.

21. Ibid.

22. Ibid.

23. Ibid., 237.

24. Turner, "Dewey, Dilthey," 42.

25. Ibid.

26. Barbara G. Myerhoff and Willard Gingerich notably avoid this error. See Barbara G. Myerhoff, "Balancing between Worlds: The Shaman's Calling," *Parabola* 1, no. 2 (1976): 6–13; and Willard Gingerich, "*Chipahuacanemiliztli*, 'the Purified Life,' in the Discourses of Book VI, Florentine Codex," in *Smoke and Mist: Mesoamerican Studies in Memory of Thelma D. Sullivan*, Part 2, ed. J. Kathryn Josserand and Karen Dakin (Oxford: British Archaeological Reports, 1988), 517–43. Myerhoff ("Balancing," 6) writes: "For most, paradox is an unnatural state, a tense transitional stage between unambiguous positions; it offers no shelter. But the shaman lives in paradox as his natural element." I contend this characterization captures the Nahua notion of nepantla and contend furthermore that nepantla characterizes the human condition per se. I believe it is erroneous to think of nepantla in terms of syncretism and hybridity.

27. Sahagún, *Florentine Codex*, VI:202; see also 175, 176, 183, 202, 206.

28. See Alfredo López Austin, *The Human Body and Ideology: Concepts of the Ancient Nahuas*, trans. Thelma Ortiz de Montellano and Bernard R. Ortiz de Montellano (Salt Lake City: University of Utah Press, 1988), I:208, 426n10; and Alfredo López Austin, *Tamoanchan, Tlalocan: Places of Mist*, trans. Bernard R. Ortiz de Montellano and Thelma Ortiz de Montellano (Niwot: University Press of Colorado, 1977), 106–8.

29. Dibble and Anderson (Sahagún, *Florentine Codex*, VI:202).

30. Josefina García Quintana, "*El baño ritual entre los nahuas según el Códice Florentino*," *Estudios de cultura náhuatl* 8 (1969): 201, 203.

31. López Austin, *Human Body*, I:208, 426n10; Alfredo López Austin, *Tamoanchan y Tlalocan* (México: Fondo de Cultura Económica, 1994), 107.

32. López Austin, *Tamoanchan, Tlalocan*, 108; López Austin, *Tamoanchan y Tlalocan*, 91.

33. López Austin, *Tamoanchan, Tlalocan*, 108; López Austin, *Tamoanchan y Tlalocan*, 91.

34. López Austin, *Tamoanchan, Tlalocan*, 108.

35. Translation by Dibble and Anderson (Sahagún, *Florentine Codex*, IX:5, 47, 55).

36. López Austin, *Tamoanchan, Tlalocan*, 108.

37. Translation by Dibble and Anderson (Sahagún, *Florentine Codex*, XII:11, 12; see also II:43).

38. See Molina, *Vocabulario*, 2:88r; López Austin, *Tamoanchan, Tlalocan*, 108.

39. López Austin, *Tamoanchan, Tlalocan*, 109, fig. 10.

40. López Austin, *Tamoanchan, Tlalocan*, 108. López Austin (*Tamoanchan, Tlalocan*, 111–12) cites Mendieta's description of the founding of Tenochtitlan at the spot "shaped like a Saint Andrew's cross" where two creeks crossed.

41. López Austin, *Tamoanchan, Tlalocan*, 108.

42. Ibid., 112.

43. Sahagún, *Florentine Codex*, XI:51.

44. Campbell, *Morphological Dictionary*, 212.

45. López Austin, *Tamoanchan, Tlalocan,* 110.

46. See "Annals of Cuauhtitlan," in *History and Mythology of the Aztecs: The Codex Chimalpopoca,* trans. John Bierhorst (Tucson: University of Arizona Press, 1992), 30; and Sahagún, *Florentine Codex,* VI:175. Sources differ over the number of celestial folds, some saying nine, others twelve. See Miguel León-Portilla, *Aztec Thought and Culture: A Study of the Ancient Nahuatl Mind* (Norman: University of Oklahoma Press, 1963) 52; López Austin, *Tamoanchan, Tlalocan;* Michel Graulich, "Creator Deities," in *The Oxford Encyclopedia of Mesoamerican Cultures: The Civilizations of Mexico and Central America,* ed. Davíd Carrasco (Oxford: Oxford University Press, 2001), 1:284–86; John D. Monaghan, "The Person, Destiny, and the Construction of Difference in Mesoamerica," *RES* 33 (Spring 1998): 137–46; and Bodo Spranz, *Los dioses en los códices mexicanos del grupo Borgia,* trans. María Martínez Peñaloza (México, DF: Fondo de Cultura Económica, 1973).

47. León-Portilla, *Aztec Thought,* 52.

48. Monaghan, "Person, Destiny," 142–43. See also Cecelia Klein, "None of the Above: Gender Ambiguity in Nahua Ideology," in *Gender in Pre-Hispanic America,* ed. Cecelia Klein (Washington, DC: Dumbarton Oaks, 2001), 187–89.

49. Nathaniel Tarn and Martín Prechtel, "Constant Inconstancy: The Feminine Principle in Atiteco Mythology," in *Symbol and Meaning: Beyond the Closed Community,* ed. Gary Gossen (Albany: SUNY Press, Institute for Mesoamerican Studies, 1986), 173.

50. See Sahagún, *Florentine Codex,* VI:141, 168, 175, 176, 183, 202; X:169; Henry B. Nicholson, "Religion in Pre-Hispanic Central Mexico," in *Handbook of Middle American Indians,* vol. 10, ed. Robert Wauchope, Gordon F. Elkholm, and Ignacio Bernal (Austin: University of Texas Press, 1971): 410–11; and Karl Taube, *Aztec and Maya Myths* (Austin: University of Texas Press, 1995), 31.

51. Juan de Torquemada, *Monarquía indiana: De los veinte y un libros rituales y monarquía indiana, con el origen y guerras de los indios occidentales, de sus poblazones, descubrimiento, conquista, conversión y otras cosas maravillosas de la mesma tierra,* 3rd ed. (México, DF: Universidad Nacional Autónoma de México, 1975–1983), 3:67.

52. See Sahagún, *Florentine Codex,* VI:41, 175; X:169; León-Portilla, *Aztec Thought,* 31–32, 80–103; Miguel León-Portilla, *La filosofía náhuatl: Estudiada en sus fuentes con un nuevo apéndice,* new ed., prologue by Angel María Garibay K. (México, DF: Universidad Nacional Autónoma de México, 2001 [1956]), 380, 382; Alfonso Caso, *The Aztecs: People of the Sun,* trans. Lowell Dunham (Norman: University of Oklahoma Press, 1958), 9; Michel Graulich, "Creation Myths," in *The Oxford Encyclopedia of Mesoamerican Cultures: The Civilizations of Mexico and Central America,* ed. Davíd Carrasco (Oxford: Oxford University Press, 2001), 1:281–84; Michel Graulich, "Creator Deities," *The Oxford Encyclopedia of Mesoamerican Cultures: The Civilizations of Mexico and Central America,* ed. Davíd Carrasco (Oxford: Oxford University Press, 2001), 1:284–86.

53. For related discussion, see Laurette Séjourné, *Burning Water: Thought and Religion in Ancient Mexico* (New York: Grove Press, 1960), 99–111. León-Portilla claims the notion of a single male~female creator is common throughout Mesoamerica (Miguel León-Portilla, "*Mitos de los origenes en Mesoamerica*," *Arqueología Mexicana* 10, no. 56 [2002]: 20–53). According to the *Popol Vuh*, the genesis of the cosmos proceeds from preexisting dual-aspect creators who are sexually dimorphic, male~female, and active~passive. "Duality belongs to the very nature of the primordial world and to anything that might be created in that world," writes Dennis Tedlock (Dennis Tedlock, "Creation in the Popol Vuh: A Hermeneutical Approach," in *Symbol and Meaning beyond the Closed Community: Essays in Mesoamerican Ideas*, ed. Gary H. Gossen [Albany, NY: Institute for Mesoamerican Studies, SUNY Press, 1986], 81). Light and darkness, sky and sea, and male and female exist before the cosmos is created. Barbara Tedlock and Dennis Tedlock contrast this with the Biblical notion of creation according to which creation proceeds from a single god who transcends sexual difference not by means of male~female unity but by means of "the suppression of the female principle" (as Dennis Tedlock puts it in "Creation in the Popol Vuh: A Hermeneutical Approach," 80). See Barbara Tedlock, *Time and the Highland Maya*, rev. ed. (Albuquerque: University of New Mexico Press, 1992); and Dennis Tedlock, "Introduction," in *Popol Vuh: The Definitive Edition of the Mayan Book of the Dawn of Life and the Glories of Gods and Kings*, intro., trans., and commentary by Dennis Tedlock (New York: Simon and Schuster, 1985), 23–66.

54. Monaghan, "Person, Destiny," 142–43; see also John D. Monaghan, "Physiology, Production and Gendered Difference: The Evidence from Mixtec and Other Mesoamerican Societies," in *Gender in Pre-Hispanic America*, ed. Cecelia F. Klein (Washington, DC: Dumbarton Oaks, 2001), 285–304.

55. Klein, "None of the Above," 189. This also applies to Oxomoco~Cipactonal.

56. Ibid.

57. Cecelia Klein, "Woven Heaven, Tangled Earth: The Weaver's Paradigm of the Mesoamerican Cosmos," in *Ethnoastronomy and Archaeoastronomy in the American Tropics*, ed. Anthony Aveni and Gary Urton, Annals of the New York Academy of Sciences, No. 38 (New York: New York Academy of Sciences, 1982), 15.

58. For related discussion see Klein, "None of the Above."

59. See Guilhem Olivier, "Tezcatlipoca," in *The Oxford Encyclopedia of Mesoamerican Cultures: The Civilizations of Mexico and Central America*, ed. Davíd Carrasco (Oxford: Oxford University Press, 2001), 3:317–19; Guilhem Olivier, *Mockeries and Metamorphoses of an Aztec God: Tezcatlipoca, "Lord of the Smoking Mirror*," trans. Michel Besson (Boulder: University Press of Colorado, 2003); Michel Graulich, "*Ochpaniztli, la fête des semailles des anciens Mexicains*," *Anales de antropología* 18 (1981): 59–100; Barbara Tedlock, *The Woman in the Shaman's Body: Reclaiming the Feminine in Religion and Medicine* (New York: Bantam Books, 2005), 227; Burkhart, *Slippery Earth*; Burkhart, "Mexica Women";

Kay A. Read, *Time and Sacrifice in the Aztec Cosmos* (Bloomington: Indiana University Press, 1998); and Kay A. Read, "More than Earth: Cihuacoatl as Female Warrior, Male Matron, and Inside Ruler," in *Goddesses Who Rule*, ed. Elisabeth Benard and Beverly Moon (Oxford: Oxford University Press, 2000), 51–68.

60. Molina, *Vocabulario*, II:34v; Rémi Siméon, *Diccionario de la lengua náhuatl o mexicana*, trans. Josefina Olivia de Coll (México, DF: Siglo Veintiuno Editores, 1977), 178; Olivier, "Tezcatlipoca," 219; Campbell, *Morphological Dictionary*, 428; and Campbell, personal correspondence, 9/07/09. Karttunen (*Analytical Dictionary*, 337) does not include "to make war" in her translation of *yecoa*. For further discussion, see Cecelia Klein, "Fighting with Femininity: Gender and War in Aztec Mexico," in *Gender Rhetorics: Postures of Dominance and Submission in Human History*, ed. Richard C. Trexler, Medieval and Renaissance Texts and Studies 113 (Binghamton: State University of New York, 1994), 219–53; Read, "More than Earth"; and Geoffrey McCafferty and Sharisse McCafferty, "The Metamorphosis of Xochiquetzal," in *Manifesting Power: Gender and the Interpretation of Power in Archaeology*, ed. Tracy L. Sweely (London: Routledge 1999), 103–25.

61. Graulich, "Ochpaniztli," 86, quoted in and translated by Olivier (*Mockeries*, 264). Read (*Time and Sacrifice*, 131–35) claims the Aztecs also likened sexual intercourse to hunting, eating, and sacrifice.

62. See Ross Hassig, *Aztec Warfare: Imperial Expansion and Political Control* (Norman: University of Oklahoma Press, 1988).

63. See Klein, "Shield Women" and "Fighting with Femininity."

64. *Historia de los mexicanos por sus pinturas*, in *Teogonía e historia de los mexicanos: Tres opúsculos del siglo XVI*, 1st ed., ed. Angel María Garibay K. (México: Editorial Porrúa, 1965), 33.

65. See Nathaniel Tarn and Martín Prechtel, *Scandals in the House of Birds: Shamans and Priests on Lake Atitlán* (New York: Marsilio, 1997), 295.

66. Durán, *Book of the Gods*, 239.

67. Quoted in Olivier, *Mockeries*, 100.

68. *Codex Fejérváry-Mayer* (Loubat: Bibliothéque Du Palais Bourbon, 1901), plate 29, http://www.famsi.org/index.html (accessed 5/19/13). For further discussion see Miguel León-Portilla, "*El Tonalámatl de los Pochtecas (Códice Fejérváry-Mayer): Estudio introductorio y comentarios*," *Arqueología Mexicana*, *Edición especial* 18 (2005): 76.

69. Mary Miller and Karl Taube, *An Illustrated Dictionary of the Gods and Symbols of Ancient Mexico and the Maya* (London: Thames and Hudson, 1993), 174–75.

70. Eloise Quiñones Keber, *Codex Telleriano-Remensis: Ritual, Divination, and History in a Pictorial Aztec Manuscript* (Austin: University of Texas Press, 1995), 187.

71. H. B. Nicholson, "Religion in Pre-Hispanic Central Mexico," in *Handbook of Middle American Indians*, vol. 10, ed. Robert Wauchope, Gordon F. Elkholm, and Igna-

cio Bernal (Austin: University of Texas Press, 1971), 395–446. See also Quiñones Keber, *Codex Telleriano-Remensis*, 163, 187.

72. Klein, "Woven Heaven," 15.

73. Nicholson, "Religion," 414, 420. See also Sahagún, *Florentine Codex*, I:23–27; VI:29–34.

74. Thelma D. Sullivan, "Tlazolteotl-Ixcuina: The Great Spinner and Weaver," in *The Art and Iconography of Late Post-Classic Central Mexico*, ed. Elizabeth Hill Boone (Washington, DC: Dumbarton Oaks, 1982), 7–36. See also Peter T. Furst, "The Thread of Life: Some Parallels in the Symbolism of Aztec, Huichol and Puebla Earth Goddesses," in *Balance y perspectiva de la antropología de Mesoamerica y del centro de México*, Mesa Redonda 13th, 1973 (México, DF: La Sociedad Mexicana de Antropología, 1975), 235–45.

75. Sullivan, "Tlazolteotl-Ixcuina," 30.

76. Ibid.

77. Quiñones Keber, *Codex Telleriano-Remensis*; Sahagún, *Florentine Codex*, I:fig. 8.

78. Quiñones Keber, *Codex Telleriano-Remensis*, 179. See also Sullivan, "Tlazolteotl-Ixcuina."

79. See Sullivan, "Tlazolteotl-Ixcuina," 15.

80. Quiñones Keber, *Codex Telleriano-Remensis*, 179f, see also folio 12r. See also Gisele Diaz and Alan Rodgers, *Codex Borgia: A Full Color Restoration of the Ancient Mexican Manuscript*, intro. and commentary by Bruce E. Byland (New York: Dover Publications, 1993), plates 12 and 23.

81. See Sullivan, "Tlazolteotl-Ixcuina"; Miller and Taube, *Illustrated Dictionary*, 149–51; Jacqueline de Durand-Forest et al., *Los elementos anexos del Códice Borbónico*, trans. Dr. Edgar Samuel Morales Sales (México, DF: Universidad Autónoma del Estado de México, 2000), 183–96.

82. Sahagún, *Florentine Codex*, I:23.

83. Sullivan, "Tlazolteotl-Ixcuina," 30.

84. Kevin Terraciano, *The Mixtecs of Colonial Oaxaca: Ñudzahui History, Sixteenth through Eighteenth Centuries* (Stanford, CA: Stanford University Press, 2001), 169. Heyden ("Metaphors, Nahualtocaitl," 39–40) discusses the symbolic connection between reeds and rulership, creation, wealth, and the gods.

85. *The Essential Codex Mendoza*, ed. Berdan and Anawalt, 25v and 26r.

86. Sahagún, *Florentine Codex*, X:86.

87. Campbell, *Morphological Dictionary*, 129.

88. Ibid.; Burkhart, *Slippery Earth*, 28.

89. For example, see Sahagún, *Florentine Codex*, III:fig. 17; IV:figs. 17, 52, 85; VII:18; VIII:figs. 1–9, 20–22, 66, 68, 82–85, 99; *Codex Laud* MS, Laud Misc, 678 (Graz: Bodleian Library, 1966): 27, http://www.famsi.org/index.html (accessed 5/9/13); Quiñones Keber, *Codex Telleriano Remensis*, 14r, 29v–32r, 34v; and *Codex Magliabechiano* (*The Book of the*

Life of the Ancient Mexicans), facsimile ed. Zelia Nuttall (Berkeley: University of California Press, 1903), plate 67.

90. Thelma Sullivan, trans., *A Scattering of Jades: Stories, Poems and Prayers of the Aztecs*, ed., comp., and intro. Timothy Knab (New York: Simon and Schuster, 1994), 258n48.

91. Campbell, *Morphological Dictionary*, 245.

92. Durán, *History of the Indies*, pls. 7–10, 15, 18, 20, 24, 37, 38.

93. Sahagún, *Florentine Codex*, IV:figs. 1, 17, 47, 52; VI:figs. 6, 12, 14–21, 28, 31.

94. Sullivan, *Scattering of Jades*, 208, 258n42.

95. Mastache, "Técnicas prehispánicas," 31.

96. Sahagún, *Florentine Codex*, XI:80–81; see figs. 261, 262.

97. Sahagún, *Primeros memoriales*, 252v and 252r, respectively.

98. Durán, *Book of the Gods*, pls. 53, 52, and 54, respectively.

99. Sahagún, *Florentine Codex*, II:78–90. For discussion, see H. B. Nicholson, "Representing the *Veintena* Ceremonies in the *Primeros Memoriales*," in *Representing Aztec Ritual: Performance, Text, and Image in the Work of Sahagún*, ed. Eloise Quiñones Keber (Boulder: University Press of Colorado, 2002), 63–106; and Philip P. Arnold, *Eating Landscape: Aztec and European Occupation of Tlalocan* (Niwot: University Press of Colorado, 1999), 92–105.

100. *Codex Magliabechiano*, 34r.

101. Sahagún, *Primeros memoriales*, 250r–53r.

102. David Freidel, Linda Schele, and Joy Parker, *Maya Cosmos: Three Thousand Years on the Shaman's Path* (New York: William Morrow, 1993), 142–43.

103. Reported in Friedel, Schele, and Parker, *Maya Cosmos*, 152.

104. Evon Z. Vogt, *Tortillas for the Gods: A Symbolic Analysis of Zinacanteco Rituals* (Cambridge, MA: Harvard University Press, 1976), 118–20.

105. Manuel Aguilar-Moreno, *Handbook to Life in the Aztec World* (Oxford: Oxford University Press, 2006), 324.

106. Rubén G. Mendoza, "The Divine Gourd Tree: Tzompantli Skull Racks, Decapitation Rituals, and Human Trophies in Ancient America," in *The Taking and Displaying of Human Body Parts as Trophies by Amerindians*, ed. Richard J. Chacon and David H. Dye (New York: Springer, 2007), 411, emphasis mine.

107. López Austin, *Tamoanchan, Tlalocan*, 108.

108. Sahagún, *Florentine Codex*, IX:5, 47, 55.

109. López Austin, *Tamoanchan, Tlalocan*, 108.

110. Sahagún, *Florentine Codex*, XII:10, 12; see also II:43.

111. Sahagún, *Florentine Codex*, II:43; Sahagún, *Primeros memoriales: Paleography*, fol. 250r. For discussion, see Arnold, *Eating Landscape*.

112. Sahagún, *Primeros memoriales*, 250r, 250v, 252v, 253r. See Nicholson, "Representing the *Veintena*," 93; López Austin, *Tamoanchan, Tlalocan*, 108.

113. Sahagún, *Florentine Codex*, XII:11, 12.

114. Martín Prechtel and Robert S. Carlsen, "Weaving and Cosmos amongst the Tzutujil Maya of Guatemala," *RES* 15 (1988): 124.

115. See Sahagún, *Florentine Codex*, II:chapter 36; Sahagún, *Primeros memoriales: Paleography*, fol. 253r; Durán, *Book of the Gods*, 463–64; Eduardo Matos Moctezuma, *Life and Death in the Templo Mayor*, trans. Bernard R. Ortiz de Montellano and Thelma Ortiz de Montellano (Niwot: University Press of Colorado, 1995), 22; Nicholson, "Religion"; and Quiñones Keber, *Codex Telleriano-Remensis*.

116. "Histoyre du Mechique," in *Teogonía e historia de los Mexicanos: Tres opúsculos del siglo XVI*, 1st ed., Angel Ma. Garibay K. (México, DF: Editorial Porrúa, 1965), 108.

117. See Durán, *Book of the Gods*, pl. 7.

118. Sahagún, *Florentine Codex*, II:125–26; Durán, *Book of the Gods*, 236–37. For graphic depictions, see Sahagún, *Primeros memoriales*, 251v; Durán, *Book of the Gods*, pl. 24; and *Codex Borbonicus* (Loubat: Bibliothéque Du Palais Bourbon, 1899), pl. 31, http://www.famsi.org/index.html (accessed 5/9/13).

119. See Durán, *Book of the Gods*, 227; Quiñones-Keber, *Codex Telleriano-Remensis*, 41v; and *Codex Vaticanus 3738 A* (*Codex Rios*) (Graz: Akademische Druck- u. Verlagsanstalt 1979), pl. 84v., http://www.famsi.org/index.html (accessed 5/9/13), depict the arrow sacrifice.

120. Eduard Seler, *Comentarios al Códice Borgia*, 3 vols. (México, DF: Fondo de Cultural Económica, 1963 [1904]), 2:74.

121. Campbell, *Morphological Dictionary*, 330–31.

122. Sahagún, *Florentine Codex*, II:29; and Molina, *Vocabulario*, 2: 154r.

123. "*palo ancho como cuchilla con que tupen y aprietan la tela quese texe*," translation by Campbell, *Morphological Dictionary*, 387.

124. Karttunen, *Analytical Dictionary*, 320.

125. Sahagún, *Florentine Codex*, II:29.

126. Quoted in McCafferty and McCafferty, "Metamorphosis of Xochiquetzal," 118.

127. Campbell, *Morphological Dictionary*, 386.

128. Ibid.

129. Ibid.

130. See Martín Prechtel and Robert S. Carlsen, "Weaving and Cosmos amongst the Tzutujil Maya of Guatemala," *RES* 15 (Spring 1988): 124; Furst, "Thread of Life"; and Barbara Tedlock, *Woman in the Shaman's Body*, 227.

131. Donald Cordry and Dorothy Cordry, *Mexican Indian Costumes*, foreword by Michael Covarrubias (Austin: University of Texas Press, 1968), 43.

132. Sahagún, *Florentine Codex*, II:chapter 35; Sahagún, *Primeros memoriales, Paleography*, 65–66.

133. Cordry and Cordry, *Mexican Indian Costumes*, 43.

134. *Pace* McCafferty and McCafferty ("Spinning and Weaving," 29), who regard them as symbols of female power and authority.

135. Monaghan, "Physiology, Production," 295.

136. *Codex Borbonicus*, pl. 36.

137. *Codex Magliabechiano*, pl. 44r.

138. See Read, "More than Earth"; and Klein, "Fighting with Femininity."

139. Durán, *Book of the Gods*, 232–33.

140. Ibid., 229, 236–37.

141. Sahagún, *Florentine Codex*, I:31.

142. Ibid., II:97.

143. Ibid., II:193.

144. Ibid., II:88.

145. Ibid., II:109, 116, 124, 130, respectively.

146. Ibid., II:149.

147. Ibid., IV:6; I:31, respectively.

148. Ibid., VII:15.

149. Ibid., I:31.

150. Ibid., II:216.

151. Ibid., II:89.

152. Ibid., II: chapter 20. See also Durán, *Book of the Gods*, 164; Richard F. Townsend, *The Aztecs* (London: Thames and Hudson, 1992), 137.

153. *"la coronilla de la mitad de la cabeza"* (Molina, *Vocabulario*, 2:85r). See also López Austin, *Human Body*, I:94; II:144.

154. Sahagún, *Florentine Codex*, X:100.

155. Ibid., IV:43.

156. Ibid., VI:202.

157. Ibid., VI:203; see also VI:38, 58, brackets mine.

158. Ibid., VI:204, brackets mine.

159. Campbell, *Morphological Dictionary*, 341. I interpret *tlallinepantli* as the middle of the earth, as opposed to *tlallitic*, which Campbell glosses as "inside the earth, or in the middle of the earth."

160. Ibid.

161. *Historia de los mexicanos por sus pinturas*, 32.

162. Quoted in López Austin, *Tamoanchan y Tlalocan* (México: Fondo de Cultura Económica, 2004), 92; see also López Austin, *Tamoanchan, Tlalocan*, 112.

163. Hernando Alvarado Tezozomoc, *Crónica Mexicayotl*, trans. A. Léon (México: Universidad Nacional Autónoma de México/Instituto de Historia, 1949), 3, 63. The above translations are by Rudolph van Zantwijk, *The Aztec Arrangement: The Social History of Pre-Spanish Mexico* (Norman: University of Oklahoma Press, 1985), 60–61. See

Berdan and Anawalt, *Essential Codex Mendoza*, 4, 6n14; Heyden, *Eagle, Cactus Rock*, 65; and Doris Heyden, *México: Orígenes de un símbolo*, versión adaptada e ilustrada (México: Dirección General de Publicaciones, INAH, 1998), 53–54, 75.

164. López Lujan, *Offerings of the Templo Mayor*, 63–69; López Austin, *Tamoanchan, Tlalocan*, 60.

165. Diego Durán, *Historia de las Indias de Nueva España e islas de tierra firme*, Vol. II, 2nd ed., ed. Angel María Garibay K. (México, DF: Editorial Porrúa, 1984), 48.

166. See López Lujan, *Offerings of the Templo Mayor*, 63–69; and Zantwijk, *The Aztec Arrangement*.

167. Sahagún, *Florentine Codex*, IV:4.

168. Ibid., IV:fig. 1; *Codex Borbonicus*, pl. 21.

169. Quoted in Elzey, "Some Remarks on the Space and Time," 318.

170. Ibid., 324, 325.

171. Elizabeth Hill Boone, *Cycles of Time and Meaning in the Mexican Books of Fate* (Austin: University of Texas Press, 2007), 60.

172. Klein, "None of the Above," 207.

173. Sahagún, *Florentine Codex*, I:19.

174. Ibid., II:37. See Sahagún, *Primeros memoriales: Paleography*, 66n41.

175. Sahagún, *Primeros memoriales: Paleography*, 266r.

176. Sahagún *Florentine Codex*, IV:10, 41, 81, 93, 107.

177. Burkhart, *Slippery Earth*, 113.

178. Sullivan, "Tlazolteotl-Ixcuina," 19. See also Sahagún, *Florentine Codex*, I:19.

179. Sullivan, "Tlazolteotl-Ixcuina," 18–19. See also Seler, *Codex Fejérváry-Mayer*, 153.

180. Sahagún, *Florentine Codex*, II:138.

181. Donald Cordry and Dorothy Cordry, *Mexican Indian Costumes* (Austin: University of Texas Press, 1968), 42.

182. Prechtel and Carlsen, "Weaving and Cosmos," 123.

183. Schaefer, *To Think*, 250.

184. Sullivan, "Tlazolteotl-Ixcuina," 19. In plate 4 of the *Codex Fejérváry-Mayer*, Tlazolteotl also lacks a spindle. She wears a headband of unspun cotton and a loop of unspun cotton from her ear. See Seler, *Codex Fejérváry-Mayer*, 42.

185. Bernardino de Sahagún, *Historia General de Las Cosas de Nueva Espana*, 10th ed., ed. Angel María Garibay K. (México: Editorial Porrúa, 1999), 95; Sahagún, *Florentine Codex*, II:37.

186. Sahagún, *Florentine Codex*, IV:chapter 33. Doris Heyden ("Sand in Ritual and History," in *Representing Aztec Ritual: Performance, Text, and Image in the Work of Sahagún*, ed. Eloise Quiñones Keber [Boulder: University Press of Colorado, 2002], 175–96) argues that sand functioned as a portal between the realms of life and death.

187. Sahagún, *Florentine Codex*, III:12. For further discussion of Tezcatlipoca and crossroads, see Olivier, *Mockeries*; Seler, *Codex Fejérváry-Mayer*, 34.

188. *Codex Fejérváry-Mayer* (Loubat, 1901), pl. 2, http://www.famsi.org/index.html (accessed 5/19/13); see also pl. 43. See also Diaz and Rodgers, *Codex Borgia*, pl. 14. For discussion, see León-Portilla, "*El Tonalámatl de los Pochtecas*," 22; and Seler, *Codex Fejérváry-Mayer*, 33–34.

189. Seler, *Codex Fejérváry-Mayer*, 141.

190. *Codex Fejérváry-Mayer* (Loubat, 1901), plates 3 and 37, respectively, http://www.famsi.org/index.html (accessed 5/19/13).

191. *Codex Laud*, pl. 43.

192. Sahagún, *Florentine Codex*, VI:247. See also Sullivan, *Scattering of Jades*, 210.

193. See also Burkhart, *Slippery Earth*, 63–63; and Sullivan, *Scattering of Jades*, 210.

194. See Burkhart, *Slippery Earth*; Sullivan, "Tlazolteotl-Ixcuina."

195. See Burkhart, *Slippery Earth*; Sullivan, "Tlazolteotl-Ixcuina"; and Heyden, "Sand in Ritual."

196. Sahagún, *Florentine Codex*, I:26–27. See Burkhart, *Slippery Earth*.

197. See Burkhart, *Slippery Earth*; Burkhart, "Mexican Women"; Sullivan, "Tlazolteotl-Ixcuina"; and Olivier, *Mockeries*, 42.

198. Sahagún, *Florentine Codex*, I:23. Here Sahagún agrees with López Austin and López Lujan that the crossing springs that marked the location of Tenochtitlan were blue and yellow.

199. *Codex Laud*, pl. 15.

200. *Codex Fejérváry-Mayer* (Loubat, 1901), plate 4, http://www.famsi.org/index.html (accessed 5/19/13).

201. León-Portilla, "*El Tonalámatl de los Pochtecas*," 26. See also Seler, *Codex Fejérváry-Mayer*, 42.

202. León-Portilla, "*El Tonalámatl de los Pochtecas*," 92.

203. Molina, *Vocabulario*, 2:76r–78r. The relevant Sahagún (*Florentine Codex*) passages are cited below. Later scholars include Seler, *Codex Fejérváry-Mayer*; Seler, *Comentarios*; Dibble and Anderson's translations of the *Florentine Codex*; Elzey, "Some Remarks on the Space and Time"; Elzey, "Nepantla"; Karttunen, *Analytical Dictionary*; Campbell, *Morphological Dictionary*; Burkhart, *Slippery Earth*; and Olivier, *Mockeries*.

204. See Elzey, "Some Remarks on the Space and Time," 324–25; and Burkhart, *Slippery Earth*.

205. León-Portilla, "*El Tonalámatl de los Pochtecas*," 22, 24, 26, 78, 92, 104; Seler, *Codex Fejérváry-Mayer*, 34, 37, 42, 141, 164, 204; and Seler, *Comentarios*, 1:27, 115, 166, 169, 172; 2:46, 73, 120, 134.

206. Reichel-Dolmatoff, "Loom of Life," 16.

207. See Molina, *Vocabulario*, 2:78r; see Dibble and Anderson's translations in the *Florentine Codex*, I:19, III:12, IV:107, VI:247.

208. Alan Sandstrom (personal communication, 10/29/10).

209. Campbell, *Morphological Dictionary*, 183.

210. Berdan, "Appendix E," 171; see the *amaxtac* glyph (*Codex Mendoza*, pl.39r).

211. Sahagún, *Florentine Codex*, XI:15, trans. by R. Joe Campbell (personal correspondence, 8/23/2010). All translations are by Campbell unless otherwise indicated.

212. Sahagún, *Florentine Codex*, XI: 113.

213. Ibid.

214. Ibid., XI:201.

215. Ibid., XI:58.

216. Ibid., XI:108. Dibble and Anderson translates this as "it has a crotch: many crotches; it is crotched."

217. Ibid., XI:110.

218. Ibid., XI:75, translated by Campbell, and Dibble and Anderson.

219. Sahagún, *Primeros memoriales: Paleography*, 263r.

220. Karttunen (*Analytical Dictionary of Nahuatl*, 141) maintains this despite a vowel length discrepancy. John Sullivan (personal communication, 10/29/10) also suggests this etymology.

221. Campbell, *Morphological Dictionary*, 183.

222. Sahagún, *Florentine Codex*, IV:50.

223. Burkhart, *Slippery Earth*, 63.

224. Eduardo De la Cruz Cruz, Zacatecas Institute for Research and Ethnography (personal correspondence, 12/10/2010).

225. James W. Dow, "Central and North Mexican Shamans," in *Mesoamerican Healers*, ed. Brad R. Huber and Alan R. Sandstrom (Austin: University of Texas Press, 2001), 66–94; and Sandstrom (personal communication, 12/13/10).

226. James M. Taggart, *Nahuat Myth and Social Structure* (Austin: University of Texas Press, 1983), 56; Burkhart, *Slippery Earth*.

227. Dow, "Central and North," 84, 86.

228. Ibid., 86.

229. Sahagún, *Florentine Codex*, II:138, translation mine; see also III:43 and VIII:49.

230. Ibid., II:44.

231. Karttunen (*Analytical Dictionary*, 318) tells us that in compounds *tzontli* sometimes has the sense of "head"; in others, "hair." Here it seems to mean "head." See also Campbell, *Morphological Dictionary*, 183.

232. While some Aztec headgear was secured to the head by means of a knot tied at the back of the head (such as the diadem or miter Aztec rulers are depicted wearing),

the maxtlatl appears to have been secured by two bands crossing at the crown of the head. It sat upon the head rather than being tied around the head. For related discussion, see H. B. Nicholson, "A Royal Headband of the 'Tlaxcalteca,'" *Revista mexicana de estudios antropológicos* 21 (1967): 71–106.

233. Prechtel and Carlsen, "Weaving and Cosmos."

234. See Molina, *Vocabulario*, 2:88r; López Austin, *Tamoanchan, Tlalocan*, 108.

235. López Austin, *Tamoanchan, Tlalocan*, 109, fig. 10a.

236. Campbell, *Morphological Dictionary*, 212.

237. Carol H. Callaway, "Pre-Columbian and Colonial Images of the Cross: Christ's Sacrifice and the Fertile Earth," *Journal of Latin American Lore* 16, no. 2 (1990): 200–201.

238. Muñoz Camargo's drawing is reproduced in Elizabeth Hill Boone, *Incarnations of the Aztec Supernatural: The Image of Huiztilopochtli in Mexico and Europe* (Philadelphia: American Philosophical Society, 1989), 69, fig. 28.

239. Reported in Callaway, "Pre-Columbian and Colonial Images," 206.

240. *Codex Telleriano-Remensis* (45v) depicts a traveller approaching a Y-shaped fork in the road. However, the probative value of this scene is questionable since it occurs in the nonritualistic portions of the text. Moreover, as Quiñones Keber (*Codex Telleriano-Remensis*, 236) and Klein (personal correspondence, 11/15/10) point out, the scene is heavily Hispanicized.

241. The same ambiguity characterizes the roads of Tepeyac, Itztapalapa, and Tlacopan. They both serve as both inward (centering) routes of communication between periphery and center and outward (peripheralizing) routes of communication between the island and the rest of the empire.

242. Antonio Serrato-Combe, *The Aztec Templo Mayor: A Visualization* (Salt Lake City: University of Utah Press, 2007), 11.

243. See Sahagún, *Florentine Codex*, I:fig. 679; for a description of gardens, see p. 200.

244. Elizabeth Brumfiel, "Towards a Middle Range Theory of Household Politics: The Standardization of Decorative Motifs in Middle Postclassic Mexico," in *The Archaeology of Politics: The Materiality of Political Practice and Action in the Past*, ed. Peter Johansen and Andrew Bauer (Newcastle upon Tyne: Cambridge Scholars Publications, 2011), 9–10, 12.

245. Brumfiel, "Towards a Middle Range Theory of Household Politics," 10.

246. Ibid.

247. Elizabeth Brumfiel, "Domestic Politics in Early-Middle Postclassic Mexico: Variability and Standardization in Decorative Motifs," presented in Estudios de género en el México antiguo, coord. M. Rodríguez-Shadow and R. García Valgaño (México, DF: Congreso International de Americanists, 2009), 5. See also Mauricio Orozpe Enríquez, *El código oculto de le greca escalonada: Tloque Nahuaque* (México, DF: UNAM, 2010).

248. Katherine E. Seibold, "Textiles and Cosmology in Choquecancha, Cuzco, Peru," in *Andean Cosmologies through Time: Persistence and Emergence*, ed. Robert V. H. Dover, John McDowell, and Katherine E. Seibold (Bloomington: Indiana Univerity Press, 1992), 186.

249. Brumfiel, "Domestic Politics"; Brumfiel, "Towards a Middle Range Theory of Household Politics."

250. John M.D. Pohl, "Weaving and Gift Exchange in the Mixtec Codices," in *Cloth and Curing: Continuity and Change in Oaxaca*, ed. Grace Johnson and Douglas Sharon (San Diego: San Diego Museum of Man, 1994), 11; Orozpe Enríquez, *El código*.

7

Teotl as Time-Place

7.1. INTRODUCTORY REMARKS ON TIME AND PLACE

TIME AS CONCRETE AND PLURAL

Fray Alonso de Molina translates the Nahuatl word *cahuitl* as "time."[1] *Cahuitl* derives from *cahua*, meaning "to leave, abandon, or relinquish something or someone; to carry something to another place; to accompany someone home."[2] Apparently *cahuitl* literally means "that which leaves, abandons, accompanies, or carries someone or something." Aztec metaphysics thus appears to conceive of time as that which leaves or abandons as well as that which carries or accompanies people and things.

Aztec metaphysics conceives the various periods of time (e.g., days, nights, thirteen-day "weeks," and twenty-day "months") as *qualitatively* different, tonalli-energy-charged burdens carried on the backs of sacred porters. These burdens were bound to the porters' backs by a malinalli-twisted tumpline (*mecapalli*).[3] Time's passing, it seems, consists of the successive comings and goings – accompanying and abandoning – of qualitatively different kinds of tonalli-energy burdens. It does not consist of a succession of qualitatively uniform, lifeless moments. Each kind of time has its own kind of energy, character, or personality depending upon its kind of tonalli-energy. Just as each period in the life of a human being – infancy, childhood, adulthood, and old age – has its own character, so too does each period of time. Some burdens contain tonalli-energy beneficial, others harmful, to humans.

Time, therefore, is heterogeneous, not homogenous. It is plural, not singular. There is no one single time; no time as such. There are many different times. Instead

DOI: 10.5876_9781607322238.c007

419

of speaking of time per se, therefore, we should speak of *times*: the qualitatively different times of the day, the thirteen-day week, and the year – just as we speak of the qualitatively different times of a person's life.

A tonalli-charged time-burden accompanies the unfolding, becoming, and processing of the cosmos. In doing so its specific kind of tonalli energy suffuses and influences the becoming of the cosmos and all its inhabitants – just as the character of infancy or old age permeates and influences the unfolding of a person's life. Each time-burden does this in a different manner. And each does so until it departs, at which time the unfolding of the cosmos comes under the influence of a new time-burden. The Aztecs imagined the cosmos and its inhabitants bound to these time-burdens by means of malinalli-twisting tumplines. As we saw in chapter 5, they believed energy is conveyed throughout the cosmos by means of vertical, malinalli-twisting currents of ascending and descending energies. Now we see that the currents convey the different tonalli-energies associated with different time-burdens. The Aztecs also conceived umbilical cords as malinalli-twisted cords. Malinalli-twisting tumplines thus express the notion that the entire cosmos is connected to, dependent on, and influenced by the specific tonalli-energies of different time-burdens in the way that babies are connected to, dependent upon, and influenced by their mother's energies.

Aztec time is *concrete*, not abstract. Just as infancy per se or in the abstract does not exist, so likewise time per se or in the abstract does not exist. There exist only specific times charged with specific powers and personalities. Time is also *locative* in the sense that it situates things within specific, concrete contexts (rather than in time generally).[4] Tewa/Santa Clara Pueblo philosopher Gregory Cajete suggests that we use a locative conception of time when we speak of timing and timeliness in creating works of art (and weaving cloth), and when we say things like "Timing is everything."[5] Since all times are locative in this sense according to Aztec metaphysics, we need to speak of specific times and not time as such.

Finally, I argue below that time is *relational* rather than *substantial*. It is not an entity but a relationship.[6] Time consists of a pattern in the becoming of teotl and hence a pattern in the unfolding of teotl's energizing of the cosmos: a pattern defined by the interrelationships between the various tonalli-energy burdens. Just as adulthood is defined in relation to childhood, infancy, and old age (and conversely), so likewise the various periods of time are defined in terms of their relationships with one another. Time is therefore aptly likened to a biological rhythm or biorhythm. Time is immanent within the unfolding of the cosmos. It is embodied, for example, in the unfolding patterns (rhythms) of life and death (or life~death cycles) of all things: insects, humans, trees, mountains, and even Sun-Earth Orderings. As Read writes, all things are "timed."[7] Time is not abstract and general, but by definition specific, concrete, embodied, and incarnate. Finally, time is not exhausted by human experience. Such an idea is far too narrow and anthropocentric.[8]

In sum, time does not consist of a uniform succession of qualitatively identical moments; nor is it a neutral frame of reference abstracted from terrestrial and celestial processes. Time is concrete, quantitative, and qualitative. It is immanent within the rhythmic becoming of the cosmos and its contents.

Place as Concrete and Plural

Aztec metaphysics conceives space in similar fashion. Space is concrete, specific, qualitative, quantitative, alive, relational (nonsubstantive), locative, and timed. It is not a general, timeless, abstract dimension, nor a neutral container, frame of reference, or football field–like grid in which events and processes take place. In order to distinguish this conception from the more abstract, wholly quantitative conceptions of space historically advocated by Western science, mathematics, religions, and metaphysics, scholars standardly use terms such as *place* or *landscape*.[9] I prefer *place* since the Aztec concept includes both terrestrial and nonterrestrial location. *Landscape* is too narrow, as it suggests only terrestrial location.

The Valley of Mexico is just such a place. It is local, concrete, and specific. It was homeplace to the Aztecs; the place where they belonged; the place that in part defined them. It is the place with which the Aztecs interacted; the place from which and in terms of which they ritually participated in the cosmos. It oriented the Aztecs to the cosmos. Like all of Tlalticpac, the Valley of Mexico is part of the unfolding of teotl. As such, it is animated and charged with power. Like all places, the Valley of Mexico is a living presence with its own character.[10] Its character is a function of the specific powers of its human and nonhuman inhabitants along with their manifold interactions and interrelationships. It is a vast, intricate web of interrelationships between humans, plants, animals, mountains, waters, and sun – all of which are animated and charged with power. And its character changes with changes in time.

All place is locative in the sense that it situates things within a unique environment rather than within uniform space. And if all places are local, then we need to speak of specific places and not place or space per se. After all, places differ from one another. The Valley of Mexico, for example, is not the Valley of Teotihuacan or Puebla Valley.

Scholars routinely observe that the Aztecs conceived time and place as inseparably fused with one another.[11] Time and place form a single seamless continuum, or what I call *time-place*.[12] Time-place tells us the *when-where* of people, happenings, processes, and things. The Valley of Mexico was the Aztecs' home time-place or when-where. *Codex Mendoza* (pl. 2r) with Tenochtitlan at its center, depicts the home time-place of the Aztecs (see Figure 4.10.) As a consequence of their fusion, time and place become locative in the additional sense of being mutually locative. *All places are timed, and all times are placed. Time literally takes place and place literally takes time.*[13]

Time-place is an aspect of the becoming and unfolding of teotl. *Time-place is how teotl moves.* It is immanent within the unfolding patterns and rhythms in the becoming of the cosmos. It is embodied in the life~death rhythms of all things: humans, insects, trees, mountains, Suns, and Sun-Earth Eras. It is not a neutral frame of reference abstracted from cosmic processes.

Codex Fejérváry-Mayer (pl.1) maps the pattern immanent within the unfolding of time-place during the Fifth Sun-Earth Era (see Figure 4.3). It is a time-place mapping that displays *where* times take place (i.e., the places of times) as well as *when* places take time (i.e., the times of places). It charts the when-where of the 260 days of the tonalpohualli. It depicts the shape of the unfolding of time-place as a combined St. Andrew's and Greek cross. Time-place during the Fifth Age divides into four groupings shaped like a Greek cross, each consisting of 65 days (one-quarter of the 260 days of the tonalpohualli) and 5 day signs of the sequence of 20 day signs, or tonallis. As Soustelle explains it, the first grouping consists of the fusion of the 5 day signs *cipactli* (caiman), *acatl* (reed), *coatl* (serpent), *olin* (movement), and *atl* (water) with the East. These 5 days *take place* in the East (defined as where the Sun rises), while the East *takes time* (occurs) during these 5 days. This is Eastern time-place. The second time-place consists of the fusion of the 5 day signs *ocelotl* (tiger), *miquiztli* (death), *tecpatl* (flint), *itzcuintli* (dog), and *ehecatl* (wind) with the North. Together they form Northern time-place. These 5 day signs *take place* in the North, while the North *takes time* (occurs) during these 5 day signs. The 5 day signs *mazatl* (deer), *quiahuitl* (rain), *ozomatli* (monkey), *calli* (house), and *cuauhtli* (eagle) fuse with West (defined as where the Sun sets) to form Western time-place. The 5 day signs *xochitl* (flower), *malinalli* (grass), *cuetzpalin* (lizard), *cozcacuauhtli* (vulture), and *tochtli* (rabbit) fuse with South to form Southern time-place.[14]

Plate 1 of *Codex Fejérváry-Mayer* also includes a second, smaller, four-petaled flower in the shape of a St. Andrew's cross. Its four petals fit between the four petals of the larger "Greek cross" and map the when-where of the four intercardinal points: summer-solstice sunrise (upper-left petal), summer-solstice sunset (lower-left petal), winter-solstice sunset (lower-right petal), and winter-solstice sunrise (upper-right petal).

Temporal seasons and years likewise fuse with place. Spring consists of five Reed months and takes place in the Eastern quadrant. Summer consists of four Rabbit months and takes place in the Southern quadrant. Autumn consists of four House months and takes place in the Western quadrant. And winter consists of five Flint months and takes place in the Northern quadrant.[15] Years divide into four kinds of time-place: Reed or Eastern time-place years; Flint or Northern time-place years; House or Western time-place years; and Rabbit or Southern time-place years.[16]

7.2. THE TONALPOHUALLI

One of the most fundamental ontological expressions of the self-unfolding and self-faceting of teotl, reality, and the cosmos is the repeating pattern of 260 *tonalli*, or *tonalpohualli* ("count of the tonalli"). This repeating 260-fold pattern characterizes *how* the cosmos move-changes and processes. Expressed less statically, the tonalpohualli is an *immanent* patterning continually disclosed and displayed in the becoming of the cosmos (teotl). If we think of the cosmos as an ongoing weaving-in-progress, then the cosmos is constantly weaving itself in the pattern of the tonalpohualli. The tonalpohualli is metaphysically objective in the sense that it existed prior to the creation of humans and will continue to exist after their demise, and also in the sense that it characterizes the cosmos independently of humans' counting-reading-interpreting of it. Its objectivity is fully compatible with the fact that skilled diviners are able to interact with it in the course of divining its significance.[17]

The Aztecs recorded the tonalpohualli in the *tonalamatl* ("book of the tonallis"). The person who used the tonalamatl to count-read-interpret the tonalpohualli was called a *tonalpouhqui*. The activity of counting-reading-interpreting was called *tonalpohualiztli*.[18] In order to avoid confusion, we need to keep distinct the tonalpouhqui and the tonalamatl from *that which* the tonalamatl records and *that which* the tonalpouhqui counts-reads-interprets. And what is that? It is the 260 tonallis of the tonalpohualli.

The concept of tonalli is one of the most complex and difficult in Aztec metaphysics, and I can only touch upon its nature here.[19] The concept of tonalli incorporates a variety of ideas, including:

(1) Solar heat, heat-energy, or power (sometimes translated as "heat").[20]

(2) Solar radiation.

(3) Inner vital energy, life force, animating power, and energy that is transmitted and sensed as heat. Tonalli as life force contributes to the functioning of the total mind-body fusion of human beings (i.e., both physiologically and psychologically). *Tonalli* in this sense is sometimes translated as "soul" or "spirit."[21]

(4) Summertime.

(5) Time-place orientation or position in the overall tonalpohualli. In this way human beings are essentially timed and placed.[22]

(6) Day.

(7) Day sign.

(8) *Mahcehualli* – that is, birth-merit; allotment of quality and quantity of energy at birth; that which is granted one; that which is one's portion; and that which one is worthy of (deserves or merits) in the sense of being adequate to, suited to, fit for, or capable of earning. *Tonalli* in this sense sometimes translated as "fate" or "destiny."[23]

(9) Personal and calendrical name.

(10) Innate physiological, psychological, and mental vigor, character, or temperament.

(11) Face (*ixtli*), overall physical visage and its "doubles" – including one's resemblance to family members, artistic image, and reflection in mirrors and water. Each of the 260 days of the tonalpohualli has its own "face" (*ixtli*) – that is, identity or character. Those born on this day partake of this face. Events and processes occurring during the day are influenced by the day's face.

(12) Coessence (alternatively but less felicitously, *nagual*, spiritual alter ego, or companion animal): consists of two apparently distinct entities (e.g., human and animal) who share the same birth time-place, hence the same birth day sign, and hence the same birth-merit or birth-destiny. According to Monaghan, if personhood consists of having a specific destiny and having a specific destiny consists of being born at a specific time-place, then there can be no essential difference between beings born at the same time-place location. They are essentially one and the same self or person. A human and her coessence may, in addition, also share a consciousness.[24]

López Austin and McKeever Furst contend the various aspects of tonalli cluster around the notion of heat-light energy that radiates upon the earthly plane, principally from Tonatiuh.[25] Hunt situates tonalli within a cluster of ideas including fire, heat, power, energy, life force ("*élan vital*"), and human soul life.[26] Read attributes the existence of a close conceptual relationship in Aztec metaphysics between sun, energy, and heat, on the one hand, and existence, on the other.[27] The foregoing suggests an equally close relationship between qualitative differences in the 260 different kinds of tonalli and qualitative differences in existence itself.[28]

On its allotted day in the 260-day sequence of the tonalpohualli, each of the 260 tonallis diffuses "over the earth's surface, bathing and infiltrating all beings in the intermediate sector."[29] In doing so it energizes, influences, and transforms everything on the earth's surface. This was called the day's "burden."[30] The Aztecs believed tonalli is absorbed by and becomes lodged in humans, animals, and plants as well as fire, statues, people's shadows and reflections in water, gemstones, brilliantly colored avian feathers, warriors' costumes, and ritual objects. According to Bernardino de Sahagún, the name for fine turquoise, *teoxihuitl*, for example, derives from *teotl* and *xihuitl* ("turquoise"). Such gems embodied *itonal in teutl* ("the *tonalli* of *teotl*").[31]

In sum, *tonalli* includes within a single concept a variety of aspects that appear by our lights as distinct: heat, irradiation, destiny or birth merit, spatiotemporal orientation, life energy (*élan vital*, soul, spirit), vigor, coessence, and character. I accordingly propose translating *tonalli* as "day-force-heat-life-energy." We must remember there are 260 different kinds of tonalli, each of which constitutes a *qualitatively* unique force or energy. Moreover, each one admits of *quantitative* differences or degrees of intensity.

The tonalpohualli is an overarching and internally complex pattern that is immanent within the becoming and self-weaving of the cosmos and teotl. It is *how* teotl becomes. The complete tonalpohualli pattern is formed by the combination of two basic patterns. The first basic pattern consists of a repeating arrangement of twenty named tonallis. Each of the twenty is a different kind of tonalli. They are depicted graphically in the tonalamatl using twenty different day signs. The twentyfold ordering of the named tonallis is: crocodile (or earth monster), wind, house, lizard, serpent, death, deer, rabbit, water, dog, monkey, twisted grass (malinalli), reed, jaguar, eagle, vulture, movement (olin), flint, rain, and flower. Given the systematic coherence of Aztec metaphysics, it is reasonable to assume that this pattern is *not* an arbitrary "grabbag of disconnected symbols" (to borrow from John Bierhorst).[32] The tonalpohualli is an irreducible, brute fact about the way the cosmos (teotl) works, just as agonistic inamic unity is. In both cases, we hit metaphysical bedrock.

The second basic pattern consists of a repeating arrangement of thirteen numerals, running from 1 to 13. This group was called a *trecena* by the Spanish chroniclers. They are depicted graphically in the tonalamatl by dots. The aforementioned patterns combine to form a complete tonalpohualli pattern of these 260 different kinds of named-and-numbered tonallis and 20 groupings of 13 different kinds of named-and-numbered tonallis.

Aztec metaphysics maintains that numbers possess specific essences or personalities, and it is these that play a determining role in the working of the cosmos.[33] Numbers are thus neither abstract, Platonic-style entities nor mere symbols (numerals). They are concrete metaphysical forces that shape the unfolding and becoming of the cosmos. Each has a unique essence or personality; each is deemed propitious or unpropitious.[34] Numbers, their manifold properties, and their manifold interrelationships (including their qualitative and semiotic interrelationships with one another) contribute essentially to the tonalpohualli and hence to the patterns, rhythms, and cycles of the cosmos (teotl). Counting-reading-interpreting the tonalpohualli required an intimate understanding of these various attributes. Numerology – that is, deciphering the qualitative and semiotic properties of time-place numbers, periods, and cycles – played an essential role in this activity, too.

The twenty named tonalli and thirteen numbers combine to form the major tonalpohualli pattern of 260 (20 × 13) named-*and*-numbered units (tonalli or days): for example, 1 Cipactli, 2 Wind, 3 House, 4 Lizard, and so on. Each unit represents a unique *kind* of tonalli or day-force-heat-life-energy. After the completion of one 260-fold pattern the pattern begins anew. Thirteen named-and-numbered days constitute a 13-day ordering, or trecena. Each trecena begins with the number 1 and ends with the number 13. Employing the Aztec vigesimal counting system, the complete 260-fold tonalpohualli divides into twenty trecenas. The twenty trecenas were also ordered into 65-day groups of five trecenas each.

A third, less well-understood pattern ran concurrently with the 260-day tonalpohualli. It consisted of a repeating sequence of nine distinct forces of influence standardly referred to as "Lords of the Night."[35] Quiñones Keber refers to the Night Lords as "a set of fundamental divinatory patrons."[36] Each Night Lord named a different kind of nighttime power, efficacious during the Sun's nocturnal journey below the Earth's surface and through the Underworld. The nine appear to have sequentially influenced the nocturnal hours of successive days and to have represented the nocturnal processing and becoming of the cosmos. They are depicted in the tonalamatls by a distinct face or glyph. The repeating sequence of nine Night Lords ran alongside each trecena, so that thirteen (nine plus four) Night Lords were gathered with each trecena. Furthermore, the nine are not numbered – unlike the 260 days of the tonalpohualli – and they do not contribute to the count of 260 days of the tonalpohualli.[37]

Each trecena was also influenced by several additional forces: for example, one of twenty patron deities, one of thirteen Lords of the Day, and one of thirteen volatiles (twelve birds and one butterfly). Each trecena was thus constituted by the complex transformational confluence or interweaving of forces and influences: named-and-numbered days, patron deity, Night Lord, Day Lord, and volatile.[38]

The basic metaphysical unit of the tonalpohualli – that is, that which the tonalpohualli counts – appears to be the individual named-and-numbered tonalli (or day). Yet we must remember that this unit is also defined in terms of its relationships with the entire assemblage of forces depicted in a trecena panel. This is consonant with the fact that the fundamental epistemological and semiotic unit was the trecena. The tonalpouhqui took into account the entire assemblage of forces depicted in a trecena panel when counting-reading-interpreting an individual named-and-numbered tonalli.

The tonalamatl recorded the 260-fold pattern of the tonalpohualli along with the manifold forces of influence associated with them. The most common way of representing the tonalpohualli in Central Mexico was by dividing it into twenty trecena panels.[39] The artist-scribes depicted in each panel the complex confluence of powerful forces influencing a thirteen-day period. The tonalamatl functioned as a preeminently practical instrument or "guide for living" well on Tlalticpac.[40] It was first and foremost practical – not theoretical or descriptive. In this respect, the tonalamatl resembles instruments such as the medieval European seafarer's compass rose, which Charles Frake characterizes as a "cognitive map" of time, tide, place, and direction.[41] Frake's discussion suggests the Aztec tonalamatl (e.g., *Codex Fejérváry-Mayer*) functions similarly as a "cognitive map" and computational device. It orients humans regarding the currents of the 260 tonalli, the Night Lords, Day Lords, and so on, with the aim of helping them navigate these currents. Its purpose is to guide life, to edify, to cultivate proper character, and to shape future behavior.[42]

The Aztecs' attitude toward the tonalamatl is revealed in the following passage from their migration story. At some moment in the deep past of their migration, the Aztecs were abandoned by all but four of their wise men and priests in a place called Tamoanchan. Those who abandoned the Aztecs took away with them "the writings, the books, the paintings. They carried the knowledge; they carried all – the song books, the flutes."[43] Of the four who remained, one was named Oxomoco, another, Cipactonal. Acknowledging that the sun would continue to rise and shine, the four nevertheless worried about the future well-being of the Aztecs:

How will the common people live, how will they dwell? He is gone; they carried away the writings. And how will the common people dwell? How will the lands, the mountains be? How will all live? What will govern? What will rule? What will show the way? What will be the model, the standard? What will be the example? From what will the start be made? What will become of the torch, the light? Then they devised the book of days [*tonalpohualli*], the book of years [*xiuhamatl*], the count of the years [*xiuhpohualli*], the book of dreams [*temic amatl*]. They arranged the reckoning just as it has been kept.[44]

What exactly is the relationship between the daily changes in the 260-day tonalpohualli, on the one hand, and the changes in the cosmos and its contents, on the other? Davíd Carrasco speaks of the relationship in terms of supernatural causal influence.[45] Austin López states the tonalli were "diffused over the earth's surface, bathing and infiltrating all beings in the intermediate sector."[46] Jacques Soustelle offers the following analogy: "The world can be compared to a great stage upon which different multi-colored lights, controlled by a tireless mechanism, project reflections that follow one another after the other and overlap, maintaining for a limitless period an unalterable sequence."[47]

I find these characterizations too dualistic, deterministic, transcendent, and externalistic. There are *not* two distinct things: tonalpohualli and cosmos. The 260-day tonalpohualli does not exist apart from the unfolding of the cosmos. It is not a separate thing, transcendent of or external to the cosmos. The relationship between the 260-fold change in tonallis and corresponding 260-fold changes in the cosmos is not a mechanical, push-and-pull, cause-and-effect relationship of the sort modern Westerners commonly associate with astrology (i.e., in which distant planets and stars exert causal influence upon earthly events).

I submit instead that the tonalpohualli is an overarching pattern *immanent* within the becoming and unfolding of the cosmos and teotl. It is *how* teotl unfolds and becomes. I thus suggest we think of it in *adverbial* terms. The cosmos unfolds *tonalpohualishly* (to coin a monstrous neologism). The tonalpohualli is not a force or thing operating from outside the cosmos that causes things to happen in the cosmos. Changes in the tonalpohualli and changes in the cosmos are co-related aspects of a single pattern of changes. The changes named in the tonalpohualli happen *in* the cosmos – not *to* the cosmos. They are defining features of how the cosmos self-unfolds and becomes. The relationship between the 260-fold change in tonalli and the 260-fold changes in the cosmos is more analogous to the constellation of regular, periodic changes that we associate with tidal or seasonal rhythms and cycles – changes that are myriad, mutually interactive, co-related, multilinear, and holistic. The changes one observes during autumn, for example, are not caused by some transcendent entity named "autumn"; rather, they are constitutive of autumn. *Autumn* is the name of the overall constellation of these changes. One might object, however, that this analogy is flawed since modern Western science regards seasonal and tidal changes as caused by distant causal agents, the sun and moon (respectively). So we might try improving Soustelle's analogy by replacing his 260 multicolored lights with 260 multicolored blushes. On the day of its ascendancy during the 260-unit sequence, each tonalli *suffuses* the cosmos. Each tonalli suffuses the cosmos *from within* – *not from without or from on high* – just as we think of the blush of a person as suffusing her face as the blood rushes within her face, or as we think of the color-changes suffusing a chameleon's skin. However, I think even this revised analogy is too dualistic.

Let's try another tack. The relationship between changes in the tonalpohualli and changes in the cosmos is more analogous to the contemporary biological understanding of biorhythms (such as annual or circadian rhythms in plants and animals) or biological cycles (such as estrous cycles in female nonprimate mammals). These consist of regular patterns of periodic changes in behavior or physiology. They are said to be regulated by the organism's own *internal* biological clock.[48] The changes are immanent; they unfold from within. They happen *in* the animals, not *to* the animals. They are an expression of the organism's own internal self-regulation, not some sort of external regulation. Earlier changes (events or stages) in cycles do not cause (at least in the mechanical sense) later changes, although it is true that the latter would not occur had the former not occurred and that the former may influence the latter.

I suggest such a biological analogy is more apt and illuminating for understanding the tonalpohualli.[49] If one thinks of the cosmos as a large organism, then the tonalpohualli represents the *internal* biological clock of the cosmos. The 260 tonallis name these changes, and the tonalamatl is a practical guide for navigating these changes. Everything happening in the cosmos, on earth, and in the lives of human beings is at one and the same time an aspect and element of the constellation of 260 tonalli changes mapped by the tonalamatl. The sequence of changes constitutes an objective pattern or design manifested by teotl in the course of its continual self-unfolding, self-faceting, and self-weaving. The tonalpohualli is therefore not imposed from outside of the cosmos or outside the Fifth Sun-Earth Age – from, say, Omeyocan. It is not transcendent. Rather, the tonalpohualli is the immanent self-disclosing of teotl: a pattern in the unfolding of teotl *out of itself.*

The analogy with biorhythms and biological clocks has the additional virtue of helping us see our way past Soustelle's view that "In such a world, change is not conceived as the result of a gradual evolving or 'becoming' in time, but rather as a brusque and complete mutation. . . . The law of the universe is the succession of different and radically separated qualities which alternately prevail, disappear and reappear without end."[50] The changes of the tonalpohualli are neither random nor "brusque"; they are elements of a periodically orchestrated pattern of changes.

For an analogy better grounded in indigenous ways of thinking, let's return to Aztec metaphysics' own root metaphors. Aztec metaphysics conceives the cosmos as a grand, ongoing weaving-in-progress. According to this way of thinking, the cosmos (teotl) is continually weaving itself in the pattern of the 260-fold tonalpohualli. Teotl discloses this pattern in the course of its self-weaving. It is *how* teotl weaves itself. Chapter 8 argues that the 260-day tonalpohualli constitutes the warp pattern in teotl's weaving of the cosmos. A textile's design is immanent. The design discloses itself in the course of weaving. (It is not added after the weaving is completed, as is the case with embroidery.)[51] What's more, the design is in a sense adverbial; that is, one weaves designedly. It is *how* one weaves – not *what* one weaves. The design is *how* the textile is woven. The tonalpohualli is thus one of the ways by which the cosmos weaves itself.

Understanding the tonalpohualli as a pattern in the ongoing self-weaving of the cosmos gains further support when we remember that Tlazolteotl-Ixcuina, the great genetrix, mother goddess, conceiver, and parturient is also the great cosmic spinner and weaver and also the patroness of the tonalpouhqui (as well as those who interpret cast grains and knotted cords).[52] After all, who better to understand the significance of the tonalpohualli than she who weaves the cosmos in a tonalpohualli way? As I earlier quoted Thelma Sullivan, "Weaving and spinning represent life, death, and rebirth in a continuing cycle that characterizes the essential nature of the Mother Goddess."[53] Now we see that the tonalpohualli is an essential aspect of her weaving of life, death, and rebirth. It is *how* she weaves the fabric of the cosmos.

7.3. THE XIHUITL OR XIUHPOHUALLI

The Aztecs counted-read-interpreted a second repeating pattern of days in addition to the tonalpohualli. Scholars commonly refer to this as the *xiuhpohualli* or *xihuitl*. The Aztecs recorded the xiuhpohualli or xihuitl in the *xiuhamatl* or "book of the years," which Fray Toribio de Benavente Motolinía calls the *xiuhtonalamatl* ("year day book").[54] These books were used to organize public festivals and as the format for the recording of historical events and personages.[55]

The xiuhpohualli consisted of the 360+5–day pattern of the vague solar year. *Xiuhpohualli* means "count of years."[56] It represents a second, fundamental onto-logical expression of and ontogenetic development in the self-unfolding and self-faceting of teotl – and thus a second, fundamental ontological expression of the continual becoming of the cosmos. Like the tonalpohualli, the xiuhpo-hualli is essentially an energy pattern continually disclosed and displayed in the becoming of the cosmos. Also like the tonalpohualli, it is an objective ordering of the cosmos: an objective fact about the path taken by some aspect of the cos-mos as the cosmos unfolds and processes. If we think of the cosmos as an ongo-ing work-of-self-weaving-in-progress, then the cosmos is continually weaving itself in the pattern of the 360+5–day xiuhpohualli. It thus constitutes a second, immanent design woven into the fabric of the cosmos; one of the ways in which and by which the cosmos weaves itself. Alternatively, if we see the cosmos as a large biological organism, then the xiuhpohualli represents a second internal biorhythm. Chapter 8 argues the 360+5–day xiuhpohualli constitutes a second warp pattern in the fabric of the cosmos.

The xiuhpohualli ran concurrently with the tonalpohualli. It employed the 260 named-and-numbered days of the tonalpohualli, as it had no independent way of referring to days.[57] It consisted of eighteen *meztli* ("moons") of twenty tonalpohualli named and numbered days. These were later called "months" and *veintenas* ("twenties") by the Spanish chroniclers. Each of the eighteen meztli was dominated by a specific "deity" (sacred force). A special feast dedicated to this deity occurred on its last day. The xiuhpohualli was used to organize the eighteen "monthly" public festivals. Their sum came to 360 days. Five days, called *nemontemi*, were added to complete the 365-day solar year. These five belonged to no twenty-day grouping and were not associated with any specific "deity" (sacred force). They were considered extremely dangerous.

Molina defines *xihuitl* as "year, turquoise, grass, comet [meteor]."[58] Campbell adds "leaf" and "heat."[59] Related constructions include *moxiuhtotia* ("for a tree to sprout leaves, or become covered with them") and *tlaxiuhcaltia* ("for a field to turn green").[60] The general concept of xihuitl thus appears to incorporate a family of notions including sun, heat, year, green plants, verdant power and growth, and preciousness.[61] The Sun generates heat and makes life possible on Tlalticpac – that precious green, middle layer of the Fifth Age. Aztec metaphys-ics thus associates the Sun with heat, energy, growth, greenness, and existence.

The tonalpohualli and xiuhpohualli run concurrently with one another and complete their respective patterns at the same point once every 52 solar years. The Aztecs called this 52-year pattern a *xiuhmolpilli* or "Binding of the Years." Teotl weaves the fabric of the cosmos in tonalpohualli and xiuhpohualli patterns in such a way that they are nested within the larger xiuhmolpilli pattern. The xiuhmolpilli "binds" tonalli and xihuitl energies together within a larger pattern. Like tonalpohualli and xiuhpohualli, the xiuhmolpilli is metaphysically objective; immanent rather than transcendent; continually disclosing and manifesting itself in the becoming of the cosmos; and a pattern of energy.

The xiuhmolpilli demonstrates another close relationship between the Sun, energy, and heat, on the one hand, and existence, on the other. The interweaving of the qualitative differences between the 260 kinds of tonalli together with the 360+5 kinds of xihuitl into the 52-year xiuhmolpilli suggests a further fine-graining of the relationship between the quality of energy and the quality of existence.[62] I suggest the 52-year xiuhmolpilli constitutes an overarching warp pattern in the fabric of the cosmos.

The addition of the xiuhmolpilli gives us a more complete idea of the complex constellation of mutually interacting energies constituting the character of time-place. As López Austin writes:

> Thus, an hour of the day had characteristics determined by being a moment of night or day; by the influence of a sign (one among the twenty day names) and a number (one among thirteen) in a cycle of 260 days; by the group of thirteen to which it belonged; by its month (among eighteen) and its position within the month (among twenty); by the year (among fifty-two), which in its turn, was marked by the destiny of a sign (among four) and a number (among thirteen); and so on, successively through the sequence of other cycles.[63]

7.4. AZTEC COSMOGONY

COSMOGONY IN THE *HISTORIA DE LOS MEXICANOS POR SUS PINTURAS*, *HISTOYRE DU MECHIQUE*, AND *LEYENDA DE LOS SOLES*

In order to understand better the nature of time-place as an aspect of teotl, we need to examine the Aztec metaphysics' account of the genesis of the cosmos. What follows relies primarily upon the *Historia de los mexicanos por sus pinturas* but at times turns to the *Histoyre du Mechique* and the *Leyenda de los soles* (*Legend of the Suns*).[64] In addition to their ritual, political, pedagogical, and literary properties, these texts contain information concerning Aztec cosmogony. I focus upon the latter with an eye for what the texts tell us about time-place.[65]

The *Historia de los mexicanos por sus pinturas* (which H. B. Nicholson characterizes as "very close to the 'official' account of Tenochtitlan") offers the following account of the history of cosmos.[66] It begins by stating that the Mexicanos had one god, whom they called Tonacatecuhtli (male aspect) and Tonacacihuatl (female aspect). This male~female deity created itself and has always existed in the thirteenth sky or heaven ("*cielo*"). Its beginning was never known.[67] Tonacatecuhtli~Tonacacihuatl constitutes a seamless agonistic inamic unity characterized by full male and female characteristics and possessing full male and female generative and regenerative powers.

Strictly speaking, therefore, there is *no beginning* to the cosmos as recounted by the *Historia*. There has always been Tonacatecuhtli~Tonacacihuatl. Since he~she is defined by agonistic inamic unity, it follows that agonistic inamic unity is a metaphysically primordial and fundamental ordering. It is primordial since it exists from the very beginning, if indeed it even makes sense to speak of a beginning. Tonacatecuhtli~Tonacacihuatl exhausts reality, and reality is processive and defined by agonistic inamic unity. The *Historia* does not speak of a time before the existence of Tonacatecuhtli~Tonacacihuatl, nor does it speak of ex nihilo creation or of the imposition of order upon nothingness or chaos. The text begins with darkness (as there exists no sun) but there is no evidence to suggest that it equates darkness with chaos or nothingness (as many world cosmogonies do). The *Historia* does not talk of a primordial or transcendent time, or of a timeless time before historical time. It speaks only of the always already existence of Tonacatecuhtli~Tonacacihuatl.

If it is appropriate to speak of there existing a cosmos at this point (and I think it is), then the cosmos is wholly identical with Tonacatecuhtli~Tonacacihuatl. And Tonacatecuhtli~Tonacacihuatl (as previous chapters have shown) is identical with Ometecuhtli~Omecihuatl and ultimately Ometeotl, the primordial, male~female unity from which everything is continually generated and regenerated – including humans, Sun-Earth Orderings, and all other "gods" – and upon which the continuing existence of everything depends. As León-Portilla puts it, Ometeotl is "root and support" of the cosmos.[68] Fray Gerónimo de Mendieta tells us this primordial, creative male~female unity was also called *moyucoyatzin áyac oquiyocux, áyac oquipic*, meaning "no one formed him or gave him existence."[69] This appellation suggests Ometeotl is self-generating and has always existed. Agonistic inamic unity and dual-aspect monism (i.e., unified twoness and twofold oneness) define Ometeotl, primordial existence, and all existing things. Dennis Tedlock writes, "Duality belongs to the very nature of the primordial world and to anything that might be created in that world."[70]

Tonacatecuhtli~Tonacacihuatl's role as progenitor~progenetrix of all things implies his~her continual sexual commingling (and interweaving) of him~her self with him~her self, hence his~her continual nepantla-defined agonistic interaction and motion-change, and hence his~her nepantla-generated unity. He~she unifies male~female inamic partners by means of a nepantla-defined process of reciprocal, back-and-forth interweaving and commingling that is continually creatively destructive, destructively creative, and hence continually transformative. In short, Tonacatecuhtli~Tonacacihuatl – and hence reality and everything he~she continually generates – are defined by *always already* nepantla-defined motion-change and processing. *Nepantla-defined agonistic inamic activity and nepantla motion-change are therefore cosmogonically primordial and metaphysically fundamental.*

From Tonacatecuhtli~Tonacacihuatl's continuing sexual commingling come all other gods and all five Sun-Earth Eras. The *Historia de los mexicanos por sus pinturas* states Tonacatecuhtli~Tonacacihuatl engendered four sons: Tlatlauhqui Tezcatlipoca ("Red Smoking Mirror," also called "Red Tezcatlipoca"), Yayauhqui Tezcatlipoca ("Black Smoking Mirror," also called "Black Tezcatlipoca"), Quetzalcoatl (also called "Yohualli Ehecatl"), and Omitecuhtli ("Lord Bone") or Maquizcoatl ("Bracelet Serpent"), called "Huitzilopochtli" by the Aztecs.[71] "These four gods," writes León-Portilla, "constitute the primary forces that activate the history of the world."[72] I interpret them as four facets in the unfolding of Tonacatecuhtli~Tonacacihuatl. The primordial twofold processing of the cosmos iterates into fourfold processing. The inamic pairs of agonistic inamic unity differentiate themselves into complementary quadruplicity.

Paragraph 11 of the *Historia* states next that 600 years ("*años*") passed during which the gods did nothing, and that the 600 years were counted by "twenties."[73] At some point apparently, Tonacatecuhtli~Tonacacihuatl generated the metaphysical pattern of twenty. This represents a further stage in the self-differentiation of the cosmos and a further stage in teotl's self-becoming. This statement contains the first explicit mention of time and the counting of time in the *Historia*. The fact that it discusses Tonacatecuhtli~Tonacacihuatl in this way suggests (1) the dynamic pair is a complete or whole unit of twenty; (2) each of the four sons equals a count of five, since their sum equals twenty, the full count represented by their parents; (3) the processive unfolding of Tonacatecuhtli~Tonacacihuatl either constitutes or occurs during vigesimally counted time; and (4) the sacred energy-in-motion of Tonacatecuhtli~Tonacacihuatl has now self-differentiated into twenty *pilli*, or units.

The statement also suggests time is being measured by twenties and hence the differentiation of sacred energy-in-motion into the pattern of twenty different kinds of tonalli counted by day signs of the tonalpohualli. However, this is deeply puzzling for several reasons. First and foremost, there is no mention of the pattern of thirteen numerical coefficients that runs concurrently with the pattern of the twenty days. But without these there can be no 260 named-and-numbered tonalli and therefore no full count and complete tonalpohualli. But without the thirteen count and without the tonalpohualli's 260 named-and-numbered days, there can be no xiuhpohualli or xihuitl and also no 52-year cycle or xiuhmopilli. Solar years cannot be properly named and counted since solar years are given names from the tonalpohualli. Second, tonalli as *day*-force-heat-life-energy is closely related to the sun. But with no sun as yet existing, how are we to understand the notion of *day* and hence tonalli itself?

In sum, are we to understand this moment in the history of the cosmos as merely an inchoate or formative stage in the generation of the complete 260-day count or tonalpohualli? The opening passage of the *Historia* states Tonacatecuhtli~Tonacacihuatl exists in the thirteen levels of the sky. Does the thirteen-day pattern of numbers derive from this? It isn't clear. The text here poses vexing questions of interpretation.

Paragraph 11 also states that "the gods did nothing" *("no hicieron cosa alguna los dioses")* during these 600 years. But what exactly does this mean? From what succeeds this statement in the text, the statement would appear to be saying the gods did not further self-differentiate or self-unfold into anything new, such as water, Underworld, humans, or Suns. Yet they did, however, remain active since they continued regenerating themselves. Tonacatecuhtli~Tonacacihuatl continued regenerating itself and his~her four sons through his~her continuous nepantla-defined sexual self-commingling, self-weaving, and inamic self-unifying. Hence, from the fact that no further self-unfolding occurred we cannot conclude (*pace* López Austin and Carrasco, as we will see below) that the 600 years were without struggle, activity, and motion-change.

After the 600 years passed, the four sons convened and decided it was time to arrange what was to follow and to establish the pattern and path to be followed. Having been assigned the task of initiating the creative process, Quetzalcoatl and Huitzilopochtli generated fire and a half-sun. However this half-sun lacked the power to cast anything but the dimmest light since it was incomplete. Did this half-sun move? What is its relationship with the twenty-day count? Did its movement create days? Is the concept of *day* defined in terms of this half-sun? The *Historia* does not say.

Quetzalcoatl and Huitzilopochtli generate the first man and woman, Oxomoco and Cipactonal, who represent a further unfolding of Tonacatecuhtli~Tonacacihuatl.[74] (Oxomoco's and Cipactonal's sexes are reversed in Sahagún, *Florentine Codex*, IV:4, and in *Codex Borbonicus*, plate 21.)[75] Oxomoco and Cipactonal give birth to *macehualtin*, human beings. The gods assign the two gender-specific activities. To Oxomoco, they assign tilling the land; to Cipactonal, spinning and weaving. They give Cipactonal the gifts of curing and divining by means of casting maize kernels. The text, curiously, makes no mention of Cipactonal's divining by means of the tonalpohualli. Paragraph 20 of the *Historia* continues: "Then they made the days and divided them into months, and gave to each one twenty days, and so they had eighteen, and 360 days in the year."[76] Carrasco interprets this as claiming that Quetzalcoatl and Huitzilopochtli created the calendar by dividing time into eighteen months of twenty days.[77] This count measures the xihuitl, or solar year, and since the xihuitl is derivative upon the tonalpohualli, this means the tonalpohualli must now exist.[78]

The *Annals of Cuauhtitlan* states, "the year count, the day sign count, and the count of each twenty-day period were made the responsibility of those humans known as Oxomoco and Cipactonal."[79] Book IV of the *Florentine Codex* likewise states, "And this count of days . . . was an invention of the two called and named Oxomoco [here, a female] and Cipactonal [here, a male], who gave it to the people. They were readers of the day signs [and] lords of all the day count."[80] The first illustration of Book IV depicts the pair facing one another engaged in the act of divining (by casting maize kernels and counting knotted cord but not by counting the tonalamatl). Annotator Hand 3 of *Codex Vaticanus 3738 A* also credits Oxomoco and Cipactonal with inventing the tonalamatl.[81] Mendieta relates that Quetzalcoatl met with Cipactonal and Oxomoco in a cave and together all three created the calendar. He gave Cipactonal the privilege of naming the first day sign.[82]

Scholars widely regard this as the beginning of the counting of the 260 days (tonalpohualli) as well as the beginning of the art of divination. Oxomoco and/or Cipactonal are the first diviners to employ the count (if not also the inventors of the count). Boone describes them as "the prototypal diviners."[83] López Austin writes, "the calendar was born with them, making Oxomoco and Cipactonal the first diviners and the first persons familiar with the chronological count."[84] They invented the day count as well as the art of divination. Because they named the periods of time and were "protectors of each of the 'months' or twenties," he writes, "they are constantly linked to time-destiny and to the calendar."[85] Furthermore, because spinning and weaving are female activities, spinning and weaving are thereby associated with counting-reading-interpreting the tonalpohualli. Finally, these passages strongly suggest that both the tonalpohualli and xihuitl existed *prior* to the series of five Suns and five Sun-Earth Ages.

The foregoing raises several additional puzzles. First, if the tonalpohualli only comes into existence with Oxomoco and Cipactonal, then how were the prior "600 years" during which "the gods did nothing" counted? This appears to contradict the *Historia* when it states earlier that the 600 years were "counted by twenties." Second, what, if anything, is the relationship between the tonalpohualli and the half-sun that exists at this point? Is the concept of tonalli as day-force-heat-life-energy defined in terms of this half-sun? What is the relevant notion of day? Is this half-sun strong enough to generate 260 different kinds of day-force-heat-life-energy and the 360-day year? Or does this task require the more complete and vigorous suns of the five Sun-Earth Ages created later? Lastly, why are Oxomoco and Cipactonal not depicted counting the tonalpohualli?

Quetzalcoatl and Huitzilopochtli then create Mictlantecuhtli~Mictecacihuatl, Lord~Lady of the Underworld ("*infierno*"), and the heavens beyond ("*allende*") the thirteenth. They make the waters in which they place the *cipactli*, a huge caiman, from whom they later form the earth. All four brothers then come together to create the paired gods of water.[86] With this, claims León-Portilla, "the gods began the history of the universe."[87] The account offered by the *Historia* reveals the basic vertical arranging of the cosmos into upper (heavens), lower (Mictlan), and middle (Earth) layers. This basic ordering exists prior to the Fifth Age and therefore is not unique to it. Upper, lower, middle layers exist in some form or another during all five Sun-Earth Ages.

Chapter 3 of the *Historia* opens: "All of the aforementioned was done and created without counting the years; it was together and without any difference of time" ("*Todo lo susodicho fue fecho y criado que en ello pongan cuenta de año, sino que fue junto y sin diferencia de tiempo*").[88] But doesn't this contradict the statements that Tonacatecuhtli~Tonacacihuatl had always existed in the thirteenth level of the sky, and that the gods did nothing for 600 years? In particular, doesn't the latter statement presuppose counting time? The possibility of internal inconsistency raises the question, "How are we to interpret the *Historia*?" Are we to do so as a straightforward (by our lights) linear chronology of the history of the cosmos; as a less straightforward (by our lights) cyclical chronology of the unfolding of the cosmos; figuratively, as a work of literature; performatively, as a ritual text or cognitive mapping; or as some combination of these? What is the status of the claim about 600 years? Are the *Historia*'s temporal claims and dates linear-historical, cyclical-historical, figurative, or ritual? I return to this issue below.

Florescano reads the passage as saying, "The first creation of the universe was done 'together and without any time difference'... when time was not yet counted, nor were the days, years, or ages."[89] He contends the *Historia* recounts three cosmogonic creations: "the first creation of the universe"; the creation of "the cyclical creation of the suns"; and "the creation of the Fifth, or Movement, Sun."[90] The first creation, "the primitive creation," which includes the creation of the half-sun, Oxomoco and Cipactonal, and the "primordial earth, heavens and waters," occurs "simultaneously" and "in a moment without time."[91]

Florescano also appears to think the first creation occurs ex nihilo. Before the creation of the first Sun (in paragraph 32 of the *Historia*), Florescano claims there is an absence of "temporality, chronological references, and movement." This, he contends, is explained by the fact that the half-sun generates insufficient energy "to give the universe full life."[92]

Although not implausible, I find Florescano's interpretation unpersuasive. First, the *Historia* strongly suggests that Tonacatecuhtli~Tonacacihuatl always existed and that no creation ex nihilo ever occurred. It suggests the cosmos underwent continual generation and regeneration – that is, movement – before and during the creation of the half-sun, Oxomoco and Cipactonal, and the "primordial earth, heavens and waters." Second, his interpretation appears to contradict the earlier statements in the *Historia* dating the creation of the tonalpohualli conjointly with the creation of Oxomoco and Cipactonal. Third, it rests upon two unsupported assumptions: first, the weakness of the half-sun explains why the events of the primordial cosmos creation lacked temporality; and second, time is materially if not also conceptually tied to the five Suns.

One might instead interpret this passage as making the far weaker claim that the period preceding the creation of the First Sun-Earth Age was not *counted* or *countable* by the tonalpohualli or xiuhpohualli. But this does not entail that time did not pass or did not exist, since it leaves open the possibility that this period was characterized by a different *kind of time*: one not patterned and countable by the tonalpohualli or xiuhpohualli. Florescano's interpretation assumes there is only one kind of time: that which is counted by the tonalpohualli. But this assumption is unwarranted. The primordial movement and hence time of Tonacatecuhtli~Tonacacihuatl was simply not metaphysically suited to be counted by the xiuhpohualli or tonalpohualli. Upon the creation of the First Sun-Earth Age, there emerged a *kind of time* that was appropriately patterned and suited. Before this point, the cosmos was nevertheless characterized by continual motion-change, process, and hence time. As for the claim about 600 years, it may represent the *Historia's* authors' anachronistic projection of the tonalpohualli and xiuhpohualli back onto the primordial past; or, the number may have ritual or figurative significance. In sum, I see no reason to embrace Florescano's interpretation.

Chapter 4 of the *Historia* opens as follows: "And because the counting commences with this first sun and the counting figures advance forward continuously, leaving behind the six hundred years, which began with the birth of the gods."[93] A new count begins with the emergence of the First Sun-Earth Age, "leaving behind" ("*dejando atras*") the last 600 years, which began with the birth of Tonacatecuhtli's~Tonacacihuatl's four sons. The counting of days thus begins with the creation of the First Sun-Earth Age. According to the text, a year consists of 360 days or eighteen 20-day "months." There are also five unnamed days. According to the new count, a "century" ("*el grande año*") consists of 52 solar years.[94] The xihuitl or xiuhpohualli begins with the creation of the first Sun. And this makes sense, seeing as the xiuhpohualli is a count of the 360+5-day vague solar year. Florescano thus appears to be correct about the xihuitl, but what about the tonalpohualli? Does it begin at this point as he claims, or does it begin earlier with the creation of Oxomoco and Cipactonal? The *Historia* does not say.

The creation and destruction of first four Ages follows next – a history defined by the agonistic struggle between the four sons. Tenochtitlan's canonical version of the four eras is preserved in the *Historia de los mexicanos por sus pinturas* and the *Leyenda de los soles* (*Legend of the Suns*).[95] The cosmos undergoes the creation and destruction of four distinct Sun-Earth Ages. Each Sun (along with its associated direction, quadrant, color, and element) defines a Sun-Earth Era. No Era lasts, as it is eventually undone by the opposition of the other brothers. Leon-Portilla writes, "with a dialectical rhythm which attempted in vain to harmonize the dynamism of opposing forces, the various Suns appeared and vanished."[96] The successive creation and destruction of the first four Eras culminates in the creation of the current Fifth Sun-Earth Era.

Chapter 4 argued in favor of characterizing these five as "Sun-Earth" ages, eras, orderings, or creations-and-destructions rather than as "cosmic," "solar," "world," or "earth" ages. All five appear divided into three major layers – upper, lower and middle – with nine minor layers (nine upper skies or heavens) above, and nine minor layers (nine places of death) below the earthly layer. What changes across eras is the nature of the Sun, the middle (earthly) layer, and the middle layer's inhabitants.[97] It is misleading, therefore, to characterize these changes as "cosmic changes" and the eras as "cosmic eras" when the entire cosmos does not undergo destruction and recreation. Since Sun and Earth are the primary objects of change, calling these *Sun-Earth Ages* seems most precise. *Sun-Earth* also emphasizes the ordering role of the Sun in the Sun-Earth fusion defining each Age.

Each Age has its own kind of Sun. The *Historia* states Black Tezcatlipoca made himself into the Sun of the first Age (apparently either replacing completely or transforming the dim, half-sun created earlier). Quetzalcoatl transformed himself into the second Sun and Tlalocantecuhtli ("Lord of the Underworld") became the third Sun while Quetzalcoatl installed Chalchiuhtlicue as the fourth.[98] Each Age had its own kind of human being or human-like being that was destroyed along with the Age and then transformed into the human-like being that emerged in the succeeding Age. Each Age is named by the tonalpo-huaili date (day sign) of its cataclysmic destruction, which also designates the force that defines the nature ("heart") of the Age and destroys the Age.[99] Each of the four first Sun-Earth Ages is associated with one of the four elemental forces of the cosmos: telluric (earth), wind (air), igneous (fire), and aqueous (water) (respectively). These four form oppositional pairs: wind and fire as male, dry, hot, and light; water and earth as female, wet, cold, and heavy.[100] They are aspects of the sacred force of teotl (Ometeotl), part of what Eva Hunt calls the "complex transformation taxonomy" of Mesoamerican thought.[101]

The *Legend of the Suns* offers an account that varies slightly from the *Historia*'s account. It states that the Sun of the first Sun-Earth Age was Ocelotonatiuh ("4 Ocelotl Sun"). The Age was destroyed on the day 4 Ocelotl by earthly energy. It was associated with the earth and destroyed by telluric energy (in this case a jaguarlike earth monster).[102] Tezcatlipoca served as the first Sun. The second age was named 4 Ehecatonatiuh ("4 Wind Sun"). It was associated with the element of wind or air, and destroyed by wind force. Quetzalcoatl served as the second Sun. The third age was 4 Tletonatiuh ("4 Fire Sun"). It was associated with the element of fire, and was destroyed by igneous power. Tezcatlipoca served as the third Sun. The Sun of the fourth age was named 4 Atonatiuh ("4 Water Sun"). It was associated with water and destroyed by aqueous force. Quetzalcoatl served as the Sun of this era.[103]

The four Suns possess the names they do because their names indicate the kind of elemental force that destroys their respective Ages. However, they also possess the names they do "because they were named according to what they did or what was attributed to them," as paragraph 12 of the *Historia* states when talking about the names and characteristics of Tonacacihuatl's~Tonacatecuhtli's four sons.[104] A thing's name indicates the nature of its power, and since a thing's power constitutes its essence, its name reveals its essence. The first Sun was therefore defined by telluric power; the second, wind power; the third, igneous power; and the fourth, aqueous power. The first four, therefore, were not Suns in the same sense as the current Sun, 4 Olin Tonatiuh Motion. Indeed, they would not appear to be Suns in a way that we can even understand. Finally, since an Age is defined by its kind of Sun, it follows that the entire First Age was defined by telluric energy; the Second, wind energy; the Third, igneous energy, and the Fourth, by aqueous energy.

The Fifth Age is named after its Sun, 4 Olin Tonatiuh ("4 Motion Sun"), of which the *Annals of Cuauhtitlan* states, "It moves, it follows its path."[105] Olin motion-change refers its essence ("heart") and its mode of destruction. 4 Olin Tonatiuh undulates and pulsates. It arranges time-place into the four horizontal (nonhierarchical) cardinal and intercardinal directions. It creates east, north, west, south, and center. Its daily and annual centered oscillating lays out the four elemental forces (colors, etc.) into the *horizontal* pattern of four cardinal directions and regions as well as creates center and periphery.[106] Susan Gillespie argues cosmograms such as *Codex Fejérváry-Mayer* (pl. 1) and *Codex Mendoza* (fol. 2r) accordingly highlight the Aztecs' concern with "the horizontality of lived space on the earth's surface" and emphasize "the location of figures, objects, or qualities in the spatial [and temporal] extension between the cosmic center and the differentiated categories of the horizontal periphery."[107] Olin motion-change assigns each place a time and each time a place. Aztec astronomy is therefore not surprisingly a "horizon astronomy."[108]

The fact that the Fifth Sun is the only Sun whose essence is motion-change, makes one wonder, did the first four Suns move-change, and if so, how? Did they move-change in the same way as 4 Olin Tonatiuh? Did they unify the four elemental forces into four cardinal directions plus a center? Neither the *Annals of Cuauhtitlan*, the *Legend of the Suns*, nor the *Historia* explicitly mentions that the first four Suns moved. The *Historia* tells us that the four Ages were counted using the xiuhpohualli and tonalpohualli, but this tells us that their Suns' moving was *counted*, not *how* the Suns moved. Since process metaphysics maintains everything move-changes, it must be the case that the first four Suns move-changed. But what did their motion-change look like? It is natural to suppose they did so according to their respective natures and hence in telluric, windy, igneous, and watery ways. But how does a telluric, windy, igneous, or aqueous Sun move-change? Does it follow a path across the sky? Does it rise and set? Does it create four directions? Because the first four Ages lacked an olin-moving Sun, it would appear they lacked the four cardinal directions and regions. There was no East, North, West, and South, just as there was neither center nor periphery. These appear to be unique to the time-place arranged by 4 Olin Tonatiuh. It thus appears time-place itself has a different face (*ixtli*) during each of the five Ages – just as it had a different face prior to the five Ages. If the first four Suns moved, it seems they did so in ways barely imaginable. In light of the foregoing I suggest *Codex Mendoza* (fol. 2r) and *Codex Fejérváry Mayor* (pl. 1) are cosmograms neither of the cosmos per se nor of the first four Ages but of the Fifth Age *only*.

Unlike the first four Ages, the Fifth is created by Quetzalcoatl and Tezcatli-poca in cooperation with one another. Unlike the preceding four Ages that are defined each by one of four elemental powers (telluric, windy, igneous, and aqueous), the Fifth is defined by motion-change.[109] Olin is not a primordial force as earth, wind, fire, and water are, and it is not uniquely associated with one of Tonacatecuhtli's~Tonacacihuatl's four sons as are earth, wind, fire, and water. Instead, 4 Olin Tonatiuh's olin motion-change brings together the four primordial forces into agonistic inamic balance with one another. Elzey claims the Fifth Age thus constitutes the "synthesis,"[110] and León-Portilla, the "harmony," of the four sons and four dominant forces of the preceding four Ages.[111] This fact also explains why the Fifth Age is so fragile. Olin introduces something else wholly novel to the sequence of Ages: the center as a fifth direction. Olin-style motion and centeredness are intrinsically connected. Center emerges as a consequence of the dynamic, agonistic balancing of the four directions. The Fifth Sun's olin-style motion centers the Fifth Age and arranges time-place into a quincunx or quatrefoil.

The creation of humankind, according to the *Historye du Mechique* and the *Legend of the Suns*, involved Ehecatl-Quetzalcoatl's traveling to Mictlan in order obtain the bones of the human-like beings of the preceding Age. After a series of trials and tribulations, Ehecatl-Quetzalcoatl brought the bones to Tamoanchan, where Cihuacoatl ground them into meal. The addition of Quetzalcoatl's penis blood, obtained through autosacrifice, transforms the bone meal into the current race of human beings.[112] Both texts state that these events transpired in darkness, as the Fifth Sun did not yet exist.[113] According to Sahagún's account of the creation of the Fifth Sun, the gods met in Teotihuacan "when it was still the dark-place time. . . . When there was not yet day."[114] The *Legend* and *Annals* likewise state it was dark for twenty-five years between the destruction of the Fourth Age and the creation of the Fifth Sun.[115] During the interstices of the Sun-Earth Eras, there were no Suns and no sunlight. The Sun of the preceding Era had been destroyed while the Sun of the succeeding Era had yet to be created.

During the dark, sunless interstices of the five Ages, did the tonalpohualli keep running? Did the cosmos continue unfolding in the pattern of the tonalpohualli? Did the 260 units (tonalli-days) of the tonalpohualli continue unfolding? And what about the xihuitl? Elzey believes these transitional "intervals stand outside measured and structured time and space."[116] In this respect they resemble other "unclassified and unstructured periods of time" such as the five unnamed days that occur at the end of each xihuitl, and the time between 52-year cycles. Elzey believes such transitional intervals are "homologous" with the period of darkness between the Fourth and Fifth Sun-Earth Ages.[117] Elzey thus believes the tonalpohualli and xiuhpohualli do not apply to these transitional periods and that therefore that which they count-read-interpret does not exist during these periods. Although he does not explicitly say, Elzey's reasoning applies mutatis mutandis to the cosmos prior to the five Suns. Neither tonalpohualli nor xihuitl would seem to have existed prior to the first Sun by

Elzey's reasoning. Both come into existence with the First Sun. Like Florescano, Elzey appears to tie the tonalpohualli (and xiuhpohualli) to the existence of complete, fully energized Suns. Both agree: "no *full* sun" means "no tonalpohualli and no xiuhpohualli."

Florescano and Elzey are correct about there being a very close relationship between tonalli energy and the tonalpohualli, on the one hand, and solar heat and energy, on the other. But when does this relationship actually emerge? Does it begin with the creation of the First Sun, as they contend, or earlier with the threefold emergence of fire, the half-sun, and Oxomoco~Cipactonal? The *Historia* appears to support both interpretations. How can we resolve this apparent contradiction? Perhaps the two day-counts existed merely in an inchoate form consonant with the weak power of the half-sun up until the moment the first Sun emerged, at which time they emerged full blown? Alternatively, perhaps the *Historia*'s statements are not literal (and chronological) but rather ritual or literary. That is, rather than attribute errors, internal incoherence, or misunderstanding to the texts or their authors, perhaps it is we who have misunderstood the text. Perhaps the *Historia* and *Annals of Cuauhtitlan* are not histories (cosmogonies) in the Western sense of linear history. If the dates and counts are used for ritual and not historical purposes, then we misunderstand them by trying to force them into the mold of Western linear history.[118]

Although it says virtually nothing regarding the period before the creation of the First Sun, the *Legend of the Suns* does clearly indicate that the days were counted between the Fourth and Fifth Suns. For example, it states that the skies were created in the year 1 Rabbit and that Tezcatlipoca smoked the skies with the new fire he created in the year 2 Reed.[119] Even more to the point, it explicitly states, "Now, it was dark for twenty-five years."[120] Darkness and the absence of a Sun therefore do not appear to entail the absence of day counting and the tonalpohualli. If this is true and the tonalpohualli continues to run during the interstices of the five Ages, then the tonalpohualli cannot be conceptually or materially bound either to any one solar entity (be it a half or full Sun) or to the solar generally. In short, if this is true, then the Florescano-Elzey principle, "no sun, no tonalpohualli," looks false. If the tonalpohualli continues to run without Suns, then it appears that the Fifth Sun can at most serve as a vehicle for the dispensation of tonalli energy during the Fifth Age. There is a significant conceptual distancing between tonalli and the tonalpohualli, on the one hand, and the sun, solar heat, summer, on the other. The latter notions are therefore not part of the meaning or concept of tonalli.[121]

Such a disconnection between Sun (the solar) and tonalpohualli is further suggested by the *Codex Borgia*. Boone argues that plates 29 through 46 advance a cosmogony that begins with two events that occur in darkness before any Sun has been created.[122] The first consists of an explosion of dark, swirling, primordial creative energy and power. The second event consists of the ordering of this primordial energy according to the twentyfold day-sign pattern of the tonalpohualli. The Sun is created *after* these two events. According to *Codex Borgia*, then, the tonalpohualli exists prior to a Sun. There is an initial separation of the tonalpohualli and Sun, their interrelationship only emerging over the course of the unfolding of the cosmos. Although of Pueblan-Tlaxcalan provenience, *Codex Borgia* nevertheless supports the general idea that the tonalpohualli and the solar are conceptually and materially separable.

The written sources also seem to suggest, *pace* Elzey, that both day counts continue running during the five nemontemi days. The five days possessed day signs and day names designated by the tonalpohualli. People obviously counted them in the sense that they knew them to be five in number and included them in the pattern of 260-day and 360+5–day counts. Granted, no one dared to count-read-interpret these five days, but this does not mean that the five days did not exist or that the two energy patterns (tonalpohualli and xiuhpohualli) ceased running. People knew there were five days and followed them closely enough to know when they began and ended. Indeed, both patterns continued to follow their ordered paths. Last and perhaps foremost, the Fifth Sun itself obviously continued moving during this five-day period. Hence if the period of five nemontemi days were homologous with the transitional intervals between Ages as Elzey maintains, then the latter would also be counted and patterned by the tonalpohualli. Elzey's claim of homology backfires on him.

In sum, the tonalpohualli is a fundamental energy pattern in the becoming of the cosmos that emerges prior to the creation of the five Suns. The five Suns subsequently unfold within its pattern and its pattern subsequently unfolds within them. From this it follows that the five Suns (either individually or collectively) are not coextensive with tonalpohualli. They fall within the scope of the tonalpohualli but do not exhaust the tonalpohualli. From this it also follows that the five Suns (either individually or collectively) are not conceptually equivalent with the tonalpohualli. The Fifth Sun is therefore not identical with the tonalpohualli. During the Fifth Age, the Fifth Sun dispenses the 260 different kinds of tonalli-days counted-read-interpreted by the tonalpohualli. This notwithstanding, because of the close association between the Fifth Sun and the tonalpohualli during the Fifth Age, the concept of tonalli appears to have become associated by humans with the ideas of sun, solar heat, and summer. Indeed, the Fifth Sun became so closely associated with the tonalpohualli that the concept of tonalli expanded to include sun, summer, and solar heat. Tonalli is an agglutinative concept: one that kept adding new meanings. Tonalli and the tonalpohualli acquired new material relationships along with these new conceptual meanings as the cosmos unfolded into the Fifth Age.

Continuing with the narrative, the *Legend* states that the Fifth Sun is created through the self-immolation and sacrificial transformation of Nanahuatzin. But the newly created Fifth Sun does not move. In fact, it does not move for four days![123] The *Legend* tells us that it takes the additional sacrifice of all the gods at Teotihuacan to set the Fifth Sun into motion. Yet according to the account offered by Sahagún, even this act does not suffice to make the Fifth Sun move. The Sun's moving requires the further effort of Ehecatl-Quetzalcoatl's fierce and forceful breathing or blowing.[124] Several features of this account merit pointing out. First, there is a disconnection between solar movement and the tonalpohualli. The Sun's immobility lasts for a count of four days. The tonalpohualli (and xihuitl) continue unfolding, but not the Sun. Second, the Fifth Sun's failure to move makes one wonder, did the first four Suns move or stand still in the sky? The fact that the Fifth Sun does not initially move shows that an immobile Sun was not inconceivable to the Aztecs. Hence the possibility that the first four Suns did not move cannot be ruled out ex hypothesi. This raises again the possibility that the Fifth Sun is unique among the five Suns in that it alone moves. What matters most about the Fifth Sun is that it olin moves-changes.

If the preceding is correct, then we need to rethink our understanding of tonalli itself. I have argued that the 260-unit tonalpohualli along with the corresponding 260 different kinds of tonalli exist before there are any Suns. This strongly suggests the following. Metaphysically speaking, tonalli is primarily associated with the tonalpohualli. In the narratives of the history of the cosmos, it is indeed initially associated exclusively with the tonalpohualli. It is only later, upon the creation of the Fifth Sun that tonalli comes to be materially associated with solar heat-energy, and hence only much later (in the Fifth Era) that the concept of tonalli comes to be semantically linked with solar heat. If this is correct, then before the emergence of the Fifth Sun-Earth Age, the term *tonalli* does not mean "day" in the sense of a *solar day*. "Tonalli" refers to a unit in the 260-unit tonalpohualli but not to a solar day as we inhabitants of the Fifth Sun-Earth Age understand it. Nor does it refer to *day* in the sense of *daylight*. The 260 tonalli of the tonalpohualli tick away in darkness before the Fifth Sun-Earth Age emerges. If this is right, our translations of *tonalli* need to be adjusted accordingly.

What, then, about *ilhuitl*, the other Nahuatl word standardly translated as "day"?[125] And what, if anything, is the relationship between tonalli and ilhuitl – that is, between tonalli as day and day sign, and ilhuitl as day? Of the written sources we have, only the *Codex Chimalpopoca* was written in Nahuatl, and it uses *ilhuitl* rather than *tonalli* when narrating the history of the cosmos.[126] It uses *tonalli* for day sign and *ilhuitl* for day. For example, side 78, line 1, reads: "But he [the Fifth Sun, 4 Olin Motion] spent four days (*nahuilhuiti*) without moving, just staying in place."[127] Only after the Fifth Sun begins to move is nightfall (*teotlac*) established (*conmanaco*).[128]

These passages suggest that *ilhuitl* is not defined in terms of solar movement and that it does not primarily mean "day" in the sense of "solar day" or "daylight." After all, four such days pass without the Sun's ever moving! Presumably, then, these four passing days are defined, and thus counted-measured, in terms of the tonalpohualli. I suggest, therefore, that *ilhuitl* refers to a single unit in the 260-count tonalpohualli, and that, like tonalli, its association with what we inhabitants of the Fifth Age think of as a solar day, or perhaps as daylight hours, emerges only with the moving of the Fifth Sun. In the unfolding of teotl and of the cosmos, the Fifth Sun moves in conformity with the tonalpohualli; the pattern of the Fifth Sun's movement conforms with the pattern of the tonalpohualli. The Sun lives out its diurnal-nocturnal life cycle within each unit of the tonalpohualli (tonalpohualli unit-day). As a consequence of the Fifth Sun's moving in conformity with the tonalpohualli, *ilhuicatl* acquires the additional meaning of solar day.

Aztec Metaphysics as Acosmogonic

The *Historia* opens with the always already self-generating and self-regenerating progenitor~progenetrix Tonacatecuhtli~Tonacacihuatl, leading us to think he~she has always been becoming and that there has never been a time when he~she was not becoming. Tonacatecuhtli~Tonacacihuatl, like Ometecuhtli~Omecihuatl and Ometeotl, is progenitor~progenetrix of everything. His~her agonistic inamic unity, twofold oneness, and unified twoness entail wholeness and completeness. Several significant consequences follow this.

First, from the fact that Tonacatecuhtli~Tonacacihuatl exists from the very start, it follows that strictly speaking *there is no start!* There is no beginning to the cosmos. There is only continual becoming and transformation. The *Historia* does not speak of a creation ex nihilo. There is no beginning to (and apparently no end) to Tonacatecuhtli~Tonacacihuatl, and hence no beginning (or end) to the cosmos. He~she has always been self-unfolding and self-transforming. His~her existence consists of becoming, that is, of the nepantla-unifying of being and nonbeing.

Second, from the fact that Tonacatecuhtli~Tonacacihuatl exists from the very start, it follows that Aztec metaphysics does *not* begin with nothingness or chaos. It does *not*, like Biblical cosmogony, start from the "confusion and chaos of a maelstrom."[129] Since there is no primordial chaos, there is no primordial divine act of imposing order upon chaos – *pace* Carrasco, who writes of a "primordial time of the gods, when order first appeared out of chaos but did not exist in action,"[130] and *pace* Florescano, who asserts "the significance of the cosmogonic creation is to avert chaos and establish order."[131] Similarly, since there is no primordial nothingness, there is no primordial divine act of transforming nothingness into existence. Tonacatecuhtli~Tonacacihuatl does not generate particular things – be they lesser gods, cosmic ages, basic elements, layers of upper and lower realms, or humans – by imposing order upon primordial disorder. All things unfold from Tonacatecuhtli~Tonacacihuatl itself, and their ordering is immanent, that is, one which already exists within Tonacatecuhtli~Tonacacihuatl before their generation.

Pantheism, according to chapter 3, upholds the identity of the sacred and the cosmos. Pantheism denies creation ex nihilo of the cosmos by a transcendent divinity or god (since there is none). Pantheists therefore do not standardly advance stories about the beginning of the cosmos. Levine writes, "Pantheism rejects the theistic creation storyline in its entirety because it rejects so much of what it is based on – like the theistic God."[132] Aztec metaphysics is a case in point. It does not offer a conventional theistic-style cosmogony, although it does offer its own pantheistic storyline – one that emphasizes regeneration rather than generation, rebirth rather than birth, and renewal (recreation) rather than creation. In short, one that emphasizes continual transformation.

This consequence is fully consonant with Tonacatecuhtli's~Tonacacihuatl's wholeness, continual becoming, and unifying of agonistic inamichuan. Because he~she is whole and complete, he~she is metaphysically all-encompassing and exhaustive. Tonacatecuhtli's~Tonacacihuatl's ceaseless nepantla-defined processing incorporates nonbeing within it. It does not deny nonbeing; it denies only its absolute existence. Being and nonbeing are inamic partners and as such are agonistically unified within Tonacatecuhtli's~Tonacacihuatl's nepantla-defined sexual commingling and interweaving. Aztec metaphysics simply has no conceptual room for absolute nonbeing and hence for absolute beginnings. In short, the very idea of an absolute beginning or ex nihilo creation *makes no sense*. It is ill-conceived. All creations are destructions (and conversely), and all acts of creation depend upon previous acts of destruction (and conversely). Creation~destruction and being~nonbeing are agonistic inamic aspects of one and the same process: Tonacatecuhtli~Tonacacihuatl. Since being~nonbeing are inamic partners, one cannot on pain of unintelligibility assign metaphysical, causal, or cosmogonical priority to one or the other. As I earlier quoted David Hall, "A polar relationship has no beginning: to claim otherwise would be to provide some concept of initiation and, thus, to give priority to one of the elements in the creative relationship."[133]

Third, time-place is identical with and hence constituted by and coextensional with the continuous becoming and transforming of Tonacatecuhtli~ Tonacacihuatl. It thus *makes no sense* to speak of time-place prior to Tonacatecuhtli~Tonacacihuatl since time-place is a modus operandi of Tonacatecuhtli~Tonacacihuatl. Fourth, the fact that time-place is identical with Tonacatecuhtli's~Tonacacihuatl's continuous back-and-forth self-interweaving suggests that time-place should be understood in terms of *weaving*.[134] Time-place is neither cyclical nor linear, yet it does have both cyclical and linear dimensions. The repetitive motion-change involved in making individual weaves of warp and weft, as well as the back-and-forth folding involved in completing successive rows of weaves, obviously display cyclical dimensions. Yet completing an individual weave and moving on to the next, as well as completing a row of weaves and moving on to the next row, obviously display linear dimensions. There is clearly a "before" and "after" each individual weave and each row of weaves. One is able to distinguish earlier and later weaves and rows. Moreover, each individual weave and each individual row of weaves occupies a *unique* locus within the larger fabric. León-Portilla's translation of *cahuitl* as "that which leaves us" also suggests a linear dimension to time-place.[135] This linear dimension does *not*, however, carry with it meanings of linear progress, teleology, or eschatology.

In sum, Aztec metaphysics is *acosmogonic*. It does not proffer a cosmogony, if by *cosmogony* one means a grand theory detailing the ex nihilo creation of the cosmos. In place of such a cosmogony, texts such as the *Historia* and *Legend of the Suns* sketch genealogical narratives of becoming and transformation. Aztec metaphysics offers a cosmology and general history of the arranging of the cosmos only.

COSMOGONY AND COSMOLOGY OF THE FIFTH AGE: THE RECEIVED VIEW

Current scholars overwhelmingly concur that the written sources speak of three different "kinds," "patterns," or "dimensions" of time, and that Aztec metaphysics is therefore committed to the existence three distinct "kinds," "patterns," or "dimensions" of time[136] that ran concurrently with one another and that "flowed together."[137] I refer to this as *the received view* of Aztec cosmogony and cosmology. Let's examine it more closely.

THE "TIME OF THE TRANSCENDENT EXISTENCE OF THE GODS"[138]

There was a first time, a "primordial time of the gods, when order first appeared out of chaos."[139] It was a "Primordial era in which gods, sometimes a dual god, existed without action, motion, or change."[140] It was peaceful, harmonious, eternal, and immutable. Nothing ever happened during this time. It was a time of *equilibrio* ("equilibrium") avers León-Portilla.[141] Florescano writes, it "was a time of absolute beginning, when chaos was exorcised. This was the preeminent sacred time."[142] For López Austin it was "the time when the gods existed peacefully without creating anything."[143] Carrasco claims it was the time of the Dual God, Ometeotl, who "dwelled peacefully in the highest heavens . . . where all was in balance and silence."[144] "This primordiality reflected modes of totality, equilibrium, prodigious potentiality, or what Mircea Eliade called an 'unhistorical primordiality.'"[145] Florescano believes it was a time during which "time was not yet counted, nor were the days, years, or ages . . . [It lacked] chronology, temporality, and movement."[146] This accords with Carrasco's remark that this "pattern of time was a kind of patternless time."[147] Florescano calls this time "primitive time," claiming it was a "perfect time, the age when the cosmos existed charged with all its vital force."[148] Finally, this temporal dimension continues to exist after the addition of two further temporal dimensions: mythic and human. It runs concurrently with them; they neither destroy nor replace it.

One wonders, however, in which temporal dimension occurs Tonacatecuhtli~Tonacacihuatl's giving birth to Tlatlauhqui Tezcatlipoca, Yayauhqui Tezcatlipoca, Quetzalcoatl, and Omitecuhtli or Huitzilopochtli. Does it take place during the first time before the second time begins, or does their birth initiate the second time, the "time of myth and of creations"?[149] On the one hand, this certainly appears to be a creative action and hence a change and happening. Yet, on the other hand, page 24 of the *Historia* states that absolutely nothing happened for 600 years *after* the four sons' birth, suggesting this first time of peaceful inactivity continued long after their birth. Carrasco, for example, writes, "The divine family lives without moving for six hundred years" after which the four sons assembled to create the cosmos.[150] One also wonders, if this birth occurred during the "patternless" time of the gods during which time was not counted, then how can the author of the *Historia* relate that nothing happened for 600 years? If days, months, and years are not yet counted, how then does this statement make any sense? Is it an anachronistic projection into the past from the current Fifth Era?

The equilibrium, peacefulness, and stasis of the first time was "broken,"[152] "shattered,"[153] and "severed"[154] by a second time: a time when "the gods engaged in tremendous activity";[155] a time of creative acts and mythical events; "the active time of the gods."[156] This time includes the creation of Cipactonal and Oxomoco, Mictlantecuhtli and Mictecacihuatl, the thirteen heavens, water, Cipactli, Tlaloc and Chalchiuhtlicue, and the earth. It is the time in which the gods' mythical actions – their struggles, games, violations, abductions, adventures, sexual intrigues, and deaths – cause the creation and destruction of the first four Sun-Earth Eras as well as creation of the Fifth. The gods' mythical actions create patterns where before there were none. They "created and transformed, divided and ranked the universe."[157]

The idea of a second kind of time, a mythical time, raises the following questions. (1) Does Tonacatecuhtli~Tonacacihuatl's giving birth to his~her four sons occur in mythic or primordial time? (2) How shall we understand this second time? Is it something over and above the tremendous activity of the gods such as a framework or container in which these actions take place? Or, is it wholly exhausted by and identical with the gods' activity? (3) What is it exactly that "breaks" the peacefulness of the first time? Is it the second time as such, or the activities of the gods? (4) In what sense does mythic time "shatter" primordial time when primordial time continues to exist alongside mythical time? (5) Does calling the time of the gods' actions "mythical" commit one to the gods' mere mythical existence? But if the gods intervene in human time, if they act upon humans beings and other earthly creatures, if they make things happen in human time, why are we calling them "mythical" as opposed to fully real?

López Austin and Carrasco maintain that both the tonalpohualli and the xiuhpohualli time counts came into existence during mythic time. The calendars were created by the gods for the purpose of governing and interacting with the third dimension of time, the time of human beings.[158] Both were also available for counting the time of the actions and events of mythic time such as the creation and destruction of the first four Sun-Earth Eras. But if so, why then think that they were invented for the exclusive purpose of ordering or patterning events in the third time? Since both time counts appear fully effective during the second time, and since what they do is order or pattern events, then it would seem that the two calendars govern mythical time as well.[159]

Florescano defends a slightly different view. He contends the counting of the years begins with the creation of the First Sun-Earth Era.[160] He cites the opening paragraph of chapter 4 of the *Historia*: "And because the counting begins with this first sun and the counting figures go forward continuously, leaving behind the six hundred years, at the beginning of which the gods were born."[161] He apparently believes this passage refers to both the tonalpohualli and the xiuhpo-hualli.[162] The creation of the "age of the suns" is one and the same as the creation of the two calendars. Both calendars are products of the divine movement that begins with the creation of the First Sun. As we saw earlier, most scholars believe the tonalpohualli came into existence with the creation of Oxomoco and Cipactonal and that this passage refers only to the xiuhpohualli.

Let's return to López Austin and Carrasco. If their view is correct, then neither the tonalpohualli nor the xiuhpohualli existed during the first time, and as a consequence, neither calendar would have been available for counting the 600 years of divine inactivity following Tonacatecuhtli~Tonacacihuatl's giving birth to their four sons. What sense then can we make of this claim in the *Historia*? On the one hand, it suggests the four sons' births must have occurred during the time of myth, while on the other hand, it seems their birth could not have taken place during the time of myth, since the time of myth was a time of "tremendous activity" that looks incompatible with the 600 years of inactivity following their birth. The *Historia* offers no easy solution to this puzzle. There is, of course, a third option: the Aztecs anachronistically projected the two calendars back into first time from the Fifth Era when making this claim.

López Austin and Carrasco maintain that mythic time, like primordial time, does not end with the creation of the First Sun-Earth Era and the creation of the third pattern of time – namely, human time, the time of the Fifth Sun-Earth Era. Both first and second times run concurrently with the third. Both first and second times continue influencing events in human time. Ometeotl, for example, while still residing in Omeyocan in the first kind of time, sends down life-energy to newborn humans and thus causally influences – in a patternless way? – events in third time. And the various gods – Quetzalcoatl, Tezcatlipoca, Huitzilopochtli, and Tlaloc, for example – likewise intervene in human time through the mediation of the 260 day signs of the tonalpohualli. They continue sending their sacred forces into human time and human affairs by way of the five sacred trees and malinalli channels of the Fifth Sun-Earth Ordering. López Austin writes, "The time of myth continued ruling, far from man's dwelling, and by means of its cycles of power over the earth it determined what would happen in the third time."[163] These divine forces impinged upon human time by means of the malinalli, double-spiraled channels.[164]

The "Time of Man" [165]

López Austin argues mythical time gave "birth" to a third dimension of time;[166] Carrasco, that the creative~destructive action of mythical actions "gave way" to a third dimension of time.[167] This third time is the time of human existence: the time of the Fifth Sun-Earth Ordering. It is the kind of time that takes place in the intermediate layers of the cosmos. Tlalticpac, 4 Olin Tonatiuh, moon, stars, human beings, and the four lower heavens all transpire during this time.[168] Human time is unique to the Fifth Sun-Earth Era and will cease when the Fifth Era ends.

The forces and energies of the gods flow into the intermediate level (Earth and four lower skies) from above and below. The dry, light, male forces originating from above oppose and struggle with the wet, dark, female forces originating from below. Their agonistic inter-twisting forms double-spiral channels. Human time is a product of these opposing paired forces.[169] Divine forces course through the intermediary level according to the order laid out in advance by the tonalpohualli and xiuhpohualli calendrical cycles.[170] In doing so, they assume "the shape of time and of destiny."[171]

7.5. AZTEC TIME-PLACE: A MONISTIC AND PROCESSIVE INTERPRETATION

Challenges Raised by the Received View

The received view is incompatible with the interpretation of Aztec metaphysics I defend here. My claim that Aztec metaphysics is ontologically and constitutionally monistic, processive, and agonistic conflicts radically with the received view's characterization of primordial time and of Omeyocan as a peaceful and harmonious time-place without struggle (*agon*); a time-place without process, motion, change, action, or creation; and a time-place during which absolutely nothing happens. My interpretation also conflicts with the received view's claim that there exist three essentially distinct kinds of time, and its commitment to the existence of two different kinds of time-place: sacred versus profane. The received view maintains sacred time is primordial, eternal, patternless, peaceful, transcendent, and immutable, and that profane time is historical, noneternal, mutable, patterned, agonistic, and in the case of the Fifth Era, human. In response, I offer the following.

Two Theories of Time-Place

Two theories of time and space have dominated Western metaphysics since the ancient Greeks: *substantivalism* and *relationalism*. Substantivalism holds that space and time are substantial entities in their own right. They are container-like entities *in which* objects exist and events take place. Relationalism denies that space and time are substantial things. They are characteristics of the *interrelationships* between actually existing things, processes, and events. In what follows I sketch each. I then argue relationalism is more congenial to Aztec metaphysics.

According to *spatial* substantivalism, space (or space-time, if one embraces relativity theory) constitutes a fixed, objectively existing, physical structure or container *in which* events and processes take place.[172] We speak, for example, of an object such as a tree as occupying a place *in space* or as having a location *in space*. Substantivalists interpret such talk literally. Space is a grand matrix in which objects occupy locations. According to *temporal* substantivalism, time constitutes an objectively existing, fixed structure or container *in which* events and processes take place. We speak, for example, of events such as a wedding as taking place *in time*; of events as occupying *a place in time*. Substantivalists interpret such talk literally. Time is a grand matrix in which events occupy locations. Substantivalism – in particular, what I call "homogenous substantivalism" below – has been the prevailing view in Western metaphysics. It also appears to be embedded in ordinary English (i.e., in ordinary ways of speaking about space and time) and to be the untutored, common sense view of most Westerners.

On this view, space and time are analogous to a basketball court. A basketball court is an objectively existing, fixed structure or container *in* which backboards, hoops, balls, and players are located, and *in* which basketball games take place. Substantivalism maintains that physical objects exist *in* space just as basketball players exist *in* ballcourts; and that world events and processes happen *in* time just as basketball games happen *in* ballcourts. Moreover, just as basketball courts exist independently of the players and games that take place within them, so likewise space and time exist independently of the objects, events, and processes that take place *within* them. Space and time are individual entities in their own right, just as basketball courts are. Accordingly, just as basketball courts continue to exist when empty and when nothing happens in them, so likewise space continues to exist even though empty and time continues to exist even though nothing happens. Substantivalism thus maintains that if one were to take an inventory of all the existing things in the universe, space and time would be counted among them. Furthermore, like basketball courts, space and time persist unchanged throughout the manifold changes in objects and events occurring within them. Which teams play or how long games last has no effect upon the objective structure of the court. Finally, just as a basketball court imposes a specific order upon the basketball games that occur within it, so likewise space and time impose a specific order or structure upon the objects and events that occur within them. The basketball court has an objective spatial structure consisting of free-throw lines, two keys, boundary lines, and so on.

The (professional) basketball game has an objective temporal structure consisting of four 12-minute periods, halftime, timeouts, overtime, and so on. These are objective features that exist independently of players and games. Analogously, space and time have objective features: space may be thought of as finite or infinite, or as having the structure of Euclidean or a non-Euclidean geometry. Time may be thought of as linear or cyclical. We speak of the structure of space or structure of time.

Isaac Newton famously defended substantivalist theories of space and time. He claimed space is an infinite, three-dimensional, Euclidean structure that persists unchanged through time and would continue to do so *even if* there were no objects or things in the universe.[73] Space is a substance that persists unchanged through changes in time. Rulers measure some *thing*, and what they measure is the structure of space. Similarly, on Newton's view there would still be moments or "instants" of time that jointly form the temporal order *even if* there were no objects or events in the universe. Time is a substance that persists unchanged through changes in space. Clocks measure some *thing*, and what they measure is the order of time.

Homogeneous substantivalism holds that space and time are qualitatively neutral media or containers. There are no qualitative differences between one point in space and another, no qualitative differences between one moment in time and another. If space and time possess mathematical or geometrical properties (e.g., Euclidean vs. non-Euclidean geometry), then these properties are treated as qualitatively homogeneous. *Heterogeneous substantivalism* holds that space and time are qualitatively diverse. There exist qualitative differences between one location in space and another, and qualitative differences between one moment in time and another. If space and time possess mathematical or geometrical properties, then these properties are regarded as qualitatively heterogeneous. On this view, not all times are the same, and not all spaces are the same. Homogenous substantivalism has been the dominant view in Western thought.

Relationalism denies that space and time are independently existing containers or orderings in which the objects, events, and processes happen. They are defined wholly in terms of, and hence exhausted by, the interrelations between actually existing substantive objects, processes, or events. Space and time are nothing over and above the order of these interrelationships. If one were to take an inventory of all existing things in the universe, space and time would *not* be counted among them. All talk of spatial and temporal relations should therefore be regarded as attributing spatial and temporal relations to actually existing things. In short: space is not a thing but a set of relationships between existing material objects. Time is not a thing but a set of relationships between actual events. Time is a function of change – where change includes change in location (or motion) and change in properties. In short, as Gottfried Leibniz expressed it, space is "an order of coexistences," and time, "an order of successions."[174] And as the late Tewa anthropologist Alfonso Ortiz expressed it, "none of the pueblos . . . has abstract terms for space and time; space is only meaningful as the distance between two points, and time cannot be understood apart from the forces and changes in nature which give it relevance and meaning."[175]

Relationalism argues that thinking of space and time as independently existing, substantive things rests upon a confusion: that of reification. Treating space and time as independently existing entities is analogous to treating sisterhood as an entity that exists over and above all actually existing female siblings. There is no such *thing* as sisterhood per se, and to think so is simply to be confused. Sisterhood consists of a relationship between actually existing female siblings. If no sisters existed, there would be no such thing as sisterhood. Analogously, space and time are wholly constituted and exhausted by the interrelationships between actually existing things. All talk of spatiality is to be regarded as talk about the relationships between actually existing objects. All talk of temporality is to be regarded as talk about the relationships between actually occurring events and processes. Talk about space and time is thus really a way of talking about the relationships between existing substances and events – not a way of talking about some *thing* called space or time. Relationalism accordingly contends that our ordinary ways of talking about space and time are deeply confused. Relationalism finds little support in ordinary English (i.e., in ordinary ways of speaking about space and time) and in the untutored, commonsense thinking of most Westerners. It also represents a minority view in the history of Western metaphysics.

Relationalism is more congenial to process metaphysics. Process metaphysics maintains reality consists a single grand macroprocess consisting of myriad microprocesses and their interrelationships. Space and time are patterns or patterned facets in the modus operandi of reality's processing. They are not transcendent matrices or structures imposed from the outside upon reality's processing but rather patterns that emerge in the unfolding of these processes. They are "process-constituted as aspects or features of the structural role of nature's processes."[176]

TIME-PLACE AS THE PATTERNED UNFOLDING OF TEOTL

I submit Aztec metaphysics conceives time-place in relationalist rather than substantivalist terms. Time-place is a pattern in the modus operandi of teotl's continual becoming, processing, and moving-changing. *Time-place* is both *how the fabric of the cosmos weaves itself* and *how the woven fabric of the cosmos is woven*. It is a *how* – not a *what*. It is not a transcendent matrix or "armature" imposed *upon* teotl's unfolding or *to which* teotl must conform.[177] It is neither metaphysically nor conceptually prior to teotl's processing, nor is it metaphysically more fundamental than teotl's processing. Time-place emerges from, and is formed by teotl's unfolding and becoming.

The temporal and spatial emerge from and are exhaustively defined in terms of the mutually interrelated and mutually correlated macroprocesses and microprocesses that comprise teotl. Borrowing Herbert Spinden's characterization of Maya thought, the Aztecs "discovered that time is neither an endless flowing nor a senseless whirligig, but an intelligible *interrelation* of changing states throughout the universe."[178] Time-place is therefore nothing more – and nothing less – than a structured aspect of the self-unfolding of teotl. It is process-constituted. Its pattern and ordering are "determined through processes of interrelation that manifest their inherently processual basis."[179]

Everything that happens in the history of the cosmos is therefore not merely *immersed in* teotl's time-place unfolding, it is also *constituted by* teotl's time-place unfolding. All things in the cosmos, from "deities," Suns, and earth, to humans, plants, and rivers, are ineliminably *timed* and *placed* or *timed-placed*. Since all things are constituted by and identical with teotl, all things have time-place coursing through them. All things participate in, embody, and express time-place.

Time-place is therefore more analogous to the rings in a cross-sectioned tree trunk or the patterns in woven fabric than it is to, for example, a basketball court, or multicolored stage lights (as Soustelle suggested above), or external "factors that combine to regulate the occurrence of cosmic events" (as León-Portilla suggested above). A tree trunk's rings emerge in the process of the tree's growing; they are a component and consequence of the tree's manifold interrelationships with its own processes and those of its environment. Its ring pattern is neither predetermined nor dictated by a structure independent of or external to the tree. Expressed more apropros, time-place is analogous to the patterns in a woven cloth. The patterns in a woven fabric emerge and disclose themselves in and through the course of weaving. Time-place is just so – a pattern that emerges in the weaving of the cosmos; a function of the interrelationships and correlations between the various fibers of the fabric. Time-place is both how the fabric of the cosmos *weaves itself* and how the woven fabric of the cosmos *is woven*.

By contrast, León-Portilla and Soustelle interpret Aztec metaphysics as embracing a heterogeneous substantivalism. León-Portilla writes, "Both space and time are conceived not as empty stage settings but as factors that combine to regulate the occurrence of cosmic events."[180] Soustelle writes, "The world can be compared to a great stage upon which different multi-colored lights, controlled by a tireless mechanism, project reflections that follow one after the other and overlap, maintaining for a limitless period an unalterable sequence."[181] Both think of time-place as an independently existing matrix that structures and acts upon what happens within it and does so according to its own intrinsic qualities. Carrasco and López Austin likewise appear to interpret the Aztecs' *cosmovisión* in these terms.[182] For the aforementioned reasons, I think this interpretation is mistaken. Relationalism is the more plausible theory of time-place for Aztec philosophy's process metaphysics.

What about the tonalpohualli and xiuhpohualli? The tonalpohualli and xiuhpohualli are two major co-related and concurrently running "rhythmic reiterative patterns" in the self-weaving of teotl, and as such do not exist apart from teotl's self-becoming. [183] They are analogous to two co-related patterns woven into a cloth. Indeed, just as the tonalpouhqui and xiuhpouhqui count the days of the tonalpohualli and xiuhpohualli, so likewise the weaver counts threads when creating and weaving patterns into a woven cloth. And just as the former take into consideration a vast web of interrelationships when counting-reading-interpreting the significance of a given day, so likewise the weaver takes into account a vast web of interrelationships when implementing each weave in her cloth.

Tonalpohualli and xiuhpohualli consist of two different patterns of interrelationships between processes and events occurring in the cosmos. The tonalpohualli pattern consists of the manifold interrelationships between the 260 tonalli units, while the xiuhpohualli pattern consists of the manifold interrelationships between 360+5 tonalli-units. Each is a patterned macroprocess consisting of a host of smaller patterned microprocesses. In light of this, they constitute two different *kinds* of time-place: tonalpohualli time-place and xiuhpohualli time-place. Time-place is therefore *relationally heterogeneous*. Not all times-places are the same. Different patterns of relationships yield different kinds of time-place. It is heterogeneous, however, *not* because it consists of heterogeneous substances or armatures (*pace* León-Portilla, Soustelle, Carrasco, Boone, and López Austin) but rather because the tonalpohualli and xiuhpohualli are two different patterns in the modus operandi of teotl. The relational heterogeneity of time-place is wholly compatible with Aztec metaphysics' ontological and constitutional monism. Tonalpohualli and xiuhpohualli run alongside one another, synchronizing every 52 years to form the larger, overarching pattern of the xiuhmolpilli. Finally, each of the 260 tonalli-units of the tonalpohualli and each of the 360+5 unit-days of the xiuhpohualli represents a unique *moment-locus* of time-place. Just as each individual weave in the making of a cloth is unique in the sense of being uniquely positioned within the overall web of interrelationships constituting the finished fabric, so analogously each moment-locus of time-place is unique in the sense of being uniquely positioned within and defined by the overall set of interrelationships constituting the tonalpohualli, xiuhpohualli, and xiuhmolpilli.

Codex Fejérváry-Mayer (pl. 1) depicts the shape of the quadripartite division of tonalpohualli-defined time-place during the Fifth Sun-Earth Ordering.[184] The tonalpohualli's *intersection with* the Fifth Sun's olin motion-change takes the shape of butterfly, quatrefoil, and quincunx. During the Fifth Age tonalpohualli time-place subdivides into four different time-place patterns consisting of the four basic quadrants or directions – East, West, North, and South – along with their respective tonalpohualli day signs, colors, reigning deities, Night Lords, cosmic trees, birds, and so on. Each of these lesser times-places is defined by its own unique set of correlations and interrelationships. It is this that makes them four different kinds of time-place – not some metaphysical time-place substance. Eastern time-place thus differs qualitatively from Western time-place, for example. Dawn-morning time-place differs from afternoon-dusk time-place, and spring time-place differs from summer time-place.

Codex Fejérváry-Mayer (pl. 1) does *not*, however, serve as a cosmogram of any of the first four Sun-Earth Ages or of the cosmos as such.[185] First, it does not depict the cosmos per se, since it includes neither the nine layers above nor the nine layers below Tlalticpac. Plate 1 depicts the fourfold division of the middle or intermediate region during the Fifth Age only. Second, what gives the figure its distinctive quincunx shape is the olin motion-change of 4 Olin Tonatiuh. The Fifth Sun-Earth Age is distinguished by the undulating motion of its Sun and by the fact that such undulating motion-change creates the fifth direction, the center. Even if the first four Suns had moved, because they are defined by Earth, Wind, Fire, and Water (respectively) they would have moved in radically different ways. There's no reason to suppose the first four Sun-Earth Orderings would have had centers or a fifth direction, or that they would have spread out the tonalpohualli into the shape of a quincunx. Moreover, as Elzey and León-Portilla argue, it is only in the Fifth Age that all four sons of Tonacatecuhtli~Tonacacihuatl and all four elements are interwoven with one another into a unified agonistic balance.[186] Hence although each of the five Sun-Earth Ages is characterized by the tonalpohualli, the exact look of time-place during each Age would appear to be different. In short, *Codex Fejérváry-Mayer* (pl. 1) serves as a time-place mapping or *chronotopogram* of the

Fifth Age.[187] It depicts what López Austin and Carrasco call "human time." It also serves as a mapping of the modus operandi of teotl. Since teotl is essentially processive and since teotl's essence is what teotl does, *Codex Fejérváry-Mayer* (pl. 1) offers insight into the nature of teotl itself. It depicts the pattern *by which* and *in which* teotl weaves the Fifth Era.

Attributing a relationalist theory of time-place to Aztec metaphysics helps us more fully understand how it is that the time-place orientations, directions, and regions of the Fifth Age are created by and so defined in relation to the Fifth Sun's olin moving-changing. Since relationalism denies the existence of substantive space-time, it denies a fortiori the existence of fixed geometric directions or regions in space-time. Consequently, the Fifth Sun does not rise "in the East" and set "in the West," as though East and West existed *before* the Sun's first rising and setting. The Sun's rising and setting *create* East and West.

Combining relationalist theory of time-place, process metaphysics, and teotl's manifold unfolding enables Aztec metaphysics to recognize the existence of as many time-places as there are patterns in the unfolding of teotl. Some of these patterns are obviously grander than others; and some are obviously more significant to human beings than others. All however are equally real, and all are nested within the single, grand macroprocess that is teotl. The 584-day Venusian cycle, for example, is one such time-place pattern in the unfolding of teotl. Less grand, the fourfold "age-growth cycle" of human beings is another time-place constituting pattern.[188] It consists of four times-places: birth and infancy; youth; adulthood and matrimony; and old age and death. Each is defined by a unique set of correlations. The time-place of childhood, for example, consists of the set of correlations including East, spring, vernal equinox, southern Sun ascending, rain beginning, the planting of the first maize crop, presexuality, and the day sign Cane (or Reed).[189] Although not a grand, overarching cosmic pattern like the tonalpohualli, the fourfold age-growth cycle of human beings represents another kind of time-place, what we might call human time-place or the time-place of lived human experience. It is constituted by the manifold interrelationships between humans, on the one hand, and other humans, their environments, tonalpohualli, xiuhpohualli, and xiuhmolpilli, on the other. It is also constituted by the manifold interrelationships between the aforementioned and the various elements, animistic energies and centers of human beings as well as the various stages of human lives. The fourfold "age-growth cycle" applies to all created things in the Fifth Age, from grasshoppers and mountains to specific ecosystems such as Lake Texcoco. Each of these is as real as the next, although perhaps not equally significant to humans. Obviously, the Aztecs paid greater attention to the grand overarching patterns such as the tonalpohualli – and rightly so, since they had a larger impact upon people's lives. In the final analysis, however, all these smaller times-places contributed to, fit into, and were defined by the grander set of interrelationships and correlations of the tonalpohualli and xiuhpohualli. They represent specific aspects of teotl's grand processual holism.

Lastly, there is Ometeotl time-place. If Ometeotl (Tonacatecutli~Tonaca-cihuatl, Ometecuhtli~Omecihuatl) has always existed and if he~she existed before the emergence of both the tonalpohualli and xiuhpohualli, and contin-ues to exist through to the present, then there appears to exist one further time-place pattern: what I call *Ometeotl (or teotl) time-place*. Ometeotl time-place is cosmogonically more primordial and metaphysically more fundamental than the other time-places.[190] And yet in keeping with ontological monism, it is not metaphysically or essentially different in kind from other time-places.

Ometeotl's nepantla-defined balancing of agonistic inamic partners, becom-ing, and transforming has always occurred and, what's more, explains every-thing else. Ometeotl time-place consists of the rhythmic, agonistic inamic patterning disclosed in the continual self-unfolding of Ometeotl. It is *how* Ometeotl unfolds. And this pattern is none other than nepantla motion-change. Ometeotl – and hence the cosmos – is a grand, ongoing nepantla process (weav-ing) in progress. The shape and look of Ometeotl time-place is therefore the look and shape of nepantla motion-change. López Austin writes, "Oxomoco and Cipactonal were personifications of the division and opposition of time's substance."[191] I interpret López Austin's remark to mean that time-place per se has always been defined by division and opposition – that is, by the continuing process of nepantla-defined agonistic inamic unification and diachronic bal-ance. Seeing as Oxomoco and Cipactonal are merely reiterations of Ometeotl, I interpret López Austin's remark to mean that Ometeotl time-place has always been characterized by nepantla-defined and -balanced *rhythmic tension*. Time-place neither flows like a river nor circles like a potter's wheel. *Time-place weaves back and forth*.

Aztec metaphysics defines Ometeotl as a single, primordial, unified male~female figure who consists of continuous unified inamic generative and regen-erative power. Ometeotl consists of the nepantla-defined commingling and weaving together of male~female powers. He~she is engaged in continuous and never-ending sexual intercourse and interweaving with him~herself, and hence continuous and never-ending activity, process, movement, and change. Since Ometeotl resides in Omeyocan, it follows that Omeyocan is a time-place when-where continual and never-ending sexual commingling and regeneration occur. It is *not* (*pace* the received view) a time-place where nothing happens.

Since sexual commingling and weaving are agonistic processes, it follows that Omeyocan is *not* one of peace, harmony, idyll, stasis, immobility, and inactivity (as claimed by the received view). Inamic partners do not coexist peacefully and harmoniously with one another. They strive to dominate one another, although never to extinguish or eliminate one another. Peace and harmony have no place amid agonistic inamic unity. The balance and equilibrium of Ometeotl and Omeyocan are the products of continual struggle – not peaceful, harmonious coexistence. Indeed, it is precisely this fact about Ometeotl's processing that accounts for his~her enduring and boundless powers of regeneration and transformation.

Omeyocan, therefore, is *neither* a time-place of peace and harmony (if one defines these to entail an absence of conflict) *nor* a time-place of inactivity, immutability, and stasis. *Pace* the received view, it is *not* a peaceful, Platonic-style transcendent realm of immutable Being, *nor* an idyllic Christian-like heaven where nothing ever changes or dies. Omeyocan is a place-time of continual nepantla-defined struggle, motion-change, and becoming. It is a time-place of continual generation, degeneration, regeneration, and thus transformation produced by continual agonistic, nepantla-defined becoming. Omeyocan is a time-place of balance, but its balance is dynamic and agonistic – not static and quietistic. In short, the received view operates from a set of metaphysical assumptions that I believe are *alien* to Aztec philosophy: first, the equating of peace, harmony, inactivity, stasis, and perfection, on the one hand, and the converse equating of disharmony, agonism, activity, opposition, and movement on the other; second, the notion that harmony, equilibrium, and balance are produced by inactivity, stasis, and peaceful coexistence rather than by inamic agonism; and third, the idea that an orderly cosmos must be created from a prior condition of absolute disorder.

Given that Ometeotl is cosmogonically primordial and metaphysically fundamental, it follows that nepantla motion-change is cosmogonically primordial and metaphysically fundamental. Nepantla motion-change is both the most primordial and the fundamental metaphysical expression of agonistic inamic activity. The processing of reality consists *essentially* of nepantla-defined agonistic activity. The cosmos is an ongoing nepantla weaving-in-progress. All other time-places are nested and integrated within the larger unifying pattern of Ometeotl time-place, forming a grand unifying "eurhythmy."[192] This unifying eurhythmy may be represented by the following diagram (see Figure 7.1). Since all other time-places are integrated within Ometeotl time-place, it follows that they, too, are characterized by rhythmic tension. Together, all time-places weave back and forth.

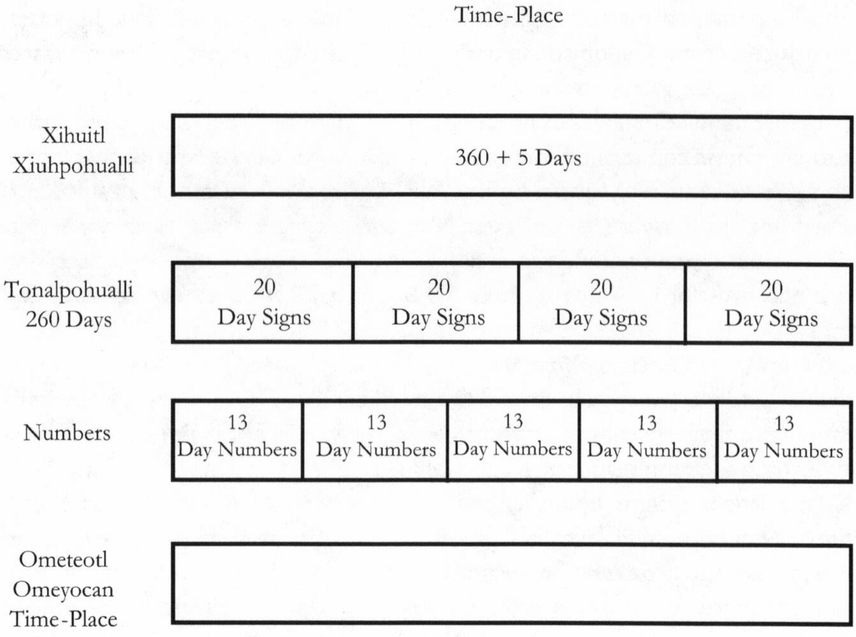

Xihuitl Xiuhpohualli	360 + 5 Days			

Tonalpohualli 260 Days	20 Day Signs	20 Day Signs	20 Day Signs	20 Day Signs

Numbers	13 Day Numbers	13 Day Numbers	13 Day Numbers	13 Day Numbers	13 Day Numbers

Ometeotl Omeyocan Time-Place					

FIGURE 7.1. *Concurrent multiple layering of time-place. (Author's drawing.)*

Ometeotl time-place does not cease to exist upon the unfolding of the tonalpohualli and xiuhpohualli, or upon the unfolding of the five Sun-Earth Orderings. It is neither displaced nor replaced by the tonalpohualli and xiuhpohualli – just as agonistic inamic unity is neither displaced nor replaced by the tonalpohualli and xiuhpohualli. Rather, the tonalpohualli and xiuhpohualli merely add complexity to the nepantla-defined macropattern of Ometeotl time-place. The tonalpohualli and xiuhpohualli as well as all lesser patterns of time-place represent micropatterns in the becoming of the cosmos that unfold within Ometeotl's macropattern. All of these patterns of interrelationships and hence times-places are as equally real as the next. While perhaps not equally useful to humans in conducting their lives, all are nevertheless manifestations of Ometeotl (teotl) and hence all are equally real. Ometeotl's (teotl's) processual unfolding may be thus counted-read-interpreted in a variety of ways. These relational patterns (and hence times-places) intermesh and overlap with one another in a variety of ways. Smaller patterns are nested within larger ones and bear interrelationships with other smaller and larger patterns, just as microprocesses are nested within macroprocesses. The fabric of the cosmos thus consists of a complex web of interrelationships and correlations. Given its primordial and fundamental metaphysical status in defining the unfolding of Ometeotl, reality, and cosmos, agonistic inamic unity must characterize and express itself within both the tonalpohualli and xiuhpohualli.

Before concluding, let's examine the Aztec notion of day. The Nahuatl word for day, *ilhuitl*, contains the prefix *il-*, which López Austin translates as "curve," "turn," and "return."[193] Other *il*-prefixed words include *ilacatzoa* ("to roll up"), *ilhuicatl* ("sky"), *ilpia* ("to tie"), *ilacatziuhqui* ("twisted thing"), *ilacatziui* ("for something like the point of an awl or something similar to twist"), *quauilacatzoa* ("to play with a rod with one's feet, or to twist and join plants together"), *ilacatzoa* ("to roll up a blanket, mat, piece of paper or something similar, or to wind up thread or string on one's finger" and "for a snake to wrap itself around a tree"), and *teteuilacachtic* ("whirlwind or something similar").[194] The semantic cluster suggests rolling, curving, circling, turning, winding up, coiling, and twisting-and-joining-together.

Like López Austin, I believe the fact that *ilhuitl* ("day") and *ilhuicatl* ("sky") are formed with the prefix *il-* tells us something important about how the Aztecs conceived time-place. López Austin and I differ, however, about what that is. López Austin believes it shows that the Aztecs conceived "the time of man" as that "which occurs by circling the intermediate world, making each day a point of return by linking it to divine time."[195] I believe "the time of man" never leaves "divine time." The former is completely woven into Ometeotl time-place since it is an iteration of Ometeotl time-place. I therefore believe that the fact that both *ilhuitl* ("day") and *ilhuicatl* ("sky") contain the prefix *il-* indicates that the Aztecs conceived time-place in terms of spinning and weaving. Rolling, curving, turning, returning twisting, coiling, and twisting-and-joining-together are all kinds of motion involved in creating cloth.

The Aztecs conceived each *ilhuitl*-as-unit-or-day-of-the-tonalpohualli in terms of twisting or spinning – and hence in terms of malinalli motion-change and transformation. The motion involved in the arriving, transpiring, and passing away of each unit-day of the tonalpohualli is a malinalli twisting-spinning. As we've seen, tonalli energy travels between intermediate *and* upper and lower levels of the Fifth Age via vertical, malinalli-shaped conduits. The Aztec apparently also conceived of ilhuicatl, the sky or skies, as rolled up or folded woven fabric. (I expand upon this in chapter 8.)

The combination of *ilhuitl* (day) and *ilhuicatl* (sky) likewise suggests the Aztecs conceived of ilhuitl-as-solar-day of the Fifth Era in terms of spinning and weaving. The Fifth Sun is the principal "porter" of tonalli in the Fifth Age. On each ilhuitl-as-unit-day-of-the-tonalpohualli, it travels over (daytime) and under (nighttime) Tlalticpac, returning the following morning in the East to begin anew. In this manner, what we think of as a solar day overlaps perfectly with each tonalpohualli day. As a result, the words *ilhuitl* and *tonalli*, originally defined exclusively in terms of the tonalpohualli, acquire the additional semantic content of solar day. In other words, ilhuitl-as-unit-day-of-the-tonalpohualli becomes conceptually associated with each ilhuitl-as-unit-solar-day. The Fifth Sun creates each time-place region of the Fifth Age; each region constituting a time-place phase in its own daily life~death cycle. As it does so, it carries with it the burden of the tonalli of that particular ilhuitl (day). These tonalli burdens represent the kind of energy the Sun radiates upon the surface of the Earth, and the kind of energy that suffuses the Fifth Age on any given "day."

What is the pattern exhibited by the moving of the Fifth Sun? It exhibits the pattern of horizontal weft threads traveling over and under the vertical warp threads on a loom. Acting as weft, the Fifth Sun interlaces with the warp threads, which exhibit the pattern of the 260-count tonalpohualli and 360+5–count xiuhpohualli. In passing over and under the tonalpohualli bearing warp threads, the Sun transmits to the intermediate region of the Fifth Era the tonalli of that day. This explains the perfect coordination of solar day and tonalpohualli day as well as the semantic expansion of *ilhuitl*. Upon doing this 260 times, the Fifth Sun completes a tonalpohualli warp pattern; upon doing it 360+5 times, it completes a xiuhpohualli warp pattern. After 52 years, it "returns" or "curves back" to begin anew. Each warp thread represents one ilhuitl-as-unit-day of the tonalpohualli, and thus one associated ilhuitl-as-solar-day. The wefting Fifth Sun oscillates over and under the tonalpohualli and xiuhpohualli patterned warp threads.

Let's look at two ideograms for *ilhuitl* ("day") (see Figure 7.2). Figure 7.2a's four smaller, outer circles together with its six internal swirling arms suggest 4 Olin Tonatiuh four-phased motion-change through the four intercardinal directions. The six swirls rotate about a center circle: the navel and fifth direction of the Fifth Age.[196] Figure 7.2a resembles one of the most common of the olin glyphs: the saltire or quincunx. Boone interprets Figure 7.2b as a single day accompanied by its mantic significance.[197] It also resembles the double-unfolding spiral examined in chapters 3 and 5 (see Figure 3.8) that represents (among other things) the Sun's birth each morning, its path both over and under the earth, and its death each dusk. A diagonal bar separates its two contrary volutes, suggesting motion-change above and below the earth's surface. The ideogram also conveys the back-and-forth, reciprocating motion-change of nepantla and nepantla-defined agonistic inamic unity.

Figure 7.2A–B. *Two ideograms for ilhuitl ("day"). (*Codex Mendoza *[1997: 19r, 70r];* courtesy of Frances F. Berdan and Patricia Rieff Anawalt.)

7.6. CONCLUSION

Time-place is an immanent pattern in the modus operandi of teotl's continual becoming and transforming. It is how teotl moves. Time-place is relational, not substantive. Since teotl has always existed, time-place has always existed. Since nepantla motion-change defines teotl, and since time-place is the modus operandi of teotl, it follows that nepantla motion-change is the modus operandi of time-place. Time-place weaves back and forth as teotl weaves the cosmos. The cosmos is a grand weaving-in-progress whose various patterns constitute various times-places.

NOTES

1. Fray Alonso de Molina, *Vocabulario en lengua castellana y mexicana y mexicana y castellana,* 4th ed., facsimile of 1571 edition (Mexico City: Porrúa, 2001), 2:13r; see also Frances Karttunen, *An Analytical Dictionary of Nahuatl* (Norman: University of Oklahoma Press, 1983), 21.

2. Karttunen, *Analytical Dictionary,* 29; and R. Joe Campbell, *A Morphological Dictionary of Classical Nahuatl: A Morpheme Index to the* Vocabulario en lengua mexicana y castellana *of Fray Alonso de Molina* (Madison: Hispanic Seminary of Medieval Studies, 1985), 45. Miguel León-Portilla ("Three Forms of Thought in Ancient Mexico," in *Studies in Symbolism and Cultural Communication,* ed. F. Allen Hanson [Lawrence: University of Kansas Press, 1982], 14) translates it as "that which leaves us."

3. See León-Portilla, "Three Forms of Thought," 15; H. B. Nicholson, "The Significance of the 'Looped Cord' Year Symbol in Pre-Hispanic Mexico," *Estudios de*

cultura náhuatl 6 (1996): 135–48; and Kay A. Read, *Time and Sacrifice in the Aztec Cosmos* (Bloomington: Indiana University Press, 1998), 89–92.

4. Philip P. Arnold, *Eating Landscape: Aztec and European Occupation of Tlalocan* (Niwot: University Press of Colorado, 1999), 45. Arnold claims time has the additional locative character of always being spatially placed.

5. Gregory Cajete, *Native Science: Natural Laws of Interdependence* (Santa Fe, NM: Clear Light Publishers, 2000), 49.

6. This fact helps us understand Franke Neumann's claim (in "The Experience of Time in Nahua Religion," *Journal of the American Academy of Religion* 44 [1976]: 259) that the word *cahuitl* was rarely used, especially in an abstract or philosophical sense.

7. Read, *Time and Sacrifice*, 28. Arnold (*Eating Landscape*, 45) also characterizes time as "embodied."

8. For related discussion, see Read, *Time and Sacrifice*; Cajete, *Native Science*; Vine Deloria Jr., and Daniel R. Wildcat, *Power and Place* (Golden, CO: American Indian Graduate Center and Fulcrum Resources, 2001); and Christopher Tilley, *A Phenomenology of Landscape: Places, Paths, and Monuments* (Oxford: Berg Publishers, 1994).

9. See Arnold, *Eating Landscape*; Read, *Time and Sacrifice*; Deloria and Wildcat, *Power and Place*; Keith H. Basso, *Wisdom Sits in Places: Landscape and Language among the Western Apache* (Albuquerque: University of New Mexico Press, 1996); Jonathan Z. Smith, *Map Is Not Territory: Studies in the History of Religions* (Chicago: University of Chicago Press, 1993); and Henri A. Frankfort and H. A. Frankfort, "Myth and Reality," in *The Intellectual Adventure of Ancient Man*, ed. Henri Frankfort et al. (Chicago: University of Chicago Press, 1977), 3–30.

10. Cajete, *Native Science*, 182. See also Arnold, *Eating Landscape*, 15. Arnold and Read (*Time and Sacrifice*) rightly place greater emphasis upon place in understanding Aztec thought than most scholars (who tend to emphasize time to the exclusion of place). Native North American philosophers such as Deloria, Wildcat, and Norton-Smith stress the absolute centrality of place in native philosophies, religions, and identities. See Vine Deloria Jr. and Wildcat, *Power and Place*; Vine Deloria Jr., *God Is Red: A Native View of Religion* (Golden, CO: Fulcrum Publishing, 1994); and Thomas Norton-Smith, *The Dance of Person and Place: One Interpretation of American Indian Philosophy* (Buffalo: SUNY Press, 2010).

11. For example, Jacques Soustelle, *El universo de los Aztecas*, trans. José Luis Martínez (chapter 1) and Juan José Utrilla (chapters 2–4) (México, DF: Fondo de Cultura Económica, 1982), 168–75; León-Portilla, *Aztec Thought*; León-Portilla, "Three Forms of Thought"; Read, *Time and Sacrifice*; Arnold, *Eating Landscape*; Cecelia Klein, "Woven Heaven, Tangled Earth: The Weaver's Paradigm of the Mesoamerican Cosmos," in *Ethnoastronomy and Archaeoastronomy in the American Tropics*, ed. Anthony Aveni and Gary Urton, Annals of the New York Academy of Sciences, No. 38 (New York: New York

Academy of Sciences, 1982), 1–35; Elizabeth Hill Boone, *Cycles of Time and Meaning in the Mexican Books of Fate* (Austin: University of Texas Press, 2007); Gordon Brotherston and Dawn Ades, "Mesoamerican Description of Space, I: Myths; Stars and Maps, and Architecture," *Ibero-Amerikanisches Archiv* I, no. 4 (1975): 279–305; and Davíd Carrasco with Scott Sessions, *Daily Life of the Aztecs: People of the Sun and Earth* (Westport, CT: Greenwood Press, 1998).

12. Read (*Time and Sacrifice*, 246n10) argues the fusion of time and place is demonstrated by the Nahuatl suffix *-yan*, which "indicates both time and place."

13. N. Scott Momaday writes: "The events of one's life take place, *take place*. How often have I used this expression, and how often have I stopped to think of what it means? Events do indeed take place" (Scott N. Momaday, *The Names: A Memoir* [New York: Harper and Row, 1976], 142).

14. Soustelle, *Universo de los Aztecas*, 168–72. See also León-Portilla, *Aztec Thought*, 55–56; Miguel León-Portilla, "*El Tonalámatl de los Pochtecas (Códice Fejérváry-Mayer): Estudio introductorio y comentarios*," *Arqueología Mexicana, Edición especial* 18 (2005): 18–21; Anthony F. Aveni, *Skywatchers: A Revised and Updated Version of Skywatchers of Ancient Mexico* (Austin: University of Texas Press, 2001), 150–51; and Read, *Time and Sacrifice*, 211–16.

15. Eva Hunt, *The Transformation of the Hummingbird: Cultural Roots of a Zinacatecan Mythical Poem* (Ithaca, NY: Cornell University Press, 1977), 111.

16. See Soustelle, *Universo de los Aztecas*, 170–71; and León-Portilla, *Aztec Thought*, 60.

17. Quiñones Keber emphasizes the interactive nature of counting-reading-interpreting the days in Eloise Quiñones Keber, "Painting Divination in the Florentine Codex," *Representing Aztec Ritual: Performance, Text, and Image in the Work of Sahagún*, ed. Eloise Quiñones Keber (Boulder: University Press of Colorado), 251–76.

18. Campbell, *Morphological Dictionary*, 256–58.

19. For in-depth examinations of tonalli, see first Alfredo López Austin, *The Human Body and Ideology: Concepts of the Ancient Nahuas*, 2 vols., trans. Thelma Ortiz de Montellano and Bernard R. Ortiz de Montellano (Salt Lake City: University of Utah Press, 1988); and Jill Leslie McKeever Furst, *The Natural History of the Soul in Ancient Mexico* (New Haven, CT: Yale University Press, 1995). Other studies include León-Portilla, *Aztec Thought*; León-Portilla, "Three Forms of Thought"; John D. Monaghan, "The Person, Destiny, and the Construction of Difference in Mesoamerica," *RES* 33 (Spring 1998): 137–46; Hunt, *Transformation*; Davíd Carrasco, *City of Sacrifice: The Aztec Empire and the Role of Violence in Civilization* (Boston: Beacon Press, 1999); and Soustelle, *Daily Life*.

20. The noun *tonalli* (or *tonal*) derives from *tona*. Karttunen (*Analytical Dictionary*, 245) glosses *tona* as "to be or make warm, for the sun to shine." Molina (*Vocabulario* 2:149r) translates *tona* as "hazer calor o sol." J. Richard Andrews and Ross Hassig gloss

it as "to be hot, to be sunny" (Andrews and Hassig, "Editor's Introduction," in *Treatise on the Heathen Superstitions that Today Live among the Indians Native to This New Spain*, by Hernando Ruiz de Alarcón [Norman: University of Oklahoma Press, 1984], 240). Humans receive *tonalli* from the cosmos at large but principally from Tonatiuh, "the Sun." The noun *tonatiuh* also derives from *tona*. Solar heat–light energy, solar radiation, life-energy perceived and transmitted as body heat, and summertime are all obviously closely related to this sense of tonalli.

21. López Austin (*Human Body and Ideology*, I:213) refers to this as "a person's animistic fortitude."

22. The relevant term in this context recorded by Molina (*Vocabulario*, 2: 150v) is *totonal*, which he glosses as "el signo, en que alguno nace, o el alma y espiritu." McKeever Furst (*Natural History*, 64) glosses the Spanish as "the sign under which one is born, or the soul or spirit." See also López Austin, *Human Body and Ideology*, I:204–5.

23. The relevant Nahuatl term is *tetonal*, which Molina (*Vocabulario*, 2:110v) translates as "racion de alguno, o cosa diputada para otro." León-Portilla ("Those Made Worthy," 46) glosses Molina's translation as "that which is granted to one, that which one deserves"; López Austin (*Human Body and Ideology*, I:205, 217) as "something meant for, or the property of, a certain person"; and McKeever Furst (*Natural History*, 64) as a "portion of each person, or a thing assigned by another."

24. For discussion, see Monaghan, "Person, Destiny," 141–43. See also López Austin, *Human Body and Ideology*; and McKeever Furst, *Natural History*.

25. López Austin, *Human Body and Ideology*, I:205; see also I:58ff.; and McKeever Furst, *Natural History*, 135–37.

26. Hunt, *Transformation*, 129.

27. Read, *Time and Sacrifice*, 262n21. This certainly seems true of the Fifth Sun-Earth Age. Whether or not it is true of the first four Sun-Earth Ages is another matter.

28. For further discussion, see Monaghan, "Person, Destiny"; and Willard Gingerich, "*Chipahuacanemiliztli*, 'the Purified Life,' in the Discourses of Book VI, Florentine Codex," in *Smoke and Mist: Mesoamerican Studies in Memory of Thelma D. Sullivan, Part II*, ed. J. Kathryn Josserand and Karen Dakin (Oxford: British Archaeological Reports, 1988), 517–43.

29. López Austin, *Human Body and Ideology*, I:205; see also 58ff.

30. See López Austin, *Human Body and Ideology*; León Portilla, *Aztec Thought*; León Portilla, "Three Forms of Thought"; Read, *Time and Sacrifice*; Quiñones Keber, *Codex Telleriano-Remensis*; and Quiñones Keber, "Painting Divination."

31. Bernardino de Sahagún, *Florentine Codex: General History of the Things of New Spain*, ed. and trans. Arthur J.O. Anderson, and Charles Dibble (Santa Fe, NM: School of American Research; Salt Lake City: University of Utah, 1953–1982), XI:224. See also McKeever Furst, *Natural History*, 72.

32. Quoted in Willard Gingerich, "Quetzalcoatl and the Agon of Time: A Literary Reading of the *Anales de Cuauhtitlan*," *New Scholar* 10 (1986): 51. Bierhorst's original statement reads, "Native American literature is coherent" and "never a grabbag of disconnected symbols." I believe Soustelle commits the error of treating the succession of twenty tonallis as a "grabbag of disconnected symbols" when writing, "The law of the universe is the succession of different and radically separated qualities which alternately prevail, disappear and reappear without end" (quoted in León-Portilla, *Aztec Thought*, 218).

33. See López Austin, *Tamoanchan, Tlalocan*, 27; Gerardo Aldana, *The Apotheosis of Janaab' Pakal: Science, History and Religion at Classic Maya Palenque* (Boulder: University Press of Colorado, 2007), 196–97; Miguel León-Portilla, *Time and Reality in the Thought of the Maya*, 2nd ed., trans. Charles Boiles, Fernanado Horcasitas, and Miguel León-Portilla (Norman: University of Oklahoma Press, 1988), 35–37; and Ross Hassig, *Time, History and Belief in Aztec and Colonial Mexico* (Austin: University of Texas Press, 2001). Each day number is also associated with Thirteen Lords of the Day, who further shape its personality.

34. See Soustelle, *Daily Life*, 111; Hunt, *Transformation*, 194–95; López Austin, *Human Body and Ideology*, I:53; and López Austin, *Tamoanchan, Tlalocan*, 27.

35. See Boone, *Cycles of Time*; Read, *Time and Sacrifice*; Quiñones Keber, *Codex Telleriano-Remensis*; and Hassig, *Time, History and Belief*.

36. Quiñones Keber, *Codex Telleriano-Remensis*, 158.

37. Read, *Time and Sacrifice*, 106–7. Read sees the nine Night Lords as a pattern of "dark" disordering energies that "counter" the "brilliant" ordering energies of the Sun. She bases this claim upon two observations. First, the odd-numbered 9-fold pattern of Night Lords does not fit neatly into the even-numbered full count of the 260-fold tonalpohualli. This remark is puzzling, however, since the two counts synchronize every even-numbered 2,340 (9 x 260) days. Second, and more persuasively, nocturnal things were regarded as *tlatlacolli*, that is, "spoiled," "messed up," and "disordered." The disorderly nocturnal forces of the nine Night Lords are paired and interlocked in an agonistic struggle with the orderly forces of the Sun, as night is paired with day (wet with dry, cold with hot, etc.). If Read is correct, here is another instance of agonistic inamic unity.

38. For further discussion, see Boone, *Cycles of Time*; Read, *Time and Sacrifice*; and Quiñones Keber, *Codex Telleriano-Remensis*.

39. Quiñones Keber, *Codex Telleriano-Remensis*, 153.

40. Elizabeth H. Boone, "*Guías para vivir: Los manuscritos adivinatorios pintados de México*," *Azteca Mexica* (1992): 333–38. See also Elizabeth H. Boone, *Stories in Red and Black: Pictorial Histories of the Aztecs and Mixtecs* (Austin: University of Texas Press, 2000); Boone, *Cycles of Time*; Wayne Elzey, "Some Remarks on the Space and Time of the 'Center' in Aztec Religion," *Estudios de cultura náhuatl* 12 (1976): 315–34; Quiñones Keber, *Codex Telleriano-Remensis*; and Quiñones Keber, "Painting Divination."

41. Charles O. Frake, "Cognitive Maps of Time and Tide among Medieval Seafarers," *Man* N.S. 20 (1985): 254–70. Elzey ("Some Remarks," 315) also likens the tonalpohualli to a compass.

42. The tonalamatl is also aptly likened to the *I Ching: Book of Changes*, trans. James Legge, ed. and intro. Ch'Chai with Winberg Chai (New Hyde Park, NY: University Books, 1964). The *I Ching* contains no specific predictions and is not a divinatory manual in the sense of foretelling the future. It functions instead as a practical action-guide for those seeking its counsel. One brings to the text a practical question. The text then offers various practical solutions to these questions.

43. Sahagún, *Florentine Codex*, X:191.

44. Ibid., X:191.

45. See, e.g., Carrasco, *Daily Life*, 60–62.

46. López Austin, *Human Body and Ideology*, I:205; see also I:58ff.

47. Quoted in León-Portilla, *Aztec Thought*, 218. See also López Austin, *Human Body and Ideology*, 1:205.

48. See Alan Isaacs, John Daintith, and Elizabeth Martin, eds., *A Dictionary of Science* (Oxford: Oxford University Press, 1999), 90, 91–92, 159, 208, 551.

49. Read (*Time and Sacrifice*) also proposes a biological conception of the cosmos.

50. Quoted in León-Portilla, *Aztec Thought*, 218.

51. See Ann Pollard Rowe, *A Century of Change in Guatemalan Textiles* (New York: Center for Inter-American Relations, 1981); Alba Guadalupe Mastache, "El tejido en el México antiguo," *Arqueología Mexicana*, Edición especial, 19 (2005): 20–28; Alba Guadalupe Mastache, "Téchnicas prehispánicas," *Arqueología Mexicana* Edición especial 19 (2005): 29–32; and Anni Albers, *On Weaving* (Middletown, CT: Wesleyan University Press, 1965).

52. Sahagún, *Florentine Codex*, I:15. For discussion, see Thelma D. Sullivan, "Tlazolteotl-Ixcuina: The Great Spinner and Weaver," in *The Art and Iconography of Late Post-Classic Central Mexico*, ed. Elizabeth Hill Boone (Washington, DC: Dumbarton Oaks, 1982), 22; and Barbara Tedlock and Dennis Tedlock, "Text and Textile: Language and Technology in the Arts of the Quiché Maya," *Journal of Anthropological Research* 41, no. 2 (1985): 121–46.

53. Sullivan, "Tlazolteotl-Ixcuina," 14.

54. Quoted in Boone, *Stories in Red and Black*, 197.

55. See ibid.

56. For further discussion, see Boone, *Cycles of Time*; Quiñones Keber, *Codex Telleriano-Remensis*; Read, *Time and Sacrifice*; León-Portilla, *Aztec Thought*; León-Portilla, "Three Forms of Thought"; and Hassig, *Time, History and Belief*.

57. Quiñones Keber, *Codex Telleriano-Remensis*, 155.

58. Molina, *Vocabulario*, 159v, brackets mine. See also Karttunen, *Analytical Dictionary*, 324; Campbell, *Morphological Dictionary*, 412–13; Read, *Time and Sacrifice*; and

López Austin, *Human Body and Ideology*. Both Karttunen and Campbell distinguish *xihuitl* from *xihuitl* ("comet").

59. Campbell, *Morphological Dictionary*, 412.

60. Ibid., 412–13.

61. Turquoise connotes preciousness (Karttunen, *Analytical Dictionary*, 324). Karttunen claims *xihuitl* functions as a modifier for heat that indicates intensity in the same way that "white" and "blue" do in English.

62. Read, *Time and Sacrifice*, 280n24. Read notes that the 52-year xiuhmolpilli and count of the nine Night Lords coincides every 468 solar years. This event was not apparently celebrated.

63. López Austin, *Human Body and Ideology*, I:65.

64. *Histoyre du Mechique* and *Historia de los mexicanos por sus pinturas* are both reproduced in *Teogonía e historia de los mexicanos: Tres opúsculos del siglo XVI*, 1st ed., ed. Angel María Garibay K. (México: Editorial Porrúa, 1965); and *Leyenda de los Soles* appears in translation in John Bierhorst, "Legend of the Suns," in *History and Mythology of the Aztecs* (Tucson: University of Arizona Press, 1992).

65. I do not mean to suggest that these characteristics are mutually exclusive by Aztec lights. A detailed discussion of these sources obviously exceeds the scope of this project. For discussion of the written texts' literal vs. figurative vs. ritual characteristics, and of their status as mytho-history vs. literature, see Gingerich, "Quetzalcoatl"; Wayne Elzey, "The Nahua Myth of the Four Suns," *Numen* (1976): 114–35; Georges Baudot, *Utopia and History in Mexico: The First Chroniclers of Mexican Civilization* (1520–1569), trans. Bernard R. Ortiz de Montellano and Thelma Ortiz de Montellano (Niwot: University Press of Colorado, 1995); Boone, *Stories in Red and Black*; Boone, *Cycles of Time*; Hassig, *Time, History and Belief*; and H. B. Nicholson, *Topiltzin Quetzalcoatl: The Once and Future Lord of the Toltecs* (Boulder: University Press of Colorado, 2001). For indigenous North American perspectives, see Norton-Smith, *Dance*; and Thurman Lee Hester and Jim Cheney, "Truth and Native American Epistemology," *Social Epistemology* (2001): 319–34.

66. Nicholson, "Religion," 397. Michel Graulich concurs (Graulich, *Myths of Ancient Mexico*, trans. Bernard R. Ortiz de Montellano and Thelma Ortiz de Montellano [Norman: University of Oklahoma Press, 1997], 75). According to Graulich, the *Historia de los mexicanos por sus pinturas* and the *Leyenda de los soles* were "commissioned by Motecuhzoma II to support his religious reforms and his revision of the myths" (Graulich, *Myths of Ancient Mexico*, 24). Nicholson ("Religion," 398) characterizes the two as preserving the "apparent canonical version of Tenochtitlan." For discussion, see also Davíd Carrasco, *Quetzalcoatl and the Irony of Empire: Myths and Prophecies in the Aztec Tradition* (Chicago: University of Chicago Press, 1982); Hassig, *Time, History and Belief*; and Elzey, "The Nahua Myth." I begin by approaching the text as literal chronology and cosmogony.

67. *Historia de los mexicanos por sus pinturas*, 23.

68. León-Portilla, *Aztec Thought*, 30, 35, 84, 90. See also Karl Taube, *Aztec and Maya Myths* (Austin: University of Texas Press, 1995), 31; and Nicholson, "Religion."

69. Quoted in León-Portilla, *Aztec Thought*, 95.

70. Dennis Tedlock, "Creation in the Popol Vuh: A Hermeneutical Approach," in *Symbol and Meaning beyond the Closed Community: Essays in Mesoamerican Ideas*, ed. Gary H. Gossen (Albany, NY: Institute for Mesoamerican Studies, SUNY Press, 1986), 81. See also León-Portilla, "Mitos de los origenes"; Dennis Tedlock, "Introduction," in *Popol Vuh: The Definitive Edition of the Mayan Book of the Dawn of Life and the Glories of Gods and Kings*, intro., trans., and commentary Dennis Tedlock (New York: Simon and Schuster, 1985), 23–66; and Barbara Tedlock, *Time and the Highland Maya*, rev. ed. (Albuquerque: University of New Mexico Press, 1992 [1982]).

71. *Historia de los mexicanos por sus pinturas*, 23–24. For discussion, see Graulich, *Myths of Ancient Mexico*; Graulich, "Creation Myths"; Graulich, "Creator Deities"; Bodo Spranz, *Los dioses en los códices mexicanos del grupo Borgia*, trans. María Martínez Peñaloza (México, DF: Fondo de Cultura Económica, 1973), 285–88; Quiñones Keber, *Codex Telleriano-Remensis*, 162–64; León-Portilla, *Aztec Thought*; and Nicholson, "Religion."

72. León-Portilla, *Aztec Thought*, 33.

73. *Historia de los mexicanos por sus pinturas*, 24.

74. Ibid., 25.

75. For discussion, see Nicholson, "Religion," 398; Michel Graulich, *Myths of Ancient Mexico*; and Quiñones Keber, *Codex Telleriano-Remensis*, 62–63.

76. *Historia de los mexicanos por sus pinturas*, 25, translation mine.

77. Carrasco, *Quetzalcoatl*, 93.

78. See Quiñones Keber, *Codex Telleriano-Remensis*, 155.

79. Bierhorst, John, trans., "Annals of Cuauhtitlan," in *History and Mythology of the Aztecs: The Codex Chimalpopoca* (Tucson: University of Arizona Press, 1992), 24. This statement does not entail that Oxomoco and Cipactonal created the count; only that they were charged with the responsibility of using the count.

80. Sahagún, *Florentine Codex*, IV:4, brackets mine. For relevant discussion, see Quiñones Keber, "Painting Divination"; Alfredo López Austin, *The Rabbit on the Face of the Moon: Mythology in the Mesoamerican Tradition*, trans. Bernard R. Ortiz de Montellano and Thelma Ortiz de Montellano (Salt Lake City: University of Utah Press, 1996), 27–28.

81. Quiñones Keber, *Codex Telleriano-Remensis*, 163.

82. See López Austin, *Tamoanchan, Tlalocan*, 92.

83. Boone, *Cycles of Time*, 24. See also Quiñones Keber, "Painting Divination," 253–54. Carrasco (*Quetzalcoatl*, 93) credits Quetzalcoatl and Huitzilopochtli with inventing the calendar.

84. López Austin, *Human Body and Ideology*, I:238; see also I:243.

85. López Austin, *Rabbit on the Face*, 104; see also Boone, *Cycles of Time*, 14–15; and Leonardo López Luján, "Old Gods," in *The Oxford Encyclopedia of Mesoamerican Cultures: The Civilizations of Mexico and Central America*, ed. Davíd Carrasco (Oxford: Oxford University Press, 2001), 404.

86. *Historia de los mexicanos por sus pinturas*, 25–26.

87. León-Portilla, *Aztec Thought*, 35.

88. *Historia de los mexicanos por sus pinturas*, 27.

89. Enrique Florescano, *Memory, Myth, and Time in Mexico: From the Aztecs to Independence*, trans. Albert G. Bork with the assistance of Kathryn R. Bork (Austin: University of Texas Press, 1994), 2.

90. Ibid., 9.

91. Ibid., 9. By "in a moment without time," does he mean "without duration" or "outside of time"? Apparently both.

92. Florescano, *Memory, Myth, and Time*, 9.

93. *Historia de los mexicanos por sus pinturas*, 29.

94. Ibid., 30.

95. Nicholson, "Religion," 398; see also Carrasco, *Quetzalcoatl*, 93. The various accounts of the four Suns differ in details. For discussion, see Nicholson, "Religion," 399.

96. León-Portilla, *Aztec Thought*, 36.

97. Only the Fifth Sun-Earth Era has four lower skies, heavens, or layers.

98. *Historia de los mexicanos por sus pinturas*, 27–31; see also Graulich, *Myths of Ancient Mexico*, 64–71. The order of these differs in the account offered in the Bierhorst, "Annals of Cuauhtitlan," 26.

99. See Carrasco, *Quetzalcoatl and the Irony of Empire*, 94; and Elzey, "The Nahua Myth," 118.

100. See Graulich, *Myths of Ancient Mexico*, 80; and López Austin, *Human Body and Ideology*, I:53.

101. Hunt, *Transformation*, 116.

102. Bierhorst, "Legend of the Suns," 142. See also León Portilla, *Aztec Thought and Culture*, 41.

103. See also Bierhorst, "Annals of Cuauhtitlan," 26. For discussion, see Graulich, *Myths of Ancient Mexico*, 64, table 4; León-Portilla, *Aztec Thought*, 38–36; and Nicholson, "Religion," 398–99.

104. "Estos dioses tenían estos nombres y otros muchos, porque según en la cosa en que se ententían, o se les atribuían, así le ponían el nombre" (*Historia de los mexicanos por sus pinturas*, 24).

105. Bierhorst, "Annals of Cuauhtitlan," 26.

106. For discussion, see León-Portilla, *Aztec Thought*, 54, 56; Elzey, "Some Remarks"; Elzey, "The Nahua Myth"; and Graulich, "Quetzalcoatl-Ehecatl," 82.

107. Susan Gillespie, "Different Ways of Seeing: Modes of Social Consciousness in Mesoamerican Two-Dimensional Artworks," *Baesler-Archiv* 55 (2007): 125, brackets mine. See also León-Portilla, *Aztec Thought*; León-Portilla, *Time and Reality*, 56–90; Elzey, "Some Remarks"; and Elzey, "The Nahua Myth."

108. Aveni, *Skywatchers*.

109. Bierhorst, "Legend of the Suns," 142–43, 147–49; and "Histoyre du Mechique," 103–4.

110. Elzey, "The Nahua Myth," 125.

111. León-Portilla, *Aztec Thought*, 54, 56.

112. Bierhorst, "Legend of the Suns," 145–46. This text states that it is Quetzalcoatl alone, bleeding his virile member. *Histoyre du Mechique* (106) states instead that all the gods bled their tongues.

113. For example, see Bierhorst, "Legend of the Suns," 145.

114. Quoted in and translated by Read, *Time and Sacrifice*, 49.

115. Bierhorst, "Legend of the Suns," 144–45; Bierhorst, "Annals of Cuauhtitlan," 26.

116. Elzey, "The Nahua Myth," 123.

117. Elzey, "Some Remarks," 324.

118. For discussion, see Gingerich, "Quetzalcoatl," and Norton-Smith, *Dance*.

119. Bierhorst, "Legend of the Suns," 144–45.

120. Ibid., 145.

121. The same would appear to hold mutatis mutandis for the xiuhpohualli and xiuhmolpilli.

122. Boone, *Cycles of Time*, 179–81.

123. Bierhorst, "Legend of the Suns," 148.

124. Sahagún, *General History*, VII:8.

125. *Ilhuitl* is also standardly translated as "festival day, holiday" (Karttunen, *Analytical Dictionary*, 104).

126. John Bierhorst, ed., *Codex Chimalpopoca: The Text in Nahuatl* (Tucson: University of Arizona Press, 1992), 78:1 (p. 90). The *Historia*, being written in Spanish, uses the word *día*.

127. Bierhorst, *Codex Chimalpopoca*, 78:1 (p. 90); see also side 77, line 56. Translation by Bierhorst, "Legend of the Suns," 148.

128. Bierhorst, *Codex Chimalpopoca*, 78:23 (p. 91) (Translation by Bierhorst, *Legend of the Suns*, 14).

129. D. Tedlock, "Creation in the Popol Vuh," 79. Brotherston and Ades ("Mesoamerican Description") argue Maya metaphysics lacks a cosmogony. See also López Austin, *Tamoanchan, Tlalocan*; and Read, *Time and Sacrifice*.

130. Carrasco, *Daily Life*, 59.

131. Florescano, *Memory, Myth, and Time*, 11.

132. Michael Levine, *Pantheism: A Non-Theistic Concept of Deity* (London: Routledge, 1994), 179.

133. Quoted in Roger T. Ames, "Putting the Te Back into Taoism," in *Nature in Asian Traditions of Thought: Essays in Environmental Philosophy*, ed. J. Baird Callicott and Roger T. Ames (Albany: State University Press of New York, 1989), 137.

134. See Tedlock and Tedlock, "Text and Textile." Burkhart ("Mexica Women," 50) reports Dennis Tedlock's suggestion that Mesoamerican calendrical periods are more aptly conceived as folds of a cloth mounted upon a loom than as wheel-like cycles.

135. León-Portilla, "Three Forms of Thought," 14.

136. Carrasco (*Daily Life*, 59) and Elzey ("The Nahua Myth," 125) characterize them as "kinds" of time, while Carrasco (in "Uttered from the Heart," 10–11) characterizes them as "patterns." López Austin (*Human Body and Ideology*, I:61) characterizes them as "dimensions." See also López Austin, *Tamoanchan, Tlalocan*; Nicholson, "Religion"; Graulich, *Myths of Ancient Mexico*; and Leonardo López Luján, *The Offerings of the Templo Mayor of Tenochtitlan*, rev. ed., trans. Thelma Ortiz de Montellano and Bernard Ortiz de Montellano (Albuquerque: University of New Mexico Press, 2005), 37–39. To my knowledge, Read (*Time and Sacrifice*) alone challenges the received view's characterization.

137. Carrasco, *Daily Life*, 59.

138. López Austin, *Human Body and Ideology*, I:61.

139. Carrasco, *Daily Life*, 59.

140. Carrasco, "Uttered from the Heart," 10–11.

141. León-Portilla, *La filosofía náhuatl*, 98; León-Portilla, *Aztec Thought*, 35. See also Nicholson, "Religion," 398.

142. Florescano, *Memory, Myth, and Time*, 25.

143. López Austin, *Tamoanchan, Tlalocan*, 18.

144. Carrasco, *Daily Life*, 59.

145. Carrasco, "Uttered from the Heart," 11.

146. Florescano, *Memory, Myth, and Time*, 9.

147. Carrasco, "Uttered from the Heart," 11.

148. Florescano, *Memory, Myth, and Time*, 25.

149. López Austin, *Human Body and Ideology*, 1:63.

150. Carrasco, *Daily Life*, 92.

151. López Austin, *Human Body and Ideology*, 1:63; see also p. 61. Carrasco ("Uttered from the Heart," 11) also uses this phrase.

152. López Austin, *Human Body and Ideology*, 1:61.

153. Carrasco, "Uttered from the Heart," 11.

154. León-Portilla, *Aztec Thought*, 36.

155. López Austin, *Tamoanchan, Tlalocan*, 18.

156. Carrasco, *Daily Life*, 59.

157. Carrasco, "Uttered from the Heart," 11. See also León-Portilla, *Aztec Thought*, 33–37.

158. López Austin, *Human Body and Ideology*, I:61; and Carrasco, *Daily Life*, 59.

159. Davíd Carrasco, *Religions of Mesoamerica: Cosmovision and Ceremonial Centers* (San Francisco: Harper and Row, 1990), 38. In this context Carrasco's remark that the First Sun-Earth Era, 4 Ocelotonatiuh, was "brought into order out of primordial chaos" is perplexing. First, the First Sun-Earth Era is created from within mythic time. Second, calendars are ordering devices, so if either of the two calendars applies to the time of myth, then the time of myth is orderly.

160. Florescano, *Memory, Myth, and Time*, 3.

161. *Historia de los mexicanos por sus pinturas*, 29 (translation by Florescano, *Memory, Myth, and Time*, 233n3).

162. See Florescano, *Memory, Myth, and Time*, 2–3.

163. López Austin, *Human Body and Ideology*, I:63; see also I:61–66.

164. Ibid., 1:65.

165. Ibid., 1:63.

166. Ibid.

167. Carrasco, *Daily Life*, 59.

168. López Austin, *Human Body and Ideology*, I:60–63. See also Carrasco, *Daily Life*, 59; and Carrasco, "Uttered from the Heart," 11.

169. See López Austin, *Human Body and Ideology*, I:60–61; López Luján, *Offerings*, 225.

170. López Austin, *Human Body and Ideology*, 1:65–66; see also López Austin, *Tamoanchan, Tlalocan*, 16.

171. López Austin, *Tamoanchan, Tlalocan*, 26.

172. The following is indebted to Lawrence Sklar, *Space, Time, and Space Time* (Berkeley: University of California Press, 1974), 161–82; Lawrence Sklar, "Space, Time, and Relativity," in *A Companion to the Philosophy of Science*, ed. W. H. Newton-Smith (Oxford: Blackwell, 2000), 461–69; Nicholas Rescher, *Process Metaphysics: An Introduction to Process Philosophy* (Albany: State University of New York Press, 1996), 94–97; and Philip Turetzky, *Time* (London: Routledge, 1998).

173. See Sklar, *Space, Time, and Space Time*, 161.

174. Quoted in Sklar, *Space, Time, and Space Time*, 168.

175. Quoted in Donald Fixico, *The American Indian Mind in a Linear World* (New York: Routledge, 2003), 12. For the indigenous peoples of North America, writes Vine Deloria Jr., place consists of "the relationships of things to each other," (Vine Deloria Jr.

and Daniel Wildcat, *Power and Place*, 23) while time is "internal to the complex relationships themselves" (Deloria, *God Is Red*, 94).

176. Rescher, *Process Metaphysics*, 96.

177. As claimed by Boone, *Cycles of Time*, 96.

178. Quoted in Hunt, *Transformation*, 47 (italics mine).

179. Rescher, *Process Metaphysics*, 96.

180. León-Portilla, *Aztec Thought*, 33.

181. Quoted in León-Portilla, *Aztec Thought*, 218, emphasis mine.

182. See López Austin, *Human Body and Ideology*; and Carrasco, *Daily Life*.

183. I borrow this phrase from Dorothy Emmet, *The Passage of Nature* (Philadelphia: Temple University Press, 1992), 68.

184. For further discussion see Read, *Time and Sacrifice*, 214–16.

185. Pace Arnold, *Eating Landscape*, 61; Carrasco, *Religions of Mesoamerica*, 68; and Carrasco, *Daily Life*, 46.

186. León-Portilla, *Aztec Thought*; Elzey, "Some Remarks"; and Elzey, "The Nahua Myth."

187. Here I follow Tedlock and Tedlock ("Text and Textile," 127), who use the term *chronotope* (which they borrow from Mikhail Bakhtin) to refer to the Mayas' fusing of space and time.

188. Hunt, *Transformation*, 109–12.

189. For the other three ages, see Hunt, *Transformation*, 111, table 2.

190. Boone, *Cycles of Time*, 181. I believe Boone mistakenly equates time itself with the tonalpohualli.

191. López Austin, *Rabbit on the Face*, 105.

192. I borrow this phrase from Quiñones Keber, *Codex Telleriano-Remensis*, 242.

193. López Austin, *Human Body and Ideology*, 1:191.

194. Campbell, *Morphological Dictionary*, 122–23; see also López Austin, *Human Body and Ideology*, 1:191.

195. López Austin, *Human Body and Ideology*, 1:191.

196. The figure is painted in four colors and stands for twenty days.

197. Boone, *Stories in Red and Black*, 35.

8

Let's tie together the arguments of the preceding chapters. Backstrap weaving is one of the principal organizing metaphors employed by Aztec metaphysics in conceiving the structure and working of reality and cosmos. Olin, malinalli, and nepantla motion-change are all involved in weaving. Backstrap weaving includes spinning, twisting, bobbing, shuttling, undulating, and interlacing. This chapter examines backstrap weaving with the aim of understanding more fully the claim that Aztec metaphysics conceives the cosmos as a grand weaving-in-progress. I first briefly review our findings regarding the nature of olin, malinalli, and nepantla motion-change.

Reality and Cosmos as Nepantla-Process

8.1. THE DYNAMICS OF THE AZTEC COSMOS

Olin, malinalli, and nepantla represent three different kinds or patterns of motion-change and transformation that explain the becoming, ordering, and diversity of the Aztec cosmos. They are *not* different *kinds* of energy but rather different *shapes* or *patterns* of teotl's single, uniform energy that characterize the self-processing, self-becoming, and self-regenerating of teotl. They are each a *how*, not a *what*. The circulation of energy and power throughout the cosmos follows these three patterns. Understanding the three is key to understanding why teotl's changes are processual – that is, regular, orderly, predictable, and transformative – rather than wholly random. Olin, malinalli, and nepantla also represent three different ways of unifying inamic partners in agonistic tension. Finally, all three are creatively destructive, destructively creative, and so transformative.

DOI: 10.5876_9781607322238.c008

Nepantla is cosmogonically primordial and metaphysically fundamental. Nepantla-defined motion-change, balancing, and reciprocity, as well as nepantla-generated agonistic inamic unity, have always existed. Teotl, Ometeotl, Ometecuhtli~Omecihuatl, and Tonacatecuhtli~Tonacacihuatl are defined by nepantla motion-change. Since they have always already existed, nepantla motion-change has always already existed. Nepantla motion-change is mutually middling, betwixt-and-betweening, and reciprocating. It unifies inamic partners in balanced agonistic tension. It is transformative – that is, both destructively creative and creatively destructive. It joins, mixes, fuses, and weaves things together, and it does so in a manner that is abundant with mutuality and reciprocity. It is middled and middling. It is orderly, ordered, and ordering. It puts stuff in place; it arranges stuff. Generally speaking generation (creation) and regeneration (renewal) involve binding together and arranging inamic partners – and this is precisely what nepantla motion-change does. Weaving and sexual commingling typify nepantla motion-change. Not being a unit-day of the tonalpohualli, nepantla has no day-sign glyph. This is wholly fitting, seeing as nepantla is cosmogonically more primordial and metaphysically more basic than the tonalpohualli and its twenty day signs. Aztec artists used ideograms such as the quincunx, quatrefoil, crossroads, and xicalcoliuhqui to convey the idea of nepantla.

Olin defines the shape of motion-change involved in cyclical continuation, completion, and renewal. Olin motion-change binds the ending of one life~death cycle with the beginning of a new life~death cycle into a single, seamless process. Olin is the defining shape of transformation *within* and *across* life~death cycles. And what holds for the inamic pair life~death holds mutatis mutandis for the various inamic pairs aligned with life~death. Olin therefore also constitutes one of the principal shapes of motion-change involved the cyclical continuation, completion, and renewal of all paired inamic forces (e.g., light~dark, east~west, and being~nonbeing).

Given that the Fifth Sun is named 4 Olin Tonatiuh and that olin motion-change therefore defines the essence of the Fifth Sun, it necessarily follows that the motion-change of 4 Olin Tonatiuh paradigmatically exemplifies olin. And how does 4 Olin Tonatiuh move-change? It moves *back-and-forth* along the horizon from winter solstice to summer solstice, as well as *over-and-above* and *down-and-under* Tlalticpac. Olin is also exemplified by bouncing rubber balls, pulsating hearts, respiring chests, earthquakes and tremors, labor contractions, the flapping of a butterfly's wings, the expanding and contracting of a spindle rod with thread, and (as we will see below) the undulating of a weaver's weft-toting bobbin during weaving. These suggest olin motion-change consists of bouncing back-and-forth, up-and-over, and down-and-under; pulsating;

throbbing; oscillating; undulating; expanding and contracting; and growing and shrinking. It is by these sorts of motion-change that olin motion-change unites the paired inamic forces of the cosmos.

Olin shaped motion-change has two additional key properties. It is four-phased and centering. First, it arranges the cyclical alternation of inamic partners around a center. Second, it arranges the cyclical alternation of inamic partners into four phases. These four phases are birth and infancy, youth, maturity, and old age and death. Olin's quaking, bouncing, throbbing, and oscillating are thus centered and four-phased. Olin is the shape of a thing's four-phased transformation from birth and infancy, to youth and maturity, to old age and death, and then from death back again to birth. It is centered and centering as well as ordered, orderly, and ordering. It defines *how* things cyclically process in the Fifth Age. All things are processes, and all processes move-change according to a specific pattern. This pattern is their *ohtli*, their *path*. Olin shapes the paths of all things in the Fifth Sun–Earth Ordering as they move through their four-phased life~death – as well as their corresponding male~female, hot~cold, being~nonbeing – cycle.

Olin motion-change is also the defining biorhythm of the Fifth Sun, the Fifth Sun–Earth Ordering, and all inhabitants of the Fifth Sun–Earth Ordering, and as such, it constitutes their "heart" or essence. It defines the Fifth Sun and therefore defines the shape of the existence *of* the Fifth Age as well as the shape of existence *in* the Fifth Age. It defines *how* things cyclically process in the Fifth Age. Finally, Aztec artists conveyed the concept of olin using quatrefoils, quincunxes, four-petaled flowers, four-winged butterflies, ballcourts, patolli boards, and the olin day sign glyph.

Malinalli motion-change is typified by twisting, spinning, spiraling, whirling, coiling, drilling, and gyrating. Malinalli motion-change, energy transmission, and transformation are exemplified by spinning fiber into thread, cooking and digesting food, blowing life into things, drilling fire, burning incense, and ritual music, speech, and song (*in xochitl in cuicatl*). It unites inamic partners into agonistic tension by twisting, spinning, whirling, and gyrating them together.

Malinalli defines the shape of motion-change, energy transmission, and transformation: *between* vertical layers of the Fifth Sun–Earth Ordering (e.g., the Above, the Below, and Tlalticpac; humans, Sun, and Earth); *between* the olin-defined life~cycles of different kinds of things (e.g., between Sun and grass, grass and rabbit, rabbit and human, human and Sun, Sun and grass, and so on); and *between* different conditions of the same thing (e.g., disorderly raw cotton and orderly thread; raw foodstuffs and cooked foodstuffs; and disorderly captives and orderly foodstuff during Tlacaxipehualiztli).

Malinalli shaped energy *initiates new* olin-defined life~death cycles as well as *feeds* and *renews* existing olin-defined life~death cycles. Malinalli-shaped energy *fuels* the four-phased, olin motion-change of the Fifth Sun and all things in the Fifth Age. It is the shape of energy that *nourishes* humans as well as plants, animals, Earth, Sun, rain, wind, fire, and Fifth Age. If olin motion-change constitutes the biorhythm of the Fifth Sun, Fifth Age, and all inhabitants of the Fifth Age, then malinalli motion-change constitutes the shape of the conveyance, circulation, and recycling of vital energies that initiate, fortify, and help complete these olin-defined biorhythms. If olin represents the pulsating heartbeat of the Fifth Age, then malinalli represents the bloodstream and foodstream – the twisting arteries, veins, and entrails – of the Fifth Age. Because one of the foremost aims of Aztec ritual is the recycling of energy in order to renew, nourish, and help complete the olin-defined life~death cycles of various processes in the Fifth Sun-Earth Ordering, malinalli-defined activities dominate Aztec rituals, and malinalli motifs and ideograms dominate Aztec ritual manuals. Aztec artists conveyed the idea of malinalli using spirals, coils, twists, double helices, double-unfolding spirals, the xicalcoliuhqui, and the malinalli day sign glyph.

Nepantla motion-change continually generates and regenerates the Fifth Sun-Earth Ordering by integrating olin and malinalli motion-change into a single process. How exactly do olin and malinalli figure into the weaving of the Fifth Age? Weaving fabric involves interlacing weft (horizontal) and warp (vertical) fibers. Olin motion-change functions as the horizontal, weft-related activities that contribute to the weaving of the Fifth Age. The weft motion of the Fifth Age is typified by the Fifth Sun's olin-defined oscillating path over and above and down and under the Earth. Malinalli motion-change functions as the vertical warp-related activities that contribute to the weaving of the Fifth Age. The tonalpohualli, xiuhpohualli, and xiuhmolpilli represent warp patterns in teotl's weaving of the Fifth Age. Nepantla motion-change weaves together malinalli and olin to form the fabric of the Fifth Age. *Together, the three kinds of motion-change define the dynamics of the Fifth Age.*

Because it is cosmogonically primordial and metaphysically fundamental, it appears nepantla motion-change precedes both olin and malinalli in the unfolding of the cosmos. Olin motion-change and malinalli motion-change appear not to emerge *at least explicitly* until Ometeotl (teotl) further unfolds and self-differentiates into the tonalpohualli.[1] If this is correct, then olin and malinalli represent further unfoldings of and differentiations within nepantla motion-change. Nepantla incorporates ollin and malinalli within a larger cosmic eurhythmy – much like a song's major musical rhythm incorporates within itself minor rhythms. Nepantla is the primordial and most fundamental pattern of generative and transformative interaction and becoming. Nepantla-defined reciprocity continually generates, orders, and defines the fabric of reality and cosmos as such. Chapter 1 argued that reality is defined by continual becoming, transforming, and processing. Now we see that this continual becoming, transforming, and processing is principally defined by nepantla. Reality is a nepantla-process in progress.

8.2. BACKSTRAP WEAVING

Backstrap weaving involves the incremental transformation of disordered raw fiber into well-ordered woven cloth.[2] Each step prepares the way for the next until finally a complete cloth is born. Becoming a woven cloth is a process of creative-destructive and destructive-creative transformation. Weaving begins with the selecting and physical seizing of raw, disorderly fiber (such as cotton, maguey, or yucca) from the periphery where it grows. This is the first step in its transformation. Transporting the fiber to the center for spinning and weaving centers it and so further orders it. The fiber is then prepared for spinning. In the case of cotton this involves cleaning the seeds, leaves, and other debris from the bolls of raw cotton. The cotton is then fluffed out and beaten with sticks into smooth even strips. These are then spun into thread (*icpatl*).[3] The raw fiber is spun onto spindle rods. Since we have already examined spinning and the role of spinning in Aztec metaphysics, I will not do so at length here. Remember, however, that the spindle is gendered male, while the spinning whorl and bowl are gendered female. Spinning is likened to sexual intercourse.[4] The complete spindle unit – rod, whorl, and bowl – thus constitutes a male~female inamic unity. Remember, too, that a spindle undergoes phases of expanding and shrinking and in so doing exhibits olin-style motion-change in addition to the malinalli motion-change of spinning itself. It begins as an empty stick. As spinning commences, the spindle expands with thread until it can hold no more. During weaving, the spindle gradually shrinks in size as the thread feeds the fabric. The spindle completes its cycle as an empty stick, only to begin anew. The expanding and contracting volume of the thread on the spindle resembles the expanding and contracting of a pulsating human heart and child-bearing woman. The spindle's physical motion also involves qualitative change, just as the woman's physical change also involves qualitative change. The spindle becomes pregnant with thread, as a woman becomes pregnant with child. Both spindle, human heart, and child-bearing woman oscillate, pulsate, and undulate with olin motion-change. Spinning fiber into thread thus evokes

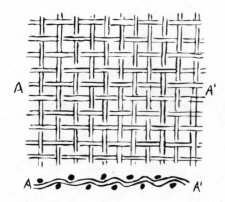

FIGURE 8.1. *Plain weave (*tafetán*). Top, top view; bottom, side view. (Redrawn from Mastache, "El Tejido en el México antiguo,"* Arqueología Mexicana, *Edición especial 19 [2005]: 29.)*

olin motion-change and reproduction.

Weaving involves the interlacing of two different sets of thread: warp and weft. Aztec metaphysics conceives the cosmos of the Fifth Sun-Earth Era as a grand weaving-in-progress and it conceives time-place as a pattern in this weaving. What are the two systems of thread involved in the weaving of the Fifth Age? The weaving of the Fifth Sun-Earth Age consists of a vertical group of tonalpohualli and xiuhpohualli warp threads and a horizontal group of 4 Olin Tonatiuh–driven olin-moving weft threads. The moving of time-place in the Fifth Age consists of interweaving these two groups. Both warp and weft threads are spun, that is, malinalli-twisted. How they differ from one another is a function of their role in making the cosmos. Thread becomes warp or weft wholly on the basis of how it is used in the weaving process. Warp and weft threads are indistinguishable, metaphysically speaking, a fact that accords nicely with Aztec metaphysics' constitutional monism. They differ neither substantively nor intrinsically.

Warp and weft threads may be interwoven in a variety of different ways, each based upon their predetermined relative ordering. The simplest weaving technique is called *plain weave* (*tafetán*), according to which the weft thread moves alternately over and under each warp thread it encounters on its horizontal course from one side of the warp to the other, at which time it reverses its direction.[5] On its way back, the weft moves under those warp threads it had earlier moved over, and moves over those it had previously moved under (see Figure 8.1).

Alba Guadalupe Mastache discusses another weaving technique called *joining* (*enlazado*). It is typically executed by hand (without bobbin or shuttle), and joins two or more weft threads with two or more warp threads. Joining is the weaving technique typically involved in simpler basket and mat weaving (see Figure 8.2).[6]

Different weaving techniques interlace warp and weft in different ways, producing fabrics of various textures, qualities, and appearances. In addition to the foregoing techniques, there is tapestry, satin, and twill.[7] Interweaving warp and weft undergoes four phases: weft repeatedly travels over, penetrates, travels under, and reemerges from warp. The Nahuatl word for warp thread is *icpatlatetectli* (*urdiembre de hilo* in Spanish).[8] *Icpatlatetectli* parses into *icpatl* ("thread") and *tlatetectli*. Molina translates *tlatetectli* as "warp of cloth (*tela urdida*) or hank of thread or something cut into pieces or sliced."[9] *Tlatetectli* parses into *tla* + *teteca* + *tli*. *Tētēca* is a reflexive verb meaning "to lie down, stretch out, to stretch something out."[10] Molina lists a second reflexive verb, *teteca*, which he translates as "to lie down with a woman," and lists a transitive verb, *teteca*, which he translates as "to warp (*urdir*) cloth or arrange a bed or platform, etc."[11]

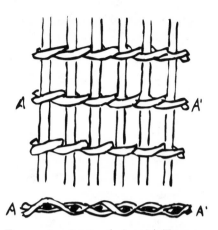

FIGURE 8.2. *Joining (enlazado). Top, top view; bottom, side view. (Redrawn from Mastache, "El Tejido en el México antiguo," Arqueología Mexicana, Edición especial 19 [2005]: 30.)*

Adding the suffix -*ni* to the verb forms the agentive noun, *tetecani*, which he translates as "one who lies down with a woman" and "one who weaves cloth or arranges a bed or platform, etc."[12] *Teteca*, in turn, derives from the verb *tēca*, meaning "to stretch oneself out, to lie down, to settle; to stretch something out, to spread something on a flat surface."[13] Joined with *tla*- (a prefix for indirect nonhuman object) and with -*tli* (a nominative suffix), we arrive at the meaning "something stretched out."

Warp thread is defined in terms of what is done to it during weaving. Warp thread is that which has been warped, that is, stretched out, laid down, and spread out on a flat surface. *Xiotia* means "to warp cloth or to dispose threads upon a loom," while *xiotl* means "scabies or mange, or thread for warping and weaving"[14] The flat surface upon which thread is warped is the warping board and/or loom. Weaving for the Aztecs is heavily laden with sexual meaning. Aztec metaphysics associates warping thread with sexual intercourse. As one lays down and stretches out thread on a frame in the course of warping, so likewise a man lays down and stretches out a woman on a bed in the course of sexual intercourse. Warping prepares the thread for penetration by the weaver's weft-toting male batten, just as bedding a woman prepares her for male penetration. The fact that warping is analogous to sexual intercourse with a woman suggests that warp threads are female-gendered.

Before being transferred to, stretched out upon, and mounted upon the loom, the warp threads are first stretched out on a warping frame or board (see Figures 5.1 and 8.3). Warping frames may be either vertical or horizontal. The purpose of this is to keep the threads from becoming entangled, to establish the length of the weaving, to establish the breadth or width of the weaving, and to arrange the threads in the order and pattern the weaver desires that they occupy on the loom. Warping involves winding the selected thread around two or more stakes or pegs while at the same time crossing the thread over itself in the shape of a butterfly, figure eight, or X. Barbara Taber and Marilyn Anderson call this process "winding a butterfly."[15] The parallel with the Aztecs' use of quincunx, floral, and butterfly motifs as chronotopograms of the Fifth Age is striking (see Figures 4.2, 4.3, 4.6, 4.7, and 4.10). This creates a cross or "lease" that fixes each warp thread in its proper position and makes it easier to distinguish even from odd threads during the weaving process. The figure eight or butterfly-shaped crossing-over of the warp threads is preserved after mounting on the loom by means of a shed rod. This creates the shed, which is the space through which the weft-thread-transporting shuttle stick (or bobbin) passes in the process of weaving over and under warp threads.

The number of times the warp thread is passed over the stakes determines the fabric's width. Bands of color in the warp threads establish the warp pattern of the fabric. Once the warp threads are ordered but before they are transferred to the loom, they are tied together using a lease string at the point where they cross over one another. This secures their ordering. Contemporary Zoque weavers in Tuxtla Gutiérez, Chiapas, according to Donald and Dorothy Cordry, refer to this tied crossing as the *corazón* ("heart") (see Figure 8.3).[16] The warp threads are tied at the heart and then removed from the warping stakes and sized in a bath of maize water. Sizing stiffens the warps, makes them easier to handle, and strengthens them for later stretching on the loom. The Tzutujil Maya of Guatemala believe the maize bath nourishes the warps, just as corn nourishes humans, and is therefore an essential part of the "birthing of cloth."[17] The entire of arrangement of warp threads is then transferred to the loom by securing each end to the loom's upper and lower loom bars.

Stretching plays an essential role in virtually every stage of the weaving process. One stretches and draws out raw fiber when spinning it into thread. Stretching helps the weaver grow the ball of thread that coils around the spindle rod. One stretches the spun threads upon the warp board and then stretches these same warp threads when mounting them upon the loom. Lastly, stretching helps maintain the proper degree of tension in the mounted warp threads. The backstrap weaver maintains the proper degree of tension for each

of the various stages of the weaving
process by leaning forward and backward, that is, by means of middling
and mutually reciprocating nepantla
motion-change. This latter motion
reproduces females' back-and forth
motion in sexual intercourse.

Stretching also figures in parturition.
With pregnancy comes the stretching of a woman's abdomen, which in
turn leaves stretch marks. In this light,
other *tititl*-related words become significant: *cuitlatitica* ("for an infected
wound or abscess to hurt before bursting"), *netititzaliztli* ("cramp in the
abdomen"), and *yollo cuitlatiticaliztli*
("to suffer in this way").[18] Abdominal
cramps and pain as well as the pain
that precedes bursting suggest pregnancy, parturition, and thus regeneration. Eduard Seler claims the *Codex
Borgia* and the *Codex Vaticanus 3773 B*
both depict the Cihuateteo (the spirits of women who died in childbirth)
with the abdominal stretch marks from pregnancy.[19]

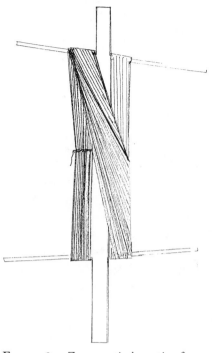

FIGURE 8.3. *Zoque vertical warping frame,
showing the "heart." (Redrawn from Cordry
and Cordry [1968: 32, photo 12].)*

What does the stretching of fiber and thread have in common with the
stretching of pregnant women's abdomens? Stretching continues the process
of ordering and arranging raw fiber, spun thread, and mounted warp threads,
and so further prepares them for their creative transformation into woven cloth,
just as stretching prepares a pregnant woman for the creative transformation
involved in giving birth to a child. Stretching also played an analogously essential role in preparing victims for creative-destructive transformation during sacrificial rituals. Aztec priests, as we saw in chapter 6, prepared victims of heart
sacrifice by stretching and arranging them upon the sacrificial stone (*techcatl*)
in an X-shape, their navels aligned with the navel of the Fifth Age (and axis
mundi) and their arms and legs aligned with the four intercardinal directions.
Stretching played an essential role in *tlacacaliliztli* ("arrow sacrifice"). Here,
too, victims were mounted upon and stretched out on a quadrilateral wooden
scaffolding into an X-shape, their four limbs oriented to the four intercardinal

directions. Finally, during Ochpaniztli priests stuffed, mounted, and stretched the skin of the Toci teixiptla on a wooden scaffold at Tocititlan, at the south causeway of Tenochtitlan. The parallels between weaving on the one hand, and tlacacaliliztli and Ochpaniztli on the other, are particularly striking. The latter's wooden scaffolds not only resemble but also function analogously to weavers' looms. Victims are mounted and stretched like warp threads upon a loom frame, arranged and prepared for nourishing the woven cloth of the cosmos. These rituals also demonstrate and enlist the creative power of nepantla-defined, X-shaped crossing of things. In short, stretching orders and arranges things and in so doing prepares them for transformation.

The transformative power of stretching is further illustrated by the *Histoyre du Mechique*. Quetzalcoatl and Tezcatlipoca formed Tlalticpac and lower skies of the Fifth Age by transforming themselves into serpents and coiling themselves around Tlaltecuhtli. One seized her right hand and left foot, the other, her left hand and right foot, thereby centering and ordering her into the shape of a figure eight or X, with her navel at its center. By constricting their coiled serpentine bodies, Quetzalcoatl and Tezcatlipoca stretched Tlaltecuhtli in opposing directions until she split down the middle, the upper half forming Tlalticpac, the lower half, the sky.[20] By stretching Tlaltecuhtli, they prepared her for subsequent stages in the Fifth Sun's ordering of the Fifth Era.

Weavers and embroiderers celebrated the festival of Tititl ("Stretching," "Wrinkled," "Contracting") during the seventeenth veintena. Scholars variously argue the festival honored Tona, Xochiquetzal, Ilamatecuhtli, and/or Cihuacoatl.[21] *Tititl* is part of a semantic cluster including *tititza* ("to stretch; to stretch something"),[22] *titicana* ("to stretch or extend what is shrunk or wrinkled"), and *tlatiticanaliztli* ("act of stretching or unwrinkling something").[23] The aforementioned honored female deities fall within Nicholson's Teteoinnan complex and are aspects of Tlazolteotl-Ixcuina, the great genetrix, spinner, and weaver. Durán's illustration for Tititl shows two youths pulling at one another while sitting in the heavens.[24] The *Tovar Calendar*'s illustration depicts what its commentators describe as "a man as one who stretches something with a cord, in order to indicate that the gods thus stretch and sustain the machine of the world so that the great violence of the winds will not destroy it."[25] Interestingly, the man pulls on a rope that is tied into a figure eight or butterfly-shaped knot of the sort described earlier. This nepantla motif occurs in the stretching and mounting of warp threads as well as in the stretching and ordering of sacrificial victims. What, then, is the significance of stretching in Tititl? Nicholson proposes "growth."[26] I propose fertility, regeneration, and transformation. One stretches things in order to prepare and guide them for transformation either within or across life~death cycles or between cosmic layers or states of being.

In sum, stretching orders and arranges things and in so doing prepares them for creative transformation. The concept of stretching plays a central role in the Aztecs' understanding of weaving, parturition, sexual intercourse, human sacrifice, the formation of the Fifth Sun's Earth and sky, and therefore generation, regeneration, and transformation. In light of these conceptual associations, the festival of Tititl is plausibly interpreted as operating on the metaphysical assumption that the Fifth Age was formed by stretching twisted cords or spun threads along a quadrilateral frame such as a loom and that the Fifth Age is a weaving-in-progress.[27] The foregoing highlights the Aztecs' conceptual association between weaving and warping with sexual intercourse (and with sacrifice). As one lays down and stretches out thread in the process of warping it and lays down and stretches out warp threads upon a loom frame in the process of weaving, so analogously a man lays down and stretches out a woman in the course of sexual intercourse, and analogously priests lay down and stretch out victims in the course of sacrificially harvesting them. The fact that warping and weaving are analogous to a man's having sexual intercourse with a woman suggests in addition that the warp threads are gendered female (just as the captive warriors stretched out for sacrifice are gendered female). The foregoing further supports the idea that the Fifth Age is a grand work of weaving – and hence a nepantla-process – in progress.

Once the warp threads have been stretched between upper and lower loom bars, backstrap weavers commonly use heddle sticks and shed rods to order, keep equidistant, and separate the warp threads.[28] These instruments are passed horizontally through the vertical warp threads in order to create sheds, or spaces, through which the batten and weft threads pass. In plain weave, shed and heddle rods create sheds made by alternatively separating even-numbered from odd-numbered warp threads. This facilitates inserting the batten and the weft-thread-toting shuttle stick. The passage of one weft involves raising the odd-numbered warp threads above the even-numbered threads, while the passage of the next weft involves raising the even-numbered threads above the odd-numbered ones. According to Ann Rowe, the backstrap weavers of Highland Guatemala refer to the interchange of the two layers of warps as "the warp cross."[29]

Molina contains two different Nahuatl words for weft ("*trama*"): *pacyotl* and *tetlanacqui*.[30] Karttunen translates *pacyotl* as "weft of cloth, fabric, web."[31] Molina defines *tetlanacqui* as "weft of cloth or one who wants to commit adultery."[32] Campbell parses *tetlanacqui* into *tetlan* and *acqui*.[33] Molina defines *tetlan* as "with others, pair of them, near them, or with another."[34] Campbell parses *tetlan* into *te*, a possessive, and *tlan*, meaning "place," suggesting that *tetlan* means something like "someone's place." Molina translates *aqui* (or *acqui*) as a verb meaning "to fit in a hole."[35] Siméon defines *aqui* as "to contain, to enter into a place, a hole, etc.,"[36] Karttunen, as "to enter, to fit in."[37]

The following related constructions from Molina offer additional insight: *aqui in tonatiuh* ("for the sun to set"), *notech aqui* ("for something to penetrate into me"), *itech aqui* ("to penetrate"), *tetlannaqui* ("to have relations with a sleeping woman"), *aquia* ("to transplant trees, drive stakes, or stick something into a hole"), *aquitia* ("to make something fit"), *ixquia* ("to work with a needle, or to mend, weaving with a needle"), and *tlaixaqui* ("one who sews up rents or fine-draws tears").[38] In sum, meaning "to enter, penetrate or fit into a hole," the Nahuatl term *acqui* forms constructions related to weaving, penetration, and sexual intercourse.

I suggest the combined word *tetlanacqui* thus means roughly "to enter, penetrate or fit into someone's place (or hole)." (Molina's definition suggests something more like "to enter into a hole with another, near others, or with others.") Entering, penetrating, and fitting into someone's place or hole aptly characterize what weft threads do. Using a shuttle stick, the weaver fits the weft threads into the space between the warp threads (the shed) that is maintained by the shed rod(s). She penetrates the shed or warp space with the weft threads. By repeating this in–and-out, under-and-below, and over-and-above motion, the weaver transforms warp and weft into cloth: she gives birth to a weaving; she creates fabric.

The parallels with sexual intercourse and reproduction abound. Recall that Molina defines *tetlanacqui* as both "weft of cloth" and as "one who wants to commit adultery." In both sexual intercourse and weaving, one fits and enters into another's place. This also suggests that warp and shed are gendered female while weft is gendered male. The warp represents the female, stretched out and laying in wait for penetration by the weft-toting shuttle rod. According to Monaghan, contemporary Nuyoo Mixtec–speakers also characterize the shed as female.[39] Gerardo Reichel-Dolmatoff's Kogi informants likewise characterize the warp as female and the shuttle as male.[40]

Before interlacing weft and warp threads, the backstrap weaver customarily spins the weft threads onto a shuttle stick or bobbin. This keeps the weft threads from getting tangled and makes it easier for the weaver to interlace them with the warp threads. Weft and warp thus differ from one another in another respect. While the warp threads are laid out and ordered on the warp board prior to weaving, the weft threads are spun again onto the shuttle stick.

The weaver then uses the weft-toting shuttle stick to penetrate the shed and warp threads, giving birth to a cloth. The weaver's shuttle stick would thus appear to be gendered male. It penetrates the warp fibers, just as the male-gendered digging stick penetrates the female-gendered Earth when planting seeds, and just as the male-gendered Fifth Sun penetrates the female-gendered Earth at dusk. Kogi metaphysics genders the shuttle stick male, for example.[41] Furthermore, we've seen that weft threads are gendered male and warp threads are gendered female.

The Nahuatl word for the shuttle stick or bobbin is *pacyo acaltontli* (Spanish: *lanzadera*).[42] *Pacyo acaltontli* combines *pacyotl* ("weft of cloth, fabric, web"[43]) and *acaltontli*. *Acaltontli* combines *acalli* ("water [*atl*] house or boat [*calli*]") with *tontli*, a compound element conveying a sense of smallness or insignificance.[44] Molina lists the related verb *acalhuia* ("to carry something across in a ship or a boat").[45] *Pacyo acaltontli* thus means "little weft boat" or "little boat used to carry weft threads." As it enters and exits the warp threads' shed spaces, the shuttle stick or bobbin literally bobs up and down. It undulates like a small boat on the water. It bounces up and down like a rubber ball. The bobbin moves up-and-over and down-and-under like the Fifth Sun's olin-defined move-ment up-and-over and down-and-under Tlalticpac. In short, it instantiates olin motion-change. The bobbing of the weft threads is nothing other than the rhythmic undulating, pulsating, and oscillating of olin-style motion. But that's not all. The shuttle stick or bobbin shuttles back and forth between right and left sides of the loom, attaining the middling and reciprocating motion-change of nepantla (see Figure 8.4).

Weavers use battens to carry out two essential activities: to open (and hold open) the shed so that they may insert the weft into the warp; and to beat down the weft into place, into the warp. The batten is a flat stick made of hard wood, usually beveled on both sides and pointed at both ends. Both Sahagún and Molina relate that the Aztecs called the batten a *tzotzopaztli*.[46] Molina defines *tzotzopaztli* as a "broad stick like a knife used to press the cloth being woven."[47] Karttunen defines it as a "weaver's reed, stick to push down and tighten the weft."[48] Sahagún describes the tzotzopaztli as an instrument "almost like a *machete*."[49] Berdan reports the batten was commonly referred to as a "weaving sword."[50]

Tzotzopaztli suggests the verbs *tzopa* ("to finish something, like weaving cloth, making a vault, putting wood on a house, or something similar")[51] and *tzopi* ("for a piece of weaving to get finished").[52] The meaning of *tzopa* is particularly appo-site. It further supports the idea of the cosmos as a woven fabric, and accords well with the idea of the sky (*ilhuicatl*) as curved or turned – that is, woven. The

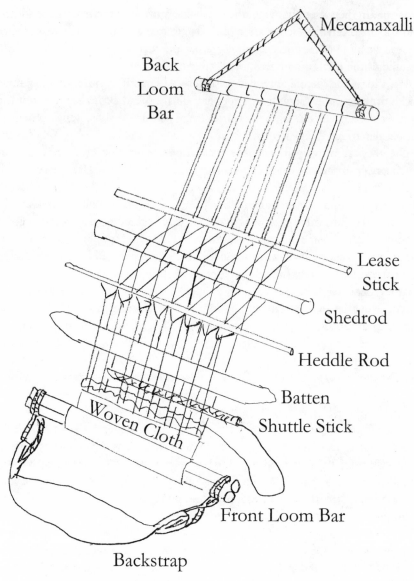

Mecamaxalli

Back
Loom
Bar

Lease
Stick

Shedrod

Heddle Rod

Batten

Woven Cloth

Shuttle Stick

Front Loom Bar

Backstrap

FIGURE 8.4. *Backstrap loom and accouterments. (Redrawn from Anderson [1978: 52].)*

Aztecs conceived weaving, sexual intercourse, and house-building in analogous terms. Finally, the related word *quicentzoptiuh* means "it is arranged perfectly or completely finished."[53] As we saw in chapter 4, olin motion is orderly and ordering. In the case of weaving, the olin-style motion of the batten, the shuttle, and the weft threads orders, arranges, and completes the cloth. In the case of the cosmos, the olin-style weft motion of the Fifth Sun orders, arranges, and completes the Fifth Sun-Earth Ordering.

The batten and its role in weaving have obvious parallels in sexual intercourse and reproduction. Using the batten to pry open the shed in order to insert the weft into the shed (the warp's place) imitates sexual intercourse, as does using the batten to beat down the weft into the warp. What's more, the weaver's pattern of leaning forward to open the shed and insert the weft, followed by her holding onto both ends of the batten and leaning backward in order to beat down and tighten the weft into the warp further parallel the motions of females in coitus and in labor contractions. Contemporary Tzutujil Maya as well as Huichol regard the weaver's forward-and-back motion as a distinctly female motion, one that simulates the transformative motion of childbirth (as well as the transformative motion of grinding corn).[54] Cordry and Cordry report that this pattern of motion is commonly used as a gesture for indicating sexual intercourse.[55] The batten and its role in weaving also have obvious parallels in planting and growing maize. Using the batten to pry open the shed in order to insert the weft into the shed (the warp's place) imitates a farmer's prying open the female earth with his digging stick. The subsequent beating down of the weft into the warp imitates the farmer's pounding down of the soil over the implanted seed.[56]

The Aztecs regarded the weaving batten as a male-gendered instrument and male fertility symbol along with sacrificial knives, swords, shuttle sticks, and the Fifth Sun. Accordingly, they regarded the wielding of a batten as a male-gendered activity along with wielding sacrificial knives, penetrating the earth with digging sticks, and moving shuttle sticks. Like shuttle sticks, weft threads, and the Fifth Sun, battens move in an olin-style, undulating manner. During the festival of Atemoztli, people made amaranth-dough figures whose hearts and heads were removed by batten-wielding Tlaloc priests. Contemporary Nuyoo Mixtec–speakers call the batten a "machete," which they consider to be a preeminently male symbol.[57]

Consequently, although weaving is a preeminently female-gendered process, weaving – like sexual reproduction and parturition – nevertheless combines and unifies *both* male- *and* female-gendered elements and activities. Indeed, it is precisely the nepantla-defined interweaving and commingling of these paired male–female inamic elements, forces, and activities that make possible and thus explain the transformative power of weaving – and indeed *transformation per se*. Not all weaving activities and instruments are therefore female. For example, battens are not, therefore, symbols of female power or authority, *pace*

Sharisse and Geoffrey McCafferty.[58] In the hands of a woman, a batten attested to her ability to successfully wield, temporarily dominate, and incorporate a preeminently male-gendered instrument and male power symbol, and therefore attested to her command of creative transformation.

Battens figured prominently in Tititl. The depictions of Tititl in the *Codex Borbonicus* (pl. 26)[59] and *Codex Magliabechiano* (pl. 45)[60] depict Cihuacoatl holding blue weaving battens and shields. Sahagún's informants describe her as carrying a "turquoise batten" (*xiuhtzotzopac*).[61] Turquoise, or blue-green, as we saw in chapter 2, is the color of balance, order, blood, maize, water, fertility, renewal, and life-energy. Illustration 6 of the *Florentine Codex* (vol. II) similarly depicts Cihuacoatl holding a weaver's batten.[62] The "Song of Cihuacoatl," however, describes her as carrying a rattle stick (*chicahuaztli*).[63] Cordry and Cordry claim the batten used in rain ceremonies was sometimes called a "rain rattle" or "rain staff." Slotted battens filled with small seeds were used for the purpose of imitating the sound of rain.[64] When moved, be it during ritual or the course of everyday weaving, they produced a noise that imitates the sound of rain and served as prayers for rain, fertility, and renewal.[65] Klein and Read contend Cihuacoatl's shield demonstrates her command over the forces of parturition, in particular, her ability as a female warrior to seize and capture babies as future foodstuffs for the gods – just as male warriors seize future food for the gods in the battlefield.[66] Cihuacoatl's shield and batten demonstrate her regenerative prowess by uniting and ordering male and female inamic forces.

Let's look finally at the backstrap loom. The backstrap loom consists of two wooden sticks, one upper and one lower, around which the ends of the prearranged, sized, and figure eight–shaped warp threads are looped. The upper stick, or loom bar, is fastened to a tree or house post by means of a bifurcating woven rope (crotch-like *mecamaxalli*), while the lower loom bar is fastened to a broad woven band that passes around the weaver's hips and waist (the backstrap). The tension on the apparatus created by the weaver's leaning away from the tree is indispensable for keeping the warp threads stretched taut while the weaver separates the warp threads to form the shed, and while she beats (or combs) the weft into the warp (see Figure 8.4).[67]

According to Cordry and Cordry, the backstrap is currently called a *mecapal*, which is related to *mecapalli*, the classical Nahuatl word for the malinalli-twisted-spun tumpline used by porters transporting goods and by the gods transporting the tonalli (day-force-heat-life-energy) burdens of the tonalpohualli.[68] Both backstrap and tumpline consist of rope connected to a band. In the former case the band goes across the weaver's waist or hips; in the latter, across the porter's forehead. *Mecapalli* derives from *mecatl* ("rope") plus the postposition -*pal* ("by means of"). Rope and cordage, of course, are malinalli-twisted. The etymology thus suggests a general Aztec metaphysical theme: *energy transmission and transformation occur by means of things that are twisted.* Just as a tumpline connects the divine porter to the burden of time-place, so the backstrap connects the weaver to the cloth to which she is giving birth. The Huichol, according to Peter Furst, see the backstrap belt as connecting the weaver and weaving as a mother and her unborn child.[69] The tumpline connects tonalli to the head, its principal location in the human body, while the backstrap connects the cloth to the weaver's midsection, the location of the unborn child. As we saw in chapter 6, the Tzutujil Maya of Santiago Atitlán characterize weaving in terms of sexual intercourse, pregnancy, and parturition. They describe completing a cloth as giving birth to a cloth. "Weavings are not just woven but in fact born."[70] Contemporary Wixárika women also speak of giving birth to cloth through weaving.[71] Woven cloth is defined by a four-phased life~death cycle. After its birth, it enjoys youth. In aging it becomes increasingly frayed, unraveled, and characterized by tlazolli. Upon death it nourishes the earth and eventually new cotton and maguey plants.

Among the female possessions burned by women about to be sacrificed during Quecholli – and also burned along with all women as part of their female funeral bundles – was their *imecamaxal* ("her divided cord which held up [the textile]") (see Figures 5.1 and 8.4).[72] Weavers use the divided cord to secure a backstrap loom to a post or tree trunk by tying the single end around the tree trunk or post and looping each of the bifurcated ends around each end of the upper loom bar. The crotch (i.e., the bifurcated space) created by the mecamaxalli is the place where the creative process of weaving occurs, just as the crotch created by the division of a woman's legs is the place where the creative process of sexual intercourse occurs.

In sum, spinning and weaving are powerful processes of transformation, and spinning and weaving instruments are literally power tools of transformation.[73] The latter empower weavers to transform the disordered into the well ordered, the disarrayed into the well arrayed, and so on. They empower weavers to join together inamic partners into a middled, mutually reciprocating, agonistically tensed unity. They also enable humans to participate in and contribute to the ongoing weaving of the Fifth Age and sacred nepantla-processing of teotl.

8.3. WEAVING THE FIFTH SUN-EARTH AGE

Aztec metaphysics conceives the processing of the Fifth Age in terms of weaving and thus nepantla motion-change, and conceives the arrangement of the Fifth Age as a grand backstrap loom. The tonalpohualli and xiuhpohualli constitute fixed, repeating patterns in the warp threads that produce a vertically banded or striped fabric. The tonalpohualli and xiuhpohualli consist of vertical malinalli motion-change and malinalli-shaped energy transmission. Malinalli motion-change thus constitutes the vertical or warp motion-change of the cosmos. It concerns the transmission of energy and motion-change between vertical layers (upper, middle, and lower) of the cosmos. The Fifth Sun's olin motion-change constitutes the weft threads in the weaving of the Fifth Age. Olin motion is horizontal, weft motion-change. The Fifth Sun's traveling across and arranging of Tlalticpac are defined by olin motion-change. Nepantla motion-change subsumes them both within the overall process of weaving (see Figures 8.5, 8.6, and 8.7).

As its name *4 Olin Tonatiuh* suggests, the Fifth Sun weaves the Fifth Age by means of olin motion-change. The olin-defined motion of the Fifth Sun represents the horizontal motion of the weft-toting shuttle stick as it trans-verses the loom, interlacing with the vertical warp bands of the tonalpohualli and xiuhpohualli. In so doing, the Fifth Sun completes the Fifth Age into woven cloth. The upper loom bar and upper unwoven warp threads separated by lease rod, shedrod, and heddle rod represent the nine layers of the heavens above the intermediate layers of the Fifth Sun-Earth Age. The Fifth Age proper consists of Tlalticpac and the lower four skies. The *warp cross* created by the interchange of shedrod and heddle rod resembles the fifth layer of the sky, *ilhuicatl mamalhuacoca* ("the sky where the whirling or gyrating is"). Here the malinalli forces twist and spin before descending to the Middle Region including Tlalticpac. The area of the loom where the actual interlacing of weft and warp takes place represents the intermediate level of the Fifth Sun-Earth Age. Here the Fifth Sun interlaces weft and warp through its daily up-and-over and down-and-below undulating motion. Lastly, the bottom loom bar represents Mictlan. The foregoing accords roughly with one of several contem-porary Wixárika (Huichol) understandings of the metaphysical significance of the loom as related by Stacy Schaefer.[74]

The wefting, olin motion-change of 4 Olin Tonatiuh undulates over and under the vertical malinalli warp threads. These vertical threads extend from upper loom bar to lower loom bar. In so doing, they connect heavens (upper layers) and underworld (lower layers) of the cosmos, "the above and the below." These vertical threads serve as malinalli-twisted veins, umbilical cords, and channels that transmit sacred energy from above and below. 4 Olin Tonatiuh creates the Fifth Sun-Earth Age by weaving together upper and lower layers (heavens and underworld) and hence the entire gamut of paired inamic forces

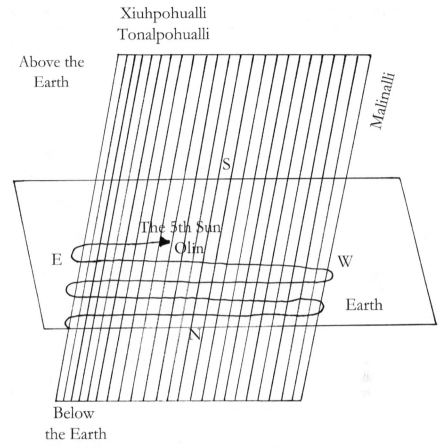

Xiuhpohualli
Tonalpohualli

Above the
Earth

Malinalli

S

Above the Earth ... The 5th Sun
E   Olin   W

Earth

N

Below
the Earth

FIGURE 8.5. *Layout of the Fifth Age. (Author's drawing.)*

associated with the above and the below: ascending influence~descending influence, light~darkness, male~female, dry~wet, and so on.

The Fifth Sun weaves the Fifth Age on this grand cosmic loom. The Fifth Age is generated by the Fifth Sun's continuous wefting and olin-defined undulating up-and-over and down-and-under the vertically arranged warp of malinalli-defined fibers constituted by the tonalpohualli and xiuhpohualli. Both the weaver's bobbin and the Fifth Sun exhibit olin motion-change. The processing of the Fifth Sun, like the processing of weft threads, is defined by a four-phased life~death cycle consisting of emerging from below, traveling over, penetrating, and traveling under Tlalticpac. The Fifth Sun oscillates up-and-down as well as shuttles back-and-forth as it travels above and below Tlalticpac and as it travels across the warp designs of the tonalpohualli and xiuhpohualli. In doing so it imitates the weft-thread-toting shuttle stick's undulating up-and-down and shuttling back-and-forth as it travels above and below the horizontal dimension of the loom and as it travels across the warp designs and width of a loom. Moreover, like the weaver's weft-thread-toting shuttle stick that penetrates, disappears into, and then reemerges from the shed (i.e., the warp threads' place or hole), the Fifth Sun penetrates and disappears into Tlalticpac at dusk and then reemerges at dawn. As a consequence, a skywatcher observes what Anthony Aveni describes as "the rhythmic oscillation"[75] of sunrise and sunset solstice points along eastern and western horizons (see Figures 4.4, 4.5, and 8.5).

The phrase *aqui in tonatiuh* ("for the sun to set") is highly suggestive in this context. The fact that the Fifth Sun's setting consists of its entering into a hole or penetrating the earth's surface (like a shuttle stick in weaving or a needle in embroidery) suggests the Aztecs conceived the movement of the Fifth Sun as a predominantly horizontal, wefting motion. The Fifth Sun travels in-and-out-of as well as over-and-under the surface of Tlalticpac. As it does, it interacts with the vertical warp threads of the tonalpohualli and xiuhpohualli, dispensing the specific tonalli of each day or unit of the tonalpohualli and xiuhpohualli. The Fifth Sun serves as a vehicle for the dispensation of tonalli energy.

The Fifth Sun's horizontal, olin-defined wefting lays out Tlalticpac's four cardinal orientations, quadrants, colors, and so on. Its olin-defined wefting centers Tlalticpac, giving it a fifth orientation and color. The Fifth Sun arranges the Fifth Age in the shape of a quincunx as depicted by *Codex Fejérváry-Mayer* (pl. 1; see Figure 4.3) and *Codex Mendoza* (pl. 2r; see Figure 4.10). As we've seen, Aztec metaphysics does not treat the four cardinal and four intercardinal orientations as fixed, preexisting directions or compass points in substantive space. Rather, it sees them as the where-whens or time-places of specific processes. West is where-when a specific process *takes place*: it is where-when the Sun sets; where-when the Sun penetrates the Earth's surface. In keeping with Mesoamerican naming practices, the Aztecs' name for West, *tonatiuh iaquian*, doubles as its essence: "the time-place or where-when (*-yan*) of the sun's (*tonatiuh*) customary entering into a hole (*aqui*)." West was also called *tonalpolihuiyampa* ("where-when the sun habitually perishes").[76] The name for westerly wind, *tonatiuh iaquiampa ehecatl*, likewise doubles as its essence: "the wind from the where-when of the sun's customary entering into a hole."[77] Aztec metaphysics named and defined East as *tonaliquizayampa* ("where-when the sun habitually emerges").[78] The Fifth Sun emerges from its journey beneath Tlalticpac and travels over Tlalticpac the same way weft threads emerge from beneath and travel over warp threads. The Fifth Sun penetrates and travels under Tlalticpac

Malinalli Pattern: Tonalpohualli & Xiuhpohualli

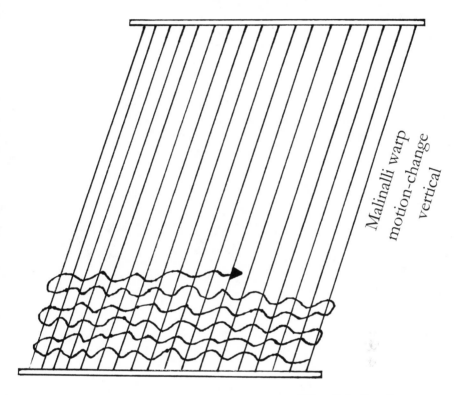

Malinalli warp
motion-change
vertical

The 5th Sun's
Olin motion-change
and weft motion-change
horizontal

Figure 8.6. *Weaving the Fifth Age. (Author's drawing.)*

the same way weft threads penetrate and travel under warp threads. Both Fifth Sun and weft threads follow olin-defined paths. Both weave something into existence – the former, the Fifth Age; the latter, cloth. The Fifth Sun's olin motion-change therefore orders and integrates the Fifth Age. Tzutujil Maya refer to the weft-toting shuttle as the *r'way kiem* or "sustenance."[79] For the Aztecs, analogously, 4 Olin Tonatiuh is the sustenance, heart, and essence of the Fifth Age.

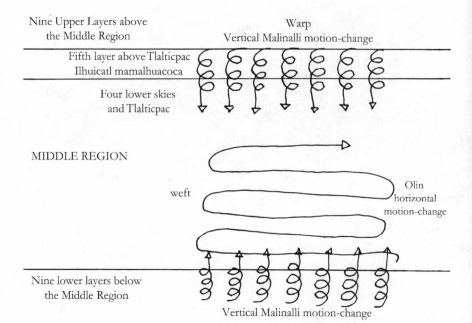

Nine Upper Layers above
the Middle Region

Warp
Vertical Malinalli motion-change

Fifth layer above Tlalticpac
Ilhuicatl mamalhuacoca

Four lower skies
and Tlalticpac

MIDDLE REGION

weft

Olin
horizontal
motion-change

Nine lower layers below
the Middle Region

Vertical Malinalli motion-change

FIGURE 8.7. *The Fifth Age as weaving-in-progress. (Author's drawing.)*

It is important to bear in mind that the Fifth Sun's wefting olin motion-change weaves *neither* the nine upper layers *nor* the lower nine layers of the cosmos. The Fifth Sun weaves *only* the intermediate layers. The upper and lower layers of the cosmos remain essentially unchanged during the five Sun-Earth Ages. Only the intermediate layers change with changes of Ages. The *cosmos of the Fifth Sun-Earth Ordering* consists of the intermediate layer unique to the Fifth Sun-Earth Ordering *in conjunction* with the upper and lower layers of the cosmos (see Figure 8.7).[80]

Understanding the cosmos of the Fifth Sun-Earth Age as a grand weaving-in-progress with the Fifth Sun as weft and tonalpohualli and xiuhpohualli as warp helps explain a number of features of Aztec metaphysics. First, it helps explain why the atl tlachinolli and the olin motifs serve as definitive ideograms of the Fifth Age. They are spinning and undulating ideograms (respectively) that refer to the two fundamental kinds of motion-change and transformation that contribute to the ordering the Fifth Age. Second, it helps explain why the Fifth Age is commonly depicted by quincunxes such as *Codex Fejérváry-Mayer* (pl. 1) and *Codex Mendoza* (pl. 2r). Both consist of crossings over and nepantla-placed planks. Both convey the "heart" or essence of the Fifth Sun-Earth Ordering.

Third, the weaving together of the weft-moving Fifth Sun and solar energy with the repeating, warp pattern of the tonalpohualli explains *why* the solar day and the ritual (tonalpohualli) day *coincide*, and explains *why* the vague 360+5 solar year (xiuhpohualli) is composed of ritual (tonalpohualli) days. The vertical malinalli conduits through which the malinalli-shaped forces of the tonalpohualli descend resemble the malinalli-twisted warp threads mounted on a loom. As the Fifth Sun moves horizontally across the loom of the cosmos, it interlaces and commingles with the 260 tonallis (day-force-heat-life-energies) of the tonalpohualli. This intermixing of solar forces and tonalpohualli forces explains the suffusing of Tlalticpac in the energies of the particular tonalpohualli day sign. It also helps explains the perfect coordination and coincidence of solar day and tonalpohualli day.

Fourth, conceiving the cosmos of the Fifth Sun-Earth Age as a grand weaving-in-progress with the Fifth Sun as weft and tonalpohualli and xiuhpohualli as warp helps explain Aztec metaphysics' relational conception of time-place as well as makes plausible the suggestion that Mesoamerican time-place is better understood in terms of weaving than in terms of intermeshing mechanical cogwheels. Time-place is a pattern disclosed in the process of the weaving of the cosmos. It is immanent, emerging in the process of weaving like a tree's rings emerge in the process of its growing. The Fifth Era is *what* is woven; time-place is *how* it is woven.

Fifth, weaving and reading-interpreting the tonalpohualli both involve *counting*. As we saw earlier, the word *pohua* means "to count, reckon, read, recount, relate, give an account, to assign something."[81] Related words include *tlahpoaliztli* ("act of counting something, or act of casting spells"), *tlalpohua* ("the act of measuring lands, or fields"), *tlalpouhqui* ("measurer of lands, or fields"), *tlatlalpalpouhqui* ("blanket which has stripes of many colors or something similar"), and the post-Contact *tlapoalteputzi* ("iron clock with a bell").[82] Just as one counts and measures the day signs of the tonalpohualli, and just as one counts and measures a milpa, so likewise one counts and measures threads when weaving.

We find parallels in contemporary Quiché Maya cosmology. According to Barbara and Dennis Tedlock, contemporary Quiché Maya see significant parallels between a backstrap loom, house, milpa, and what they call "skyearth" (what I call "Sun-Earth Ordering").[83] All have four sides and four corners. Constructing them involves stretching, counting, and measuring. One stretches out measuring ropes when measuring and establishing the four sides and corners of loom, house, milpa, and skyearth. The *Popol Vuh* states:

Siding by fours, cornering by fours,
measuring, staking by fours,
cording by halves, cording by wholes,
in the sky, on the earth,
the four sides, the four corners.[84]

The fact that measuring out and constructing the skyearth is analogous to measuring out and constructing the backstrap-weaver's loom supports understanding the cosmos as weaver's loom. The Wixárika similarly see the full length of the warp between top and bottom loom bars as a flat, horizontal a field or *milpa*, according to Schaefer.[85] Reichel-Dolmatoff reports Kogi cosmological thinking consists of similar views. The Kogi interpret the cosmos in terms of weaving and looms.[86]

The foregoing parallels hold true for Aztec metaphysics. One uses malinalli-twisted cords when setting up a house, milpa, and loom. One measures and counts time-place and the Fifth Sun-Earth Ordering using the malinalli-twisted day-units of the tonalpohualli. According to this way of thinking, the chronotopogram depicted on plate 1 of the *Codex Fejérváry-Mayer* depicts *how* the Fifth Age is woven. It is essentially a weaver's pattern that is continually and repeatedly disclosed in the weaving of the Fifth Sun-Earth Era.

Sixth, conceiving the cosmos of the Fifth Sun-Earth Age as a grand weaving-in-progress, with the Fifth Sun as weft and tonalpohualli and xiuhpohualli as warp, sheds further light on how Aztec metaphysics is pantheistic (chapter 2); how Aztec metaphysics is a process metaphysics (chapter 1); how reality is defined by agonistic inamic unity (chapter 3); how all things are interrelated, interdependent, correlated, and interactive with one another (chapter 1); how the reality is an artistic-shamanic process and product (chapter 1); and the holistic nature of reality (chapter 1).

8.4. THE FIRST FOUR SUN-EARTH AGES AS NEPANTLA-PROCESS

The Fifth Sun-Earth Age is unique. What distinguishes it from the preceding four Ages is the fact that its Sun, 4 Olin Tonatiuh, is defined by olin motion-change. It is the wefting, olin motion-change of 4 Olin Tonatiuh that arranges the middle layers that constitute and further distinguish the Fifth Age from its four predecessors.

But how are we to understand the nature and organization of the first four Ages? If the cosmos is a grand nepantla-process in progress, then the first four Ages must also be nepantla-processes. But these four Sun-Earth Orderings lack an olin-wefting Sun, so in what sense may they be said to be nepantla-processes? Our sources provide few details concerning their makeup and working. The *Legend of the Suns* and *Historia de los mexicanos por sus pinturas* tell us the names and natures of their Suns, the nature of their inhabitants, how long they lasted, and how they were destroyed.[87] We know Tezcatlipoca and Quetzalcoatl alternately created, dominated, and defined the first four Ages, and that they also alternately destroyed one another's Ages. This succession of creations and destructions represents the back-and-forth, nepantla-defined struggle (*agon*) between the inamic forces of Quetzalcoatl~Tezcatlipoca. However, since each of the four Ages is dominated by one or the other inamic at the expense of its partner, it follows that none of the four is *by itself* nepantla-balanced. None of the first four is *individually* nepantla-woven. This is key. Instead, each constitutes a dialectical moment in the overall nepantla-balancing *of all four*. It is the *entire series* of four Ages that is nepantla-woven. Nepantla-balance is attained *diachronically* by the succession of the four Ages.

After these four creations and destructions, Quetzalcoatl and Tezcatlipoca cooperate with one another to create the Fifth Age. *Only* the Fifth Age *individually* attains and embodies the nepantla-middling and -unifying of agonistic Quetzalcoatl forces and Tezcatlipoca forces. The Fifth Age alone *centers* and *unifies* all four of Tonacatecuhtli~Tonacacihuatl's four sons (Tlatlauhqui Tezcatlipoca, Yayauhqui Tezcatlipoca, Quetzalcoatl, and Omitecuhtli or Huitzilopochtli) and all four elemental forces (earth, wind, fire, water), directions, quadrants, colors, and so on.[88]

8.5. THE FIFTH AGE AS NEPANTLA-GENERATED WOVEN HOUSE

The fact that nepantla motion-change is fundamental to the cosmos and the fact that the Fifth Age is a grand weaving-in-progress accords well with the claim that Aztec metaphysics conceives the Fifth Age as a woven house or container (*calli*): "bounded, defined, and contained by long, thin, essentially supple objects of a basically cord-like form."[89] According to Siméon, malinalli grass was plaited or braided "without doubt for the construction of houses" ("*trenjada sin duda para la construcción de casas*").[90] The festival of Tititl further supports the idea that Aztec metaphysics conceives the Fifth Age as formed at least partly by the stretching of twisted cords or spun threads along a loom frame or house frame. As we saw in chapter 6, Sahagún's informants reported, "The people of old . . . thought and took as truth that the heavens were just like a house; it stood resting in every direction, and it extended reaching to the water. It was as if the water walls were joined to it."[91] Common Aztec wattle-and-daub houses are constructed by interweaving warp (vertical poles and stakes) and weft (horizontal supple reeds) components. The *Florentine Codex* (Book XI) contains several relevant illustrations. Illustration 902 depicts a wattle-and-daub straw house that Sahagún's informants describe as "a reed hut (*tolxacalli*) or grass hut (*zacaxalli*), etc., mud-plastered, with chinks filled."[92] Illustration 405 shows the wall beams of a house joined together with X-shaped, intercrossing grass cords.[93] Klein reports contemporary Mayas describing the walls of their houses as "woven or braided" and "interwoven as in a braid or mat."[94] Mesoamerican houses, especially wattle-and-daub houses, are literally woven together using twisted cords and vines.

The notion that the Fifth Age is a woven house also accords with chapter 1's claim that Aztec metaphysics is nonhierarchical. A woven house is ontologically homogenous since its layers consists of qualitatively identical stuff. Upper and lower layers are constructed from one and the same thing: cane, twining, and mud. The notion that the Fifth Age is a woven house also accords with chapter 5's claim that vital forces and energies circulate vertically throughout the cosmos by means of malinalli-twisted-spun channels (called "the malinalli" by López Austin and Carrasco).[95] The malinalli serve as vertical spun filaments connecting various parts of the cosmic house.

8.6. THE VERTICAL FOLDING OF THE COSMOS AND OF THE FIFTH AGE

Aztec metaphysics sees the vertical ordering of the cosmos during each of the five Sun-Earth Ages as consisting of three basic regions: upper, middle, and lower.[96] However, the cosmos was not always ordered in this way. As we saw in chapter 7, at first the cosmos consisted entirely of the primordial inamic male~female unity: Ometeotl, Ometecuhtli~Omecihuatl, or Tonacatecuhtli~Tonacacihuatl. Neither middle layer (Sun, Earth) nor lower layer (Mictlan) existed. Over the course of Ometeotl's self-unfolding, the cosmos became vertically layered and its vertical layering became more complex. There became three basic regions.

The three regions of the cosmos of the Fifth Sun-Earth Ordering are counted in several different ways. According to one, the three regions consist of thirteen upper or celestial layers, Tlalticpac (the earthly layer), and nine lower layers (Mictlan).[97] According to a second, the upper region consists of nine layers. The first four layers above Tlalticpac – Ilhuicatl of Tlalocan and Metztli (the Moon), Ilhuicatl of Citlalicue (Skirt of Stars), Ilhuicatl of Tonatiuh (the Sun), and Ilhuicatl of Huixtotlan (Salt-Fertility Goddess)[98] – are not genuinely celestial but assigned instead to the middle region along with Tlalticpac.[99] By this reckoning, the nine layers above the middle realm parallel the nine layers below. By yet another way of reckoning, the earth constitutes the first layer of both the ascending and the descending counts. The earth is the first layer of the upperworld as well as the first layer of the underworld.[100] This manner of reckoning nicely captures the inamic ambiguity of the earth as nepantla-defined confluence of ascending~descending forces along with its parallel inamic partners. The earthly layer, the habitat of humans, is constantly awash in two kinds of sacred forces: those originating in and descending from the upper realm (male, dry, hot, etc.) and those originating in and ascending from the under realm (female, wet, cold, etc.). These are none other than the basic agonistic inamic pairs of Aztec metaphysics. They constitute those forces creative of and essential to life (e.g., tonalli, heat, teyolia, sunshine, spring water, agricultural fertility, and rain) as well as those forces detrimental to and destructive of life (e.g., drought, heat wave, agricultural infertility, flood, and disease).

Scholars routinely interpret the illustrations on *Codex Vaticanus 3738 A* (fol. IV and 2r) as depicting the vertical layering of the Fifth Age.[101] Each layer has its own name and kind of power. Folio IV depicts the celestial layers beginning with the Sky-Place of the Sun, while folio 2r depicts the nine layers under the Earth. Scholars also routinely base their claims about the *hierarchical* nature of the Aztec cosmos upon these two illustrations and their accompanying text.[102] Chapter 1 however argued Aztec philosophy embraces a monistic and nonhierarchical metaphysics. How does this square with the apparent hierarchical organization of the cosmos suggested by the illustrations on *Codex Vaticanus 3738 A* (fol. IV and 2r)?

First, illustrations such as these are rather rare among the artwork of both Postclassic and post-Contact central Mexico. In fact, Gillespie argues the two-dimensional Postclassic artworks of central Mexico such as the chronotopograms of *Codex Fejérváry-Mayer* (pl. 1) and *Codex Mendoza* (fol. 2r) emphasize the nonhierarchical as opposed to the hierarchical structure of the cosmos of the Fifth Age.[103]

Second, this artistic emphasis upon the nonhierarchical at the expense of the hierarchical corresponds neatly with the emphasis in Aztec sociopolitical philosophy, moral philosophy, aesthetics, and epistemology upon nonhierarchical horizontal space over hierarchical vertical space. As Louise Burkhart and Wayne Elzey show, Aztec sociopolitical and moral (etc.) notions are configured primarily in terms of the opposition between center and periphery.[104] These emphases upon the nonhierarchical are, in turn, consonant with Aztec metaphysics' emphasis upon immanence over transcendence, becoming over being, and process over substance.

Third, nothing in the aforementioned *Codex Vaticanus 3738 A* illustrations themselves – as opposed to the commentaries accompanying them – logically entails a metaphysical hierarchy. Interpreting their visual vertical ordering as a *metaphysical* hierarchical ordering would appear to rest upon a tacit metaphysical assumption deeply rooted in Western metaphysics and theology: namely, the equivalence of the vertical with the hierarchical.[105] According to the latter, higher means better, more real, and more perfect, whereas lower means worse, less real, and less perfect. Yet I see no reasons for attributing this assumption to Aztec metaphysics.[106]

But if not hierarchically, how then does Aztec metaphysics interpret the vertical ordering of the cosmos? Aztec metaphysics conceives the vertical layers of the cosmos as folded layers or lengths of a single cloth or blanket, and therefore as ontologically homogenous. The vertical layers of the cosmos are nothing more than folds in a single, ontologically homogeneous stuff: teotl as energy-in-motion. The thirteen celestial levels above and nine levels below Tlalticpac do not constitute a hierarchy of ontologically graded levels or degrees of being, purity, perfection, mutability, and inactivity. Each fold represents a different aspect of teotl's energy. Higher folds are not *more* real or *more* sacred than lower folds. The respective names for upper and lower realms – *chicnauhtopan* ("nine that are above us") and *chicnauhmictlan* ("nine places of death") – by no means entail a hierarchy.[107] Nor, for that matter, does the name, *topan, mictlan* ("what is above us, what is below us" or "the beyond" (*el más allá*).[108] Aztec metaphysics does not therefore construe the layers along the lines of Arthur Lovejoy's notions of "the great chain of being" or "great scale of being" – an organizing metaphor that has influenced Western religious and secular metaphysics since Plato.[109] Briefly put, altitude (up, down) does not translate into qualitative metaphysical difference; and vertical layering does not entail a hierarchical metaphysics.

Durán reports that Nezahualpilli spoke of the "nine folds of the heavens" in a speech addressed to Moctezuma II.[110] Molina however explains that heavens (*cielos*) are among the items that are counted using the special Nahuatl numeral classifier *tlamantli* ("a thing that has been set down"), which is used for counting things that can be doubled over, layered, or piled upon one another.[111] Other things in this category are blankets, bowls, pairs of sandals, plates, conversations, and sermons. Such things are typically but not exclusively flat. The use of this numeral classifier supports the idea that Aztec cosmologists conceived the vertical ordering of the cosmos as a single homogeneous stuff folded over upon itself in the manner of cloth or blanket – rather than as a set of ascending and hierarchically ordered heterogeneous substances stacked on top of one another.

What does the linguistic evidence suggest? The Nahuatl term meaning "to line or cover something, or fold a blanket, or to join one with another" is *ixnepanoa*.[112] Given the centrality of nepantla-processes in the making of the cosmos, it should not surprise us that *ixnepanoa* is a member of the nepantla semantic cluster. Chapter 6 quoted a speech delivered by a midwife upon the occasion of the ritual bathing of a newborn. In it she declares the newborn to have been conceived in *Omeyocan* (the place of duality), *Chicnauhnepaniuhcan*, the residence of Omecihuatl and Ometecuhtli.[113] The speech identifies Chicnauhnepaniuhcan with Omeyocan, the double heaven occupying the twelfth and thirteenth layers of the cosmos that, according to López Austin, is sometimes identified with Tamoanchan.[114] Chapter 6 argued that nepantla motion-change defines Chicnauhnepaniuhcan, Tamoanchan, and Omeyocan; that nepantla motion-change functions as the crucial element in creation miracles; and that nepantla motion-change defines Tamoanchan's process of "marvelous crossing" and hence the highest level of the cosmos, Omeyocan. I interpreted the series of nine superimposed, united, and continuous figures suggested by the name *Chicnauhnepaniuhcan* as a series of nine, nepantla-defined interweavings. I suggest we now add *foldings-over*. There is no evidence here of an ontologically graded hierarchy.

Let's look more closely at the word *ilhuicatl*, which is routinely translated as "sky" and in early post-Conquest literature is standardly used to mean "heaven" and "celestial."[115] As we saw in chapter 7, López Austin translates *il* as "curve," "turn," and "return."[116] Other *il*-prefixed words include *ilacatzoa* ("to roll up"), *ilpia* ("to tie"), *ilacatziuhqui* ("twisted thing"), *ilacatziui* ("for something like the point of an awl or something similar to twist"), *quauilacatzoa* ("to play with a rod with one's feet, or to twist and join plants together"), *ilacatzoa* ("to roll up a blanket, mat, piece of paper or something similar or to wind up thread or string on one's finger" and "for a snake to wrap itself around a tree"), and *teteuilacachtic* ("whirlwind or something similar").[117] This semantic cluster suggests the Aztecs conceived the cosmos as a single, ontologically uniform substance that is folded, rounded, or rolled up like a blanket or mat.

In light of such considerations Klein writes, "In the end the infinite strands of the universe [were] seen as integrated into a giant pile of cloth."[118] She includes a figure that I interpret as illustrating the cosmos of the Fifth Age (see Figure 8.8). Contemporary indigenous women in Mexico fold their wrap-around skirts using a variety of methods resembling Klein's illustration. Cordry and Cordry

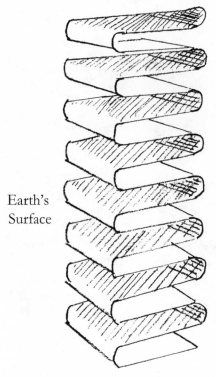

Earth's
Surface

FIGURE 8.8. *The folds of the cosmos.*
(Redrawn from Klein [1982: Figure 16].)

record some fifteen of these.[119] One that is especially suggestive is depicted in Figure 8.9.

Matos Moctezuma suggests the vertical architectural arrangement of the Templo Mayor reproduced the vertical arrangement of the cosmos.[120] The pyramid rested upon a platform that was raised above the floor of the Sacred Precinct. This platform represented the earthly plane, Tlalticpac. The pyramid's superstructure represented the levels above the earthly plane. The topmost level represented Omeyocan. The lower levels of the Underworld extend from the platform to the floor of the Sacred Precinct, upon which the platform rested. The Templo Mayor's vertical arrangement, however, does not entail that the Aztecs conceived these levels as an ontologically graded hierarchy. According to Félix Báez-Jorge and Arturo Gómez Martínez, contemporary Nahuatl-speakers in Chicontepec similarly reproduce the vertical arrangement of the cosmos with quadrangular altars. The altar's top layer represents the heavens, its middle represents the earth, and the floor represents the underworld.[121] There is no indication that they conceive the cosmos in an ontologically hierarchical manner.

8.7. COSMOS AND REALITY AS NEPANTLA-PROCESS

Eliade writes, "The symbolism of [spinning and weaving] crafts is highly significant; in the final phases of culture we find them raised to the rank of a principle explaining the world."[122] Erich Neumann writes, "the Great Mother . . . weaves the web of life and spins the threads of fate. . . . The *crossing of threads* is the symbol of sexual union."[123] Aztec metaphysics is clearly a case in point. It raises weaving – or more precisely, nepantla motion-change – to the rank of a metaphysical principle that explains the arrangement as well as becoming, processing, and transforming of reality and cosmos. As Thelma Sullivan argues, "Weaving and spinning represent life, death, and rebirth in a continuing cycle that characterizes the essential nature of the Mother Goddess."[124] Reality as weaving-in-progress is thus characterized by a four-phased life~death cycle as indicated by the quadruplicity of Tlazolteotl-Ixcuina, the Mother Goddess, and hence Ometeotl and ultimately teotl. Weaving joins together the agonistic inamic forces of the cosmos – life~death, male~female,

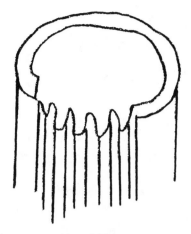

FIGURE 8.9. *Skirt-folding pattern. (Redrawn from Cordry and Cordry [1968: 106, Figure 11f].)*

being~nonbeing, and so on – in a never-ending succession of cycles that generates and regenerates the endless becoming, processing, and transforming of reality and cosmos. Moreover, all things – Sun, Earth, humans, trees, birds, insects and stones – are consequently interrelated as moments or loci in this grand cosmic fabric.

Weaving thus functions as one of the principal root metaphors of Aztec metaphysics.[125] The cosmos is a grand weaving-in-progress. However, given the nature of Ometeotl (and other primordial progenitor~progenetrix pairs such as Ometecuhtli~Omecihuatl and Tonacatecuhtli~Tonacacihuatl), Teteoinnan, Toci, Tonantzin, and Tlazolteotl-Ixcuina, the close parallels between weaving and sexual commingling, and the male- and female-gendering of weaving activities and tools, it is clear that Aztec metaphysics also embraces sexual commingling as a root metaphor. The cosmos is also a continual grand sexual commingling that unites male~female, order~disorder, being~nonbeing, and so on.[126] All things are consequently interrelated as siblings generated by this cosmic sexual commingling. In sum, the Aztecs' world hypothesis is generated from, determined by, and organized around the root metaphors and basic analogies of weaving and sexual commingling.

Since both weaving and sexual commingling are nepantla-processes, it follows that Aztec metaphysics conceives the cosmos as a grand nepantla-process. Nepantla-defined balancing, middling, and mutually reciprocating motion-change, and hence nepantla-defined processing, becoming, and transforming, are cosmogonically primordial and metaphysically fundamental. Nepantla-generated agonistic inamic unity is likewise cosmogonically primordial and metaphysically fundamental. Chapter 1 argued Aztec metaphysics embraces a process metaphysics that conceives reality in terms of continual becoming. Now we can be more specific: Aztec metaphysics conceives reality's continual becoming and transforming as a nepantla-process. Chapter 1 also argued Aztec metaphysics regards the cosmos as teotl's grand artistic-shamanic self-transformation, and it defended the association between weaving, artistic creation, shamanism, and metaphysical transformation. Now we can be more specific: Aztec metaphysics conceives teotl's artistic-shamanic self-transformation in terms of nepantla-processing.

However, nepantla motion-change – unlike its more familiar everyday instantiations, weaving and sexual commingling – is no mere metaphor. Nepantla motion-change *literally* defines, generates, and constitutes reality. It constitutes what López Austin calls the "unifying nucleus" of the Aztecs' *cosmovisión*.[127] Since nepantla-motion change defines, orders, and constitutes reality and the cosmos per se, it follows that nepantla motion-change defines, organizes, and constitutes the cosmos *prior to* the unfolding of the tonalpohualli, xiuhpohualli, and five Sun-Earth Ages. This stretch in the history of the cosmos, like all others, is defined by the always already nepantla-processing of primordial progenitor~progenetrix pairs such as Ometecuhtli~Omecihuatl and ultimately teotl.

Barbara and Dennis Tedlock contend the *Popol Vuh* likewise conceives weaving as a primordial activity in creating the cosmos. They interpret the opening passage of the *Popol Vuh* as alluding to weaving: "The actions referred to by the stem -*tz'iba*- include the creation of designs by means of weaving, while those referred to by -*tiqui*- include brocading, the principal technique by which highland Mayan textile designs were (and are) actually realized. This suggests the following reinterpretation of the second sentence: 'Here we shall design, we shall brocade the Ancient Word.'"[128]

Creation and fertility goddesses are not only associated with spinning and weaving but also with the arts of divination, soothsaying, and prophecy. The association is fitting, seeing as the goddesses weave the tonalli-defined life-energies, personalities, and fate-destinies of humans as they weave the fabric of the cosmos. Sahagún reports that Teteoinnan, an aspect of Tlazolteotl-Ixcuina, was worshipped by those who read-count-interpret the future (*tlapouhque*), those who cast auguries by looking upon water (*atlan teitani*) or by scattering maize kernels (*tlaolchauauhque*), and "by those who read fortunes by knotted cords" (*mecatlapouhque*).[129] He also relates that the primordial male~female couple, begetters of all human beings, Cipactonal and Oxomoco, invented the

260-day ritual count and became "lords of the day count." [130] *Codex Borbonicus* (pl. 19) depicts the couple sitting face-to-face (befitting of an inamic pair) while divining by casting maize kernels. [131] Neumann writes, "the Great Mother . . . *weaves the web of life and spins the threads of fate.* . . . Because 'reality' is wrought by the Great Weaver, all such activities as plaiting, weaving, and knotting belong to the fate-governing activity." [132] According to a Huichol creation story recorded by Peter Furst, the mother goddess Nakawé – who invented spinning and weaving, who spins and weaves herself, and who is patroness of all spinners and weavers – played a game of fate by throwing spindles fully laden with thread or balls of thread in order to determine the fate of the first people. [133]

Both weaving fabric and reading the tonalpohualli involve counting, judging, and interpreting. Just as the weaver counts and measures the threads, interprets their relationships to the other threads and patterns of the cloth, and assigns them a significance in the whole cloth, so analogously the tonalpouhqui counts the days of the tonalpohualli, interprets their relationship to the other days and patterns of the tonalpohualli, and assigns them a significance. The tonalpouhqui tries to discern the patterns by means of which the processes, forces, and events of the cosmos are woven together. The "fortune-teller" who counts-reads-interprets maize kernels, according to Hernando Ruíz de Alarcón, casts the kernels upon a cloth which he "*spreads out* in front of himself . . . *doubled* and well *stretched out* so that it does not wrinkle." [134] Spreading out, stretching, and doubling over evoke weaving-related activities. Given the parallels between divination and weaving, it does not seem accidental that such activities figure in divination. Contemporary Nahuatl-speaking shamans continue the practice of divining by casting maize kernels on a spread out, unwrinkled cloth. [135] After casting the maize, the diviner reads-counts-interprets their pattern – much, I suggest, as the weaver reads-counts-interprets the pattern of the threads. Shamans also divine by reading-counting-interpreting the patterns in incense smoke and crystals. Mesoamericans standardly regarded divination as a process of recreation since divination invokes and brings together the forces of primordial creation at a specific time-place. [136]

The Aztecs not surprisingly conceived well-rooted, authentic, and genuinely human existence in terms of nepantla-balanced processes and place-times. Woven cloth signified well-balanced and hence well-rooted and true (*nelli*) human existence. [137] Woven cloth was both the most highly prized tribute good and most common in the Aztec state. [138] Thirty-two out of the thirty-four tribute-paying provinces paid tribute to Tenochtitlan in woven cloth (in the form of mantles, skirts, blouses, and loincloths). [139] According to Berdan, tribute-paying provinces sent 147,000 to 248,000 items of cloth each year. [140] Cloth was prized as a religious offering,[141] seen as a desirable spoil of war,[142] and served as currency in marketplaces. The Aztecs distributed cloth as a way of marking transitional moments such as birth, admission into the calmecac, marriage, and death, as well as the assumption of political, military, and religious positions.[143] They rewarded successful warriors with fine cloaks. They distinguished themselves (and their households) from one another socially, politically, and religiously in terms of woven fabric. Hunt writes, "Clothing . . . was the major symbol in the presentation of the self as a social being, identifying age and sex status, social class, ethnic group, profession, and special privileges."[144] For Mesoamericans, adds Klein, "life has always been structured, contained, and bettered by the strands and folds of the spinner and weaver." [145]

The significance of weaving and woven products in Aztec metaphysics is further underscored by the role of woven cloth in making sacred bundles (*tla-quimilolli*) and mortuary bundles, in adorning deity statues, in ritual human sacrifice, and in creating teixiptla. Sacred bundles stand out in Aztec religious thought and ritual practices and in Aztec migration stories. They were one of the Aztecs' most valuable possessions. *Tlaquimilolli* ("something wrapped or bundled") derives from *quimiloa,* meaning "to tie or wrap up something in a piece of fabric or blanket" and "to put a shroud on a dead person, or to wrap someone in a blanket, or to dress someone."[146] Sacred bundles consisted of powerful objects associated with a divinity enwrapped by fabric. They served as receptacles of sacred power, materializations of sacred presence, instruments for communicating with the "gods," and symbols of political power and authority. The Aztecs made mortuary bundles (usually for cremation) using woven cloth.[147] *Quimiloa* also refers to dressing someone. Dressing someone in the appropriate woven vestment such as the *quemitl* (a biblike apron tied around the neck) contributed to his/her transformation into a teixiptla or sacrificial victim.[148] The Aztecs saw the quemitl as a "bib of the gods," claims Anawalt.[149] The quemitl conveyed the concept of godliness and also symbolized human sacrifice. Lastly, the Aztecs portrayed deities in the codices wearing woven vestments, a practice reflecting their custom of dressing deity statues and effigies in woven vestments.[150] The quemitl, for example, was closely associated with Tlaloc. Contemporary Nahuas, Tepehuas, and Otomís continue this practice by clothing ritual cut-paper figures.[151] In sum, woven cloth orders, balances, and transforms.

8.8. CONCLUSION

Aztec metaphysics conceives the cosmos as a grand nepantla-defined process in progress. Nepantla-processing is the primordial and fundamental pattern of reality's ceaseless becoming and transforming. Nepantla-processes create an agonistic contact point, crossroads, or confluence of middled creative-destruction, destructive-creation, and transformation. Nepantla-processes commingle and weave together reality's various agonistic inamic partners – life~death, male~female, dry~wet, and so forth – into a process of continual becoming and transformation. They unite reality's agonistic inamic partners within a single, rhythmic, back-and-forth, and mutually reciprocating process that preserves them while middling them and balancing them off against one another. Nepantla-processes commingle and interweave order~disorder, being~nonbeing, and so on to form a continuing succession of cyclical alternations. In doing so they generate and regenerate the continuous becoming, processing, and transforming of reality. Nepantla-processes weave together agonistic inamic partners into balanced unity, and moreover do so in a way that is continuously fertile, productive, sustaining, nourishing, regenerative, and transformative. Reality (teotl) thus consists of a single, grand, ontologically homogenous, all-encompassing, holistically interrelated, and nepantla-defined *macroprocess* that subsumes and incorporates the multitude of mutually interdependent and reciprocally influencing agonistic *microprocesses* that we experience about us (e.g., life~death and day~night cycles).

Teotl's nepantla-processing also interweaves, commingles, unites, and balances more abstract agonistic inamic pairs such as order~disorder, arrangement~derangement, and being~nonbeing. Teotl's nepantla-balancing is dynamic and diachronic: it is generated by the ceaseless, back-and-forth alternation of two *imbalances* – just as becoming is generated by the back-and-forth alternation of being~nonbeing. Balancing is *not* an inamic but rather a process that unites inamic partners. Teotl's nepantla-processing orders, integrates, and arranges them. Teotl's nepantla-balancing therefore constitutes a second-order, non-inamically defined *ordering* of first-order, inamically defined orderings~disorderings, and similarly, a second-order, non-inamically defined *arranging* of first-order, inamically defined arrangings~derangings. Like teotl's balancing, teotl's *second-order* ordering and *second-order* arranging are *not* themselves inamic pairs since they unite and subsume within themselves reality's *first-order* inamic pairs. Equally important, teotl's balancing and second-order ordering and arranging are immanent and nonhierarchical (like patterns woven into fabric, waves upon the ocean's surface, and tree rings within a tree trunk). In the final analysis, teotl is simultaneously the weaver of reality, the weaving of reality, and woven reality itself.

NOTES

1. Elizabeth Hill Boone (*Cycles of Time and Meaning in the Mexican Books of Fate* [Austin: University of Texas Press, 2007], 181) argues that *Codex Borgia* (pl. 30) depicts the emergence of the tonalpohualli.

2. I owe my understanding of backstrap weaving to Anni Albers, *On Weaving* (Middletown, CT: Wesleyan University Press, 1965); Frances F. Berdan, "Cotton in Aztec Mexico: Production, Distribution, and Uses," *Mexican Studies* 3, no. 2 (1987): 235–62; Donald Cordry and Dorothy Cordry, *Mexican Indian Costumes* (Austin: University of Texas Press, 1968); Alba Guadalupe Mastache, "El tejido en el México antiguo," Edición especial, *Arqueología mexicana* 19 (2005): 20–28; Alba Guadalupe Mastache, "Téchnicas prehispánicas," *Arqueología mexicana, Edición especial* 19 (2005): 29–32; Stacy B. Schaefer, *To Think with a Good Heart: Wixárika Women, Weavers, and Shamans* (Salt Lake City: University of Utah Press, 2002); Marilyn Anderson, *Guatemalan Textiles Today* (New York: Watson-Guptill Publications, 1978); Barbara Taber and Marilyn Anderson, *Backstrap Weaving* (New York: Watson-Guptill Publications, 1975); Patricia Rieff Anawalt, *Indian Clothing before Cortés: Mesoamerican Costumes from the Codices* (Norman: University of Oklahoma Press, 1981); Patricia Rieff Anawalt, "Weaving," in *The Oxford Encyclopedia of Mesoamerican Cultures: The Civilizations of Mexico and Central America*, ed. Davíd Carrasco (Oxford: Oxford University Press, 2001), 3: 324–28; Patricia Rieff Anawalt, "*Atuendos del México antiguo*," *Arqueología mexicana, Edición especial* 19 (2005): 8–20; and Ann Pollard Rowe, *A Century of Change in Guatemalan Textiles* (New York: Center for Inter-American Relations, 1981).

3. Frances Karttunen, *An Analytical Dictionary of Nahuatl* (Norman: University of Oklahoma Press, 1983), 95.

4. The Kogi make the same gender assignment. See Gerardo Reichel-Dolmatoff, "The Loom of Life: A Kogi Principle of Integration," *Journal of Latin American Lore* 4, no. 1 (1978): 13.

5. Mastache, "Téchnicas prehispánicas," 29.

6. Ibid., 30.

7. Ibid., 30–31.

8. Fray Alonso de Molina, *Vocabulario en lengua castellana y mexicana y mexicana y castellana*, 4th ed., facsimile of 1571 edition (Mexico City: Porrúa, 2001), 2:33v; see also Rémi Siméon, *Diccionario de la lengua náhuatl o mexicana*, trans. Josefina Olivia de Coll (México, DF: Siglo Veintiuno Editores, 1977), 174.

9. R. Joe Campbell, *A Morphological Dictionary of Classical Nahuatl: A Morpheme Index to the* Vocabulario en lengua mexicana y castellana *of Fray Alonso de Molina* (Madison, WI: Hispanic Seminary of Medieval Studies, 1985), 298.

10. Karttunen, *Analytical Dictionary*, 233.

11. Campbell, *Morphological Dictionary*, 298.

12. Ibid., 298.

13. Karttunen, *Analytical Dictionary*, 215.

14. Campbell, *Morphological Dictionary*, 411.

15. Taber and Anderson, *Backstrap Weaving*, 45f. The same crossing over occurs with the warping board of the Tzutujil Maya (Martin Prechtel and Robert S. Carlsen, "Weaving and Cosmos amongst the Tzutujil Maya of Guatemala," *RES* 15 [1988]: fig. 1).

16. Cordry and Cordry, *Mexican Indian Costumes*, 32.

17. Prechtel and Carlsen, "Weaving and Cosmos," 123.

18. Campbell, *Morphological Dictionary*, 330–31.

19. Eduard Seler, *Comentarios al Códice Borgia*, 3 vols. (México, DF: Fondo de Cultura Económica, 1963 [1904]), II:74.

20. "Histoyre du Mechique," in *Teogonía e historia de los mexicanos: Tres opúsculos del siglo XVI*, 1st ed., ed. Angel María Garibay K. (México, DF: Editorial Porrúa, 1965), 108.

21. See Bernardino de Sahagún, *Florentine Codex: General History of the Things of New Spain*, ed. and trans. Arthur J.O. Anderson and Charles Dibble (Santa Fe, NM: School of American Research; Salt Lake City: University of Utah Press, 1953–82), II:31–32, 155–58); Sahagún, *Primeros memoriales*. Paleography of Nahuatl Text and English Translation, by Thelma Sullivan (Norman: University of Oklahoma Press, 1997), fol. 253r; Diego Durán, *Book of the Gods and Rites* and *The Ancient Calendar*, trans. and ed. Fernando Horcasitas and Doris Heyden (Norman: University of Oklahoma Press, 1971), 463–64; Henry B. Nicholson, "Religion in Pre-Hispanic Central Mexico," in *Handbook of Middle American Indians*, vol. 10, ed. Robert Wauchope, Gordon F. Elkholm, and Ignacio Bernal (Austin: University of Texas Press, 1971), table 4; Eloise Quiñones Keber, *Codex Telleriano-Remensis: Ritual, Divination, and History in a Pictorial Aztec Manuscript* (Austin: University of Texas Press, 1995), 149–50; *The Tovar Calendar: An Illustrated Mexican Calendar ca. 1585*, reproduction and comment by G. Kubler and C. Gibson, Memoirs of the Connecticut Academy of Arts and Sciences, XI (New Haven: Connecticut Academy of Arts and Sciences, 1951), 34. Durán (*Book of the Gods*, 463) translates *tititl* as "to stretch"; Caso, as *arrugado* ("wrinkled" or "crumbled") (as reported by Cecelia Klein, "Woven Heaven, Tangled Earth: The Weaver's Paradigm of the Mesoamerican Cosmos," in *Ethnoastronomy and Archaeoastronomy in the American Tropics*, ed. Anthony Aveni and Gary Urton, Annals of the New York Academy of Sciences, No. 38 [New York: New York Academy of Sciences, 1982], 12); Ross Hassig (*Time, History, and Belief in Aztec and Colonial Mexico* [Austin: University of Texas Press, 2001], 14) as "wrinkled or shrunk"; and Nicholson ("Religion," table 4) as "'Contraction'? 'Stretching'? 'Wrinkled'?"

22. Karttunen, *Analytical Dictionary*, 241.

23. Campbell, *Morphological Dictionary*, 331.

24. Durán, *Book of the Gods*, pl. 54.

25. Kubler and Gibson, "The Tovar Calendar," 34. See plate 13.

26. Nicholson, "Religion," table 4.

27. Kogi metaphysics entertains a similar view according to Reichel-Dolmatoff ("Loom of Life").

28. See Anderson, *Guatemalan Textiles Today*, fig. 4.2; Rowe, *Century of Change*, 19 and fig. 36; Schaefer, *Think with a Good Heart*, 44, 277, fig. 9.

29. Rowe, *Century of Change*, 19.

30. *Pacyotl* occurs only in the Spanish-to-Nahuatl side of Molina's dictionary (Molina, *Vocabulario*), whereas *tetlanacqui* occurs in both (see page 114v of the Spanish-to-Nahuatl side and page 108v of the Nahuatl-to-Spanish). Siméon's *Diccionario*, 369, contains *pacyotl* but not *tetlanacqui*.

31. Karttunen, *Analytical Dictionary*, 183.

32. Molina, *Vocabulario*, 2:108v.

33. Campbell, *Morphological Dictionary*, 346.

34. "[C]on otros, o par dellos, o cerca dellos, o con otro" (Molina, *Vocabulario*, 2:109).

35. "[C]aber en agujero" (Molina, *Vocabulario*, 2r:7).

36. "[C]ontener, entrar en un lugar, un agujero, etc." (Siméon, *Diccionario*, 35).

37. Karttunen, *Analytical Dictionary*, 12.

38. Collated and translated by Campbell, *Morphological Dictionary*, 13–14.

39. John D. Monaghan, "Physiology, Production and Gendered Difference: The Evidence from Mixtec and Other Mesoamerican Societies," in *Gender in Pre-Hispanic America*, ed. Cecelia Klein (Washington, DC: Dumbarton Oaks, 2001), 295.

40. Reichel-Dolmatoff, "Loom of Life," 14.

41. Ibid., 14.

42. The Spanish-to-Nahuatl side of Molina, *Vocabulario*, 1:76v. Karttunen (*Analytical Dictionary*, 134) translates *malacatl* as "spindle, bobbin, spiral." This is fitting, seeing as the weft threads are spun onto the bobbin much as rough fiber is spun onto the spindle.

43. Karttunen, *Analytical Dictionary*, 183.

44. Ibid., 1, 247.

45. Campbell, *Morphological Dictionary*, 6.

46. Sahagún, *Florentine Codex*, II:29; Molina, *Vocabulario*, 2:154r.

47. "[P]alo ancho como cuchilla con que tupen y aprietan la tela quese texe," translation by Campbell (*Morphological Dictionary*, 387).

48. Karttunen, *Analytical Dictionary*, 320.

49. Sahagún, *Florentine Codex*, II:29.

50. Quoted in Geoffrey McCafferty and Sharisse McCafferty, "The Metamorphosis of Xochiquetzal," in *Manifesting Power: Gender and the Interpretation of Power in Archaeology*, ed. Tracy L. Sweely (London: Routledge, 1999), 118.

51. Campbell, *Morphological Dictionary*, 386.

52. Ibid.

53. Ibid.

54. Prechtel and Carlsen, "Weaving and Cosmos," 124. See also Peter T. Furst, "The Thread of Life: Some Parallels in the Symbolism of Aztec, Huichol, and Puebla Earth Goddesses," in *Balance y perspectiva de la antropolgía de Mesoamerica y del centro de México*, Mesa Redonda 13th, 1973 (México, DF: La Sociedad Mexicana de Antropolgía, 1975); and Barbara Tedlock, *The Woman in the Shaman's Body: Reclaiming the Feminine in Religion and Medicine* (New York: Bantam Books, 2005), 227.

55. Cordry and Cordry, *Mexican Indian Costumes*, 43.

56. For parallels in contemporary Wixárika understanding of weaving, see Schaefer, *Think with a Good Heart*, 211.

57. Monaghan, "Physiology, Production and Gendered Difference," 295.

58. McCafferty and McCafferty, "Spinning and Weaving," 29; see also Geoffrey McCafferty and Sharisse McCafferty, "The Metamorphosis of Xochiquetzal," in *Manifesting Power: Gender and the Interpretation of Power in Archaeology*, ed. Tracy L. Sweely (London: Routledge, 1999), 103–25.

59. *Codex Borbonicus* (Loubat: Bibliothéque du Palais Bourbon, 1899), 26, http://www.famsi.org/index.html (accessed 5/18/2013).

60. *Codex Magliabechiano* (*The Book of the Life of the Ancient Mexicans*), facsimile ed. by Zelia Nuttall (Berkeley: University of California Press, 1903), 45.

61. Sahagún, *Florentine Codex*, I:11. See the illustration in Sahagún, *Primeros memoriales: Facsimile*, 264r.

62. Sahagún, *Florentine Codex*, II:illus. 6.

63. Sahagún *Florentine Codex*, II:appendix 236.

64. Cordry and Cordry, *Mexican Indian Costumes*, 44.

65. Ibid., 44, 49.

66. Cecelia Klein, "Fighting with Femininity: Gender and War in Aztec Mexico," in *Gender Rhetorics: Postures of Dominance and Submission in Human History*, Medieval and Renaissance Texts and Studies 113, ed. Richard C. Trexler (Binghamton: State University of New York, 1994), 219–53; and Kay A. Read, "More than Earth: Cihuacoatl as Female Warrior, Male Matron, and Inside Ruler," in *Goddesses Who Rule*, ed. Elisabeth Benard and Beverly Moon (Oxford: Oxford University Press, 2000), 51–68.

67. See also Taber and Anderson, *Backstrap Weaving*, 12; Cordry and Cordry, *Mexican Indian Costumes*, 35; and Schaefer, *Think with a Good Heart*, 42.

68. Cordry and Cordry, *Mexican Indian Costumes*, 43; Karttunen, *Analytical Dictionary*, 142.

69. Furst, "Thread of Life," 236.

70. Prechtel and Carlsen, "Weaving and Cosmos," 123.

71. Schaefer, *Think with a Good Heart*, 250.

72. Sahagún, *Florentine Codex*, II:138; see also III:43 and II:38.

73. This view is shared by contemporary Tzutujil Maya (Prechtel and Carlsen, "Weaving and Cosmos") and Wixárika (Schaefer, *Think with a Good Heart*).

74. Schaefer, *Think with a Good Heart*, 213 and fig. 40. See also Reichel-Dolmatoff, "Loom of Life," 16.

75. Anthony F. Aveni, *Skywatchers: A Revised and Updated Version of Skywatchers of Ancient Mexico* (Austin: University of Texas Press, 2001), 63.

76. See Campbell, *Morphological Dictionary*, 15. I follow Read (*Time and Sacrifice*, 246n10) by interpreting the postposition *-yan* as including both time and place.

77. See Campbell, *Morphological Dictionary*, 15.

78. See ibid., 288.

79. Prechtel and Carlsen, "Weaving and Cosmos," 126.

80. Chapters 4 and 7 discussed the distinction between cosmos per se, Sun-Earth Ordering, and the cosmos of a Sun-Earth Ordering.

81. Karttunen, *Analytical Dictionary*, 201.

82. Campbell, *Morphological Dictionary*, 256–58.

83. Barbara Tedlock and Dennis Tedlock, "Text and Textile: Language and Technology in the Arts of the Quiché Maya," *Journal of Anthropological Research* 41, no. 2 (1985): 127–28.

84. Ibid., 127.

85. Schaefer, *Think with a Good Heart*, 211.

86. Reichel-Dolmatoff, "Loom of Life." Kogi metaphysics conceives the loom as the horizontal surface of the earth and conceives each cosmic layer above the earth as an additional horizontal loom.

87. *Historia de los mexicanos por sus pinturas*, 30–31; Bierhorst, "Legend of the Suns," 142–44.

88. Wayne Elzey, "Some Remarks on the Space and Time of the 'Center' in Aztec Religion," *Estudios de cultura náhuatl* 12 (1976): 316, 320. Elzey thus claims the Fifth Sun is the "synthesis," "recapitulation," and "culmination" of the preceding Four Suns. See also Miguel León-Portilla, *Aztec Thought and Culture: A Study of the Ancient Nahuatl Mind*, trans. Jack Emory Davis (Norman: University of Oklahoma Press, 1963); Jacques Soustelle, *El universo de los Aztecas*, trans. José Luis Martinez (chapter 1) and Juan José Utrilla (chapters 2–4) (México, DF: Fondo de Cultura Económica, 1982); and Susan Gillespie, "Different Ways of Seeing: Modes of Social Consciousness in Mesoamerican Two-Dimensional Artworks," *Baesler-Archiv* 55 (2007): 103–42.

89. Klein, "Woven Heaven," 2–4.

90. Siméon, *Diccionario*, 251, translation mine.

91. Sahagún, *Florentine Codex*, XI:247.

92. Ibid., XI:273. They describe the straw-covered wooden house depicted in illustration 901 as "bound with thongs" (*tlamecacuialli*).

93. Sahagún, *Florentine Codex*, XI:fig. 405.

94. Klein, "Woven Heaven," 4–6.

95. See Alfredo López Austin, *The Human Body and Ideology: Concepts of the Ancient Nahuas*, trans. Thelma Ortiz de Montellano and Bernard R. Ortiz de Montellano (Salt Lake City: University of Utah Press, 1988), I:65, 251; Alfredo López Austin, *The Myths of the Opossum: Pathways of Mesoamerican Mythology*, trans. Bernard R. Ortiz de Montellano and Thelma Ortiz de Montellano (Salt Lake City: University of Utah Press, 1993), 275; López Austin, *Tamoanchan, Tlalocan*, 98–101; Davíd Carrasco, *Religions of Mesoamerica: Cosmovision and Ceremonial Centers* (San Francisco: Harper and Row, 1990), 51; Davíd Carrasco, "Uttered from the Heart: Guilty Rhetoric among the Aztecs," *History of Religions* 39 (1999): 9–10.

96. See López Austin, *Human Body and Ideology*, I:54–55, 209; López Austin, *Myths of the Opossum*, 51–60; López Austin, *Tamoanchan, Tlalocan*, 12–15, 17, 98–101, 105–12; Carrasco, *Religions of Mesoamerica*; Carrasco, "Uttered from the Heart"; and Carrasco, with Scott Sessions, *Daily Life of the Aztecs: People of the Sun and Earth* (Westport, CT: Greenwood Press, 1998).

97. For example, see Carrasco with Sessions, *Daily Life*, 44–45.

98. Nicholson, "Religion," 409 and table 2; and Carrasco with Sessions, *Daily Life*, 44–45.

99. López Austin (*Human Body and Ideology*, I:52–58) and López Austin (*Tamoanchan, Tlalocan*, 17) discusses two alternative ways of counting the heavens. See also Eduardo Matos Moctezuma, *Life and Death in the Templo Mayor*, trans. Bernard R. Ortiz de Montellano and Thelma Ortiz de Montellano (Niwot: University Press of Colorado, 1995), 25.

100. Nicholson, "Religion," 406–7.

101. *Codex Vaticanus 3738 A* (Graz 1979).

102. See León-Portilla, *Aztec Thought*; López Austin, *Tamoanchan, Tlalocan*; Carrasco with Sessions, *Daily Life*; and Matos Moctezuma, *Life and Death*.

103. Gillespie, "Different Ways of Seeing," 125; see also 126.

104. Louise M. Burkhart, *The Slippery Earth: Nahua-Christian Dialogue in Sixteenth-Century Mexico* (Tucson: University of Arizona Press, 1989), chapter 3; Elzey, "Some Remarks." For discussion of the role of center and periphery in contemporary Nahua thought, see Alan R. Sandstrom, "Center and Periphery in the Social Organization of Contemporary Nahuas of Mexico," *Ethnology* 35, no. 3 (1996): 161–80; and James M. Taggart, *Nahuat Myth and Social Structure* (Austin: University of Texas Press, 1983).

105. As Arthur O. Lovejoy (*The Great Chain of Being: A Study of the History of an Idea* [New York: Harper and Row, 1960]) points out, this assumption dates back at least as far as Plato in Western philosophy and later finds its way into Christian theology and metaphysics by way of neo-Platonism.

106. One might argue the foregoing considerations cast doubt upon the faithfulness of the illustrations themselves. There are, after all, grounds for worrying that the illustrations were skewed by post-Contact indigenous concerns (such as trying to make indigenous cosmology appear more Christian) or by Christian metaphysical concepts (such as the existence of a hierarchical cosmology). For further discussion of these issues, see Read, *Time and Sacrifice*, 138–39; and for discussion of the provenience of *Codex Vaticanus 3778 A*, see Quiñones Keber, *Codex Telleriano-Remensis*.

107. López Austin, *Tamoanchan, Tlalocan*, 17.

108. León-Portilla, *La filosofía náhuatl*, 58, 70.

109. Lovejoy, *Great Chain of Being*.

110. Diego Durán, *The History of the Indies of New Spain*, trans., annot., and intro. Doris Heyden (Norman: University of Oklahoma Press, 1994), 391.

111. Molina, *Vocabulario*, 1:119. This translation of *tlamantli* is from J. Richard Andrews, *Introduction to Classic Nahuatl*, rev. ed. (Norman: University of Oklahoma Press, 2003), 315. See also Karttunen, *Analytical Dictionary*, 281.

112. Campbell, *Morphological Dictionary*, 146, 212.

113. Sahagún, *Florentine Codex*, VI:202; see also 175, 176, 183, 202, 206.

114. López Austin, *Human Body and Ideology*, I:208, 426n10; López Austin, *Tamoanchan, Tlalocan*, 106–8.

115. See Karttunen, *Analytical Dictionary*, 104; Burkhart, *Slippery Earth*, 49; and Campbell, *Morphological Dictionary*, 122.

116. López Austin, *Human Body and Ideology*, 1:191.

117. Campbell, *Morphological Dictionary*, 122–23; see also López Austin, *Human Body and Ideology*, 1:191.

118. Klein, "Woven Heaven," 25.

119. Cordry and Cordry, *Mexican Indian Costumes*, 106, fig. 11.

120. Eduardo Matos Moctezuma, *Life and Death in the Templo Mayor*, trans. Bernard R. Ortiz de Montellano and Thelma Ortiz de Montellano (Niwot: University Press of Colorado, 1995), 23, 61–65.

121. Félix Báez-Jorge and Arturo Gómez Martínez, "Los equilibrios del cielo y de la tierra: Cosmovisión de los nahuas de Chicontepec," *Desacatos* 5 (Winter 2000): 85–86. See also Alan R. Sandstrom, "Sacred Mountains and Miniature Worlds: Altar Design among the Nahua of Northern Veracruz, Mexico," in *Mesas and Cosmologies in Mesoamerica*, ed. Douglas Sharon, San Diego Museum of Man Papers 42 (San Diego: San Diego Museum of Man, 2003), 51–70.

122. Mircea Eliade, *Rites and Symbols of Initiation: The Mysteries of Birth and Rebirth*, trans. Willard R. Trask (New York: Harper and Row, 1958), 45.

123. Erich Neumann, *The Great Mother: An Analysis of the Archetype*, trans. Ralph Mannheim (Princeton, NJ: Princeton University Press, 1963), 227, emphasis mine. For

relevant discussion, see also Prechtel and Carlsen, "Weaving and Cosmos"; B. Tedlock, *Woman in the Shaman's Body*; Schaefer, *Think with a Good Heart*; and Reichel-Dolmatoff, "Loom of Life." Abigail E. Adams and James E. Brady, "Ethnographic Notes on Maya Q'eqchi' Cave Rites: Implications for Archaeological Interpretation," in *In the Maw of the Earth Monster: Mesoamerican Ritual Cave Use*, ed. James E. Brady and Keith M. Prufer (Austin: University of Texas Press, 2005). According to Adams and Brady ("Ethnographic Notes," 319), the presence of cotton, needles, and spindle whorls in Santiago Atitlán's image of San Juan Carajo suggests the creation of the world by weaving. Furst ("Thread of Life") argues this same association holds true in Huichol and Pueblo thought.

124. Thelma D. Sullivan, "Tlazolteotl-Ixcuina: The Great Spinner and Weaver," in *The Art and Iconography of Late Post-Classic Central Mexico*, ed. Elizabeth Hill Boone (Washington, DC: Dumbarton Oaks, 1982), 14; see also 30. According to Schaefer (*Think with a Good Heart*, 229), for the Wixáritari "spinning yarn is like giving life." The great genetrix, Takutsi, "breathed" life into all her creations when she spun yarn. See also B. Tedlock, *Woman in the Shaman's Body*, chapter 15. For similar parallels between weaving and sexual intercourse in contemporary Atitlán, see Nathaniel Tarn and Martin Prechtel, *Scandals in the House of Birds: Shamans and Priests on Lake Atitlán* (New York: Marsilio Publishers, 1979), 298–300.

125. Aztec metaphysics embraces a "weaver's paradigm," as Klein ("Woven Heaven," 1) puts it.

126. According to Sandstrom (Sandstrom, Alan R. "The Tonantsi Cult of the Eastern Nahua." In *Mother Worship: Themes and Variations*, edited by James J. Preston, 25–50. Chapel Hill, University of North Carolina Press, 1982), contemporary southern Huastecan Nahuas believe Tonantsi ("our sacred mother") combines both male and female principles in a "productive unity" associated with germination, fertility, birth, growth, well-being, food, generosity, and the unity of siblings.

127. López Austin, *Tamoanchan, Tlalocan*, 8.

128. B. Tedlock and D. Tedlock, "Text and Textile," 126. According to Reichel-Dolmatoff ("Loom of Life"), the Kogi view the cosmos in terms of weaving and looms.

129. Sahagún, *Florentine Codex*, I:15.

130. Ibid., IV:4.

131. *Codex Borbonicus*, 19.

132. Neumann, *The Great Mother*, 227 (emphasis mine).

133. Furst, "Thread of Life," 238. See also Schaefer, *Think with a Good Heart*.

134. Hernando Ruiz de Alarcón, *Treatise on the Heathen Superstitions that Today Live among the Indians Native to This New Spain*, trans., ed., and intro. J. Richard Andrews and Ross Hassig (Norman: University of Oklahoma Press, 1984), 153 (emphasis mine).

135. Sandstrom, *Corn Is Our Blood*, 235–36.

136. Mary Miller and Karl Taube, *An Illustrated Dictionary of the Gods and Symbols of Ancient Mexico and the Maya* (London: Thames and Hudson, 1993), 80. See also Alfredo López Austin, "*Los ritos: Un juego de definiciones*," *Arqueología Mexicana* 6, no. 34 (1988): 4–37.

137. Rosemary A. Joyce (*Gender and Power in Prehispanic Mesoamerica* [Austin: University of Texas Press, 2000], 164) claims that "woven cloth signified civilized existence" for the Aztecs.

138. Berdan, "Cotton in Aztec Mexico," 242; Frances Berdan, "Trade and Tribute in the Aztec Empire," in *Current Topics in Aztec Studies: Essays in Honor of Dr. H. B. Nicholson*, ed. Alana Cordy-Collins and Douglas Sharon, San Diego Museum of Man, vol. 30 (San Diego: San Diego Museum of Man, 1993) 71–84; Joyce, *Gender and Power*, 164; and Durán, *History*, 162, 165, 177, 200, 204, 342.

139. Elizabeth M. Brumfiel, "Tribute Cloth Production and Compliance in Aztec and Colonial Mexico," *Museum Anthropology* 21, no. 2 (1997), 57. See also Berdan, "Cotton in Aztec Mexico," 252; Berdan, "Trade and Tribute."

140. Cited in Brumfiel, "Tribute Cloth Production," 5.

141. Berdan, "Cotton in Aztec Mexico," 239.

142. Durán, *History*, 95, 317.

143. Brumfiel, "Tribute Cloth Production," 64; Durán, *History*, 293.

144. Eva Hunt, *The Transformation of the Hummingbird: Cultural Roots of a Zinacatecan Mythical Poem* (Ithaca, NY: Cornell University Press, 1977), 159.

145. Klein, "Woven Heaven," 29.

146. Guilhem Olivier, "Bundles," in *The Oxford Encyclopedia of Mesoamerican Cultures: The Civilizations of Mexico and Central America*, ed. Davíd Carrasco (Oxford: Oxford University Press, 2001), 1:105; and Campbell, *Morphological Dictionary*, 283. What follows is indebted to Olivier, "Bundles"; and Miller and Taube, *Illustrated Dictionary*, 47–48, 119.

147. Berdan, "Cotton in Aztec Mexico," 239.

148. Anawalt, "Memory Clothing," 166.

149. Ibid., 169–70.

150. Anawalt, "Memory Clothing"; and Berdan, "Cotton in Aztec Mexico."

151. Alan Sandstrom and Pamela Effrein Sandstrom, *Traditional Papermaking and Paper Cult Figures of Mexico* (Norman: University of Oklahoma Press, 1986), 66–67, 295–96.

The Aztecs' world, the fifth and last Sun-Earth Ordering in the history of the cosmos, is *a world in motion*. It is a world of ceaseless nepantla-defined becoming and transformation. The Aztecs' world is also nonhierarchical: one without transcendent deities, purpose, truths, norms, or commandments. In such a world, Aztec tlamatinime asked, what is the correct path (*ohtli*), the right way of life, for human beings to follow? What enables humans to follow and further this path, and what disables them? How did Aztec tlamatinime, in other words, conceive what Western philosophers call ethics, political philosophy, epistemology, and aesthetics? This question obviously requires another study. By way of conclusion, I sketch the following answer.

Given the centrality of nepantla in Aztec metaphysics, it is not surprising that Aztec philosophy defines human existence in terms of nepantla.[1] Human existence is, in short, both *in* nepantla and *of* nepantla. It is *in* nepantla in the sense that it is defined by ceaseless and ineluctable betwixt-and-betweenness. Life takes time-place in the cyclical back-and-forth struggle of cosmic inamic pairs such as order~disorder, being~nonbeing, life~death, and male~female. Trapped in the tension-ridden, reciprocating balance between being~nonbeing, human existence is defined by inescapable processing, becoming, and transformation. Human life is consequently unstable, fragile, perilous, fleeting, and evanescent.

Human existence is also *of* nepantla. Life itself is a nepantla-process consisting of continual nepantla-defined becoming and transformation as well as the nepantla-defined interweaving of agonistic inamic forces. Human beings (the complete, energy-constituted

DOI: 10.5876_9781607322238.c009

mind-body fusion) are not only generated and sustained by, but also consist of, the nepantla-defined intersecting and middling of inamic forces – indeed, the selfsame nepantla intersecting and middling that generate and sustain the Fifth Sun and Fifth Age. As a consequence, human life is unstable, fragile, perilous, fleeting, and evanescent.

Because it is by definition both in and of nepantla, human existence is also by definition both *in* and *of* the crossroads. Life takes place and takes part in the crucible of crossing cosmic arms depicted so clearly by *Codex Mendoza* (pl. 2r; see Figure 4.10) and *Codex Fejérváry-Mayer* (pl. 1; see Figure 4.3). After all, it is in the crossroads – that is, the middled and balanced commingling and interweaving of agonistic inamic forces – that all regeneration, all degeneration, and all olin-defined life~death occur in the Fifth Sun-Earth Ordering. Human beings are no exception. Teotl's nepantla-processing situates human existence in nepantlatli, that is, in the dynamic betwixt-and-between of agonistic inamic partners.

Understanding and embracing the foregoing holds the key to wisdom and living a good (*cualli*) human life. The Aztecs looked to their metaphysics for guidance concerning how to conduct their lives and to follow a path in a cosmos defined by nepantla. Given its defining role in Aztec metaphysics, they turned to teotl, or more precisely, *teotl-as-nepantla-process*. They regarded teotl-as-nepantla-process as the ideal normative model *for* human behavior because they regarded teotl-as-nepantla-process as the ideal descriptive model *of* nepantla-behavior. They did *not* however turn to teotl because they saw teotl as transcendent, supernatural, omniscient, or benevolent, or because they saw teotl as sacred while seeing themselves as profane. Instead, they turned to teotl because human beings are *in* and *of* teotl. Aztec tlamatinime accordingly enjoined people to live their lives in a teotl-like, nepantla-middling manner, and they based their prescriptions regarding how humans ought to conduct their lives upon teotl's example. The concept of nepantla thus figures prominently in Aztec prescriptions concerning how humans ought to walk, speak, eat, drink, think, feel, bathe, dance, perform rituals, and sexually commingle, for example. Nepantla, in other words, defines the Aztecs' understanding of what Western philosophers call ethics, epistemology, aesthetics, and social and political philosophy.[2]

Aztec tlamatinime apparently reasoned that since reality and human existential condition are inescapably middled, humans must therefore act and live middlingly. In a cosmos defined by nepantla, one must live a life defined by nepantla. Ideograms such as the quincunx, four-petaled flower, and butterfly therefore functioned both descriptively *and* prescriptively. *Codex Mendoza* (pl. 2r) and *Codex Fejérváry-Mayer* (pl. 1) both *describe* the nature of human existence and *prescribe* a way for humans to exist. They describe the way things *are* as well as prescribe how things *ought* to be – that is, how humans *ought* to behave and what their way of life and path *ought* to be. Aztec philosophy consequently rejects modern Western philosophy's *fact* vs. *value* and *is* vs. *ought* distinctions.[3] The same seamless descriptive-cum-prescriptive role characterizes other common ideograms such as twilling, quatrefoils, ballcourts, reciprocal-motion motifs, and *xicalcoliuhqui*. As a Kogi priest declares, "We must have this [quincunx-shaped] loom constantly before our eyes [and heart-minds]. It is to remind us always, everywhere, day and night, of the need to live well. . . . We must think of this all the time."[4]

The seamless descriptive-cum-prescriptive role of nepantla should not surprise us, given nepantla's role as a fundamental organizing metaphor in Aztec philosophy. Indeed, the role of weaving – that is, nepantla-defined balancing, middling, mutuality, and reciprocity – in Aztec philosophy clearly illustrates chapter 3's claim that a "culture's most fundamental values and value system cohere with the metaphorical structure of the most fundamental concepts of that culture."[5] As root metaphor, weaving plays a defining role in Aztec "cognitive processes, belief systems, affective-motivational processes, value systems, and everyday practices."[6]

The Aztecs likened the human condition to walking down a narrow, jagged path along a mountain peak. As a Nahuatl proverb recorded by Sahagún puts it, "*Tlaalahui, tlapetzcahui in tlalticpac*" ("It is slippery, it is slick on the earth").[7] Humans invariably lose hold of whatever balance they momentarily attain while walking down the path of life. They inevitably lose their footing on the earth's slippery surface. The well-balanced and well-ordered in human life ineluctably slips into imbalance and disorder, causing misfortune, pain, suffering, hunger, sorrow, disease, and death. The well-woven life ineluctably becomes unraveled and frayed. All things inevitably fall apart. Death, disintegration, derangement, disorder, and nonbeing are inescapable, and so life is by nature unstable, fragile, perilous, and ultimately fleeting and evanescent.

The *in huehuetlatolli* ("old, old spoken words") recorded by Sahagún include the following address from a mother to her daughter: "On earth we walk, we travel along a mountain peak. Over here there is an abyss, over there is an abyss. If thou goest over here, or if thou goest over there, thou wilt fall."[8] Following this description, the mother advises her daughter: "*zan tlanepantla in uiloa, in nemoa*" ("only in or through the middle doth one go, doth one live").[9] Her advice invokes *tlanepantla* ("in or through the middle"). A father likewise advises his son: "*xonmimattinemi in tlalticpac, ca oticcac in zan tlanepantlacayotl monequi*" ("continue with caution on earth, for thou hast heard that moderation is necessary").[10] Nahuatl uses the suffix -*yotl* to form abstract nouns, suggesting we interpret *tlanepantlacayotl* as referring to "middleness" or "middlehood."[11] One's conduct must be *middled* and *middling*. This advice is echoed by the Aztec adage, *tlacoqualli in monequi* ("the middle good is necessary").[12] Molina offers two related entries, *tlanepantla yeliztli* and *tlanepantla nemiliztli*, which he glosses as "*mediano estado, o manera de vivir*."[13] I suggest we gloss these as "living or being middlingly" or "middled way of being or living." Those striving to walk in balance upon the slippery earth must pursue a middle footing, a middled way of being and living.

Aztec tlamatinime accordingly aimed at teaching humans how, like skilled mountaineers, to maintain their balance upon the narrow, jagged summit of the earth. They sought to instruct humans how to gain a *middle footing* on the path of life, how to middle themselves in all endeavors. They sought to teach humans to behave as accomplished weavers who weave together the various agonistic inamic forces constituting both the cosmos and their lives into a well-balanced fabric.[14] Aztec philosophy thus embraces an *ethics – as well as epistemology, politics, and aesthetics – of nepantla:* one of reciprocity and balance, and of middling mutuality. Aztec wisdom enjoins humans to weave together into a well-balanced fabric one's feelings, thoughts, words, and actions as well as one's relationships with family, community, and indeed all things (including plants, animals, rocks, springs, and cosmos). In order to live wisely, live well, live artfully, and live a genuine human life, one's living must embody nepantla-middling and nepantla-balancing. One's life must be an artfully crafted nepantla-process.

The Aztecs accordingly endeavored to *weave a nepantla-balanced way of life*. They lived and died within a woven way of life and within a woven cosmos. They were born on woven mats, married on woven mats, fabricated cloth on woven mats, divined the *tonalpohualli* on woven mats, and ruled from woven mats. They slept in woven mats, had sexual relations on woven mats, and commonly died on woven mats. They lived in woven houses and conducted important religious rituals on woven mats in temples with woven roofs. They grew agricultural foodstuffs in woven fields (*chinampas*). They inserted their bloody autosacrificial thorns and spines in woven grass balls. They wove words together to form ritual speech and song-poems; they wove musical notes together to form ritual music. Equally if not more significantly, they defined themselves in terms of weaving and woven cloth. They dressed themselves, *teixiptla*, statues, sacred bundles, and the dead in woven cloth. They distinguished themselves from outsiders and from one another ethically, socially, politically, and religiously in terms of woven fabric. In short, Aztec tlamatinime conceived genuine, authentic, and well-rooted human existence in terms of nepantla-balanced and nepantla-middled processes, activities, and time-places. Well-balanced living enjoyed such earthly benefits as greater stability, longevity, health, happiness, and pleasure.

Aztec tlamatinime contrasted this with the poorly rooted and inauthentically human existence of wayward peoples such as the Chichimecs, whom they likened to deer and rabbits and regarded as unstable, skittish, erratic, disordered, uncentered, self-indulgent, and lacking in moderation and self-discipline.[15] Such people followed the wild, crooked, and wandering path of vagabondage – as opposed to the straight, centered, and middled path of well-balancedness. They lived in the periphery – that is, in the plains, the forests, the crags – not the center, the middle, and the navel. They wore raw hides and skins, or like the Huastecs, wore no breechcloths at all.[16] Imbalanced living suffered such earthly costs as greater instability, expiry, ill health, hunger, sorrow, and pain.

In closing, nepantla organizes the Aztecs' understanding of their lifeway. Wise living embraces, implements, and masters nepantla motion-change. It seeks neither to avoid, minimize, nor escape nepantla. Nepantla is the norm, not the exception. Human existence takes place in the crossroads. Wisdom consists of embracing and mastering the ineliminable ambiguity of the crossroads and hence the ineliminable ambiguity of life – not trying to deny, minimize, or escape it.

NOTES

1. In speaking of the human existential condition I am not likening Aztec thought to twentieth-century European philosophical existentialism. The nature of human existence is a common theme in world philosophies. European existentialism represents merely *one* culture's understanding of and response to this condition. Furthermore, in saying that Aztec philosophy defines the human existential condition in terms of nepantla it is imperative to remember that nepantla is *not* to be understood in terms of Turner's liminality (Victor Turner, "Betwixt and Between: The Liminal Period in Rites of Passage," in *Reader in Comparative Religion: An Anthropological Approach*, 4th ed., ed. William A. Lessa and Evon Z. Vogt [New York: Harper and Row, 1979], 234–42).

2. The Aztecs sought to behave "cosmogonically," as Girardot puts it when discussing the Daoist aim to model human behavior upon the Dao (Norman J. Girardot, "Behaving Cosmogonically in Early Taoism," in *Cosmogony and Ethical Order: New Studies in Comparative Ethics*, ed. Robin W. Lovin and Frank E. Reynolds [Chicago: University of Chicago Press, 1985]). Aztec philosophy draws no principled distinction between the sagely, ethical, political, epistemological, and aesthetic dimensions of human conduct, institutions, and relationships. These are *our* distinctions, not theirs. In this respect, it resembles indigenous North American philosophies and classical Daoism and Confucianism.

3. For discussion of the *fact* vs. *value* and *is* vs. *ought* distinctions in Western philosophy, see Robert Audi, ed., *The Cambridge Dictionary of Philosophy* (Cambridge: Cambridge University Press, 1995).

4. Quoted in Gerardo Reichel-Dolmatoff, "The Loom of Life: A Kogi Principle of Integration," *Journal of Latin American Lore* 4, no. 1 (1978), 23, brackets mine. Elizabeth Brumfiel discusses the normative aspects of artistic motifs in Brumfiel, "Towards a Middle Range Theory of Household Politics: The Standardization of Decorative Motifs in Middle Postclassic Mexico," in *The Archaeology of Politics: The Materiality of Political Practice and Action in the Past*, ed. Peter Johansen and Andrew Bauer (Newcastle upon Tyne: Cambridge Scholars Publications, 2011).

5. George Lakoff and Mark Johnson, *Metaphors We Live By* (Chicago: University of Chicago Press, 1980), 22.

6. Ibid., 3.

7. Bernardino de Sahagún, *The Florentine Codex: General History of the Things of New Spain*, ed. and trans. Arthur J.O. Anderson and Charles Dibble (Santa Fe, NM: School of American Research; Salt Lake City: University of Utah Press, 1953–1982), VI:228; translated by Louise M. Burkhart, *The Slippery Earth: Nahua-Christian Dialogue in Sixteenth-Century Mexico* (Tucson: University of Arizona Press, 1989), 58.

8. Sahagún, *Florentine Codex*, VI:101.

9. Ibid., VI:126.

10. Ibid.

11. See Frances Karttunen, *An Analytical Dictionary of Nahuatl* (Norman: University of Oklahoma Press, 1983), 339.

12. Sahagún, *General History*, VI:231, translation by Burkhart, *Slippery Earth*, 134. Burkhart (*Slippery Earth*, 210n6) observes that *tlacoqualli* derives from two words, *tlaco* ("middle, center, half") and *cualli* ("something good").

13. Alonso de Molina, *Vocabulario en lengua castellana y mexicana y mexicana y castellana*, 4th ed. (Mexico City: Porrúa, 2001), 2:128r.

14. For related discussion, see Willard Gingerich, "Chipahuacanemiliztli, 'the Purified Life,' in the Discourses of Book VI, Florentine Codex," in *Smoke and Mist: Mesoamerican Studies in Memory of Thelma D. Sullivan*, Part 2, ed. Kathryn Josserand and Karen Dakin, 517–43 (Oxford: British Archaeological Reports, 1988); Barbara G. Myerhoff, *Peyote Hunt: The Sacred Journey of the Huichol Indians* (Ithaca, NY: Cornell University Press, 1974); and James Maffie, "*In Huehue Tlamanitiliztli* and *la Verdad*: Nahua and European Philosophies in Fray Bernardino de Sahagún's *Colloquios y doctrina cristiana*," *Inter-America Journal of Philosophy* 3 (2012): 1–33. According to Reichel-Dolmatoff ("Loom of Life," 12–13, 20), the Kogi sing of weaving the "fabric" of their lives. Life is to be organized by a set of simple rules symbolized by spinning and weaving.

15. Sahagún, *Florentine Codex*, X:171ff. For discussion, see Louise Burkhart, "Moral Deviance in Sixteenth Century Nahua and Christian Thought: The Rabbit and the Deer," *Journal of Latin American Lore* 12 (1986); Burkhart, *Slippery Earth*; and James Maffie, "To Walk in Balance: An Encounter between Contemporary Western Science and Pre-Conquest Nahua Philosophy," in *Science and Other Cultures: Philosophy of Science and Technology Issues*, ed. Robert Figueroa and Sandra Harding (New York: Routledge, 2003), 70–91.

16. Sahagún, *Florentine Codex*, X:186. See the depiction of a Huastec man in Sahagún, *Florentine Codex*, IX:figure 43.

Bibliography

Adams, Abigail E., and James E. Brady. "Ethnographic Notes on Maya Q'eqchi' Cave Rites: Implications for Archaeological Interpretation." In *In the Maw of the Earth Monster: Mesoamerican Ritual Cave Use*, edited by James E. Brady and Keith M. Prufer, 301–27. Austin: University of Texas Press, 2005.

Aguilar-Moreno, Manuel. *Handbook to Life in the Aztec World*. Oxford: Oxford University Press, 2006.

Aguilera, Carmen. "Templo Mayor: Dual Symbol of the Passing of Time." In *The Imagination of Matter: Religion and Ecology in Mesoamerican Traditions*, edited by Davíd Carrasco, 129–35. BAR International Series 515. Oxford: BAR, 1989.

Albers, Anni. *On Weaving*. Middletown, CT: Wesleyan University Press, 1965.

Aldana, Gerardo. *The Apotheosis of Janaab' Pakal: Science, History and Religion at Classic Maya Palenque*. Boulder: University Press of Colorado, 2007.

Allen, Paula Gunn. *The Sacred Hoop: Recovering the Feminine in American Indian Traditions*. Boston: Beacon Press, 1986.

Allen, R. E., ed. *The Concise Oxford English Dictionary*. 8th ed. Oxford: Clarendon Press, 1990.

Alvarado Tezozomoc, Hernando. *Crónica mexicayotl*. Translated by A. Léon. Mexico: Universidad Nacional Autonoma de Mexico/Instituto de Historia, 1949.

Ames, Roger T. "Confucius and the Ontology of Knowing." In *Interpreting across Boundaries: New Essays in Comparative Philosophy*, edited by Gerry Larsen and Eliot Deutsch, 265–79. Princeton, NJ: Princeton University Press, 1988.

Ames, Roger T. "Images of Reason in Chinese Culture." In *Introduction to World Philosophies*, edited by Eliot Deutsch, 254–59. Upper Saddle River, NJ: Prentice-Hall, 1997.

Ames, Roger T. "Putting the *Te* Back into Taoism." In *Nature in Asian Traditions of Thought: Essays in Environmental Philosophy*, edited by J. Baird Callicott and Roger T. Ames, 113–43. Albany: SUNY Press, 1989.

DOI: 10.5876_9781607322238.c010

Ames, Roger T. *"Yin* and *Yang."* In *Encyclopedia of Chinese Philosophy*, edited by Antonio S. Cua, 846–47. New York: Routledge, 2003.

Ames, Roger T., and Henry Rosemont Jr. *The Analects of Confucius: A Philosophical Translation*. New York: Ballantine Books, 1998.

Anawalt, Patricia Rieff. "Analysis of the Aztec Quechquemitl: An Exercise in Inference." In *The Art and Iconography of Late Post-Classic Central Mexico*, edited by Elizabeth Boone, 37–72. Washington, DC: Dumbarton Oaks, 1982.

Anawalt, Patricia Rieff. "Atuendos del México antiguo." *Arqueología Mexicana, Edición especial* 19 (2005): 8–20.

Anawalt, Patricia Rieff. "A Comparative Analysis of the Costumes and Accoutrements of the *Codex Mendoza."* In *The Essential Codex Mendoza*, edited by Frances Berdan and Patricia Rieff Anawalt, 1:103–50. Berkeley: University of California Press, 1992.

Anawalt, Patricia Rieff. *Indian Clothing before Cortés: Mesoamerican Costumes from the Codices*. Norman: University of Oklahoma Press, 1981.

Anawalt, Patricia Rieff. "Memory Clothing: Costumes Associated with Aztec Human Sacrifice." In *Ritual Human Sacrifice in Mesoamerica*, edited by Elizabeth Boone, 165–93. Washington, DC: Dumbarton Oaks, 1984.

Anawalt, Patricia Rieff. "Weaving." In *The Oxford Encyclopedia of Mesoamerican Cultures: The Civilizations of Mexico and Central America*, edited by Davíd Carrasco, 3:324–28. Oxford: Oxford University Press, 2001.

Anders, Ferdinand, Maarten Jansen, and Luis Reyes García. *El Libro de Tezcatlipoca, Señor del Tiempo, libro explicative del llamado Códice Fejérváry-Mayer*. Graz: Akademische Druck- und Verlagsanstalt, 1994.

Anderson, Marilyn. *Guatemalan Textiles Today*. New York: Watson-Guptill Publications, 1978.

Andrews, J. Richard. "Aztec Medical Astrology." In *Smoke and Mist: Mesoamerican Studies in Memory of Thelma D. Sullivan*, Part 2, edited by J. Kathryn Josserand and Karen Dakin, 605–27. Oxford: British Archaeological Reports, 1988.

Andrews, J. Richard. *Introduction to Classic Nahuatl*. rev. ed. Norman: University of Oklahoma Press, 2003.

Andrews, J. Richard, and Ross Hassig. "Editor's Introduction." In *Treatise on the Heathen Superstitions That Today Live among the Indians Native to This New Spain*, by Hernando Ruiz de Alarcón, 3–36. Norman: University of Oklahoma Press, 1984.

Arnold, Philip P. *Eating Landscape: Aztec and European Occupation of Tlalocan*. Niwot: University Press of Colorado, 1999.

Asad, Talal. *Genealogies of Religion: Discipline and Reasons of Power in Christianity and Islam*. Baltimore: Johns Hopkins University Press, 1993.

Audi, Robert, ed. *The Cambridge Dictionary of Philosophy*. Cambridge: Cambridge University Press, 1995.

Aveni, Anthony F. *Skywatchers: A Revised and Updated Version of Skywatchers of Ancient Mexico*. Austin: University of Texas Press, 2001.

Aveni, Anthony, and Gary Urton, eds. *Ethnoastronomy and Archaeoastronomy in the American Tropics. Annals of the New York Academy of Sciences, No. 38.* New York: New York Academy of Sciences, 1982.

Báez-Jorge, Félix, and Arturo Gómez Martínez. "Los equilibrios del cielo y de la tierra: Cosmovisión de los nahuas de Chicontepec." *Desacatos* 5 (Invierno 2000): 79–94.

Báez-Jorge, Félix, and Arturo Gómez Martínez. *Tlacatecolotl y el Diablo: La cosmovisión de los nahuas de Chicontepec.* Xalapa: Gobierno del Estado de Veracruz, 1998.

Baquedano, Elizabeth. "Aspects of Death Symbolism in Aztec Tlaltecuhtli." In *The Symbolism in the Plastic and Pictorial Representations of Ancient Mexico: A Symposium of the 46th International Congress of Americanists, Amsterdam 1988,* edited by Jacqueline de Durand-Forest and Marc Eisinger, 157–80. Bonner Amerikanistische Studien, vol. 21. Bonn: Bonner Amerikanistische Studien, 1993.

Baquedano, Elizabeth. "Earth Deities." In *The Oxford Encyclopedia of Mesoamerican Cultures: The Civilizations of Mexico and Central America,* edited by Davíd Carrasco, 1:350–51. Oxford: Oxford University Press, 2001.

Barnes, Jonathan. *The Presocratic Philosophers.* London: Routledge, 1970.

Barrera Rodríguez, Raúl, and Gabino López Arenas. "Hallazgos en el recinto ceremonial de Tenochtitlan." *Arqueología Mexicana* 16, no. 93 (2008): 18–25.

Bassie-Sweet, Karen. *At the Edge of the World: Caves and Late Classic Maya World View.* Norman: Oklahoma University Press, 1996.

Basso, Keith H. *The Cibecue Apache.* New York: Holt, Rinehart, and Winston, 1970.

Basso, Keith H. *Wisdom Sits in Places: Landscape and Language among the Western Apache.* Albuquerque: University of New Mexico Press, 1996.

Baudot, Georges. *Utopia and History in Mexico: The First Chroniclers of Mexican Civilization (1520–1569).* Translated by Bernard R. Ortiz de Montellano and Thelma Ortiz de Montellano. Niwot: University Press of Colorado, 1995.

Beaney, Michael. "Analysis." In *The Stanford Encyclopedia of Philosophy (Summer 2011 Edition),* edited by Edward N. Zalta, 2011. http://plato.stanford.edu/archives/sum2011/entries/analysis/. (accessed 5/19/2013.)

Beck, Peggy V., Anna Lee Walters, and Nia Francisco. *The Sacred: Ways of Knowledge, Sources of Life,* redesigned ed. Tsaile, AZ: Navajo Community College Press, 1992.

Berdan, Frances F. "Appendix E: The Place-Name, Personal Name, and Title Glyphs of the *Codex Mendoza*: Translations and Comments." In *The Codex Mendoza,* edited by Frances F. Berdan and Patricia Rieff Anawalt, 1:163–238. Berkeley: University of California Press, 1992.

Berdan, Frances F. *The Aztecs.* New York: Chelsea House Publications, 1989.

Berdan, Frances F. "Cotton in Aztec Mexico: Production, Distribution, and Uses." *Mexican Studies* 3, no. 2 (1987): 235–62. http://dx.doi.org/10.2307/1051808. (accessed 5/19/2013.)

Berdan, Frances F. "Trade and Tribute in the Aztec Empire." In *Current Topics in Aztec Studies: Essays in Honor of Dr. H. B. Nicholson,* edited by Alana Cordy-Collins and Douglas Sharon, 71–84. San Diego Museum Papers, vol. 30. San Diego: San Diego Museum of Man, 1993.

Berdan, Frances F., and Patricia Rieff Anawalt, eds. *The Codex Mendoza*, 4 vols. Berkeley: University of California Press, 1992.

Berdan, Frances F., and Patricia Rieff Anawalt, eds. *The Essential Codex Mendoza*. Berkeley: University of California Press, 1997.

Bernasconi, Robert. "African Philosophy's Challenge to Continental Philosophy." In *Postcolonial African Philosophy: A Critical Reader*, edited by Emmanuel Chukwadi Eze, 183–93. Oxford: Blackwell, 1997.

Beyer, Hermann. "El origen, desarollo y significado de la greca escalonada." *El México antiguo* 10 (1965): 53–104.

Beyer, Hermann. *Mito y simbología del México antiguo*. vol. 10. México: Sociedad Alemana Mexicanista, 1965.

Bierhorst, John, ed. "Annals of Cuauhtitlan." In *History and Mythology of the Aztecs: The Codex Chimalpopoca*. 17–138. Tucson: University of Arizona Press, 1992.

Bierhorst, John, transcription and trans. *Ballads of the Lords of New Spain: The Codex Romances de los Señores de la Nueva España*. Austin: University of Texas Press, 2009.

Bierhorst, John, ed., intro., and commentary. *Cantares Mexicanos: Songs of the Aztecs*. Stanford, CA: Stanford University Press, 1985.

Bierhorst, John, ed. *Codex Chimalpopoca: The Text in Nahuatl*. Tucson: University of Arizona Press, 1992.

Bierhorst, John, "Legend of the Suns." In *History and Mythology of the Aztecs: The Codex Chimalpopoca*, translated by John Bierhorst, 139–62. Tucson: University of Arizona Press, 1992.

Bierhorst, John. *History and Mythology of the Aztecs: The Codex Chimalpopoca*. Tucson: University of Arizona Press, 1992.

Bierhorst, John. "Annals of Cuauhtitlan." In *History and Mythology of the Aztecs: The Codex Chimlpopoca*, translated from the Nahuatl by John Bierhorst, 17–138. Tucson: University of Arizona Press, 1992.

Boone, Elizabeth Hill, ed. *The Art and Iconography of Late Post-Classic Central Mexico*. Washington, DC: Dumbarton Oaks, 1982.

Boone, Elizabeth Hill, ed. *The Aztec Templo Mayor*. Washington, DC: Dumbarton Oaks, 1987.

Boone, Elizabeth Hill. *The Aztec World*. Washington, DC: Smithsonian Books, 1994.

Boone, Elizabeth Hill. *Cycles of Time and Meaning in the Mexican Books of Fate*. Austin: University of Texas Press, 2007.

Boone, Elizabeth Hill. *Incarnations of the Aztec Supernatural: The Image of Huiztilopochtli in Mexico and Europe*. Philadelphia: American Philosophical Society, 1989. http://dx.doi.org/10.2307/1006524. (accessed 5/19/2013.)

Boone, Elizabeth Hill. *Guías para vivir: Los manuscritos adivinatorios pintados de México.*, 333–38. Azteca Mexica, 1992.

Boone, Elizabeth Hill. *Stories in Red and Black: Pictorial Histories of the Aztecs and Mixtecs*. Austin: University of Texas Press, 2000.

Bowker, John, ed. *The Oxford Dictionary of World Religions*. Oxford: Oxford University Press, 1997.

Boyd, James W., and Ron G. Williams. "Artful Means: An Aesthetic View of Shinto Purification Rituals." *Journal of Religious Studies* 13, no. 1 (1999): 37–52.

Boyd, James W., and Ron G. Williams. "The Art of Ritual in Comparative Context." In *Zoroastrian Rituals in Context: Proceedings of the Conference at the Internationales Wissenschaftsforum*, University of Heidelberg, April 2002, edited by Michael Stausberg, 137–51. Leiden: Brill, 2004.

Boyd, James W., and Ron G. Williams. "Japanese Shinto: An Interpretation of a Priestly Perspective." *Philosophy East & West* 55, no. 1 (2005): 33–63. http://dx.doi.org /10.1353/pew.2004.0039. (accessed 5/19/2013.)

Boyd, Richard. "The Current Status of Scientific Realism." In *Scientific Realism*, edited by Jarrett Leplin. Berkeley: University of California Press, 1984.

Brady, James E. "In My Hill, in My Mountain: The Importance of Place in Ancient Maya Ritual." In *Mesas and Cosmologies in Mesoamerica*, edited by Douglas Sharon, 83–92. San Diego Museum of Man Papers 42. San Diego: San Diego Museum of Man, 2003.

Bright, William. "'With One Lip, with Two Lips': Parallelism in Nahuatl." *Language* 66, no. 3 (1990): 437–52. http://dx.doi.org/10.2307/414607. (accessed 5/19/2013.)

Broda, Johanna. "Astronomical Knowledge, Calendrics, and Sacred Geography in Ancient Mesoamerica." In *Astronomies and Cultures*, edited by Clive N. Ruggles and Nicholas J. Saunders, 253–95. Niwot: University Press of Colorado, 1993.

Broda, Johanna. "Astronomy, *Cosmovisión*, and Ideology in Pre-Hispanic Mesoamerica." In *Ethnoastronomy and Archaeoastronomy in the American Tropics*, edited by Anthony Aveni and Gary Urton, 81–110. Annals of the New York Academy of Sciences, No. 38. New York: New York Academy of Sciences, 1982. http://dx.doi.org /10.1111/j.1749-6632.1982.tb34260.x. (accessed 5/19/2013.)

Broda, Johanna. "Templo Mayor as Ritual Space." In *The Great Temple of Tenochtitlan: Center and Periphery in the Aztec World*, edited by Johanna Broda, David Carrasco, and Eduardo Matos Moctezuma, 61–123. Berkeley: University of California Press, 1987.

Broda, Johanna, David Carrasco, and Eduardo Matos Moctezuma, eds. *The Great Temple of Tenochtitlan: Center and Periphery in the Aztec World*. Berkeley: University of California Press, 1987.

Broda de Casas, Johanna. "Tlacaxipehualiztli: A Reconstruction of an Aztec Calendar Festival from 16th Century Sources." *Revista española de antropología americana* 5 (1970): 197–274.

Brotherston, Gordon. *Feather Crown: The Eighteen Feasts of the Mexican Year*. London: The British Museum, 2005.

Brotherston, Gordon. *Image of the New World: The American Continent Portrayed in Native Texts*. London: Thames & Hudson, 1979.

Brotherston, Gordon. "Mesoamerican Description of Space, II: Signs for Directions." *Ibero-Amerikanisches Archiv* 2, no. 1 (1976): 39–62.

Brotherston, Gordon. "Native Numeracy in Tropical America." *Social Epistemology* 15, no. 4 (2001): 299–317. http://dx.doi.org/10.1080/02691720110093324. (accessed 5/19/2013.)

Brotherston, Gordon, and Dawn Ades. "Mesoamerican Description of Space, I: Myths, Stars and Maps, and Architecture." *Ibero-Amerikanisches Archiv* 1, no. 4 (1975): 279–305.

Brumfiel, Elizabeth M. "Asking about Gender: The Historical and Archaeological Evidence." In *Gender in Prehispanic America*, edited by Cecelia Klein, 57–86. Washington, DC: Dumbarton Oaks, 2001.

Brumfiel, Elizabeth M. "Aztec Women: Capable Partners and Cosmic Enemies." In *The Aztec World*, edited by Elizabeth M. Brumfiel and Gary M. Feinman, 87–104. New York: Harry N. Abrams, 2008.

Brumfiel, Elizabeth M. "Cloth, Gender, Continuity and Change: Fabricating Unity in Anthropology." *American Anthropologist* 108, no. 4 (2006): 862–77. http://dx.doi.org/10.1525/aa.2006.108.4.862. (accessed 5/19/2013.)

Brumfiel, Elizabeth M. "Domestic Politics in Early-Middle Postclassic Mexico: Variability and Standardization in Decorative Motifs." Paper presented in Estudios de género en el México antiguo, coordinated by M. Rodríguez-Shadow and R. García Valgañon. Congreso International de Americanists, México, DF, 2009.

Brumfiel, Elizabeth M. "Towards a Middle Range Theory of Household Politics: The Standardization of Decorative Motifs in Middle Post-Classic Mexico." In *The Archaeology of Politics: The Materiality of Political Practice and Action in the Past*, edited by Peter G. Johansen and Andrew M. Bauer, 245–82. Newcastle upon Tyne: Cambridge Scholars Press, 2011.

Brumfiel, Elizabeth M. "Tribute Cloth Production and Compliance in Aztec and Colonial Mexico." *Museum Anthropology* 21, no. 2 (1997): 55–71. http://dx.doi.org/10.1525/mua.1997.21.2.55. (accessed 5/19/2013.)

Brumfiel, Elizabeth M., and Gary M. Feinman, eds. *The Aztec World*. New York: Harry N. Abrams, 2008.

Brundage, Burr Cartwright. *The Fifth Sun: Aztec Gods, Aztec World*. Austin: University of Texas Press, 1979.

Burkhart, Brian Yazzie. "The Physics of the Spirit: The Indigenous Continuity of Science and Religion." In *The Routledge Companion to Religion and Science*, edited by James W. Hagg, Gregory R. Peterson, and Michael L. Spezio, 34–42. New York: Routledge, 2011.

Burkhart, Louise M. "The Amanuenses Have Appropriated the Text: Interpreting a Nahuatl Song of Santiago." In *On the Translation of Native American Literatures*, edited by Brian Swann, 339–55. Washington, DC: Smithsonian Institute Press, 1992.

Burkhart, Louise M. "Flowery Heaven: The Aesthetic of Paradise in Nahuatl Devotional Literature." *RES* 21 (Spring 1991): 89–109.

Burkhart, Louise M. "Mexica Women on the Home Front: Housework and Religion in Aztec Mexico." In *Indian Women of Early Mexico*, edited by Susan Schroeder, Stephanie Wood, and Robert Haskett, 25–54. Norman: University of Oklahoma Press, 1997.

Burkhart, Louise M. "Moral Deviance in Sixteenth-Century Nahua and Christian Thought: The Rabbit and the Deer." *Journal of Latin American Lore* 12, no. 2 (1986): 107–39.

Burkhart, Louise M. *The Slippery Earth: Nahua-Christian Dialogue in Sixteenth-Century Mexico.* Tucson: University of Arizona Press, 1989.

Cajete, Gregory. *Native Science: Natural Laws of Interdependence.* Santa Fe, NM: Clear Light Publishers, 2000.

Callaway, Carol H. "Pre-Columbian and Colonial Images of the Cross: Christ's Sacrifice and the Fertile Earth." *Journal of Latin American Lore* 16, no. 2 (1990): 199–231.

Campbell, R. Joe. *A Morphological Dictionary of Classical Nahuatl: A Morpheme Index to the* Vocabulario en lengua mexicana y castellana *of Fray Alonso de Molina.* Madison: Hispanic Seminary of Medieval Studies, 1985.

Campbell, R. Joe. Concordance to the *Florentine Codex.* (Various portions of this work were provided by Campbell through personal correspondence, 8/4/2005), n.d.

Campbell, R. Joe, and Frances Karttunen. *Foundation Course in Nahuatl Grammar,* 2 vols. Missoula: University of Montana, 1989.

Carlsen, Robert S., and Martin Prechtel. "The Flowering of the Dead: An Interpretation of Highland Maya Culture." *Man* 26, no. 1 (1991): 23–42. http://dx.doi.org /10.2307/2803473. (accessed 5/19/2013.)

Carrasco, Davíd. *City of Sacrifice: The Aztec Empire and the Role of Violence in Civilization.* Boston: Beacon Press, 1999.

Carrasco, Davíd, ed. *The Imagination of Matter: Religion and Ecology in Mesoamerican Traditions. BAR International Series.* Oxford: BAR, 1985.

Carrasco, Davíd. "Introduction." In *The Great Temple of Tenochtitlan: Center and Periphery in the Aztec World,* edited by Johanna Broda, Davíd Carrasco, and Eduardo Matos Moctezuma, 1–14. Berkeley: University of California Press, 1987.

Carrasco, Davíd. "Myth, Cosmic Terror, and the Templo Mayor." In *The Great Temple of Tenochtitlan: Center and Periphery in the Aztec World,* edited by Johanna Broda, Davíd Carrasco, and Eduardo Matos Moctezuma, 124–62. Berkeley: University of California Press, 1987.

Carrasco, Davíd, ed. *The Oxford Encyclopedia of Mesoamerican Cultures: The Civilizations of Mexico and Central America.* 3 vols. Oxford: Oxford University Press, 2001.

Carrasco, Davíd. *Quetzalcoatl and the Irony of Empire: Myths and Prophecies in the Aztec Tradition.* Chicago: University of Chicago Press, 1982.

Carrasco, Davíd. *Religions of Mesoamerica: Cosmovision and Ceremonial Centers.* San Francisco: Harper and Row, 1990.

Carrasco, Davíd. "The Sacrifice of Tezcatlipoca: To Change Place." In *To Change Place: Aztec Ceremonial Landscapes,* edited by Davíd Carrasco, 32–57. Niwot: University Press of Colorado, 1991.

Carrasco, Davíd. "The Sacrifice of Women in the *Florentine Codex*: The Hearts of Plants and the Players in War Games." In *Representing Aztec Ritual: Performance, Text, and Image in the Work of Sahagún,* edited by Eloise Quiñones Keber, 197–226. Niwot: University Press of Colorado, 2002.

Carrasco, Davíd, ed. *To Change Place: Aztec Ceremonial Landscapes*. Niwot: University Press of Colorado, 1991.

Carrasco, Davíd. "Toward the Splendid City: Knowing the Worlds of Moctezuma." In *Moctezuma's Mexico: Visions of the Aztec World*, edited by Davíd Carrasco and Eduardo Matos Moctezuma, 99–148. Niwot: University Press of Colorado, 1992.

Carrasco, Davíd. "Uttered from the Heart: Guilty Rhetoric among the Aztecs." *History of Religions* 39, no. 1 (1999): 1–31. http://dx.doi.org/10.1086/463571. (accessed 5/19/2013.)

Carrasco, Davíd, Lindsay Jones, and Scott Sessions, eds. *Mesomerica's Classic Heritage: From Teotihuacan to the Aztecs*. Boulder: University Press of Colorado, 2000.

Carrasco, Davíd, and Eduardo Matos Moctezuma. *Moctezuma's Mexico: Visions of the Aztec World*. Niwot: University Press of Colorado, 1992.

Carrasco, Davíd, with Scott Sessions. *Daily Life of the Aztecs: People of the Sun and Earth*. Westport, CT: Greenwood Press, 1998.

Carrasco, Davíd, and Scott Sessions. "Middle Place, Labyrinth, and Circumambulation: Cholula's Peripatetic Role in the *Mapa de Cuauhtinchan* No.2." In *Cave, City, Eagle's Nest: An Interpretive Journey through the* Mapa de Cuauhtinchan No. 2., edited by Davíd Carrasco and Scott Sessions, 427–54. Albuquerque: University of New Mexico Press, 2007.

Caso, Alfonso. *The Aztecs: People of the Sun*. Translated by Lowell Dunham. Norman: University of Oklahoma Press, 1958.

Caso, Alfonso. *Los calendarios prehispánicos*. México, DF: Universidad Nacional Autónoma de México, Instituto de Investigaciones Históricas, 1967.

Caso, Alfonso. "Calendrical Systems of Central Mexico." In *Handbook of Middle American Indians*. vol. 10, edited by Robert Wauchope, Gordon F. Elkholm, and Ignacio Bernal, 333–48. Austin: University of Texas Press, 1971.

Castellón Huerta, Blas. "Cúmulo de símbolos: La serpiente emplumada." *Arqueología Mexicana* 9, no. 53 (2002): 28–35.

Ceramic Disk Featuring a Temple Surmounted by a Christian Cross. Chicago, The Field Museum, 2007. http://archive.fieldmuseum.org/aztecs/popups/CON4.html. (accessed 5/19/2013.)

Ch'en, Ku-ying. *Lao Tzu: Text, Notes, and Comments*. Introduction, adaptation, and translation by Rhett Y. W. Young and Roger T. Ames. San Francisco: Chinese Materials Center, 1977.

Christenson, Allen J. "Dancing in the Footsteps of the Ancestors." In *Lords of Creation: The Origin of Sacred Maya Kingship*, edited by Virginia Fields and Dorie Reents-Budet, 92–96. London: Scala Publications, 2005.

Clendinnen, Inga. *Aztecs: An Interpretation*. Cambridge: Cambridge University Press, 1991.

Codex Becker. Graz: Akademische Druck -u. Verlagsanstalt, 1961. http://www.famsi.org/index.html.

Codex Borbonicus. Loubat: Bibliothéque Du Palais Bourbon, 1899. http://www.famsi.org/index.html.

Codex Fejérváry-Mayer. Loubat: Bibliothéque Du Palais Bourbon, 1901. http://www
.famsi.org/index.html.

Codex Laud MS. Laud Misc. 678. Graz: Bodleian Library, 1966. http://www.famsi.org
/index.html.

Codex Magliabechiano (The Book of the Life of the Ancient Mexicans). Facsimile edited by
Zelia Nuttall. Berkeley: University of California Press, 1903.

The Codex Nuttall: A Picture Manuscript from Ancient Mexico, edited by Zelia Nuttall,
introduction by Arthur G. Miller. New York: Dover, 1975.

Codex Tonalamatl Aubin. Loubat, 1901. http://www.famsi.org/index.html.

Codex Vaticanus 3738 A (*Codex Rios*). Graz: Akademische Druck - u. Verlagsanstalt,
1979. http://www.famsi.org/index.html.

Codex Vaticanus 3773 B. Graz: Akademische Druck - u. Verlagsanstalt, 1972. http://www
.famsi.org/index.html.

Coggins, Clemency. "New Fire Drill at Chichen Itza." In *Memorias del Primer Coloquio
Internacional de Mayistas,* 427–44. México, DF: UNAM, 1987.

Coggins, Clemency. "The Shape of Time: Some Political Implications of a Four-Part
Figure." *American Antiquity* 45, no. 4 (1980): 727–39. http://dx.doi.org/10.2307/280144.
(accessed 5/19/2013.)

Cohodas, Marvin. *The Great Ball Court at Chichen Itza, Yucatan, Mexico.* New York:
Garland Publishing, 1978.

Cooper, David A. *God Is a Verb: Kabbalah and the Practice of Mystical Judaism.* New
York: Riverhead Books, 1997.

Cordova, Viola. "Approaches to Native American Philosophy." In *American Indian
Thought: Philosophical Essays,* edited by Anne Waters, 27–33. Oxford: Blackwell,
2004.

Cordova, Viola "Ethics: The We and the I." In *American Indian Thought,* edited by
Anne Waters, 173–81. Oxford: Blackwell, 2004.

Cordova, Viola. "The European Concept of *Usen*: An American Aboriginal Text." In
Native American Religious Identity: Unforgotten Gods, edited by Jace Weaver, 26–32.
Maryknoll, NY: Orbis Books, 1998.

Cordry, Donald, and Dorothy Cordry. *Mexican Indian Costumes. Foreword by Miguel
Covarrubias.* Austin: University of Texas Press, 1968.

Curcio-Nagy, Linda A. "Faith and Morals in Colonial Mexico." In *The Oxford History
of Mexico,* edited by Michael C. Meyer and William H. Beezly, 151–82. Oxford:
Oxford University Press, 2000.

Davies, Nigel. "Dualism as a Universal Concept: Its Relevance to Mesoamerica." In
Mesoamerican Dualism/Dualismo Mesoamericano, edited by R. van Zantwijk, R. de
Ridder, and E. Braahuis, 8–14. Utrecht: RUU-ISOR, 1990.

Deleuze, Gilles. *Spinoza: Practical Philosophy.* Preface and translation by Robert Hurley.
San Francisco: City Lights Books, 1988.

Deloria, Barbara, Kristen Foehner, and Sam Scinta, eds. *Spirit and Reason: A Vine
Deloria, Jr., Reader.* Golden, CO: Fulcrum Publishers, 1999.

Deloria, Vine, Jr. *God Is Red: A Native View of Religion.* Golden, CO: Fulcrum Publishing, 1994.

Deloria, Vine, Jr. "Philosophy and the Tribal Peoples." In *American Indian Thought,* edited by Anne Waters, 3–11. Oxford: Blackwell, 2004.

Deloria, Vine, Jr., and Daniel R. Wildcat. *Power and Place.* Golden, CO: American Indian Graduate Center and Fulcrum Resources, 2001.

Deutsch, Eliot. *Advaita Vedanta: A Philosophical Reconstruction.* Honolulu: East-West Center Press, 1969.

Deutsch, Eliot. *On Truth: An Ontological Theory.* Honolulu: University of Hawaii Press, 1979.

Díaz, Gisele, and Alan Rodgers. *Codex Borgia: A Full Color Restoration of the Ancient Mexican Manuscript.* With introduction and commentary by Bruce E. Byland. New York: Dover Publications, 1993.

Díaz Balsera, Viviana. *The Pyramid under the Cross: Franciscan Discourses of Evangelization and the Nahua Christian Subject in Sixteenth-Century Mexico.* Tucson: University of Arizona Press, 2005.

DiCesare, Catherine. *Sweeping the Way: Divine Transformation in the Aztec Festival of Ochpaniztli.* Niwot: University Press of Colorado, 2009.

Dover, Robert V. H., John McDowell, and Katherine E. Seibold, eds. *Andean Cosmologies through Time: Persistence and Emergence.* Bloomington: Indiana University Press, 1992.

Dow, James W. "Central and North Mexican Shamans." In *Mesoamerican Healers,* edited by Brad R. Huber and Alan R. Sandstrom, 66–94. Austin: University of Texas Press, 2001.

Durán, Diego. *Book of the Gods and Rites* and *The Ancient Calendar,* translated and edited by Fernando Horcasitas and Doris Heyden, with a foreword by Miguel León-Portilla. Norman: University of Oklahoma Press, 1971.

Durán, Diego. *Historia de las Indias de Nueva España e Islas de la tierra firme,* vol. 2, 2nd ed., edited by Angél Ma. Garibay K. México, DF: Editorial Porrúa, 1984.

Durán, Diego. *The History of the Indies of New Spain,* translated, annotation, and introduction by Doris Heyden. New York: Orion Books, 1994.

Durand-Forest, Jacqueline de, Françoise Rousseau, Madeleine Cucuel, and Sylvie Szpirglas. *Los elementos anexos del Códice Borbónico.* Translated by Dr. Edgar Samuel Morales Sales. México, DF: Universidad Autónoma del Estado de México, 2000.

Edmonson, Munro S. "Foreword." In *The Mixe of Oaxaca: Religion, Ritual and Healing,* by Frank J. Lipp, vii–ix. Austin: University of Texas Press, 1991.

Edmonson, Munro S. "The Mayan Faith." In *South and Meso-american Spirituality: From the Cult of the Feathered Serpent to the Theology of Liberation,* edited by Gary H. Gossen, in collaboration with Miguel León-Portilla, 65–85. New York: Crossroads, 1993.

Edwards, Paul, ed. *Encyclopedia of Philosophy.* 8 vols. New York: Macmillan Publishing, 1967.

Eliade, Mircea. *The Myth of the Eternal Return, or Cosmos and History.* Princeton, NJ: Princeton University Press, 1954.

Eliade, Mircea. *Patterns of Comparative Religion.* Translated by Rosemary Sheed. Lincoln: University of Nebraska Press, 1996.

Eliade, Mircea. *Rites and Symbols of Initiation: The Mysteries of Birth and Rebirth.* Translated by Willard R. Trask. New York: Harper and Row, 1958.

Eliade, Mircea. *Shamanism: Archaic Techniques of Ecstasy.* Princeton, NJ: Princeton University Press, 1964.

Elzey, Wayne. "The Nahua Myth of the Four Suns." *Numen* 23, no. 2 (1976): 114–35. http://dx.doi.org/10.1163/156852776X00021. (accessed 5/19/2013.)

Elzey, Wayne. "Nepantla." In *The Oxford Encyclopedia of Mesoamerican Cultures: The Civilizations of Mexico and Central America*, edited by Davíd Carrasco, 2:365–66. Oxford: Oxford University Press, 2001.

Elzey, Wayne. "Some Remarks on the Space and Time of the 'Center' in Aztec Religion." *Estudios de cultura náhuatl* 12 (1976): 315–34.

Emmet, Dorothy. *The Passage of Nature.* Philadelphia: Temple University Press, 1992.

Enciso, Jorge. *Design Motifs of Ancient Mexico.* New York: Dover Publications, 1953.

Ermine, Willie. "Aboriginal Epistemology." In *First Nations Education in Canada: The Circle Unfolds*, edited by Marie Battiste and Jean Barman, 101–112. Vancouver: University of British Columbia Press, 1995.

Farriss, Nancy M. *Maya Society under Colonial Rule: The Collective Enterprise of Survival.* Princeton, NJ: Princeton University Press, 1984.

Fay, Brian. *Contemporary Philosophy of Social Science.* Oxford: Blackwell, 1996.

Filloy, Laura. "Rubber." Translated by Scott Sessions. In *The Oxford Encyclopedia of Mesoamerican Cultures: The Civilizations of Mexico and Central America*, edited by Davíd Carrasco, 3: 92–93. Oxford: Oxford University Press, 2001.

Fixico, Donald. *The American Indian Mind in a Linear World.* New York: Routledge, 2003.

Flannery, Kent, and Joyce Marcus, eds. *The Cloud People: Divergent Evolution of the Zapotec and Mixtec Civilizations.* New York: Academic Press, 1983.

Florescano, Enrique. *Memory, Myth, and Time in Mexico: From the Aztecs to Independence.* Translated by Albert G. Bork with the assistance of Kathryn R. Bork. Austin: University of Texas Press, 1994.

Florescano, Enrique. *The Myth of Quetzalcoatl.* Translated by Lisa Hochroth. Baltimore: Johns Hopkins University Press, 1999.

Fogelson, Raymond D. "Person, Self, and Identity: Some Anthropological Retrospects, Circumspects, and Prospects." In *Psychosocial Theories of the Self*, edited by Benjamin Lee, 67–109. New York: Plenum Press, 1982. http://dx.doi.org/10.1007/978-1-4684-4337-0_5. (accessed 5/19/2013.)

Fogelson, Raymond D., and Amelia B. Walker. "Self and Other in Cherokee Booger Masks." *Journal of Cherokee Studies* 5 (1980): 88–102.

Forrest, Peter. "Pantheism and Science." *Monist* 80, no. 2 (1997): 307–19. http://dx.doi.org/10.5840/monist199780213. (accessed 5/19/2013.)

Frake, Charles O. "Cognitive Maps of Time and Tide among Medieval Seafarers." *Man* n.s. 20 (1985): 254–70. http://dx.doi.org/10.2307/2802384. (accessed 5/19/2013.)

Frankfort, Henri A., and H. A. Frankfort. "The Emancipation of Thought from Myth." In *The Intellectual Adventure of Ancient Man*, edited by Henri Frankfort, H. A. Frankfort, John A. Wilson, Thorkild Jacobsen, and William A. Irwin, 363–88. Chicago: University of Chicago Press, 1977.

Frankfort, Henri A., and H. A. Frankfort. "Myth and Reality." In *The Intellectual Adventure of Ancient Man*, edited by Henri Frankfort, H. A. Frankfort, John A. Wilson, Thorkild Jacobsen, and William A. Irwin, 3–30. Chicago: University of Chicago Press, 1977.

Frankfort, Henri, H. A. Frankfort, John A. Wilson, Thorkild Jacobsen, and William A. Irwin. *The Intellectual Adventure of Ancient Man*. Chicago: University of Chicago Press, 1977. Published in 1960 by Penguin Press as *Before Philosophy*.

Freidel, David, Linda Schele, and Joy Parker. *Maya Cosmos: Three Thousand Years on the Shaman's Path*. New York: William Morrow, 1993.

Furst, Peter T. "Huichol." In *The Oxford Encyclopedia of Mesoamerican Cultures: The Civilizations of Mexico and Central America*, edited by Davíd Carrasco, 2:19–21. Oxford: Oxford University Press, 2001.

Furst, Peter T. "Introduction: An Overview of Shamanism." In *Ancient Traditions: Shamanism in Central Asia and the Americas*, edited by Gary Seaman and Jane S. Day, 1–28. Niwot: Denver Museum of Natural History and University Press of Colorado, 1994.

Furst, Peter T. "The Roots and Continuities of Shamanism." In *Stones, Bones, and Skin: Ritual and Shamanic Art*, edited by Anne T. Bodsky, Rose Danesewich, and Nick Johnson, 1–28. Toronto: Society for Art Publications, 1977.

Furst, Peter T. "Shamanistic Survivals in Mesoamerican Religion." *Actas del XLI Congreso Internacional de Americanistas*, vol. 3: 149–57. Mexico: Instituto Nacional de Antropología e Historia, 1976.

Furst, Peter T. "The Thread of Life: Some Parallels in the Symbolism of Aztec, Huichol and Puebla Earth Goddesses." In *Balance y perspectiva de la antropología de Mesoamerica y del centro de México*, 235–45. Mesa Redonda 13th, 1973. México, DF: La Sociedad Mexicana de Antropología, 1975.

Galinier, Jacques. *The World Below: Body and Cosmos in Otomí Indian Ritual*. Boulder: University Press of Colorado, 1997.

García Quintana, Josefina. "El baño ritual entre los Nahuas según el Códice Florentino." *Estudios de cultura náhuatl* 8 (1969): 189–214.

Garza, Mercedes de la. *El universo sagrado de la serpiente entre los mayas*. México, DF: Universidad Nacional Autónoma de México, 1984.

Garza, Mercedes de la. "The Harmony between People and Animals in the Aztec World." In *The Aztec Empire*, curated by Felipe R. Solís Olguín, 70–75. New York: Solomon Guggenheim Foundation, 2004.

Garza, Mercedes de la. "Time and World in Maya and Nahuatl Thought." In *Cultural Relativism and Philosophy: North and Latin American Perspectives*, edited by Marcelo Dascal, 105–27. Leiden: E. J. Brill, 1991.

Gill, Sam D. *Native American Religions: An Introduction*. Belmont, CA: Wadsworth Publishing, 1982.

Gill, Sam D. *Native American Religious Action: A Performance Approach to Religion*. Columbia: University South Carolina Press, 1987.

Gillespie, Susan. *The Aztec Kings: The Construction of Rulership in Mexica History*. Tucson: University of Arizona Press, 1989.

Gillespie, Susan. "Different Ways of Seeing: Modes of Social Consciousness in Mesoamerican Two-Dimensional Artworks." *Baesler-Archiv* 55 (2007): 103–42.

Gingerich, Willard. "*Chipahuacanemiliztli*, 'the Purified Life,' in the Discourses of Book VI, Florentine Codex." In *Smoke and Mist: Mesoamerican Studies in Memory of Thelma D. Sullivan, Part 2*, edited by J. Kathryn Josserand and Karen Dakin, 517–43. Oxford: British Archaeological Reports, 1988.

Gingerich, Willard. "Heidegger and the Aztecs: The Poetics of Knowing in Pre-Hispanic Nahuatl Poetry." In *Recovering the Word: Essays on Native American Literature*, edited by B. Swann and A. Krupat, 85–112. Berkeley: University of California Press, 1987.

Gingerich, Willard. "Quetzalcoatl and the Agon of Time: A Literary Reading of the *Anales de Cuauhtitlan*." *New Scholar* 10 (1986): 41–60.

Girardot, Norman J. "Behaving Cosmogonically in Early Taoism." In *Cosmogony and Ethical Order: New Studies in Comparative Ethics*, edited by Robin W. Lovin and Frank E. Reynolds, 67–97. Chicago: University of Chicago Press, 1985.

Gómez Martínez, Jorge. *Tlaneltokilli: La espiritualidad de los nahuas chicotepecanos*. México, DF: Ediciones del Programa de Desarrollo Cultural de la Huasteca, 2002.

Gonlin, Nancy, and Jon C. Lohse. *Commoner Ritual and Ideology in Ancient Mesoamerica*. Boulder: University Press of Colorado, 2007.

Gossen, Gary H. "Mesoamerican Ideas as a Foundation for Regional Synthesis." In *Symbol and Meaning beyond the Closed Community: Essays in Mesoamerican Ideas*, edited by Gary H. Gossen, 1–8. Albany: Institute for Mesoamerican Studies, SUNY Press, 1986.

Gossen, Gary H. "The Religious Traditions of Mesoamerica." In *The Legacy of Mesoamerica: History and Culture of a Native American Civilization*, edited by Robert Carmack, Janine Gasco, and Gary H. Gossen, 290–320. Upper Saddle River, NJ: Prentice Hall, 1996.

Gossen, Gary H., ed. *Symbol and Meaning beyond the Closed Community: Essays in Mesoamerican Ideas*. Albany, NY: Institute for Mesoamerican Studies, SUNY Press, 1986.

Gossen, Gary H., in collaboration with Miguel León-Portilla, eds. *South and Mesoamerican Spirituality: From the Cult of the Feathered Serpent to the Theology of Liberation*. New York: Crossroads, 1993.

Graham, Angus. *Disputers of the Tao: Philosophical Argument in Ancient China*. LaSalle, IL: Open Court, 1989.

Graulich, Michel. "Creation Myths." In *The Oxford Encyclopedia of Mesoamerican Cultures: The Civilizations of Mexico and Central America*, edited by Davíd Carrasco, 1:281–84. Oxford: Oxford University Press, 2001.

Graulich, Michel. "Creator Deities." In *The Oxford Encyclopedia of Mesoamerican Cultures: The Civilizations of Mexico and Central America*, edited by Davíd Carrasco, 1:284–86. Oxford: Oxford University Press, 2001.

Graulich, Michel. *Mitos y rituales del México antiguo*. Madrid: Ediciones Istmo, 1990.

Graulich, Michel. *Myths of Ancient Mexico*. Translated by Bernard R. Ortiz de Montellano and Thelma Ortiz de Montellano. Norman: University of Oklahoma Press, 1997.

Graulich, Michel. "Ochpaniztli, la fête des semailles des anciens Mexicains." *Anales de antropologia* 18, no. 2 (1981): 59–100.

Graulich, Michel. "Quetzalcoatl-Ehecatl, the Bringer of Life." In *Ancient America: Contributions to New World Archaeology*, edited by Nicholas J. Saunders, 33–38. Oxford: Oxbow Books, 1992.

Gregory, R. L. *Eye and Brain: The Psychology of Seeing*. 3rd ed., revised and updated. New York: McGraw-Hill, 1978.

Gruzinski, Serge. *Man-Gods in the Mexican Highlands: Indian Power and Colonial Society, 1520–1800*. Translated by Eileen Corrigan. Stanford, CA: Stanford University Press, 1989.

Gupta, Bina, and J. N. Mohanty, eds. *Philosophical Questions East and West*. Lanham, MD: Rowman and Littlefield, 2000.

Hall, David L. "Just How Provincial *Is* Western Philosophy? 'Truth' in Comparative Context." *Social Epistemology* 15, no. 4 (2001): 285–97. http://dx.doi. org/10.1080/02691720110093315. (accessed 5/19/2013.)

Hall, David L. "Process and Anarchy: A Taoist View of Creativity." *Philosophy East & West* 28, no. 3 (1978): 271–86. http://dx.doi.org/10.2307/1398237. (accessed 5/19/2013.)

Hall, David L., and Roger T. Ames. *Anticipating China: Thinking through the Narratives of Chinese and Western Culture*. Albany: SUNY Press, 1995.

Hall, David L., and Roger T. Ames. *Thinking from the Han: Self, Truth and Transcendence in Chinese and Western Culture*. Albany: SUNY Press, 1998.

Hall, David L., and Roger T. Ames. *Thinking through Confucius*. Albany: State University of New York Press, 1987.

Hall, David L., and Roger T. Ames. "Understanding Order: The Chinese Perspective." In *From Africa to Zen*, edited by Robert Solomon and Kathleen Higgins, 1–23. Lanham, MD: Rowman and Littlefield, 1993.

Hallen, Barry. "'Philosophy Doesn't Translate': Richard Rorty and Multiculturalism." *SAPINA* 8, no. 3 (1995): 1–42.

Hallowell, A. Irving. *Contributions to Anthropology: Selected Papers of A. Irving Hallowell*. Chicago: University of Chicago Press, 1976.

Haly, Richard. "Bare Bones: Rethinking Mesoamerican Divinity." *History of Religions* 31, no. 3 (February 1992): 269–304. http://dx.doi.org/10.1086/463285. (accessed 5/19/2013.)

Hampshire, Stuart. *Spinoza*. Harmondsworth, UK: Penguin Books, 1951.

Hanks, William F. *Referential Practice: Language and Lived Space among the Maya*. Chicago: University of Chicago Press, 1990.

Hansen, Chad. *A Daoist Theory of Chinese Thought: A Philosophical Interpretation.* Oxford: Oxford University Press, 1992.

Harding, Sandra. *Is Science Multicultural? Postcolonialisms, Feminisms, and Epistemologies.* Bloomington: Indiana University Press, 1988.

Harvey, Herbert R. "Household and Family Structure in Early Colonial Tepetlaoztoc: An Analysis of the *Códice de Santa María Asunción.*" *Estudios de cultura náhuatl* 18 (1986): 275–94.

Hassig, Ross. *Aztec Warfare: Imperial Expansion and Political Control.* Norman: University of Oklahoma Press, 1988.

Hassig, Ross. *Time, History and Belief in Aztec and Colonial Mexico.* Austin: University of Texas Press, 2001.

Henry, Paget. *Caliban's Reason: Introducing Afro-Caribbean Philosophy.* London: Routledge, 2000.

Hester, Thurman Lee, and Jim Cheney. "Truth and Native American Epistemology." *Social Epistemology* 15 (2001): 319–34.

Hester, Thurman Lee, Jr., and Dennis McPherson. "Editorial: The Euro-American Philosophical Tradition and Its Ability to Examine Indigenous Philosophy." *Ayaangwaamizin: International Journal of Indigenous Philosophy* 1 (1997): 3–9.

Heyden, Doris. "Caves, Gods, and Myths: World-View and Planning in Teotihuacan." In *Mesoamerican Sites and World-Views*, edited by Elizabeth P. Benson, 1–35. Washington, DC: Dumbarton Oaks, 1981.

Heyden, Doris. "Las cuevas de Teotihuacán." *Arqueología Mexicana* 6, no. 34 (1998): 18–27.

Heyden, Doris. "La Diosa Madre: Iztpapalotl." *Boletín Instituto Nacional de Antropología e Historia* 2, no. 11 (1974): 3–14.

Heyden, Doris. *The Eagle, the Cactus, the Rock: The Roots of Mexico-Tenochtitlan's Foundation Myth and Symbol.* BAR International Series 484. Oxford: BAR, 1989.

Heyden, Doris. "Metaphors, Nahualtocaitl, and other 'Disguised' Terms among the Aztecs." In *Symbol and Meaning beyond the Closed Community: Essays in Mesoamerican Ideas*, edited by Gary H. Gossen, 35–43. Albany: Institute for Mesoamerican Studies, SUNY Press, 1986.

Heyden, Doris. *México: Orígenes de un símbolo; Versión adaptada e ilustrada.* México, DF: INAH Dirección General de Publicaciones, 1998.

Heyden, Doris. *Mitología y simbolismo de la flora en el México prehispánico.* México, DF: UNAM, Instituto de Investigaciones Antropológicas, 1984.

Heyden, Doris. "Rites of Passage and Other Ceremonies in Caves." In *In the Maw of the Earth Monster*, edited by James E. Brady and Keith M. Prufer, 21–34. Austin: University of Texas Press, 2005.

Heyden, Doris. "Sand in Ritual and History." In *Representing Aztec Ritual: Performance, Text, and Image in the Work of Sahagún*, edited by Eloise Quiñones Keber, 175–196. Boulder: Colorado University Press, 2002.

Heyden, Doris. "Sellos con el símbolo ollin." *Boletín del INAH* 25 (1966): 39.

Heyden, Doris. "The Skin and Hair of Tlaltecuhtli." In *The Imagination of Matter: Religion and Ecology in Mesoamerican Tradition*, edited by Davíd Carrasco, 211–24. BAR International Series 515. Oxford: BAR, 1989.

Heyden, Doris. "Trees and Wood in Life and Death." In *Chipping away on Earth: Studies in Prehispanic and Colonial Mexico in Honor of Arthur J. O. Anderson and Charles Dibble*, edited by Eloise Quiñones Keber, 143–62. Lancaster, CA: Labyrinthos, 1994.

Heyden, Doris. "Xipe Totec." In *The Oxford Encyclopedia of Mesoamerican Cultures: The Civilizations of Mexico and Central America*, edited by Davíd Carrasco, 3:353–54. Oxford: Oxford University Press, 2001.

Hickman, Larry A., and Thomas M. Alexander, eds. *The Essential Dewey: Ethics, Logic, Psychology*. vol. 1. Bloomington: Indiana University Press, 1998.

Hill, Jane H. "The Flower World of Old Uto-Aztecan." *Journal of Anthropological Research* 48, no. 2 (1992): 117–44.

Hill, Jane H. "Today There Is No Respect: Nostalgia, 'Respect,' and Oppositional Discourse in Mexicano (Nahuatl) Language Ideology." In *Language Ideologies: Practice and Theory*, edited by Bambi B. Schieffelin, Kathryn A. Woolard, and Paul Kroskrity, 68–86. New York: Oxford University Press, 1998.

Hinz, Eike. "Aspectos sociales del calendarios de 260 dias en Mesoamerica." *Estudios de cultura náhuatl* 14 (1980): 203–24.

Historia de los mexicanos por sus pinturas. In *Teogonía e historia de los mexicanos: Tres opúsculos del siglo XVI*, 1st ed., edited by Angel María Garibay K., 23–79. México: Editorial Porrúa, 1965.

Histoyre du Mechique. In *Teogonía e historia de los mexicanos: Tres opúsculos del siglo XVI*, 1st ed., edited by Angel María Garibay K., 91–116. México: Editorial Porrúa, 1965.

Hochberg, Julian. "Gestalt Theory." In *The Oxford Companion to the Mind*, edited by Richard L. Gregory, 288–91. Oxford: Oxford University Press, 1987.

Horcasitas, Fernando, and Doris Heyden. "Fray Diego Durán: His Life and Works." In *Book of the Gods and Rites* and *The Ancient Calendar, by Fray Diego Durán*. Translated and edited by Fernando Horcasitas and Doris Heyden, 3–47. Norman: University of Oklahoma Press, 1971.

Houston, Stephen, and David Stuart. "The Ancient Maya Self: Personhood and Portraiture in the Classic Period." *RES* 33 (1998): 73–101.

Houston, Stephen, and David Stuart. "Of Gods, Glyphs, and Kings: Divinity and Rulership among the Classic Maya." *Antiquity* 70 (1996): 289–312.

Huber, Brad R., and Alan R. Sandstrom, eds. *Mesoamerican Healers*. Austin: University of Texas Press, 2001.

Humboldt, Alexander von, and Aimé Bonpland. *Researches Concerning the Institutions and Monuments of the Ancient Inhabitants of America*, vols. 1–2. Translated by Helen Maria Williams. Amsterdam: Theatrum Orbis Terrarum and Da Capo Press, 1972.

Hume, David. *Enquiries Concerning Human Understanding and Concerning the Principles of Morals*, edited by L. A. Selby-Bigge. Oxford: Clarendon Press, 1902.

Hunt, Eva. *The Transformation of the Hummingbird: Cultural Roots of a Zinacatecan Mythical Poem*. Ithaca, NY: Cornell University Press, 1977.

Hvidtfeldt, Arild. *Teotl and *Ixiptatli: Some Religious Conceptions in Ancient Mexico*. Copenhagen: Munksgaard, 1958.

I Ching: Book of Changes. Translated by James Legge, edited and introduction by Ch'Chai with Winberg Chai. New Hyde Park, NY: University Books, 1964.

Isaacs, Alan, John Daintith, and Elizabeth Martin, eds. *A Dictionary of Science*. Oxford: Oxford University Press, 1999.

Isbell, Billie Jean. *To Defend Ourselves: Ecology and Ritual in an Andean Village*. Prospect Heights, IL: Waveland Press, 1978.

Iwasaki, Takashi. "Man-Gods." In *The Oxford Encyclopedia of Mesoamerican Cultures: The Civilizations of Mexico and Central America*, edited by Davíd Carrasco, 2:163–64. Oxford: Oxford University Press, 2001.

Jímenez Estrada, Vivian M. "The Tree of Life as a Research Methodology." *Australian Journal of Indigenous Education* 34 (2005): 44–52.

Joyce, Arthur A. *Mixtecs, Zapotecs, and Chatinos: Ancient Peoples of Southern Mexico*. Oxford: Wiley-Blackwell, 2010.

Joyce, Rosemary A. *Gender and Power in Prehispanic Mesoamerica*. Austin: University of Texas Press, 2000.

Jullien, François. *Vital Nourishment: Departing from Happiness*. Translated by Arthur Goldhammer. Cambridge, MA: Zone Books, 2007.

Karttunen, Frances. *An Analytical Dictionary of Nahuatl*. Norman: University of Oklahoma Press, 1983.

Karttunen, Frances, and James Lockhart. "La estructura de la poesía náhuatl vista por sus variantes." *Estudios de cultura náhuatl* 14 (1980): 15–64.

Kasulis, T. P. "Truth and Zen." *Philosophy East & West* 30, no. 4 (1980): 453–64. http://dx.doi.org/10.2307/1398971. (accessed 5/19/2013.)

Keen, Benjamin. *The Aztec Image in Western Thought*. New Brunswick, NJ: Rutgers University Press, 1971.

Kellogg, Susan. "From Parallel and Equivalent to Separate but Unequal: Tenocha Mexica Women, 1500–1700." In *Indian Women of Early Mexico*, edited by Susan Schroeder, Stephen Wood, and Robert Haskett, 123–43. Norman: University of Oklahoma Press, 1997.

Kelso, J. A. Scott, and David A. Engstrøm. *The Complementary Nature*. Cambridge, MA: MIT Press, 2006.

Kendall, Timothy. *Patolli: A Game of Ancient Mexico*. Newton, MA: Whitehall Games, 1983.

Kidwell, Clara Sue, Homer Noley, and George E. "Tink" Tinker. *A Native American Theology*. Maryknoll, NY: Orbis, 2002.

Kim, Jaegwon. *Philosophy of Mind*. Boulder, CO: Westview Press, 1996.

Kim, Jaegwon, and Ernest Sosa, eds. *A Companion to Metaphysics*. Oxford: Blackwell, 1995. http://dx.doi.org/10.1111/b.9780631199991.1995.x

King, Cecil. "Here Come the Anthros." In *Indians and Anthropologists: Vine Deloria, Jr., and the Critique of Anthropology*, edited by Thomas Biolsi and Larry J. Zimmerman, 115–19. Tucson: University of Arizona Press, 1997.

King, Lord Edward, and Viscount Kingsborough, eds. *Codex Boturini: Antiquities of Mexico.* 9 vols. London: Robert Havell, 1831.

Kitcher, Philip. *Abusing Science: The Case against Scientific Creationism.* Cambridge, MA: MIT Press, 1982.

Klein, Cecelia. "Autosacrifice." In *The Oxford Encyclopedia of Mesoamerican Cultures: The Civilizations of Mexico and Central America*, edited by Davíd Carrasco, 1:64–66. Oxford: Oxford University Press, 2001.

Klein, Cecelia. "Fighting with Femininity: Gender and War in Aztec Mexico." In *Gender Rhetorics: Postures of Dominance and Submission in Human History*, edited by Richard C. Trexler, 219–53. Medieval and Renaissance Texts and Studies 113. Binghamton: State University of New York, 1994.

Klein, Cecelia, ed. *Gender in Pre-Hispanic America.* Washington, DC: Dumbarton Oaks, 2001.

Klein, Cecelia. "The Ideology of Autosacrifice at the Templo Mayor." In *The Aztec Templo Mayor*, edited by Elizabeth Hill Boone, 293–370. Washington, DC: Dumbarton Oaks, 1987.

Klein, Cecelia. "None of the Above: Gender Ambiguity in Nahua Ideology." In *Gender in Pre-Hispanic America*, edited by Cecelia Klein, 183–254. Washington, DC: Dumbarton Oaks, 2001.

Klein, Cecelia. "Post-Classic Mexican Death Imagery as a Sign of Cyclic Completion." In *Death and Afterlife in Pre-Columbian America*, edited by Elizabeth P. Benson, 69–84. Washington, DC: Dumbarton Oaks, 1975.

Klein, Cecelia. "The Shield Women: Resolution of a Gender Paradox." In *Current Topics in Aztec Studies: Essays in Honor of Dr. H. B. Nicholson*, edited by Alana Cory and Douglas Sharon, 39–64. San Diego Museum of Man Papers 30. San Diego: San Diego Museum of Man, 1993.

Klein, Cecelia. "*Teocuitlatl*, 'Divine Excrement': The Significance of 'Holy Shit' in Ancient Mexico." *Art Journal* 52, no. 3 (1993): 20–27. http://dx.doi.org/10.2307/777364. (accessed 5/19/2013.)

Klein, Cecelia. "Woven Heaven, Tangled Earth: The Weaver's Paradigm of the Mesoamerican Cosmos." In *Ethnoastronomy and Archaeoastronomy in the American Tropics*, edited by Anthony Aveni and Gary Urton, 1–35. Annals of the New York Academy of Sciences, No. 38. New York: New York Academy of Sciences, 1982. http://dx.doi.org/10.1111/j.1749-6632.1982.tb34257.x. (accessed 5/19/2013.)

Klor de Alva, J. Jorge, ed. and trans. "The Aztec-Spanish Dialogue of 1524." *Alcheringa/Ethnopoetics* 4, no. 2 (1980): 52–193.

Klor de Alva, J. Jorge. "Christianity and the Aztecs." *San Jose Studies* 5 (1979): 7–21.

Klor de Alva, J. Jorge. "Spiritual Conflict and Accommodation in New Spain: Toward a Typology of Aztec Responses to Christianity." In *The Inca and Aztec States:*

1400–1800, edited by George A. Collier, Renato Rosaldo, and John D. Walsh, 345–66. New York: Academic Press, 1982.

Knab, Timothy J. *The Dialogue of Earth and Sky: Dreams, Souls, Curing and the Modern Aztec Underworld*. Tucson: University of Arizona Press, 2004.

Knab, Timothy J. "Metaphors, Concepts, and Coherence in Aztec." In *Symbol and Meaning beyond the Closed Community: Essays in Mesoamerican Ideas*, edited by Gary H. Gossen, 45–56. Albany: Institute for Mesoamerican Studies, SUNY Press, 1986.

Knab, Timothy J., ed. *A Scattering of Jades: Stories, Poems, and Prayers of the Aztecs*. Translated by Thelma D. Sullivan, and introduction and commentary by Timothy J. Knab. New York: Simon and Schuster, 1994.

Knab, Timothy J. *A War of Witches: A Journey into the Underworld of the Contemporary Aztecs*. Boulder, CO: Westview Press, 1995.

Köhler, Ulrich. "On the Significance of the Aztec Day Sign 'Olin.'" In *Proceedings of the Symposium [on] Space and Time in the Cosmovisíon of Mesoamerica*, edited by Franz Tichy, 111–28. Munich: Wilhelm Fink, 1982.

Krickeberg, Walter. *Las antiguas culturas mexicanas*. México: Fondo de Cultura Económica, 1961.

Kuhn, Thomas. *The Structure of Scientific Revolutions*, 2nd enlarged edition. Chicago: University of Chicago Press, 1970.

Kurath, Gertrude Prokosch, and Samuel Martí. *Dances of Anahuac: The Choreography and Music of Precortesian Dances*. New York: Wenner-Gren Foundation for Anthropological Research, 1964.

Lakoff, George, and Mark Johnson. *Metaphors We Live By*. Chicago: University of Chicago Press, 1980.

Lee, Jongsoo. "Westernization of Nahuatl Religion: Nezahualcoyotl's Unknown God." *Latin American Indian Literatures Journal* 19, no. 1 (2003): 19–48.

Leibsohn, Dana. *Script and Glyph: Pre-Hispanic History, Colonial Bookmaking, and the Historia Tolteca-Chichimeca*. Washington, DC: Dumbarton Oaks, 2009.

León-Portilla, Miguel. "Appendix B: Recent Contributions on the Theme of this Book." In *Time and Reality in the Thought of the Maya*, 2nd enlarged ed., by Miguel León-Portilla, 161–205. Norman: University of Oklahoma Press, 1988.

León-Portilla, Miguel. *The Aztec Image of Self and Society: An Introduction to Nahua Culture*, edited with an introduction by J. Jorge Klor de Alva. Salt Lake City: University of Utah Press, 1992.

León-Portilla, Miguel. *Aztec Thought and Culture: A Study of the Ancient Nahuatl Mind*. Translated by Jack Emory Davis. Norman: University of Oklahoma Press, 1963.

León-Portilla, Miguel. *Bernardino de Sahagún: First Anthropologist*. Translated by Mauricio J. Mixco. Norman: University of Oklahoma Press, 2002.

León-Portilla, Miguel. "*El Tonalámatl de los Pochtecas (Códice Fejérváry-Mayer): Estudio introductorio y comentarios*." *Arqueología Mexicana Edición especial*, 18 (2005).

León-Portilla, Miguel. *Endangered Cultures*. Translated by Julie Goodson-Lewis. Dallas: Southern Methodist University Press, 1990.

León-Portilla, Miguel. *Fifteen Poets of the Aztec World*. Norman: University of Oklahoma Press, 1992.

León-Portilla, Miguel. *La filosofía náhuatl: Estudiada en sus fuentes con un nuevo apéndice*, new ed., prologue by Angel María Garibay K. México, DF: Universidad Nacional Autónoma de México, 2001 [1956].

León-Portilla, Miguel. "¿Hay composiciones de origen prehispánico en el manuscrito de cantares mexicanos?" *Estudios de cultura náhuatl* 33 (2002): 141–7.

León-Portilla, Miguel. "Mitos de los origenes en Mesoamerica." *Arqueología Mexicana* 10, no. 56 (2002): 20–53.

León-Portilla, Miguel. "Ometeotl, el supremo díos dual, y Tezcatlipoca." *Estudios de cultura náhuatl* 30 (1999): 133–52.

León-Portilla, Miguel. "Those Made Worthy by Divine Sacrifice: The Faith of Ancient Mexico." In *South and Meso-American Native Spirituality: From the Cult of the Feathered Serpent to the Theology of Liberation*, edited by Gary H. Gossen in collaboration with Miguel León-Portilla, 41–74. New York: Crossroads, 1993.

León-Portilla, Miguel. "Three Forms of Thought in Ancient Mexico." In *Studies in Symbolism and Cultural Communication*, edited by F. Allen Hanson, 9–24. Lawrence: University of Kansas Press, 1982.

León-Portilla, Miguel. *Time and Reality in the Thought of the Maya*, 2nd enlarged ed., foreword by Sir Eric S. Thompson, appendices by Alfonso Villa Rojas and Miguel León-Portilla, translated by Charles Boiles, Fernanado Horcasitas, and Miguel León-Portilla. Norman: University of Oklahoma Press, 1988.

León-Portilla, Miguel. "¿Una nueva interpretación de los cantares mexicanos?" *Estudios de cultura náhuatl* 18 (1986): 385–400.

Levine, Michael. *Pantheism: A Non-Theistic Concept of Deity*. London: Routledge, 1994.

Lévy-Bruhl, Lucien. *How Natives Think*. Translated by Lilian A. Clare with an introduction by Ruth L. Bunzel. New York: Washington Square Press, 1966.

Libura, Krystyna M. *Los días y los dioses del Códice Borgia*. México, DF: Ediciones Tecolote, 2000.

Limón Olvera, Silvia. "Fire Deities." In *The Oxford Encyclopedia of Mesoamerican Cultures: The Civilizations of Mexico and Central America*, edited by Davíd Carrasco, 1: 409–10. Oxford: Oxford University Press, 2001.

Lipp, Frank. *The Mixe of Oaxaca: Religion, Ritual and Healing*. Austin: University of Texas Press, 1991.

Lloyd, Genevieve. *Part of Nature: Self-Knowledge in Spinoza's Ethics*. Ithaca, NY: Cornell University Press, 1994.

Lloyd, Genevieve. *Spinoza and the Ethics*. London: Routledge, 1996.

Lockhart, James. *The Nahuas after the Conquest: A Social and Cultural History of the Indians of Central Mexico, Sixteenth through Eighteenth Centuries*. Stanford, CA: Stanford University Press, 1992.

Lockhart, James. *Nahuatl Studies Series 3*. vol. 76. *Nahuas and Spaniards: Postconquest Central Mexican History and Philology*. UCLA Latin American Studies. Stanford, CA: Stanford University Press, 1991.

Lok, Rossana. "The House as Microcosm." In *The Leiden Tradition in Structural Anthropology: Essays in Honor of P. E. de Josselin de Jong*, edited by R. De Ridder and J. A. J. Karremans, 211–23. Leiden: Brill, 1987.

Looper, Matthew G. "Dance Performance at *Quiriguá*." In *Landscape and Power in Ancient Mesoamerica*, edited by Rex Koontz, Kathryn Reese-Taylor, and Annabeth Headrick, 113–36. Boulder: Westview Press, 2001.

López Austin, Alfredo. "Complementos y composiciones." *Ojarasca* 5 (1992): 40–2.

López Austin, Alfredo. "Cosmovision." Translated by Scott Sessions. In *The Oxford Encyclopedia of Mesoamerican Cultures: The Civilizations of Mexico and Central America*, edited by Davíd Carrasco, 1: 268–74. Oxford: Oxford University Press, 2001.

López Austin, Alfredo. "Cuarenta clases de magos del mundo náhuatl." *Arqueología Mexicana* 7 (1967): 87–117.

López Austin, Alfredo. *Cuerpo humano e ideología: Las concepciones de los antiguos Nahuas*, 2nd ed. 2 vols. México, DF: Universidad Autónoma de México, 1984.

López Austin, Alfredo. *Hombre-dios: Religión y política en el mundo náhuatl*, 3rd ed. México, DF: Universidad Autónoma de México, 1998 [1973].

López Austin, Alfredo. *The Human Body and Ideology: Concepts of the Ancient Nahuas*, 2 vols. Translated by Thelma Ortiz de Montellano and Bernard R. Ortiz de Montellano. Salt Lake City: University of Utah Press, 1988.

López Austin, Alfredo. "The Masked God of Fire." In *The Aztec Templo Mayor*, edited by Elizabeth Hill Boone, 257–92. Washington, DC: Dumbarton Oaks, 1987.

López Austin, Alfredo. *The Myths of the Opossum: Pathways of Mesoamerican Mythology.* Translated by Bernard R. Ortiz de Montellano and Thelma Ortiz de Montellano. Albuquerque: University of New Mexico Press, 1993.

López Austin, Alfredo. "The Natural World." In *Aztecs*, edited by Eduardo Matos Moctezuma and Felipe Solís Olguín, 141–42. London: Royal Academy of the Arts, 2002.

López Austin, Alfredo. *The Rabbit on the Face of the Moon: Mythology in the Mesoamerican Tradition.* Translated by Bernard R. Ortiz de Montellano and Thelma Ortiz de Montellano. Salt Lake City: University of Utah Press, 1996.

López Austin, Alfredo. "Los ritos: Un juego de definiciones." *Arqueología Mexicana* 6, no. 34 (1988): 4–37.

López Austin, Alfredo. "Tamoanchan." In *The Oxford Encyclopedia of Mesoamerican Cultures: The Civilizations of Mexico and Central America*, edited by Davíd Carrasco, 3:184–85. Oxford: Oxford University Press, 2001.

López Austin, Alfredo. *Tamoanchan, Tlalocan: Places of Mist.* Translated by Bernard R. Ortiz de Montellano and Thelma Ortiz de Montellano. Niwot: University Press of Colorado, 1997.

López Austin, Alfredo. *Tamoanchan y Tlalocan.* México, DF: Fondo de Cultura Económica, 1994.

López Luján, Leonardo. *The Offerings of the Templo Mayor of Tenochtitlan*, rev. ed., translated by Bernard R. Ortiz de Montellano and Thelma Ortiz de Montellano. Albuquerque: University of New Mexico Press, 2005.

López Luján, Leonardo. "Old Gods." In *The Oxford Encyclopedia of Mesoamerican Cultures: The Civilizations of Mexico and Central America*, edited by Davíd Carrasco, 2:403–5. Oxford: Oxford University Press, 2001.

Lovejoy, Arthur O. *The Great Chain of Being: A Study of the History of an Idea*. New York: Harper and Row, 1960.

Loy, David. *Nondualism: A Study in Comparative Philosophy*. Amherst, NY: Humanities Books, 1988.

MacIntyre, Alasdair. "Ontology." In *Encyclopedia of Philosophy*, edited by Paul Edwards, 5:542–43. New York: Macmillan, 1967.

MacIntyre, Alasdair. "Pantheism." In *Encyclopedia of Philosophy*, edited by Paul Edwards, 6:31–35. New York: Macmillan, 1967.

Madsen, William. "Christo-Paganism: A Study of Mexican Religious Syncretism." In *Nativism and Syncretism* 19:105–79. New Orleans: Middle American Research Institute, Tulane University Press, 1957.

Maffie, James. "The Centrality of Nepantla in Conquest-Era Nahua Philosophy." *Nahua Newsletter* 44 (2007): 11–31.

Maffie, James. "Ethnoepistemology." *The Internet Encyclopedia of Philosophy*. 2005. http://www.iep.utm.edu/ethno-ep.

Maffie, James. "*In Huehue Tlamanitiliztli* and *la Verdad*: Nahua and European Philosophies in Fray Bernardino de Sahagún's *Colloquios y doctrina cristiana*." *Inter-America Journal of Philosophy* 3 (2012): 1–33.

Maffie, James. "To Walk in Balance: An Encounter between Contemporary Western Science and Pre-Conquest Nahua Philosophy." In *Science and Other Cultures: Philosophy of Science and Technology Issues*, edited by Robert Figueroa and Sandra Harding, 70–91. New York: Routledge, 2003.

Maffie, James. "'Whatever Happens, We Have the Gatling Gun, and They Have Not': Future Prospects for Indigenous Knowledges." In "Futures of Indigenous Knowledges." Special issue, *Futures: The Journal of Policy, Planning, and Futures Studies* 41 (2009): 53–65.

Maffie, James. "Why Care about Nezahualcoyotl? Veritism and Nahua Philosophy." *Philosophy of the Social Sciences* 32, no. 1 (2002): 71–91. http://dx.doi.org/10.1177/004839310203200104.

Marcus, Joyce. "Zapotec Religion." In *The Cloud People: Divergent Evolution of the Zapotec and Mixtec Civilizations*, edited by Kent Flannery and Joyce Marcus, 345–50. New York: Academic Press, 1983.

Marcus, Joyce, Kent V. Flannery, and Ronald Spores. "The Cultural Legacy of the Oaxacan Preceramic." In *The Cloud People: Divergent Evolution of the Zapotec and Mixtec Civilizations*, edited by Kent Flannery and Joyce Marcus, 36–39. New York: Academic Press, 1983.

Martinich, A. P. "Pantheism." In *The Cambridge Dictionary of Philosophy*, edited by Robert Audi, 556. Cambridge: Cambridge University Press, 1995.

Mastache, Alba Guadalupe. "'El tejido en el México antiguo." *Arqueología Mexicana* Edición especial, 19 (2005): 20–28.

Mastache, Alba Guadalupe. "'Técnicas prehispánicas de tejido." *Arqueología Mexicana* Edición especial, 19 (2005): 29–31.

Mastache, Alba Guadalupe. "'Weaving in Ancient Mexico." Translated by Debra Nagao. *Arqueología Mexicana* Edición especial, 19 (2005): 86–8.

Matos Moctezuma, Eduardo. "The Aztec Calendar." In *The Aztec Calendar and Other Solar Monuments*, by Eduardo Matos Moctezuma and Felipe Solís Olguín, 13–75. México, DF: Conaculta-Instituto Nacional de Antropología e Historia, 2004.

Matos Moctezuma, Eduardo. "Aztec History and Cosmovision." In *Moctezuma's Mexico: Visions of the Aztec World*, edited by Davíd Carrasco and Eduardo Matos Moctezuma, 3–98. Niwot: University Press of Colorado, 1992.

Matos Moctezuma, Eduardo. *Life and Death in the Templo Mayor*. Translated by Bernard R. Ortiz de Montellano and Thelma Ortiz de Montellano. Niwot: University Press of Colorado, 1995.

Matos Moctezuma, Eduardo. *Muerte a filo de obsidiana: Los nahuas frente a la muerte.* México, DF: Fondo de Cultura Económica, 2008.

Matos Moctezuma, Eduardo. "The Templo Mayor of Tenochtitlan: History and Interpretation." In *The Great Temple of Tenochtitlan: Center and Periphery in the Aztec World*, edited by Johanna Broda, Davíd Carrasco, and Eduardo Matos Moctezuma, 15–60. Berkeley: University California Press, 1987.

Matos Moctezuma, Eduardo, and Felipe R. Solís Olguín. *The Aztec Calendar and Other Solar Monuments*. México, DF: Conaculta-Instituto Nacional de Antropología e Historia, 2004.

Maxwell, Judith M., and Craig A. Hanson. *Of the Manners of Speaking That the Old Ones Had: The Metaphors of Andrés de Olmos in the TULAL Manuscript,* Arte para aprender la lengua mexicana. 1547. Salt Lake City: University of Utah Press, 1992.

McCafferty, Geoffrey, and Sharisse McCafferty. "The Metamorphosis of Xochiquetzal." In *Manifesting Power: Gender and the Interpretation of Power in Archaeology*, edited by Tracy L. Sweely, 103–25. London: Routledge, 1999.

McCafferty, Sharisse, and Geoffrey McCafferty. "Spinning and Weaving as Female Gender Identity in Post-classic Mexico." In *Textile Traditions of Mesoamerica and the Andes: An Anthology*, edited by Margot Blum Schevil, Janet Catherine Berlo, and Edward B. Dwyer, 19–46. Austin: University of Texas Press, 1991.

McKeever Furst, Jill Leslie. *Codex Vindobonesis Mexicanus: A Commentary*. Albany: SUNY and Institute for Mesoamerican Studies, 1978.

McKeever Furst, Jill Leslie. "Duality." In *The Oxford Encyclopedia of Mesoamerican Cultures: The Civilizations of Mexico and Central America*, edited by Davíd Carrasco, 1:344–45. Oxford: Oxford University Press, 2001.

McKeever Furst, Jill Leslie. *The Natural History of the Soul in Ancient Mexico*. New Haven, CT: Yale University Press, 1995.

McKeever Furst, Jill Leslie. "Skeletonization in Mixtec Art: A Revaluation." In *The Art of Iconography of Late Post-Classic Central Mexico*, edited by Elizabeth P. Benson and Elizabeth H. Boone, 207–25. Washington, DC: Dumbarton Oaks, 1982.

McKeever Furst, Jill Leslie. "Soul." In *The Oxford Encyclopedia of Mesoamerican Cultures: The Civilizations of Mexico and Central America*, edited by Davíd Carrasco, 3:155–56. Oxford: Oxford University Press, 2001.

McLaughlin, Brian P. "Philosophy of Mind." In *The Cambridge Dictionary of Philosophy*, edited by Robert Audi, 597–606. Cambridge: Cambridge University Press, 1995.

Mendieta, Gerónimo de. *Historia eclesiástica indiana*. 2nd ed. Mexico City: Editorial Porrúa, 1971. (Original work published 1870).

Mendoza, Rubén G. "*The Divine Gourd Tree*: Tzompantli Skull Racks, Decapitation Rituals, and Human Trophies in Ancient America." In *The Taking and Displaying of Human Body Parts as Trophies by Amerindians*, edited by Richard J. Chacon and David H. Dye, 400–43. New York: Springer, 2007.

Meyer, Leroy N., and Tony Ramirez. "'*Wakinyan Hotan*'*: The Inscrutability of Lakota/ Dakota Metaphysics. *The Thunder Beings Call Out." In *From Our Eyes: Learning from Indigenous Peoples*, edited by Sylvia O'Meara and Douglas A. West, 89–105. Toronto: Garamond Press, 1996.

Mignolo, Walter D. "Philosophy and the Colonial Difference." In *Latin American Philosophy*, edited by Eduardo Mendieta, 80–86. Bloomington: Indiana University Press, 2003.

Miller, Arthur G. "The Iconography of the Painting in the Temple of the Diving God, Tulum, Quintana Roo, Mexico: The Twisted Cords." In *Mesoamerican Archaeology: New Approaches*, edited by Norman Hammond, 167–86. Austin: University of Texas Press, 1974.

Miller, Mary, and Karl Taube. *An Illustrated Dictionary of the Gods and Symbols of Ancient Mexico and the Maya*. London: Thames and Hudson, 1993.

Mills, Charles W. *The Racial Contract*. Ithaca, NY: Cornell University Press, 1997.

Molina, Alonso de. *Vocabulario en lengua castellana y mexicana y mexicana y castellana*, 4th ed. Facsimile of 1571 edition. Mexico City: Porrúa, 2001.

Momaday, N. Scott. *The Names: A Memoir*. New York: Harper and Row, 1976.

Monaghan, John D. *The Covenants with Earth and Rain: Exchange, Sacrifice and Revelation in Mixtec Sociality*. Norman: University of Oklahoma Press, 1995.

Monaghan, John D. "The Person, Destiny, and the Construction of Difference in Mesoamerica." *RES* 33 (Spring 1998): 137–46.

Monaghan, John D. "Physiology, Production and Gendered Difference: The Evidence from Mixtec and Other Mesoamerican Societies." In *Gender in Pre-Hispanic America*, edited by Cecelia Klein, 285–304. Washington, DC: Dumbarton Oaks, 2001.

Monaghan, John D. "Sacrifice, Death, and the Origins of Agriculture in the *Codex Vienna*." *American Antiquity* 55, no. 3 (1990): 559–69. http://dx.doi.org/10.2307/281286. (accessed 5/19/2013.)

Monaghan, John D. "Theology and History in the Study of Mesoamerican Religions." In *Supplement to the Handbook of Middle American Indians*. vol. 6. edited by John D. Monaghan, 24–49. Austin: University of Texas Press, 2000.

Moore, Kathleen Dean, Kurt Peters, Ted Jojola, and Amber Lacy, eds. *How It Is: The Native American Philosophy of V. F. Cordova*. Foreword by Linda Hogan. Tucson: University of Arizona Press, 2007.

Morris, Brian. *Anthropological Studies of Religion: An Introductory Text.* Cambridge: Cambridge University Press, 1987.

Motolinía, Toribio de Benavente. *Motolinía's History of the Indians of New Spain.* Translated and annotated by Francis Borgia Steck. Washington, DC: Academy of American Franciscan History, 1951.

Mountjoy, Joseph B. "Patolli." In *The Oxford Encyclopedia of Mesoamerican Cultures: The Civilizations of Mexico and Central America,* edited by Davíd Carrasco, 2:448. Oxford: Oxford University Press, 2001.

Murashige, Stanley. "Philosophy of Art." In *Encyclopedia of Chinese Philosophy,* edited by Antonio S. Cua, 511–17. New York: Routledge, 2003.

Myerhoff, Barbara G. "Balancing between Worlds: The Shaman's Calling." *Parabola* 1, no. 2 (1976): 6–13.

Myerhoff, Barbara G. "The Huichol and the Quest for Paradise." *Parabola* 1, no. 1 (1976): 22–9.

Myerhoff, Barbara G. *Peyote Hunt: The Sacred Journey of the Huichol Indians.* Ithaca, NY: Cornell University Press, 1974.

Nettleship, Richard Lewis. *Lectures on the Republic of Plato.* 2nd ed. London: MacMillan and Co, 1963.

Neumann, Eric. *The Great Mother: An Analysis of the Archetype,* translated by Ralph Mannheim. Princeton, NJ: Princeton University Press, 1963.

Neumann, Franke J. "The Experience of Time in Nahua Religion." *Journal of the American Academy of Religion* 44 (1976): 256–63.

Neumann, Franke J. "The Flayed God and His Rattle Stick: A Shamanic Element in Pre-Hispanic Mesoamerican Religion." *History of Religions* 15, no. 3 (1976): 251–63. http://dx.doi.org/10.1086/462746. (accessed 5/19/2013.)

Newton-Smith, W. H., ed. *A Companion to the Philosophy of Science.* Oxford: Blackwell, 2000.

Nicholson, Henry B. "The Cult of Xipe Totec in Mesoamerica." In *Religión en Mesoamérica, XII Mesa Redonda,* edited by Jaime Litvak King and Noemí Castillo Tejero, 213–18. México, DF: Sociedad Mexicana de Antropología, 1972.

Nicholson, Henry B. "Religion in Pre-Hispanic Central Mexico." In *Handbook of Middle American Indians.* vol. 10. edited by Robert Wauchope, Gordon F. Elkholm, and Ignacio Bernal, 395–446. Austin: University of Texas Press, 1971.

Nicholson, Henry B. "Representing the *Veintena* Ceremonies in *The Primeros Memoriales.*" In *Representing Aztec Ritual: Performance, Text, and Image in the Work of Sahagún,* edited by Eloise Quiñones Keber, 63–106. Niwot: University Press of Colorado, 2002.

Nicholson, Henry B. "A Royal Headband of the 'Tlaxcalteca.'" *Revista mexicana de estudios antropológicos* 21 (1967): 71–106.

Nicholson, Henry B. "The Significance of the 'Looped Cord' Year Symbol in Pre-Hispanic Mexico." *Estudios de cultura náhuatl* 6 (1966): 135–48.

Nicholson, Henry B. *Topiltzin Quetzalcoatl: The Once and Future Lord of the Toltecs.* Niwot: University Press of Colorado, 2001.

Nicholson, Irene. *Firefly in the Night: A Study of Ancient Mexican Poetry and Symbolism*. London: Faber and Faber, 1959.

Noguez, Xavier. "Códice de la Cruz-Badiano." *Arqueología Mexicana* 16, no. 94 (2008): 84–5.

Norton-Smith, Thomas M. *The Dance of Person and Place: One Interpretation of American Indian Philosophy*. Buffalo: SUNY Press, 2010.

Nowotny, Karl Anton. *Tlacuilolli: Style and Contents of the Mexican Pictorial Manuscripts with a Catalog of the Borgia Group*. Edited and translated by George A. Everett Jr. and Edward Sisson. Norman: University of Oklahoma Press, 2005.

Nuttall, Zelia. *The Book of the Life of the Ancient Mexicans Containing an Account of Their Rites and Superstitions*. Facsimile reproduction. Introduction, translation, and commentary by Zelia Nuttall. Berkeley: University of California Press, 1903.

Olivier, Guilhem. "Aztec Human Sacrifice as Expiation." In *The Strange World of Human Sacrifice*, edited by Jan N. Bremmer, 9–29. Leuven: Peeters, 2007.

Olivier, Guilhem. "Bundles." In *The Oxford Encyclopedia of Mesoamerican Cultures: The Civilizations of Mexico and Central America*, edited by Davíd Carrasco, 1:105–6. Oxford: Oxford University Press, 2001.

Olivier, Guilhem. *Mockeries and Metamorphoses of an Aztec God: Tezcatlipoca, "Lord of the Smoking Mirror."* Translated by Michel Besson. Niwot: University Press of Colorado, 2003.

Olivier, Guilhem. "Tezcatlipoca." In *The Oxford Encyclopedia of Mesoamerican Cultures: The Civilizations of Mexico and Central America*, edited by Davíd Carrasco, 3:217–19. Oxford: Oxford University Press, 2001.

Olivier, Guilhem, and Leonardo López Luján. "Images of Moctezuma and His Symbols of Power." In *Moctezuma: Aztec Ruler*, edited by Colin McEwan and Leonardo López Luján, 78–123. London: British Museum Press, 2009.

Olmos, Andrés de. *Arte de la lengua mexicana y vocabulario*. Introduction and appendixes by Thelma D. Sullivan; edited by René Acuña. México. DF: Universidad Autónoma de México, 1985.

Orozpe Enríquez, Mauricio. *El código oculto de le greca escalonada: Tloque Nahuaque*. México, DF: UNAM, 2010.

Orr, Heather S. "Ballgame." In *The Oxford Encyclopedia of Mesoamerican Cultures: The Civilizations of Mexico and Central America*, edited by Davíd Carrasco, 1:75–78. Oxford: Oxford University Press, 2001.

Ortiz de Montellano, Bernard R. *Aztec Medicine, Health, and Nutrition*. New Brunswick, NJ: Rutgers University Press, 1990.

Pace, Edward. "Pantheism." *The Catholic Encyclopedia*. Vol. 11. New York: Robert Appleton Company, 1911. http://www.newadvent.org/cathen/11447b.htm. (accessed 5/19/2013).

Pagden, Anthony. *The Fall of Natural Man*. Cambridge: University of Cambridge Press, 1982.

Pasztory, Esther. *Aztec Art*. Norman: University of Oklahoma Press, 1983.

Payne, Stanley E., and Michael Closs. "A Survey of Aztec Numbers and Their Uses." In *Native-American Mathematics*, edited by Michael P. Closs, 215–35. Austin: University of Texas Press, 1986.

Pepper, Stephen. *World Hypotheses: A Study in Evidence*. Berkeley: University of California Press, 1970.

Pereboom, Derek. "Early Modern Philosophical Theology." In *A Companion to Philosophy of Religion*, edited by Philip L. Quinn and Charles Taliaferro, 103–10. Oxford: Blackwell, 1997.

Peterson, Jeanette Favrot. *The Paradise Garden Murals of Malinalco: Utopia and Empire in Sixteenth-Century Mexico*. Austin: University of Texas Press, 1993.

Peterson, Jeanette Favrot. "Sacrificial Earth: Iconography and Function of Malinalli Grass in Aztec Culture." In *Flora and Fauna Imagery in Precolumbian Cultures: Iconography and Function*, edited by Jeanette Favrot Peterson, 133–48. BAR International Series, 171. Oxford: BAR, 1982.

Piña Chan, Román. *Cacaxtla: Fuentes históricas y pinturas*. México, DF: Fondo de Cultura Económico, 1998.

Plato. *Plato: The Collected Dialogues including the Letters*, edited by Edith Hamilton and Huntington Cairns. Princeton, NJ: Princeton University Press, 1961.

Plato. *The Republic of Plato*. Translated, introduction, and notes by Francis M. Cornford. Oxford: Oxford University Press, 1971.

Pohl, John M. D. "Weaving and Gift Exchange in the Mixtec Codices." In *Cloth and Curing: Continuity and Change in Oaxaca*, edited by Grace Johnson and Douglas Sharon, 3–13. San Diego: San Diego Museum of Man, 1994.

Pomar, Juan Bautista de. "Relación de Tezcoco." In *Relaciones geográficas del siglo XVI: Mexico*, vol. 3, edited by Rene Acuma, 23–113. México, DF: UNAM, 1986.

Popol Vuh: The Definitive Edition of the Mayan Book of the Dawn of Life and the Glories of Gods and Kings. Introduction, translation and commentary by Dennis Tedlock. New York: Simon and Schuster, 1985.

Prechtel, Martin, and Robert S. Carlsen. "Weaving and Cosmos amongst the Tzutujil Maya of Guatemala." *RES* 15 (1988): 122–32.

Quezada, Noemí. "Creencias tradicionales sobre embarazo y parto." *Anales de antropología* 14 (1977): 307–26.

Quezada, Noemí. "Mito y génera en la sociedad mexica." *Estudios de cultura náhuatl* 26 (1966): 21–40.

Quine, W. V. O. *From a Logical Point of View*, 2nd ed., rev. Cambridge, MA: Harvard University Press, 1961.

Quine, W. V. O. *Word and Object*. Cambridge, MA: MIT Press, 1960.

Quiñones Keber, Eloise. "Codex Borbonicus." In *The Oxford Encyclopedia of Mesoamerican Cultures: The Civilizations of Mexico and Central America*, edited by Davíd Carrasco, 91–94. Oxford: Oxford University Press, 2001.

Quiñones Keber, Eloise, ed. *Codex Telleriano-Remensis: Ritual, Divination, and History in a Pictorial Aztec Manuscript*. Austin: University of Texas Press, 1995.

Quiñones Keber, Eloise. "Mayahuel and Maguey: Sustenance and Sacrifice in Aztec Myth." *Latin American Indian Literatures Journal* 5, no. 2 (1989): 72–83.

Quiñones Keber, Eloise. "Painting Divination in the Florentine Codex." In *Representing Aztec Ritual: Performance, Text, and Image in the Work of Sahagún*, edited by Eloise Quiñones Keber, 251–76. Niwot: University Press of Colorado, 2002.

Quiñones Keber, Eloise, ed. *Representing Aztec Ritual: Performance, Text, and Image in the Work of Sahagún*. Niwot: University Press of Colorado, 2002.

Quiñones Keber, Eloise. "Xolotl: Dogs, Death, and Deities in Aztec Myth." *Latin American Indian Literatures* 7, no. 2 (1991): 229–39.

Radin, Paul. *Primitive Man as Philosopher*. New York: Dover Publications, 1957.

Rappaport, Roy A. *Ritual and Religion in the Making of Humanity*. Cambridge: Cambridge University Press, 1999. http://dx.doi.org/10.1017/CBO9780511814686. (accessed 5/19/2013.)

Read, Kay A. "More than Earth: Cihuacoatl as Female Warrior, Male Matron, and Inside Ruler." In *Goddesses Who Rule*, edited by Elisabeth Benard and Beverly Moon, 51–68. Oxford: Oxford University Press, 2000.

Read, Kay A. *Time and Sacrifice in the Aztec Cosmos*. Bloomington: Indiana University Press, 1998.

Reichel-Dolmatoff, Gerardo. "The Loom of Life: A Kogi Principle of Integration." *Journal of Latin American Lore* 4, no. 1 (1978): 5–17.

Rescher, Nicholas. *Process Metaphysics: An Introduction to Process Philosophy*. Albany: State University of New York Press, 1996.

Rescher, Nicholas. "Process Philosophy." In *A Companion to Metaphysics*, edited by Jaegwon Kim and Ernest Sosa, 417–19. Oxford: Blackwell, 1995.

Ripinsky-Naxon, Michael. "Shamanistic Knowledge and Cosmology." In *Tribal Epistemologies: Essays in the Philosophy of Anthropology*, edited by Helmut Wautischer, 119–61. Aldershot: Ashgate, 1998.

Robicsek, Francis, and Donald Hales. "Maya Heart Sacrifice: Cultural Perspectives and Surgical Technique." In *Ritual Human Sacrifice in Mesoamerica*, edited by Elizabeth H. Boone, 49–90. Washington, DC: Dumbarton Oaks, 1984.

Rodríguez-Alegría, Enrique. "The Aztecs after the Conquest." In *The Aztec World*, edited by Elizabeth M. Brumfiel and Gary M. Feinman, 195–208. New York: Harry N. Abrams, 2008.

Rorty, Richard. *Objectivity, Relativism, and Truth*. Cambridge: Cambridge University Press, 1991.

Rorty, Richard. "A Pragmatist View of Rationality and Cultural Difference." *Philosophy East & West* 42, no. 4 (1992): 581–89. http://dx.doi.org/10.2307/1399670. (accessed 5/19/2013.)

Rorty, Richard. "Stories of Difference: A Conversation with Richard Rorty," edited by Gaurav Desai. *SAPINA Bulletin* 2–3 (1993): 23–45.

Rosenbaum, Brenda. "Women and Gender in Mesoamerica." In *The Legacy of Mesoamerica: History and Culture of a Native American Civilization*, edited by Robert

Carmack, Janine Gasco, and Gary H. Gossen, 221–78. Upper Saddle River, NJ: Prentice Hall, 1996.

Rowe, Ann Pollard. *A Century of Change in Guatemalan Textiles*. New York: Center for Inter-American Relations, 1981.

Ruiz de Alarcón, Hernando. *Treatise on the Heathen Superstitions that Today Live among the Indians Native to This New Spain*. Translated, edited, and introduction by J. Richard Andrews and Ross Hassig. Norman: University of Oklahoma Press, 1984.

Sahagún, Bernardino de. *Coloquios y doctrina cristiana con que los doce frailes de San Francisco enviados por el papa Adriano VI y por el emperador Carlos V convirtieron a los indios de la Nueva España, en lengua mexicana y española. Los diálogos de 1524, dispuestos por fray Bernardino de Sahagún y sus colaboradores . . .* Edición facsimilar, introducción, paleografía, versión del náhuatl y notas de Miguel León-Portilla. Instituto de Investigaciones Históricas, Facsímiles de lingüística y filosofía nahuas, 4. México, DF: Universidad Nacional Autónoma de México, 1986.

Sahagún, Bernardino de. *Florentine Codex: General History of the Things of New Spain*. Translated and edited by Arthur J.O. Anderson and Charles Dibble. 12 vols. Santa Fe, NM: School of American Research; Salt Lake City: University of Utah Press, 1953–1982.

Sahagún, Bernardino de. *Historia General de Las Cosas de Nueva Espana*, 10th ed., edited by Angel María Garibay. México, DF: Editorial Porrúa, 1999.

Sahagún, Bernardino de. *Primeros memoriales:* Facsimile Edition. Photographs by Ferdinand Anders. Códice Matritense de la Biblioteca del Real Palacio. *Historia de las cosas de Nueva España por Fr. Bernardino de Sahagún*, edited by Francisco del Paso y Troncoso. vol. 6. Norman: University of Oklahoma Press, 1993.

Sahagún, Bernardino de. *Primeros memoriales*, Paleography of Nahuatl text and English translation by Thelma D. Sullivan. Norman: University of Oklahoma Press, 1997.

Said, Edward. *Orientalism*. New York: Vintage, 1978.

Sandstrom, Alan R. "The Cave-Pyramid Complex among the Contemporary Nahua of Northern Veracruz." In *In the Maw of the Earth Monster: Mesoamerican Ritual Cave Use*, edited by James E. Brady and Keith M. Prufer, 35–68. Austin: University of Texas Press, 2005.

Sandstrom, Alan R. "Center and Periphery in the Social Organization of Contemporary Nahuas of Mexico." *Ethnology* 35, no. 3 (1996): 161–80. http://dx.doi.org/10.2307/3773916. (accessed 5/19/2013.)

Sandstrom, Alan R. *Corn Is Our Blood: Culture and Ethnic Identity in a Contemporary Aztec Indian Village*. Norman: University of Oklahoma Press, 1991.

Sandstrom, Alan R. "Divination." In *The Oxford Encyclopedia of Mesoamerican Cultures: The Civilizations of Mexico and Central America*, edited by Davíd Carrasco, 1:327–29. Oxford: Oxford University Press, 2001.

Sandstrom, Alan R. "Sacred Mountains and Miniature Worlds: Altar Design among the Nahua of Northern Veracruz, Mexico." In *Mesas and Cosmologies in Mesoamerica*, edited by Douglas Sharon, 51–70. San Diego Museum of Man Papers 42. San Diego: San Diego Museum of Man, 2003.

Sandstrom, Alan R. "The Tonantsi Cult of the Eastern Nahua." In *Mother Worship: Themes and Variations*, edited by James J. Preston, 25–52. Chapel Hill: University of North Carolina Press, 1982.

Sandstrom, Alan, and Pamela Effrein Sandstrom. *Traditional Papermaking and Paper Cult Figures of Mexico*. Norman: University of Oklahoma Press, 1986.

Santana, Alejandro. "Did the Aztecs Do Philosophy?" *American Philosophical Association Newsletter on Hispanic/Latino Issues in Philosophy* 8, no. 1 (2008): 2–9.

Sasao, Michiyo. "New Fire Ceremony." In *The Oxford Encyclopedia of Mesoamerican Cultures: The Civilizations of Mexico and Central America*, edited by Davíd Carrasco, 2:366–68. Oxford: Oxford University Press, 2001.

Saunders, Nicholas J. "Shamanism: Pre-Hispanic Cultures." In *The Oxford Encyclopedia of Mesoamerican Cultures: The Civilizations of Mexico and Central America*, edited by Davíd Carrasco, 3:141–42. Oxford: Oxford University Press, 2001.

Schaefer, Stacy B. *To Think with a Good Heart: Wixárika Women, Weavers, and Shamans*. Salt Lake City: University of Utah Press, 2002.

Scharfstein, Ben-Ami. *A Comparative History of World Philosophy: From the Upanishads to Kant*. Albany: SUNY Press, 1998.

Schele, Linda, and Peter Mathews. *The Code of Kings: The Language of Seven Sacred Maya Temples and Tombs*. New York: Touchstone, 1998.

Schele, Linda, and Ellen Miller. *The Blood of Kings: Dynasty and Ritual in Maya Art*. Fort Worth, TX: Kimbell Art Museum, 1986.

Scott, James C. *Domination and the Arts of Resistance: Hidden Transcripts*. New Haven, CT: Yale University Press, 1990.

Seibold, Katherine E. "Textiles and Cosmology in Choquecancha, Cuzco, Peru." In *Andean Cosmologies through Time: Persistence and Emergence*, edited by Robert V. H. Dover, John McDowell, and Katherine E. Seibold, 166–201. Bloomington: Indiana Univerity Press, 1992.

Séjourné, Laurette. *Burning Water: Thought and Religion in Ancient Mexico*. New York: Grove Press, 1960.

Séjourné, Laurette. *El universo de Quetzalcoatl*. Preface by Mircea Eliade. 7th ed. Mexico City: Fondo de Cultural Económica, 2003.

Seler, Eduard. *Codex Fejérváry-Mayer: An Old Mexican Picture Manuscript in the Liverpool Free Public Museums (12014/M)*. German edition, 1901–1902. Berlin: T. and A. Constable, 1902.

Seler, Eduard. *Comentarios al Códice Borgia*. 3 vols. México, DF: Fondo de Cultura Económica, 1963 [1904].

Sellars, Wilfrid. *Science, Perception and Reality*. London: Routledge and Kegan Paul, 1963.

Sepasi-Tehrani, Homayoon, and Janet Flesch. "Persian Philosophy." In *From Africa to Zen: An Invitation to World Philosophy*, edited by Robert C. Solomon and Kathleen Higgins, 151–86. Lanham, MA: Roman and Littlefield, 1993.

Serrato-Combe, Antonio. *The Aztec Templo Mayor: A Visualization*. Salt Lake City: University of Utah Press, 2007.

Sharon, Douglas, ed. *Mesas and Cosmologies in Mesoamerica*. San Diego Museum of Man Papers 42. San Diego: San Diego Museum of Man, 2003.

Siméon, Rémi. *Diccionario de la lengua náhuatl o mexicana*. Translated by Josefina Olivia de Coll. México, DF: Siglo Veintiuno Editores, 1977.

Sklar, Lawrence. "Space, Time, and Relativity." In *A Companion to the Philosophy of Science*, edited by W. H. Newton-Smith, 461–69. Oxford: Blackwell, 2000.

Sklar, Lawrence. *Space, Time, and Spacetime*. Berkeley: University of California Press, 1974.

Smart, Ninian. "Symbol and Myth." *Monist* 50, no. 4 (1966): 475–87. http://dx.doi.org /10.5840/monist196650434. (accessed 5/19/2013.)

Smith, Andrea. "Walking in Balance: The Spiritual-Liberation Praxis of Native Women." In *Native American Religious Identity: Unforgotten Gods*, edited by Jace Weaver, 178–98. Maryknoll, NY: Orbis Books, 1998.

Smith, Jonathan Z. *Map Is Not Territory: Studies in the History of Religions*. Chicago: University of Chicago Press, 1993.

Smith, Michael E. *Aztec City-State Capitals*. Gainesville: University of Florida Press, 2008.

Smith, Michael E. *The Aztecs*. Oxford: Blackwell, 1996.

Solís Olguín, Felipe R., curator. *The Aztec Empire*. New York: Guggenheim Museum Publications, 2004.

Solís Olguín, Felipe R., with Roberto Velasco Alonso. "Monuments of Sun Worship." In *The Aztec Calendar and Other Solar Monuments*, Eduardo Matos Moctezuma and Felipe R. Solís Olguín, 79–151. México, DF: Conaculta-Instituto Nacional de Antropología e Historia, 2004.

Solomon, Robert C. *The Big Questions: A Short Introduction to Philosophy*. 5th ed. New York: Harcourt Brace College Publishers, 1998.

Soustelle, Jacques. *Daily Life of the Aztecs on the Eve of the Spanish Conquest*. Translated by Patrick O'Brien. Stanford, CA: Stanford University Press, 1970.

Soustelle, Jacques. *El universo de los Aztecas*. Translated by José Luis Martinez (ch. 1) and Juan José Utrilla (chs. 2–4). México, DF: Fondo de Cultura Económica, 1982.

Spinoza, Benedict de. *Ethics*. Edited and introduction by James Gutman. New York: Hafner Publishing, 1949.

Spores, Ronald L. "Mixtec Religion." In *The Cloud People: Divergent Evolution of the Zapotec and Mixtec Civilizations*, edited by Kent Flannery and Joyce Marcus, 342–45. New York: Academic Press, 1983.

Spranz, Bodo. *Los dioses en los códices mexicanos del Grupo Borgia*. Translated by María Martínez Peñaloza. México, DF: Fondo de Cultura Económica, 1973.

Stresser-Péan, Guy. *The Sun God and the Savior: The Christianization of the Nahua and Totonac in the Sierra Norte de Puebla, Mexico*. Boulder: University Press of Colorado, 2009.

Stuart, David. "Kings of Stone: A Consideration of Stelae in Ancient Maya Ritual and Representation." *RES* 29/30 (Spring/Autumn 1996): 147–71.

Sullivan, Thelma D. "The Mask of Itztlacoliuhqui." In *Actas del XVI Congreso Internacional de Americanistas* [1974], 2: 252–62. México, DF: Instituto Nacional de Antropología e Historia, 1976.

Sullivan, Thelma D. "The Rhetorical Orations, or *Huehuetlatolli*, Collected by Sahagún." In *Sixteenth-Century Mexico: The Work of Sahagún*, edited by Munro S. Edmonson, 79–109. Albuquerque: University of New Mexico Press, 1976.

Sullivan, Thelma D. *A Scattering of Jades: Stories, Poems and Prayers of the Aztecs*. Edited, compiled, and introduction by Timothy Knab. New York: Simon and Schuster, 1994.

Sullivan, Thelma D. "A Scattering of Jades: The Words of the Aztec Elders." In *Symbol and Meaning beyond the Closed Community: Essays in Mesoamerican Ideas*, edited by Gary H. Gossen, 9–17. Albany: Institute for Mesoamerican Studies, 1986.

Sullivan, Thelma D. "Tlazolteotl-Ixcuina: The Great Spinner and Weaver." In *The Art and Iconography of Late Post-Classic Central Mexico*, edited by Elizabeth Hill Boone, 7–36. Washington, DC: Dumbarton Oaks, 1982.

Swann, Brian, ed. *On the Translation of Native American Literatures*. Washington, DC: Smithsonian Institution Press, 1992.

Taber, Barbara, and Marilyn Anderson. *Backstrap Weaving*. New York: Watson-Guptill Publications, 1975.

Taggart, James M. *Nahuat Myth and Social Structure*. Austin: University of Texas Press, 1983.

Tarn, Nathaniel, and Martin Prechtel. "Constant Inconstancy: The Feminine Principle in Atiteco Mythology." In *Symbol and Meaning: Beyond the Closed Community*, edited by Gary Gossen, 173–84. Albany: SUNY Press, Institute for Mesoamerican Studies, 1986.

Tarn, Nathaniel, and Martin Prechtel. *Scandals in the House of Birds: Shamans and Priests on Lake Atitlán*. New York: Marsilio Publishers, 1979.

Taube, Karl. *Aztec and Maya Myths*. Austin: University of Texas Press, 1995.

Taube, Karl. "Maize: Iconography and Cosmological Significance." In *The Oxford Encyclopedia of Mesoamerican Cultures: The Civilizations of Mexico and Central America*, edited by Davíd Carrasco, 2:150–152. Oxford: Oxford University Press, 2001.

Taube, Karl. "The Turquoise Hearth: Fire, Self Sacrifice, and the Central Mexican Cult of War." In *Mesoamerica's Classic Heritage*, edited by Davíd Carrasco, Lindsay Jones, and Scott Sessions, 269–340. Niwot: University Press of Colorado, 2000.

Tedlock, Barbara. *Time and the Highland Maya*. rev. ed. Albuquerque: University of New Mexico Press, 1992. (Original work published 1982).

Tedlock, Barbara. *The Woman in the Shaman's Body: Reclaiming the Feminine in Religion and Medicine*. New York: Bantam Books, 2005.

Tedlock, Barbara, and Dennis Tedlock. "Text and Textile: Language and Technology in the Arts of the Quiché Maya." *Journal of Anthropological Research* 41, no. 2 (1985): 121–46.

Tedlock, Dennis. "Creation in the *Popol Vuh*: A Hermeneutical Approach." In *Symbol and Meaning beyond the Closed Community: Essays in Mesoamerican Ideas*, edited by

Gary H. Gossen, 77–82. Albany, NY: Institute for Mesoamerican Studies, SUNY Press, 1986.

Tedlock, Dennis. "Introduction." In *Popol Vuh: The Definitive Edition of the Mayan Book of the Dawn of Life and the Glories of Gods and Kings*, introduction, translated, and commentary by Dennis Tedlock, 23–66. New York: Simon and Schuster, 1985.

Tedlock, Dennis. *The Spoken Word and the Work of Interpretation*. Philadelphia: University of Pennsylvania Press, 1983.

Tena, Raphael. "La religión mexica: Catálogo de dioses." *Arqueología Mexicana Edición especial*, 30 (2009.

Terraciano, Kevin. *The Mixtecs of Colonial Oaxaca: Ñudzahui History, Sixteenth through Eighteenth Centuries*. Stanford, CA: Stanford University Press, 2001.

Thompson, J. Eric S. *Maya Hieroglyphic Writing: An Introduction*. Norman: University of Oklahoma Press, 1960.

Tilley, Christopher. *A Phenomenology of Landscape: Places, Paths, and Monuments*. Oxford: Berg Publishers, 1994.

Tinker, George. "Jesus, Corn Mother, and Conquest: Christology and Colonialism." In *Native American Religious Identity: Unforgotten Gods*, edited by Jace Weaver, 134–54. Maryknoll, NY: Orbis, 1998.

Tinker, George. "Religion." In *Encyclopedia of North American Indians*, edited by Frederick E. Hoxie, 537–40. Boston: Houghton Mifflin, 1996.

Torquemada, Juan de. *Monarquía indiana: De los veinte y un libros rituales y monarquía indiana, con el origen y guerras de los indios occidentales, de sus poblazones, descubrimiento, conquista, conversión y otras cosas maravillosas de la mesma tierra*, 3rd ed. 7 vols. Coordinated by Miguel León-Portilla. México, DF: Universidad Nacional Autónoma de México, 1975–1983.

The Tovar Calendar: An Illustrated Mexican Calendar ca. 1585. Reproduction and commentary by G. Kubler and C. Gibson. Memoirs of the Connecticut Academy of Arts and Sciences, 11: 1–82. New Haven, CT: Connecticut Academy of Arts and Sciences, 1951.

Townsend, Richard F. *The Aztecs*. London: Thames and Hudson, 1992.

Townsend, Richard F. "Coronation at Tenochtitlan." In *The Aztec Templo Mayor*, edited by Elizabeth Hill Boone, 371–410. Washington, DC: Dumbarton Oaks, 1987.

Townsend, Richard F. "Malinalco and the Lords of Tenochtitlan." In *The Art and Iconography of Late Postclassic Central Mexico*, edited by Elizabeth H. Boone, 111–40. Washington, DC: Dumbarton Oaks, 1982.

Townsend, Richard F. "Moctezuma and the Renewal of Nature." In *Moctezuma: Aztec Ruler*, edited by Colin McEwan and Leonardo López Luján, 124–44. London: British Museum Press, 2009.

Townsend, Richard F. "Pyramid and Sacred Mountain." In *Ethnoastronomy and Archaeoastronomy in the American Tropics*, edited by Anthony Aveni and Gary Urton, 371–410. Annals of the New York Academy of Sciences, no. 38. New York: New York Academy of Sciences, 1982.

Townsend, Richard F. *State and Cosmos in the Art of Tenochtitlan*. Washington, DC: Dumbarton Oaks, 1979.

Trask, Huanani-Kay. *From a Native Daughter: Colonialism and Sovereignty in Hawai'i*. Honolulu: University of Hawaii Press, 1999.

Turetzky, Philip. *Time*. London: Routledge, 1998. http://www.ebookstore.tandf.co.uk /html/searchresult.asp. (accessed 5/19/2013.)

Turner, Victor. "Betwixt and Between: The Liminal Period in Rites of Passage." In *Reader in Comparative Religion: An Anthropological Approach*. 4th ed., edited by William A. Lessa and Evon Z. Vogt, 234–42. New York: Harper and Row Publishers, 1979.

Turner, Victor. "Dewey, Dilthey, and Drama: An Essay in the Anthropology of Experience." In *The Anthropology of Experience*, edited by Victor Turner and Edward Bruner, 33–44. Urbana: University of Illinois Press, 1986.

Turner, Victor. *Dramas, Fields and Metaphors: Symbolic Action in Human Society*. Ithaca, NY: Cornell University Press, 1974.

Vaillant, Georg Clapp. *Aztecs of Mexico*. Revised by Suzannah B. Vaillant. New York: Penguin Books, 1944.

Vega Sosa, Constanza. "El curso del sol en los glifos de la cerámica azteca tarde." *Estudios de cultura náhuatl* 17 (1984): 125–70.

Velasco Lozano, Ana María, and Debra Nagao. "Mitología y simbolismo de las flores." *Arqueología Mexicana* 13, no. 78 (2006): 28–35.

Villa Rojas, Alfonso. "Appendix A: The Concepts of Space and Time among the Contemporary Maya." In *Time and Reality in the Thought of the Maya*, 2nd enlarged ed., by Miguel León-Portilla, 113–59. Norman: University of Oklahoma Press, 1988.

Vogt, Evon Z. "Cardinal Directions and Ceremonial Circuits in Mayan and Southwestern Cosmology." *National Geographic Society Research Reports* 2 (1985): 487–96.

Vogt, Evon Z. *Tortillas for the Gods: A Symbolic Analysis of Zinacanteco Rituals*. Cambridge, MA: Harvard University Press, 1976.

Watanabe, John M. "In the World of the Sun: A Cognitive Model of Mayan Cosmology." *Man* 18, no. 4 (1983): 710–28. http://dx.doi.org/10.2307/2801904. (accessed 5/19/2013.)

Waters, Anne, ed. *American Indian Thought: Philosophical Essays*. Oxford: Blackwell, 2004.

Waters, Anne. "Language Matters: Nondiscrete Nonbinary Dualism." In *American Indian Thought: Philosophical Essays*, edited by Anne Waters, 97–115. Oxford: Blackwell, 2004.

Watts, Alan. *Tao: The Watercourse Way*. New York: Pantheon Books, 1975.

Weaver, Jace, ed. *Defending Mother Earth: Native American Perspectives on Environmental Justice*. Maryknoll, NY: Orbis Books, 1996.

Weaver, Jace. "Introduction: Notes from a Miner's Canary." In *Defending Mother Earth: Native American Perspectives on Environmental Justice*, edited by Jace Weaver, 1–28. Maryknoll, NY: Orbis Books, 1996.

Weaver, Jace. "Preface." In *Native American Religious Identity: Unforgotten Gods*, edited by Jace Weaver, ix–xii. Maryknoll, NY: Orbis Books, 1988.

Weaver, Jace, ed. *Native American Religious Identity: Unforgotten Gods*. Maryknoll, NY: Orbis Books, 1988.

Whitt, Laurie Ann. "Indigenous Peoples and the Cultural Politics of Knowledge." In *Issues in Native American Cultural Identity*, edited by Michael K. Green, 223–71. New York: Peter Lang, 1995.

Wolters, Clifton. *The Cloud of Unknowing*. Baltimore: Penguin Books, 1961.

Wylie, Alison. *Thinking from Things: Essays in the Philosophy of Archaeology*. Berkeley: University of California Press, 2002.

Zantwijk, Rudolph van. *The Aztec Arrangement: The Social History of Pre-Spanish Mexico*. Norman: University of Oklahoma Press, 1985.

Atemoztli festival, 377, 379, 382, 493

atl tlachinolli (flaming water) ideogram, 257n228, **320–21**, *321*, 500. *See also* Fifth Age; warfare or combat

Aveni, Anthony, 227, *229*, 233, 346n305, 498

axis mundi: as channel of *malinalli* energy, 317–19 (*see also* fire, drilling; spinning); as stabilizing center or navel, 100, 105, 110, 298, 301, 316–17, 385–86, 487 (*see also* center or centering; navel or umbilicus); as *yollo* (axis), 222. *See also* Templo Mayor; *teyolia* (vital force)

Ayocuan Cuetzpaltzin, 5

Aztec philosophers: as Nahua *tlamátiquetl* (person of knowledge), 42; as *tlamatinime* (knowers of things), 1, 15, 29, 38, 152, 155, 523, 524, 526–27; as *tlateumatini* (knowledgeable of *teotl*), 108. *See also* epistemology; metaphysics or philosophy

Aztec priests or *tolmatinime* (those who are wise in words), 105, 106. *See also* religion or theology

Aztec process metaphysics, **43–62**; as agonistic *inamic* unity, **137–83**; as ambiguous, 27, **157–59**, 165 (*see also olin* motion-change); approach to understanding, **1–20**, 185–86; assumptions alien to, 4, 7, 16n5, 40, 47, 60, 117, 135n196, 438, 461, 506; as atheistic, 119 (*see also* deity); as biological organism or ecosystem, 28–29, 87, 142, 178n57, 420, 429, 431; as ceaseless movement, change, or transformation, 12–13, 24, 27, 140, 153, 242n1, 242n5, 252n169, 252n171, 254n182, 523; as a cosmogonic, 24, **466–48** (*see also* cosmogony); defined by adverbs (*e.g.,* how, not what), or gerunds (*e.g.,* becoming), 25, 56, 57, 64n10, 102, 140, 153, 170, 360–64, 428–30; defined as balanced or centered, **137–40**, **168–69**, **224–27**, **479–83** (*see also* balance or balancing; center or centering; middle or middling; *nepantla* motion-change); defined by chance, 202; defined by qualitative intensity, 99, 271, 419, 425, 471n61; defined by relationalism, vs. substantivalism, 148, 150, 420–21, **452–65** (*see also* time-place); as holistic, 28–29, **148–52**, 460, 502, 513; importance of metaphors or kennings in, 2, 3, 28, 81, 84, 85, 87, 141–43, 173n12, 178n52, 178n57, 273, 370, 506, 509, 510, 525;

importance of pattern or shape in, 139–40, 189, 403, 479; as macroprocess, 28, 87, 88, 168, 185, **455–64**, 513; as monism (ontological, constitutional, dual-aspect), 12, 13, 21–22, 33, 40, 42, **47–62**, **79–80**, 87, 92, 101–4, 111–14, 118, 120, 126n83, **137–40**, 143, 147, **169–70**, 433, **452–60**, 484, 505 (*see also* dualism; Ometeotl; *teixiptla*); as noneschatological, 23, 91, 143, 151, 152, 448; as nonteleological, 13, 23, 28–29, 91, 151, 152, 448; as ontologically nonhierarchical or pantheistic, **100–13**, **504–8** (*see also* pantheism); as unity, wholeness, or oneness, 153 (*see also* numbers or numerology); as weaving in progress, 509; as web of dynamic interrelationships, crossing threads, or belief, 8–9, 66n66, 149, 421, 457–58, 462, 489, 491, 508, 511; as world in motion, 523–29; as woven way of life, 526. *See also* metaphysics or philosophy; religion or theology; *teotl* (cosmos)

Aztecs, terms for, 1–2. *See also* Nahua

backstrap weaving. *See* weaving

Báez-Jorge, Félix, 221, 508

balance or balancing: as diachronic and dynamic, 152–53, 165–66, 168, 171, 212, 368, 460, 503, 513 (*see also* agonistic *inamic* unity); and imbalance, characterized as slipping, **168–69**, 181n76, 401; as nonhierarchical ordering, 105; as triadic vs. *inamic*, 168–69; as walking, 135, 138–39; as well-balanced or *nepantla*-middled, 383; as well-twilled, 377–78. *See also* middle or middling; *nepantla* motion-change; well-rootedness (*neltiliztli*)

ballcourts: basketball, as time-place, 453–54; sacred (*teotlachtli*), 197–98, *237*; symbolic associations of, 231, 234, 238, 239, 402, 481, 525

ballgame: and balls (*see* rubber); ideogram, 231; as metaphor for cyclical completion, **197–99**, 202, 205; and players, in *inamic* relationship, 149–50, 153; and sweeping, 282; and Xolotl, 204, 207. *See also* chance; *olin* motion-change

banners, sacrificial, 309, 312; spattered with rubber, 197; symbolism of, 324, *325*, 327, 328–29. *See also* paper

Basso, Keith, 36

battens. *See* weaving

Beck, Peggy, 93

being~nonbeing, defined, 153, **164–68**, 447. *See also* dualism, ontology; *inamic* pairs

Berdan, Frances, xiii, 328, 329, 381, 385, 395, 491, 511

Bernasconi, Robert, 5

Beyer, Hermann, 80, 116, 198, 238

Bible, 5, 24

Bierhorst, John, 45, 46, 47, 60, 61, 62, 72n113, 75n142, 76n151, 425, 469n32

Binding of the Years ceremony. *See* xiuhmolpilli

biorhythm. *See* motion-change

birth or childbirth, 100; and birth-merit, 214, 271, 424, 425 (*see also tonalli*); contractions, or fetus stirring, 13, 188, 190, 193, 194, 210, 249n122, 480, 493; death in, 195, 199, 380, 387–88, 398, 487; inducing, 249n122; on mats, 276, 375; and postpartum ritual bathing, 210, 293, 364, 384, 387, 507; as weaving, 171, 359, 372, 379, 382, 483; and womb, uterus, or birth canal, 193, 207, 209, 210, 232, 268, 278, 289, 322–23, 373, 387. *See also* children; midwives or midwifery; navel or umbilicus; pregnancy

Blackfoot, 36

blood, human: as condensed *olin* motion-change, 194; as fiery liquid, 93; and *malinalli* grass, 276; as precious, like water, 197, 209, 306, 315, 328; recycling energy through, 225; as rich in *tonalli*, 271; and symbolic associations of bloodletting, 277, 307, 309, 328; vessels, as rope or cordage, 319. *See also* hearts; rubber; *teyolia* (life force)

blowing. *See* breath or breathing

books: Aztec, 106, 427; of days, 62, 428 (*see also tonalpohualli*); of dreams, 62, 428; and readers, 386; sacred, 39, 141; of *tonallis*, 423 (*see also tonalamatl*); of years, 62, 428, 430 (*see also xiuhamatl*)

Boone, Elizabeth, 33, 249n127, 259n247, 325, 387, 436, 443, 457, 464, 477n190, 514n1

Boyd, Richard, 10

Brady, James, 132n168, 521n123

Brahman, 56–57, 75n143

braiding or plaiting. *See* hair

breath or breathing: or blowing, of newborns, 285, 293; as breath on the mirror (*see* human

perception); energy, 37, 52 (*see also qi*); and kindling fire, 287–88; as life or respiration, and *yol*-rooted words, 190, 191–92 (*see also* blood); as measured blowing, by Ehecatl-Quetzalcoatl, 285; and prayer, 286 (*see also* speaking); and wind-breath-air associations, 286–89; and wind instruments, 285, 287, 288, 293. *See also* creation; *names of vital life forces*

Bright, William, 94

Broda, Johanna, 110–11, 132, 164, 238, 254n180

brooms, 261, 273, 274, **279–82**, 281. *See also* sweeping

Brotherston, Gordon, 198–99, 221, 251n150, 253n173, 253n174, 253n177, 254n180, 474n129

Brumfiel, Elizabeth, xiii, 159, 160, 235, *237*, 257n223, 301, 344, 402, 528n4

Brundage, Burr, 80–81, 198, 205

bundles, sacred. *See* ritual practice

burden, time or energy. *See tonalli* (vital force)

Burkhart, Brian Yazzie, 49

Burkhart, Louise, xi, 30, 33, 82, 93, 224, 405, 475n134, 505; on order~disorder or *tlazolli*, 98–99, 166, 226, 331n25, 395, 396; on sweeping, 281, 337n135

butterfly: as design motif or ideogram, 159, 231, 232, *233*, 238, 239, 240, 241, 343n224, 458, 480, 481, 524; as volatile, 427; as winding of warp thread, 486, 488. *See also* crosses, figure-eight; flint; Itzpapalotl

Cajete, Gregory, 36, 420

calendar. *See* time and calendars

Callaway, Carol, 399

Camaxtli (Lord of Hunting), 305, 313–14, 379. *See also* Mixcoatl

Campbell, R. Joe, xiii, 100, 369, 431, 489–90; and *Florentine Codex*, 77n164; on *inamic*, 144, 146; on *malinalli*, 263–64, 331n14, 332n31, 353n420; on *nepantla*, 357, 362, 404n8, 413n159

Cantares mexicanos, 43, 46, 47, 60, 72n109, 76n149, 76n151, 109, 287, 290

Carlsen, Robert, 63n8, 229, 379, 388, 399

Carrasco, Davíd, xi, xiii, 96, 224, 231, 242n6, 351n389, 504; on cosmic time, 255n194, 428, 435, 436, 447, 449–51, 459, 472n83, 475n136, 476n159; on cosmo-magical cosmovision, 135n196, 457; on sacred vs. profane, *axis mundi*, or Templo Mayor, 33, 100, 103, 110–11, 164, 256n202, 317

Caso, Alfonso, 16, 119, 120, 121–22n6, 188, 254n184
causality: or causal explanations, 1, 3, 8, 9, 21, 89, 115, 428, 429, 448, 451; vs. correlationality, 65–66n19, 178n52; and objects or practices, as causally potent, 230, 257n223, 279, 286, 287, 291, 306, 403. *See also* philosophy of science
caves, as portals, 352n393; symbolic associations of, 232, 267
Celestial Creativity-Divine Paternalism deity complex, 88–89, 283, 285, 295
center or centering: and ambiguity of fifth orientation, **224–27**, 320, 325, 417n241; cellular-modular model of, 105–6, 109; and circumambulation, 299–300, 306, 346n305; of corncob, 189; as earth-navel-center, 316, 386 (*see also axis mundi*); of jade bead, 231 (*see also* ideograms, four-petal); of *patolli* board and Fifth Sun movement, 200–1 (*see also* crosses; crossroads); and periphery, as triadic vs. *inamic* relationship, 137, **168–69**, 222, 281, 314, 390, 483, 505–6, 519n104, 527 (*see also tlazolli*); as shape and centeredness of oscillating energy, 13, 193, 223, 241, 398, 400, 442 (*see also olin* motion-change); as zenith, 222. *See also* balance or balancing; middle or middling
centipedes, 33, 95, 267–68, 372, 388, *389*, 391, 395; as frayed mat snake, 373
Chalchiuhtlicue (She of Jade Skirt), 85, 90, 157, 323–24, 439, 450
chance, luck, or gaming: and the Fifth Age, 202, 226–27; and rubber balls, 198–99; and Tezcatlipoca factor, 168, 202, 226. *See also* ballgame; *patolli*
Chantico (In the House), 295
Chatino, 34
Cherokee, 36, 40
Chichimeca, 62, 297, 313–14, 527
Chicnauhnepaniuhcan (Place of the Nine Heavens), 364–67, 507. *See also* Omeyocan
Chicomecoatl (Seven Snake), 160, 282
Chicomexochitl (Seven Flower), 372
Chicontepec, Veracruz, 116, 221, 224, 508
children, 48, 280, 379, 384, 387, 401, 495; and childrearing or childhood, 1, 213, 419, 420, 459; newborn or infant, 188, 213, 285–86, 293, 295, 364, 384–85, 451, 507; sacrifice of, 197. *See also* birth or childbirth

chinampas (agricultural plots), as woven fields, 378, 526
Cihuacoatl (Woman-Snake), 208, 274, 379, 383, 442, 488; Song of, 282, 494
Cihuateteo (angry goddesses) or Cihuapipiltin (Noble Women), 387–88; with centipede, *389*, 391; and Cihuateocalli (Shrine of the Women), 383, 389; and Cihuatlampa (Place of Women), 387; and power of forked or crossing roads, 387–90, 390–91, 393, 395, 396, 398, 400 (*see also* crossroads); as women unfulfilled as weavers, 388; as women who died giving birth, 380, 387, 388, 487 (*see also* birth or childbirth)
Cinteotl (God of Corn), 98, 160, 273, 283, 334n63. *See also* maize or corn
Cipactli (primordial caiman), 51, 380, 437, 450; as day sign 422, 426
Cipactonal~Oxomoco. *See* Omoxoco~Cipactonal
circumambulation. *See* center or centering
cleansing or cleaning. *See tlazolli* (filth or pollution)
cloth or clothing: cotton preferred over maguey, 273; as folded skirt or blanket, 30, *509* (*see also* folds or folding); loincloth or breechcloth, 399; production of fabricated textile or woven, 87, 141, 273, 308, 372, 375, 376, 356, 456, 457, 483, 495, 506, 522n137; as sacrificial vestment or ritual garment (*teoquemitl*), 31, 283, 379, 383, 512 (*see also teixiptla*); as tied together, in marriage ritual, 357. *See also* cotton; headgear; tribute; weaving
Coatlicue (Skirt of Serpents), 162–63, 207
Codex Borbonicus, 107, 160, *161*, 206, 233, *234*, *239*, 279, 282, *287*, 309, 311, 312, 324, *325*, 373, 383, 386, 412n118, 435, 494, 511
Codex Borgia, 160, *162*, 170, 206, 210, *239*, *241*, 259n247, 291, 312, *326*, *327*, 328, 380, 388, *389*, 391, 393, 443–44, 487, 514n1
Codex Chimalpopoca, 446
Codex Cruz, 261
Codex Dresden, 288
Codex Fejérváry-Mayer, 110, 160, 233, 235, 238, 296, 312, 316, 319, *326–27*, 372, 390, *391–92*, 393, 400, 401, 422, 423, 427, 498, 500, 502, 505, 524; as cosmogram, *202*, 441, 458–59. *See also tonalamatl* (book of days)

uncreated patterns or things, vs. created, 50, 139–40, 151. *See also* birth or childbirth; breath or breathing; Celestial Creativity-Divine Paternalism deity complex; fertility; fire; Rain, Moisture, and Agricultural Fertility deity complex; ritual sacrifice; sexual intercourse

crosses: Greek or Christian (+-shaped), 230, 321; Maltese, 233; St. Andrews (X-shaped), 230, 233; symbolic associations of, or cruciforms generally, 365–67, 378–79, 385–86, 399–401, *402*, 422. *See also* ideograms; quatrefoil; quincunx

crossroads: ambiguity of, 361, **386–87, 393–94**, 397, 400–2, 527; comparing *nepan-* vs. *maxatl-*rooted words, **393–97**; contrasting intersecting vs. forking, as metaphor for *tlazolli*, **397–401**; and forked (*otlamaxac*) or Y-shaped bifurcating roads, **393–401**; ideogram, 402; as *nepantla* or *onepanco*, 361–62, **386–402**, 524, 527; as regenerative, 390–91. *See also* agonistic *inamic* unity; *nepantla* motion-change; *ohtli* (path or road); quincunx

dance or dancing: as *inamic*, 153, 180n73; of monkey, 309; as *nepantla*-middled, 383, 524; ritual or sacred, 297, 298, 303–4, 306, 346n294, 378, 384, 401; of spindle, 266, 290, 302, 323

dao (formative energy), 25, 37–38, 91, 118, 120, 166; and Taoist/Daoist metaphysics, 4, 64n12, 97, 527n2

Davies, Nigel, 143

day or days: and dawn, twilight, or sun-night, 311; as deathday~birthday, of 4 Olin (Fifth Sun), 212–14, 227 (see also *xiuhmolpilli*); four (*nahuilhuiti*), and movement of Fifth Sun, 446 (*see also* numbers or numerology); as *ilhuitl* or *ilhuicatl* units, in daylight, sky, solar-day concepts, 215, 445–46, 463–64, *465* (*see also* sky); and Maya sun-day-time (*see kinh*); and midday, midnight, sunrise, or sunset, 222, 227, *228, 229*, 384, 387, 390 (*see also* astronomy; zenith); *nemontemi* (uncounted, unnamed), 226, 431, 439, 442, 444; as *tonalli* and *xihuitl* units, in daycount, day-name, day-sign, time-place concepts, **212–19, 423–46**, 457, 463–64, 494,

498, 501 (*see also* day name *or* day sign *under subjects*). *See also* time-place; *tonalli* (vital force); *tonalpohualli*; *xiuhpohualli*

death. *See* life~death

deity: as god, saint, demon, or *hombre-dios*, 31–32, 82, 132n154, 133n178, 196; as naming convention for complex, cluster, or pantheon, 80–81, 84, **86–91**, 97, 98, 124n37, 149, 157, 204, 208, **215–19**, 217, 218, 226, 283, 339n154, 372, 427, 431, 433, 488; as nonpersonal, nonminded, nonintentional agent or being, 12, 22–23, 25, 36, 80. *See also* dualism; pantheism; religion or theology; sacred; *teixiptla* (deity impersonator or image); *teotl* (cosmos)

Deloria, Vine, Jr., 35–36, 37, 49, 63n3, 64n14, 65n19, 93, 136n218, 347n305, 466n10, 476n175

Descartes, René, 7

Dewey, John, 7

Dibble, Charles, 61, 299, 362, 364, 390, 400

digging sticks, 382, 491, 493

directions, cardinal: and cosmic East, West, North, South, 203, 217–18, 221–23, 374, 422, 441, 458–59, 498 (*see also* time-place); and importance of intercardinal orientations and center, 169, 200, 222, 346n305, 442, 464, 487–88 (*see also* center or centering; solstice or equinox); not as fixed compass points, 221, 222, 223, 253n177, 498 (*see also* astronomy); symbolic associations of, 105, 107, 110, 164, 231–32, 235, 238–39, 296, 297, 298, 300, 303, 306, 307, 380–81, 385, 427, 439, 503 (*see also* axis mundi; crossroads; *patolli*; quincunx; ritual sacrifice); and two directions, or bidirectionality, 276, 317, 318, 488 (*see also* numbers or numerology, twoness)

divination: as casting auguries or divining future, 85, 116, 209, 226, 275, 278, 423, 435–36, 510–11; and counting-reading-interpreting (*see* time and calendars); and first diviners, 376, 436 (*see also* tonalamatl). *See also* maize; shamans or shamanism; water

divine. *See* sacred

Dōgen, Zen master, 57

dogs: as day sign, 422; symbolic associations of, 204. *See also* Xolotl

Dow, James, 74n140, 115, 396

dreams or dreaming: book of (*temicamatl*), 62, 428; as dreamlike or out-of-body visions, 42, 93, 96; as source of knowledge, 10, 45–46, **59–62**; or *temiqui*-rooted words, 61, 62, 77n164, 145; and *tonalli* leaving sleeping body, 60–61. *See also* divination; epistemology; human perception; *tonalli* (vital force)

drilling. *See* fire, drilling

dualism: Christian, 29–30; vs. constitutional monism, 11, 47–54, 138; as dichotomy of sacred or supernatural, vs. profane, 80, 92, 96, 100 (*see also* sacred); as hierarchical, vs. nonhierarchical ordering, 100–1, 104, 112, 113; Mesoamerican or Native American, 143, 171, 174–75n20; as metaphysical relationalism, immanence, or permanence, 148, 170, 256n202, 428, 429 (*see also* agonistic *inamic* unity); vs. ontological monism, 11, 54–59, 59–62, 118; as ontology of Being (*i.e,* Plato's Reality), vs. of Becoming, 4, 11–12, 24–27, 30, 40–41, **43–47**, 55, 75n143, 87, 96, 165, 371, 506 (*see also* Aztec process metaphysics, monism); Zoroastrian or Manichean, 143, 155. *See also* metaphysics or philosophy; religion or theology

Duhem, Pierre, 9

Durán, Fray Diego, 11, 94, 120, 187, 192, 196, 199, 203, 224, 232, 238, 276, 282, 299, 307, 313, 323–24, 324, 355, 372, 376, 377, 378, 380, 383, 386, 488, 506; and *Book of the Gods and Rites* and *The Ancient Calendar*, 200, 301, 302; and *History of the Indies of New Spain (Historia de las Indias de Nueva España)*, 95, 231, 302, 345n267

Durkheim, Émile, 96

dwarves, 204

eagle, 39, 321, 386; day sign, 387, 389, 422, 425; feathers, 270, 301; foot, 207; mat, 376; men, as captives, 298, 302; and ocelot, 153–54; vessel (*cuauhxicalli*), 196, 237, 298, 302, 309; warriors, 232, 306, 376. *See also atl tlachinolli* (flaming water) ideogram; warfare or combat

earth: monster, 51, 207, 231, 380, 390, 425, 440, 521n123; navel (*tlalxicco*) or center, 224–25, 316–17 (*see also* navel or umbilicus); as slippery, 167, 181n76, 525–26; or *tlalli*, and *tlal*-rooted words, 109, 113, 191–2, 208, 225, 255n191, 292, 316, 351n378, 385. *See also* Fifth

Sun-Earth Ordering; Rain, Moisture, and Agricultural Fertility deity complex; *tlalticpac* (earth's surface)

earthquakes, 13, 34, 186, 188, 189, 192, 193, 194, 213, 214, 480

earwigs, 395

Ehecatl (Wind) or Ehecatl-Quetzalcoatl: and blowing, **284–89** (*see also* breath or breathing); breathing Fifth Age to life, 206, 286–89, 445; creating humans 442; day sign, 422; as Ehecatl-Ozomatli, 309, *310*, 311; and incantations, 314; and Pahtecatl, 310, 311; as Rain-Moisture-Agricultural Fertility deity complex, 86, 283, 324, 339n154; spiral temples or shell ideograms, 285, 289, 321–23; and sweeping or blowing, drilling, kindling fire, 280, 281, 283, **284–89**; and Tlalteotl, 317. *See also malinalli* motion-change; Ometeotl; Quetzalcoatl

Eliade, Mircea, 71n91, 96, 100, 133n178, 256n202, 449, 508

Elzey, Wayne, 224, 252n169, 254n185, 355, 361, 386, 442–44, 458, 505, 518n88

epistemology: xi, 2, 4, 5, 8–9, 10, 15, 20n32; as comprehension or perceptual ability, 29, **50–54**, 167 (*see also* human perception); and deception, 40–41, 42 (*see also* masks or masking); and dreams, **59–62**; as epistemological strategy, **54–59**, 86; as knowable reality, vs. unknowable, 96, 100, **116–18** (*see also* sacred); as praxis or ritual time-place, 1, 275, 377, 401, 427, 505, 523, 524, 526 (*see also* ritual practice). *See also* Aztec philosophers; Aztec process metaphysics; dreams or dreaming; dualism; human perception

equinox. *See* solstice or equinox

Ermine, Willie, 36

eschatology. *See* Aztec process metaphysics

Estrada, Viviana Jímenez, 153

ethics or conduct, 2, 178n53, 277, **523–29**; and morality of good and evil, 23, 155, 178n53; of *nepantla*, 526; as path, 1, 313, 350n368, 399; Western vs. Aztec prescriptive, 525. *See also* balance or balancing; human existence; middle or middling; reciprocity

ethnography. *See* Nahua, ethnographic studies

Etzalcualiztli (Eating of Etzalli), 378

eyes, 53, 56, 111, 163, 208–9, 216, 238, 267; extruded, and sacrifice, 325–26, *327*, 328;

layers or layering, of cosmos: 14, 30, 215–16, **219–20**, 225, 283, 287, 289–90, 292, 295–97, 311, 317–19, 329, 364, 367, 377, 437, 439, 447, 452, 458, 500, 502; concurrent multiple, as time-place, *462*; as vertical, nonhierarchical, 481, **504–8**. *See also* Fifth Sun-Earth Ordering; folds or folding; layers *under subjects*

Lee Jongsoo, 120

Legend of the Suns (*Leyenda de los soles*), 158, 203, 212, 213, 214, 248n98, 284, 289, 292, 295, 309, 343n223, **432–46**, 448, 503

Leibniz, Gottfried, 455

León-Portilla, Miguel: on Aztec philosophy and *La Filosofía Náhuatl* (*Aztec Thought and Culture: A Study of the Ancient Nahuatl Mind*), xi, 5, 6–7; on cosmograms and cardinal directions, 251n150, 252n171, 254n188, 307; on crossroads, 393, 400; on deity or sacred, cosmology, and time-place, 48–49, 95, 408n53, 433–34, 437, 439, 442, 448, 449, 456–57, 458; on dreams, 60–62; on heart, 108, 190, 191, 194; on *inamic*, 144; on *nepantla*, 368; on *olin*, 223, 224, 258n232; on pan-chronotheism, pantheism, or Ometeotl, 84, **116–21**, **169–72**; on *patolli*, 202, 235; on song-poems, 39, 43–47; on sweeping, 391; on *tonalli*, 468n23; on transcendence, 117; on well-rootedness, 101–2

Levinas, Emmanuel, 5

Levine, Michael, 91–92, 116–17, 119, 121n2, 447; and *Pantheism: A Nontheistic Concept of Deity*, 79

Lévy-Bruhl, Lucien, 37

life~death: as ambiguous creative/alive/fleshed, vs. destructive/dead/skeletal, **157–59**, **164–68**, 194; as biological metaphor, 178n57; as cyclical completion, or single process, 208, 480–82; as mutually dependent, 147. *See also* Fifth Sun-Earth Ordering; *inamic* pairs (complementary polarities); life~death *under subjects*; masks or masking; *olin* motion-change; Xolotl

lightning, 32, 81, 89, 90, 93, 283, 291, 292, 351–52n389; bolts, 157

liminality. *See nepantla* motion-change

Lipp, Frank, 215, 226

Lloyd, Genevieve, 49, 65n19, 92

Locke, John, 7

Lockhart, James, 105, 106, 109, 264

loom, backstrap. *See* weaving

López Austin, Alfredo, xi, xiii; on animism or sacred essences, 115, 124n37; on color symbolism, 107; on cosmology, on cosmovision, 141, 457, 510; counting time, or *Tamoanchan, Tlalocan*, 32, 432, 435, 436, 449, 450, 451, 459, 460, 463, 475n136, 507, 519n99; on dreams, 60–61; on dualism, binary categories, or *inamic* pairs, **50–54**, 138, 143, **148–55**, 164, 170, 177n50, 215–16; on human body or navel, 225, 315, 316, 319; on *ixiptla* (image), 113; on *ixtli* (face), 48; on *malinalli*, 262, 277, 317, 318, 320, 325, 504; on Mesoamerican pantheon or polytheism, 83, 84, 90; on *nepantla* or crosses, **364–68**, 386, 394, 399; on *olin* or center, 189, 190, 193, 198, **224–27**, 239, 242n6; on Quetzalcoatl, 283, 286, 348n333; on *tonalli*, 270, 424, 468n23

López Luján, Leonardo, 100, 110, 239, 260n272, *268*, 297, 386, 415n198

Lovejoy, Arthur, 30, 506, 519n105

Macuilxochitl (Five Flower), 226, 384

Madsen, William, 149

magic, 31; as problematic term, 116, 71n91, 135n196, 350n365. *See also* shamans or shamanism

maguey: fiber (*ixtle*), 262, 269, 273, 283, 308, 309, 383, 483 (*see also* cloth or clothing); hat, 348n338 (*see also* headgear); and *malinalli* transformation, 206, 262, 308–9, 314, 383; sap fermented as *octli* (*pulque*), 87, 308, 348n338; thorns, 248n103, 277, 309, 312, 373

Maimonides, 7

maize or corn, 27, 85, 283; casting kernels of, 209, 436, 510–11 (*see also* divination); as Chicomecoatl or Xilonen, 282; as Cinteotl, or mature, 98, 160, 273, 283, 334n63; grinding, as transformative process, 218, 315, 382, 493; as metaphor for sustenance, 302; and phases of maturation, 218; silk, 273; stew of victim's thigh, 298, 304; symbolic associations of, 107, 108, 211, 459, 493, 494; tortillas, 24, 27, 33, 54, 95, 100, 149, 297; water, 486; as Xolotl, 204, 206

male~female: as bride~groom or newlyweds, *145*, 148, 357 (*see also* marriage); and direction of Fifth Age, 198; as father/man~mother/woman partners, 51, **154–58**, 164, 170, 369, 375,

140, 148, 150, 165, 256n202, 363, 426, 461, 506, 519n105; Mesoamerican or North American indigenous, 4–8, **35–37**, 49, 143, 174–75n20, 466n10; and methods, **8–12**, 186; as ontology of Being vs. Becoming (*see* dualism); as ontology of the ambiguous, 13, 23, 27, 37, 48, 89–90, 99, **157–59**, 321, 363 (*see also* agonistic *inamic* unity; ambiguity *under subjects*; being~nonbeing; dualism; masks or masking; *tlazolli*); substantivalist vs. relationalist theories in, **452–65** (*see also* time-place); as way-centered or way-finding, vs. truth-seeking, 19n21, 97, 102, 106, 526 (*see also* well-rootedness); Western assumptions and prejudices of, xi, 4–12, 15n1, 17n12, 38, 54–55, 135n196, 155. *See also* Aztec process metaphysics; epistemology

Mexica-Tenocha, 2. *See also* Tenochtitlan

Meyer, Leroy, 36

Mictlan (Underworld, Land of the Dead), 110, 158, 198, 203, 341n186, 442; as *chicnauhmictlan*, or nine-layered, 216, 504, 506; as layer of cosmos, 65n16, 437, 504; as loom bar, 496; and Xolotl, 204–6, 283–84

Mictlantecuhtli, 149, 238, 289, 292, 390, 341n186, 390; deity complex, 89; and Mictlantecuhtli-Mictecacihuatl, 437, 450; as Mictlantecuhtli-Quetzalcoatl, 160, *162*; 238, 259n247

middle or middling, **168–69**; as levels or regions of cosmos, **219–20**, 431, 437, 439, 458, 488, 496, 502, **504–8**; and middle age, 211, 282, 374 (*see also* layers or layering); as mutuality, moderation, or caution, **523–29**; as *nepantla* processing, 14, **172**, **355–64**, 371, 376, 377, **383–86**, 403, 480, 487, 491, 495, 503, 509, 513. *See also* balance or balancing; center or centering; ethics or conduct; reciprocity; well-rootedness (*neltiliztli*)

midwives or midwifery, 208, 210, 275, 278, 285–86, 293, 295, 364, 379, 384–85, 507. *See also* birth or childbirth; children

military struggle. *See* warfare or combat

Miller, Arthur, 230

Miller, Ellen, 35

milpas (cultivated fields), 105, 106, 109, 129, 275, 501–2

Mixcoatl (Cloud Serpent), 89, 324; drilling original fire, 291, 293, 294; as

Mixcoatl-Camaxtli (Lord of Hunters) 296–97, 313–14

Mixe, 68n64, 215

Mixtec (Nuyoo), 22, 34–35, 276, 375, 382, 490, 493; conceptions of religion or *yii* (sacred principle), 34, 49, 64n14, 69n73, 120, 293

Moctezuma II or Motecuhzoma Xocoyotzin, 313, 376, 378, 379, 471n66, 506

Molina, Alonso de, 11, 95, 106, 118, 128n94, 245n70, 324, 331n14, 336n111; on counting, 506; on crossroads, 393, 394, 395, 400; on dreams, 61, 76n158; on fire, 290, 292; on hearts, 190, 192, 225; on *inamic*, 144–45; on *malinalli*, 262, 264, 279, 332n25; on navels, 315, 316, 350n371, 350n373; on *nepantla*, 355, 356, 357, 361, 362, 526; on *ollin*, 187, 196; on time, 419, 431; on *tonalli*, 485n20, 468n22, 468n23; and *Vocabulario en lengua castellana y mexicana y mexicana y castellana*, 76n156, 187; 516n30; on warfare, 369; on weaving, 376, 381, 404n8, 485, 489–90, 491, 516n42

Momaday, N. Scott, 467n13

Monaghan, John: on animism, pantheism, or the sacred, 34, 49, 63n8, 85, 86, 92, 93, 115, 133n178, 135n199; on personhood or destiny, 424; on twoness, 171, 368–69; on weaving, 490

monism, ontological. *See* Aztec process metaphysics, monism

monkeys, 309, 311; day sign, 422

monotheism. *See* religion or theology

moon (*meztli*), 49, 85, 208, 295, 429, 431, 452, 504; crescent-shaped, nosepiece, 312

morality. *See* ethics or conduct

mother-goddess. *See* Rain, Moisture, and Agricultural Fertility deity complex

motion-change: as backstrap weaving, **483–95** (*see also* weaving); as becoming, 465, 512 (*see also* time-place); as biorhythm of Fifth Age, 14, 194, 213–14, 232, 241, 329, 420, 429, 431, 481, 482 (*see also* Fifth Sun-Earth Ordering); comparing *malinalli*, *nepantla*, *olin*, 359, 365–67, **479–83**; as dynamics of cosmos, **479–83** (*see also* Aztec process metaphysics); as how things move-change, 193–94, 213–14, 218, 223, 263, 241, 371, 423, 441, 481; as interlacing, vs. coiling, 367; as *nepantla* eurhythmy, 482; as ordering, of macro- and micro-processes, 513 (*see also* balance or balancing; center or centering; middle or middling); as processing, of Sun-Earth Ages, **495–504** (*see also* Fifth Sun-Earth Ordering); as sacred energy-in-motion, 62 (*see also teotl*); as shape, pattern, or path, 139, 185, 188, 189, 190, 229, 241, 260n259, 329, 403, 479; as struggle, **172** (*see also* agonistic *inamic* unity; *inamic* pairs); as transformation within/across, vs. betwixt/between, or back/forth, over/above, down/under *tlaticpac*, 13–15, 186, **241**, 266, **329–30, 403**, 480–82, 491, 495–96, *497, 499, 500* (*see also* Tonatiuh); as vertical folding, of cosmos, **504–8** (*see also* folds or folding). *See also malinalli* motion-change; *nepantla* motion-change; *olin* motion-change

Motolinía, Toribio de Benavente, 11, 120, 196, 279, 308, 430

Muñoz Camargo, Diego: and *Historia de Tlaxcala*, 399

music, 93, 108, 115, 285, 372, 383, 401, 481, 482–83, 526; and musical instruments, 50, 288–89, 324; and musicians, 287. *See also in xochitl in cuicatl* (flower and song)

Myerhoff, Barbara, 96, 168, 406n26

Nahua: ethnographic studies of contemporary, 11, 34, 62, 65n16, 77n170, 83, 116, 157, 186, 191, 221, 224–25, 332n38, 395, 396, 508, 511; as Mexica-Tenocha, or Aztecs, 1–2

nahual (also *nahualli, nagual*), 39–42, 58, 204, 248n100, 284; and *nahuallatolli* (secret or hidden words), 115, 274, 287; as *tonalli*, coessence, or companion animal, 424. *See also* shamans or shamanism; *teotl* (cosmos)

Nahuatl language-speakers, 107, 186–88, 355

Nanahuatzin (Little Pustule Covered One), 107, 206, 248n103, 286, 295, 445

nature: as alive, 115; as earth's things, 65n16; as face (*ixtli*), 48; forces or processes of, 32, 32; as Great, 37; as spiritual, vs. material, 36. *See also* earth; sacred; *teotl* (cosmos); *tlaticpac* (earth's surface)

Navajo, 36, 135n196

navel or umbilicus: of captive, in sacrifice, 298, 301, 487; of earth (*tlalxicco*), 107, 224–25, 301, **315–19**, 385; and human umbilical cord (*ximecayotl*), 225, 315–16. *See also axis mundi*; birth or childbirth

neltiliztli. See well-rootedness

nepantla motion-change, **355–418**; compared to liminality or paradox, 362–64, 406n26, 527n1; and crossroads, **386–401, 401–2**; defined as dynamics of Aztec cosmos, and *nepan*-rooted words, 13–15, 185, **355–68**, **479–522**; ideograms and symbolic associations of, **401–3** (*see also* crosses; reciprocity; spinning; twilling; weaving); and middling, **355–63, 383–86** (*see also* marriage; middle or middling; sexual intercourse); and Ometeotl/*teotl* (cosmos), **368–75**; and Omeyocan, **364–68**; and stretching, **380–83** (*see also* center or centering; stretching); as weaving, **371–75, 379–83, 495–502**; (*see also* Tlazolteotl-Ixcuina); woven house or way of life, balanced by, 106, **375–79, 503–4, 512–13, 523–29**. *See also* motion-change

Neumann, Erich, 508, 511

Neumann, Franke, 466n6

New Fire ceremony, 107, 195, 233, *234*, 256n213, 282, 288, 291, 293–94, 384, 385. *See also xiuhmolpilli*

Newton, Isaac, 182n92, 454

Nezahualcoyotl, 5, 39, 43–47, 120, 122n6

Nezahualpilli, 506

Nicholson, Henry B., xi; on cosmology, 432, 473n95; on deity complexes or clusters, 88, 89, 120, 124n44, 157, 169, 170, 208, 209, 268, 283, 295, 305, 347n312, 372, 379, 488; on fire, 318; on numbers, 215, 226

Nicholson, Irene, 163

Night Lords, or Lords of the Night, 216, 390, 426, 427, 458, 469n37, 471n62

Nowotny, Karl Anton, 207

numbers or numerology: as concrete metaphysical forces, 215, 426; and five, as excess or uncertainty, 224–27 (*see also* Tezcatlipoca); and four (*nahui*) or quadruplicity, as metaphysical completeness, 177n50, 215–19, 373–74, 385–86, 391, 402, **422–23**, 427, 434, 439–42, 458, 459, 464, 481, 501–2, **502–3** (*see also* day or days; directions, cardinal; *tonalpohualli*); and nine, as cross-shaped or inauspicious, 30, 215–16, 364–67, 506–7; and oneness, 153, 171–72, 217, 419, 368, 397, 433, 466; and thirteen or *trecena*, as auspicious, 30, 203, 206–7, 208, 215, 309, 364, 419, 420, 425–27, 432, 434–35, 469n33, 506–7; and twenty, 203, 219, 432, 434 (*see also* time and calendars); and two or twoness, as wholeness, 51, 147, 153, 162, 169, 171–72, 217, 219, 317, 318, 368, 397 (*see also* agonistic *inamic* unity; Omeyocan); and use of numeral classifier (*tlamantli*), 506–7; as vertical folding of cosmos, **504–8**; Maya, 215. *See also* folds or folding; *nepantla* motion-change

obsidian: butterfly, 208, 232, 343n224; knives or knife-tongue, 232–33, 327; place (underworld), 318; as sacred, 93; symbolic associations of, 297; war club, 299
Ochpaniztli (Sweeping the Path or Way) ritual. *See* sweeping
Ockham, William of, 7
octli (pulque), 87, 226, 299, 306, 307–10, 313, 314, 348n338; and divine intoxication, 87, 308; and Ehecatl-Quetzalcoatl, as inventor of, 348n338; vessels for, 311; and war or sacrifice, 303, 311–12
ohtli (path or road), 241, 338n146, 361, 393–94, 481, 523; of the dead, 221. *See also* crossroads; ethics or conduct; motion-change; sweeping; path *under subjects*
olin motion-change, **185–260**; and ambiguity of fifth orientation, **224–27** (*see also* agonistic *inamic* unity; center or centering); and ballgame or *patolli*, **197–99**, **199–202**; day name (4 Olin) glyph, and symbolic associations, 195–96, 206, **212–19**, 222, *229*, *234*, **236–41**, *239*, *240*, *241*, 301, 464, 481 (*see also* Fifth Sun-Earth Ordering, 4 Olin Tonatiuh); day sign (Olin), **203–12**, 213, 366, 384 (*see also* directions, cardinal; Tlazolteotl; *tonalpohualli*; Xolotl); defined, and *ollin* or *olli*-rooted words, 13–15, **172**, **185–96**, 212–14, 218, **229–30**, 296, 329–30, 374, 480–82; and heart energy, **194–96** (*see also* hearts; ritual sacrifice; *teyolia*); and *olli*, **196–99** (*see also* rubber); and weaving, 210–11, 218, 228, 235, 240, *265*, 266, **495–502** (see also battens; spindle; spinning; weaving). *See also* motion-change
Olivier, Guilhem, 115, 286, 288, 369, 522n146
Olmec, 108, 237
Olmos, Andrés de, 188, 262, 264, 285, 286
Ometeotl (Two Sacred Energy, Two-Teotl, God of Duality) deity complex, 51, 82,

88–89, 116–20, 137, **169–72**, 225, 283, 295, 316, **368–75**, 397, 433, 440, 449, 451, 480, 482, 504, 509; as appropriate sexuality, 397 (*see also* sexual intercourse); as interchangeable with *teotl* and time-place; 116, 460–63; also Ometecuhtli~Omecihuatl (Two-Lord~Two-Lady), 149, 285–86, 293, 433; as progenitor~progenetrix of cosmos, 446. *See also* Celestial Creativity-Divine Paternalism deity complex; creation; male~female; numbers or numerology; teotl (cosmos)
Omeyocan (Two-Place, Place of Unified Twoness), 51, 171–72, 370, 371, 429, 451, 452, 460–61, 507–8; as *nepantla* motion-change, **364–68**. *See also* Chicnauhnepaniuhcan; Tamoanchan
Omitecuhtli (Bone Lord), 119, 217, 434, 449, 503
order~disorder, **153–55**, **164–67**; as nonhierarchical ordering, 99, **100–13**. *See also inamic* pairs; *tlazolli* (filth or pollution)
Orozpe Enríquez, Mauricio, 180n70, 403
Orr, Heather, 198, 205
Ortiz, Alfonso, 455
Otomí, 34, 42, 82, 84, 85, 114, 323, 512
Owen, H. P., 92
Oxomoco~Cipactonal: as first diviners, 376, 436 (*see also* divination; *tonalamatl*); giving birth to humans (*macehualtin*), 435; as plural singularity, 408n55 (*see also* Ometeotl); as primordial man and woman, 62, 160, 427, 435–39, 443, 437, 450, 451; as time-place, 460; as *tonalpohualli* creators (lords of the day count), 386, 472n79, 510–11

Pace, Edward, 119–20
Pahtecatl, **307–12**, 313–14. *See also octli* (pulque)
painting-writing, 39, 141
paired opposites. *See inamic* pairs (complementary polarities)
pantheism, 11, 16–17n5, **79–136**, 502; compared to panentheism or panpsychism, 79, 92, 121; compared to polytheism, **86–92**; defined as *teotl* (cosmos), **79–85**; as nonsalvific, 155; as non-theistic, 79, 80, 81, 91, 119, 447; as pan-chronotheism, 84; as syncretic, 82, 83, 406n26. *See also* animism; time-place
Pantitlan, 323–24, 379, 384. *See also* spirals or spiraling

paper, 141, 264, 309, 463, 507; Aztec offerings of, and liquid rubber, 187, 196, 197; clothing, 365, 379, 391; ritual cutting of, 42, 82, 83–84, 114, 379, 396, 512. *See also* banners; books; cloth or clothing

Pasztory, Esther, 159–60

path. *See ohtli* (path or road)

patolli (board game), **199–202**: as *olin*, 199, 200, 201–2; symbolic associations of, 161, 226, 231, 235, 238, 239, 402, 454, 481. *See also* chance; directions, cardinal

pattern or patterning: as first-order ordering~disordering, 139–40; of rhythmic *olin* and *malinalli* motion-change, 355, 376–77, 382, 383, 402, 403; of time-place, **455–65**; of *tonalpohualli* and *xiuhpohualli*, **423–32**; in weaving, **140–43**. *See also nepantla* motion-change; time and calendars; weaving

Peñafiel, Antonio, 274, 338n150

Pepper, Steven, 141, 142, 173n12

perception. *See* human perception

periphery. *See* center or centering

Peterson, Jeanette Favrot, 258n229, 261, 262, *267, 268*, 274, 277, 282, 328

philosophy. *See* metaphysics or philosophy

philosophy of science, xi, **8–12**. *See also* causality

place, landscape, or space. *See* time-place

poetry or poets, xiii, 39, 81, 106, 109, 230. *See also in xochitl in cuicatl* (flower and song)

Pohl, John, 403

polarities. *See inamic* pairs (complementary polarities)

pollution. *See tlazolli* (filth or pollution)

polytheism. *See* religion or theology

Pomar, Juan Bautista, 120

Popol Nah (Maya council house), 378

Popol Vuh 24, 53, 59, 66n26, 112, 198, 378, 474n129, 501, 510

power. *See* sacred

Prechtel, Martin, 63n8, 171, 229, 368, 369, 379, 388, 399, 521n124

pregnancy, 210, 278, 372, 381, 388; and gestation of fetus, 204, 207–8, 210, 225, 315–16, 363, 387 (*see also* navel or umbilicus); and miscarriage, 278; or parturition, and symbolic associations, 98, 211, 266, 268, 323, *324*, 374, 383, 387–88, 430, 483; and stretch marks, 380–81, 487; 210–11, 266, 323, *324*, 480, 483.

See also birth or childbirth; sexual intercourse; spindle; spinning; stretching

Primeros memoriales, 62, 149, 209, 238, 284, 285, 308, 377–78, 379, 387, 395

process metaphysics. *See* Aztec process metaphysics

Pueblo (Laguna, Tewa, or Santa Clara), 93, 420, 455, 521n123

qi (breath-energy), in Chinese metaphysics, 37–38, 49, 52, 65n14, 120. *See also* breath or breathing

quatrefoil, 202, 230–31, 233–35, 238–41, 402, 442, 458, 480, 481, 525. *See also* crosses; ideograms; quincunx

Quetzalcoatl: deity complex, 86, 97, 149, 167, **283–90**, 299, 309, 311, 434; and Mictlantecuhtli, *162*, 238, 259n247, 292, 437; priests, 95, 108; and role in Aztec cosmogony, 51, 158, 295, 380, **432–46**, 488, 503; symbolic associations of, 291, **321–23**, 370, 379, 392; and Tezcatlipoca, 160, *161*, 199, 226, 281–82, 503; and Xolotl, **204–8**, 295, 324. *See also* Ehecatl (Wind) or Ehecatl-Quetzalcoatl; *malinalli* motion-change; Venus; *Yohualli Ehecatl*

Quezada, Noemí, 278

quincunx, 159, 161, 200, *201, 202*, **222–24**, 230–31, 233–34, *235, 236, 237*, 238–41, 301, 316, 338n141, 366, 402, 442, 458, 464, 480, 481, 498, 500, 524–25; as figure-eight or butterfly shape, 486, 488, 494. *See also* center or centering; crosses; ideograms; *patolli*; quatrefoil

Quine, W. V. O., 8, 9

Quiñones Keber, Eloise, 120, 207, 207, 242n3, 309, 311, 414n186, 417n240, 426, 467n17, 477n192, 520n106; on pantheism, 136n222; on Tlazolteotl, 209, 373

rabbits: day sign, 422; and Gestalt figure-ground phenomenon, 57, *58*; 161, 403; and Ometochtli deity complex 87, 89; symbolic associations of, 14, 87, 246n77, 297, 303, 307–8, 309, 311, 313–14, 330, 422; as year sign (Tochtli), 217. *See also* fertility; *octli* (pulque)

rain: and Cihuateteo, 387, 388; as *inamic* partner of drought or dry season, 147, 153–54, 328; as manifestation of sacred, 24, 34, 35, 36, 37, 49, 85, 93, 505; and North, 221; praying for, 257n223, 382; and Quetzalcoatl, 284; as rainbows, 81; as raining or rainstorm, 25, 31; sacrifice of children for, 197; staff or rattle, 494; as swirling clouds, 324; and Tlaloc, 281. *See also* fertility; Rain, Moisture, and Agricultural Fertility deity complex; water

Rain, Moisture, and Agricultural Fertility deity complex, 88, 89, 157, 208, 283, 305, 347n312; and mother-goddess, earth-goddess, earth-mother, creation-, fertility-, or genetrix-related entities, 39, 89, 98, 208–9, 210, 217, 218, 232, 267, 268, 270, 274, 282, 327, 332n40, 372–74, 379, 383, 388, 391–92, 430, 433, 446, 488, 504, 509, 510, 521n124, 521n126. *See also* deity complex *under names of forces or processes*; earth; fertility

Ramírez, Tony, 36

Rappaport, Roy, 96–97

Read, Kay, xi, 204, 208, 254n185, 256n202; on sacrifice, 100, 195, 294, 315, 409n61, 494; on *teotl* and sacred cosmos, 28, 33, 67n30, 68n50, 115, 126n83, 127n86, 128n98, 421, 425; on time and place, 466n10, 467n12, 469n37, 470n49, 471n62, 475n136, 518n76, 520n106; on weaving, 141

rebirth: emphasis on renewal or regeneration, vs. birth or creation, 91, 204, 208, 210, 281, 284, 311, 312, 327, 379, 447. *See also* birth or childbirth; creation; fertility

reciprocity: design motifs symbolizing, 160–61, 162, 164, 402–3; as discharging debt or completing gift cycle, 94; as ethics or conduct, 277; or mutuality, as dynamic of *nepantla*, 355–57, 359, 361, 362, 364, 394, 403, 480, 483, 525, 526. *See also* agonistic *inamic* unity; crossroads; middle or middling; *nepantla* motion-change

Reed (Acatl), year sign, 217

Reichel-Dolmatoff, Gerardo, 394, 404n9, 490, 502

religion or theology: as animistic or animism, 114–16; approach to understanding, 1–8; Bible or Biblical in, 5, 24, 408n53, 447; Christian or Judeo-Christian, 23, 24, 29, 30, 34, 46, 48, 66n24, 76n151, 82, 83, 91, 98, 115, 119–20, 135n196, 225, 355, 461, 519–20n105–6; dogma, doxology, orthodoxy, or orthopraxy in, 5, 6, 96, 97; Greek or Roman, 81; hierophany in, 100–1; as monotheism, 80,

81, 84, 119, 121–22n6, 135n196; Nahua or Mesoamerican, as *teoyoism* (generalized sacred), 32–33, 34; as pantheism, 79–136; as polytheism, 11, 12, 16n5, 33, 79, 80, 81, 82, 83, 84, 85, 86–92, 119, 121; as sacred vs. profane dichotomy, 30, 113–14. *See also* animism; Aztec priests; Aztec process metaphysics; crosses; deity; dualism; pantheism; ritual practice; sacred; *teotl* (cosmos)

ritual practice: aims of, 1–2, 11, 31, 32–33, 83, 482, 512, 524 (*see also* sacred); and amaranth effigies, 31, 32, 95, 113, 382, 401, 493; cleansing or cleaning, 210, 282, 383–85, 396, 400 (*see also* sweeping); and cut-paper figures, 42, 82–4, 114, 396, 512 (*see also* paper); funeral or mortuary, 495, 512; and sacred bundles, 293, 512, 526. *See also names of rituals or ceremonies*; religion or theology; ritual sacrifice

ritual sacrifice: as arrow sacrifice (*tlacacaliliztli*), 380, 381, 383, 385, 487–88; Aztec conception of, 99–100; and captive binding-rope (*tonacamecatl*), 301–2; as centering energy from four directions, 195, 306 (*see also* center or centering; directions, cardinal); of children, 197; and *cuauhxicalli* (eagle vessel, place of sacrifice), 196, 237, 298, 301, 302, 309, 312, 345n267; and deity impersonators (*see teixiptla*); and feeding captives *octli* (pulque), 299, 303, 306, 312; and flaying (*see* Tlacaxipehualiztli; Xipe Totec); as gifts for Sun, 216–17; and gladiatorial striping or incising, 298, 299, 300, 302, 303, 305; heart, 194–96 (*see also* hearts); as metamorphosis, 305–6; and Montezuma's Cuauhxicalli, Sun Stone, Stone of Tizoc, or ex-Archibishop's Palace Stone, 220, 236, 238, 240, 245n59, 299, 302, 344n259; as self- or autosacrifice, 248n103, 277, 295, 307, 309, 312, 526 (*see also malinalli* grass, balls); as stretching, 380–81 (*see also* Tititl ritual); and *techcatl* (sacrificial stone), 195–96, 237, 298, 373, 385, 487; and *temalacatl* (gladiatorial stone), 236, 298, 299, 300, 301–4, 306, 318; timing of, 272. as twisting-spinning victims, 298–99, 300–1, 302, 304–5, 306, 309, 312 (*see also* seizing; spinning); of victims, as *nepantla*-middled, 383; *See also* warfare or combat

rivers: as force, energy, or process, 23, 34, 37, 90, 189, 190, 191, 194 (*see also* water); as

nepantla-processed, or confluence, 361, 364, 366, 394–95; symbolic associations of, 89, 267, 283, 324; as time-place, 456, 460
Romances de los señores de la Nueva España, 43–44, 46, 47, 71n87
rootedness. *See* well-rootedness
ropes or cordage: symbolic associations of, **274–79**, 301, 305, 308, 312, 314, 315, 319, 495, 501. *See also malinalli* grass; navel or umbilicus
Rorty, Richard, 5, 6
Rowe, Ann, 489
rubber: balls, 186–89, 193, **196–99**, 202, 222, 227–28, 241, 245n63, 248n103, 480, 491; properties and symbolism of liquid, 194, 196–97, 200, 201, 209, 235, 373. *See also* ballgame; *olin* motion-change
Ruiz de Alarcón, Hernando, 274, 511
Russell, Bertrand, 4, 49

sacred: anthropomorphism, 36, 82, 83, 84, 85, 90, 119, 136n218, 159; as ascending~descending forces, 505 (*see also* agonistic *inamic* unity); books (*amoxtli*), 39, 62, 141; as deity, divinity, god, or spiritual force (*see* deity); as dual or dichotomous sacred/spiritual/supernatural, vs. profane/secular/natural concepts, 29–30, 104, 106, 111, **113–14**, 121, 127n86, 133n178, 256n202, 452, 524 (*see also* dualism; Ometeotl); as eternal Being, 26; as everywhere and everything, or immanent, 29–30, 32; as genuine, or *neltiliztli*, **100–13** (*see also* well-rootedness); indigenous concepts of, **35–38**, 119–20, 135n196, 185, 508; knowledge of, 100, 117–18 (*see also* epistemology); as nonhierarchical vertical ordering, 506 (*see also* folds or folding); as pollution, filth, or excrement, 98, 99, 103, 106, 281 (*see also tlazolli*); as power, 35, 93, 95, 103, 106; precinct, 197, 233, 279, 317, 318, 378, 385, 402; as precious gemstones or minerals, 98; as sanctity or sacred postulates, 96; as single unity, or *teotl* (cosmos), 13, 22, 24, 25, **31–33**, **92–100**; as sunlight, 22, 352n393. *See also* deity; *kinh* (sun-day-time); *mana* (power or influence); *qi* (breath-energy); religion or theology; ritual practice; *teotl* (cosmos); *usen* (power); *wakan tanka* (power or force)

sacrifice or sacrificial stone. *See* ritual sacrifice
Sáenz, César, 238
Sahagún, Bernardino de, 11; on the Aztec gods or *teotl*, 120, 170, 197, 204, 208, 211, 281, 391, 425, 510; on crossroads, 387, 389–90, 391, 393, 395, 400; on dreams, 61, 62; on drunkards, *269, 270*; on Fifth Sun, 107, 203, 216, 218, 225, 286, 295, 442, 445; on *malinalli*, 261; on *nepantla*, 362, 364, 366, 386; on New Fire ceremony, 291, 293; on nobility, 275, 384; on Pahtecatl or pulque, 226, 307, 308, 309; on riddles, figures of speech, or proverbs, 109, 110, 111, 113, 167, 213, 265–66, 327, 525; on the sacred, 94, 98; on sacrifice, 192, 271, 298, 299, 303, 304, 325, 380, 398–99; on sweeping, 282, 284, 396; on weaving, *265*, 276, 277, 375–79, 381–82, 397, 435, 491, 494, 503–4; on *yollotl*, 108, 233. *See also Florentine Codex*
Śamkara (Shankara), 56–57
Sandstrom, Alan, xi, xiii, 16n5, 42, 65n16, 191, 336n108, 521n126; on center vs. periphery, 224–25, 394–95, 396; on pantheism or cave-pyramid complex, 34, 82–85, 90, 116, 191
Sandstrom, Pamela Effrein, xi, xiii, 42, 82–83
Schaefer, Stacey, 42, 72, 141, 332n40, 496, 502, 517, 521n124
Scharfstein, Ben-Ami, xi, 37
Schele, Linda, 35, 354n432
scorpions, 267, 395
sculpture or sculptors, 81, *160*, 162, 196, 209, 372
seasons: as *inamic* partners, 186; as metaphor for *teotl* and motion-change, 23, 25, 27, 88, 220; temporal, 423; winter or dry (*tonalco*), 314. *See also* solstice or equinox
Seibold, Katherine, 180n70, 403
seizing: captive's female energy, 294, 305, 306; enemy's topknot, 271, *272* (*see also* hair); hearts, as cosmic food, 195, 303, 314 (*see also* ritual sacrifice); from the middle, 385; raw fiber, 262, 483. *See also* spinning
Séjourné, Laurette, 222, 230, 237, 238, *240, 323*
Seler, Eduard, 215, 206n262, 301, 308, 311, 312, 327, 328, 380, 389, 487; on crossroads 387, 390, 393, 400; on *olin*, 188, 216, 238, 249n136; on Xolotl, 204–5, 206
Sellars, Wilfred, 7
Seneca, 40
Serna, Jacinto de la, 218, 282
Serrato-Combe, Antonio, 233, 401–2

sexual intercourse: or commingling, as root metaphor of Aztec metaphysics, 14, 142–43, 171, 370–71, 509–10, 524; as crossing of threads, 508; and excess, promiscuity, or deviance, as *tlazolli*, 97, 99, 204, 209, 210, 309, 313, 395–96, 397, 399; as fire drilling, 291, 292; as flower motif, 230; and Ometeotl complex, 283, 375, 460–61; of partners, as agonism, 171, 153, 311, 357, 360, 369–70; and reproduction, 2, 142–43, 174, 490, 492, 495 (*see also* birth or childbirth); as sacrifice, by stretching, 380–81, 489; and semen, 387; as weaving, or *nepantla* processing, 265–66, 276, 323, 357–69, 371–72, 375, 381–82, 388, 480, 483, 485, 490, 492, 508 (*see also* spindle). *See also* creation

shamans or shamanism: and artistic-shamanic self-transformation, 21, **38–42**, 62, 63n8, 502, 510 (*see also nahual*); and curing, 396; and divination, 511; as managing segments of sacred unity, 83, 84; as manipulating unseen forces, 75n140; as shamanic balance, or tension, 168–69, 406n26; as shamanic-epistemological strategy, 58. *See also* dreams or dreaming; epistemology; *teotl* (cosmos)

shells, conch, 204, 207, 285, 288–89, 292, 322, *323*

Shinto, Japanese, 64n12, 121n4; and *musubi* (generative force), 37

Siméon, Rémi, 61, 144, 176, 188, 190, 262, 263, 369, 490, 503

Sioux, 18n16, 35–36, 93, 120, 135n196

skulls, 158, 325, *326*, 327, 373; and mandible, as *malinalli* glyph, *326*–27; and skeletonization, 158; and skull rack (*tzompantli*), 298, 373, 378–79. *See also* human body; ritual sacrifice

sky (*ilhuicatl*): and layers of cosmos, 65n16, 110, 318–19, 367, 504–5, 507; as sky-earth, 220; as Sky-Place of the Sun, 505; as skywatching (*see* astronomy); and solar day, 446, 463; as woven fabric or house, 381, 463, 491, 496. *See also* day or days; time-place

Smart, Ninian, 101

Smith, Andrea, 96

snakes or serpents: and *coatl*-rooted words, 264, 282, 299, 350n363, 373, 376, 395, 463, 507; and ropes, 274; and snakely perception, 56–57; symbolic associations of, 162–63, 257n223, 309, 329, 350, 372

Socrates, 5, 46

Solís Olguín, Felipe, 195, 198, 205, 236, 239, 246n72, 299, 302

Solomon, Robert, 92, 93

solstice or equinox: 193, 203, 218, 221, 222, 227, *228–29*, 307, 480, 498; and ballgame, 198, 234; and *patolli*, 200; as quincunx or flower motif, *201*, 238, 422. *See also* astronomy; directions, cardinal; seasons

song-poems. *See in xochitl in cuicatl* (flower and song)

Sophists, 5

sorcery or sorcerers, 215, 216, 390, 393; as problematic terms, 116

souls. *See names of vital life forces*

Soustelle, Jacques, 386, 422, 428, 429, 456–57, 469

Soyaltepec, 158, *159*

space: and place or landscape, as concrete and plural, 421; and spatialization, as motion-change, 223; and theories of time, 454. *See also* time-place

speaking: and figures of speech, 390, 399; as *huehuetlatolli* (addresses), 525; by midwives, 285, 286, 364, 507; as *nahuallatolli* (secret words), 274, 287; as *nepantla*-middled or balanced, 383; as ritualized, noble speech or song, 287, 526; by sages, 105; as speech-breath, sung prayer, incantation, or invocation, 61, 115, **286–89**, 314 (*see also* breath or breathing); and speech scrolls, 287, *288* (*see also* volutes); and spoken words, as *inamic*, 146; symbolic associations of, 230, 287, 324; as *teotlahtolli* (sacred words), 109–10. *See also in xochitl in cuicatl* (flower and song)

Spinden, Herbert, 456

spindle: as *axis mundi*, 317; as male~female gendered, 292, 483; as pregnant, or fetus coagulating, 211, 266, 323, *324*, 483 (*see also* birth or childbirth; pregnancy); rods, shafts, or spindles, 210, 228, 241, 262, 263–64, *265*, 290, 309, 319, 372, 373–74, 480, 483, 486, 516n42; as sacrificial victim, 300, 301, 302, 306 (*see also* ritual sacrifice); whorls, 210, 235, *237*, 262, 264, *265*, 283, 381, 388, 403, 521n123; wind, 284. *See also* spinning; weaving

spinning: bowl, 264, *265*, 302; as gendered activity, 435, 436; and good and bad spinners, 332n39; as *malinalli*-twisting-spinning or fire drilling, 14, **172**, 266, 280–82, 285, 292,

(*see also* day or days; sky); as monistic and processive, **452–65**; as *nepantla*-middled, ritually powerful, 384, 401; as relationalist and heterogeneous, **419–21**, 454–57. *See also* Aztec process metaphysics; cosmology; day or days; *malinalli* motion-change; *olin* motion-change; *nepantla* motion-change; *teotl* (cosmos); time and calendars; *tonalpohualli*; *xiuhpohualli*

Tinker, George, 36, 183n95

Tititl (stretching) ritual, or *tititl*-rooted words, 270, 377, 379–80, 381, 487, 488–89, 494, 503, 515n21. *See also* ritual sacrifice; stretching

Tlacaxipehualiztli (Flaying of Men) ritual, 276, 293, **297–307**, 305–7, 325, 379. *See also* ritual sacrifice; stretching

Tlaelquani (Eater of Ordure), 98, 209–10, 373. *See also* Tlazolteotl

Tlahuahuanaliztli (striping) ritual, 298, 305, 344n243. *See also* ritual sacrifice, gladiatorial striping or incising

Tlalchitonatiuh (Sun Going into the Earth), 90, 206–7. *See also* Tonahtiuh (Sun)

Tlaloc, 81, 164, 197, 207, 217, 378, 450, 451; deity complex, 86, 89, 90, 157, 283, 347n312; fourfold aspects of, 218; priests, 382, 493; and *tlaloque* (rain helpers), 157, 197, 218, 270–71, 281, 284; as Tlaloque-Tepictonton, 157; and woven *quemitl*, 512; and Xochiquetzal, 372. *See also* rain; water

Tlalocan, 504; and Tlalocantecuhtli (Lord of the Underworld), 439

Tlaltecuhtli (Earth Lord~Lady), 51, 207, 220, 233, *235*, *267–68*, 269, 301, 313, 314, 316, 327–28, 377, 380, 488; hair of, as *tonalli*, **267–74**, 272–74, 276, 277, 279, 288; as Tlalteotl (Earth Goddess), 231, 317; as Tlaltetecui, 62

tlalticpac (earth's surface): and earthly existence, or living well, 62, 427, 431, 452 (*see also* time-place); as earthly layers, ordered by Fifth Sun, 193, 198, 205, 221–22, 227–28, 230–32, 233–34, 238, 458, 463, 480, 491, 496 (*see also* Sun-Earth Ordering); as nature, 65n16; as nonhierarchical, 30, 106, 109; as slippery, 167, 181n76, 525–26; and Templo Mayor, or Valley of Mexico, 110, 421 (*see also* axis mundi); as vertical ordering, of cosmos, 504–5, 506, *508* (*see also* folds or folding); as vivified, by *malinalli* energy, 225, 292, 317, 318,

330, 481, 488, 496; as weaving, of Fifth Age, 496–98, 501. *See also* directions, cardinal; earth; time-place

Tlatelolco, 94, 105

Tlatilco, 158

tlatoani (speaker-ruler-king), 16, 110, 219, 298, 304

Tlaxcala or Tlaxcalteca, 2, 149, 314, 399, 402, 444

tlazolli (filth or pollution): and arts or crafts, 113; as entropy, 280, 281; as organic humus (earth filth), 98, 209, 281, 373; as sacred power, 97, 99, 103, 106, 209 (*see also* sacred); as stuff out of place, 97, 376; symbolic associations of 97–98, 267–68, 373; as *tlatlacolli* (damaged, spoiled, disordered), or *tlazolli*-rooted words, 97, 376, 387, 388, 469n37 (*see also* Tlazolteotl); transformed by sweeping, 279–82, 282–83 (*see also* Ochpaniztli); transmitted to periphery, 279, 280, 281, 287 (*see also* center or centering); and twisting, 263, 495. *See also* order~disorder; sweeping

Tlazolteotl (Sacred Humus-Filth-Refuse) deity complex: confessing transgressions to, 98, 330, 391; and healing or medicine, 210; symbolic associations of, 97–98, 281, 390, 391, *392*, 393, 395–99, 400; as Teteoinnan (Mother of the Gods), 208, 274; as Tlazolteotl-Ixcuina or Ixcuina (Filth Goddess-Lady Cotton), 87, 90, 98, 204, **208–12**, 232, 235, 270, 274, 282, 284, **371–75**, 379, 383, 388, 391–92, 430, 488, 509–10; as Tlazolteotl-Tlaelquani (Eater of Ordure), 98, 209–10, 373. *See also* cotton; crossroads; earth; fertility; Ochpaniztli; Rain, Moisture, and Agricultural Fertility deity complex; sexual intercourse; sweeping; *tlazolli* (filth or pollution)

Tochihuitzin Coyolchiuhqui, 5, 45, 46, 47, 60, 61, 62, 76n151, 76n152

Toci (Our Grandmother), 208, 274, 282–83, 299, 380, 383, 388, 488, 509. *See also* Rain, Moisture, and Agricultural Fertility deity complex; *teixiptla* (deity impersonator or image)

Tonacatecuhtli~Tonacacihuatl, 80, 89, 120, 149, 151, 160, 170, 171, 286, 368–71, 385, 458, 460, 480, **503–4**, 509; four sons of, 217, 434, 449–51; as progenitor~progenetrix of